The text that will help your students become more skillful writers and active, critical readers.

The Longwood Reader
Second Edition

by
Edward A. Dornan
and
Charles W. Dawe

Wouldn't you like a text that involved your students from the very first page?

Continuing a strong tradition of success, *The Longwood Reader*, now in its second edition, is filled with valuable information, intriguing reading selections, and challenging assignments to keep your students interested with the turn of every page. *Every* unique feature is geared to helping your students improve their reading and writing techniques.

In this new edition, Professors Dornan and Dawe have maintained the rhetorical arrangement of the first edition but also include several new features to make both the teaching *and* the learning experience more *effective* and *enjoyable*. Just take a look through the following pages to see how *The Longwood Reader* can help make the difference in your composition classroom.

A text written by teachers... with your beginning students in mind.

The Student Edition

Here are 49 balanced readings — plus annotated student writing examples; abundant illustrative examples; biographical and reading notes; and questions on Meaning and Purpose, Strategy and Structure, and Style and Language — all designed to help ensure that your students master the fundamentals of the common organizational techniques.

Authors Edward Dornan and Charles Dawe are classroom teachers who know what your students need for a full understanding of the concepts of effective writing. It's evident in this revision, which includes **many new features** to benefit both you and your students...

❖ **A new chapter, "The Writing Process,"** defines the essay, places the essay in the college classroom context, and discusses the composing process. It introduces students to the methods of prewriting, drafting, and revising with a work-in-progress writing example. It also presents students with guidelines for maintaining unity and coherence, and for developing content. Five useful tips for revision conclude this well-rounded chapter.

---

36 *The Writing Process*

advantage. Instead of "What should I write about?" ask, "How can I find a subject to write about?" The rephrased question gives you direction. You can stop chewing the pencil eraser and go to work.

Here's how to start.

Begin by keeping this writing principle firmly in mind: You will write your best essays on subjects you know and care about. We urge you, therefore, to examine your own experience for subjects. Look at your interests, your work, your values, your leisure activities. Watch the news, a film, or a television show for ideas. Browse through a newspaper or magazine for subject possibilities. Any of these sources can give you plenty to write about.

You must pursue this search actively. Engage yourself in the process by picking up a pencil and going to work. Try one of the following strategies:

1. *Create idea lists.* Time management experts urge busy people to keep lists of commitments—action lists. Action lists begin as random collections of upcoming events, commitments, or tasks. Once the list is complete, the list maker evaluates the entries, ranks them, and establishes a work schedule. The list provides the person with some clarity and direction for his or her activities.

   An idea list like an action list helps to bring your activity into focus. In this case the activity is writing. You can use an idea list to compile possible writing topics. Begin by setting a minimum time limit—perhaps thirty, forty, sixty minutes—and stick to it. Your goal is to develop a *spontaneous* series of brief entries that capture your ideas and responses to them.

2. *Use a journal.* If you have kept a journal at anytime in your life, browse through it for ideas. There is always a good chance that if an entry engages your interest you can develop it into a full essay that will engage a reader's interest.

3. *Record from memory.* If a recent class discussion or lecture stimulated your curiosity or stirred a strong opinion you

❖ **New Essays!**

One-third of the essays are new in the Second Edition. Chosen for their superior writing style and their effectiveness with composition students, the selections represent *a unique balance* of classic and contemporary pieces, academic and popular subjects, and male and female authors from diverse cultures. Included as an added convenience for instructors is a Thematic Table of Contents that groups the text's essays under fifteen subject areas. The authors also include a list of paired essays for assignment purposes.

❖ **Intriguing photographs**

have been added to each chapter in a special new section entitled *Responding to Photographs.* This section offers students more varied discussion and writing assignments.

❖ **Succinct prompts**

at the beginning of each essay help initiate attentive reading for students.

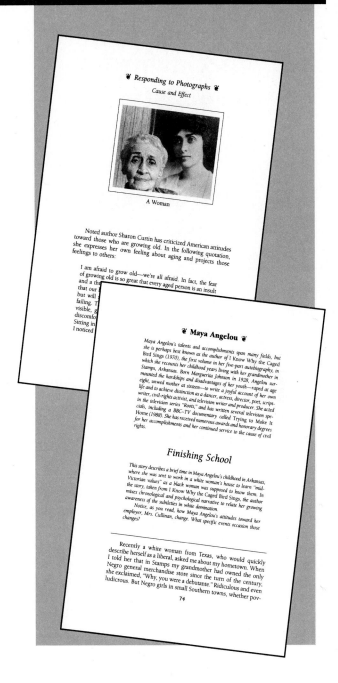

❦ *Responding to Photographs* ❦
Cause and Effect

A Woman

Noted author Sharon Curtin has criticized American attitudes toward those who are growing old. In the following quotation, she expresses her own feeling about aging and projects those feelings to others:

I am afraid to grow old—we're all afraid. In fact, the fear of growing old is so great that every aged person is an insult and a th[...] that our [...] but will [...] failing. T[...] visible, g[...] discomfo[...] Sitting in [...] I noticed [...]

❦ **Maya Angelou** ❦

Maya Angelou's talents and accomplishments span many fields, but she is perhaps best known as the author of I Know Why the Caged Bird Sings (1970), the first volume in her five-part autobiography, in which she recounts her childhood years living with her grandmother in Stamps, Arkansas. Born Marguerita Johnson in 1928, Angelou surmounted the hardships and disadvantages of her youth—raped at age eight, unwed mother at sixteen—to write a joyful account of her own life and to achieve distinction as a dancer, actress, director, poet, scriptwriter, civil-rights activist, and television writer and producer. She acted in the television series "Roots," and has written several television specials, including a BBC-TV documentary called Trying to Make It Home (1988). She has received numerous awards and honorary degrees for her accomplishments and her continued service to the cause of civil rights.

Finishing School

This story describes a brief time in Maya Angelou's childhood in Arkansas, where she was sent to work in a white woman's house to learn "mid-Victorian values" as a black woman was supposed to know them. In the story, taken from I Know Why the Caged Bird Sings, the author mixes chronological and psychological narrative to relate her growing awareness of the subtleties in white domination.

Notice, as you read, how Maya Angelou's attitudes toward her employer, Mrs. Cullinan, change. What specific events occasion those changes?

Recently a white woman from Texas, who would quickly describe herself as a liberal, asked me about my hometown. When I told her that in Stamps my grandmother had owned the only Negro general merchandise store since the turn of the century, she exclaimed, "Why, you were a debutante." Ridiculous and even ludicrous. But Negro girls in small Southern towns, whether pov-

74

Special features help your students understand the relationship between reading and writing.

The Longwood Reader begins with an introductory unit on the reading process that helps students develop an awareness of the importance of sound reading strategies and their relationship to effective writing. The chapter also describes how students should use critical reading skills to determine and examine the author's purpose, organizational strategy, and style. Five tips for the first reading of an essay are included as well as five tips for rereading the essay.

Following a new Chapter Two on the writing process, the nine remaining chapters concentrate on the specific organizational strategies — narration; description; examples; comparison and contrast; cause and effect; process analysis; classification and division; definition; and persuasion and argument.

The text has retained many other popular features from the first edition that appealed to students and teachers alike...

❖ Chapter Introductions
Each chapter begins with a detailed discussion of the writing method, offers suggestions for its use, and presents a student's sample to illustrate the method at work in college writing.

The Method

To describe is to picture in words—the people we meet, the places we visit, the conversations we hear, the infinite number of things we encounter. Description, like narration, is often associated with imaginative literature: children's tales, short stories, and novels. In fiction, narrative events provide a story's bones; description adds flesh to the skeletal structure, helping a reader to imagine the narrative events: "The wind rattled the windows . . . a tall figure wearing a cape emerged from the darkness . . . a pasty white face . . . black hair plastered like a swimmer's cap to his head . . . red lips curled in a sneer . . . the air smelling of rotting meat. . . ." For a descriptive passage to be effective, fiction writers know they must involve their readers' senses to create a reaction to the words. This requirement also applies to essayists who use description as a dominant essay pattern. They, too, must involve a reader's senses—that is, make their readers see, hear, smell, feel, and taste.

Sight

The streets boiled with shoppers . . .
His sunburned face looked grim, heavily lined, and ringed with a gray beard . . .
Flames lashed the sky . . .

Sound

The breath rasped from his lungs . . .
Water trickled from the faucet in a steady beat . . .
The silence was broken by clicks of forks against plates and the crunching of lettuce . . .
The soft lilt of Asian voices carried across the river . . .

Smell

The streets smelled of ripe fruit and straw . . .
The aroma of curry floated above the cooking pots . . .
The perfume was full of musk . . .

124

❖ **Full Apparatus With Each Selection**

Essays are introduced with a brief biography of the author and comments that place the essay in context. *New prompts* at the beginning of each selection focus student attention, and a variety of questions and writing assignments ask students to comment on Meaning and Purpose, Strategy, and Style.

❖ **A Unique Editing Appendix**

A Guide to Editing and Revising Sentences offers practical advice to students on improving their writing skills, with no need to go to a separate handbook. Arranged by rules, this handy reference section covers topics such as eliminating pretentious language, placing modifiers, and considering denotation and connotation of words.

❖ **Additional Writing Tasks**

At the end of each chapter, these writing assignments challenge students to write about personal and academic subjects, using the rhetorical strategies learned. Students can choose from a variety of stimulating topics on which to focus their writing.

A Guide to Editing and Revising Sentences

This guide will help you revise your sentences to make them more readable and interesting. Unfortunately, no one has invented a clear procedure to follow when editing and revising prose. Some writers revise as they carefully work their way through a first draft; others swoop through the first draft and then revise during a second or third draft. Each writer, it seems, devises his or her own approach.

Two preliminary steps in revision do seem to be adopted by all writers. First, they must learn what makes writing effective. We offer this guide as a source of suggestions you can use to gain that knowledge. Second, they must pick up a pencil and go to work on their sentences. We must now stand aside and wish you the best of luck.

Eliminate pretentious language.

Pretentious writing draws attention to itself. The vocabulary is unnecessarily complex, perhaps because the writer has thumbed through a thesaurus replacing simple words with difficult words. Always try to select simple words over fancy ones. If you want to indicate that dogs make good pets, do not write, "Domesticated canines will contribute felicity to anyone's life."

The earthqu

destroyed th

Children li

these fears.

---

120   *Narration*

Displayed on a wall are hundreds of photographs, many of African-American and Native-American leaders, perhaps each embodying a story of its own. Behind his head, slightly obscured, are the words of Martin Luther King, "I have a dream."

This storyteller stands in the classroom, but where are the students who might be eager to hear a meaningful story? He is looking and pointing outside the photographic frame, but at what or whom? From the viewer's perspective he is alone . . . . or is he?

In a unified narrative respond to one of the following writing tasks. Before you begin the first draft, review effective narrative conventions described at the beginning of the chapter.

1. Create your own tale about the storyteller in this photograph. Begin by studying the photograph. Imagine how the storyteller feels in his attire. Imagine how he feels during his performance. Imagine what his life is like when he is not being a storyteller. What does he do? Where does he live? What do his friends think of his storytelling? Is he a fulfilled person? A happy person? A sad person?

   As you imagine the storyteller, list your observations. Once this exploratory phase of the assignment is complete, review your observations and determine what dominant impression you wish to create.

   Finally, to start your first draft, you might begin this way: "Once upon a time an ordinary man who lived in our city decided to become a storyteller." Throughout your draft integrate physical details from the photograph.

2. Imagine that the storyteller in the photograph is fully aware that ancient mysteries have been clarified scientifically. He is still compelled to tell tales, meaningful tales designed to give people insight into a society which some see as growing more and more chaotic.

   For this task, tell how the storyteller became successful. Include in your narrative a summary of one tale that gave his listeners insight into contemporary life.

_D_esigned to make your job as a teacher of writing a little easier.

The Annotated Instructor's Edition

The Annotated Instructor's Edition (AIE) was developed to let you concentrate on what you do best — teach! This integrated, easy-to-use teaching tool combines the student text and helpful annotations for the instructor in one paperbound volume. No longer will you have to refer to a separately bound instructor's manual and other related information.

For each of the 49 readings in the text, you will find a series of easy-to-identify, second-color annotations designed to help you plan a teaching approach, lead class discussions, and evaluate your students' responses to the questions included in the text. The annotations appear only in the AIE, not in the student text, and include the following...

❖ **Teaching Suggestions** are detailed plans to help you approach the reading selections in class. The emphasis here, as exemplified throughout the text, is placed on teaching students to fully understand the selection as an example of effective writing.

TEACHING SUGGESTIONS

Change brings further change, sometimes not entirely foreseen. Shari Miller Sims carefully and expansively defines aggression, assertiveness, and several lesser but contextually important concepts to show that we should interest ourselves in the possible residue of a major change in traditional (or old-fashioned) society. Her thesis—that more women are accepting violence as a means of expression—is primarily developed with examples and by examining cause and effect.

Was the collapse of the Eastern Bloc a global change for the better? Of course. And we have seen better relations between the Soviet republics and the United States. Another change for the better.

But what of the changes that grow from those two alterations in the politics of the planet? Some economists believe that our country will experience strong competition from abroad in the goods and services and manufacturing sectors of our economy. We could have a difficult time of it, all the way down to the personal, financial level.

MARGINAL NOTES

Sims opens her essay with two journalistic anecdotes, designed to get readers' attention at once by engaging them in lightly detailed particulars from interesting events specifically appropriate to her topic.

❦ Shari Miller Sims ❦

Born in New York in 1956, Shari Sims, soon after graduating from Kenyon College, joined the staff at McCall's magazine, where she was an associate editor. She then spent six years as a staff writer and editor for Vogue. She began working for Self magazine in 1987 and is executive editor of Health and Beauty there. She is coauthor, with Lia Schorr, of two beauty books: Lia Schorr's Skin Care Guide for Men (1985) and Seasonal Skin Care (1988). She has also contributed to Working Woman magazine.

Violent Reactions

Domestic violence, reports Sims in an essay from the March 1989 issue of Self, appears increasingly to be considered an "acceptable" form of communication within families and couples. In her essay she probes the changes in sex roles for possible causes, seeking a new definition for "violence."

Sims uses psychological and sociological observations to support her definition. As you read this essay, note how she uses the opinions of experts to strengthen her own statements.

A thirty-year-old man moved out of a New York City apartment it had taken him months to find. Nothing unusual, except for the reason: the couple, just about his age, who lived next door. Their fights were getting progressively louder, more intense, and what he'd heard was more than words. The shouting seemed to have escalated into all-out warfare, and lately additional noises—breaking glass, the crash of objects being thrown echoed into his apartment. What was even more disturbing to him was their source: He was convinced it was the woman who was starting the fights, who was screaming the words of abuse and hurling things across the apartment—all aimed at the man.

A reporter recently asked a karate champion how she hap-

512

❖ Marginal Notes

consist of brief comments and observations that help illuminate and enrich each reading. There are marginal notes on writing strategies; allusions, which explain references that typically require some library research; background material relevant to the reading; and cultural reflections.

❖ Possible Answers

are positioned adjacent to questions on Meaning and Purpose, Strategy, and Style posed in response to each reading. These suggested answers will help you use the questions more effectively in class.

All information is accurate as of date of printing. Subject to change without notice.

---

382   *Process Analysis*

man doesn't buy a cow if he can get milk for free, our mothers tell us in dire tones. We don't point out that we're not cows, and we don't fight against girdles, which apparently do a good job of discouraging wandering hands, since most of the single girls I know are virgins.

But which girdle should I wear? If I pick the panty girdle, I'll 8 need 10 minutes' advance notice before going to the toilet. If I wear the two-way stretch, it will ride up and form a sausage around my waist. Either way, my flesh will be marked with welts and stripes when, at that delirious moment in my bedroom, I can strip off my clothes and scratch and scratch.

I pick the two-way stretch but, born compromiser that I am, 9 put underpants over it.

Next comes the bra. I don't dare look at myself in the mirror 10 as I put it on. This is the era of the pinup girl, the heyday of Lana Turner and Betty Grable, when breasts bubble and froth over the rims of C-cups and a flat chest is considered about as exciting as flat champagne. Not until Twiggy appears on the scene in the 1960's will thinness become acceptable in a girl, much less desirable—but how am I supposed to survive until then? The answer is the garment I've just put on, the confession of my disgrace—a padded bra. If I wear a strapless gown, I pin foam-rubber bust pads, which are known as "falsies," in place. Occasionally one of these breaks loose during a particularly ardent conga or mambo and rises above my dress like the rim of the sun peering over a hilltop.

At least the bra won't show under my silk slip. Silk is ex- 11 pensive, of course, and no male will see my underwear unless he marries me or I'm carried off to a hospital emergency room—but

Lana Turner and Betty Grable, voluptuous American movie stars and pinup girls during World War II, predated Twiggy, the British model thin almost to emaciation, by more than twenty years. The padded bra was first advertised in nineteenth-century Paris. The first modern bra was designed and made by socialite Mary Phelps Jacobs, in 1913. Notice the mother's warning. Some things never change.

Nylon stockings were again available in 1950. Gould reminisces about "stockings" during World

---

244   *Examples*

that will be solved only when a great many people have given it a great deal of thought.

Meaning and Purpose

1. What is your first response to Nilsen's essay? Are you aware of sexist language? Explain.
2. An argument is a reason or reasons stated for or against something. What is the author arguing for? What is she arguing against? Find one sentence from the essay that shows each position.
3. Where does Nilsen state her purpose in this essay? What is her point in each of the three sections, and how are these points related to the thesis?
4. The first three paragraphs tell about Nilsen's experiences in another culture. Why are those experiences included in this essay?
5. Nilsen fills her essay with examples of words and phrases that support her assertions about language. As a reader, how do you react to her using so many examples? Do you feel overwhelmed with information, or does she need the many examples to make her meaning clear?

Strategy

1. Does Nilsen use specific, typical, or hypothetical examples? How effective is her choice?
2. Paragraph 33 lists examples of the differences in job descriptions between the jobs women hold in civilian life and those men hold in the armed services. What role do you believe Nilsen thinks the language of these examples has in people's attitudes toward the jobs?

Annotated Instructor's Edition

The Longwood Reader
Second Edition

Edward A. Dornan
Charles W. Dawe

Orange Coast Community College

Allyn and Bacon

Boston   London   Toronto   Sydney   Tokyo   Singapore

Editor in Chief, Humanities: Joseph Opiela
Series Editorial Assistant: Brenda Conaway
Production Administrator: Rowena Dores
Editorial-Production Service: York Production Services
Text Designer: Pat Torelli
Cover Administrator: Linda Dickinson
Composition and Manufacturing Buyer: Louise Richardson
Photo Researcher: Laura Frankenthaler
Cover Designer: Studio Nine

ISBN 0-205-14751-8

Acknowledgments

"Living Well Is the Best Revenge—Just Ask the Urban Coyote" reprinted by permission of the author, Michelle Huneven.

Acknowledgments continue on page 709, which constitutes an extension of the copyright page.

Printed in the United States of America

10 9 8 7 6 5 4 3 2 1   97 96 95 94 93 92

A Note about
the Instructor's Edition

We hope this special instructor's edition of THE LONG-WOOD READER pleases you. We have tried to make it as interesting as possible. As you thumb through it, you will quickly see that it is much different from the traditional "Instructor's Manual." Furthermore, its size is clearly larger than the student edition (which, by the way, you can order from Allyn and Bacon if you prefer it for classroom use).

The complete text of the student edition is printed in this outsized instructor's edition, but because of the additional space, we were able to pack the margins with commentary. This format has a clear advantage over a traditional instructor's manual: the commentary is where it should be—next to whatever it refers to instead of being tucked away at the end of the text or in a separate booklet.

The commentary is arranged under three headings: Teaching Suggestions, Marginal Notes, and Possible Answers. Our suggestions for teaching are just that—merely suggestions. You will find that they often give some background information to help set the stage for class discussion and then refer directly to the essay itself.

Marginal Notes are chock-full of observations on writing strategies, comments about allusions, information about references, and musings on culture. Sometimes the commentary may seem a bit esoteric. Would you know, for example, that the figure of speech Gretel Erlich uses in the opening of "About Men" is called *hysteron proteron*, a passage in which something that should logically come first comes last? Othertimes the commentary embodies what may be well known. You probably know, for example, that the Chisholm Trail, named after an American scout, Jesse Chisholm (1806–1868), led from San Antonio, Texas, to Abilene, Kansas, serving as a cattle trail for twenty years after the Civil

War. But do you know that Marlboro cigarette ads were once directed at women and that Marlboros once had red filter tips so lipstick traces would not show on them? Well, one of us didn't. In any case we hope the marginal notes, whether the information is esoteric or commonly known, interests you and enriches your experience with the essays and in the classroom.

Possible Answers offers answers to the questions that follow each essay.

E.A.D
C.W.D

Contents

11/Persuasion and Argument　Convincing a Reader　545

"Much is made of the pain inflicted on . . . animals in the name of medical science. The animal-rights activists contend that this is evidence of our malevolent and sadistic nature."

"The fact is, the chief attraction of hunting is the pursuit and murder of animals—the meat-eating aspect of it is trivial."

"As we talked of freedom and justice one day for all, we sat down to steaks. I am eating misery, I thought, as I took the first bite. And spit it out."

". . . it is only during the cessation of work that we nurture our family bonds, educate our children, nourish our friendships; it is in 'recreation' that we literally re-create, renew, restore ourselves after the wear of labor."

"I have been assured by a very knowing American of my acquaintance in London, that a young healthy child well nursed is at a year old a most delicious, nourishing, and wholesome food, whether stewed, roasted, baked, or boiled. . . ."

"We know through painful experience that freedom is never voluntarily given by the oppressor; it must be demanded by the oppressed."

Thematic Table of Contents

Growing Up

Health, Nature, and the Environment

History

Human Behavior

Humor and Satire

Politics and Government

Work

Pairs of Essays

Although the selections in *The Longwood Reader* are arranged by rhetorical patterns, we have included a Thematic Table of Contents grouping the selections under fifteen subject areas.

In addition, we offer the following suggestions for those who wish to assign pairs of essays. Such pairing may be useful for discussion of contrary and/or complementary views of similar subjects or situations, choices of style and presentation strategies, as well as different ways of using a particular rhetorical strategy.

Individual teachers will, of course, discover additional pairings equally valid and informative.

Preface to the Second Edition

The second edition of *The Longwood Reader* maintains the rhetorical arrangement of the first edition but also includes several new features. We have added prompts at the beginning of each essay to initiate attentive reading. We have also included photographs to offer students more varied discussion and writing assignments. But most significantly, we have added a chapter titled "The Writing Process."

The centerpiece of the "The Writing Process" is a student essay, one we use throughout the chapter to illustrate key concepts. In "The Writing Process" we define the essay, place essay writing in the college classroom context, and then discuss the composing process. The discussion begins with ways to find subjects and follows with an explanation of prewriting techniques that help writers explore their subjects.

We then offer methods for sorting and grouping information in rough form by using clusters or informal outlines. Next we explain the thesis statement—how to find one and shape it to serve as an essay's guiding principle. We go on to explain and illustrate formal planning with a clear sense of a reader in mind (a step many students resist). We then discuss essay structure in detail—a discussion that concentrates on strategies for writing introductions, discussions, and conclusions. We also present guidelines for maintaining unity, coherence, and for developing content.

We conclude "The Writing Process" with Five Tips for Revision. These are practical tips, ones we believe will not overwhelm student writers with technical detail but still provide them with enough direction to polish their essays.

In this edition, one-third of the essays are new to *The Longwood Reader*. While selecting these essays, we were guided by the same principle that guided our selections for the first edition: the assumption that "good reading influences good writing."

By "good reading" we mean the activity that engages a reader's imagination when he or she picks up a text. We mean the ability to question an author's ideas, to subject an author's argument to skeptical scrutiny, to use a pencil to note disagreements and counterpoints in a text's margins. By good reading we also mean the ability to read with a "critical eye," that is, to read with the ability to see an author's strategies: the way paragraphs are shaped, the way sentences create rhythm and impact, and the way images create feeling. Every writing course must then also be a course in reading with a second sight that sees beneath a text's skin to examine its bones and vital organs. Unfortunately, reading like a writer, reading with a critical eye, does not come naturally; students must acquire the ability.

How?

They must gather information about the writing craft, and they must study the craft at work. As we perceive the process, student writers must go into "training" much like student actors, dancers, musicians, or painters must train. A vital part of this training is studying the works of those who have mastered the art of writing, writers like Maya Angelou, E. B. White, Alice Walker, George Orwell, Maxine Hong Kingston, Gretel Ehrlich, and others represented in *The Longwood Reader.*

You will notice that Chapter 1 of *The Longwood Reader* not only prepares students to write an essay but also prepares them to read with a critical eye. We explain the reader–writer contract: a reader must assume that a writer has created an understandable work; a writer must assume that a reader wants to understand the work. Together the reader and writer create meaning, relying on writing conventions to aid their effort. We explain the importance of reading to understand a writer's purpose, strategy, and style, a framework that establishes the pattern for the discussion questions that follow each essay. We also present five tips for the first reading of an essay. We then illustrate the practice of reading with a pencil in hand with Michelle Huneven's "Living Well Is the Best Revenge—Just Ask the Urban Coyote" accompanied by student notes. We close the Introduction with five tips for rereading an essay.

We arranged the nine chapters that follow the first two according to traditional writing methods, beginning with narration and ending with argumentation. We believe there is a slight risk in teaching rhetorical modes. When misunderstood, they may generate "cookie-cutter" prose, but we believe the benefit of mastering rhetorical modes outweighs the risk. When students understand these common development patterns, they can examine them at work in professional essays, thus sharpening their critical reading skills. By way of caution, however, throughout *The Longwood Reader* we discuss essays as having a dominant mode. We point out that during the composing process writers respond primarily to their material by selecting paragraph and essay patterns that best suit their subject and purpose instead of trying to fit their material into preselected patterns.

Each chapter begins with a detailed discussion that explains a writing method, offers strategies for using the method, and presents a sample of student work, several paragraphs in length, that illustrates the method at work in college writing. Here we wish to emphasize "detailed," for *The Longwood Reader* offers a thorough, though economical, discussion of each rhetorical mode and uses ample examples to illustrate major concepts. In Chapter 3, Narration, for instance, you will find an explanation of narrative effect illustrated by a brief tale from Zen Buddhist lore. You will find advice on writing the opening, body, and climax of a narrative as well as a discussion of conflict, point of view, chronological and psychological time, and scene and summary. We use several examples to illustrate these concepts to help students understand them in the essays that comprise this chapter. In Chapter 5, Examples, you will find a detailed discussion of specific, typical, and hypothetical examples as well as the practice of mixing different types of examples in an essay. The discussion is amply illustrated by eight paragraph examples. We continue this practice throughout the text. Moreover, the student examples that conclude each chapter are fully annotated to reveal the writer's strategy.

Eight chapters have five essays each and the final chapter,

Persuasion and Argument, has eight. Each essay is introduced with a brief biography of the author, brief comments to place the essay in context, and a prompt to initiate attentive reading. Each essay is followed by questions grouped under the headings of Meaning and Purpose, Strategy, and Style. Two writing assignments follow the study questions, and each chapter closes with additional writing assignments designed to challenge students with a wide range of essay topics from which to choose.

The Longwood Reader offers several important reference features. The Glossary defines rhetorical terms that appear throughout the text. When a term first appears, it is highlighted in bold type to signal its appearance in the Glossary. *The Longwood Reader* also offers a thematic table of contents for readers who wish to read several essays on a common subject and a list of paired readings for those who wish to read for similarities or differences in perspective and style.

Of all the reference features, A Guide to Editing and Revising Sentences will have the most direct influence on a student's writing. The guide is arranged by rules: "Eliminate pretentious language," "Use technical language with care," "Consider the denotation and connotation of words," "Revise for proper coordination," "Place modifiers with care," "Provide variety in your sentences," and so on. Each of the rules is fully explained and illustrated, thus allowing students to use this appendix independently.

Once again we thank those colleagues from colleges and universities around the country who advised us on the first edition of *The Lonqwood Reader*:

Kathleen L. Bell, Old Dominion University; Michael Bobkoff, Westchester Community College; Judith M. Boschult, Phoenix College; Shirley Curtis, Polk Community College; Charles Dodson, University of North Carolina—Wilmington; Jane Dugan, Cleveland State University; Janet Eber, County College of Morris; Leslie Harris, Georgia State University; Elaine Sheridan Horne, Manchester Community College; Gloria Johnson, Broward Community College; Peggy Jolly, University of Alabama—Birmingham;

Robert A. Kelly, Macon College; Joseph LaBriola, Sinclair Community College; Russell R. Larson, Eastern Michigan University; Barry Maid, University of Arkansas—Little Rock; Thomas E. Martinez, Villanova University; Jerry McElveen, Richland College; Gratia Murphy, Youngstown State University; Beth Richards, University of Nebraska; Connie Rothwell, University of North Carolina—Charlotte; Gerald Schiffhorst, University of Central Florida; David E. Schwalm, Arizona State University; Carole M. Sherman, College of DuPage; Laurence J. Starczyk, Kent State University; Jo Koster Tarvers, Rutgers University; Eugene Wright, University of North Texas.

We also thank the professionals at Allyn and Bacon who guided the first edition through the production process: Alicia Reilly, Amy Capute, and Rowena Dores. And we continue to appreciate Kathy Daniel's and David Lynch's fine work on the final manuscript for the first edition.

For the second edition, as well as the first, we owe a special debt of gratitude to our sponsoring editor Joe Opiela for his advice throughout the process. We also thank Editorial Assistant Brenda Conaway, Permissions Editor Laurie Frankenthaler, and Production Administrator Rowena Dores for their help in preparing the second edition manuscript for publication.

We also wish to acknowledge an immense debt to our colleagues Don Pierstorff and Mike Finnegan for their extensive contributions to both the first and second editions of *The Longwood Reader*. Finally, a special thank you is due John Finnegan for his ability to translate illegible handwriting into finished copy.

The Longwood Reader

1

The Reading Process

We heard a story recently about an event that occurred at a nearby campus. Campus officials, faculty members, and a contingent of dissatisfied students had been haggling over curriculum changes. Months of negotiation ended in deadlock. Frustrated, the students called a rally. A representative from administration began to speak, offering the "official" view. Suddenly, a student leader leaped to the platform and grabbed the microphone. Veins pulsed in his neck; his face turned crimson; his eyes spurted with anger. Everyone became excited, ready for a fiery attack on the administration and faculty, but instead he shouted, "Words, Words, Words! I'm sick of words!" He dug into a bag and began tossing lecture notes, essay shreds, and pages torn from textbooks at the astonished crowd. "If words were feathers," he bellowed, "everyone on this campus would smother before anything changed." And then he stormed to the admissions office and promptly withdrew from his classes.

Or so the story goes.

A true story? Who knows for sure? It does, nevertheless, illustrate a common belief that words slow action. Indeed, taking direct action seems much easier than agonizing over a thoughtful, well-reasoned argument. But education relies primarily on words, written words—words *you* read and words *you* write. Reading and writing are sometimes slow, frustrating activities that at first glance may seem to oppose each other. On the contrary, though, reading and writing complement each other. The better reader you are, the better writer you can become.

Of course, you've been reading since grammar school. You probably spend some leisure time reading for pleasure, perhaps becoming engrossed in the psychological twists and turns of a popular thriller or enthralled by the intricate social weaving of a historical narrative. But you probably spend more time reading for information, gleaning facts from history, psychology, and science textbooks. While reading textbooks, you probably concentrate on a goal, which often has something to do with a midterm or final examination. In other words, you've learned efficient reading techniques. You've learned to approach a textbook as if it were a lake in which you troll for facts and theories instead of bass or trout.

Certainly, reading in this way helps you prepare for tests. It will also help after graduation when you face the heaps of memoranda, reports, and research every profession generates. It won't, however, help you become a better writer. For your writing to improve, you must learn to read like a writer. You can begin by learning to read with a "critical eye." The critical eye reveals a writer's purpose and strategies. It scrutinizes the way in which words work in sentences. The critical eye pierces a work's surface and reveals its bones and heart.

We offer the essays in this anthology as a means to help you develop a critical eye. The essay is often described as a well-organized nonfiction composition in which the author concentrates on a single aspect of a subject. Usually this kind of essay is written in formal English and designed to convey information. But essays as a group cover a much broader territory. Many are impressionistic or exploratory. Often they express personal feelings or attitudes based on the writer's experience.

Because essays are so varied, these selections represent a great range, all the better, we believe, to help you sharpen your critical eye. They include works by such well-known essayists as George Orwell, Joan Didion, and E. B. White, as well as works by less-known, rising essayists, such as Gretel Ehrlich and Phyllis Rose. The essays are from varied sources: newspapers, magazines, academic and scientific journals, and nonfiction books. They cover many subjects: crime and violence, men and women, work and play, country and city life, even culture and customs. The collection embodies several styles, ranging from the newswriter's objective report to the poet's subjective expression. Some are serious. Some are playful. All are worth your attention. As you study them, hold one idea in mind: you are reading like a writer; that is, reading to develop your writing skill—reading with a critical eye.

The Writer–Reader Contract

Pause for a moment. Imagine an essayist pushing back from a typewriter desk. The writer stretches and yawns before slipping a final manuscript into an envelope and sending it off for publication. You might think this is the critical moment—when the essay is completed and in the mail to the publisher.

But it isn't.

The critical moment comes when the work falls into a reader's hands—your hands. To begin reading an essay is the first act in a dynamic interaction—not between you and the writer, as you might guess—but between you and the essay itself.

This is not to deny that a relationship connects you and the writer. In fact, readers and writers are joined by an implicit agreement, a "contract" between writer and reader. A reader must assume that a writer has created an understandable work; a writer must assume that a reader wants to understand the work.

Unfortunately, communicating in written language is often difficult. A writer cannot gaze over your shoulder and whisper into your ear to make understanding an essay any easier. Only the essay speaks to you. To fulfill the writer–reader contract, a writer employs principles known as "conventions" to help you understand the essay. Even if the essay is difficult, you must trust that the writer has kept the reader in mind during the writing. You must trust that the writer has seen the essay through *your* eyes. In other words, you must trust that the writer has used the conventions of essay writing to help you understand the work.

Generally, these conventions dictate that essays have a purpose, use clear strategies to achieve the purpose, and employ an appropriate style. Understanding these conventions will help you decipher most nonfiction texts. Indeed, understanding the conventions will help sharpen your critical eye.

Reading for Purpose

Writers know that readers expect to understand the purpose behind an essay. Purpose gives an essay direction. It provides a destination. It keeps a reader on the track. Some writers, especially when the primary intent is to convey information, state a purpose: "My purpose is to explain the ways in which human beings have decorated their bodies through the ages: by tattooing, by scarring, and by reshaping bone structure." Other writers, especially those writing personal narration and description, do not state a purpose as directly, thus encouraging the reader to become more deeply involved in interpretation. You must then formulate the purpose in your own way: "The writer narrates an early childhood experience to show how important imaginative play is." When an essay is rich enough to invite interpretation, much like a careful reading of an intricate poem or short story, then all that you have heard, tasted, touched, smelled, seen, and thought; all your knowledge of people, books, music, art, culture, and language; literally everything you have lived through, is the raw material at your disposal. Drawing on that rich resource, you apply your knowledge to interpret the essayist's purpose.

Consider a short passage from Norman Mailer's *Fire on the Moon,* a work in which he concentrates on America's space program. In this passage astronauts Neil Armstrong and Buzz Aldrin have completed their historic moon walk on the Sea of Tranquility. The event takes place at the end of their first day on the moon.

It was about three-thirty in the morning when the astronauts finally prepared for sleep. They pulled down the shades and Aldrin stretched out on the floor, his nose near the moon dust. Armstrong sat on the cover of the ascent engine, his back leaning against one of the walls, his legs supported in a strap he had tied around a vertical bar. In front of his face was the eyepiece of the telescope. The earth was in its field of view, and the earth "like a big blue eyeball" stared back at him. They could not sleep. Like the eye of a victim just murdered, the earth stared back at him.

One clear purpose is to describe the astronauts' preparations for sleep, but toward the end of the passage, Mailer compares the earth to a murder victim. Moreover, he suggests that Armstrong is haunted by the image of the earth "like the eye of a victim" staring at him. Is the comparison merely a dramatic flourish? We doubt it. The description will lead a sensitive reader to explore the deeper purpose in Mailer's comparison. Mailer does not spell out what the passage means. Instead he invites the reader to interpret it. That puts the reader in an interesting spot, for just as Mailer has drawn on his knowledge and experience to create the image, readers must draw on theirs to interpret it, to find a meaning.

The meaning may vary from reader to reader, depending on each one's knowledge and experience. One reader may recall Edgar Allan Poe's macabre tale of murder, "The Tell-Tale Heart." In Poe's story the murder victim's eye—"a pale blue eye"—haunted the murderer, as the blue earth seems to haunt Armstrong. Does the image suggest, therefore, that the earth has been abandoned like a corpse by astronauts who seek other worlds?

Another reader may explore technological associations. The 1969 Apollo II flight was history's most advanced scientific achievement. But at what price? Isn't the human thirst for scientific achievement and the technology it generates sapping mother earth's natural resources? In a metaphorical sense, therefore, isn't technology killing the earth? And couldn't Mailer be using the moon landing to suggest that "ecological crime"? Who, then, are the perpetrators? Perhaps all humankind, represented by the astronaut who, Mailer suggests, feels accused by the "big blue eyeball" staring at him.

Not all essays invite a careful interpretation of purpose, but the many that do are rich in detail and express a personal vision.

Reading for Strategy

A writer must develop strategies to execute the purpose. The writer might first develop a sense of the audience and a strategy for addressing them: To whom is the essay directed? How much do they know about the subject? How much time are they likely to spend with the essay? Will they want a straightforward treatment of the subject or an exploration through richly textured prose? Answering questions such as these will give a writer a sense of the audience, a feel for the person sitting at a desk or in an easy chair reading the essay.

Having acquired a sense of the audience, the writer may next develop a strategy for the essay's structure, knowing that readers want essays to have clear organization. Usually writers choose a dominant rhetorical pattern to organize their work, such as development by narration, description, examples, comparison and contrast, or definition. Rhetorical patterns are not formulas. They don't offer a magic recipe for success in writing. Moreover, professional writers seldom stick to any one pattern, choosing instead to use several within a dominant structure. We suggest you see rhetorical patterns as a tool to guide your writing and to provide an effective way of fulfilling a reader's desire for structure.

To see how rhetorical patterns can work, imagine that you are a film critic and want to compare and contrast two movies. You pick thrillers and narrow your subject to plot structure. You decide to explain the similarities and differences in each director's way of hooking an audience, generating suspense, building to a climax, and constructing the resolution. Thorough knowledge of comparison-and-contrast patterns will help you balance the similarities and differences in your analysis.

While composing your essay, however, you find yourself bringing the plot of a third movie into the discussion, one that represents still another structure. A warning light flashes in the back of your mind. You pause to think through what you're doing. Your knowledge of rhetorical patterns helps you realize you're drifting into classification, which is a pattern different from comparison and contrast, perhaps one best avoided for this writing situation. You stop. You return to your original strategy or reconsider, and in fact move to classification.

At still another stage, you drift into discussing the effects of thriller plots on an audience. It makes sense—an exciting plot does affect an audience, right? Of course it does. But you would be employing yet another rhetorical pattern, cause and effect. After some thought, though, you may decide to explore the effect on the audience, but you will do it in another section of your paper, and you will arrange it according to cause-and-effect technique.

Our point is quite simple: Knowledge of rhetorical patterns helps writers organize their work. These aren't cookie-cutter patterns that writers press into the dough of their thought. They are effective strategies that writers use to organize their material and guide a reader through an essay. They also help writers remain flexible, shifting smoothly from pattern to pattern according to the demands of the subject. The best way we know for you to build knowledge of rhetorical patterns is to examine how professional writers use them—that is, to read with a critical eye.

Reading for Style

People usually think of style as appearance. Imagine a punk rocker walking across your campus. To what kinds of things are you referring when you speak of his or her "style"? Perhaps it's the black leather jacket and silver studs; the hair dyed black, swept into a peak, and shaved at the sides; the defiant swagger; even the throaty voice, rasping across the quad—all these details, and more, create the image, the "style" this person generates.

Writing also embodies many details that work together to generate a "style." To identify a writer's style, you might begin by examining word selection. Are the words abstract or concrete? Do the words lull you into inattention like the speech of a politician trying to obscure past transgressions, or do they catch your attention like pebbles pinging against a window? Are the words common, found in everyone's vocabulary? Or are they scholarly, obscure words used by specialists? Or does the writer mix common with scholarly language?

You might also study a writer's sentences. Notice how the writer builds sentences and varies their structure. We have no simple rules for this technique. Writers learn a feel for sentences, as potters develop a feel for clay. They shape them. They vary their length. They alter their rhythm to increase or slow the pace of reading for emphasis.

Writers use sentences to create figures of speech, the bits and pieces of colorful language sparkling through the essay. A writer may use figurative language to compare two things that are essentially different but alike in some way. With a crisp simile, Flannery O'Connor compares a woman's determination to a truck: Mrs. Freeman's "forward expression was steady and driving like the advance of a heavy truck." In another memorable simile, Ralph Waldo Emerson offers a fresh way to see a child: "A sleeping child gives me the impression of a traveler in a very far country." With figurative language, writers not only help their readers understand what is being said but also add vigor to their prose.

Word choice, sentence variety, and figurative language combine to create another element of style—tone. Begin to think of tone as an expression of a writer's attitude, much as tone of voice may reflect a speaker's attitude. Imagine, for a moment, that you have given a speech. The next day you receive this note:

> That was an effective speech. You carefully covered the main points. We all thank you.

A straightforward compliment? We think so, don't you? But with a few word substitutions and additions and by altering emphasis, the tone changes dramatically:

> That was . . . *some* speech. You *lingered* on all the points—at least three times each. Thanks a lot.

The message no longer expresses appreciation. It now expresses snide criticism. In other words, the tone has changed.

Some kinds of writing are dominated by well-defined tones. News reporters seem to share a tone, an objective presentation of events—just the facts, please. Thriller and romance writers seem to favor a breathless, frenzied tone. Essayists, however, struggle to find the exact tone to fit the subject, audience, and attitude. The same writer may use one tone for one subject and another tone for another subject. The tone may be formal, informal, flippant, conversational, intimate, solemn, playful, or ironic. The tone may even reveal the writer's awe of the subject. Consider the opening lines from Richard Selzer's essay on skin:

> I sing of skin, layered fine as baklava, whose colors shame the dawn, at once the scabbard upon which is writ our only signature, and the instrument by which we are thrilled, protected, and kept constant in our natural place.

Selzer brings to his essay years of experience as a surgeon and medical-school teacher. A reader with knowledge of Selzer's background might expect him to treat the skin in a matter-of-fact way, as merely a thin barrier that must be sliced through to reach the vital organs. But this is clearly not his attitude. He writes rhapsodically, "I sing of skin"; he makes a rich comparison, "layered fine as baklava"; and he claims its "colors shame the dawn." The sentence is a tribute to skin, and the tone expresses his sense of awe.

Style is difficult territory to explore, no doubt about it. If you devote time to reading for style, you will achieve a *feel* for it. Study a writer's words and you will learn to choose the right words. Study a writer's sentences and you will learn to shape your sentences. Study a writer's figurative language and you will soon be writing colorfully. Study a writer's tone and soon a voice will rise from your pages.

Five Tips for a First Reading

When reading to improve your writing, you cannot sweep through an essay and then set it aside. You should be prepared to read it several times. The first reading may be quick, designed to give you a view of the content, a sense of the purpose, and a feeling for the style. When you begin the first reading, we suggest you keep five tips in mind.

1. *Know the Writer*

Whatever you learn about an author will help you anticipate his or her biases. If the author is identified as a liberal politician and the subject is poverty, then you might anticipate an argument supporting government aid to the poor. If the author is an environmentalist and the subject is the greenhouse effect, then you might expect a plea to save the world's rain forests. Many periodicals and essay anthologies include information about an author, usually on the first page of the essay or in a section often titled "Notes on Contributors." In this collection, each essay is introduced by a headnote, which includes an author profile and brief comments on the essay. Read each profile with care; it will prepare you for your first reading of the essay.

2. *Consider the Place and Year of Publication*

Knowing where the essay was first published is necessary in establishing a writer's credentials. An essay titled "Bigfoot: Hoax or Hysteria?" would have more credibility if published in *Media, Culture, and Society,* a highly respected periodical for people interested in the influence exerted by newspaper, television, and film on readers' and viewers' perceptions, than it would if published in *The National Enquirer,* a popular tabloid known for its sensationalism. Knowing when an essay was first published will also give you clues about the social environment it was written in. Certainly an essay on civil liberty written in the early 1960s is going to display different assumptions from those in one written in the late 1980s.

3. *Examine the Title*

Sounds obvious, right? Well, you would be surprised at how many readers mistakenly believe an essay begins with its first line. It doesn't. It begins with a title.

A title can help you anticipate what is to follow. It may announce the writer's subject, suggest the dominant rhetorical pattern, or hint at the writer's attitude. The title "A Hanging" lets you know you won't be going to a tea party. It makes sense to anticipate an essay about an execution, which will not be a pretty experience. The title "Cyclone! Rising to the Fall" is a little more ambiguous. Does "cyclone" refer to the destructive natural phenomenon? Or does it mean a roller coaster? Or could "Cyclone" be the name of a bronco? Anyway, you probably expect a description of a thrilling, or even frightening, experience: get a tight grip on the book. "I Want a Wife" seems like a straightforward title. But if you know that a feminist author wrote the essay, you might expect an ironic tone.

4. Take Quick Notes

Always read with a pencil in hand. Don't just chew on the eraser: star key passages, underline startling images, bracket shifts in thought, and scribble notes in the margins. Roughly trace your reactions to the text, questions that come to mind, even disagreements with the writer. Ah yes, circle words you don't know so that you can refer to a dictionary for their meaning before the second reading.

Why go to all this trouble for a first reading? We don't suggest that you linger on any page for very long, but a first reading is like traveling in new territory. Much like markings on a map, markings on an essay will help your exploration during the return visit.

5. Record Your First Impression

We urge you to record your first impressions after the first reading and before going on to a second reading. Write down what you think the writer was trying to achieve—the purpose. Identify the dominant strategies. Describe the audience. Jot down your thoughts on style. Record any impressions you have.

Now let's look at an essay, Michelle Huneven's "Living Well Is the Best Revenge—Just Ask the Urban Coyote."

Huneven is a rising writer who concentrates on southern California's transformation from a "suburban dream" in the 1950s to an "urban nightmare" in the 1990s. Her essay conveys preoccupation with adapting in an urban world, not just human adaptation but also that of wild creatures.

Before reading Huneven's essay, you should know that several coyote attacks on children had been reported in southern California at about this time. These were not attacks in the wilderness as you might expect but attacks on front lawns and at the edges of vacant lots. Huneven also draws on common knowledge of the coyote, information that can be found in any encyclopedia, such as this excerpt from *World Book Encyclopedia:*

> **Coyote,** *KY oht* or *ky OH tee,* is a wild member of the dog family. It is known for its eerie howl, usually heard during the evening, night, or early morning.
>
> Coyotes once lived only in western North America. However, they now inhabit much of the United States, Canada, and Mexico, and even parts of Central America. The coyote lives in a variety of environments, including deserts, mountains, and prairies. It is sometimes called the *prairie wolf* or *brush wolf.*
>
> Adult coyotes vary in color from light yellow or yellowish-gray to brownish-yellow. Their fur may be tipped with black. The coyote has large, pointed ears and a bushy tail. An adult coyote measures about 4 feet (1.2 meters) long, including its 11- to 16-inch (28- to 41-centimeter) tail. It stands about 2 feet (0.6 meter) high and weighs from 25 to 30 pounds (11 to 14 kilograms). Most coyotes live alone or in pairs, but some form groups of three or more.
>
> Coyotes eat more kinds of food than do many other animals. They feed chiefly on rabbits and such rodents as gophers, mice, prairie dogs, rats, and squirrels. Coyotes also prey on antelope, goats, sheep, and other animals. The coyote eats various insects and reptiles as well. During the winter, many coyotes in northern regions feed on the re-

mains of large dead animals, such as cattle, deer, and elk. In some areas, coyotes eat juniper berries, mesquite beans, watermelons, and other fruits for a few weeks of the year.

Some ranchers dislike coyotes because the animals kill cattle, sheep, and other livestock. Other people, however, think coyotes help keep rodent populations under control and are valuable for that reason. Some people hunt and trap coyotes for sport. Coyote pelts are used to make coats and to trim parkas or other clothing.

You probably noticed that the purpose of the *World Book* entry is clear—the writer gives you the bare-bones facts about coyotes in general. This is the kind of writing you would read strictly for information. Huneven's purpose is different. She takes the information, limits her focus to coyotes living in urban areas, and writes in a style that lifts her subject well above the facts.

Huneven's essay is also annotated according to the suggestions in "Five Tips for a First Reading." Glance at the annotations to see how one writer recorded questions and impressions while reading the essay for the first time.

❦ **Michelle Huneven** ❦

*Living Well Is the Best Revenge—
Just Ask the Urban Coyote*

Canis latrans, God's dog, the song dog of the west, the trickster. The coyote is a wild canid, larger and more brazen than the fox, smaller and less social than the wolf. He's easy to spot in any pack of dogs; he's the one with the guilty look and sidling gait. Over the past hundred years or so he's acquired a bad reputation by raiding henhouses and rustling sheep. He ruined so many ranchers and gorged on so many wooly innocents that he became the target of the largest and longest predator-control program in history. He survived, of course. Proved himself indestructible. And refused to be banished into the wilderness. Even as cities encroach on his territory, he holds his ground, adapts and, frankly, flourishes. The new urban coyote is strong, healthy and busy compounding his bad reputation by plundering Southern California towns for garbage, house pets and, recently, a small child. Brother Coyote can't help himself; he *likes* man—maybe not to talk to or play with, but definitely to live next door to. And exploit.

Professionally the coyote is both scavenger and predator, sanitation engineer and ro-

15

Handwritten annotations:

Associations:
1. Cliché: Once saw a "Yuppie" Poster that featured a Rolls Royce with this phrase.
2. "Urban Coyote": Is this a metaphor for humans? "Urban Cowboy" comes to mind.
3. Coyotes run undocumented workers across Mexican border.

Huneven describes an actual coyote—a new kind of coyote that exploits people. Ironic? Because people "exploit" the natural world.

Purpose: to describe a new breed of coyote. Coyote described as a professional, with a job.

→ Why Brother Coyote?

dent-control specialist. (His job) is to eat anything that needs to be eaten and to check any exploding population of smaller animals. He's designed to consume; form follows function. It's impossible to see a coyote without thinking of hunger. Mark Twain dubbed him "a living, breathing allegory of Want."

He looks like a German shepherd—a starving German shepherd with a long family history of malnutrition. Standing 20 to 24 inches tall at the shoulder, the coyote matches a German shepherd in height, but his average 20 to 30 pounds ranks him among beagles in weight. His long-limbed skeleton creates the illusion of greater size, but his hide seems shrunken over his frame in such a way that his nose appears unusually pinched and pointed, his ears and eyes and tail disproportionately large. He's grayish red, his forehead and feet a darker cinnamon or rust color. For a few months in the winter his fur can look quite respectable, with the soft, woolly undercoat thick and luxurious beneath longer, coarse, water-repellent hair. The rest of the year he's fading, molting, growing in, plagued by fleas and mange and, in general, a scruffy, sorry exterior. His long, black-tipped tail is always fluffy and could be his crowning glory, if only he'd untuck it from between his legs. If he ever did unfurl that tail he'd measure four feet from its tip to his nose.

Begins physical description

Huneven compares coyotes to familiar animals.

Vivid description

Tales of enormous, 50-, 60-, 80-pound coyotes abound—the creature seems to have a curious, expansive effect on the human imagination—but the largest coyote on record (a New Yorker) weighed around 50 pounds, and the largest Southern California specimen tipped the scales at 34 pounds. The standard female urban coyote weighs about 20 pounds, the male 5 pounds more.

The coyote's eyes are slanted, black-lidded, amber-colored, though they're said to glow greenish gold at night. Homeowners in L.A. County have complained of coyotes staring through front windows with their large yellow eyes, glaring at poodles or house cats. His eyes and ears are fine, sensitive instruments, but the coyote relies on his nose, takes his cues from and acts upon olfactory information; he often will not flee danger until he gets the enemy's scent.

*Strategy—
Huneven moves
from the general
to the
particular—
coyote's nose,
mouth, teeth ...*

The coyote's hardworking mouth holds 42 specialized teeth. Small nibblers up front are perfect for currying fleas, lice and ticks from his fur, uncaking mud, pulling foxtails from between his toes and scraping every last shred of meat from a bone. The sharp tusks that lend the lurid aspect to his smile do the heavy work of snagging and holding prey. Midmandible, the coyote's top and bottom teeth just meet for easy cutting and still more holding power. (In ranching country a coyote will grab a sheep by the throat and hang on for thirteen minutes until the animal suffocates; house pets are fast food by comparison.) His rear teeth are "scissor" teeth; they pass each other close to the jaw muscle and are ideal for shredding gristle, pulverizing big bones and, when necessary, chewing through PVC pipe to get to water. The only teeth the

*House pets as
fast food!!!*

Urban hunt?

coyote lacks are close-set, wide, chunky teeth, like our own molars, teeth that grind grain and break down vegetable matter. But don't worry, the coyote gets his fiber and complex carbohydrates. He eats his fruits and vegetables whole—just gulps them down. This practice indirectly gives him yet another ecological function: scatterer of seeds. Not only are fruit seeds dispersed in his scat, the seeds' pericarp dissolves in his digestive tract, increasing the chance of germination by 85 percent.

No molars—an interesting detail: a meat eater.

A coyote's breath is rumored to be so rank he can stun his prey with it.

A memorable image—UGH! Why a separate paragraph? Drama?

Most people may never see a coyote—especially if they go looking for one—but everyone can hear them at night. They're most vocal from December to February, during mating season. The famous racket consists of eleven different calls: the growl, the huff, the whine, the yelp, the woof, the bark, the bark-yip, the lone howl, group howl, group howl-up and the greeting song. The lone howl is the cry of an individual separated from mate or chums; the greeting song, soft and quavering, is produced when a lesser male appears near more dominant males. Coyotes sing to declare their territory and because they love to sing—alone or with friends. A single coyote can make several noises at once and achieve all kinds of ventriloquistic effects in the process. Often what sounds like several song-dog armies scattered in the foothills is one or two coyotes really cutting loose. A passing siren triggers a spirited response.

Effective transition Uneven shifts to coyote's voice.

Urban hunt—

Most animals are specialized in their eating habits: cougars as carnivores, rodents as vegetarians. Coyotes are "specialized generalists," i.e., specialized to eat *everything*. Coyotes have no problem recognizing dinner—they'll eat anything from grasshoppers to grapefruit, coleslaw to carrion, mice to Minute Rice.

Shifts to eating habits

A coyote also eats avocados, oranges, melons, berries, chickens, small dogs, livestock and fowl with relish. The rare but rising number of attacks on small children indicates that once certain coyotes overcome their inherent fear of man, very young human specimens also look like food. And if his own offspring or mate is killed, he might well snack off the carcass. A meal's a meal.

Grim humor— "young human specimens" sounds scientific but seems ironic.

"A meal's a meal"— nice touch. This urban coyote is a real survivor.

To Brother Coyote, it's truly a dog-eat-dog world.

Coyotes, it was discovered, are so intelligent they can learn from their own mistakes and the mistakes of fellow coyotes. Remarkably, they also teach their young to avoid those mistakes.

Shifts to coyote intelligence

Ultimately, man learned a few things, too. He learned coyotes step up their reproduction to compensate for losses in population—when they are threatened, litter size doubles and females breed at an earlier age. A community of coyotes can lose 70 percent of its number and replenish itself *within one year*. Killing millions of coyotes merely culled the species—the whole predator-control program effected an accelerated exercise in evolution in which the fittest survived, and reproduced.

A new housing tract in the hills initially may disorient and disturb coyotes displaced by the construction, but within a year they relax and learn to appreciate the urban development for what it is: coyote paradise. In Southern California, ground squirrels and gophers flourish in disturbed, developing environments. This profusion of rodents delights indigenous coyotes; imagine snoozing in the shade all day, then, come evening, nipping down to town for drinks and dinner. It's a wild dog's life.

H uneven picks up adaptation theme—coyotes adjust.

There's such a concentration and diversity of food available in suburban neighborhoods that the opportunistic coyote no longer has to spend long hours ranging over great distances to meet his dietary requirements. The urban coyote finds he has much more leisure time on his hands. Having yet to develop a taste for television, movies or alcohol, the coyote is still very much a family dog. He uses the extra hours in his day for courtship, mating and playing with his children. Since much of this play is instructional, each new generation of urban coyote is better educated and craftier than the last.

Irony increases: coyote becomes more human.

Human characteristics ironic. One thought: like coyotes, humans came from the wilderness and settled in cities... Strange parallel.

Over the years homeowners have complained of coyotes drinking from swimming pools, eating from outdoor pet bowls, of a big mangy coyote routinely sleeping on a backporch chaise lounge, a coyote chasing a small dog through a doggy door and around the kitchen, a coyote tightrope walking down a fence rail, coyotes living in freeway landscaping, a coyote eating a poodle in public.

Coyotes have bad manners. An unwanted house guest.

Small domestic animals can't protect themselves from a coyote because it attacks so swiftly. When confronted by a stalking coyote, a pet rarely takes constructive action; a cat will bunch up and hiss, a poodle may snarl or charge. Pets don't think like wild animals. When they see a coyote coming they think: uh-oh, there's going to be a fight. The coyote thinks: lunch.

Conclusion — Humans and their domesticated pets are no match for the urban coyote.

{ Is this the end? { Very abrupt.

FINAL NOTES —

Purpose: Huneven gives the reader a new slant on coyotes. No longer creatures hunting in the distant hills, they are city dwellers; coyotes flourish in urban areas.

Strategy: Mostly a description, but not a scientific description — it's lively, full of fun, yet full of facts. Huneven begins with an overview of the coyote, then moves to the parts.

Style: The tone is ironic and witty. Huneven's coyote, a wily creature, seems to be the opposite of the coyote in the Road Runner cartoons — a survivor, not a victim. Her style suggests a cartoon — well detailed, rich in images, dark humor.

After the first reading you should be familiar with the essay's content and purpose. You should have a sense of the strategies and the tone. You also should have jotted down general impressions and responses to the essay. In other words, you've left your markings. Now you're ready to return to the territory.

Five Tips for Rereading

Before reading the essay, review your notes and reconsider the title: Did it accurately reflect the content or purpose of the essay? Did it embody the tone? If not, how does it function? Then you're ready to begin. Once again you should read with a pencil in hand, ready to expand or change your previous observations and make new ones. Remember, too, that you're attempting to read like a writer examining another writer's techniques—that is, you're reading with a critical eye.

1. Review the Beginning and End

The beginning and end are critical sections. The opening paragraphs usually will, directly or indirectly, establish the purpose of the essay. Sometimes the purpose will be immediately clear, as it is in Huneven's "Living Well Is the Best Revenge— Just Ask the Urban Coyote." Clearly, her purpose is to describe "a new breed" of coyote, one that thrives in urban and suburban environments. The end will often restate, or in a narrative, dramatize the purpose. Huneven's essay ends abruptly, but the end reinforces her primary purpose: People provide a very good living for the urban coyote.

2. Read with the Purpose in Mind

The purpose can serve as a beacon that will guide you as you read through the essay. Knowing the purpose will clarify the strategies the writer uses to achieve that purpose. Huneven's dominant rhetorical pattern is description. She begins with a general description of the coyote, then follows with a series of paragraphs concentrated on parts of the coyote—the eyes, the jaws and teeth, the howl. After the physical description, she shifts to what coyotes eat (everything, it seems), their intelligence, their ability to adapt. As you reread, mark the transitional points and underline topic sentences. Gradually the essay's skeleton will appear, much as an x-ray reveals human bone structure.

3. *Examine the Style*

You'll already have a sense of the style from the first reading. Now's the time to pin it down. Notice the selection of words. Pay close attention to the shapes and rhythms of sentences. Underline phrases that embody the tone. Huneven uses words that are common in almost everyone's vocabulary. Perhaps only two—*pericarp* and *trickster*—would send you to the dictionary. *Pericarp,* from botany, refers to the three layers that surround the seed in ripe fruit. *Trickster* has a special meaning in folklore: a supernatural figure that appears in many guises and engages in mischievous activities, usually considered a culture hero. In other words, it is adaptable and tough to control.

Huneven's language is crisp and vivid, but many of the sentences are lengthy:

> Over the years homeowners have complained of coyotes drinking from swimming pools, eating from outdoor pet bowls, of a big mangy coyote routinely sleeping on a back-porch chaise lounge, a coyote chasing a small dog through a doggy door and around the kitchen, a coyote tightrope walking down a fence rail, coyotes living in freeway landscaping, a coyote eating a poodle in public.

She expects her readers to concentrate, demanding that they exert the patience to follow the twists and turns of sentences that often seem as unpredictable as the coyote itself.

Huneven uses humor and irony, both hard to miss. She seems to draw a great deal of pleasure from knowing that an uncontrollable creature lives at the heart of our civilization. She personifies the coyote; that is, she gives it human qualities—it has a profession; it likes its leisure, using its "extra hours for courtship, mating and playing with his children." At times she suggests that the urban coyote leads a comfortable life similar to that of a 1980s Yuppie, a young, ambitious, and well-educated city dweller with a professional career and an affluent life-style. But she also gleefully reports that this Yuppie coyote will violate social decorum by "eating a poodle in public"—a nasty *hombre,* after all.

4. *Linger on Interesting Passages*

Stop your reading to examine passages that catch your attention. What's an interesting passage? That's a judgment call. Perhaps the passage will be rich in figurative language. Perhaps it will be an interestingly structured paragraph or series of paragraphs. Later, you might want to use it as a model to emulate in your writing practice.

In one passage that deserves some attention Huneven makes use of contrast and of hyperbole, the technique of dramatic exaggeration with which writers make a point.

> Most animals are specialized in their eating habits: cougars as carnivores, rodents as vegetarians. Coyotes are "specialized generalists," i.e., specialized to eat *everything*. Coyotes have no problem recognizing dinner—they'll eat anything from grasshoppers to grapefruit, coleslaw to carrion, mice to Minute Rice.

One writer who bracketed this passage used it as a model for practicing style. The result is the following paragraph:

> Most appointed officials specialize in one area of government: the Secretary of Defense on weapons, the Attorney General on law. Elected officials are "specialized generalists"; that is, specialized to speak on any subject. Senators and members of Congress are quick to pounce on all controversial issues—they'll speak on anything from abortion to prayer, peace to war, human rights to animal rights.

Of course, using passages from professional writers as models for practice comes later, after you've finished reading the essay.

5. *Record Your Closing Impressions*

Your impressions may be related to purpose, strategy, and style. They may also include your associations with the essay: Does it bring to mind any experiences you've had? Do you associate it with something you've learned or something you've seen or heard about? Does it stir a specific meaning in you? And, perhaps most important, does it call to mind any ideas you might like to explore in writing?

2

The Writing Process

The situation has changed. The writer–reader roles are reversed. You are no longer the reader. You are now the writer, in this case the essayist. The writer–reader contract still applies to the situation, but now you must meet the obligation you have to your reader, which is to compose an understandable work. You, in other words, will be using writing conventions to guide your reader, and your reader will rely on these conventions to decipher your essay. Bluntly, you, like every successful writer, must fulfill your half of the writer–reader contract—you must use what you have learned from reading with a critical eye.

Remember, essays are relatively brief nonfiction compositions. Essays concentrate on a single aspect of a topic. Effective essays always have well-defined purposes, use clear strategies to achieve their purpose, and employ an appropriate style. Sometimes essays, especially in college writing, integrate research, but usually they tend to be personal, embodying a writer's voice and analyzing or interpreting a subject from a writer's personal perspective. Keep in mind, however, that even though an essay embodies a writer's perspective, it is not necessarily about the writer. Instead, essays gain their personal character from the individual writer's insights and values as manifested in the discussion.

Although a writer may combine several rhetorical patterns in an essay (each discussed in a separate chapter in this text), one of nine common patterns will usually dominate the overall work, depending on the subject and the writer's approach.

1. *Narration* relates events. Narration shows what happened, when and where it took place, who was involved, and why it happened. (See Chapter 3.)
2. *Description* captures the sense of an experience. Description renders what something looks like, its characteristics, the impressions it makes. (See Chapter 4.)
3. *Examples* illustrate ideas. Examples offer typical cases and concrete instances to develop a point. (See Chapter 5.)
4. *Comparison and Contrast* presents similarities and differences. Comparison relates how something is like something else. Contrast relates how something is different from

26

something else. Combined, the pattern relates how two things are both alike and different. (See Chapter 6.)

5. *Cause and Effect* identifies reasons and results. Cause and effect explores why something happened, what the consequences are, how something is related to something else. (See Chapter 7.)

6. *Process Analysis* explains experience step by step. Process analysis shows how something happens, how it works, how it is made. (See Chapter 8.)

7. *Classification and Division* establishes categories. Classification and division sorts things by their common components and characteristics. (See Chapter 9.)

8. *Definition* limits meaning. Definition explains what something is, what it means, how it is alike and different from other members in its class. (See Chapter 10.)

9. *Persuasion and Argument* convinces readers. Persuasion and argument attempts to move people to action or to convince them to change their opinions. (See Chapter 11.)

Writers use rhetorical patterns to help them make writing choices. Imagine, for a moment, that you have been assigned an essay on advertising. Once you decide on your essay's purpose, you will then decide on which rhetorical pattern would best help to achieve the purpose; thus the pattern dominates the essay's development. For example, if your purpose is to relate consumer stories, you would choose narration. If your purpose is to reveal the subliminal messages in advertising images, you would choose description. If your purpose is to explain the similarities and differences between two advertising campaigns, you would choose comparison and contrast. Or if your purpose is to convince a reader that film directors should stop including "disguised" cigarette advertisements in movies, then you would choose argumentation. No matter which choice you make, your final essay will reflect the rhetorical conventions of the pattern you choose, thus helping the reader trace the development of the essay's central purpose.

Once you decide on a dominant rhetorical pattern and are

ready to write, you can employ another conventional essay strategy by structuring your essay with a clear introduction, discussion, and conclusion.

Introductions are composed of one or more paragraphs, all designed to introduce an essay's central purpose. An introduction should arouse a reader's curiosity, provide appropriate background information, and clarify any questions the reader might need answered to understand the central purpose. An introduction should also display the thesis, which is a clear, limited statement of the essay's general purpose. You might think of the thesis statement as a direct promise to a reader, a promise that clearly sets the course for the rest of the essay.

Discussions fulfill the promise made in the thesis. An essay's discussion should be several paragraphs in length, all organized by topic sentences that identify subpoints of the thesis statement. The topic sentences should also *echo* the thesis to show the promise is being fulfilled and to rivet the reader's attention to the essay's central purpose.

Conclusions bring an essay to a satisfactory close. At the very least, a conclusion should show that the promise made in the thesis statement has been fulfilled. One point to keep in mind: A conclusion should never apologize for covering the subject inadequately.

Typically, a college essay is between 500 and 1,500 words, but more appropriately the length should be determined by the complexity of the subject and the amount of detailed discussion necessary to support the thesis.

Please don't get the wrong impression. Effective essays are not as mechanically contrived as our brief description might suggest, a fact you can quickly substantiate by thumbing through several selections in this text. Our purpose here, before discussing the process involved in composing an essay, is to emphasize that writers employ a few common conventions to help them meet their part of the writer–reader contract. How well writers use those conventions depends on their skills.

Now, with this brief description in mind, study the following essay on one aspect of the topic *propaganda*. The student author Lane Williams has the following to say about his essay:

> For me composing an essay is a chaotic activity. Whenever I reread a final draft and it makes sense, I'm always surprised. The development of this essay was especially chaotic. I created it from my own ideas, class notes, and by looking at magazine and television advertisements.
>
> One major problem I had to overcome was to think about an essay in more complicated ways than I had been taught in high school where I learned to write five-paragraph essays. For this project I had too much information to fit into a simple five-paragraph structure, so I needed to work very hard at organization. But once I had all my material gathered, the central purpose emerged and the actual writing process began to organize itself. What is my purpose? I wanted to explain some ways advertisers use propaganda devices to trick us into spending our money. Clearly my essay had to define some important terms, but overall I knew the rhetorical pattern would be dominated by examples.

Now study Williams's essay. After reading the essay through once, reread it along with the marginal notes, which point out some of the conventional strategies Williams uses.

Title suggests subject—advertising

Who's Come a Long Way, Consumers?

Opens with a dramatic catalogue

No doubt you have seen advertisements such as these: A savings and loan company claiming that an investment in a retirement account is an investment in "the American way"; a food producer associating its cake mix with "motherhood"; a men's clothing manufacturer relating its *roughware* to "manhood." "The American way," "motherhood," and "manhood" are all abstract concepts that elicit emotional responses in our

Explains how
abstract
terms work

psyches. Many other concepts create a similar response: "liberty," "freedom," "constitutional rights," "free speech," "the democratic process," "the right to life," "freedom of choice." All these words suggest a virtue or quality most Americans hold dear. Sometimes their use is designed to trigger an unexamined response that bypasses intellectual analysis. Among people who manipulate this kind of language these virtue words are called glittering generalities. Glittering generalities are often used to gain unquestioned support for a cause or product. In fact, glittering generality is one among several potent propaganda devices.

glittering
generalities
named

Opening
sentence
sets up
propaganda
definition.

When most of us think of propaganda, we think of politicians or dictators, people who want to control the masses. We might even think of official or political lying. But propaganda does not have to be used to perpetuate lies. It can also be used for positive ends, such as moving people to protect endangered species or rain forests or voting rights. Nevertheless, whether in support of a good cause or a bad cause, the propagandist appeals to a target audience's emotion rather than to its powers of reason, unlike an educator who explores all sides of an issue. In other words, the propagandist works by tricking us, not by informing us.

Begins to define
propaganda
Introduces
Key word, "trick"

This paragraph
links propaganda
to advertising.
General purpose
begins to
emerge

For good or evil, propaganda pervades our daily lives, helping to shape our attitudes on thousands of subjects. Nowhere is the propagandist more active than in the advertising business. For example, why is investing in a retirement account an investment in "the American way?" Or how can buying a cake mix confirm a sense of "motherhood?" Or how can a feeling of "manhood" be gained

Ties back to glittering generalities

Thesis statement makes a promise to the reader. Reuses key word, "trick"

Topic sentence presents one subpoint of thesis.

Bandwagon briefly defined

Example 1

Example 2

This brief paragraph

from wearing a brand of clothes? When examined critically, these advertisements have no relationship between the service or product they offer and the glittering generalities associated with them. They are merely an advertiser's obvious attempts to manipulate consumers by appealing to emotion rather than to reason. Glittering generality is only one propaganda device. Advertisers use several other propaganda devices to trick consumers into buying their products.

Bandwagon is another technique advertisers use to trick consumers into buying their products. Through bandwagon, they urge people to buy a product because it is popular—that is, because everyone is doing it together. This call to "get on the bandwagon" appeals to the strong desire to join the crowd rather than be an outsider. A recent television advertisement for Plymouth's mini van uses bandwagon to motivate car buyers. The advertisement features a group of people working out in a gym. A message over the loudspeaker announces, "There is a Plymouth mini van parked in the street." The message is clear: If you want to be part of the crowd, buy a mini van. A recent magazine advertisement for Cuervo Gold tequila also makes use of bandwagon. The advertisement features sixteen young party people either sitting on the edge or standing in an empty swimming pool. They are clearly enjoying themselves, each holding a margarita and toasting the viewer outside the advertisement. Clearly, a Cuervo Gold party is fun. The message is that the consumer can join the party. How? Quite obviously, buy Cuervo Gold . . . and hop on the bandwagon.

The Cuervo Gold tequila advertisement also features a prominent television person-

links bandwagon discussion with next subpoint, testimonial

Brief definition of testimonial }

ality—Dennis Miller. Miller stands in the group's center and also holds a Cuervo margarita. His presence adds prestige to the product, suggesting that if Cuervo Gold is good enough for a celebrity like Dennis Miller, it certainly is good enough for the average consumer. The technique of using a celebrity to sell a product is called testimonial, another method advertisers use to entice consumers.

Opening sentence sets up a more detailed discussion of testimonial

}
↓

presents a catalogue of celebrities

Testimonial is a commonly used advertising ploy. Many celebrities from motion pictures, music, and sports lend (more accurately, sell) the use of their names to pitch products: music performer Michael Jackson for soft drinks, basketball star Michael Jordan for athletic shoes, former halfback and sports commentator O. J. Simpson for luggage, retired actress June Allyson for adult diapers, comedienne Martha Raye for denture cleaner, and, among advertising's more clever use of testimonial, former Jets quarterback Broadway Joe Namath for pantyhose. What do these celebrities know about the products they pitch? Probably very little, but advertisers bank on consumers being attracted to products because a celebrity claims to use it. The appeal is to emotion, not to reason.

This paragraph begins with a clear topic sentence and defines "Plain folks" with a brief comparison to testimonial

Another device advertisers use to trick consumers is plain folks. In one way plain folks is like testimonial. Both involve someone standing up to praise a product, urging consumers to rely on his or her word, not on sound evidence, to make a product decision. But whereas testimonial features a respected celebrity, plain folks features someone "just like ourselves" to promote confidence in a product. Often plain folks takes the form of a dentist praising a toothpaste or a friendly

Examples of "Common folks" who praise products.

neighbor recommending a brand of coffee or a Little League coach explaining that a detergent is powerful enough to remove grass stains. Of course what advertisers do not reveal is that these are all actors who are paid (just as celebrities are paid) to pitch the toothpaste, coffee, and detergent.

This opening sentence signals that the "plain folk" discussion will continue

An extended example

A recent advertisement for Solgar Vitamin Supplements features a potent use of the plain folks device. This advertisement features a young attractive working mother, who is obviously a single parent trying to make ends meet. In the middle of the advertisement, she stands behind her son, smiling with her arms wrapped around him in a protective embrace, and looks directly at the viewer. The son, about eight years old, is also smiling and holding on to his mother's arm. Both seem to be healthy and to care deeply for each other. Above the photograph is the phrase "First Things First," suggesting that loved ones come first. Below the photograph, the son is quoted as saying, "You're the most important thing to me, Mom. Please take care of yourself." Featured next to the comment is a bottle of Solgar vitamins. Implicitly, the average working mother and son are testifying to the power of Solgar Vitamins to maintain their health and their loving relationship.

Effective transition into next paragraph
Briefly defines transfer

Also at work in this Solgar advertisement and in most advertisements, for that matter, is another propaganda device called transfer. Through transfer advertisers attempt to lure consumers into buying their products by associating them with something consumers love, desire, or respect. No manufacturer uses transfer more effectively than Philip Morris, Inc. For over two decades

Example 1

Philip Morris has effectively transferred the desire for the rugged cowboy's outdoor life to smoking Marlboro cigarettes. Marlboro advertisements feature images of cowboys herding cattle or riding horses across open spaces. More recently, Marlboro has concentrated less on cowboys at work and more on equipment these Marlboro men use: worn boots, spurs, lariats, saddles—each item designed to remind the reader of a life spent on open prairies with snow capped mountains in the background. And, in case the consumer misses the point, Marlboro advertisements usually include the slogan, "Come to Marlboro Country." How can consumers reach "Marlboro Country?" By lighting up a Marlboro cigarette, of course, thus completing the transfer.

Opening sentence connects with previous discussion of transfer

Example 2 of transfer (echoes title)

Philip Morris also makes effective use of transfer in its Virginia Slims magazine campaign. Each advertisement features a beautiful woman staring boldly into the camera. Clearly, she is in charge of her life, the embodiment of the 1990s image of an independent woman. In a box placed in the corner of these advertisements is a contrasting image, a photograph of a woman from an earlier historical period serving a man. An ironic slogan links the two images, "You've come a long way, baby" (ironic because "baby" echoes sexism). Without much analysis the advertiser's ploy here is clear. Philip Morris hopes to entice women into smoking Virginia Slims by transferring a desire for personal independence to its product.

Conclusion opens with a "question"

Do these propaganda ploys work? Can advertisers actually trick unwary consumers into buying their products? When subjected to critical examination, propaganda seems to

*Emphasizes
Critical thinking*

*Echoes title
"A long way"*

*Ends with
a provocative
question*

be obvious perhaps even ludicrous . . . certainly too clumsy to allow any manufacturer to pick a consumer's pocket. But the power of propaganda is emotional. Advertisers use propaganda techniques to operate beneath the level of intellect where images and concepts are not subjected to critical analysis. They work through suggestion, association, image. They seduce and their seductions have taken advertisers "a long way." Why else would they use these propaganda tactics to trick consumers year after year and decade after decade?

Williams's essay is effectively executed. He has established a strong purpose and expressed it in a clear thesis statement, which serves as his promise to the reader. He develops an ample discussion section by arranging his information around subpoints of the thesis statement, thus fulfilling his promise. And his conclusion successfully brings the essay to a close. In other words, Williams has met his part of the writer–reader contract.

Let's now examine the process Williams and other writers follow to create their essays. We don't want to give you the impression that experienced writers sit down and write a perfect first draft—they don't. They struggle with subjects, shuffle rough notes, doodle with outlines, all in an effort to shape their material effectively into finished form. Generally, a finished essay unfolds according to a writer's unique composing methods—that is, the phases of the composing process that begin with finding a subject and end with a final draft.

Find a Subject

"What should I write about?" is an all too familiar question that often signals a writer is blocked. If you find yourself asking this question, you must immediately turn the question to your advantage. Instead of "What should I write about?" ask, "How can I find a subject to write about?" The rephrased question gives you direction. You can stop chewing the pencil eraser and go to work.

Here's how to start.

Begin by keeping this writing principle firmly in mind: You will write your best essays on subjects you know and care about. We urge you, therefore, to examine your own experience for subjects. Look at your interests, your work, your values, your leisure activities. Watch the news, a film, or a television show for ideas. Browse through a newspaper or magazine for subject possibilities. Any of these sources can give you plenty to write about.

You must pursue this search actively. Engage yourself in the process by picking up a pencil and going to work. Try one of the following strategies:

1. *Create idea lists.* Time management experts urge busy people to keep lists of commitments—action lists. Action lists begin as random collections of upcoming events, commitments, or tasks. Once the list is complete, the list maker evaluates the entries, ranks them, and establishes a work schedule. The list provides the person with some clarity and direction for his or her activities.

   An idea list like an action list helps to bring your activity into focus. In this case the activity is writing. You can use an idea list to compile possible writing topics. Begin by setting a minimum time limit—perhaps thirty, forty, sixty minutes—and stick to it. Your goal is to develop a *spontaneous* series of brief entries that capture your ideas and responses to them.

2. *Use a journal.* If you have kept a journal at anytime in your life, browse through it for ideas. There is always a good chance that if an entry engages your interest you can develop it into a full essay that will engage a reader's interest.

3. *Record from memory.* If a recent class discussion or lecture stimulated your curiosity or stirred a strong opinion you

hold, record the details you recall. Either the discussion or lecture could inspire an essay.

4. *Browse through current reading material.* Glance through a newspaper or magazine until a subject catches your attention, perhaps merely a headline or an article title. Jot down your responses. A response to an article can make an effective essay, especially if the article ignites a strong value you hold.

Often college writing is initiated by class assignments. At first, you might think an assignment makes the writing task simple, but it usually does not. In fact, an assigned task might be harder to complete than one you generate yourself. It might create a sense of false security by leading you to skip the exploration process and plunge directly into the first draft.

As a way of defending yourself from this mistake, remember a second writing principle: An assignment is not a subject. You must create a subject from the assignment.

For example, consider Lane Williams's essay. He wrote it in response to the following assignment: "In four to five typed pages, discuss the role of propaganda in political or commercial communication." To the experienced writer this assignment is much too large to be addressed successfully in a single essay. It must be placed in a more limited focus, reduced to a manageable subject. So instead of plunging into a first draft without exploring the assignment, he used the assignment wisely. Williams says,

> The assignment was just too broad to cover in a five-page essay. I would have to write about propaganda in politics and advertising. I immediately knew it had to be narrowed to manageable size so I decided to explore the assignment by writing an idea list. I knew if I listed enough of my interests I would eventually find something that would give me more direction.

Williams's idea list took the form of phrases capturing the flow of his thought. He put down whatever came to mind. Later he would judge the entries to see how they related.

Politicians and lying . . .
Campaign propaganda in the presidential race . . .
Local council members and land developers . . .
Advertisements and the consumer . . .
Why do people vote for politicians?
Why do people buy certain products?
How do advertisements get attention?
What propaganda techniques are effective in ads?
How can we protect ourselves from propaganda?
    In political decisions?
    In the marketplace?
I'm the victim of propaganda.
    In voting?
    In buying products?
What do advertisements reveal about consumers?
What does propaganda use reveal about politicians?
Propaganda undermines the democratic process.
Master propagandists—political "spin doctors."

Writing the list helped Williams place his subject in focus. Although no single entry represented a clear subject, he was able to combine several ideas to shape a general subject, the role of propaganda in advertising.

Use Prewriting Techniques to Explore a Subject

You, like all writers, must place your subject in focus and clarify your purpose, often a long and difficult process. The most effective way to start the process is by using prewriting techniques to discover what you know and do not know about the subject.

What is prewriting and how does it work?

Well, prewriting is easy to understand. But first, consider how some writers talk about the mind in relation to writing—a simplified view, but one that will help you understand the writing process.

When discussing how they compose their works, writers often talk of intuition and intellect. They associate intuition with creativity. The creative part of the mind generates ideas, events, and metaphors, the raw material that makes fresh, interesting writing. In contrast, they associate intellect with criticism. The critical part of the mind judges content, organization, and logic, the refined evaluation that makes accurate, coherent writing. Intuition fuels the creative process; intellect guides the critical process. Through the creative process writers *invent* their material; through the critical process they evaluate and organize it for readers.

Both creative and critical abilities are necessary to write successfully. The creative process, however, is less self-conscious than the critical process. As a consequence, prewriting activities use the creative process while restraining the more self-conscious critical process.

Freewriting

Freewriting, or brainstorming, is valuable during any phase of the writing process. Freewriting is a method of free association for generating ideas. Freewriting can help you frame a subject more accurately, generate material, clarify a purpose, and even develop a thesis. But perhaps its most important use is to start the actual writing process.

Once you have a subject, no matter how tentative, set aside some time for a writing session (as we advised you to do when compiling a memory list). While freewriting, abandon the urge to criticize yourself and let the creative process take over, especially if you have a little voice in your head that automatically judges your writing efforts.

To direct the process, write your subject at the top of the page. Then go at it. Write down everything that comes to mind. Associate one idea to another. Don't judge your ideas or shut them out. Often the unexpected will present itself, ideas connecting to ideas in ways you could have never planned. Don't be concerned with the technical aspects of writing—grammar, punctuation, sentence structure, or logic. Merely enter the creative flow of your own thought, excluding the critical process. Remember—this draft is for your eyes only, not for you reader's. It is a rough map of your thought process, a chart of your mental meanderings, not a paper to be criticized or graded. About his freewriting process, Lane Williams says,

> Freewriting helps me gain perspective on my subject. The process releases a great deal of information I have somehow stored in my memory. By free writing, that is, merely following the pattern of my thought, I gain access to that information. The hard part, of course, is sorting through all that I have written.

The examination of freewriting can be difficult. You will quickly discover that much of your freewriting will not help you develop an effective essay, such as obvious observations, clichéd thinking, dead-end ideas, stalled musings, odd digressions, but other parts will be valuable—"hot" ideas you can pursue. Evaluating the material in freewriting involves the intellect more directly; that is, now apply the "critical eye" to decide what material will help develop an effective paper and what will not.

While reading your prewritten draft, mark passages that seem to be hot leads for further exploration. Once you have the leads, you can use them to start another freewriting session to generate more new material.

Freewriting will also reveal what you do not know about a subject. This knowledge can direct your search to the library, to class notes, to discussions with relatives, friends, or teachers, to any number of sources that will be helpful. All these activities will help define a general purpose and generate material for your final essay.

Sort and Group Your Material

The freewriting is complete. Now is the time to sort and group your ideas in a logical arrangement. Here, one of two common strategies will help—clustering and informal outlining.

Clustering

Clustering visually shows the relationship between ideas. Often freewriting appears to create a hodgepodge of unrelated material, but if you rearrange the material around the central purpose that emerges from the free written draft, then you can begin to see connections. In one sense, a cluster brings order to the creative chaos.

Begin a cluster in a simple fashion. Write what you have determined to be your essay's purpose in the center of the page. Draw a circle around the purpose. As you examine the prewritten draft, arrange major ideas around the central purpose in "orbits" connected by lines. Also circle the major ideas. As you discover (or develop) ideas related to the major ideas, create another orbiting system. All this is done in single words or brief phrases. Remember you can always return to the prewritten draft to examine the full entry. Through this process, you are simply dividing and subdividing your roughly drafted material, becoming more specific as you isolate facts, opinions, examples, and specific details that could be used effectively to develop your purpose.

Here is a tip: Be prepared to create more than one cluster. Clustering, like freewriting, often generates even more material. We also suggest you develop your cluster on a large piece of drawing paper, or at least be prepared to tape several sheets of notebook paper together to accommodate all your material.

Lane Williams created a cluster from his prewritten material. Examine part of it reproduced on page 42.

Informal Outlining

The second approach to sorting and grouping your material involves arranging the major ideas related to your purpose under broad headings in an informal fashion. The complexity of the outline depends on how you like to work. It may include only the broadest heading or it may include broad headings followed by more specific points, even phrases that capture specific information.

You may create several drafts of informal outlines, each be-

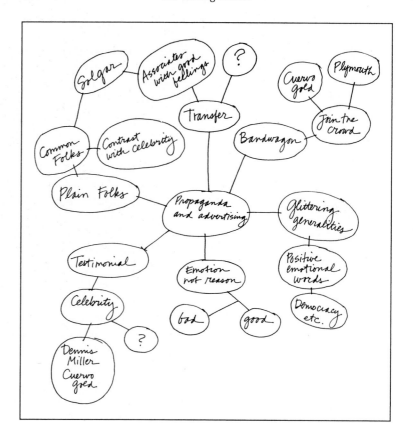

coming more specific. Gradually drafts of informal outlines may suggest your essay's final development pattern.

If you find yourself dissatisfied with your outlines, rather than spending a great deal of time rewriting them, photocopy them and then cut and paste the photocopies until you have one that satisfies you.

The following example shows part of the detailed informal outline Lane Williams developed from his cluster. About this informal outline Williams says,

Propaganda and advertising
What is it: appeals to emotion
  rather than reason.
  Use for good and bad causes.

Methods:
  ① Glittering Generalities: Positive words to
      stir strong values.
                    ⎧ "Motherhood"
  Develop a   ⎨ "Manhood"
  list of   ⎩ "American Way"
  G.G.

  ② Bandwagon: Invites consumers to
      join the crowd.
          Plymouth minivan — Health Club
          Cuervo gold — Yuppie crowd standing
             in an empty pool, drinking margaritas
  link to — Dennis Miller
  testimonial
  ③ Testimonial: Celebrities praise products
          Dennis Miller / Cuervo gold — two methods
          working together.
          Develop extensive list of celebrities .....
          include old Joe Namath ad for laughs.

I wasn't happy with just clustering. Eventually I have to develop a sense of my material as I imagine it will unfold in the essay. I'm not obsessed with detail or perfection at this stage of the writing process, but I do need to create a strong impression of how the development takes place. The cluster didn't give me the space to add the detail I wanted. For me, an informal outline is a strong preliminary plan that helps me to see where I need to delete information or develop more information.

Develop a Thesis Statement

Always keep in mind that any essay you write unfolds through a process. Although throughout this discussion we describe the writing process as if it follows a predictable pattern, in actual practice you will find it does not always do so. An essay evolves, often changing its direction as you encounter new information and uncover new relationships in your material. Nevertheless, if there is a point where an essay's final direction and shape become clear, it is at the point where you form a clear thesis statement.

A thesis statement embodies your essay's central purpose. It is the statement that all the following paragraphs support, argue for, or illustrate. The thesis statement should be broad enough to serve as an umbrella for the discussion that follows it while at the same time it should limit the discussion to a manageable size. In other words, the thesis statement marks the territory of the essay.

Pause for a moment to consider how useful a clearly stated thesis statement is for writers and readers.

For writers, a thesis statement articulates the central purpose and keeps the essay unified. Once you have a clear thesis statement, you will find it easier to make decisions about what to include and exclude. If you have trouble developing your thesis statement, then you know you must seek more information to flesh out your content.

For readers, a thesis statement tells where the essay is headed. A clearly phrased thesis statement helps them put your discussion paragraphs in perspective. Imagine the burden you place on a reader if you develop several paragraphs but fail to provide the perspective to understand their purpose. A thesis statement provides that perspective.

What are the characteristics of an effective thesis statement?

An effective thesis statement, usually expressed in a single sentence, limits the central purpose of your essay. If you were writing about crime, for example, and tried to develop this thesis statement, "Crime is destroying the social fabric of America," you would soon discover the impossibility of your task. This thesis statement is much too broad for a three-or four-page essay. At best you could only develop a few general—very general—observations, all unsupported by specific detail.

This thesis statement could be limited, however. Writers limit their thesis statements in two ways. First, they limit the subject. As it now stands, the subject of this thesis statement is "crime." But "crime" covers a large territory—murder, robbery, swindles, shoplifting, and so on. If the writer was to concentrate on one aspect of crime, then the subject would be limited. For example, "Violent crime is destroying the social fabric of America" or "Gang crime is destroying the social fabric of America" or "Crime against children is destroying the social fabric of America."

These thesis statements are still too broad, much too broad for a brief essay even though the subjects are now narrow. Another way to limit a thesis is to narrow the predicate part, in this example the part that reads "is destroying the social fabric of America." "The social fabric of America" covers a great deal of territory, but if the writer were to write about his or her direct experience, this might be narrowed to a city, town, or neighborhood. After narrowing the predicate part, the thesis statement might read, "Violent crime is destroying the social fabric of my neighborhood" or "Gang crime is destroying the social fabric of my hometown" or "Crime against children is destroying the social fabric of schools."

These thesis statements are now manageable. A writer could develop them from personal observation, police reports, and newspaper articles.

An effective thesis statement is always stated precisely and lends itself to development. Vague language and overly general assertions misguide your reader. Use precise language, not fuzzy words, to phrase your thesis statement.

Not: The study of people in prisons is fascinating.

But: Psychological studies of imprisoned murderers reveal that the death penalty is no deterrent to killers.

The second example, phrased precisely in specific language, leaves no room for the reader to be confused about the purpose of this paper.

Finally, an effective thesis statement makes a promise to the reader to fulfill the essay's purpose, a promise the writer must keep or risk writing an unsuccessful essay.

For example, consider the following three thesis statements:

If a thug has the firepower, holding up a mom and pop grocery store is a simple process.

The promise: to explain the easy process of robbing the innocent.

Although there were over 450 arrests in my neighborhood last year, crime can be categorized into three groups.

The promise: to classify local crime.

Some people think the political buzz phrase "law and order" has something to do with putting criminals behind bars, but in reality it has a racist definition.

The promise: to redefine the political phrase "law and order."

Lane Williams developed his thesis statement in several phases. He says,

By the time I had finished freewriting and grouping my material, I had a pretty clear idea of my general purpose. I wanted to expose how some advertisers misguide consumers. After I developed more material by reviewing class notes and finding some typical advertisements, I decided it was time to formulate a more specific purpose, that is, a thesis statement that would keep me on track.

I began with this statement: "The public needs to become aware of how advertisers deceive them." Sounds lame, doesn't it? At least that's what I thought. Just too vague. I rephrased it: "The public needs to know how advertisers use propaganda to deceive them." I didn't like this either. What was I, the public guardian? Mr. District Attorney? The statement made me feel pretentious. But when I had written the word "propaganda," my mind started firing. The assignment called for a discussion of propaganda so the word had to be in my thesis. Moreover, the word stirred up my anger. I hate to be tricked by people, and bottom line, that's what advertisers do—they trick people. So now I was on to my thesis, which finally became "Advertisers use propaganda devices to trick consumers into buying their products." I wasn't sure this statement would be phrased this way in my final draft, but I knew it would help me arrange my paper—and announce what to expect to the reader.

Develop a Formal Plan with a Reader in Mind

If you have not done so already, now is the time to imagine your reader. The reader you conceive in your imagination will influence choices you make about the content and vocabulary of your essay. If you were separately to report the events at an accident scene to a friend, your parents, a police officer, an insurance agent, or as a witness in court you would select different details and words for each occasion. In speech you make this adjustment quite easily. In writing you have to give this adjustment some thought. It is essential, therefore, that before you get too far into the writing process, you imagine who your reader will be so you can determine how much he or she might already know about your subject, which will help you decide what to include and exclude.

For example, although Lane Williams was writing a paper for a critical thinking course, he decided his reader would be the "average consumer," one who did not know the meaning of propaganda and would not understand the way advertisers use it. This decision and the formulation of his thesis statement meant that he was ready to develop a more formal plan for his essay.

One method to plan your essay is to create a formal outline. Whereas an informal outline will help you sort and group pre-writing around ideas, a formal outline will help you see the final arrangement of the material. A formal outline will include the thesis statement, the subpoints, and various levels of detail depending on the subject's complexity.

A formal outline can be written in topic or sentence form. The main items will be identified by roman numerals, the first sublevel of items by capital letters, the second sublevel by arabic numerals, the third sublevel by lowercase letters, the fourth sublevel by arabic numerals enclosed in parentheses, and the fifth sublevel by lowercase letters enclosed in parentheses. All letters and numbers at the same level are indented to fall directly under one another.

I. _____
   A. _____
   B. _____
      1. _____
      2. _____
         a. _____
         b. _____
            (1) _____
            (2) _____
               (a) _____
               (b) _____
II. _____

You will rarely need all six levels, especially for college essays. But notice that each level is a division of the level above it. Therefore, there must be two items at every level because, logically, a topic cannot be divided into one item. You cannot have an A without a B or a 1 without a 2, for example. Of course, there may be more than two items at any level.

Also keep in mind that all items at the same level must be expressed in parallel grammatical structure and the first word in each item must be capitalized. The following example is a formal topic outline for "Who's Come a Long Way, Consumers?" Thesis: Advertisers use propaganda devices to trick consumers into buying their products.

I. Propaganda appeals to emotion not reason
  A. Glittering generalities
  B. Good and bad propaganda
  C. Advertisers and propaganda

II. Bandwagon says join the crowd
  A. Plymouth mini van
  B. Cuervo Gold and bandwagon

III. Testimonial features celebrities
  A. Cuervo Gold and Dennis Miller
  B. All-star list
    1. Michael Jackson for soft drink
    2. Michael Jordan for shoes
    3. O. J. Simpson for luggage
    4. June Allyson for diapers
    5. Martha Raye for denture cleaner
    6. Joe Namath for pantyhose

IV. Plain folks features the common people
  A. Common folks list
    1. Dentist for toothpaste
    2. Neighbor for coffee
    3. Coach for detergent
  B. Solgar Vitamin Supplements

V. Transfer associates with good feelings
  A. Marlboro cigarettes and the outdoors
    1. Cowboys
    2. Western gear
  B. Virginia Slims and female independence
    1. Today's woman
    2. Yesterday's woman

VI. Advertising works

Developing a formal outline forces you to arrange your material for a reader. Throughout the process of constructing a formal outline, you will draw on the informal outline you constructed earlier, your prewritten material, and any other material you collected. About his outlining process, Williams says,

> This is the first outline I have written. Before I finished I had my first outline, prewriting, class notes, and the advertisements I planned to use as examples in a pile on my desk. I kept moving through the material, thinking how it should be arranged. I ended up with some surprises.
>
> For instance, I had planned to use glittering generalities as the topic for a discussion paragraph, but while outlining, I realized I didn't have enough material for a full discussion. As a result, I used it in the introduction.
>
> I decided to discuss transfer last because I thought my readers would be familiar with the Marlboro and Virginia Slims advertisements and I also found them to be the most interesting.
>
> All in all, I discovered that writing a formal outline forced me to think through the actual essay before I started my first full draft. Looking back on the experience, I believe it saved me time overall.

Too often beginning writers want to skip formal planning, yet it is an important part of the writing process, one that will force you to figure out the final arrangement of your material.

Develop Parts of the Essay

At this point in the writing process you should be aware of your reader and the conventions you will use to guide your reader. In other words, you are consciously trying to meet the writer–reader contract by seeing and shaping your material with a "critical eye."

To start, reread the final draft of Lane Williams's essay (pp. 29–35). Study how the material from his formal plan was developed into a full essay. Clearly, his initial strategy was to arrange his material in a traditional fashion—that is, to structure his essay with a clear introduction, discussion, and conclusion.

Write the Introduction

The introduction presents the thesis statement. Actually, "presents" is not dramatic enough. Let's say the introduction "showcases" a thesis statement, because to showcase is to display in a way the reader cannot miss. Remember your thesis statement is your promise to the reader. Don't let the reader miss the promise.

Also remember the introduction is your chance to grab the reader's interest, but too often student writers waste their introductions. They offer sweeping generalizations. They write aimless, dull comments. They end the sequence with an ill-phrased thesis statement. You should make your introductions do much more. Professional writers tend to use one of six strategies to begin their essays.

1. Relate a dramatic anecdote;
2. Expose a commonly held belief;
3. Present surprising facts and statistics;
4. Use a provocative quotation or question;
5. Create a dramatic narrative example;
6. Define a key term.

Any of these is an effective strategy to begin your essay—if it fits your purpose. That's the key to writing an effective introduction: It must grow from the essay's purpose and lead to the thesis statement.

Often introductions are only a paragraph long and end with the thesis statement. But an introduction can be one, two, three, or any number of paragraphs in length. We suggest, however, that it be no longer than a fifth of the length of your entire essay, a reasonable length which should be determined by the complexity of your purpose.

For example, the introduction Lane Williams wrote for his final draft of "Who Has Come a Long Way, Consumers?" is three paragraphs long and ends with the thesis statement. About his final introduction Williams says,

> I expected to write a single-paragraph introduction, a convention I had learned in high school. I imagined that introduction would formally define propaganda and end with the thesis statement that claimed advertisers use propaganda devices to trick consumers into buying their products.
>
> But while planning the introduction I saw I would have to cover too much territory. I would have had trouble making the leap from the general use of propaganda to advertising. So I decided to integrate my material on glittering generalities, which was skimpy anyway, into the introduction while preparing my reader for the thesis statement, which now comes after paragraph 3.

Whatever approach you choose for your introduction, remember it is an integral part of the essay. It should grow from your purpose, arouse a reader's interest, and showcase the thesis statement, usually by placing it in the closing sentences of the introduction.

Write the Discussion

The discussion develops the thesis statement. The discussion paragraphs present the subpoints and supporting detail necessary to convince your reader that the thesis statement is reasonable. In other words, the discussion keeps the promise implied in the thesis.

To be effective, discussion paragraphs should follow three paragraph conventions—they should be unified, coherent, and well developed.

Unity.   Discussion paragraphs are unified when the information they present is clearly related to the main idea in the paragraph, which some writers shape in the form of a topic sentence. For example, consider the following paragraph from Olivia Vlahos's *Human Beginnings*. Vlahos opens with a clearly stated topic sentence, "Nearly all living creatures manage some form of communication," and follows with a series of examples, each clearly related to the topic sentence.

Topic sentence sets a direction

Series of examples clearly relates to the main idea

Nearly all living creatures manage some form of communication. The dance patterns of bees in their hive help to point the way to distant flower fields or announce successful foraging. Male stickleback fish regularly swim upside-down to indicate outrage in a courtship contest. Male deer and lemurs mark territorial ownership by rubbing their own body secretions on boundary stones or trees. Everyone has seen a frightened dog put his tail between his legs and run in panic. We, too, use gestures, expressions, postures, and movement to give our words point.

Keep in mind also that the main idea or topic sentence is one step in fulfilling your promise to the reader. It identifies one subpoint of the thesis and supports that subpoint. For example, Lane Williams begins this process in his first discussion paragraph. He clearly relates his opening topic sentence to his thesis statement, which maintains that advertisers use propaganda devices to trick consumers into buying their products.

Williams' topic sentence establishes the subpoint "bandwagon".

Bandwagon is another technique advertisers use to trick consumers into buying their products. Through bandwagon, they urge people to buy a product because it is popular—that is, because everyone is doing it to-

Brief definition of "bandwagon"

gether. This call to "get on the bandwagon" appeals to the strong desire to join the crowd rather than be an outsider. A recent television advertisement for Plymouth's mini van uses bandwagon to motivate car buyers. The advertisement features a group of people working out in a gym. A message over the loudspeaker announces, "There is a Plymouth mini van parked in the street." The message is clear: If you want to be part of the crowd, buy a mini van. A recent magazine advertisement for Cuervo Gold tequila also makes use of bandwagon. The advertisement features sixteen young party people either sitting on the edge or standing in an empty swimming pool. They are clearly enjoying themselves, each holding a margarita and toasting the viewer outside the advertisement. Clearly, a Cuervo Gold party is fun. The message is that the consumer can join the party. How? Quite obviously, buy Cuervo Gold . . . and hop on the bandwagon.

Bandwagon example 1

Bandwagon example 2

While this paragraph is unified because the entire discussion relates to its topic sentence, it also adds to the overall unity of the essay because the topic sentence refers back to the thesis statement. Echoing the thesis statement in topic sentences is an effective strategy to use throughout an essay. The technique reminds the reader of your thesis and shows how the subpoints are connected.

Coherence.   Guide your readers smoothly and logically from one sentence to another. Don't let them stray from the direction you establish in the paragraph's opening. If they do stray, you risk losing their attention. When a paragraph flows smoothly and logically, the paragraph is coherent; that is, the main idea advances from sentence to sentence in a well-constructed verbal web.

You can create coherence in your paragraphs in three conventional ways.

1. By repeating and rephrasing key words and concepts;
2. By using pronouns to refer to key nouns in previous sentences;
3. By using transitional expressions that guide your reader through a paragraph.

Poet and novelist Erica Jong repeats a key word to create coherence in the following paragraph from "The Artist as House-wife." The paragraph's main idea deals with a poet's problem of creating a personal voice in her work. Jong then associates with *authenticity* in the second sentence. She then repeats or rephrases the key word *authenticity* throughout the paragraph.

Writer maintains Coherence by effectively repeating "Key word".

Rephrase this "Key idea"

The main problem of the poet is to raise a voice. We can suffer all kinds of kinks and flaws in a poet's work except lack of <u>authenticity</u>. <u>Authenticity</u> is a difficult thing to define, but roughly it has to do with our sense of the poet as a mensch, a human being, an author (with the accent on authority). Poets arrive at <u>authenticity</u> in very different ways. Each poet finds her own road by walking it—sometimes backward, sometimes at a trot. To achieve <u>authenticity</u> you have to know who you are and approximately why. You have to know yourself not only as defined by the roles you play but also as a creature with an inner life, a creature built around an inner darkness. Because women are always encouraged to see themselves as role players and helpers ("help-mate" as a synonym for "wife" is illuminating here), rather than as separate beings, they find it hard to grasp this <u>authentic sense of self</u>. They have too many easy cop-outs.

In the following paragraph, conservationist Cleveland Amory repeats a key noun—coyotes—and uses pronouns to refer back to it.

Coherence is created by the effective use of key nouns and their pronouns.

The <u>coyote's</u> only hope lies in his cleverness. And stories of <u>coyotes</u> outwitting hunters are legion. <u>Coyotes</u> will work in teams, alternately resting and running to escape dogs set upon <u>them</u>. <u>They</u> have even been known to jump on automobiles and flat cars to escape dogs. And <u>they</u> have also successfully resisted bombing. Lewis Nordyke reports that once when a favorite <u>coyote</u> haunt in Texas became a practice range for bombing, the <u>coyotes</u> left— temporarily. Soon <u>they</u> were back to investigate and found that the bombing kept people out. <u>They</u> decided to stay. Meanwhile, <u>they</u> learned the bombing schedule and avoided bombs.

Conscious and careful repetition of key words and ideas is a subtle way to keep a paragraph coherent. A more direct strategy is to use transitional words and phrases. In "Who's Come a Long Way, Consumers'?" Lane Williams uses overt transitions effectively in one paragraph.

Williams uses overt transitions to create coherence.

A recent advertisement for Solgar Vitamin Supplements features a potent use of the plain folks device. This advertisement features a young attractive working mother, who is obviously a single parent trying to make ends meet. <u>In the middle</u> of the advertisement, she stands behind her son, smiling with her arms wrapped around him in a protective embrace, and looks directly at the viewer. The son, about eight years old, is also smiling and holding on to his mother's arm. Both seem to be healthy and to care deeply for each other. Above the photograph is the phrase "First Things First," suggesting that loved ones come first. Below the photograph, the son is quoted as saying, "You're the most important thing to me, Mom. Please take care of yourself." Featured next to the comment is a bottle of Solgar vitamins. Implicitly, the average working mother and son are testifying to the power of Solgar Vitamins to maintain their health and their loving relationship.

No matter what strategy you use to create coherence, remember the purpose is to direct the reader's attention as he or she reads from sentence to sentence.

Development.   Beginning writers often ask the question, how long should a paragraph be? Paragraph length depends on several considerations: the complexity of material, the rhetorical method, and the length of preceding and following paragraphs. But most importantly, a paragraph should be developed enough to do justice to the main idea.

Well-developed paragraphs might contain examples, definitions, comparisons, causes, effects, facts, statistics—all presented in enough detail to make a paragraph several hundred words long, or a paragraph might serve as a transition between subpoints of a thesis statement and be only a sentence or two long. When a paragraph becomes exceptionally long, writers will often separate the material into two or more paragraphs to ease the reading process, even though the information amplifies the main idea in a single subpoint. For example, Williams breaks up several exceptionally long paragraphs in "Who's Come a Long Way, Consumers?" as the following example illustrates.

Topic sentence introduces transfer

Also at work in this Solgar advertisement and in most advertisements, for that matter, is another propaganda device called transfer. Through transfer advertisers attempt to lure consumers into buying their products by associating them with something consumers love, desire, or respect. No manufacturer uses transfer more effectively than Philip Morris, Inc. For over two decades Philip Morris has effectively transferred the desire for the rugged cowboy's outdoor life to smoking Marlboro cigarettes. Marlboro advertisements feature images of cowboys herding cattle or riding horses across open spaces. More recently, Marlboro has effectively transferred the desire for the rugged cowboy's outdoor life to smoking Marlboro cigarettes. Marlboro advertisements feature images of cowboys herding cattle or riding horses across open spaces. More recently, Marlboro has concentrated less on cowboys at work and more on equipment these Marlboro men use: worn boots, spurs, lariats, saddles—each item designed to remind the reader of a life spent on open prairies with snow-capped mountains in the background. And, in case the consumer misses the point, Marlboro advertisements usually include the slogan, "Come to Marlboro Country." How can consumers reach "Marlboro Country?" By lighting up a Marlboro cigarette, of course, thus completing the transfer.

Philip Morris also makes effective use of transfer in its Virginia Slims magazine campaign. Each advertisement features a beautiful woman staring boldly into the camera. Clearly, she is in charge of her life, the embodiment of the 1990s image of an independent woman. In a box placed in the corner of these advertisements is a contrasting image, a photograph of a woman from an earlier historical period serving a man. An ironic slogan links the two images, "You've come a long way, baby" (ironic because "baby" echoes

---

Marginal annotations:

First extended example of transfer.

Opening sentence continues the main idea

Second extended example of transfer

sexism). Without much analysis the advertiser's ploy here is clear. Philip Morris hopes
to entice women into smoking Virginia Slims
by transferring a desire for personal independence to its product.

In the opening sentence, Williams sets up the transition from
one paragraph to another by referring to the previous discussion
of Solgar Vitamin Supplements. He then develops the main paragraph idea with a brief definition of the transfer device. He follows
with the analysis to two extended examples to show transfer at
work in advertisements. But since the examples are long, he breaks
the paragraph into parts, yet both parts amplify a single main
idea—that is, advertisers use the transfer device to trick consumers. Williams is careful to begin the second paragraph with
an opening statement that clearly shows the discussion of transfer
is continuing, even though he has begun a new paragraph.

While composing an essay, you might discover that you need
more information to develop an effective paragraph. You have
three actions to take. First, you can return to your freewriting
draft for an idea. Second, you can actually develop more freewriting. Third, you can consult outside sources for more information. The process of inventing and acquiring material continues
until the final draft is complete.

Write the Conclusion

Too often beginning writers treat their conclusions in a per-
functory manner—a couple of general statements about the subject and a rapid "That's all, folks" to close. Experienced writers,
in contrast, use a different strategy based on the simple principle
that readers remember best what they read last. They, therefore,
treat their conclusions as a challenge, one that demands skill and
concentration. Generally, writers use one of four common strategies to close their essays:

1. They review the subpoints and restate the essay's thesis
   statement.

2. They recommend a course of action.
3. They offer a prediction based on the discussion.
4. They present an appropriate quotation or anecdote that leads a reader to reflect about the subject.

Keep in mind that a conclusion must flow logically from the essay. If it does not, it will merely seem tacked on.

Create a Title

Titles are not afterthoughts, a phrase hastily typed at the top of the page before rushing to class. A title actually begins the essay. Titles should suggest the general subject and serve as an invitation to read the essay.

The best time to compose a title is after you have written your essay. Only then will you know the complete content. The title should be brief but interesting and may be taken directly from the essay. Often, however, it will echo a thought that runs through the essay. About his title, "Who's Come a Long Way, Consumers?" Lane Williams says,

> I usually have a hard time thinking of titles, but if I reread the essay or parts of it enough, a title will eventually come to mind . . . persistence, I guess, is my method.
>
> The title "Who's Come a Long Way, Consumers?" is my way of reworking the Virginia Slims slogan. I hope it is read ironically, since my essay's purpose is to make unaware consumers conscious of ploys advertisers use to get their hard-earned cash.

So how should you proceed in composing a title? Well, we can offer no clear guidelines because the process involves more intuition than logic. But once you have a title follow this rule: Never underline or place quotation marks around your own title. Use quotation marks or underlining for other people's titles, not yours.

Revise Your Essay for Style and Clarity

Once you have a well-structured essay in hand, you can begin the revision process that will lead to the final draft. You might think each phase of the writing process refines the material for the final draft . . . and each does . . . but the final draft is the only part of the process your reader will see. We suggest, therefore, that you approach revision with care.

During the early phases of the composing process, we mentioned that you should imagine your reader. Now the reader becomes a major part of the process, as if he or she is sitting on your shoulder as you make revision decisions.

As you reread your essay with a eye toward revision, consider its style (see p. 22). Style, as you probably recall, has to do with work selection, sentence length and variety, and tone. For college papers, we suggest you employ a plain style that communicates your purpose clearly and directly. You should write in standard American English, which is taught in schools and used in mainstream magazines and newspapers. In most writing situations, standard English is appropriate.

Standard American English can be formal or informal. Informal writing is characterized by common expressions taken from spoken English and makes use of contractions such as "don't," "can't," "won't," and "could've," which are contractions of "do not," "cannot," "will not," and "could have." Formal written English seldom uses contractions and avoids other characteristics of informal writing, such as abbreviations and the personal point of view. About his style decision, Lane Williams says,

> I tried to conform to my instructor's view of English, which leans toward the formal. You may have noticed for instance that I avoided using some common abbreviations. I wrote out "television" and "advertisement" instead of using the more common "TV" and "ad." I also avoided using contractions, which helps create a more formal tone. I did, however, address my reader as "you" now and then and

used the personal pronouns "we" and "our" several times, decisions some instructors might discourage.

To further develop your sense of style, consult "A Guide to Editing and Revising Sentences" (pp. 683–708). We offer the Guide along with the following tips with the hope that they will help you meet your bargain with the reader.

Five Tips for Revision

1. Reread to see if your purpose is clear. Examine the thesis statement. Does it suggest a rhetorical pattern? Does it make a promise to the reader?
2. Reread to determine if your strategy is effective. Does your paper have an introduction, a discussion, and a conclusion? Have you organized your discussion paragraphs around topic sentences or main ideas? Do you use transitions to connect paragraphs?
3. Reread the discussion paragraphs. Are they clearly unified? Are they coherent? Are they adequately developed?
4. Reread for style. Have you selected words for accuracy? Are the sentences varied? Is the tone consistent?
5. Reread to correct technical errors. Is the grammar correct? Are punctuation marks used correctly? Is the spelling correct?

3

Narration

Relating Events

The Method

Once upon a time is the phrase that begins countless childhood narratives. *To narrate* is to tell a story. Our lives are full of stories, some exciting, some dull. These stories might be as brief as an anecdote—"A funny thing happened to me today while dissecting a frog in biology." They might seem as simple as a fairy tale, such as "Little Red Riding Hood," or as complex as a novel, such as James Joyce's *Ulysses*.

Narratives are so common in human experience that some psychologists have claimed that their patterns are etched on the human psyche, that people actually *need* stories. Absurd? It is difficult to imagine that some people might require stories in the same way as they require affection. One fact, though, is certain: effective narratives embody a few known characteristics, and good writers keep this fact in mind when composing their stories.

The most common of these characteristics is the **narrative effect**, or, as some writers call it, the "payoff." Readers want a payoff—a moral, an insight, a message, a point, or just good entertainment. Often the narrative effect will be subtle, nothing more than getting the reader to utter a soft "Aha!" Consider this narrative, a teaching tale from Zen Buddhist lore. At first glance, it may seem to lack a narrative effect.

> A man traveling across a field encountered a tiger. He fled, the tiger after him. Coming to a precipice, he caught hold of the root of a wild vine and swung himself down over the edge. The tiger sniffed at him from above. Trembling, the man looked down to where, far below, another tiger was waiting to eat him. Only the vine sustained him.
>
> Two mice, one white and one black, little by little started to gnaw away the vine. The man saw a luscious strawberry near him. Grasping the vine with one hand, he plucked the strawberry with the other. How sweet it tasted!

What is the payoff? is a fair question that every reader has the right to ask. Clearly the narrative effect the storyteller might wish to achieve is not spelled out; the story reveals no thesis. But it certainly has something to do with being involved in the present and, perhaps, not worrying about what can't be controlled. One student suggests that fear of the past (represented by the first tiger pacing above the man, who is a monk) or fear of the future (the second tiger pacing below the monk) should not interfere with our enjoyment of the present (the strawberry). But what about the mice? They're a detail that needs to be considered in any interpretation. Soon they will gnaw through the vine, sending the monk to his death. Perhaps the tale suggests that when death is imminent, life becomes inordinately sweet.

Why create a story to illustrate a point, you might ask, even one as brief as this Zen tale? Why not just hold up a finger, smile sagely, and directly state a purpose? "Do not let fear of the past or present interfere with your enjoyment of the moment" or "Enjoy life now, for death may be near." In other words, "Why all the mystery?"

Not all narratives are packed with hidden meanings or intended to provoke emotional responses. Many are factual reports, such as news reports or police reports, which simply recount events as they unfold, but narrative essays often deal with subjects that go beyond the limits of a report. Like the treasures in many children's tales, the purpose in many narratives—especially works of fiction such as tales, short stories, and novels—is therefore buried. In this way, the narrative essay offers its readers the opportunity to experience anything the storyteller has experienced—love, anger, fear, hate, prejudice, outrage, confusion, hope, disappointment—all the emotional states we encounter in life. The events, therefore, must be dramatized, not explained, thus recreating, rather than reporting, events: first you live through a string of related experiences and then you get the meaning—well, maybe you get the meaning.

Strategies

Because of the nature of narrative essays, the relationship between you and the storyteller is complex. Storytellers will entice you to use your imagination to re-create the story. You should join, not resist, a writer in this effort. If the effort fails, then you will not make the creative leap that allows a narrative essay to achieve its emotional effect. Even if the purpose behind a narrative essay seems murky after a first reading, trust that the writer who chooses narration as a dominant essay pattern will always keep an eye on the purpose, usually dramatizing rather than stating it.

Narrative Structure

Every storyteller knows that readers crave order, a sense of direction, movement. To meet this need, many narrative essays are divided in three parts:

1. The **opening.** The beginning sentences usually arouse your interest without giving away the outcome. The opening may suggest the purpose of the story about to unfold, but not reveal it.
2. The **body.** The story moves forward through scenes that dramatize the events, without explaining them, using such devices as description, dialogue, conflict, and suspense.
3. The **climax.** All stories should end with a memorable conclusion. Here in the story the purpose usually lurks just beneath the surface. An effective climax may send you back to the story so that you can study how all the parts fit together.

You will find that most effective narrative essays follow this loose pattern. You can usually count on a storyteller to establish a story's situation in the opening by providing information that answers these questions: Who? What? Where? and When? They will suggest a **conflict** as well. Consider this opening from Martin Gansberg's "Thirty-eight Who Saw Murder Didn't Call the Police."

For more than half an hour thirty-eight respectable, law-abiding citizens in Queens watched a killer stalk and stab a woman in three separate attacks in Kew Gardens.

Twice their chatter and the sudden glow of their bedroom lights interrupted him and frightened him off. Each time he returned, sought her out, and stabbed her again. Not one person telephoned the police during the assault; one witness called after the woman was dead.

That was two weeks ago today.

Whom does the situation involve? A murder victim, the murderer, and, most important, the "thirty-eight respectable, law-abiding citizens" who didn't call the police. What does the situation involve? Crime in the streets. Where did it take place? An area in Queens, a New York City borough. When did it happen? Two weeks before the date of the newspaper narrative. And the conflict? Gansberg clearly suggests a conflict related to social obligation—the indifference of the thirty-eight bystanders who fail to meet their legal and moral responsibility.

Point of View

Also in the opening of narrative essays, writers establish the **point of view**—that is, they reveal who is telling the story. As generally used in narrative essays, point of view is easy to understand. Stories are told either by a participant in the events (first-person point of view) or by a nonparticipant—third-person point of view.

Most often readers associate stories with the first-person point of view, which seems to give narrative essays authenticity: "I swear this is true—I was there! I lived it!" Often the events have directly affected the first-person storyteller in some emotional or intellectual way. At other times, the storyteller acts as a spectator, reporting events he or she saw others experience. In either case, first-person narratives usually are more subjective than third-person narratives. They embody the storyteller's attitudes throughout the essay, directly in overt statements or indirectly in style. Writers almost always establish the point of view in the first paragraph. Consider the opening paragraph in Flannery O'Connor's essay, "The King of Birds."

> When I was five, I had an experience that marked me for life. Pathé News sent a photographer from New York to Savannah to take a picture of a chicken of mine. This chicken, a buff Cochin Bantam, had the distinction of being able to walk either forward or backward. Her fame had spread through the press, and by the time she reached the attention of Pathé News, I suppose there was nowhere left for her to go—forward or backward. Shortly after that she died, as now seems fitting.

O'Connor's opening paragraph illustrates one more bit of advice we can give you when reading first-person narratives: watch for the storyteller's own perspective. Notice that O'Connor begins by relating the emotional effect of an event that took place when she was five, but the first and last sentences clearly indicate that she is writing from an adult's perspective, not a five-year-old's, thus adding complexity, perhaps even irony, to the tone.

A writer who uses the third-person point of view usually relates events as accurately, and sometimes objectively, as possible. As a nonparticipant, the third-person narrator develops the story from reports by others, much as a journalist collects information for a story. This approach doesn't mean a third-person narration lacks power or drama. It merely means that the storyteller is not part of the action. Consider the opening paragraph in Maxine Hong Kingston's brief narrative "The Wild Man of the Green Swamp."

> For eight months in 1975, residents on the edge of Green Swamp, Florida, had been reporting to the police that they had seen a Wild Man. When they stepped toward him, he made strange noises as in a foreign language and ran back into the saw grass. At first, authorities said the Wild Man was a mass hallucination. Maneating animals lived in the swamp, and a human being could hardly find a place to rest without sinking. Perhaps it was some kind of a bear the children had seen.

Kingston's point of view is clearly **objective**, even dispassionate. We don't want to leave you with the impression, though, that third-person narrations are always objective and dispassionate. Review the opening from Gansberg's "Thirty-eight Who Saw Murder Didn't Call the Police," presented above. Gansberg's attitude toward the "thirty-eight respectable, law-abiding citizens" who watched a killer stalk his victim is clearly **subjective** and very passionate.

Chronological and Psychological Time

Because narratives unfold in time, storytellers must arrange the events so that the connections between them are clear. As you begin to read a narrative, notice the writer's narrative arrangement: Are the events arranged according to **chronological time**; that is, in sequence as they happened, step by step? Or are they arranged according to **psychological time**; that is, the way in which events might be connected in memory, shifting back and forth in time while keeping a sense of forward movement?

The decision a writer makes about the arrangement of a narrative essay is often determined by the subject. A historical essay, such as a narrative about a battle, usually marches along in chronological time. But if the subject comes from personal experience then the essay may be arranged in psychological time, beginning *in medias res,* "in the middle of things," with an event that comes near the end of the actual chronology. This opening event can be highly dramatic, designed to keep you in suspense until the essay closes, when its purpose becomes clear.

Whichever arrangement the writer chooses, he or she is obliged to guide you through the story. While reading with a critical eye, you should, therefore, watch for transitions in time. They may be complete sentences designed to smooth your way from one event to another: "My social life began to crumble into pieces like a stale oatmeal cookie after we settled in Santa Fe." They may take the form of brief phrases: "Two weeks later," "Only one year ago," "Soon I was to learn." Or they may be single words that help a writer cut through time: "Now, Then," "Before, Today." Identifying the transitional tactics will help you follow the most complex narrative.

Scene and Summary

While crafting a narrative essay, the storyteller has two methods to use in presenting the events: **scene** and **summary**. You'll recognize scene because it directly portrays an event on the page. Like a scene in film or drama, a narrative-essay scene is played before your eyes. Summary is a synopsis of an event. It relates the high points but leaves out much of the specific detail that a scene usually includes. Many narratives include both scene and summary, with summary serving as the glue that holds the scenes together. It might help if you think of scene and summary as showing and telling: scene shows, summary tells. Consider this scene from a student's narrative that shows the writer's battle with fear:

> I stood paralyzed on the dock, my hands clenched and my knees locked tight. Bobby was flailing at the water, trying to pull himself to the overturned boat. He shouted for help, his voice rising to a shrill pitch and carrying beyond the boathouse and into the empty woods.
>
> I wanted to plunge into the lake, but my body would not unlock, and the horrible, empty spot in my mind threatened me like a black pit I might fall into. It was the water and all it symbolized—darkness, suffocation, a murky death.

The narrator presents this dramatic moment as if it were taking place before your eyes. He is showing it to you. Now compare this scene to a summarized version:

> When my brother Bobby overturned the rowboat and fell into the lake, I panicked. You see, I had almost drowned once in this very lake. The experience left me with the deep, irrational fear that if I ever swam in it again, I would be swallowed up. Although I knew he needed help, seeing Bobby flailing in the water paralyzed me.

Here the writer tells about the event. This summary lacks the immediacy of the scenic version, yet it, too, is effective. Whether a writer uses scene or summary, or both, depends on the effect he or she wishes to create. Often narrative essayists present the dramatic moments in scenes and use summary to move from scene to scene.

Narration in College Writing

Informal narration based on personal experience is a frequent assignment in college courses. In cultural anthropology or social psychology you may be assigned a narrative report that requires your own observations. In history you may be asked to write from imagination a narrative about a historical event from a historical figure's point of view. In English you may be assigned an informal narrative essay based on a personal experience that brought you some insight. More often, college writers work brief narrative passages into an essay with other dominant patterns. In such papers, narrative passages may be used to create an interesting opening or to illustrate a point. In either case, the narrative must have a clear structural purpose to justify its use, the events must be carefully arranged, and the point of view must be clear.

The following four paragraphs function as an introduction to an essay exploring the psychological implications of living in a hostile urban environment. Raymond Luu, who grew up in San Francisco, uses personal experience to develop his subject. He opens with this narrative passage to establish the essay's psychological **mood** and to suggest his purpose:

Opening sentence state Luu's purpose—his life is dominated by need for security." It also sets the point of view—first person.

I am beginning to feel as if my life is dominated by a need for security. I am not talking about the kind of security most people hope to achieve by retirement or the kind that comes from a trusting relationship. I am talking about the kind that comes from living in a dangerous world. My day begins at the

Luu clearly marks the transitions from the one narrative point to another: "My day begins," "before I leave for work," and "when I walk to my car."

bathroom sink. When I open a new bottle of mouthwash, I must pry loose a tight plastic shrink-wrap seal. This nuisance takes some time, but the seal is necessary so that a psychopath does not poison my mouthwash and kill me as I gargle.

Before I leave for work I switch on the burglar-alarm system that lets out a loud klaxon before informing the police whenever anyone passes through the perimeter of my house. The alarm is absolutely necessary because homes in my neighborhood have become piggy banks for drug addicts.

When I walk up to my car, I must deactivate the alarm system or it will shriek and the lights will begin to blink. If I did not have the alarm system, thieves would smash in the window and make off with my radio and CD player that cost me a week's pay.

He ends by driving home the narrative effect—there's no escape; he even dreams of security measures.

It is only 7:30 A.M., yet preoccupation with security measures has been at the center of my thought. This absorption will continue through the rest of the day, into the night, and even manifest itself in my dreams.

. . .

Luu's narrative passage is simple and direct. He concentrates on three moments in his morning to dramatize his need for security. He could have included a great deal more in this passage—rising from bed, showering, brushing his teeth, eating breakfast, and so on—but he selected only the details he needed to achieve the narrative effect: There is no escape from the dangers of a hostile world, not even in sleep.

Now read the narrative essays that follow. Apply the information you have acquired in this introduction. Identify each essay's structure: the opening, the body, and the climax. Is the essay arranged according to chronological or psychological time? What is the point of view, first person or third person? Mark the passages in which the author uses summary and scene. Remember, you are reading as a writer reads; you are reading to learn the craft of writing.

❧ Maya Angelou ❧

Maya Angelou's talents and accomplishments span many fields, but she is perhaps best known as the author of I Know Why the Caged Bird Sings *(1970), the first volume in her five-part autobiography, in which she recounts her childhood years living with her grandmother in Stamps, Arkansas. Born Marguerita Johnson in 1928, Angelou surmounted the hardships and disadvantages of her youth—raped at age eight, unwed mother at sixteen—to write a joyful account of her own life and to achieve distinction as a dancer, actress, director, poet, scriptwriter, civil-rights activist, and television writer and producer. She acted in the television series "Roots," and has written several television specials, including a BBC–TV documentary called* Trying to Make It Home *(1988). She has received numerous awards and honorary degrees for her accomplishments and her continued service to the cause of civil rights.*

Finishing School

This story describes a brief time in Maya Angelou's childhood in Arkansas, where she was sent to work in a white woman's house to learn "mid-Victorian values" as a black woman was supposed to know them. In the story, taken from I Know Why the Caged Bird Sings, *the author mixes chronological and psychological narrative to relate her growing awareness of the subtleties in white domination.*

Notice, as you read, how Maya Angelou's attitudes toward her employer, Mrs. Cullinan, change. What specific events occasion those changes?

TEACHING SUGGESTIONS

One possible lead-in to assigning this selection is to briefly discuss how much personal names matter: How do we feel when people mispronounce or forget our names? Do some names suggest personality or character traits? Do our names influence our behavior? Do the names parents select for children suggest (at least to the parents) qualities the parents want their children to have? Why are names so important? Such a discussion should help prepare students for reading Maya Angelou's narrative.

After students have read the story, discussion might turn to structure. Have students notice the careful and thorough attention the narrator gives to presenting background information: first, about herself in paragraphs 1 and 2, and then about Mrs. Cullinan, her house, and her family in paragraphs 3 through 12. After setting up this background, the narrator presents three brief incidents: the speckled-faced woman's suggestion that "Margaret" be shortened to "Mary," Mrs. Cullinan's first use of the name "Mary," and the climactic incident of Marguerita's breaking the china. Have students discuss the purposes of each. Finally, have them discuss how effective the last two paragraphs are.

MARGINAL NOTES

Paragraphs 1 and 2 set the stage for the narration by contrasting early training of white girls with that of black girls.

Recently a white woman from Texas, who would quickly describe herself as a liberal, asked me about my hometown. When I told her that in Stamps my grandmother had owned the only Negro general merchandise store since the turn of the century, she exclaimed, "Why, you were a debutante." Ridiculous and even ludicrous. But Negro girls in small Southern towns, whether pov-

1

74

"munching along": just getting by

"mid-Victorian values": values of middle-class respectability, which would include a high degree of class consciousness.

The physical description of Mrs. Cullinan, though brief, allows the reader to picture her quite accurately.

Students should notice the value attached to things and their names at Mrs. Cullinan's house, an ironic contrast to the way in which names of the servants are changed for convenience.

erty-stricken or just munching along on a few of life's necessities, were given as extensive and irrelevant preparations for adulthood as rich white girls shown in magazines. Admittedly the training was not the same. While white girls learned to waltz and sit gracefully with a tea cup balanced on their knees, we were lagging behind, learning the mid-Victorian values with very little money to indulge them. . . .

2 We were required to embroider and I had trunkfuls of colorful dishtowels, pillowcases, runners and handkerchiefs to my credit. I mastered the art of crocheting and tatting, and there was a lifetime's supply of dainty doilies that would never be used in sacheted dresser drawers. It went without saying that all girls could iron and wash, but the finer touches around the home, like setting a table with real silver, baking roasts and cooking vegetables without meat, had to be learned elsewhere. Usually at the source of those habits. During my tenth year, a white woman's kitchen became my finishing school.

3 Mrs. Viola Cullinan was a plump woman who lived in a three-bedroom house somewhere behind the post office. She was singularly unattractive until she smiled, and then the lines around her eyes and mouth which made her look perpetually dirty disappeared, and her face looked like the mask of an impish elf. She usually rested her smile until late afternoon when her women friends dropped in and Miss Glory, the cook, served them cold drinks on the closed-in porch.

4 The exactness of her house was inhuman. This glass went here and only here. That cup had its place and it was an act of impudent rebellion to place it anywhere else. At twelve o'clock the table was set. At 12:15 Mrs. Cullinan sat down to dinner (whether her husband had arrived or not). At 12:16 Miss Glory brought out the food.

5 It took me a week to learn the difference between a salad plate, a bread plate and a dessert plate.

6 Mrs. Cullinan kept up the tradition of her wealthy parents. She was from Virginia. Miss Glory, who was a descendant of slaves that had worked for the Cullinans, told me her history. She had married beneath her (according to Miss Glory). Her

husband's family hadn't had their money very long and what they had "didn't 'mount to much."

As ugly as she was, I thought privately, she was lucky to get   7
a husband above or beneath her station. But Miss Glory wouldn't let me say a thing against her mistress. She was very patient with me, however, over the housework. She explained the dishware, silverware and servants' bells. The large round bowl in which soup was served wasn't a soup bowl, it was a tureen. There were goblets, sherbet glasses, ice-cream glasses, wine glasses, green glass coffee cups with matching saucers, and water glasses. I had a glass to drink from, and it sat with Miss Glory's on a separate shelf from the others. Soup spoons, gravy boat, butter knives, salad forks and carving platter were additions to my vocabulary and in fact almost represented a new language. I was fascinated with the novelty, with the fluttering Mrs. Cullinan and her Alice-in-Wonderland house.

All mentions of Mr. Cullinan remark on his in-significance to the girl and even to Mrs. Cullinan.

Her husband remains, in my memory, undefined. I lumped   8
him with all the other white men that I had ever seen and tried not to see.

The next few paragraphs establish the girl's con-sideration and loyalty until Mrs. Cullinan does the unforgivable.

On our way home one evening, Miss Glory told me that Mrs.   9
Cullinan couldn't have children. She said that she was too delicate-boned. It was hard to imagine bones at all under those layers of fat. Miss Glory went on to say that the doctor had taken out all her lady organs. I reasoned that a pig's organs included the lungs, heart, and liver, so if Mrs. Cullinan was walking around without those essentials, it explained why she drank alcohol out of un-marked bottles. She was keeping herself embalmed.

When I spoke to Bailey about it, he agreed that I was right,   10
but he also informed me that Mr. Cullinan had two daughters by a colored lady and that I knew them very well. He added that the girls were the spitting image of their father. I was unable to remember what he looked like, although I had just left him a few hours before, but I thought of the Coleman girls. They were very light-skinned and certainly didn't look very much like their mother (no one ever mentioned Mr. Coleman).

My pity for Mrs. Cullinan preceded me the next morning like   11
the Cheshire cat's smile. Those girls, who could have been her daughters, were beautiful. They didn't have to straighten their

hair. Even when they were caught in the rain, their braids still hung down straight like tamed snakes. Their mouths were pouty little cupid's bows. Mrs. Cullinan didn't know what she missed. Or maybe she did. Poor Mrs. Cullinan.

For weeks after, I arrived early, left late and tried very hard 12 to make up for her barrenness. If she had her own children, she wouldn't have had to ask me to run a thousand errands from her back door to the back door of her friends. Poor old Mrs. Cullinan.

Then one evening Miss Glory told me to serve the ladies on 13 the porch. After I set the tray down and turned toward the kitchen, one of the women asked, "What's your name, girl?" It was the speckled-faced one. Mrs. Cullinan said, "She doesn't talk much. Her name's Margaret."

The suggestion of a name change in this incident is the turning point in the girl's sympathy for Mrs. Cullinan.

"Is she dumb?" 14

"No. As I understand it, she can talk when she wants to but 15 she's usually quiet as a little mouse. Aren't you, Margaret?"

I smiled at her. Poor thing. No organs and couldn't even 16 pronounce my name correctly.

"She's a sweet little thing, though." 17

"Well, that may be, but the name's too long. I'd never bother 18 myself. I'd call her Mary if I was you."

I fumed into the kitchen. That horrible woman would never 19 have the chance to call me Mary because if I was starving I'd never work for her. . . .

That evening I decided to write a poem on being white, fat, 20 old and without children. It was going to be a tragic ballad. I would have to watch her carefully to capture the essence of her loneliness and pain.

This incident illustrates Mrs. Cullinan's thoughtfulness about her white neighbors and her casual disregard of her black servants.

The very next day, she called me by the wrong name. Miss 21 Glory and I were washing up the lunch dishes when Mrs. Cullinan came to the doorway. "Mary?"

Miss Glory asked, "Who?" 22

Mrs. Cullinan, sagging a little, knew and I knew. "I want Mary 23 to go down to Mrs. Randall's and take her some soup. She's not been feeling well for a few days."

Miss Glory's face was a wonder to see. "You mean Margaret, 24 ma'am. Her name's Margaret."

"That's too long. She's Mary from now on. Heat that soup 25

from last night and put it in the china tureen and, Mary, I want you to carry it carefully."

Every person I knew had a hellish horror of being "called out of his name." It was a dangerous practice to call a Negro anything that could be loosely construed as insulting because of the centuries of their having been called niggers, jigs, dinges, blackbirds, crows, boots and spooks. 26

Miss Glory had a fleeting second of feeling sorry for me. Then as she handed me the hot tureen she said, "Don't mind, don't pay that no mind. Sticks and stones may break your bones, but words . . . You know, I been working for her for twenty years." 27

She held the back door open for me. "Twenty years. I wasn't much older than you. My name used to be Hallelujah. That's what Ma named me, but my mistress give me 'Glory,' and it stuck. I likes it better too." 28

I was in the little path that ran behind the houses when Miss Glory shouted, "It's shorter too." 29

For a few seconds it was a tossup over whether I would laugh (imagine being named Hallelujah) or cry (imagine letting some white woman rename you for her convenience). My anger saved me from either outburst. I had to quit the job, but the problem was going to be how to do it. Momma wouldn't allow me to quit for just any reason. 30

"She's a peach. That woman is a real peach." Mrs. Randall's maid was talking as she took the soup from me, and I wondered what her name used to be and what she answered to now. 31

For a week I looked into Mrs. Cullinan's face as she called me Mary. She ignored my coming late and leaving early. Miss Glory was a little annoyed because I had begun to leave egg yolk on the dishes and wasn't putting much heart in polishing the silver. I hoped that she would complain to our boss, but she didn't. 32

Then Bailey solved my dilemma. He had me describe the contents of the cupboard and the particular plates she liked best. Her favorite piece was a casserole shaped like a fish and the green glass coffee cups. I kept his instructions in mind, so on the next day when Miss Glory was hanging out clothes and I had again been told to serve the old biddies on the porch, I dropped the 33

This paragraph emphasizes how greatly names affect a sense of personal dignity.

Miss Glory's acceptance of her name change represents the older ways of accommodation. In contrast, the girl finds the name change intolerable and resolves to leave.

Two paragraphs of transition lead to the last incident.

The final incident, the result of a deliberate plan to get fired, once again reveals Mrs. Cullinan's values. It also illustrates Bailey's wise understanding of how vulnerable these values are.

The two short, last paragraphs, 39 and 40, close the narrative on a defiant and triumphant note.

empty serving tray. When I heard Mrs. Cullinan scream, "Mary!" I picked up the casserole and two of the green glass cups in readiness. As she rounded the kitchen door I let them fall on the tiled floor.

I could never absolutely describe to Bailey what happened 34 next, because each time I got to the part where she fell on the floor and screwed up her ugly face to cry, we burst out laughing. She actually wobbled around on the floor and picked up shards of the cups and cried, "Oh, Momma. Oh, dear Gawd. It's Mamma's china from Virginia. Oh, Momma, I sorry."

Miss Glory came running in from the yard and the women 35 from the porch crowded around. Miss Glory was almost as broken up as her mistress. "You mean to say she broke our Virginia dishes? What we gone do?"

Mrs. Cullinan cried louder. "That clumsy nigger. Clumsy little 36 black nigger."

Old speckled-face leaned down and asked, "Who did it, Viola? 37 Was it Mary? Who did it?"

Everything was happening so fast, I can't remember whether 38 her action preceded her words, but I know that Mrs. Cullinan said, "Her name's Margaret, goddamn it, her name's Margaret." And she threw a wedge of broken plate at me. It could have been the hysteria which put her aim off, but the flying crockery caught Miss Glory right over her ear and she started screaming.

I left the front door wide open so all the neighbors could 39 hear.

Mrs. Cullinan was right about one thing. My name wasn't 40 Mary.

Meaning and Purpose

1. The message you take from this selection will be influenced by your own experiences and attitudes. Think of an experience from your life, a movie or television program, reading, or knowledge

Possible Answers

Meaning and Purpose

1. Give students time to explore their experiences of being angered or humiliated when treated unfairly. Did they feel powerless? Did they seek revenge? Be sure they compare their experiences with Angelou's.
2. Before Mrs. Cullinan calls her Mary, Marguerita is critical but cooperative, and even sympathetic, about her inability to have children ("For weeks after I arrived early, left late and tried very hard to make up for her barrenness" [12]). After Mrs. Cullinan calls her Mary, Marguerita is justifiably angry and deliberately breaks precious dishes to take revenge and get herself fired.
3. Angelou wants readers to feel as she feels about Mrs. Cullinan. Angelou also gives information about how a young black girl was expected to be trained and what she had to deal with in the world of privileged whites.
4. Angelou's audience could be people of all colors who want to hear about her experiences and perhaps be made to think about how blacks were—and are—treated. They are people who want to understand why Angelou writes what she writes. Her readers are educated and aware.
5. Angelou says that blacks "had a hellish horror" of not being called by their correct names because of the abusive names they have been called for centuries. Even in calling her Margaret, Mrs. Cullinan doesn't use Angelou's correct name.
6. Glory accepted and even preferred having her name changed by whites, just as most blacks then were docile and submissive. Marguerita rebelled against being called Mary and would not

accept the role Glory accepted. The contrast between the two women emphasizes Angelou's point about names.

Strategy

1. The payoff for the reader is the lesson in how prejudice affects one young black girl, and, by extension, all minorities. The moral is that prejudice is evil and should be rebelled against.

2. The introduction recounts for readers first how Angelou gets into the story she tells (a white woman asked Angelou about her hometown and then made the remark about a "debutante" [1]). Then Angelou gives general information about the differences between how white and black girls were trained in domestic arts. The second paragraph has some details about what black girls learned and then gets Angelou into the setting of her narrative. After reading these two paragraphs, readers know something about the larger context for the story that begins in paragraph 3.

3. Obviously Angelou is telling this story from the perspective of an adult looking back on herself at age ten. Her memory is perhaps fuzzy because the events happened a long time ago, and they happened fast. Her credibility is not in question because an adult is usually a more reliable narrator than a child. Rather, her saying she can't remember exactly what happened is honest, and true to her adult perspective.

4. Some transitional phrases are: "On our way home one evening" (9); "For weeks after" (12); "That evening I decided" (20); "Then Bailey solved my dilemma" (33). These and others keep the story flowing through its chronological order.

5. The last sentence emphasizes that Mrs. Cullinan is in fact not right in most things she says about her young black servant, including her correct name, which is not Margaret. Mrs. Cullinan does not understand her own actions and Marguerita's feelings. The one thing she finally does understand—that Marguerita's name is not going to be Mary—is a victory for Marguerita. This sentence reminds readers of the differences

of others' experiences, which in some way parallels Marguerita's experience. In what ways was this experience similar and different?

2. How would you describe Marguerita's feelings about Mrs. Cullinan before Mrs. Cullinan calls her Mary, and then after? What actions or events does Angelou use in her narrative to show those feelings?

3. Do you think Angelou's primary purpose is to give information or to evoke emotion? Examine your own response to this selection as you decide. What words and sentences convince you of your choice?

4. How would you describe Angelou's intended audience? Does she expect that audience to be empathetic with the young black girl? How do you know?

5. What does Angelou reveal about the significance of being "called out of [one's] name" (26)?

6. Why do you think Angelou included the story about Hallelujah's name being changed to "Glory"?

Strategy

1. What is the payoff in this narrative essay—that is, the moral, point, or message?

2. The first two paragraphs in this selection serve as introduction to the narrative, which begins in the third paragraph. How does this introduction prepare you for the narrative?

3. In the last scene, how does Angelou's telling you she has trouble remembering exactly what happened affect the credibility of the narrative? How does this admission help establish point of view?

4. The entire narrative covers several weeks. List some of the transitional phrases that Angelou uses to help her readers follow the passage of time.

5. What significance has the last sentence? How does it pull the essay together and conclude it?

in training between white and black girls that Angelou talks about in her first two paragraphs.

Style

1. Paragraph 30 is a good example of Angelou's telling us Marguerita's thoughts. They reveal that Marguerita understands, even at age ten, the abuse and unfairness in Glory's not being called by her given name. And the thoughts show that Marguerita plans to get out of her job for good cause. Marguerita is shrewd and smarter than her employer.

2. a. The irony is that the white woman's kitchen could never teach Marguerita how to be a "debutante"; she also makes sure she is "finished" with this finishing school.

b. Marguerita would not expect to have a home herself in which she would use such fancy china and utensils or live the life-style that goes with them.

c. Mrs. Cullinan is melodramatic about her situation, and in fact is probably not lonely and in pain. Marguerita's sympathy is misdirected toward someone who cannot sympathize with her not wanting to be called Mary.

d. Mrs. Cullinan doesn't get the point at all about the broken dishes. She is disturbed only about losing something she valued that Marguerita scorned.

3. In paragraph 9, "She was keeping herself embalmed" refers, in a humorous and sad way, to Mrs. Cullinan's drinking habit. Marguerita's explanation of the habit fits the perspective of a ten-year-old. Paragraph 11 is a humorous description of what Marguerita thinks Mr. Cullinan's daughters must look like—beautiful and with straight hair, unlike herself. That Marguerita says "Poor Mrs. Cullinan" shows her naiveté, and the reader gets the benefit of the humor.

Style

1. Several times Angelou presents the thoughts of the young girl. In paragraph 16, after being called Margaret instead of Marguerita, the girl thinks "Poor thing. No organs and couldn't even pronounce my name correctly." Find other examples of Marguerita's thoughts and discuss what they tell us about her.

2. Irony describes our recognizing a reality different from the one that appears to us. It can be expressed in words that actually mean the opposite of what they say. Explain the irony in these items:

   a. "During my tenth year, a white woman's kitchen became my finishing school."

   b. The careful attention to lists of names Marguerita had to learn (soup spoons, gravy boat, butter knives, and so on).

   c. "I would have to watch her carefully to capture the essence of her loneliness and pain."

   d. Mrs. Cullinan's reaction to Marguerita's breaking the dishes.
   Can you find other ironies in the selection?

3. How does humor work in this essay? Find examples.

Writing Tasks

1. Consider whether you think Mrs. Cullinan has learned a lesson from Marguerita's actions at the end of the selection. Write a narrative essay about an event in which the "payoff " (moral, point) involves a subordinate or "weaker" person's taking revenge on an authority figure or "stronger" person. End your narrative so that the person in authority either learns a lesson or not, according to whether or not you think Mrs. Cullinan does.

2. Write an essay expressing your feelings about the way in which Marguerita deals with prejudice. Before writing, consider these questions and others of your own: What choices do you think Marguerita had? Was she naive to empathize with Mrs. Cullinan's lack of children? Is Mrs. Cullinan merely a product of her culture's attitudes toward blacks? What responsibility do you think she has for what happens in the final scene?

❦ George Orwell ❦

George Orwell is the pen name of Eric Arthur Blair, who was born in Bengal, India, the son of a British civil servant. At age four, he was sent to England, where he attended prestigious schools, but before finishing his university education he returned to India to serve in the British Imperial Police in Burma. Already scornful of British high society, he was soon disillusioned with imperialism as well. He returned to Europe in 1927 to spend several impoverished years in Paris and London before his writing began to bring him financial and critical rewards. His experience living among and writing about the poor workers and coal miners in urban northwest England confirmed his political stand as a socialist, which led him to fight in the Spanish Civil War against the fascists. Many of his essays and his nonfiction works relate in narrative form the first-hand experiences that shaped his political views, and in his best-known novels, Animal Farm *(1945) and* 1984 *(1949), he uses fiction to elaborate the dangers of totalitarianism.*

TEACHING SUGGESTIONS

The simplicity and subject of this essay will appeal to most students. After they discuss the idea of the essay—what it says about executions and their effect on those involved—you can profitably turn to Orwell's style of presentation. Understated, matter of fact, but rich in descriptive detail—it is a good example of the power of words to create vivid images in our minds. Ask students to notice the ease with which each scene can be visualized, as if they were watching a movie.

A Hanging

In "A Hanging," Orwell uses a simple story to examine the complexity of his personal involvement in the British imperialistic occupation of India early in the twentieth century. Taken from the collection, Shooting an Elephant and Other Essays *(1950), it is a straight chronological narrative that conveys Orwell's deep sympathy for the oppressed in society.*

   Notice the simplicity and understatement of Orwell's language and how it contrasts with the enormity of the event it describes. Notice, too, how this contrast emphasizes and dramatizes that event.

MARGINAL NOTES

Like a movie camera moving from a long shot, to a medium shot, to a close-up, Orwell begins with the jail yard, moves to the row of cells, and finally comes to the description of a prisoner, the one to be executed today.

It was in Burma, a sodden morning of the rains. A sickly light, like yellow tinfoil, was slanting over the high walls into the jail yard. We were waiting outside the condemned cells, a row of sheds fronted with double bars, like small animal cages. Each cell measured about ten feet by ten and was quite bare within 1

82

except for a plank bed and a pot for drinking water. In some of them brown, silent men were squatting at the inner bars, with their blankets draped round them. These were the condemned men, due to be hanged within the next week or two.

One prisoner had been brought out of his cell. He was a Hindu, a puny wisp of a man, with a shaven head and vague liquid eyes. He had a thick, sprouting mustache, absurdly too big for his body, rather like the mustache of a comic man on the films. Six tall Indian warders were guarding him and getting him ready for the gallows. Two of them stood by with rifles and fixed bayonets, while the others handcuffed him, passed a chain through his handcuffs and fixed it to their belts, and lashed his arms tight to his sides. They crowded very close about him, with their hands always on him in a careful, caressing grip, as though all the while feeling him to make sure he was there. It was like men handling a fish which is still alive and may jump back into the water. But he stood quite unresisting, yielding his arms limply to the ropes, as though he hardly noticed what was happening.

The bugle call and the superintendent's voice get the narration under way.

Eight o'clock struck and a bugle call, desolately thin in the wet air, floated from the distant barracks. The superintendent of the jail, who was standing apart from the rest of us, moodily prodding the gravel with his stick, raised his head at the sound. He was an army doctor, with a grey toothbrush mustache and a gruff voice. "For God's sake, hurry up, Francis," he said irritably. "The man ought to have been dead by this time. Aren't you ready yet?"

"Dravidian": a speaker of one of a family of languages used in southern India.

Francis, the head jailer, a fat Dravidian in a white drill suit and gold spectacles, waved his black hand. "Yes sir, yes sir," he bubbled. "All iss satisfactorily prepared. The hangman iss waiting. We shall proceed."

"Well, quick march, then. The prisoners can't get their breakfast till this job's over."

We set out for the gallows. Two warders marched on either side of the prisoner, with their rifles at the slope; two others marched close against him, gripping him by arm and shoulder, as though at once pushing and supporting him. The rest of us, magistrates and the like, followed behind. Suddenly, when we

The dog's natural behavior contrasts sharply with the official military solemnity of the march to the gallows. His picking the prisoner for a special greeting links the man and the dog and reminds all of the prisoner's human worth.

"pariah": literally a drum beater; now a member of any oppressed social class, particularly in India. The dog is of mixed breed, probably unkempt, perhaps a stray.

The prisoner's natural movements and his sidestepping the puddle lead the narrator to thoughts on the wrongness of taking a human life.

had gone ten yards, the procession stopped short without any order or warning. A dreadful thing had happened—a dog, come goodness knows whence, had appeared in the yard. It came bounding among us with a loud volley of barks and leapt around us wagging its whole body, wild with glee at finding so many human beings together. It was a large woolly dog, half Airedale, half pariah. For a moment it pranced around us, and then, before anyone could stop it, it had made a dash for the prisoner, and jumping up tried to lick his face. Everybody stood aghast, too taken aback even to grab the dog.

"Who let that bloody brute in here?" said the superintendent angrily. "Catch it, someone!"   7

A warder detached from the escort, charged clumsily after the dog, but it danced and gambolled just out of his reach, taking everything as part of the game. A young Eurasian jailer picked up a handful of gravel and tried to stone the dog away, but it dodged the stones and came after us again. Its yaps echoed from the jail walls. The prisoner, in the grasp of the two warders, looked on incuriously, as though this was another formality of the hanging. It was several minutes before someone managed to catch the dog. Then we put my handkerchief through its collar and moved off once more, with the dog still straining and whimpering.   8

It was about forty yards to the gallows. I watched the bare brown back of the prisoner marching in front of me. He walked clumsily with his bound arms, but quite steadily, with that bobbing gait of the Indian who never straightens his knees. At each step his muscles slid neatly into place, the lock of hair on his scalp danced up and down, his feet printed themselves on the wet gravel. And once, in spite of the men who gripped him by each shoulder, he stepped lightly aside to avoid a puddle on the path.   9

It is curious; but till that moment I had never realized what it means to destroy a healthy, conscious man. When I saw the prisoner step aside to avoid the puddle, I saw the mystery, the unspeakable wrongness, of cutting a life short when it is in full tide. This man was not dying, he was alive just as we are alive. All the organs of his body were working—bowels digesting food,   10 skin renewing itself, nails growing, tissues forming—all toiling away in solemn foolery. His nails would still be growing when he stood on the drop, when he was falling through the air with a tenth-of-a-second to live. His eyes saw the yellow gravel and the grey walls, and his brain still remembered, foresaw, reasoned—even about puddles. He and we were a party of men walking together, seeing, hearing, feeling, understanding the same world; and in two minutes, with a sudden snap, one of us would be gone—one mind less, one world less.

Orwell returns to objective description following the meditative thoughts in the preceding paragraph.

The gallows stood in a small yard, separate from the main grounds of the prison, and overgrown with tall prickly weeds. It was a brick erection like three sides of a shed, with planking on top, and above that two beams and a crossbar with the rope dangling. The hangman, a greyhaired convict in the white uniform of the prison, was waiting beside his machine. He greeted us with a servile crouch as we entered. At a word from Francis the two warders, gripping the prisoner more closely than ever, half led, half pushed him to the gallows and helped him clumsily up the ladder. Then the hangman climbed up and fixed the rope around the prisoner's neck.   11

We stood waiting, five yards away. The warders had formed in a rough circle round the gallows. And then, when the noose was fixed, the prisoner began crying out to his god. It was a high, reiterated cry of "Ram! Ram! Ram! Ram!" not urgent and fearful like a prayer or cry for help, but steady, rhythmical, almost like the tolling of a bell. The dog answered the sound with a whine. The hangman, still standing on the gallows, produced a small cotton bag like a flour bag and drew it down over the prisoner's face. But the sound, muffled by the cloth, still persisted, over and over again: "Ram! Ram! Ram! Ram! Ram!"   12

"Ram": Rama, an incarnation of the Hindu god Vishnu, the Preserver.

The hangman climbed down and stood ready, holding the lever. Minutes seemed to pass. The steady, muffled crying from the prisoner went on and on, "Ram! Ram! Ram!" never faltering for an instant. The superintendent, his head on his chest, was slowly poking the ground with his stick; perhaps he was counting the cries, allowing the prisoner a fixed number—fifty, perhaps, or a hundred. Everyone had changed colour. The Indians had   13 gone grey like bad coffee, and one or two of the bayonets were wavering. We looked at the lashed, hooded man on the drop, and listened to his cries—each cry another second of life; the same thought was in all our minds; oh, kill him quickly, get it over, stop that abominable noise!

Suddenly the superintendent made up his mind. Throwing up his head he made a swift motion with his stick. "Chalo!" he shouted almost fiercely.

"Chalo": Hindu; a command to let the prisoner drop through the gallows.

There was a clanking noise, and then dead silence. The prisoner had vanished, and the rope was twisting on itself. I let go of the dog, and it galloped immediately to the back of the gallows; but when it got there it stopped short, barked, and then retreated into a corner of the yard, where it stood among the weeds, looking timorously out at us. We went round the gallows to inspect the prisoner's body. He was dangling with his toes pointed straight downwards, very slowly revolving, as dead as a stone.

The superintendent reached out with his stick and poked the bare brown body; it oscillated slightly. "*He's* all right," said the superintendent. He backed out from under the gallows, and blew out a deep breath. The moody look had gone out of his face quite suddenly. He glanced at his wrist-watch. "Eight minutes past eight. Well, that's all for this morning, thank God."

The execution completed, the men turn to other activities, with exaggerated alacrity to relieve the tension.

The warders unfixed bayonets and marched away. The dog, sobered and conscious of having misbehaved itself, slipped after them. We walked out of the gallows yard, past the condemned cells with their waiting prisoners, into the big central yard of the prison. The convicts, under the command of warders armed with lathis, were already receiving their breakfast. They squatted in long rows, each man holding a tin pannikin, while two warders with buckets marched around ladling out rice; it seemed quite a homely, jolly scene, after the hanging. An enormous relief had come upon us now that the job was done. One felt an impulse to sing, to break into a run, to snigger. All at once everyone began chattering gaily.

"lathis": wooden police sticks.
"pannikin": a metal cup or dish.

The Eurasian boy walking beside me nodded towards the way we had come, with a knowing smile: "Do you know, sir, our friend (he meant the dead man) when he heard his appeal had

"boxwallah": a jewelry-box merchant.

been dismissed, he pissed on the floor of his cell. From fright. Kindly take one of my cigarettes, sir. Do you not admire my new silver case, sir? From the boxwallah, two rupees eight annas. Classy European style."

Several people laughed—at what, nobody seemed certain. 19

Francis was walking by the superintendent, talking gar- 20
rulously: "Well, sir, all has passed off with the utmost satisfactoriness. It was all finished—flick! Like that. It iss not always so—oah, no! I have known cases where the doctor was obliged to go beneath the gallows and pull the prissoner's legs to ensure decease. Most disagreeable!"

"Wriggling about, eh? That's bad," said the superintendent. 21

"Ach, sir, it iss worse when they become refractory! One man, 22
I recall, clung to the bars of hiss cage when we went to take him out. You will scarcely credit, sir, that it took six warders to dislodge him, three pulling at each leg. We reasoned with him, 'My dear fellow,' we said, 'think of all the pain and trouble you are causing to us!' But no, he would not listen! Ach, he wass very troublesome!"

I found that I was laughing quite loudly. Everyone was laugh- 23
ing. Even the superintendent grinned in a tolerant way. "You'd better all come out and have a drink," he said quite genially. "I've got a bottle of whisky in the car. We could do with it."

We went through the big double gates of the prison into the 24
road. "Pulling at his legs!" exclaimed a Burmese magistrate suddenly, and burst into a loud chuckling. We all began laughing again. At that moment Francis' anecdote seemed extraordinarily funny. We all had a drink together, native and European alike, quite amicably. The dead man was a hundred yards away.

The matter-of-fact last sentence is more effective than a moralistic caution against cruelty would be.

Meaning and Purpose

Meaning and Purpose

1. The simple title is effective because it fits the solemn, matter-of-fact tone and the lack of emotion in the descriptions. The title implies no judgment, as the essayist makes no explicit judgment. "*The* Hanging" is specific, but "A Hanging" says this is one of many similar hangings—unremarkable. He wants readers to figure out his point themselves.

2. The leaping, barking dog is too painful and sharp a contrast to the subdued prisoner, and the somber observers, to be comfortable.

3. The narrator sees clearly that the prisoner has a life "in full tide" (10) when he avoids the puddle. The narrator feels a connection among all the men there, "together, seeing, hearing, feeling, understanding the same world." And the death of one would mean "one mind less, one world less." The narrator sees the condemned man as an individual and understands that taking his life will demean us all.

4. After the hanging, the men are relieved and even jubilant, chattering and laughing. They are suddenly past the burden of anticipating and carrying out the execution or of taking moral responsibility for it. They need to distance themselves emotionally from it.

5. Orwell questions the morality of capital punishment and the colonial rule that imposed it, as well as the small value placed on one Indian life. His specific story illustrates how Indians were oppressed under British rule and his sympathy for them.

Strategy

1. Orwell uses first person and refers to the group of men he is with as "we." Because he and the others are spectators, the first-person voice has an objective and detached sound. Orwell is

1. Orwell titles his essay simply "A Hanging." How effective is this title? Is it different in meaning from "*the* hanging"? Would a more descriptive title, such as "A Horrible Experience in Burma" or "The Cruelty of Capital Punishment," be better? Why or why not?
2. Why do you think the narrator describes the sudden presence of the dog as a "dreadful thing"?
3. Why does the condemned man's sidestepping a puddle make the narrator realize "what it means to destroy a healthy, conscious man"?
4. How would you characterize the behavior of the men after "the job was done"? How do you explain the behavior?
5. What is the purpose of Orwell's essay? Is it just a riveting story, or does it have a larger meaning?

Strategy

1. What is the point of view in this essay, and how well does it work?
2. What time order does Orwell use in telling his story? Does he depart from this order anywhere?
3. Why do you think Orwell doesn't tell us the crime the man is being hanged for? Does it matter? Why or why not?

Style

1. How would you describe the tone established in the first paragraph? What words create it? Is this tone sustained throughout the essay, or does it change? Explain.
2. Understatement is a form of irony that represents something as less than it actually is. Find some sentences that are examples

participant and spectator at the same time. This voice understates the situation and makes it all the more stark.

2. Orwell uses chronological order, beginning with his "waiting outside the condemned cells" (1), right through the hanging, and having a drink afterward. In paragraph 10 Orwell briefly stops the forward movement to reflect on "what it means to destroy a healthy, conscious man."

3. The crime is unimportant because, under British rule, the Indians had little or no value as individuals. The hanged man is simply one example of an execution. That his identity and specific crime make no difference expresses Orwell's point about injustice.

Style

1. The tone is somber and solemn, even depressing. Words such as "sodden morning of the rains," "sickly light," and "brown, silent men" establish the mood. Later in the essay, "desolately thin" (3), and "The Indians had gone grey like bad coffee" (13) carry this tone through the hanging. Then the words change to describe the men's elation and laughter, beginning in paragraph 17. But the somber mood lurks under the gaiety. Orwell's emotionless descriptions maintain the original tone.

2. The sentence, "We set out for the gallows" in paragraph 6 is understatement because it carries no emotion, yet suggests a somber and horrible journey. And, "The superintendent reached out with his stick and poked the bare brown body; it oscillated slightly" in paragraph 16 is also understatement. Orwell shows the lack of feeling in this scene, and emphasizes the emotional and moral detachment.

3. The next-to-last sentence describes the men drinking together "amicably," "native and European alike," when the reality is that one group rules the other and considers them of little value as people. In fact, the British have just executed one of them, and yet they drink together. The last sentence heightens starkly the contrast between the execution and the moral detachment of the men that allows them to be jolly.

of understatement. How does this technique serve Orwell's purpose?

3. Explain the irony in the last two sentences.

Writing Tasks

1. In "A Hanging," Orwell uses narrative to communicate ideas without stating them directly. Write a brief narrative in which you make a point without explicitly stating it. Tell the story of an event that illustrates your point, such as how a stylish wedding shows that we care too much about money and appearance, or how a charismatic speaker shows that we are easily persuaded to believe something.

2. Write a first-person narrative in which you tell about an exciting or moving event in a detached, dispassionate voice. Let understatement emphasize the excitement or other emotion in the story.

❦ Art Harris ❦

Art Harris is an award-winning journalist based in Atlanta. After graduating from Duke University, he began his journalism career with the Atlanta Constitution. *He later worked for the* San Francisco Examiner *before joining the staff of the* Washington Post, *the paper for which he has since covered the South. His articles have appeared in* Reader's Digest, GQ, Esquire, *and* Rolling Stone. *Harris covered the downfall of evangelical preacher Jimmy Swaggart for the* Washington Post *and wrote the well-known article about Swaggart's demise for* Penthouse *magazine. He has won two National Headliner Awards for outstanding feature writing. He is on the staff at CNN news as a contributing correspondent for their investigative unit.*

Trapped in Another Life

This newspaper article, from the Los Angeles Times, *February 23, 1989, tells the story of a woman who led two distinctly separate lives, one as a drug-abusing prostitute with a criminal record and the other as a model wife and mother. Because of the remarkable turnaround in this woman's life, the story raises questions about justice and punishment.*

Harris carefully outlines the causes that led the woman who is the subject of this essay to live two diametrically opposed lives. Pay particularly close attention to those causes.

TEACHING SUGGESTIONS

Students will find this story of Pamela Rodgers's two lives engrossing. Undoubtedly, they will have differing opinions about the proper disposition of the case. After discussing the content and the law-enforcement dilemma, you may wish to have students examine the way in which Harris uses different rhetorical patterns—comparison and contrast, cause and effect, description, and chronological narration—to tell Pamela's story. It is a good time to emphasize that essays are not usually written in one "pure" rhetorical pattern. In any one essay a writer may use many patterns as they become appropriate.

MARGINAL NOTES

Harris begins with a contrast between prison life and life outside and between Kay and her former self.

JESSUP, MD.   She stares out the window past twin 12-foot fences topped with razor wire, watchtowers manned by armed guards, steel electronic gates, past the stand of hardwoods, the nearby men's prison and up the road. 1

It's dusting snow, cold, bleak. Just over the hill, a 10-minute drive if she could just drive out of here, and she would be home in her split-level house with a devoted but baffled brood: her husband, Ray, two teen-age sons. 2

Kay Smith was the very model of a Severn, Md., housewife 3

and working mother, so perfect that no one around here can believe she was once a hard-drinking, pill-popping criminal with a gun.

Dark Secrets Come to Light

Beginning here, Harris goes to the more distant past, then relates her recent past in paragraphs 5–9.

But for a decade, until her capture last spring, she was a fugitive from a South Carolina mill town. She had been imprisoned for a string of armed robberies until she walked away from work release and disappeared. Her first husband was a convicted killer. 4

These were secrets Kay Smith buried deep as she recast her life. Over the years, she had become a doting mom to her two boys and foster daughters. She ferried her sons to school and sports, took courses at Anne Arundel Community College. As a real estate agent for Gary Hart Realty in Glen Burnie, she sold house after house—$1 million in sales last year. 5

Who could have suspected that she really was an outlaw named Pamela Rodgers? 6

Kay Smith wore subdued suits and slacks, a bare wisp of Max Factor. In her home, she warned her sons about drinking. She spurned even a glass of wine, and politely insisted that friends take half-empty bottles home after parties. 7

"I can't imagine for the life of me how this woman could do anything remotely resembling what happened," says Bill Cashman, who coached her sons in track at Old Mill High. "She'd ask me what I thought about her sons' grades, their sports performance, the people they hung around with. Her family was always first." 8

Somehow, she managed to keep it together as she lived in fear and hid her past, even from her husband. "I just wanted to get my boys through school," she says, "then I was going to straighten it all out." 9

Continuing the chronological sequence, Harris relates the most immediate past and describes her present situation.

But detectives disrupted her plan last May. And when they came for her, she had run so long and hard, she barely knew the woman, handcuffed and under arrest. All at once, she again was 10

Pamela Rodgers—the woman she thought she had left behind. In three months, she was on her way back to prison in South Carolina.

Just before Christmas, a routine interstate swap allowed her   11
to serve out the rest of her 12-year sentence for armed robbery near home. She found herself in this stark red-brick campus, the Maryland Correctional Institute for Women.

"At least I don't have to carry that terrible secret any more,"   12
she says, wrapping a sweater about her to ward off the chill. Suddenly she looks panicked. "Oh, God, I'm so sorry my sons were cheated."

She wears a purple prison jumpsuit, works in the prison   13
library, clips recipes and frets about her family. Figuring "someday they'll want honest answers," she writes letters she never mails.

Based on her record of violent crime and escape, Kay Smith   14
was classified by Maryland prison officials as a security risk. So she awaits the outcome of early release pleas—by her reckoning she could be here until March, 1993, unless authorities grant an unlikely pardon, premature parole or work release.

Family and friends have canvassed the community, collecting   15
at least 3,000 signatures petitioning South Carolina's Pardon and Parole Board for leniency.

The next four paragraphs contrast two views about her possible pardon.

"I'm not saying she ought to get a medal, but she's paid her   16
debt to society," argues John Hassett, a former prosecutor, who took her case for expenses only.

In South Carolina, former prosecutor Dick Harpootlian took   17
up her cause too, saying, "I take other cases for money. Kay's case is among those I take because I believe in the folks."

But sniffs Jim Anders, the South Carolina prosecutor who put   18
Kay Smith back in jail: "Don't make me cry. If we cut slack for her, we encourage people to escape."

Jean Gilbert, Kay Smith's mother, says of her daughter in a   19
telephone interview from Greenville, S.C.: "If people could just understand what brought her to this point. She was just a woman desperate to have her kids, who was terrorized by bad men."

Returning to the chronological, Harris now goes to the far distant past, relating her background up to her committing criminal acts, using a cause-and-effect pattern.

Kay Smith was born Pamela Annette Gilbert on Oct. 1, 1951, [20] the second of six children raised by a trucker and a grocer's daughter in the Blue Ridge foothills of Greenville, S.C. She remembers her father's belt, his guns, his whiskey, his temper.

Her father declines to discuss the past, but other family members confirm her memories; her mother recalls stepping in to take [21] "many of those licks."

"I watched him whip her . . . when she was just 15 months [22] old," says her grandmother, Mary Hinton, 83.

Kay says of her father: "He just didn't know how to show [23] affection. I can't remember ever hearing him say 'I love you.' "

When Kay was a 10th-grader, she dropped out and took a [24] job at a convenience store, where she met stock boy Danny Rodgers, another dropout.

"I knew I didn't love Danny," Kay reflects. "I married him to [25] get out. I thought I could make it work."

She was 16. [26]

Bouncing between Rodgers' modest family farm in Cullman, [27] Ala., and her hometown in Greenville, they moved into a dinky Greenville trailer.

"First time I ever saw him slap her," Kay's mother says, "I hit [28] him back. He said, 'You hit me,' and I said, 'You hit my daughter.' So he informed me, 'It's not your daughter any more; it's my wife.' "

They moved to Florida, where Danny found construction [29] work at Disney World, but preferred hanging out. Danny Jr. was born Dec. 17, 1969, as Pam was learning fast about her mercurial husband, who relished "playing with guns and knives, very nice one day and the next day beating the heck out of you."

Six months later, out of work, he ran off with a neighbor's [30] wife, she says. So Pam headed home again, hired on the midnight shift as a cotton mill weaver. Danny returned, but she refused to make up.

Then, one night, when she was at work, he snatched the baby [31] and ran, a tactic he repeatedly used to keep her in line. And it worked: She kept going back to him. "It was the only way to keep my baby," she says. Another son, James, was born in September, 1972, but life was only getting worse.

Kay moved home to Greenville, and in 1973 won temporary custody of the boys. Rodgers stalked her, she says, and one day showed up and fired a pistol into the roof of her trailer. Days later, he snatched the boys again. Only this time Pam couldn't find them. 32

"She had dreams he'd drowned them because he swore he'd do it before he'd let her have them," her mother says. "She woke up at night screaming and fell into drugs and alcohol." 33

Paragraphs 34–39 continue the cause-and-effect pattern leading up to her jail sentence and her escape.

She boxed up their toys, reminders of her "failure," and dumped them at Goodwill. She reported her husband to the police, but no one offered any hope. 34

She found a kind of solace at the Little Darling, a Greenville bar that drew hustlers such as Arthur Broome Jr., a distant cousin. 35

She was 22. 36

Broome was 43, owned a tile company, but never seemed to work. He promised to help track her boys, and she moved into his trailer—a place police say attracted the local criminal fringe. Broome, she says, had money, and drugs to kill her pain. 37

Life was going badly for her. During the 1974 Masters golf tournament, she drove to Augusta, Ga., to hang out with a bar mate—a former hooker, she says. A man approached them at a local restaurant. They began flirting. Suddenly, she says, she was under arrest for possessing amphetamines and soliciting an undercover cop for prostitution. Police records suggest that case was never prosecuted. 38

Meanwhile, back home, Broome was teaching her how to use a gun—and everything a country girl needed to know about stickups. Together they held up stores in the Greenville area. 39

"I didn't really care if I got caught," she says. "I thought if I got in enough trouble, Danny would tell me where the boys were. I wasn't thinking straight." 40

On Sept. 14, 1974, they hit Paces Jewelers just before closing. Pulling a pistol from a large black bag, she ordered customers to the floor and grabbed 18 watches and $400 in cash. 41

Because witnesses had caught her license plate numbers, po- 42
lice easily tracked her to Broome's trailer, where both were arrested. But she got out on bail, and, high on uppers, hit a liquor
store alone. Later, she drove the rolling countryside for hours,
realizing she would never get her sons back now. She went home
and gobbled pills to end it all, then raced to find her mother.

"She said, 'Mama, I took a handful of pills and I'm gonna 43
die,'" her mother recalls. "I called an ambulance, they pumped
her stomach and took her to the state hospital."

Rodgers got the news at his California apartment, where he 44
had taken the boys. He phoned, invited his wife to join him and
try again. Ignoring bail rules against leaving the state, her mother
put her on a plane. "I had to do it to save her," she says.

But it didn't work out. 45

Danny began knocking her around, but for the first time, she 46
fought back. When she called the police for help, Danny told
them his wife was a bail jumper from South Carolina.

Detectives flew her home, where she pleaded guilty in state 47
court to five armed robberies. In October, 1975, she drew a 12½-
year sentence. Broome got 25 years; Kay wound up in Columbia's
women's prison.

Rodgers filed for divorce and won permanent custody of the 48
children, but in March, 1977, he shot a man in California, for
which he was convicted of second-degree murder and sentenced
to five years in prison. The boys, 6 and 8, were dispatched to
live with his family in Alabama.

Pam, who was told Danny was in a hospital, was being a 49
model inmate. After 18 months, she made work release and labored in a printing plant. But she fell off the wagon on the job—
using pills and whiskey, she says. And she feared further setbacks
would let Danny keep her children forever. There was only one
way out: Take a walk.

This next section, to paragraph 69, details the recent past and her new life.

With six or so months left to serve, in January, 1978, she 50
hitched as far as Glen Burnie, Md., rented a room, took a job as
a waitress in a Greek diner. To avoid confusion with a waitress
named Pam, she became Kay Smith. Days later, just after mid-

night, a short, balding trucker plopped down, spied the sad-eyed brunette in a white apron and fell in love.

She was crying. A cook was screaming at her. The trucker asked her name. 51

"Ray and Kay," Ray Smith joked. "Pretty neat. We ought to get along fine. We got the same names." 52

He was gentle, optimistic. He told her he had two daughters by a woman he never had married, that he was lonely on the road and looking for a co-pilot. At quitting time, she threw down her apron and climbed aboard his snorting '74 Peterbilt. 53

High in the cab, hauling steel and furniture over the next three months, they became friends. Ray talked of a hardscrabble life, raised by grandparents in the West Virginia hollows. She was amazed. He had suffered, yet was so happy. Kay hedged about her past. 54

After three months on the road, he proposed marriage at the Truck Stop of America in Knoxville. Her dilemma was right out of some country song: How could she let someone she loved marry an outlaw with a fake name? She had forged a birth certificate, gotten a Social Security card and a Maryland driver's license. "There was no right answer," she says. "So I just decided to block out the past." 55

On July 1, 1978, Ray's family and drinking buddies, about 500 in all, crowded into a Pasadena, Md., church, and went from there to a dance hall. "I was happier than anyone could be," he says. "I knew she loved me." 56

Kay was determined to change her life. That Christmas, gambling on her former in-laws to keep her secret, she drove to Alabama with Ray to see her boys. 57

Studying on the road, she passed a high school equivalency exam, enrolled in Anne Arundel Community College, began driving on her own. 58

In 1980, the Smiths bought a three-bedroom house in Severn, outfitting bedrooms for the boys. Life without them still drove her into the bedroom with a bottle. 59

When Ray drew the line over her drinking, she found a therapist in Baltimore, and her story tumbled out for the first 60 time. She looked inside, read Norman Vincent Peale, tried bio-feedback and stopped drinking.

She made friends, becoming close to neighbor Cathy Moore, 61 a divorced mother who once rescued her dog. When Moore's daughter left to live with her father in Wyoming, Kay "reassured me," she says. "I wondered, 'How comes she's so smart about life?' "

On one visit to Alabama, she learned her former husband was 62 in prison. But she knew there was nothing she could do to get her boys back without giving herself away.

And there was nothing she could do when Danny got out, 63 remarried, reclaimed the boys and resettled in his new wife's hometown, Boise, Idaho.

But she stayed in touch, sent money, opened local charge 64 accounts for the boys, saw them at Boise's Flying J truck stop on trips west.

Meanwhile, she hired a Baltimore attorney to square her past. 65 But he reported there was no record, raising her hopes. Only later did she discover her name had been misspelled in the search.

She grew more concerned for her sons. They had told her 66 that Danny had recruited them to steal from the Salvation Army to furnish his yard sales. Then, in January, 1985, James attempted suicide; young Dan got into a fight with his father. One night, James sneaked out for a ride with a teen-ager who wrapped his car around a telephone pole, killing the driver.

Rodgers threw in the towel. "Come get them," he told his 67 former wife. "They're yours."

She flew west the next day to claim them before he changed 68 his mind. Back in Severn, the boys made friends quickly, reveled in their rooms, Reeboks and new jeans. When Ray wheeled in, they sat grinning at the kitchen table. For the first time, he saw Kay was happy. Curfews were set; grades improved. It was a "Leave It to Beaver" home, they liked to say.

She seized on real estate as a way to sock away money for 69 college.

Paragraphs 70–78 report the events leading to her arrest again.

But she remained haunted by the past and present. In 1987, 70 her former husband was charged again with murder for shooting a 21-year-old Boise man over a drug deal, chopping him into 13 pieces and dumping them into a reservoir. Now he was calling collect from jail; he wanted to see the boys, afraid he might get the chair.

After Rodgers was convicted last March, an Idaho pre-sentencing investigator ran a routine computer check of his former wife, discovered she was a fugitive and alerted South Carolina. 71

But the investigator, puzzling over an unlisted Maryland phone number in the killer's wallet, dialed it. He reached James, who confirmed his mother's maiden name and her hometown without knowing what he had done. 72

Now police had the tip they had been after. The phone rang and when she answered, it was Danny. "I guess we're in the same boat," he said. "They know about you." 73

She was numb, near hysterics. 74

Without alarming the boys, she hinted she "might have to go away for a little while" and phoned her attorney, who suggested she find a criminal lawyer. She found Hassett. 75

Then, on May 10, 1988, a patrolman knocked on her door. After her arrest, with handcuffs on, she turned white, broke into tears. "It's been 10½ years," she said. "Why now?" 76

Ray was loading in New Jersey when he got the word. The boys were in school. The next day, out on $25,000 bail, she told the boys the rest of the story, then sat down with Ray, alone. 77

"She told me everything," he says. "She was crying. She said, 'I hope this doesn't break us up. I love you so much.' " 78

Now the house feels empty. Danny, a well-mannered 6-footer who has briefly curtailed college to work in a hospital billing department, cheers on James, who takes his anger out on a punching bag and works to stay afloat at Old Mill. Most Saturdays, they visit their mother for an hour in a communal room at the prison. 79

With Ray on the road, working double time to pay the bills, friends like Pam McLane, an Old Mill senior, drop by to fix dinner, help clean up and remember Kay. 80

As for Kay herself, "there wasn't any freedom for the last 10 81

The final section relates the present situation as she and her family await word of a possible parole.

POSSIBLE ANSWERS

Meaning and Purpose

1. Crime doesn't pay, but neither is our justice system always fair. Even though Kay seemed to have left her criminal life behind, the law caught up with her. Harris's purpose is to show her struggle to live a decent life after her misguided early life and to question the justice of her returning to prison. Perhaps Harris hopes that telling Kay's story sympathetically in the newspaper will rally support for her release and pardon.

2. Though Kay changed her life when she married Ray, she "remained haunted by the past and present" (70). Back in prison, she says, "There wasn't any freedom for the last ten years, not for anyone with a conscience" (81). The two lives she had were starkly different, and her earlier life kept her trapped.

3. Harris draws a sympathetic portrait of Kay in the first fifteen paragraphs and so leads readers to favor Hassett's statement. Harris describes Kay's exemplary life and quotes a person who says how conscientious she was. Being taken back to prison seems wrenching and unfair after these descriptions.

4. Max Factor is a cosmetics company. The phrase refers to makeup and how little Kay wore. Harris equates her use of little makeup with her new life of decency and moral uprightness.

5. Each description sounds like fiction, a stereotype. They contrast sharply, and readers will feel disbelief that both could describe the same person, will feel intrigued, even skeptical, and will want to know more.

Strategy

1. Paragraphs 1–3 describe a scene and place readers in it. Enough mystery hovers about the scene ("a devoted but baffled brood") to arouse interest. Not calling Kay by name till paragraph 3 delays this necessary information and gives Harris time to create an impression before readers know who she is. The contrasting descriptions of her in paragraph 3 have readers interested enough to read on.

2. This is a newspaper article and readers want information fast. A survey of Kay's life lets readers know the gist, then they can read on for details. If Harris had begun with her early life, readers would have a harder time sympathizing with her, and Harris's points would not be as effectively—and dramatically—made.

years, not for anyone with a conscience," she reflects on this bleak Maryland winter day. "You overcome depression, drinking and negative forces, but you're not free. I was 21 when it happened. I made a terrible, terrible mistake. I feel horrible about it. . . ."

But, she adds, "I am not Pam Rodgers any more. I just don't want my children destroyed. That's my sense of urgency. Why destroy a family when it's on the verge of changing the cycle?"   82

Meaning and Purpose

1. Taking the entire article into consideration and paying close attention to the last section (79–82), what do you think Harris's purpose is in this article?
2. How does the title relate to the story?
3. Examine the statements by John Hassett in paragraph 16 and Jim Anders in paragraph 18. Which statement more closely agrees with your thinking about reformed criminals in general? About Kay Smith-Pamela Rodgers in particular? Has Harris led you to a specific view? If so, how?
4. What does Harris mean by "a bare wisp of Max Factor" in paragraph 7?
5. What is the emotional effect of describing Kay as both "the very model of a Severn, Md., housewife and working mother," and "a hard-drinking, pill-popping criminal with a gun" in the same paragraph (3)?

Strategy

1. How do the first three paragraphs pull the reader into Kay Smith's story?
2. Harris summarizes Kay's life in paragraphs 4–19, then begins her story again at an earlier time and in more detail, starting

3. The essay is mostly a summary of events, giving highlights and leaving out a lot of details. The two sentences, "She remembers her father's belt, his guns, his whiskey, his temper" (20), and "With six or so months left to serve, in January, 1978, she hitched as far as Glen Burnie, Maryland, rented a room, took a job as a waitress in a Greek diner" (50) summarize events but do not dramatize them in a scene.

4. Harris is careful to put present events in the present tense, as in the opening scene in prison. He tells of her past life in past tense ("Somehow she managed to keep it together as she lived in fear and hid her past, even from her husband" [9]), but he again intersperses the present tense for her present life ("She wears a purple prison jumpsuit" [13] and "Family and friends have canvassed the community" [17]). The direct quotations are in present tense ("Kay says of her father" [23]).

Style

1. Harris sympathizes with Kay from the start when he paints a stark, lonely picture of her in prison. He highlights events that show her a victim, as in paragraph 28 when Danny slaps her, and in paragraph 31. When Harris describes her reformed life, he tells of good and generous things she did. The tipoff to her identity as a fugitive is inadvertently given by her son—she did nothing to draw the attention of the law. All these details arouse sympathy in readers and question the justice of putting Kay back in prison.

2. Though these words are fairly understandable in context, they are jargon, and Harris's audience might be readers unfamiliar with trucking. But any audience could understand this essay.

3. The language is concise and fast-paced, but Harris doesn't care about being objective. He portrays Kay as victimized in her young life, now trying to live a decent life, and recently yanked away from her family and thrust back into prison. Harris intends readers to see the irony when he reports that Kay "was classified by Maryland prison officials as a security risk" (14). Clearly, Harris thinks she should be released and pardoned, and his article is like a plea for this action.

with paragraph 20. Why does he choose this order of events? Why doesn't he begin the article with "Kay Smith was born Pamela Annette Gilbert on Oct. 1, 1951 . . . " (20)?

3. Does Harris use the scene or summary method to present the events of the story? Give examples to support your answer.

4. Harris alternates between present and past tense in this essay. What logic do you think he uses in choosing tenses?

Style

1. What is Harris's attitude toward Kay's situation? How does he establish this attitude in the tone of the essay?

2. What do words in paragraphs 53–56 such as "co-pilot," "snorting," and "hardscrabble" tell you about Harris's intended audience? This article originally appeared in a mass-circulation newspaper. Does that background explain his choice of words?

3. This essay is a news article, and most news writers try to claim objectivity in reporting. Does Harris care about objectivity? How do you know?

Writing Tasks

1. The Kay Smith-Pamela Rodgers article begins in the present and then goes back in time to retrace her history. Write a narrative beginning with a description of a present situation as Harris does. Then go back to record the events leading to that situation. At the end of your narrative, return to the present.

2. Write an essay in which you compare style and effectiveness of the opening situations in this chapter's first four selections. Ask yourself how well each author grabs readers, establishes a situation and a conflict, and begins to create a mood. If necessary, read the chapter introduction again for some elements of narrative openings.

❦ **Richard Rodriguez** ❦

Richard Rodriguez was born in San Francisco in 1944 to Mexican-American parents who spoke only Spanish at home. Rodriguez none-theless mastered the English language and went on to study at Stanford, Columbia, and the University of California at Berkeley, where he earned a Ph.D. in English literature. He also received a Fulbright fellowship to study English literature in London. In spite of several offers for teaching positions, Rodriguez made writing and journalism his profession. In The Hunger of Memory *(1982), a collection of autobiographical essays, he examines the American educational system from the point of view of an immigrant who has gone all the way through it, and he strongly opposes bilingual education.*

Los Pobres

In this autobiographical essay from The Hunger of Memory, *Rodriguez describes his first experience of working at hard labor. The summer after he graduates from Stanford University, he takes a construction job that leads him to a vital insight about his relationship to the Mexican immigrant community he "left behind" because of his education.*

Be aware as you read how closely Rodriguez examines himself, particularly how he examines himself in relation to others.

I went to college at Stanford, attracted partly by its academic reputation, partly because it was the school rich people went to. I found myself on a campus with golden children of western America's upper middle class. Many were students both ambitious for academic success *and* accustomed to leisured life in the sun. In the afternoon, they lay spread out, sunbathing in front of the library, reading Swift or Engels or Beckett. Others went by in convertibles, off to play tennis or ride horses or sail. Beach boys dressed in tank-tops and shorts were my classmates in under-graduate seminars. Tall tan girls wearing white strapless dresses

101

sat directly in front of me in lecture rooms. I'd study them, their physical confidence. I was still recognizably kin to the boy I had been. Less tortured perhaps. But still kin. At Stanford, it's true, I began to have something like a conventional sexual life. I don't think, however, that I really believed that the women I knew found me physically appealing. I continued to stay out of the sun. I didn't linger in mirrors. And I was the student at Stanford who remembered to notice the Mexican-American janitors and gardeners working on campus.

It was at Stanford, one day near the end of my senior year,   2
that a friend told me about a summer construction job he knew was available. I was quickly alert. Desire uncoiled within me. My friend said that he knew I had been looking for summer employment. He knew I needed some money. Almost apologetically he explained: It was something I probably wouldn't be interested in, but a friend of his, a contractor, needed someone for the summer to do menial jobs. There would be lots of shoveling and raking and sweeping. Nothing too hard. But nothing more interesting either. Still, the pay would be good. Did I want it? Or did I know someone who did?

I did. Yes, I said, surprised to hear myself say it.   3

In the weeks following, friends cautioned that I had no idea   4
how hard physical labor really is. ("You only *think* you know what it is like to shovel for eight hours straight.") Their objections seemed to me challenges. They resolved the issue. I became happy with my plan. I decided, however, not to tell my parents. I wouldn't tell my mother because I could guess her worried reaction. I would tell my father only after the summer was over, when I could announce that, after all, I did know what "real work" is like.

The day I met the contractor (a Princeton graduate, it turned   5
out), he asked me whether I had done any physical labor before. "In high school, during the summer," I lied. And although he seemed to regard me with skepticism, he decided to give me a try. Several days later, expectant, I arrived at my first construction site. I would take off my shirt to the sun. And at last grasp desired

sensation. No longer afraid. At last become like a *bracero*. "We need those tree stumps out of here by tomorrow," the contractor said. I started to work.

This passage is required for the reader's understanding that it is not distaste for manual labor that separates the narrator from *los pobres*.

I labored with excitement that first morning—and all the days after. The work was harder than I could have expected. But it was never as tedious as my friends had warned me it would be. There was too much physical pleasure in the labor. Especially early in the day, I would be most alert to the sensations of movement and straining. Beginning around seven each morning (when the air was still damp but the scent of weeds and dry earth anticipated the heat of the sun), I would feel my body resist the first thrusts of the shovel. My arms, tightened by sleep, would gradually loosen; after only several minutes, sweat would gather in beads on my forehead and then—a short while later—I would feel my chest silky with sweat in the breeze. I would return to my work. A nervous spark of pain would fly up my arm and settle to burn like an ember in the thick of my shoulder. An hour, two passed. Three. My whole body would assume regular movements; my shoveling would be described by identical, even movements. Even later in the day, my enthusiasm for primitive sensation would survive the heat and the dust and the insects pricking my back. I would strain wildly for sensation as the day came to a close. At three-thirty, quitting time, I would stand upright and slowly let my head fall back, luxuriating in the feeling of tightness relieved.

The brief incident recalled in paragraphs 7, 8, and 9 gives the narrator the insight that a summer job will not really admit him to the world of the laborer and prepares the reader for the larger insight that follows in paragraphs 20–24.

Some of the men working nearby would watch me and laugh. Two or three of the older men took the trouble to teach me the right way to use a pick, the correct way to shovel. "You're doing it wrong, too fucking hard," one man scolded. Then proceeded to show me—what persons who work with their bodies all their lives quickly learn—the most economical way to use one's body in labor.

"Don't make your back do so much work," he instructed. I stood impatiently listening, half listening, vaguely watching, then noticed his work-thickened fingers clutching the shovel. I was annoyed. I wanted to tell him that I enjoyed shoveling the wrong

6

7

8

way. And I didn't want to learn the right way. I wasn't afraid of back pain. I liked the way my body felt sore at the end of the day.

I was about to, but, as it turned out, I didn't say a thing. 9
Rather it was at that moment I realized that I was fooling myself if I expected a few weeks of labor to gain me admission to the world of the laborer. I would not learn in three months what my father had meant by "real work." I was not bound to this job; I could imagine its rapid conclusion. For me the sensations of exertion and fatigue could be savored. For my father or uncle, working at comparable jobs when they were my age, such sensations were to be feared. Fatigue took a different toll on their bodies—and minds.

The narrator discovers the diversity among American workers and finds himself at ease in their company. The comfort contrasts with the coming description of his uneasiness in addressing the Mexican aliens.

It was, I know, a simple insight. But it was with this realization 10
that I took my first step that summer toward realizing something even more important about the "worker." In the company of carpenters, electricians, plumbers, and painters at lunch, I would often sit quietly, observant. I was not shy in such company. I felt easy, pleased by the knowledge that I was casually accepted, my presence taken for granted by men (exotics) who worked with their hands. Some days the younger men would talk and talk about sex, and they would howl at women who drove by in cars. Other days the talk at lunchtime was subdued; men gathered in separate groups. It depended on who was around. There were rough, good-natured workers. Others were quiet. The more I remember that summer, the more I realize that there was no single *type* of worker. I am embarrassed to say I had not expected such diversity. I certainly had not expected to meet, for example, a plumber who was an abstract painter in his off hours and admired the work of Mark Rothko. Nor did I expect to meet so many workers with college diplomas. (There were the ones who were not surprised that I intended to enter graduate school in the fall.) I suppose what I really want to say here is painfully obvious, but I must say it nevertheless: The men of that summer were middle-class Americans. They certainly didn't constitute an oppressed society. Carefully completing their work sheets; talking about the fortunes of local football teams; planning Las Vegas

vacations; comparing the gas mileage of various makes of campers—they were not *los pobres* my mother had spoken about.

On two occasions, the contractor hired a group of Mexican aliens. They were employed to cut down some trees and haul off debris. In all, there were six men of varying age. The youngest in his twenties, the oldest (his father?) perhaps sixty years old. They came and they left in a single old truck. Anonymous men. They were never introduced to the other men at the site. Immediately upon their arrival, they would follow the contractor's directions, start working—rarely resting—seemingly driven by a fatalistic sense that work which had to be done was best done as quickly as possible.   11

I watched them sometimes. Perhaps they watched me. The only time I saw them pay me much notice was one day at lunchtime when I was laughing with the other men. The Mexicans sat apart when they ate, just as they worked by themselves. Quiet. I rarely heard them say much to each other. All I could hear were their voices calling out sharply to one another, giving directions. Otherwise, when they stood briefly resting, they talked among themselves in voices too hard to overhear.   12

The contractor knew enough Spanish, and the Mexicans—or at least the oldest of them, their spokesman—seemed to know enough English to communicate. But because I was around, the contractor decided one day to make me his translator. (He assumed I could speak Spanish.) I did what I was told. Shyly I went over to tell the Mexicans that the *patrón* wanted them to do something else before they left for the day. As I started to speak, I was afraid with my old fear that I would be unable to pronounce Spanish words. But it was a simple instruction I had to convey. I could say it in phrases.   13

The dark sweating faces turned toward me as I spoke. They stopped their work to hear me. Each nodded in response. I stood there. I wanted to say something more. But what could I say in Spanish, even if I could have pronounced the words right? Perhaps I just wanted to engage them in small talk, to be assured of their confidence, our familiarity. I thought for a moment to ask them where in Mexico they were from. Something like that. And maybe   14

I wanted to tell them (a lie, if need be) that my parents were from the same part of Mexico.

I stood there.   15

Their faces watched me. The eyes of the man directly in front   16 of me moved slowly over my shoulder, and I turned to follow his glance toward *el patrón* some distance away. For a moment I felt swept up by that glance into the Mexicans' company. But then I heard one of them returning to work. And then the others went back to work. I left them without saying anything more.

When they had finished, the contractor went over to pay   17 them in cash. (He later told me that he paid them collectively— "for the job"—though he wouldn't tell me their wages. He said something quickly about the good rate of exchange "in their own country.") I can still hear the loudly confident voice he used with the Mexicans. It was the sound of the *gringo* I had heard as a very young boy. And I can still hear the quiet, indistinct sounds of the Mexican, the oldest, who replied. At hearing that voice I was sad for the Mexicans. Depressed by their vulnerability. Angry at myself. The adventure of the summer seemed suddenly ludicrous. I would not shorten the distance I felt from *los pobres* with a few weeks of physical labor. I would not become like them. They were different from me.

After that summer, a great deal—and not very much really—   18 changed in my life. The curse of physical shame was broken by the sun; I was no longer ashamed of my body. No longer would I deny myself the pleasing sensations of my maleness. During those years when middle-class Black Americans began to assert with pride, "Black is beautiful," I was able to regard my complexion without shame. I am today darker than I ever was as a boy. I have taken up the middle-class sport of long-distance running. Nearly every day now I run ten or fifteen miles, barely clothed, my skin exposed to the California winter rain and wind or the summer sun of late afternoon. The torso, the soccer player's calves and thighs, the arms of the twenty-year-old I never was, I possess now in my thirties. I study the youthful parody shape in the mirror: the stomach lipped tight by muscle; the shoulders rounded by chin-ups; the arms veined strong. This man. A man. I meet him. He laughs to see me, what I have become.

The man's glance over the narrator's shoulder toward *el patrón* tells the narrator that he is seen only as a messenger from the boss and dashes his hopes for a bond between him and the Mexican workers.

These paragraphs take us to a more recent past and confirm the narrator's acceptance of his membership in a privileged class.

The dandy. I wear double-breasted Italian suits and custom-made English shoes. I resemble no one so much as my father— the man pictured in those honeymoon photos. At that point in life when he abandoned the dandy's posture, I assume it. At the point when my parents would not consider going on vacation, I register at the Hotel Carlyle in New York and the Plaza Athénée in Paris. I am as taken by the symbols of leisure and wealth as they were. For my parents, however, those symbols became taunts, reminders of all they could not achieve in one lifetime. For me those same symbols are reassuring reminders of public success. I tempt vulgarity to be reassured. I am filled with the gaudy delight, the monstrous grace of the nouveau riche. [19]

The final paragraphs sum up his understanding of what the earlier experience means. The fundamental distinction between the narrator and *los pobres* is an attitude that grows from different experiences.

In recent years I have had occasion to lecture in ghetto high schools. There I see students of remarkable style and physical grace. (One can see more dandies in such schools than one ever will find in middle-class high schools.) There is not the look of casual assurance I saw students at Stanford display. Ghetto girls mimic high-fashion models. Their dresses are of bold, forceful color; their figures elegant, long; the stance theatrical. Boys wear shirts that grip at their overdeveloped muscular bodies. (Against a powerless future, they engage images of strength.) Bad nutrition does not yet tell. Great disappointment, fatal to youth, awaits them still. For the moment, movements in school hallways are dancelike, a procession of postures in a sexual masque. Watching them, I feel a kind of envy. I wonder how different my adolescence would have been had I been free. . . . But no, it is my parents I see—their optimism during those years when they were entertained by Italian grand opera. [20]

The registration clerk in London wonders if I have just been to Switzerland. And the man who carries my luggage in New York guesses the Caribbean. My complexion becomes a mark of my leisure. Yet no one would regard my complexion the same way if I entered such hotels through the service entrance. That is only to say that my complexion assumes its significance from the context of my life. My skin, in itself, means nothing. I stress the point because I know there are people who would label me "disadvantaged" because of my color. They make the same mistake [21]

I made as a boy, when I thought a disadvantaged life was circumscribed by particular occupations. That summer I worked in the sun may have made me physically indistinguishable from the Mexicans working nearby. (My skin was actually darker because, unlike them, I worked without wearing a shirt. By late August my hands were probably as tough as theirs.) But I was not one of *los pobres.* What made me different from them was an attitude of *mind,* my imagination of myself.

I do not blame my mother for warning me away from the 22 sun when I was young. In a world where her brother had become an old man in his twenties because he was dark, my complexion was something to worry about. "Don't run in the sun," she warns me today. I run. In the end, my father was right—though perhaps he did not know how right or why— to say that I would never know what real work is. I will never know what he felt at his last factory job. If tomorrow I worked at some kind of factory, it would go differently for me. My long education would favor me. I could act as a public person— able to defend my interests, to unionize, to petition, to speak up—to challenge and demand. (I will never know what real work is.) I will never know what the Mexicans knew, gathering their shovels and ladders and saws.

Their silence stays with me now. The wages those Mexicans 23 received for their labor were only a measure of their disadvantaged condition. Their silence is more telling. They lack a public identity. They remain profoundly alien. Persons apart. People lacking a union obviously, people without grounds. They depend upon the relative good will or fairness of their employers each day. For such people, lacking a better alternative, it is not such an unreasonable risk.

Their silence stays with me. I have taken these many words 24 to describe its impact. Only: the quiet. Something uncanny about it. Its compliance. Vulnerability. Pathos. As I heard their truck rumbling away, I shuddered, my face mirrored with sweat. I had finally come face to face with *los pobres.*

Beginning the last two paragraphs with the same sentence emphasizes the Mexican workers' compliance and vulnerability and leaves us with wonder at the chasm between the classes.

POSSIBLE ANSWERS

Meaning and Purpose

1. Rodriguez is observant of his fellow students and believes they are wealthier and more privileged than he. He feels inferior, more kin to the Mexican-American janitors and gardeners, and he is sensitive about his dark skin. He doesn't think he is appealing physically: he "didn't linger in mirrors" (1).

2. Rodriguez had never done hard physical labor, as his father had. Wanting to rise above the working class, he was surprised when "desire uncoiled" (2) in him for the construction job. Challenged by physical labor, he didn't want his parents to think he'd taken a job beneath him, or that he had no ambition.

3. Rodriguez's main point is realizing what makes people *los pobres*. In paragraph 22 he says, "What made me different from them was an attitude of *mind*, my imagination of myself." He worked with white laborers who had college degrees and with Mexican laborers who were silent, compliant, and vulnerable (24). It was not occupation but his perception of himself, and the voice his education had given him, which would keep him from ever being one of *los pobres* (21).

4. The insight is that Rodriguez cannot "gain admission to the world of the laborer" (9) just by working at a summer construction job. He was not bound to the job and could savor the sensation of fatigue. The connection with "But I was not one of *los pobres*" (21) is that his body might be capable of physical labor and his hands as "tough as theirs" (21), but his "attitude of *mind*" (21) and his education keep him from being poor.

5. Being paid as a group eliminates their individuality as men. The contractor takes advantage of their alien status and their inability to bargain for themselves.

6. The Mexican workers are silent because they have no union, no grounds, no "public identity" (23). They depend on others' good will. Finally their silence brings Rodriguez "face to face with *los pobres*."

Strategy

1. The order is chronological, so that Rodriguez can show his early naiveté about class and lifestyle, then his later sophistication and ability to understand his summer.

2. The summer job, core of the narrative, requires details to make the point about Rodriguez's realizing what it means to be poor. Sections two and three compress time and summarize the life-style he later lived and now lives. These two sections don't describe just one event but show Rodriguez looking back through postcollege experiences that help him understand that summer.

Meaning and Purpose

1. What picture of Rodriguez do you get from the first paragraph? How does he see himself?
2. Why is he surprised to hear himself say yes (3) to the offer of a summer job at manual labor? What is his motive for taking the job? Why doesn't he tell his parents?
3. Rodriguez talks about many things in this essay: being a student at Stanford, physical labor, the Italian suits he wears, and ghetto high-school students. What do you think his main point is, and where does he state it?
4. Paragraph 10 begins with "It was, I know, a simple insight." What is the insight and what triggers it? How does this insight connect with his later statement, "But I was not one of *los pobres*"?
5. Is it significant that the Mexican workers were paid as a group rather than individually? Explain.
6. Rodriguez begins paragraphs 23 and 24 with the words, "Their silence stays with me." What does the silence signify?

Strategy

1. Rodriguez's narrative begins with one summer while he is a student at Stanford, then jumps to the vague time frame of "After that summer" (18), then to "In recent years" (20). Why does he choose to arrange the events and skip to the periods that he does?
2. Why does Rodriguez draw out details of his summer construction job and compress the details of the longer periods in sections 2 and 3?
3. Does Rodriguez use summary or scene to tell his story? Give examples.
4. What is Rodriguez's point of view? Give evidence from the essay of how effective it is.

3. Rodriguez uses both summary and scene. The summer job is presented more as scene, a drama acted out with characters and dialogue. (" 'Don't make your back do so much work,' he instructed. I stood patiently listening" [8]). But some of it is summarized: "I labored with excitement the first morning—and all the days after" (6). Section two is summary about his physical condition and the clothes he wears (18–19). And in section three, he also summarizes (20). The summary parts have little or no dialogue and no scenes are acted out.

4. Rodriguez uses first person to tell his own story, but he is looking back from his thirties on the summer job in college. With this point of view he can show how he came to understand what it is to be poor. Examples that show this effectiveness are: "The more I remember that summer, the more I realize that there was no single *type* of work" (10); "And I can still hear the quiet, indistinct sounds of the Mexican, the oldest, who replied . . ." (17).

Style

1. In the last sentence of paragraph 10, *los pobres* is what the middle-class construction workers just described are not. A *bracero* (5) is "no longer afraid," but a strong worker. The *patrón* (13), or the contractor, gives orders to the Mexicans. *Gringo* (17) comes right after the description of how the contractor pays the Mexicans, and how "loudly confident" his voice is. *Gringo* is a disparaging name for whites.
2. Three fragments in the first two paragraphs are: "Less tortured perhaps"; "But still kin"; "Nothing too hard." These fragments create the informal, conversational tone of the opening, and they are emphatic in their brevity.
3. Rodriguez re-creates life, especially in describing the Mexican workers, who seem immediate and real, even in their anonymity.

Style

1. Locate the words *los pobres, bracero, patrón,* and *gringo* in the text. Can you define them using only the context of the narrative?
2. Rodriguez occasionally uses sentence fragments purposely. Find at least three in the first two paragraphs and explain how they affect the tone of the introduction.
3. A good narrative re-creates life. Does "Los Pobres" do so? Explain.

Writing Tasks

1. At some time in your life you have undoubtedly been an "outsider." It may have been in another country or at a new school, in a new neighborhood, or on a new job. Write a narrative about that time. As Rodriguez does in "Los Pobres," blend the details of the situation with your thoughts and insights from a later perspective.
2. Choose an event to narrate, and write it in two ways. In one version, use the scene method to dramatize the event and make it immediate. In the other version, use summary to tell more than show. Which version is more effective?

❦ Harry Mark Petrakis ❦

Harry Mark Petrakis was born in 1923 in St. Louis of Greek parents, his father an Eastern Orthodox priest. Before becoming a full-time writer he worked as a laborer, a steelworker, a speech writer, and a sales correspondent. He has taught in both fiction and nonfiction writing workshops. He has won several writing awards and was nominated for the National Book Award for two of his novels, Pericles on 31st Street *(1965) and* A Dream of Kings *(1966). In 1986 he published his* Collected Stories. *The following selection is an excerpt from a non-fiction work,* Stelmark:? A Family Recollection *(1970).*

Barba Nikos

In this essay Harry Mark Petrakis narrates an incident from his child-hood that demonstrates the strains which can arise between first and second generation immigrants when the young are desperately trying to prove both to themselves and others that they are now really Americans.

Petrakis often writes about Greek Americans and immigrants. At the beginning of this excerpt he shows what can happen when young people feel embarrassed about their parents' ethnic background because they so strongly desire to be accepted in their new culture. Because the story is about how a first generation Greek American boy (Petrakis) learned respect for his culture and heritage from an immigrant (Barba Nikos), pay close attention as you read to both how and what he learned.

TEACHING SUGGESTIONS

This is a good piece to encourage your own first and second generation students to recount their own and their families' experiences in adjusting to their new culture. Some will probably describe the problems they personally had in adapting. Encourage native students to recall the problems they had when finding themselves in alien situations or in being pressured to do things they didn't want to do by peer expectations. Point out that it is these kinds of tensions on which much good narration is based. You might want to use the essay in conjunction with Maya Angelou's "Finishing School" or Richard Rodriguez's "Los Pobres" or his "Los Otros, Mis Hermanos." All have adult narrators looking back at childhood experiences.

MARGINAL NOTES

Petrakis clearly establishes both point of view and conflict in this opening paragraph (see pp. 66–69). The incident to be narrated is a youthful indiscretion and the subsequent knowledge gained from it viewed from an adult perspective. The conflict is between recent immigrants and first and, possibly, second generation Americans trying to separate themselves from their ethnic pasts to embrace and become part of their new, national future.

There was one storekeeper I remember above all others in my youth. It was shortly before I became ill, spending a good portion of my time with a motley group of varied ethnic ancestry. We contended with one another to deride the customs of the old country. On our Saturday forays into neighborhoods beyond our own, to prove we were really Americans, we ate hot dogs and drank Cokes. If a boy didn't have ten cents for this repast he went hungry, for he dared not bring a sandwich from home made of the spiced meats our families ate. 1

111

The second paragraph gives a general example of one of the things the youthful "motley group" would do to assert their break with their old cultures.

The narrative begins here with a series of summary paragraphs, 3 through 6 (see pp. 70–71).

Paragraphs 7–20 constitute a scene, made up primarily of dialogue, but with enough description to root that dialogue in a palpable place and situation.

One of our untamed games was to seek out the owner of a pushcart or a store, unmistakably an immigrant, and bedevil him with a chorus of insults and jeers. To prove allegiance to the gang it was necessary to reserve our fiercest malevolence for a storekeeper or peddler belonging to our own ethnic background. 2

For that reason I led a raid on the small, shabby grocery of old Barba Nikos, a short, sinewy Greek who walked with a slight limp and sported a flaring, handlebar mustache. 3

We stood outside his store and dared him to come out. When he emerged to do battle, we plucked a few plums and peaches from the baskets on the sidewalk and retreated across the street to eat them while he watched. He waved a fist and hurled epithets at us in ornamental Greek. 4

Aware that my mettle was being tested, I raised my arm and threw my half-eaten plum at the old man. My aim was accurate and the plum struck him on the cheek. He shuddered and put his hand to the stain. He stared at me across the street, and although I could not see his eyes, I felt them sear my flesh. He turned and walked silently back into the store. The boys slapped my shoulders in admiration, but it was a hollow victory that rested like a stone in the pit of my stomach. 5

At twilight when we disbanded, I passed the grocery alone on my way home. There was a small light burning in the store and the shadow of the old man's body outlined against the glass. Goaded by remorse, I walked to the door and entered. 6

The old man moved from behind the narrow wooden counter and stared at me. I wanted to turn and flee, but by then it was too late. As he motioned for me to come closer, I braced myself for a curse or a blow. 7

"You were the one," he said, finally, in a harsh voice. 8

I nodded mutely. 9

"Why did you come back?" 10

I stood there unable to answer. 11

"What's your name?" 12

"Haralambos," I said, speaking to him in Greek. 13

He looked at me in shock. "You are Greek!" he cried. "A Greek boy attacking a Greek grocer!" He stood appalled at the 14 immensity of my crime. "All right," he said coldly. "You are here because you wish to make amends." His great mustache bristled in concentration. "Four plums, two peaches," he said. "That makes a total of 78 cents. Call it 75. Do you have 75 cents, boy?"

I shook my head. 15

"Then you will work it off," he said. "Fifteen cents an hour into 75 cents makes"—he paused—"five hours of work. Can you come here Saturday morning?" 16

"Yes," I said. 17

"Yes, Barba Nikos," he said sternly. "Show respect." 18

"Yes, Barba Nikos," I said. 19

"Saturday morning at eight o'clock," he said. "Now go home and say thanks in your prayers that I did not loosen your impudent head with a solid smack on the ear." I needed no further urging and fled. 20

Saturday morning, still apprehensive, I returned to the store. I began by sweeping, raising clouds of dust in dark and hidden corners. I washed the windows, whipping the squeegee swiftly up and down the glass in a fever of fear that some member of the gang would see me. When I finished I hurried back inside. 21

For the balance of the morning I stacked cans, washed the counter, and dusted bottles of yellow wine. A few customers entered, and Barba Nikos served them. A little after twelve o'clock he locked the door so he could eat lunch. He cut himself a few slices of sausage, tore a large chunk from a loaf of crisp-crusted bread, and filled a small cup with a dozen black shiny olives floating in brine. He offered me the cup. I could not help myself and grimaced. 22

"You are a stupid boy," the old man said. "You are not really Greek, are you?" 23

"Yes, I am." 24

"You might be," he admitted grudgingly. "But you do not act Greek. Wrinkling your nose at these fine olives. Look around this store for a minute. What do you see?" 25

"Fruits and vegetables," I said. "Cheese and olives and things like that." 26

He stared at me with a massive scorn. "That's what I mean," 27

Paragraphs 21 and 22 again summarize experience.

Paragraphs 23–40 constitute a long scene in which Barba Nikos teaches the youthful Petrakis about the richness of his cultural heritage through Greek food.

he said. "You are a bonehead. You don't understand that a whole nation and a people are in this store."

I looked uneasily toward the storeroom in the rear, almost expecting someone to emerge. 28

"What about olives?" he cut the air with a sweep of his arm. "There are olives of many shapes and colors. Pointed black ones from Kalamata, oval ones from Amphissa, pickled green olives and sharp tangy yellow ones. Achilles carried black olives to Troy and after a day of savage battle leading his Myrmidons, he'd rest and eat cheese and ripe black olives such as these right here. You have heard of Achilles, boy, haven't you?" 29

"Yes," I said. 30

"Yes, Barba Nikos." 31

"Yes, Barba Nikos," I said. 32

He motioned at the row of jars filled with varied spices. "There is origanon there and basilikon and daphne and sesame and miantanos, all the marvelous flavorings that we have used in our food for thousands of years. The men of Marathon carried small packets of these spices into battle, and the scents reminded them of their homes, their families, and their children." 33

He rose and tugged his napkin free from around his throat. "Cheese, you said. Cheese! Come closer, boy, and I educate your abysmal ignorance." He motioned toward a wooden container on the counter. "That glistening white delight is feta, made from goat's milk, packed in wooden buckets to retain the flavor. Alexander the Great demanded it on his table with his casks of wine when he planned his campaigns." 34

He walked limping from the counter to the window where the piles of tomatoes, celery, and green peppers clustered. "I suppose all you see here are some random vegetables?" He did not wait for me to answer. "You are dumb again. These are some of the ingredients that go to make up a Greek salad. Do you know what a Greek salad really is? A meal in itself, an experience, an emotional involvement. It is created deftly and with grace. First, you place large lettuce leaves in a big, deep bowl." He spread his fingers and moved them slowly, carefully, as if he were arranging 35

Achilles, the prototype of ancient Greek bravery and masculine beauty, was the hero of Homer's *Iliad,* the epic poem about the war between the Greek city-states and Troy. He was the Greek's most renowned hero in the Trojan War and, in that war, slew the Trojan hero, Hector. As an infant he was dipped in the river Styx by his mother. This made him invulnerable, except for his heel, the place where his mother had held him. He was fatally wounded there by an arrow shot by Hector's younger brother, Paris. In another version of the story it is the god Apollo disguised as Paris who shot the arrow. Thus the term *Achilles heel* refers to the vulnerable point in the character of a person or nation.

In Greek mythology the Myrmidons were a savage and brutal people of Thessaly, a region of eastern Greece.

Marathon is a city northeast of Athens where the Athenians won a major battle against the invading Persians. According to tradition, the news of the victory was brought back to Athens by an armor-clad runner, Pheidippedes, who, after the run, collapsed and died from the strain. The feat is commemorated in modern marathon races, usually fixed at 26 miles, 385 yards, the distance from Marathon to Athens.

Alexander the Great (356–323 B.C.), the son of Philip of Macedon, an ancient country in the Balkan Peninsula north of ancient Greece, and conqueror of the civilized world, extended Greek civilization eastward, as far as India. He was admired for his frequent generous and humane acts.

Here the loving description of a Greek salad serves as its definition.

Zeus was the supreme god of the ancient Greeks who lived on Olympus with the other gods.

In Greek mythology Pan was an Arcadian god of pastures, forests, flocks, and herds who was pictured with the lower part of a goat and the upper part of a man. An oracle was the answer of a god or an inspired priest to an inquiry regarding the future. It also refers to the place where the deity could be consulted. There were many oracles in ancient Greece, Delphi the most famous. Nymphs were lesser deities conceived of as beautiful maidens inhabiting the sea, rivers, woods, trees, and mountains, and frequently mentioned as attending a superior deity.

the leaves. "The remainder of the lettuce is shredded and piled in a small mound," he said. "Then comes celery, cucumbers, tomatoes sliced lengthwise, green peppers, origanon, green olives, feta, avocado and anchovies. At the end you dress it with lemon, vinegar, and pure olive oil, glinting golden in the light."

He finished with a heartfelt sigh and for a moment closed his eyes. Then he opened one eye to mark me with a baleful intensity. "The story goes that Zeus himself created the recipe and assembled and mixed the ingredients on Mount Olympus one night when he had invited some of the other gods to dinner." 36

He turned his back on me and walked slowly again across the store, dragging one foot slightly behind him. I looked uneasily at the clock, which showed that it was a few minutes past one. He turned quickly and startled me. "And everything else in here," he said loudly. "White beans, lentils, garlic, crisp bread, kokoretsi, meat balls, mussels and clams." He paused and drew a deep, long breath. "And the wine," he went on, "wine from Samos, Santorini, and Crete, retsina and mavrodaphne, a taste almost as old as water . . . and then the fragrant melons, the pastries, yellow diples and golden loukoumades, the honey custard galatobouriko. Everything a part of our history, as much a part as the exquisite sculpture in marble, the bearded warriors, Pan and the oracles at Delphi, and the nymphs dancing in the shadowed groves under Homer's glittering moon." He paused, out of breath again, and coughed harshly. "Do you understand now, boy?" 37

He watched my face for some response and then grunted. We stood silent for a moment until he cocked his head and stared at the clock. "It is time for you to leave," he motioned brusquely toward the door. "We are square now. Keep it that way." 38

I decided the old man was crazy and reached behind the counter for my jacket and cap and started for the door. He called me back. From a box he drew out several soft, yellow figs that he placed in a piece of paper. "A bonus because you worked well," he said. "Take them. When you taste them, maybe you will understand what I have been talking about." 39

I took the figs and he unlocked the door and I hurried from 40

Meaning and Purpose

1. Petrakis overtly states that the reason for displaying their "fiercest malevolence for a storekeeper or peddler belonging to our own ethnic background" was "to prove allegiance to the gang"(2). The implied reason for this and their derision for the customs of the old country was to cut themselves off psychologically from their cultural pasts in order to perceive themselves more securely as Americans. Their hostility to the past, then, is prompted by their current insecurity.

2. Nikos registered shock when Petrakis told him his name was Haralambas (anglicized later to Harry Mark) in paragraph 14. He is appalled that a Greek boy would display such incivility to him and such hostility to his cultural heritage.

3. Barba Nikos insists the young Petrakis respectfully and formally recite Nikos's full name when the boy answers his question (18), and he repeats this lesson in respect as he begins to teach the boy about Greek culture (31).

4. Petrakis shows sensitivity to the immorality of his behavior when he returns to the grocery "goaded by remorse" (6). This sensitivity prepares us for his responsiveness to Nikos's lesson.

5. Like most good teachers Nikos is able to make abstractions palpable. In teaching Petrakis about the food all around them, he shows how that food connects with the long and rich Greek heritage they both share. Petrakis carries the figs home with him and when he tastes them the pervasive richness of their flavor is like the pervasive richness of the history and culture he had learned earlier in the day. And as the flavor remains with him into the next day, so the lesson he learned stays with him the rest of his life. The metaphoric significance of the figs is explained in the final paragraph.

the store. I looked back once and saw him standing in the doorway, watching me, the swirling tendrils of food curling like mist about his head.

I ate the figs late that night. I forgot about them until I was in bed, and then I rose and took the package from my jacket. I nibbled at one, then ate them all. They broke apart between my teeth with a tangy nectar, a thick sweetness running like honey across my tongue and into the pockets of my cheeks. In the morning when I woke, I could still taste and inhale their fragrance. 41

I never again entered Barba Nikos's store. My spell of illness, which began some months later, lasted two years. When I returned to the streets I had forgotten the old man and the grocery. Shortly afterwards my family moved from the neighborhood. 42

Some twelve years later, after the war, I drove through the old neighborhood and passed the grocery. I stopped the car and for a moment stood before the store. The windows were stained with dust and grime, the interior bare and desolate, a store in a decrepit group of stores marked for razing so new structures could be built. 43

I have been in many Greek groceries since then and have often bought the feta and Kalamata olives. I have eaten countless Greek salads and have indeed found them a meal for the gods. On the holidays in our house, my wife and sons and I sit down to a dinner of steaming, buttered pilaf like my mother used to make and lemon-egg avgolemono and roast lamb richly seasoned with cloves of garlic. I drink the red and yellow wines, and for dessert I have come to relish the delicate pastries coated with honey and powdered sugar. Old Barba Nikos would have been pleased. 44

But I have never been able to recapture the halcyon flavor of those figs he gave me on that day so long ago, although I have bought figs many times. I have found them pleasant to my tongue, but there is something missing. And to this day I am not sure whether it was the figs or the vision and passion of the old grocer 45

Strategy

1. The brief but vivid description of Barba Nikos gives him some distinguishing characteristics so that the reader can more easily picture him as the narration progresses. The "flaring, handlebar mustache" emphasizes his Greekness.

2. Petrakis not only describes his insensitive act but implies his guilt for doing it by both his diction and use of contrast and simile. The juice left on Nikos's cheek is a "stain," and Petrakis felt the old man's stare "sear" his flesh. And while he feels his "hollow victory" rest "like a stone in his stomach," he is congratulated by his friends.

3. The mention of illness in the first paragraph both foreshadows and sets up its functional use several paragraphs later. The illness in paragraph 42 separates the narrator and, therefore, the reader, in time from the main narration and leads to the present reflection that serves as the essay's conclusion.

4. The first three paragraphs set the scene and situation for the narrative that is to follow. The narrator is looking back on his callow, insensitive behavior. Paragraphs 42–43 bring the reader to the chronological present and show how part of the past is gone forever. But the last two paragraphs show how the past lesson of Barba Nikos lives now in the mature narrator's present and will always live in his future, thereby enriching him the rest of his life.

5. In paragraph 3 Nikos's lameness gives him a distinguishing characteristic and emphasizes his vulnerability before he is assaulted. The latter two times it is mentioned create a contrast between this disability and the strength of his moral character, thereby emphasizing the latter.

Style

1. Words such as *motley, deride, forays, repast, bedevil, malevolence,* and *epithets* remind us of the maturity of the narrator and point forward to the formality of Barba Nikos and the importance of the lesson he will teach.

2. The term probably means elaborate invective as opposed to short angry curses.

that coated the fruit so sweetly I can still recall their savor and fragrance after almost thirty years.

Meaning and Purpose

1. What stated and unstated reasons does Petrakis give for his gang attacking immigrants, with particular vehemence directed against those with the same ethnic background as their own?

2. Why does Barba Nikos register shock to learn that Petrakis is Greek? Where in the essay does Nikos again mention the author's ethnicity? Why is it mentioned twice?

3. How does Nikos establish respect for himself? How does this establish respect for Greek culture?

4. What clue does Petrakis give that he will be ultimately responsive to the richness of his heritage?

5. How and why does Barba Nikos connect food with Greek myth and history? What particular significance do the figs have in paragraphs 39-41?

Strategy

1. What function does the description in paragraph 3 serve?

2. How, specifically, does paragraph 5 prepare the reader for paragraph 6?

3. Petrakis mentions his illness in paragraphs 1 and 42. Why would he choose these particular places to do so?

4. Reread the paragraphs that frame the narrative: 1–3; 42–45. How do they differ in tone? Why?

5. Petrakis mentions Barba Nikos's lameness in paragraphs 3, 35, and 37. Why does he repeat this fact? What has happened to change the reader's attitude from the first mention to the second and third?

3. The physicality of the simile has a more forceful impact on the reader than a mere declaration of guilt would have, and the "stone" is like that of the plum that Petrakis threw to initiate the guilt.

4. *Halcyon,* meaning calm or peaceful, is derived from the Greek word for kingfisher. It is also the name of a mythical bird usually identified with the kingfisher, said to breed about the time of the winter solstice in a nest floating on the sea, and to have the power of charming winds and waves into calmness.

5. *Motley*: exhibiting a great diversity of elements; *deride*: to laugh at in scorn or contempt; *forays*: quick raids, usually for the purpose of taking plunder; *repast*: a quantity of food taken for one occasion of eating, a meal; *bedevil*: to torment or harass maliciously; *malevolence*: ill will, malice, hatred; *epithet*: a word, phrase or expression used invectively as a form of abuse or contempt; *mettle*: courage and fortitude; *goaded*: prodded, incited as by a goad, a pointed stick; *brine*: a salt and water solution for pickling; *baleful*: full of menacing or malign influence; *halcyon*: 1. calm, peaceful; 2. rich, wealthy; 3. happy, joyful.

Style

1. In the first four paragraphs the author uses diction that is more formal than a young boy would use. What are the words and why does he use them?
2. In paragraph 4 Petrakis calls Nikos's Greek "ornamental." What does he mean by this?
3. Examine the simile in the last sentence of paragraph 5. Why is it particularly appropriate here?
4. Look up both the meaning and etymology of "halcyon" in paragraph 45. What makes this word particularly appropriate?
5. If necessary look up these words in a dictionary: *motley, deride, foray, repast* (1); *bedevil, malevolence* (2); *epithet* (4); *mettle, goaded* (5); *brine* (22); *baleful* (36); *halcyon* (45).

Writing Tasks

1. Narrate an incident in your life in which you came in conflict with someone or something and were forced to resolve the conflict in some way.
2. Narrate an incident in which you gave in to peer pressure and acted in a way that you yourself disapproved. How did you feel then? Now? Or write a piece on how you resisted such pressure.
3. Write a reflective narrative in which you look back on a childhood incident with adult eyes. Use "Barba Nikos" as a narrative model and frame the main narrative by establishing the setting and situation in the introduction and giving the reader a payoff in the conclusion.

The Storyteller

Ancient cultures viewed storytellers as being touched with divine madness. These storytellers had tales that explained life's mysteries.

But times have changed.

Astronauts have soared through space. The deepest rainforests amd highest mountain peaks have been photographed. What mysteries need to be explained? What lessons need to be taught? What is the role of the storyteller in an age when movie and television production companies create visual stories by formula?

Is the photograph "The Storyteller" commenting on the role of storytellers today?

The Storyteller's outfit suggests he indeed might be touched by divine madness. He wears ribbons, balloons, streamers, a whimsical laurel around his head, and a banner that identifies him.

119

Displayed on a wall are hundreds of photographs, many of African-American and Native-American leaders, perhaps each embodying a story of its own. Behind his head, slightly obscured, are the words of Martin Luther King, "I have a dream."

This storyteller stands in the classroom, but where are the students who might be eager to hear a meaningful story? He is looking and pointing outside the photographic frame, but at what or whom? From the viewer's perspective he is alone . . . or is he?

In a unified narrative respond to one of the following writing tasks. Before you begin the first draft, review effective narrative conventions described at the beginning of the chapter.

1. Create your own tale about the storyteller in this photograph. Begin by studying the photograph. Imagine how the storyteller feels in his attire. Imgine how he feels during his performance. Imagine what his life is like when he is not being a storyteller. What does he do? Where does he live? What do his friends think of his storytelling? Is he a fulfilled person? A happy person? A sad person?

    As you imagine the storyteller, list your observations. Once this exploratory phase of the assignment is complete, review your observations and determine what dominant impression you wish to create.

    Finally, to start your first draft, you might begin this way: "Once upon a time an ordinary man who lived in our city decided to become a storyteller." Throughout your draft integrate physical details from the photograph.

2. Imagine that the storyteller in the photograph is fully aware that ancient mysteries have been clarified scientifically. He is still compelled to tell tales, meaningful tales designed to give people insight into a society which some see as growing more and more chaotic.

    For this task, tell how the storyteller became successful. Include in your narrative a summary of one tale that gave his listeners insight into contemporary life.

❧ Additional Writing Tasks ❧

Narration

1. All of us have had experiences that can be retold in narrative form. Often these experiences stay with us much longer than impersonal events we have merely observed. For this writing task, select an incident from your early years that involves a simple action that you can recall clearly and vividly. The incident does not have to be exceptionally dramatic, but it should be interesting enough to move from the opening through the body to the climax—the major components of narrative. The incident may involve you alone or it may involve others as well. It must have enough action with connected events to be developed as a narration.

    Because this is to be an incident from your early years, you might begin by setting aside time to explore your past. Begin by spontaneously jotting down memories from your early past as a way to begin the selection procedure. Make a list by devoting no more than three or four sentences to each experience you recall. These three entries are from one student's memory list:

    > I remember walking home from school one June morning. Hot. Humid. A man with a Bible and wearing a black suit stopped me and asked, "Have you been saved, Sonny?" I was frightened.
    >
    > When I was ten I visited my grandfather in the hospital. He was very ill, dying. I recalled all the wonderful and all the horrible fishing trips we took together.
    >
    > Why was my dog shot? The killer was never found. I remember searching the faces of strangers for looks of guilt.

    Each writer, of course, will have his or her own memories: an automobile accident, a mystery, a sudden appearance, a victory, a defeat, a meeting with a famous person, and so on.

    Once you have compiled a list, select one of the memories, perhaps the one that stirs the most emotion in you when you recall it, and use it as the basis for your narration. Before starting your first draft, take at least an uninterrupted hour to compose a rough sketch of the incident, capturing the movement of events and the people. Then you will be prepared to start the first draft. Begin by arranging the material in dramatic order to serve as a loose outline.

2.   Select an incident to narrate that you have not directly experienced yourself. The incident may come from what you have seen, heard, or read. Perhaps you will select an incident from a television show, film, short story, news article, or friend's experience. If you select a newspaper article as your source, you may want to retell it as though you had witnessed the incident. If you want to convey a friend's story, you may add observations of your own. If you select an incident from a film or short story, you may want to concentrate on an incident involving one character and rearrange the events to suit your purpose. Keep in mind, though, that your task is not to merely summarize the story line; your task is to select material for your own narrative.

4

Description

Capturing Sensory Details

The Method

To describe is to picture in words—the people we meet, the places we visit, the conversations we hear, the infinite number of things we encounter. Description, like narration, is often associated with imaginative literature: children's tales, short stories, and novels. In fiction, narrative events provide a story's bones; description adds flesh to the skeletal structure, helping a reader to imagine the narrative events: "The wind rattled the windows . . . a tall figure wearing a cape emerged from the darkness . . . a pasty white face . . . black hair plastered like a swimmer's cap to his head . . . red lips curled in a sneer . . . the air smelling of rotting meat. . . ." For a descriptive passage to be effective, fiction writers know they must involve their readers' senses to create a reaction to the words. This requirement also applies to essayists who use description as a dominant essay pattern. They, too, must involve a reader's senses—that is, make their readers see, hear, smell, feel, and taste.

Sight

The streets boiled with shoppers . . .
His sunburned face looked grim, heavily lined, and ringed with
*   a gray beard . . .*
Flames lashed the sky . . .

Sound

The breath rasped from his lungs . . .
Water trickled from the faucet in a steady beat . . .
The silence was broken by clicks of forks against plates and the
*   crunching of lettuce . . .*
The soft lilt of Asian voices carried across the river . . .

Smell

The streets smelled of ripe fruit and straw . . .
The aroma of curry floated above the cooking pots . . .
The perfume was full of musk . . .

*His breath, laced with garlic and onions, could stop a blood-
hound . . .*

Touch

The fur, soft and silky, touched my skin . . .
Sharp pebbles covered the path . . .
The cold shower felt like a gust of Arctic air . . .
His fingers said the wound was gaping . . .

Taste

The potion had a sharp, coppery flavor . . .
*She held the bite of sweet melon in her mouth, then began
to chew, the juice, like rich syrup, trickling down her
throat . . .*

Beyond the specific senses is a source that writers also use
to involve their readers in a descriptive passage. It might be called
a writer's "impression" of an experience, his or her own reaction
or perception. Or more simply, a writer's *feelings*.

Feelings

*The air was fresh, cool, and clean, as I walked up the trail,
feeling as if I had been reborn . . .*
*Around and around the park the motorcyclists buzzed like deadly
black bees, and I was afraid to move . . .*
I feel happy when I am curled up in bed with a good book . . .

Strategies

When reading with a critical eye, study the techniques writers
use to involve your senses. Remember that serious writers calculate each detail in a descriptive passage, shaping the words to

touch a circuit in your imagination. Study this passage from "In the Jungle" by naturalist and essayist Annie Dillard. Dillard describes a jungle encampment by appealing to our senses of sight, touch, sound, and smell. She closes by expressing her feelings about the site.

> It was February, the middle of summer. Green fireflies spattered lights across the air and illuminated for seconds, now here, now there, the pale trunks of enormous, solitary trees. Beneath us the brown Napo River was rising, in all silence; it coiled up the sandy bank and tangled its foam in vines that trailed from the forest and roots that looped the shore.
>
> Each breath of night smelled sweet, more moistened and sweet than any kitchen, or garden, or cradle. Each star in Orion seemed to tremble and stir with my breath. All at once, in the thatch house across the clearing behind us, one of the village's Jesuit priests began playing an alto recorder, playing a wordless lyric, in a minor key, that twined over the village clearing, that caught in the big trees' canopies, muted our talk on the bankside, and wandered over the river, dissolving downstream.
>
> This will do, I thought. This will do, for a weekend, or a season, or a home.

Dillard describes a concrete scene full of details directly perceived by the senses. But writers don't limit their descriptive passages to that which can be perceived. Often they describe abstract experiences, such as love, hate, joy, or anger. But to fire a reader's imagination, they must describe the abstract in concrete words. Anger might be described as "a fire in the blood." In this passage from *Dispatches*, a collection of essays about the Vietnam War, Michael Herr captures the fear that comes when an enemy-filled jungle suddenly goes silent. Notice how Herr uses concrete words to describe the abstract and weaves his feelings and earlier experiences into the descriptive fabric.

> There were times during the night when all the jungle sounds would stop at once. There was no dwindling down

or falling away, it was all gone in a single instant as though some signal had been transmitted out to the life; bats, birds, snakes, monkeys, insects, picking up on a frequency that a thousand years in the jungle might condition you to receive, but leaving you as it was to wonder what you weren't hearing now, straining for sound, one piece of information. I had heard it before in other jungles, the Amazon and the Philippines, but those jungles were "secure," there wasn't much chance that hundreds of Viet Cong were coming and going, moving and waiting, living out there just to do you harm. The thought of that one could turn any sudden silence into a space that you'd fill with everything you thought was quiet in you, it could even put you on the approach to clairvoyance. You thought you heard impossible things: damp roots breathing, fruit sweating, fervid bug action, the heartbeat of tiny animals.

Subjective and Objective Description

Descriptive writing is likely to be either subjective or objective. The passage above from Herr's *Dispatches* is subjective. Herr describes a personal encounter with fear, trying to picture his response to the threat an utterly silent jungle foreshadows in a war zone. Objective description, by contrast, is factual, impersonal, thoroughly scrubbed of the writer's impressions. An objective report on yesterday's weather might read like this:

> Westerly ten-mile-an-hour winds blew across the beach. The swells reached fifteen feet.

Rewritten from a subjective angle—that is, with a writer's impressions coloring the facts—the description might read like this:

> Kicked up by ten-mile-an-hour winds, waves rose to mountainous crests before crashing like an avalanche of water onto body surfers.

Purely objective writing is rare in essays with description as the dominant pattern. It is mainly found in scientific reports and encyclopedias. Of course, we find degrees of subjectivity and objectivity. Most descriptive essays, as your reading will confirm, fall somewhere between the extremes.

Dominant Impression

To create an effective description, you might think writers do nothing more than record all they perceive. They do much more. As a critical reader, keep in mind that descriptive writing is not a haphazard activity. With so much detail available for any description, writers must select descriptive details with care and shape them with precision to achieve a **dominant impression.**

In subjective description, selecting detail to create a dominant impression is even more critical than in objective description. Writers must not only select but also embellish descriptive details to create the impression they want. When describing a desert, a writer might want to show that the land is hostile: "the harsh sunlight reflecting from the bleached sand like needles plunging into the hiker's eyes." Describing a politician, a writer might want to show him to be untrustworthy: "his face heavily lined from years of calculating behind closed doors, his eyes skipping around the crowd like those of a criminal about to be exposed." Writers seldom directly state the dominant impression they wish to create; they suggest it.

Consider this passage from Gretel Ehrlich's "A Season of Portraits." Ehrlich, who is an essayist, a novelist, and a Wyoming rancher, describes the dry summer of 1988, when raging fires consumed much of Yellowstone National Park forests. In this passage she concentrates on the wind, suggesting that it is a wind from hell, savage and ghostly, perhaps even isolating her as souls are isolated in a mythical underworld.

> A breeze stiffens. Gusts are clocked at forty-five, sixty, eighty-five miles per hour. Rainless thunderclouds crack above, shaking pine pollen down. *La bufera infernale*—that's

what Dante calls winds that lashed at sinners in hell. I decide to go out in the infernal storm. "This is hell," a herder moving his sheep across the mountain says, grinning, then clears his parched throat and rides away. Wind carries me back and forth, twisting, punching me down.

I'm alone here for much of the summer, these hot winds my only dancing partner. The sheep and their herder vanish over the ridge. I close my eyes, and the planet is auditory only: tree branches twist into tubas and saxes, are caught by large hands that press down valves, and everywhere on this ranch I hear feral music—ghostly tunes made not by animals gone wild but by grasses, sagebrush, and fence wire singing.

Once writers decide on a dominant impression and select the appropriate details to suggest it, they must arrange the details in an effective order. Often a structure will become visible during the writing and revision, one that will be unique for that passage. Ehrlich arranges the passage above in two parts: the world she sees and the world she hears, which are clearly separated when she writes, "I closed my eyes." She continues by suggesting that the wind plays the branches of trees like musical instruments and creates ghostly music by rushing through grasses, sagebrush, fence wire. By shutting her eyes, and yours as a sensitive reader, she transforms the world into a mysterious place.

Arrangement of Details

But you will find no strict formulas for arranging descriptive details; writers do, however, follow some general principles. In visual description, a writer will usually structure the details in the way that the eye would record them; that is, by spatial arrangement—from left to right, right to left, near to far, far to near, center outward. A writer might begin with a broad picture and narrow to the particulars, like a film opening with a panoramic view of a landscape or city and gradually moving into the scene, finally focusing on one specific image.

To describe a person, a writer might begin with a general descriptive statement: "She looked as if she had stepped from the pages of *Vogue,* a stylish woman," and then moved downward from head to toe, "Her hair was the color of straw and cropped short; her neck seemed carved from ivory. . . ." Or this writer might begin by describing an unusual physical feature and work from there: "Her nose didn't fit her stylish appearance: it was a bit long and bent slightly to the left, as if it had stopped a boxer's left cross. Otherwise, she was unflawed. . . ." As you read descriptive passages, keep in mind that writers have many ways in which to organize a description. Critical readers examine writers' varied ways of structuring descriptive details and applying the techniques.

Description in College Writing

Vivid description is embedded in all but the most scientifically objective papers, bringing life to reports, arguments, explanations, even essay examinations. Often you may want to use a descriptive passage to add color and drama to an essay that is developed around a dominant pattern other than description. The principles of description for such a passage still apply. Above all, you must establish a clear purpose for such a passage and clearly understand your audience to determine how much descriptive detail to include in the passage.

This descriptive passage begins an extended student essay analyzing the ways in which people use their physical appearance to communicate a message. Debra Carlson wrote twelve paragraphs to complete the project, but only the first two paragraphs are pure description. The third brief paragraph here establishes the purpose of the descriptive passage.

Carlson's opening sentences suggest the

At first glance, Tom does not look like a typical teenager in advertisements for the Gap

purpose—Tom's appearance is clearly not in the "mainstream." She begins the description at Tom's head and moves to his feet, following a clear structure. She selects her details carefully to reinforce her purpose. It might help to imagine what she has excluded—color of Tom's hair and eyes, his physical size, and so on. She doesn't need these details to achieve the dominant impression she wants to create.

Carlson opens paragraph 2 by responding to Tom's appearance, defining it for the reader.

She reviews some of the details she had recorded, recasting them, suggesting that Tom is not what he appears to be.

This paragraph clearly sets the purpose of the passage and leads to the discussion that follows.

and Polo. In fact, his appearance contrasts sharply with the image of the typical upper-middle-class teen splashed on the pages of mainstream magazines. His hair is twisted into finger-sized dreadlocks and hangs in long strands below his shoulders, like the hair of Jamaican musicians. He wears an earring, sometimes a gold post that twinkles in the light, at other times a peace symbol that dangles from the end of a chain. He wears "tie-dyed" shirts, a popular sixties style that comes in bright oranges, greens, reds, purples, and yellows, with psychedelic patterns. His trousers are usually faded jeans with threadbare knees and strategically placed rips held together with safety pins, "A carryover from punk days," he says. When he is not wearing hiking boots, well worn and split on the sides, he wears sandals.

His appearance might be described as "scruffy" today; twenty-five years ago, it would have been described as "counterculture." But on closer examination, it is clear that Tom's earring is not gold plated, it is fourteen karat, his T-shirt did not come from the local thrift shop, it came from a unisex boutique with high price tags, and his jeans were not made by Levi, they were made by a high-fashion designer company. His appearance might suggest he lives in a low-rent apartment, but in reality he lives in an expensive suburb, attends a private high school, and has a straight A grade average. Although he listens to reggae music while his peers listen to rock, he is quick to set aside his Sony Walkman and discuss his recent spiritual conversion.

What explains Tom's appearance? Why is his dress so dramatically different though his behavior reflects conservative middle-class values? Tom's appearance is sending a message that says, "I'm different, I'm unique." Appearance—or style—always communicates a message.

. . .

Carlson has applied the principles of description effectively. She has carefully selected the details to create the impression she wants. She arranges the details in a sensible structure and sticks to it. She achieves what description should achieve when used with another dominant essay pattern—she invigorates her essay by adding color to a passage that might have been a colorless analysis.

Most of us share senses—sight, sound, smell, touch, taste—and we have feelings. Professional writers know that by evoking sensory experience and feelings in their readers' minds, they will enrich the reading experience. Read the essays in this section. See how the authors evoke the senses; analyze their selection of descriptive details; and examine how they shape descriptive passages to achieve a dominant impression. Take notes as you read, mark an interesting passage, underline a vivid phrase. When you write your own descriptive passages, apply the principles you've learned from reading as a writer. Don't be timid about using a professional writer's passage for a model. The techniques of effective description are universal—available for everyone to use. Professional writers are challenged by the demands of description; certainly you, the beginning writer, should also feel challenged.

Rarely will an author attempt to develop an essay by focusing readers' attention on description primarily, as Kingston does in "Photographs of My Parents." Ostensibly describing meager biographical artifacts, Kingston outlines her mother's life, from young adult to aged matriarch, obliquely including remnants of her own life.

Archeology scientifically studies ancient lives and cultures, in part by examining artifacts excavated at the sites of ancient civilizations. You might begin an "archeological exercise" by asking the class to discuss one famous person: a politician, a movie star, a world leader, or the like. Then ask them to imagine that thousands of years from now, archeologists discover the site where this famous person thrived. The question for discussion is this: "What five artifacts—any objects made by human beings—would best represent or symbolize this person's qualities?"

After such a discussion, students see that much can be learned about people by scrutinizing their possessions; they can create a carefully contrived descriptive essay by concentrating on the artifacts that go into the essay, rather than on characters, actions, or settings.

MARGINAL NOTES

The word *joy* is represented in "abstract" Chinese ideographs; that is, the classical ideographs themselves have been shaped into a form combining message and ornamentation.

During the Chinese Civil War (1945–1949) between the communist troops of Mao Tse-Tung and the nationalist troops of Chiang Kai-Shek, many Chinese fled China for Hong Kong.

❦ Maxine Hong Kingston ❦

Maxine Hong Kingston was born and raised in a Chinese-American community in Stockton, California, where her parents ran a laundry. She grew up listening to stories about China from her parents and relatives, who were first-generation immigrants. She attended the University of California at Berkeley and currently teaches creative writing at the University of Hawaii. Her stories, essays, and poems have been published in Ms., The New Yorker, *and* American Heritage. The Woman Warrior: Memoirs of a Girlhood among Ghosts *(1975), Kingston's award-winning autobiography, describes her memories and retells the stories she heard as a child. Her second book,* China Men *(1980), won the National Book Award.*

Photographs of My Parents

In this selection from The Woman Warrior, *Kingston looks at much more than photographs. Her searching descriptions of mundane objects reveal some of the deep differences between the culture she grew up in and the China her parents left. In writing of both the familiarity and the strangeness in the photographs of her parents, she reaches into the past to better understand the present.*

Try to visualize as vividly as you can the differences between the Chinese and the Chinese-American photographs that Kingston describes. Consider how these differences contribute to the essay's central meaning.

Once in a long while, four times so far for me, my mother brings out the metal tube that holds her medical diploma. On the tube are gold circles crossed with seven red lines each—"joy" ideographs in abstract. There are also little flowers that look like gears for a gold machine. According to the scraps of labels with Chinese and American addresses, stamps, and postmarks, the family airmailed the can from Hong Kong in 1950. It got crushed in the middle, and whoever tried to peel the labels off stopped because the red and gold paint came off too, leaving silver scratches

In China, the bat is emblematic of happiness and long life.

Kingston mentions four predominantly Chinese regions in the Far East, each having its distinct politics and customs; all are Chinese, nonetheless.

The National Republic of China, under Chiang Kai-Shek, was formally recognized by the United States in 1928.

The stork-brings-the-baby myth can be traced to an Old Norse legend. To account for the mother's bed rest after giving birth, children were told that the stork bit the mother just before he departed. The stork has long been a symbol of filial devotion: The Romans enforced *Lex Ciconaria*, the "Stork's Law," compelling children to care for their aged parents. "Ex-assistant étranger . . .": literally, "Former foreign teacher (ex-assistant) at the surgical and maternity clinic of the University of Lyons." *Chop* is from Hindi *chap*, "impression, stamp." A chop is an official stamp or seal; also, a person's "signature stamp," used in many parts of Asia.

The small mystery about the mother's true age heightens interest in this descriptive passage.

that rust. Somebody tried to pry the end off before discovering that the tube pulls apart. When I open it, the smell of China flies out, a thousand-year-old bat flying heavy-headed out of the Chinese caverns where bats are as white as dust, a smell that comes from long ago, far back in the brain. Crates from Canton, Hong Kong, Singapore, and Taiwan have that smell too, only stronger because they are more recently come from the Chinese.

Inside the can are three scrolls, one inside another. The largest says that in the twenty-third year of the National Republic, the To Keung School of Midwifery, where she has had two years of instruction and Hospital Practice, awards its Diploma to my mother, who has shown through oral and written examination her Proficiency in Midwifery, Pediatrics, Gynecology, "Medecine," "Surgary," Therapeutics, Ophthalmology, Bacteriology, Dermatology, Nursing and Bandage. This document has eight stamps on it: one, the school's English and Chinese names embossed together in a circle; one, as the Chinese enumerate, a stork and a big baby in lavender ink; one, the school's Chinese seal; one, an orangish paper stamp pasted in the border design; one, the red seal of Dr. Wu Pak-liang, M.D., Lyon, Berlin, president and "Ex-assistant étranger à la clinique chirugicale et d'accouchement de l'université de Lyon"; one, the red seal of Dean Woo Yin-kam, M.D.; one, my mother's seal, her chop mark larger than the president's and the dean's; and one, the number 1279 on the back. Dean Woo's signature is followed by "(Hackett)." I read in a history book that Hackett Medical College for Women at Canton was founded in the nineteenth century by European women doctors.

The school seal has been pressed over a photograph of my mother at the age of thirty-seven. The diploma gives her age as twenty-seven. She looks younger than I do, her eyebrows are thicker, her lips fuller. Her naturally curly hair is parted on the left, one wavy wisp tendrilling off to the right. She wears a scholar's white gown, and she is not thinking about her appearance. She stares straight ahead as if she could see me and past me to her grandchildren and grandchildren's grandchildren. She has spacy eyes, as all people recently from Asia have. Her eyes do not focus on the camera. My mother is not smiling; Chinese do not smile for photographs. Their faces command relatives in foreign lands—"Send money"—and posterity forever—"Put food in front of this picture." My mother does not understand Chinese-American snapshots. "What are you laughing at?" she asks.

The second scroll is a long narrow photograph of the graduating class with the school officials seated in front. I picked out my mother immediately. Her face is exactly her own, though forty years younger. She is so familiar, I can only tell whether or not she is pretty or happy or smart by comparing her to the other women. For this formal group picture she straightened her hair with oil to make a chinlength bob like the others'. On the other women, strangers, I can recognize a curled lip, a sidelong glance, pinched shoulders. My mother is not soft; the girl with the small nose and dimpled underlip is soft. My mother is not humorous, not like the girl at the end who lifts her mocking chin to pose like Girl Graduate. My mother does not have smiling eyes; the old woman teacher (Dean Woo?) in front crinkles happily, and the one faculty member in the western suit smiles westernly. Most of the graduates are girls whose faces have not yet formed; my mother's face will not change anymore, except to age. She is intelligent, alert, pretty. I can't tell if she's happy. 4

The graduates seem to have been looking elsewhere when they pinned the rose, zinnia, or chrysanthemum on their precise black dresses. One thin girl wears hers in the middle of her chest. A few have a flower over a left or right nipple. My mother put hers, a chrysanthemum, below her left breast. Chinese dresses at that time were dartless, cut as if women did not have breasts; these young doctors, unaccustomed to decorations, may have seen their chests as black expanses with no reference points for flowers. Perhaps they couldn't shorten that far gaze that lasts only a few years after a Chinese emigrates. In this picture too my mother's eyes are big with what they held—reaches of oceans beyond China, land beyond oceans. Most emigrants learn the barbarians' directness—how to gather themselves and stare rudely into talking faces as if trying to catch lies. In America my mother has eyes as strong as boulders, never once skittering off a face, but she has not learned to place decorations and phonograph needles, 5

The white chrysanthemum has a long and fabled history in both China and Japan. The famous haiku poet Basho wrote that the white chrysanthemum "remains immaculate," even under intense scrutiny.

In tailoring, a dart is a short, stitched fold meant to make a garment fit closely while conforming to the natural shape of the body.

Earlier, Kingston's mother had "spacy eyes, as all people recently from Asia have." Now the eyes have become "accustomed" to America, and the description gives Kingston a chance to comment obliquely on her mother's life.

nor has she stopped seeing land on the other side of the oceans. Now her eyes include the relatives in China, as they once included my father smiling and smiling in his many western outfits, a different one for each photograph that he sent from America.

He and his friends took pictures of one another in bathing suits at Coney Island beach, the salt wind from the Atlantic blowing their hair. He's the one in the middle with his arms about the necks of his buddies. They pose in the cockpit of a biplane, on a motorcycle, and on a lawn beside the "Keep Off the Grass" sign. They are always laughing. My father, white shirt sleeves rolled up, smiles in front of a wall of clean laundry. In the spring he wears a new straw hat, cocked at a Fred Astaire angle. He steps out, dancing down the stairs, one foot forward, one back, a hand in his pocket. He wrote to her about the American custom of stomping on straw hats come fall. "If you want to save your hat for next year," he said, "you have to put it away early, or else when you're riding the subway or walking along Fifth Avenue, any stranger can snatch it off your head and put his foot through it. That's the way they celebrate the change of seasons here." In the winter he wears a gray felt hat with his gray overcoat. He is sitting on a rock in Central Park. In one snapshot he is not smiling; someone took it when he was studying, blurred in the glare of the desk lamp.

There are no snapshots of my mother. In two small portraits, however, there is a black thumbprint on her forehead, as if someone had inked in bangs, as if someone had marked her.

"Mother, did bangs come into fashion after you had the picture taken?" One time she said yes. Another time when I asked, "Why do you have fingerprints on your forehead?" she said, "Your First Uncle did that." I disliked the unsureness in her voice.

The last scroll has columns of Chinese words. The only English is "Department of Health, Canton," imprinted on my mother's face, the same photograph as on the diploma. I keep looking to see whether she was afraid. Year after year my father did not come home or send for her. Their two children had been dead for ten years. If he did not return soon, there would be no more children. ("They were three and two years old, a boy and a girl.

The beginning of a *flashback*, a device with which writers present a scene or incident that happened before some preceding scene or incident in the work.

Fred Astaire (1899–1987) starred in such musical comedies as *Top Hat* (1935) and *Shall We Dance?* (1937). His graceful and original tap dancing was famous.

The photographs are described as if they were ordinary identification or passport photos.

6

7

8

9

They could talk already.") My father did send money regularly, though, and she had nobody to spend it on but herself. She bought good clothes and shoes. Then she decided to use the money for becoming a doctor. She did not leave for Canton immediately after the children died. In China there was time to complete feelings. As my father had done, my mother left the village by ship. There was a sea bird painted on the ship to protect it against shipwreck and winds. She was in luck. The following ship was boarded by river pirates, who kidnapped every passenger, even old ladies. "Sixty dollars for an old lady" was what the bandits used to say. "I sailed alone," she says, "to the capital of the entire province." She took a brown leather suitcase and a seabag stuffed with two quilts.

A sea bird painted on a ship's bow may be a traditional emblem of protection, but it is also interesting that a bird, according to Jungian theory, is a beneficent creature representing spirits or angels, supernatural aid, or thoughts and flights of fancy.

Notice that Kingston's mother took one quilt for each of them.

Meaning and Purpose

1. Have you ever looked through old photographs of your parents or grandparents? What feelings did you have when you looked at them? What questions did you ask? What do the photographs tell you about yourself?
2. What are the contrasts between Chinese and Chinese-American photographs and what do these contrasts suggest about the meaning of "Photographs of My Parents"?
3. In paragraph 3, Kingston writes that "the school seal has been pressed over a photograph of my mother"; in paragraph 7, Kingston describes a small portrait of her mother, "there is a black thumbprint on her forehead . . . as if someone had marked her"; and in paragraph 9, she reports that another photograph has the English words, "Department of Health, Canton," printed over her face. How do these descriptive details work in the essay?
4. What does paragraph 6 reveal about Kingston's father?
5. Discuss the significance of flowers pinned awkwardly on the graduates' dresses.

POSSIBLE ANSWERS

Meaning and Purpose

1. Encourage students to discuss how they feel about old photographs. Ask them to describe some photographs in as much detail as Kingston does.

2. The Chinese in the photographs are nearly expressionless because "Chinese do not smile for photographs" (3), and Kingston "can't tell if [her mother] is happy" (4). The Chinese-Americans in the photographs are "always laughing" (6), and they pose as westerners do.

3. The seals and words over the photographs of Kingston's mother show that the photographs were official. They are not taken for pleasure, or to capture fun or happiness, as those of Kingston's father are.

4. Kingston's father is happy-go-lucky in some photographs. He works in a laundry, watches American movies, adapts an American custom about "stomping on straw hats" (6), and pursues a course of study. He seems to combine fun, work, and ambition.

5. The women were unaccustomed to decoration, and the dresses did not conform to the female figure. The flowers therefore seem out of place, and were pinned on awkwardly.
6. The bat is a symbol of happiness and long life in China.

Strategy

1. Kingston organizes her essay as the contents of the metal tube are organized: she describes the three scrolls as they appear, one inside another. The transitions from one section to the next are the second sentence in paragraph 2, and the first sentences in paragraphs 4 and 9.
2. Some examples of sensory details are: *smell*—"The smell of China flies out, a thousand-year-old bat . . . brain" (1) (metaphor); *sight*—"Her naturally curly hair is parted on the left, one wavy wisp tendrilling off to the right" (3) (image); and "flowers that look like gears for a gold machine" (1) (simile). Examples of *impression* or *feeling* are: "Most of the graduates are girls whose faces have not yet formed . . . happy" (4), and "She wears a scholar's white gown and she is not thinking about her appearance" (3).
3. This is a subjective essay, told from the author's point of view.
4. Kingston describes the tube in careful details that evoke China: the "joy" ideographs, the flowers, and the stamps. The tube was damaged in the mail but still carries the smell of China. These details already suggest a contrast between East and West and prepare readers for the depth of detail that follows.

Style

1. Kingston is nostalgic about the China of her mother's younger life when she describes, in paragraph 1, the smell flying out of the tube, and in paragraph 9, "In China, there was time to complete feelings." She describes her mother with affectionate detail.

6. In the first paragraph, what does the "thousand-year-old bat" signify?

Strategy

1. What is Kingston's general organizational strategy for description? Where are the three transition points at which Kingston moves from one section to another?
2. Identify some descriptions that involve the senses, and some that evoke impressions or feelings. What kinds of figures of speech are they—metaphor, simile, personification, descriptive image?
3. Is this descriptive essay subjective or objective, and how do you know?
4. What impression does Kingston give of the metal tube in the first paragraph? How does her description prepare you for the rest of the essay?

Style

1. How would you describe the tone of the essay or the narrator's feelings about the contents of the metal tube?
2. Consider the metal tube to be a symbol for Kingston's mother. What qualities does it suggest about her?
3. Kingston uses some medical terms. Be sure you know their meanings: *ophthalmology, pediatrics, gynecology, dermatology, therapeutics* (2).

Writing Tasks

1. Study Kingston's essay to see how she uses photographs to reveal bits and pieces of her parents' history. Then select photographs

2. Kingston's mother embodies the essence of China, as the tube does. She is rigid and contained, and her Chinese customs are "damaged" by life in the West, like the tube.

3. *Ophthalmology,* specialty in eyes; *pediatrics,* specialty in children's medicine; *gynecology,* specialty in women's medicine; *dermatology,* specialty in the skin; *therapeutics,* specialty in remedies.

of two friends or relatives who have both similar and opposing character traits. Use the photographs to write a description that reveals their character traits without stating them directly.

2. Describe a significant possession of someone you know, and show how it characterizes the person.

This evocative essay deals with time: its delightful past, its pleasant present, and its tragic future—when the author finally acknowledges its passing.

The subject intrigues students, mainly because it has not often been taken seriously: time is now, to many of us. Only as our days close do we realize that time is not constantly on the sidelines. It's here and we are its products. Hemingway said to Lillian Ross, "Time is the least thing we have of."

Instructors have energized a conversation on time by asking students, "How old is *old*?" Experience suggests that answers will vary, from "Five years older than I am right now," to "Forty." These answers will help to establish the chronological climate in which students approach this essay, which was written when White was about forty-one, about the age that is still considered a time for reflection.

After students have discussed age well enough to establish that no one has a definitive answer, instructors have asked, "How far back can you remember?" Again, answers range from five years to whenever, depending on how long students think about their answers.

The third and fourth questions lead in to White's essay: "How far back can you remember a pleasant experience that has *meaning* for you now?" followed quickly by "Has the meaning of the experience changed for you, over the years?" These two questions are not lightly answered, for they require much memory-searching, which one student calls "scratching the bottom of the database barrel."

When White visited the lake as a boy, the experience had no meaning for him except as a trigger: Lake = joy. No more. With age, however, his experience took on hitherto unsuspected meaning. Students often see that the past event, plus time, equals a new meaning for the event—after they have thought over their class discussion about time.

❦ E. B. White ❦

Born in Mount Vernon, New York, in 1899, Elwyn Brooks White is considered one of America's finest essayists. At Cornell University he studied English composition with Edmund Strunk, and years later revised Strunk's concise book of writing guidance, now known as Strunk and White's Elements of Style. *He was for many years a staff writer at* The New Yorker, *where he first earned his reputation as a master essayist. He also wrote a regular column for* Harper's *magazine for several years. His essay collections include* One Man's Meat *(1944),* The Second Tree from the Corner *(1953), and* The Essays of E. B. White *(1977). Two of his books—*Stuart Little *(1945) and* Charlotte's Web *(1952)—have become classics of children's literature. He died in 1985 at his farm in coastal Maine, to which he had retired in 1957.*

Once More to the Lake

In this essay, first published in Harper's *in 1941 and collected in* One Man's Meat *(1944), White uses the force of reminiscence to enhance a meticulous description of a recent event. On a fishing trip to a lake in Maine with his young son, the author recalls his own childhood summers at the same lake. He inevitably begins to see himself in his son and is jolted into awareness of his own mortality.*

White, in this essay, ranges in time—from the present, to the past, to the present, and back again. Be alert to those changes.

August 1941

One summer, along about 1904, my father rented a camp on a lake in Maine and took us all there for the month of August. We all got ringworm from some kittens and had to rub Pond's Extract on our arms and legs night and morning, and my father rolled over in a canoe with all his clothes on; but outside of that the vacation was a success and from then on none of us ever thought there was any place in the world like that lake in Maine.

MARGINAL NOTES

Born in 1899, White would have been about five years old at the time of the earlier excursion.

Here, nostalgia, a longing for former happy times, is White's stimulus to return to the lake to "revisit old haunts," after almost forty years.

White combines light tension and reverie in this paragraph. First, he worries about how the lake might have been changed by encroaching civilization. Next, he recounts memories of his early days on the lake.

White reminds us that we can remember our calm moments of joy if we allow ourselves to pursue the mental paths of least resistance, letting one memory softly lead into another.

Notice White's combining an image of nature (the lake) with a symbol of religion.

White gives us the larger picture of the lake, pointing out its general virtues, and then he mentions how those virtues appear through the eyes of a child—as "primeval"; that is, "of the earliest times or ages."

We returned summer after summer—always on August 1 for one month. I have since become a salt-water man, but sometimes in summer there are days when the restlessness of the tides and the fearful cold of the sea water and the incessant wind that blows across the afternoon and into the evening make me wish for the placidity of a lake in the woods. A few weeks ago this feeling got so strong I bought myself a couple of bass hooks and a spinner and returned to the lake where we used to go, for a week's fishing and to revisit old haunts.

I took along my son, who had never had any fresh water up his nose and who had seen lily pads only from train windows. On the journey over to the lake I began to wonder what it would be like. I wondered how time would have marred this unique, this holy spot—the coves and streams, the hills that the sun set behind, the camps and the paths behind the camps. I was sure that the tarred road would have found it out, and I wondered in what other ways it would be desolated. It is strange how much you can remember about places like that once you allow your mind to return into the grooves that lead back. You remember one thing, and that suddenly reminds you of another thing. I guess I remembered clearest of all the early mornings, when the lake was cool and motionless, remembered how the bedroom smelled of the lumber it was made of and of the wet woods whose scent entered through the screen. The partitions in the camp were thin and did not extend clear to the top of the rooms, and as I was always the first up I would dress softly so as not to wake the others, and sneak out into the sweet outdoors and start out in the canoe, keeping close along the shore in the long shadows of the pines. I remembered being very careful never to rub my paddle against the gunwale for fear of disturbing the stillness of the cathedral.

The lake had never been what you would call a wild lake. There were cottages sprinkled around the shores, and it was in farming country although the shores of the lake were quite heavily wooded. Some of the cottages were owned by nearby farmers, and you would live at the shore and eat your meals at the farmhouse. That's what our family did. But although it wasn't wild, it was a fairly large and undisturbed lake and there were places in it that, to a child at least, seemed infinitely remote and primeval.

I was right about the tar; it led to within half a mile of the shore. But when I got back there, with my boy, and we settled into a camp near a farmhouse and into the kind of summertime I had known, I could tell that it was going to be pretty much the same as it had been before—I knew it, lying in bed the first morning, smelling the bedroom and hearing the boy sneak quietly out and go off along the shore in a boat. I began to sustain the illusion that he was I, and therefore, by simple transposition, that I was my father. This sensation persisted, kept cropping up all the time we were there. It was not an entirely new feeling, but in this setting it grew much stronger. I seemed to be living a dual existence. I would be in the middle of some simple act, I would be picking up a bait box or laying down a table fork, or I would be saying something, and suddenly it would be not I but my father who was saying the words or making the gesture. It gave me a creepy sensation.

We went fishing the first morning. I felt the same damp moss covering the worms in the bait can, and saw the dragonfly alight on the tip of my rod as it hovered a few inches from the surface of the water. It was the arrival of this fly that convinced me beyond any doubt that everything was as it always had been, that the years were a mirage and that there had been no years. The small waves were the same, chucking the rowboat under the chin as we fished at anchor, and the boat was the same boat, the same color green and the ribs broken in the same places, and under the floorboards the same fresh-water leavings and débris—the dead hellgrammite, the wisps of moss, the rusty discarded fish-hook, the dried blood from yesterday's catch. We stared silently at the tips of our rods, at the dragonflies that came and went. I lowered the tip of mine into the water, tentatively, pensively dislodging the fly, which darted two feet away, poised, darted two feet back, and came to rest again a little farther up the rod. There had been no years between the ducking of this dragonfly and the other one—the one that was part of memory. I looked

4

5

Throughout the essay, the boy is never clearly described; he is never identified beyond mere "boy." William Wordsworth's lines from *My Heart Leaps Up* (1807) are worth reviving here, as capturing the essence of White's "boy":

The child is father of the man;
And I could wish my days to be
Bound each to each by natural piety.

White approaches an almost instinctual, innate need to see himself as the boy.

The beginning of the adventure, the reliving of White's childhood. His years fall away, he becomes the boy again, and the water remains as when he had first seen it.

Water as symbol has a venerable history. Limitless and immortal in the eyes of the ancients, water is the beginning of all life. Homer, in book IV of *The Iliad,* speaks of "Ocean, who is the source of all." Modern psychology sees water as symbolizing the unconscious: the nonformal, dynamic, motivating, female side of the personality.

To enchant is "to cast a spell over," "to charm greatly," and more. An enchantment is a reduction to an inferior state, as in a person changing into an animal, for which see the story of Circe, as told in *The Odyssey*. White's "sea" enchants; that is, in mysterious ways the lake itself has its effect on White, causing him in a way to "be" his childhood self.

A cult is a system of ritual. White's passing comment is that some things never change. We will always have the pseudo-cultists of nature with us, who despoil nature by using it, this time to bathe with scum-producing soap.

White is no longer in 1904 or thereabout. Horse-drawn wagons produce three tracks, the middle one made by the horse. Now that the automobile has replaced the horse, the middle track has disappeared. For that matter, middle alternatives in people's lives also disappear with passing time, White suggests, but life itself goes on, "there having been no passage of time, only the illusion of it."

at the boy, who was silently watching his fly, and it was my hands that held his rod, my eyes watching. I felt dizzy and didn't know which rod I was at the end of.

We caught two bass, hauling them in briskly as though they were mackerel, pulling them over the side of the boat in a businesslike manner without any landing net, and stunning them with a blow on the back of the head. When we got back for a swim before lunch, the lake was exactly where we had left it, the same number of inches from the dock, and there was only the merest suggestion of a breeze. This seemed an utterly enchanted sea, this lake you could leave to its own devices for a few hours and come back to, and find it had not stirred, this constant and trustworthy body of water. In the shallows, the dark, water-soaked sticks and twigs, smooth and old, were undulating in clusters on the bottom against the clean ribbed sand, and the track of the mussel was plain. A school of minnows swam by, each minnow with its small individual shadow, doubling the attendance, so clear and sharp in the sunlight. Some of the other campers were in swimming, along the shore, one of them with a cake of soap, and the water felt thin and clear and unsubstantial. Over the years there had been this person with the cake of soap, this cultist, and here he was. There had been no years. 6

Up to the farmhouse to dinner through the teeming, dusty field, the road under our sneakers was only a two-track road. The middle track was missing, the one with the marks of the hooves and the splotches of dried, flaky manure. There had always been three tracks to choose from in choosing which track to walk in; now the choice was narrowed down to two. For a moment I missed terribly the middle alternative. But the way led past the tennis court, and something about the way it lay there in the sun reassured me; the tape had loosened along the backline, the alleys were green with plantains and other weeds, and the net (installed in June and removed in September) sagged in the dry noon, and the whole place steamed with midday heat and hunger and emptiness. There was a choice of pie for dessert, and one was blueberry and one was apple, and the waitresses were the same country girls, there having been no passage of time, only the illusion of 7 it as in a dropped curtain—the waitresses were still fifteen; their hair had been washed, that was the only difference—they had been to the movies and seen the pretty girls with the clean hair.

Summertime, oh summertime, pattern of life indelible, the fade-proof lake, the woods unshatterable, the pasture with the sweetfern and the juniper forever and ever, summer without end; this was the background, and the life along the shore was the design, their tiny docks with the flagpole and the American flag floating against the white clouds in the blue sky, the little paths over the roots of the trees leading from camp to camp and the paths leading back to the outhouses and the can of lime for sprinkling, and at the souvenir counters at the store the miniature birch-bark canoes and the postcards that showed things looking a little better than they looked. This was the American family at play, escaping the city heat, wondering whether the newcomers in the camp at the head of the cove were "common" or "nice," wondering whether it was true that the people who drove up for Sunday dinner at the farmhouse were turned away because there wasn't enough chicken. 8

It seemed to me, as I kept remembering all this, that those times and those summers had been infinitely precious and worth saving. There had been jollity and peace and goodness. The arriving (at the beginning of August) had been so big a business in itself, at the railway station the farm wagon drawn up, the first smell of the pine-laden air, the first glimpse of the smiling farmer, and the great importance of the trunks and your father's enormous authority in such matters, and the feel of the wagon under you for the long ten-mile haul, and at the top of the last long hill catching the first view of the lake after eleven months of not seeing this cherished body of water. The shouts and cries of the other campers when they saw you, and the trunks to be unpacked, to give up their rich burden. (Arriving was less exciting nowadays, when you sneaked up in your car and parked it under a tree near the camp and took out the bags and in five minutes it was all over, no fuss, no loud wonderful fuss about trunks.) 9

Peace and goodness and jollity. The only thing that was wrong now, really, was the sound of the place, an unfamiliar nervous 10

In ancient Greece, a paean was a hymn of thanksgiving to the gods, especially to Apollo, the god of music, poetry, prophecy, and medicine, represented as exemplifying manly youth and beauty. In this paragraph of unrestrained and timeless joy, White has written his own modern paean.

The less frequently we see something, the less likely we are to recognize it because of familiarity alone. In this paragraph, White dwells on the sheer excitement a boy feels (or felt) at the moment when the family arrived at the lake. These times were worth saving in the storehouse of his memory, from which other times have long since faded. (Nothing nowadays is as exciting as memories of past excitement.)

The paragraph begins with a complaint: the new outboard motors are too loud. Then it drifts into the past, when the older motors were comparatively silent and depended more on the operator. White as a boy had more control over machines; he could tinker with them, experiment, attain complete mastery. The man could control more of his life when he and machines were young.

sound of the outboard motors. This was the note that jarred, the one thing that would sometimes break the illusion and set the years moving. In those other summertimes all the motors were inboard; and when they were at a little distance, the noise they made was a sedative, an ingredient of summer sleep. They were one-cylinder and two-cylinder engines, and some were make-and-break and some were jump-spark, but they all made a sleepy sound across the lake. The one-lungers throbbed and fluttered, and the twin-cylinder ones purred and purred, and that was a quiet sound, too. But now the campers all had outboards. In the daytime, in the hot mornings, these motors made a petulant, irritable sound; at night, in the still evening when the afterglow lit the water, they whined about one's ears like mosquitoes. My boy loved our rented outboard, and his great desire was to achieve single-handed mastery over it, and authority, and he soon learned the trick of choking it a little (but not too much), and the adjustment of the needle valve. Watching him I would remember the things you could do with the old one-cylinder engine with the heavy flywheel, how you could have it eating out of your hand if you got really close to it spiritually. Motorboats in those days didn't have clutches, and you would make a landing by shutting off the motor at the proper time and coasting in with a dead rudder. But there was a way of reversing them, if you learned the trick, by cutting the switch and putting it on again exactly on the final dying revolution of the flywheel, so that it would kick back against the compression and begin reversing. Approaching a dock in a strong following breeze, it was difficult to slow up sufficiently by the ordinary coasting method, and if a boy felt he had complete mastery over his motor, he was tempted to keep it running beyond its time and then reverse it a few feet from the dock. It took a cool nerve, because if you threw the switch a twentieth of a second too soon you would catch the flywheel when it still had speed enough to go up past center, and the boat would leap ahead, charging bull-fashion at the dock.

We had a good week at camp. The bass were biting well and the sun shown endlessly, day after day. We would be tired at night and lie down in the accumulated heat of the little bedrooms

As he does with the other paragraphs in this essay, White is playing with time. Halfway through this paragraph, he abruptly shifts from past to present, from "what it had felt like to think about girls then" to "After breakfast we [he and his boy] would go up to the store." This strategy reinforces his earlier claim that things remain the same, timeless in his eyes, a point that he makes clear in the last line of this paragraph, where the boy and he become indivisible.

11

after the long hot day and the breeze would stir almost imperceptibly outside and the smell of the swamp drift in through the rusty screens. Sleep would come easily and in the morning the red squirrel would be on the roof, tapping out his gay routine. I kept remembering everything, lying in bed in the mornings—the small steamboat that had a long rounded stern like the lip of a Ubangi, and how quietly she ran on the moonlight sails, when the older boys played their mandolins and the girls sang and we ate doughnuts dipped in sugar, and how sweet the music was on the water in the shining night, and what it had felt like to think about girls then. After breakfast we would go up to the store and the things were in the same place—the minnows in a bottle, the plugs and spinners disarranged and pawed over by the youngsters from the boys' camp, the Fig Newtons and the Beeman's gum. Outside, the road was tarred and cars stood in front of the store. Inside, all was just as it had always been, except there was more Coca-Cola and not so much Moxie and root beer and birch beer and sarsaparilla. We would walk out with the bottle of pop apiece and sometimes the pop would backfire up our noses and hurt. We explored the streams, quietly, where the turtles slid off the sunny logs and dug their way into the soft bottom; and we lay on the town wharf and fed worms to the tame bass. Everywhere we went I had trouble making out which I was, the one walking at my side, the one walking in my pants.

One afternoon while we were there at that lake a thunderstorm came up. It was like the revival of an old melodrama that I had seen long ago with childish awe. The second-act climax of the drama of the electrical disturbance over a lake in America had not changed in any important respect. This was the big scene, still the big scene. The whole thing was so familiar, the first feeling of oppression and heat and a general air around camp of not wanting to go very far away. In mid-afternoon (it was all the same) a curious darkening of the sky, and a lull in everything that had made life tick; and then the way the boats suddenly swung the other way at their moorings with the coming of a breeze out of the new quarter, and the premonitory rumble. Then the kettle drum, then the snare, then the bass drum and cymbals, then

12

Typically, a melodrama ended happily, after the second-act *climax*, which describes the intensity of interest in the audience. White remains with the "timelessness motif," saying that "The whole thing was so familiar." The storm itself is indeed timeless: It is melodramatic, with its kettle, snare, and bass drums, and ancient Greece with its "gods grinning and licking their chops." It ends with the eternal comedian, who is out of place yet strangely appropriate—the two conditions of comedy.

crackling light against the dark, and the gods grinning and licking their chops in the hills. Afterward the calm, the rain steadily rustling in the calm lake, the return of light and hope and spirits, and the campers running out in joy and relief to go swimming in the rain, their bright cries perpetuating the deathless joke about how they were getting simply drenched, and the children screaming with delight at the new sensation of bathing in the rain, and the joke about getting drenched linking the generations in a strong indestructible chain. And the comedian who waded in carrying an umbrella.

When the others went swimming, my son said he was going in, too. He pulled his dripping trunks from the line where they had hung all through the shower and wrung them out. Languidly, and with no thought of going in, I watched him, his hard little body, skinny and bare, saw him wince slightly as he pulled up around his vitals the small, soggy, icy garment. As he buckled the swollen belt, suddenly my groin felt the chill of death.

13

The shock of recognition. White suddenly realizes that time in fact passes, and that he will pass with time as part of his life—his boy—goes on. No stores of imagination or memory can erase the knowledge that sooner or later one reaches the point of no return.

POSSIBLE ANSWERS

Meaning and Purpose

1. Let students share experiences about places for which they feel nostalgia. Ask them how they look at the changes time has made in the place and in themselves, and how their feelings compare to White's.
2. White states that he wants to return to the lake to fish and "revisit old haunts" (1). He longs for "the placidity of a lake in the woods" (1), and to reconnect with his youth. This paragraph sets the scene for the return.
3. The title has a poetic ring that suits White's descriptions of nature. The words "Once More" are not final and suggest that this may not be White's last visit to the lake.
4. White understands that time at the lake has stood still because so many things are the same

Meaning and Purpose

1. Have you a special place about which you feel nostalgic that you've visited recently? If so, has anything changed? If not, what are you afraid might have changed? Do any of White's descriptions remind you of this place?
2. As you read the opening paragraph of "Once More to the Lake," what do you understand White's purpose to be?
3. How does the title relate to the essay? After you've read the essay, does the title become more significant?
4. What do you think White comes to understand about time and change during his visit to the lake?
5. In the closing paragraph, White describes his son pulling on his wet swimming trunks. At that moment, White says he feels "the chill of death." What do you believe he means? Has anything in the essay prepared you for this conclusion?

as when he was a boy—"The small waves were the same, chucking the rowboat under the chin as we fished at anchor, and the boat was the same boat, the same color green and the ribs broken in the same places . . ." (5). He even confuses his identity with his son's in paragraph 4. At the same time, White notices changes all around him—"The middle track was missing, the one with the marks of the hooves and the splotches of dried, flaky manure" (7)—and understands that change is inevitable.

5. White is suddenly confronted with his own death and the relentless march of time. Readers are prepared only in little ways as White records each change he sees.

Strategy

1. In paragraph 12, White creates the impression of a storm as a natural drama played out. First it is oppressive, then percussive, then calm. White manipulates language to create impressions. "It was like the revival of an old melodrama"—a simile. The approach of the storm creates a "feeling of oppression," "a curious darkening of the sky," and a "lull in everything." Comparing the storm to the sound of drums is a metaphor. The language that describes the lake after the storm is quite different: "return of light and hope and spirits," "joy and relief," and "bright cries."

2. White uses many transitions to avoid confusion about time. In paragraph 2, thinking about returning to the lake with his son, he slips into a memory: "I guess I remembered clearest of all. . . ." In paragraph 5, he describes fishing with his son and says, "There had been no years between the ducking of this dragonfly and the other one—the one that was part of memory." Another shift to memory occurs in paragraph 9 with, "It seemed to me, as I kept remembering all this, that those times and those summers had been infinitely precious and worth saving." Let students find other transitions between past and present.

3. The more specific the writing, the more nearly universal the meaning. Most students will have

Strategy

1. What is the dominant impression that White creates in paragraph 12? How does he use language to create it?
2. White mixes description of his recent trip to the lake with details from past trips. How does he avoid confusion? What transitions does he use to go back and forth in time?
3. Could White's essay have significance for you even if you have never been to Maine, or camped by a lake, or fished? Does the essay transcend its subject? If so, how does White accomplish this feat? Does the lake have a larger meaning?
4. Why does White call his son his "boy" and not name him or give him strong identifying characteristics?

Style

1. Identify in the opening three paragraphs the words that White uses to describe the lake. What impressions do they create? How does the closing sentence in paragraph 3 reinforce this impression?
2. White's essay is clearly subjective, amply mixing descriptive details about the lake with his personal thoughts. How would you describe the essay's tone? What frame of mind does White seem to be in?
3. If necessary, check the dictionary for the meaning of these words: *gunwale* (2); *primeval* (3); *transposition* (4); *hellgrammite* (5); *undulating* (6); *petulant* (10); *premonitory* (12); *languidly* (13). What do these words reveal about White's intended audience?

Writing Tasks

1. Describe a place such as a camp, a farm home, a relative's house, or a childhood haunt, to which you returned after long absence. Structure your description so that it captures how the place

had some experience to help them identify with White's lake. But he goes beyond the specific, as in paragraph 8, when he talks about "summer without end" and "the American family at play," and also in paragraph 9, "There had been jollity and peace and goodness." White offers his lake as a symbol of natural goodness and American family values, the necessary retreat from the ills of the city.

4. White's "boy" becomes himself as White remembers his boyhood summers at the lake (5). If he had given the boy a more specific identity, it would have been harder for White to sustain the illusion that he becomes the boy.

Style

1. Some of the descriptive words about the lake are "Placidity" (1); in paragraph 2, "holy spot," "cool and motionless," "sweet outdoors," "the stillness of a cathedral." These words show the lake as a sacred place, undisturbed and natural, respected and held in awe, almost in a religious way. In paragraph 3, "remote and primeval" reinforces these impressions, as if to say the lake is prehistoric, without the imprint of people.

2. The essay is nostalgic and affectionate in tone, a little sad and peaceful, like a reverie. White seems to need reconnecting with the lake before it's too late, before he, too, passes on. He delights in what he finds on his return: "I could tell it was going to be pretty much the same as it had been before" (4). And he feels sad and "jarred" by some changes (see sentences 2 and 3 of paragraph 10).

3. *Gunwale,* the upper edge of a ship's or boat's side; *primeval,* existing from the beginning; *transposition,* a changing of the normal order; *helgramite* (also *hellgrammite*), the dark brown aquatic larva of a fly, used as fish bait; *undulating,* moving in a wavy or flowing manner; *petulant,* rude, or capriciously ill-humored; *premonitory,* giving warning; *languidly,* sluggishly or listlessly. White expects his audience to be fairly well educated.

appears in your memory and how it appears now. Select the descriptive details carefully and include your subjective thoughts.

2. Write a short descriptive essay (about any subject) in which you appeal to all five senses.

Reportorial description, the "see-it, write-it" detached yet energetic prose of the experienced observer, appeals to the reader's imagination because it displays little of the writer's own imaginative commentary, allowing readers to explore freely their own reactions. The fewer the writer's remarks about descriptions, the more readers can conjure their own remarks, a vital force behind all "appearance-versus-reality" prose.

Sometimes we look, but we do not see. Instructors can take advantage of this fact when introducing the article by asking students to look around, to *see* the classroom itself, often for the first time. How would the room seem to the outside observer?

Students often reply that the room is no more than "just a room." "Yes," you can reply, "and to medical personnel experienced in trauma, a battered woman is just a battered woman, a corpse is just a corpse, and a gunshot wound or a stabbing is just that. No more." To illustrate your point, you can then introduce this essay.

❧ George Simpson ❧

Born in Virginia in 1950, George Simpson studied journalism at the University of North Carolina. He wrote for the Carolina Financial Times *in North Carolina and for the* News-Gazette *in Virginia before joining the staff at* Newsweek *in 1972. In 1978 he was appointed* Newsweek's *director of public affairs. For a series of articles about the football program at the University of North Carolina, he won the Sigma Delta Chi Best Feature Writing Award in 1972. He has contributed stories to* The New York Times, Sport, Glamour, *and other major publications.*

The War Room at Bellevue

In this essay, first published in New York *magazine in 1983, George Simpson uses objective description of events during one night at Bellevue Hospital to achieve immediacy. Arranging the emergency-room scenes in strict (by-the-clock) chronological order creates the impression of a minute-by-minute account and contributes to the power of the description.*

Simpson describes the staff at the Bellevue trauma center speedily responding to emergencies with both efficiency and care. Notice how they maintain commonplace relationships among themselves even amid the chaos.

The author lists the word's *connotations,* the implications or emotional surroundings that words in context carry, as distinguished from their denotative or lexical meanings. Simpson reinforces the connotations by quoting a nurse about Bellevue's rumored reputation.

In London, an old insane asylum, later a hospital for the mentally ill.

Bellevue. The name conjures up images of an indoor war zone: the wounded and bleeding lining the halls, screaming for help while harried doctors in blood-stained smocks rush from stretcher to stretcher, fighting a losing battle against exhaustion and the crushing number of injured. "What's worse," says a long-time Bellevue nurse, "is that we have this image of being a hospital only for . . ." She pauses, then lowers her voice; "for crazy people." 1

Though neither battlefield nor Bedlam is a valid image, there is something extraordinary about the monstrous complex that spreads for five blocks along First Avenue in Manhattan. It is said 2

150

Bellevue has a world-class reputation for its trauma center.

A "typical" Friday night in Bellevue begins and all is routine, down to deciding who will go for coffee.

Simpson foreshadows events by showing the shock and seriousness of what has already happened.

A stiletto's blade is slender and tapering, designed for use as a weapon.

In trauma-care jargon, *emergent* means "sudden, or unforeseen."

A tube passed through the body for evacuating or injecting fluids from or into body cavities. This paragraph mirrors the standard operating procedure for trauma victims, which includes first aid for shock, test for blood type, and quick evaluation of internal organs.

best by the head nurse in Adult Emergency Service: "If you have any chance for survival, you have it here." Survival—that is why they come. Why do injured cops drive by a half-dozen other hospitals to be treated at Bellevue? They've seen the Bellevue emergency team in action.

9:00 P.M. It is a Friday night in the Bellevue emergency room. The after-work crush is over (those who've suffered through the day, only to come for help after the five-o'clock whistle has blown) and it is nearly silent except for the mutter of voices at the admitting desk, where administrative personnel discuss who will go for coffee. Across the spotless white-walled lobby, ten people sit quietly, passively, in pastel plastic chairs, waiting for word of relatives or to see doctors. In the past 24 hours, 300 people have come to the Bellevue Adult Emergency Service. Fewer than 10 percent were true emergencies. One man sleeps fitfully in the emergency ward while his heartbeat, respiration, and blood pressure are monitored by control consoles mounted over his bed. Each heartbeat trips a tiny bleep in the monitor, which attending nurses can hear across the ward. A half hour ago, doctors in the trauma room withdrew a six-inch stiletto blade from his back. When he is stabilized, the patient will be moved upstairs to the twelve-bed Surgical Intensive Care Unit.

9:05 P.M. An ambulance backs into the receiving bay, its red and yellow lights flashing in and out of the lobby. A split second later, the glass doors burst open as a nurse and an attendant roll a mobile stretcher into the lobby. When the nurse screams, "Emergent!" the lobby explodes with activity as the way is cleared to the trauma room. Doctors appear from nowhere and transfer the bloodied body of a black man to the treatment table. Within seconds his clothes are stripped away, revealing a tiny stab wound in his left side. Three doctors and three nurses rush around the victim, each performing a task necessary to begin treatment. Intravenous needles are inserted into his arms and groin. A doctor draws blood for the lab, in case surgery is necessary. A nurse begins inserting a catheter into the victim's penis and continues to feed in tubing until the catheter reaches the bladder. Urine flows through the tube into a plastic bag. Doctors are glad not

Medically, shivers are slight tremors of the skin, as from cold or fear. To a nonmedical person like Simpson, perhaps it suggests shock, which is marked by paleness of skin.

The doctor tries to determine the depth of the wound and its nearness to bone, nerves, and other parts or systems of the human body. The yellow disinfectant probably is a tincture of iodine.

Juxtaposing the wounded man and the derelict suggests the spectrum of patients treated by Bellevue's staff.

Again, coupling examination of the Hispanic girl with that of the old white woman helps illustrate the kinds of patients who go to Bellevue. Notice that each woman is attended by a specialist.

Despite one's condition, one is treated carefully.

to see blood in the urine. Another nurse records pulse and blood pressure.

The victim is in good shape. He shivers slightly, although the trauma room is exceedingly warm. His face is bloodied, but shows no major lacerations. A third nurse, her elbow propped on the treatment table, asks the man a series of questions, trying to quickly outline his medical history. He answers abruptly. He is drunk. His left side is swabbed with yellow disinfectant and a doctor injects a local anesthetic. After a few seconds another doctor inserts his finger into the wound. It sinks in all the way to the knuckle. He begins to rotate his finger like a child trying to get a marble out of a milk bottle. The patient screams bloody murder and tries to struggle free.

Meanwhile in the lobby, a security guard is ejecting a derelict who has begun to drink from a bottle hidden in his coat pocket. "He's a regular, was in here just two days ago," says a nurse. "We checked him pretty close then, so he's probably okay now. Can you believe those were clean clothes we gave him?" The old man, blackened by filth, leaves quietly.

9:15 P.M. A young Hispanic man interrupts, saying his pregnant girl friend, sitting outside in his car, is bleeding heavily from her vagina. She is rushed into an examination room, treated behind closed doors, and rolled into the observation ward, where, much later in the night, a gynecologist will treat her in a special room—the same one used to examine rape victims. Nearby, behind curtains, the neurologist examines an old white woman to determine if her headaches are due to head injury. They are not.

9:45 P.M. The trauma room has been cleared and cleaned mercilessly. The examination rooms are three-quarters full—another overdose, two asthmatics, a young woman with abdominal pains. In the hallway, a derelict who has been sleeping it off urinates all over the stretcher. He sleeps on while attendants change his clothes. An ambulance—one of four that patrol Manhattan for Bellevue from 42nd Street to Houston, river to river—delivers a middle-aged white woman and two cops, the three of them soaking wet. The woman has escaped from the psychiatric

Tetanus is an acute infectious disease that causes painful muscle spasms. Because its first sign is stiffness of the jaw, it is sometimes called "lock-jaw." It is usually, but not always, fatal. Gamma globulin is a protein formed in the blood; it and other proteins, concentrated, resist infection.

Methadone hydrochloride is a habit-forming, synthetic, analgesic drug with potency equal to that of morphine, but with weaker narcotic action. Under careful supervision, methadone hydrochloride is used to treat people who are dependent on drugs derived from opium, such as heroin.

In hospital jargon, a person who has overdosed on drugs is an "O.D."

Notice that "alleged perpetrator" is used to describe a crime suspect. This jargon expression has become standard in police work.

floor of a nearby hospital and tried to drown herself in the East River. The cops fished her out. She lies on a stretcher shivering beneath white blankets. Her eyes stare at the ceiling. She speaks clearly when an administrative worker begins routine questioning. The cops are given hospital gowns and wait to receive tetanus shots and gamma globulin—a hedge against infection from the befouled river water. They will hang around the E.R. for another two hours, telling their story to as many as six other policemen who show up to hear it. The woman is rolled into an examination room, where a male nurse speaks gently: "They tell me you fell into the river." "No," says the woman, "I jumped. I have to commit suicide." "Why?" asks the nurse. "Because I'm insane and I can't help [it]. I have to die." The nurse gradually discovers the woman has a history of psychological problems. She is given dry bed-clothes and placed under guard in the hallway. She lies on her side, staring at the wall.

The pace continues to increase. Several more overdose victims arrive by ambulance. One, a young black woman, had done a striptease on the street just before passing out. A second black woman is semiconscious and spends the better part of her time at Bellevue alternately cursing it and pleading with the doctors. Attendants find a plastic bottle coated with methadone in the pocket of a Hispanic O.D. The treatment is routinely the same, and sooner or later involves vomiting. Just after doctors begin to treat the O.D., he vomits great quantities of wine and methadone in all directions. "Lovely business, huh?" laments one of the doctors. A young nurse confides that if there were other true emergencies, the overdose victims would be given lower priority. "You can't help thinking they did it to themselves," she says, "while the others are accident victims."

10:30 P.M. A policeman who twisted his knee struggling with an "alleged perpetrator" is examined and released. By 10:30, the lobby is jammed with friends and relatives of patients in various stages of treatment and recovery. The attendant who also functions as a translator for Hispanic patients adds chairs to accommodate the overflow. The medical walk-in rate stays steady—between

9

10

eight and ten patients waiting. A pair of derelicts, each with battered eyes, appear at the admitting desk. One has a dramatically swollen face laced with black stitches.

The story of the suicide continues. Simpson shows that Bellevue becomes one setting for the drama of many people's lives.

11:00 P.M. The husband of the attempted suicide arrives. He thanks the police for saving his wife's life, then talks at length with doctors about her condition. She continues to stare into the void and does not react when her husband approaches her stretcher. 11

Emergency room. Simpson's descriptions of people include a representative spectrum from military personnel to members of minority groups to children to battered women.

Meanwhile, patients arrive in the lobby at a steady pace. A young G.I. on leave has lower-back pains; a Hispanic man complains of pain in his side; occasionally parents hurry through the adult E.R. carrying children into the pediatric E.R. A white woman of about 50 marches into the lobby from the walk-in entrance. Dried blood covers her right eyebrow and upper lip. She begins to perform. "I was assaulted on 28th and Lexington, I was," she says grandly, "and I don't have to take it *anymore*. I was a bride 21 years ago, and, God, I was beautiful then." She has captured the attention of all present. "I was there when the boys came home—on Memorial Day—and I don't have to take this kind of treatment." 12

While preparing for a shift change, the conversations are normal. No one recounts a specific incident that happened during her shift. The implication is that no matter what happens, it is "normal" for Bellevue.

As midnight approaches, the nurses prepare for the shift change. They must brief the incoming staff and make sure all reports are up-to-date. One young brunet says, "Christ, I'm gonna go home and take a shower—I smell like vomit." 13

A triage nurse screens and classifies sick and injured people to determine the most efficient way of using medical and nursing personnel, equipment, and facilities. In emergency rooms, the triage nurse ranks patients in order of importance for treatment.

11:50 P.M. The triage nurse is questioning an old black man about chest pains, and a Hispanic woman is having an asthma attack, when an ambulance, its sirens screaming full tilt, roars into the receiving bay. There is a split-second pause as everyone drops what he or she is doing and looks up. Then all hell breaks loose. Doctors and nurses are suddenly sprinting full-out toward the trauma room. The glass doors burst open and the occupied stretcher is literally run past me. Cops follow. It is as if a comet has whooshed by. In the trauma room it all becomes clear. A half-dozen doctors and nurses surround the lifeless form of a Hispanic man with a shotgun hole in his neck the size of your fist. Blood pours from a second gaping wound in his chest. A respirator is slammed over his face, making his chest rise and fall as if he were breathing. "No pulse," reports one doctor. A nurse jumps on a 14

This paragraph illustrates how Bellevue has earned its high reputation as a trauma center. Despite the man's condition, no medical person gives up treating him until his death is clinically determined.

stool and, leaning over the man, begins to pump his chest with her palms. "No blood pressure," screams another nurse. The ambulance driver appears shaken. "I never thought I'd get here in time," he stutters. More doctors from the trauma team upstairs arrive. Wrappings from syringes and gauze pads fly through the air. The victim's eyes are open yet devoid of life. His body takes on a yellow tinge. A male nurse winces at the gunshot wound. "This guy really pissed off somebody," he says. This is no ordinary shooting. It is an execution. IV's are jammed into the body in the groin and arms. One doctor has been plugging in an electrocardiograph and asks everyone to stop for a second so he can get a reading. "Forget it," shouts the doctor in charge. "No time." "Take it easy, Jimmy," someone yells at the head physician. It is apparent by now that the man is dead, but the doctors keep trying injections and finally they slit open the chest and reach inside almost up to their elbows. They feel the extent of the damage and suddenly it is all over. "I told 'em he was dead," says one nurse, withdrawing. "They didn't listen." The room is very still. The doctors are momentarily disgusted, then go on about their business. The room clears quickly. Finally there is only a male nurse and the still-warm body, now waxy-yellow, with huge ribs exposed on both sides of the chest and giant holes in both sides of the neck. The nurse speculates that this is yet another murder in a Hispanic political struggle that has brought many such victims to Bellevue. He marvels at the extent of the wounds and repeats, "This guy was really blown away."

Midnight. A hysterical woman is hustled through the lobby into an examination room. It is the dead man's wife, and she is nearly delirious. "I know he's dead, I know he's dead," she screams over and over. Within moments the lobby is filled with anxious relatives of the victim, waiting for word on his condition. The police are everywhere asking questions, but most people say they saw nothing. One young woman says she heard six shots, two louder than the other four. At some point, word is passed that the man is, in fact, dead. Another woman breaks down in hysterics; everywhere young Hispanics are crying and comforting each other. Plainclothes detectives make a quick examination of

Intravenous infusions. Solutions such as those containing saline, dextrose, or potassium chloride are injected into veins in an attempt to produce immediate results, when treating hemorrhage, shock, or collapse.

This casual comment is not to be taken as a cold, unfeeling statement. People who work daily in trauma centers have learned to mask their feelings. The alternative is to destroy their careers by becoming psychologically involved with their work.

An appearance-versus-reality paragraph. The midnight episode quickly reminds other patients that their problems, in the harsh, comparative light of reality, may not be so serious after all.

15

the body, check on the time of pronouncement of death, and begin to ask questions, but the bereaved are too stunned to talk. The rest of the uninvolved people in the lobby stare dumbly, their injuries suddenly paling in light of a death.

Another appearance-versus-reality paragraph, this time comparing patients' view of the various emergencies with the Bellevue staffers' view of them.

12:30 A.M. A black man appears at the admission desk and says he drank poison by mistake. He is told to have a seat. The ambulance brings in a young white woman, her head wrapped in white gauze. She is wailing terribly. A girl friend stands over her, crying, and a boyfriend clutches the injured woman's hands, saying, "I'm here, don't worry, I'm here." The victim has fallen downstairs at a friend's house. Attendants park her stretcher against the wall to wait for an examination room to clear. There are eight examination rooms and only three doctors. Unless you are truly an emergency, you will wait. One doctor is stitching up the elbow of a drunk who's been punched out. The friends of the woman who fell down the stairs glance up at the doctors anxiously, wondering why their friend isn't being treated faster. 16

Just as the drama of the suicide had a follow-up paragraph earlier, the murder drama has its follow-up—Simpson's method of showing that life goes on, desperately or otherwise, despite the deaths at Bellevue.

1:10 A.M. A car pulls into the bay and a young Hispanic asks if a shooting victim has been brought here. The security guard blurts out, "He's dead." The young man is stunned. He peels his tires leaving the bay. 17

Simpson compares the quickness of the Bellevue trauma staff with that of an automobile that can accelerate from 0 to 60 miles an hour in five seconds, which is remarkably fast.

Although normal in a fetus, a collapsed lung in a mature adult is serious, often caused (though not in this case) by the rupture of a bleb (an "internal blister") on the pleural (membrane) surface of the lung, which then becomes airless or nearly so.

Again, the nurses deal realistically with their lives while treating the lives of others. This healthy way of handling a job that could be emotionally painful distinguishes expert trauma-center personnel from those who do not last long as employees there.

1:20 A.M. The young woman of the stairs is getting stitches in a small gash over her left eye when the same ambulance driver who brought in the gunshot victim delivers a man who has been stabbed in the back on East 3rd Street. Once again the trauma room goes from 0 to 60 in five seconds. The patient is drunk, which helps him endure the pain of having the catheter inserted through his penis into his bladder. Still he yells, "That hurts like a bastard," then adds sheepishly, "Excuse me, ladies." But he is not prepared for what comes next. An X-ray reveals a collapsed right lung. After just a shot of local anesthetic, the doctor slices open his side and inserts a long plastic tube. Internal bleeding had kept the lung pressed down and prevented it from reinflating. The tube releases the pressure. The ambulance driver says the cops grabbed the guy who ran the eight-inch blade into the victim's back. "That's not the one," says the man. "They got the wrong guy." A nurse reports that there is not much of the victim's 18

The last paragraph strongly reinforces what Simpson has been describing and commenting about all along: Although unnerving for lay visitors, emergencies are routine for the medical experts at a trauma center, particularly at Bellevue.

type blood available at the hospital. One of the doctors says that's okay, he won't need surgery. Meanwhile blood pours from the man's knife wound and the tube in his side. As the nurses work, they chat about personal matters, yet they respond immediately to orders from either doctor. "How ya doin'?" the doctor asks the patient. "Okay," he says. His blood spatters on the floor.

So it goes into the morning hours. A Valium overdose, a woman who fainted, a man who went through the windshield of his car. More overdoses. More drunks with split eyebrows and chins. The doctors and nurses work without complaint. "This is nothing, about normal, I'd say," concludes the head nurse. "No big deal."   19

POSSIBLE ANSWERS

Meaning and Purpose

1. Give students a chance to relate their own experiences in hospital emergency rooms and compare theirs to those Simpson describes.
2. Simpson's purpose is to expose a vital feature of Manhattan representing its people, violence, and trauma. He also wants to praise the emergency team by showing them in action.
3. At Bellevue injured people have a good chance for survival (2). Bellevue is a "monstrous complex" (2) like an "indoor war zone" (1). Some think it's only "for crazy people" (1). The emergency staff are highly trained and efficient. Simpson's details of the varied cases that come to them illustrate their expertise. " 'This is nothing, about normal, I'd say,' concludes the head nurse. 'No big deal' " (19).
4. From the emergency ward Manhattan looks like a violent, harsh city with a wide racial and ethnic mixture. "A policeman . . . twisted his knee struggling with an 'alleged perpetrator.' " (10). "A Hispanic man complains of pains in his side." (12).

Meaning and Purpose

1. Have you ever been in a hospital emergency room? How would you describe the experience? Were you aware of the attitude of the doctors and nurses? Of the people waiting with the patients? Do any of Simpson's descriptions compare to what you saw?
2. What do you believe to be Simpson's purpose in "The War Room at Bellevue"?
3. What impressions of the hospital and its staff grow from the description? What details give you that impression?
4. Although Simpson does not describe the city that surrounds the hospital, what impression of the city does he leave you with? Support your answer with details from the essay.
5. Why does Simpson capitalize "Bedlam" in paragraph 2? What are the denotation and connotation of the word?

Strategy

1. What is the structure of this descriptive essay?
2. Many internal workings of "The War Room at Bellevue" are

5. "Bedlam" is capitalized because it is a variant of "Bethlehem"—the Hospital of St. Mary of Bethlehem, an old insane asylum in London. Bedlam: a state of uproar and confusion, a wild and frantic condition.

Strategy

1. Two introductory paragraphs set the scene and describe the hospital's reputation. Paragraphs 3–18 describe the typical activity of the emergency room from 9:00 **P.M.** Friday to 1:20 **A.M.** Saturday. The suicide story (8) has a follow-up in paragraph 11, and the gunshot victim (14–15) in paragraph 17. The final paragraph telescopes the activity till morning. This structure is clear and easy to follow. The sections by time suggest the methodical and orderly running of the emergency room.
2. Other stimulus-response patterns: the gunshot victim arrives (14), and the stab victim arrives (18).
3. Transitions indicating simultaneous action: "Meanwhile in the lobby" (6); "A Young Hispanic man interrupts" (7); "The pace continues to increase" (9); and "Meanwhile, patients arrive in the lobby" (12).
4. The present tense creates an immediacy that conveys the quick action and intensity of the emergency room.
5. A panoramic view of admitting desk, waiting room, and emergency room, where "one man sleeps fitfully" (3). A far-to-near arrangement shows when the ambulance arrives, the "glass doors burst open," and a man is put on the treatment table (4). Another visual sweep takes the eye from trauma room to examination rooms to hallway (8).

Style

1. The intense emergency-room activity shows in the depth of detail—"After a few seconds another doctor inserts his finger into the wound. It sinks in all the way to the knuckles" (5). Simpson is objective and detached; "Another

constructed on a "stimulus-response" pattern—that is, an event takes place and people respond. You'll find a stimulus-response pattern in paragraph 4: it opens with the arrival of an ambulance; a patient is rolled into the lobby on a mobile stretcher; a nurse screams "Emergent!" and the scene explodes with action. Find a stimulus-response pattern in other passages of the essay.
3. Often Simpson has to describe simultaneous events—that is, separate actions that take place at the same time. Find at least four overt transitions at the beginning of paragraphs that capture the sense of simultaneous action.
4. Simpson describes the Bellevue emergency room in the present tense. What is the effect of using this tense?
5. Comment on the spatial arrangement of some of the descriptions. Is it broad to narrow? near to far? center outward? Give examples.

Style

1. How would you describe the narrator of "The War Room at Bellevue"? Is the material presented objectively or subjectively?
2. What words and images help create the sense of a battle in the first two paragraphs?
3. How does the tone of the final paragraph differ from the tone Simpson creates through most of the essay?
4. Identify phrases that help create the sense of sound in paragraph 3. Find words that create a dominant sense impression in one or two other paragraphs.

Writing Tasks

1. Describe a scene in which a great deal of action takes place—a sports event, a shopping mall, an intersection, a park, or a school yard. Keep your description objective, carefully selecting the details to create, without emotion or judgment, a dominant impression.

woman breaks down in hysterics; everywhere young Hispanics are crying and comforting each other" (15), and "The young woman of the stairs is getting stitches in a small gash over her left eye" (18).

2. Words suggestive of battle are "war zone," "wounded and bleeding," "harried doctors," "rush from stretcher to stretcher," "crushing number of injured," "battlefield," and "survival."

3. The closing paragraph quickly surveys the time from 1:20 A.M. to "the morning hours." Simpson catalogues the cases even more dispassionately, not even specifying who has which injuries. This activity is routine. The tone conveys a less harried, less immediate, less alarming atmosphere. The narrator has pulled back from the situation.

4. The sound words are "whistle has blown," "mutter of voices," "sit quietly," "tiny bleep," and "nurses can hear." Paragraph 4 has mostly touch words, and paragraph 14, sound words.

2. Compare the subjective description in "Once More to the Lake" with the objective description in "The War Room at Bellevue." What words make the essays predominantly subjective or objective? What is the overall effectiveness of each strategy and its suitability to the subject? Could each essay be told from the other point of view?

Unless they live there, few students know much about Kansas. The state is sparsely populated, having approximately 2.4 million residents on 82,276 square miles of land, or about thirty people per square mile. Its population comprises about 1 percent of the U.S. total. The name *Kansas* comes from the Sioux Indian word meaning the "south wind people" of their territory, which was mainly Wisconsin, Iowa, Minnesota, and North and South Dakota. Kansans place high value on individualism: They advocate the liberty, rights, and independent actions of each person, while at the same time they cooperate with one another. Urge your students to find descriptive examples of cooperation in this piece, as well as examples of individualism. Ask them to note where the descriptions of individual activities coincide with the descriptions of cooperative activities.

❦ William Least Heat-Moon ❦

William Trogdon, who writes under the name of William Least Heat-Moon, was born in Kansas City, Missouri, in 1939. Of Osage, English, and Irish ancestry, William Trogdon earned a bachelor's degree in photojournalism and a doctorate in English from the University of Missouri. Blue Highways, *his first book, was named a notable book of 1983 by the American Library Association and by the* New York Times. *It was also named one of the best non-fiction books of 1983 by* Time *magazine. The following selection is taken from his book* PrairyErth *(1991). The book describes, chapter by chapter, the lives of many of the people who live in a sparsely populated area of 744 square miles near the center of Kansas. The word* prairyerth *is an old term in geology that described the soils of the grasslands in the center of the United States, which was once covered by a natural prairie of tall grass. Part of that natural prairie still exists in Chase County.*

On the Town: The Emma Chase

This descriptive piece details what happened to the Emma Chase Café and its owner, in terms of history, biography, and setting. It contains three integrated portraits: one of "Emma Chase," one of the café and its customers, and one of the feminist-owner of the café, Linda Thurston.

William Least Heat-Moon traveled to Chase County, Kansas, with a notebook, which he used to record detail after detail. He later converted those details, with the help of his memory, into a fully dimensional descriptive piece of writing. This episode weaves subjective and objective description (see p. 127) into a tapestry of facts and impressions about the people and their surroundings.

After you read the descriptions of the owner, the café, and its patrons, decide whether you would like to have known Linda Thurston and to have eaten at the Emma Chase Café during its heyday.

Broadway, west side, a storefront window, and painted on the plate glass a cup of steaming coffee, morning, Cottonwood

1

appearance of the café, the time of day, the town's name, and the year, almost as if he were focusing and refocusing an imaginary microscope. The opening moves from large details to small ones, and then back to larger ones.

The café is more or less socially segregated, by choice it seems, with its "men's table" and its "women's table."

Rutherford B. Hayes (1822–1893), born in Ohio, was the nineteenth president of the United States (1877–1881).

Salmon P. Chase (1808–1873), born in New Hampshire, was prominent in defending fugitive slaves. He was U.S. Secretary of the Treasury (1861–1864) under President Lincoln and later served as Chief Justice of the Supreme Court (1864–1873).

A humorous confusion with the popular story that Lincoln jotted down the Gettysburg Address on the back of an old envelope while on the train to Gettysburg.

"A-Cookie-in-Every-Jar" is reminiscent of "A chicken in every pot," which was the Republican Party's campaign slogan in 1932. This slogan, in turn, resembles "I hope to make France so prosperous that every peasant will have a chicken in his pot on Sunday," spoken by Henry IV, King of France (1589–1610), at his coronation.

Falls, the Emma Chase Café, November 1984: I'm inside and finishing a fine western omelet and in a moment will take on the planks of homemade wheat-bread—just as soon as the shadow from the window coffee cup passes across my little notebook. The men's table (a bold woman sometimes sits at it, but rare is the man who sits at the women's table) has already emptied, and now the other one too. On the west wall hangs a portrait of a woman from the time of Rutherford B. Hayes, and she, her hair parted centrally, turns a bit to the left as if to answer someone in the street, her high collar crisp, her eyebrow ever so slightly raised, her lips pursed as if she's about to speak. (Someone calls out from the kitchen to the new waitress, *On your ticket, what's this U.P.?* and the girl says, *Up,* and from the kitchen, *You can't have scrambled eggs up.*) The portrait is of *the woman history forgot,* Emma Chase, who said, *You can't start a revolution on an empty stomach.* She was not wife, daughter, sister, or mother of Salmon P. Chase, the great enemy of slavery and Lincoln's chief justice, whose name the county carries. Emma stands in no man's shadow but in the dark recess that the past mostly is. In this county, she's famous for having been forgotten; after all, who remembers it was on the back of one of Emma's envelopes that Lincoln outlined his Emancipation Proclamation? That's been the story in the Falls, anyway.

Most countians now understand that Emma "A Cookie-in-Every-Jar" Chase has the reality of an idea and an ideal. When Linda Pretzer Thurston decided to open the café a couple of years ago, she cast about for a name, something local, something feminine, and she searched the volumes of the *Chase County Historical Sketches* for an embodiment of certain values but came away unsatisfied by or unaware of the facts, such as those of 1889 about Minnie Morgan of Cottonwood, one of the first women in the county elected mayor and *the* first—and probably the only one—to serve with an all-female city council. Minnie has stood in a few dark historical corridors herself: her daughter's biography of the family in the *Historical Sketches* speaks of wild plums and a neighbor who threw her family's clothes down the cistern to save them from a prairie fire, and it mentions her father's founding of the county newspaper the *Leader,* but it says not one word about Minnie's mayoralty or her advocacy of woman suffrage. There has not been a female mayor since.

So, the café had no name until one night at the family supper table Linda and her identical twin said simultaneously in response to something she's now forgotten, *The Emma Chase!* Soon, newspaper ads for the café printed Emma's chocolate chip cookie recipe, and they asked townspeople to search their attic trunks for information about her. One day Whitt Laughridge came in with a large, framed portrait of an unidentified woman he'd found in the historical society vault. Thurston said, *Yes! At last we've got Emma!* Unsatisfied with history, she had invented a persona and then had to invent ways to get people to accept the name. Her ads and fabricated history worked so well that she, who grew up five miles west in Elmdale, *she* became to the citizens *Emma down at the café,* and she doesn't mind.

3

Two of Thurston's values and beliefs are briefly illustrated.

There are other things she does object to, such as the racist joke a fellow told a while ago at the men's table and to which she said loudly from across the room, *Did you hear that one at church, Ray?* and sometimes to sexist comments she'll recite from the café refrigerator, covered with stick-on slogans like a large, upright bumper: THE ROOSTER CROWS BUT THE HEN DELIVERS or WOMEN'S RIGHTS—REAGAN'S WRONGS.

4

Note the capsule description of a multitalented, worldly person: Thurston, a Ph.D. in child psychology, is training her new waitress.

Linda Thurston is trim and pretty, a dark strawberry blonde given to large, swinging earrings; today she wears a pair of silvery stars almost of a size to be hoisted atop the courthouse cupola for Christmas. She sits down across from me to see what I'm scratching in my notebook. Now I'm copying what is on her coffee mug:

5

I HAVE A B.A., M.A., PH.D.

ALL I NEED NOW IS A GOOD J.O.B.

"Aunt Jemima": *The Random House Dictionary of the English Language,* Second Edition, Unabridged (New York: Random House, 1987) has this to say about "Aunt Jemima": *"Slang (dis-*

Her doctorate is in child psychology, she is thirty-nine, divorced, and has a son, John. She calls across the little café to the new waitress, *We can't do scrambled eggs over easy.*

We talk, and then she brings the guest book to me. In it are names from many states and also from Russia, Italy, Israel, and

6

paraging and offensive): a black woman considered by other blacks to be subservient to or to curry favor with whites . . . after the trade-marked name of a brand of pancake mixes and associated products, featuring a picture of a black female cook on the packaging."

This one-sentence paragraph condenses the descriptions of a man, an action, and Linda's reaction, giving us an insight into her attitude towards tax.

she says, *My friends say I'm the white Aunt Jemima of the women's movement, a radicalized, storefront feminist whose job is to get cowboys to eat quiche Lorraine even if they call it quick lorn. I'm an aproned militant known for scratch pies, soups, and breads, the one who's taught a waitress Lamaze-breathing on a café floor.*

A man, his spine crumbling with age, his eyesight almost gone, comes up and holds out a palm of change for his coffee, and Linda takes out thirty-five cents, forget the tax.   7

Three years ago she and her young son lived near Kansas City, Kansas, where she worked with battered women and handicapped children, some of whose fathers couldn't remember their child's name; they all were poor city people who lived anonymously. She was also president of a large chapter of the National Organization for Women, and she campaigned and typed and marched. When Ronald Reagan became president and inner-city social programs started disappearing, she found herself depressed and beginning to wonder who the enemy was, where the battlefield was, and she didn't understand why ideas so apparently democratic and humane were so despised and thwarted, and she was no longer sure what it meant to help the disadvantaged or to be a feminist. Women seemed in retreat from action to the easier, safer battles of awareness. Things were retrogressing.   8

On a trip home to Elmdale she learned that the old and closed Village Inn Café was for sale, and she looked it over, found a broken-down and fouled building, and, suddenly, a fight against dirt and dilapidation, enemies you could lay your rubber-gloved hands on, looked good, especially when she heard the county-seat citizens wanted a pleasant place once again to sit down with a coffee and find out whose cattle it was that went through the ice, whose horse had sent him over the fence. A group of Broadway businesspeople met in Bell's western clothing store and offered to buy the café building and lease it to her until she could pay for it—after all, she was a native—and so Linda Thurston decided to live out her fantasy of running a little homey restaurant, and she moved back to Chase County, where, she hoped, *the Hills could heal.* Her friend Linda Woody, a state lobbyist for NOW, had also wearied of the struggle against Reaganism, and joined   9 her, and the once dingy, moribund café became unofficially the Retreat for Burned-Out Social Activists, a place where the women could serve homilies, history, and cold pasta salad.

Linda Thurston says: *I saw it as a haven of rest from political struggles, a place I'd have time to write up my research. If we could undermine a few stereotypes along the way and wake up a few people, that was fine too. I've never seen my return as going home so much as going forward to my roots, but I don't think I'll stay long enough to grow old here—unless I already have. I believe when the time comes to go back to whatever, I'll know where that is. I've learned you can go home again, but I don't know whether you can stay home again.* 10

Refurbishing the café became a community task: the seventy-eight-year-old furniture dealer power-sanded the chipped floor, the clothier painted, a drywaller showed the women how to mud plasterboard. They came to love the exhaustion of such work. Then they got to the Wolf stove, which yielded its encrusted grease to no woman, man, or method from scrapers to torches. One day two fellows came in with an idea: they dismantled the range, put it in the back of a pickup, hauled it to the county highway yard, turned a steam hose on it, and reassembled it into the beauty of new sculpture, and someone happily wrote on the blackboard Thurston had set up to list possible names for the place: the Clean Stove Café. Also on the board were the Double L, the Quarthouse, and Soup and Psychological Services, this last already beginning to have some meaning. 11

The women did not flaunt their politics, and the town was enough impressed with their hard work to ignore their ERA NOW! bumper stickers, and strollers stopped in to watch the work or help out or just pour themselves a cup of free coffee. After six weeks of reconstruction, the women papered over the street windows to create suspense for the opening a couple of days later while they completed last details. In a county where beef stands second only to Christianity, where gravy and chicken-fried steak are the bases from which all culinary judgments proceed, the women offered eggplant parmigiana, linguine with clams, gazpacho, fettuccine Alfredo—and chicken-fried steak. Business was 12

"you can go home again": Compare with the title of Thomas Wolfe's famous novel, *You Can't Go Home Again* (1940). The hero in that book is disillusioned when he returns to his hometown after experiencing the outside world.

Members of the community turned out to help her, including helping to clean her Wolf stove, a large industrial stove designed for heavy use.

"Soup and Psychological Services": At least one person in the community knew of Thurston's academic or political background.

"eggplant parmigiana": eggplant cooked and served with Parmesan cheese; "linguine with clams": clams in a flavorful sauce, accompanied by a pasta in long, slender flat strips; "gazpacho": a soup made of chopped tomatoes, onions, cucumbers, garlic oil and vinegar, and served cold; "fettuccine Alfredo": cooked pasta cut in flat, narrow strips, in a cream sauce made with Parmesan cheese, said to be named after *Alfredo all'Augusteo*, a restaurant in Rome where it was first served; "pasta primavera": pasta served with chopped or minced vegetables.

excellent, and the first day they sold out of pasta primavera, and the women were certain they could keep their pledge never to serve french fries or factory white bread. All their eggs came from Chase farms; on weekends, in season, they prepared calf fries fresh from county pastures (and tolerated jokes attendant to feminists grilling ballocks), and they catered meals to businessmen in lodge meetings and ranch hands at corrals.

"calf fries" and "ballocks": vulgar terms for calf testes. Beef cattle are castrated when they are calves. Also called prairie oysters.

Linda says to me: *Scratch cooking all the way. The highest* 13 *compliment is a woman saying, "This is as good as I make at home." But the men bitched all the time about no french fries or white bread so we gave in and cut our own fry potatoes and baked our own white bread, but, still today, if you want a grilled cheese between a couple of slices of Rainbo, you'll just have to go someplace else. That's the only little thing we haven't compromised on.*

"Rainbo": a commercial brand of bread popular in the Midwest.

We've never changed our deeper values because we refuse to 14 *divorce being café owners from our feminism. We're tolerated for it and sometimes we're defined by it: I heard a man ask his friend what a crêpe was and why something like that would even be on the menu, and the waitress told him, "They're for the ERA." And that's right. We employ only women, and we try to bring to them what we've learned. In the first days of the café, a wealthy lady told me there were no battered women in the county, and she believed that, but she's been misled—the problem is just buried. Not long ago at the health fair in the school gym we sponsored a display about services for abused women and children, and we found out later that some people were afraid to stand in front of it because a neighbor might think they were abused. And one day a woman said to me, she was holding back tears, "You ought to get out of here—the longer you stay, the worse you'll feel about yourself as a woman." Maybe that's a minority view, but it's valid. The other side is that people here are still close to their pioneer ancestors, and they all can tell stories about strong and capable grandmothers. For a long time women have owned businesses in the county, so we're accepted, but then the café isn't a hardware store or a transmission shop.*

"Crêpe": a thin, light, delicate pancake.

"ERA": Equal Rights Amendment, the proposed 27th amendment to the U.S. Constitution that would prohibit discrimination on the basis of sex.

The young waitress has just given a single check to a man 15 sitting with two women, and Linda explains to her to give each person one, and she says, *Don't assume the male always pays, and* to me, *Separate checks also protect privacy—people watch and read something into who picks up the tab.* I ask whether lack of privacy isn't the worst thing about a small town, and she says, *And also the best. I love going to the post office in the morning and knowing everybody. The only time we honk a car horn is with a wave. It's touching when somebody asks about my son or my dad's health. We can't afford not to care about other people in a place this small. Our survival, in a way, depends on minimizing privacy because the lack of it draws us into each other's lives, and that's a major resource in a little town where there aren't a thousand entertainments. There's an elderly man who lost his little granddaughter to a drunk, a hit-and-run driver, a few months ago. Every time the old gentleman comes into the Emma Chase, he retells the story, and every time people listen. What's that worth to a person? Or to a community? A café like this serves to bond us.*

"bond": to establish a close emotional relationship with another person or with other people. The Emma Chase Café is a psychological magnet for the people of the area.

I'm scribbling things down, and she watches and says, *Growing up in this county I learned not to ask questions. If people want you to know something, they'll tell you.* I say that I must be a popular fellow, what with a question mark in every sentence, and she says, *You don't count. You don't live here. Besides, the word is out that you're in the county. You'll be tolerated even if they do think you're about a half bubble off plumb.* She watches me write that down, and she says, *We can't afford to ostracize each other just because we don't like this one's politics or the way that one raises her kids. You can get away with it in a city—picking and choosing—but here we're already picked. Participation by everybody discourages change, and the radical gets cut off. But if we give aberrant behavior a wide berth we don't usually reject it completely. Every merchant on Broadway can tell a story about some petty shoplifter whose pilfering has been ignored to avoid a bigger problem. For an outsider it's different: if you—yourself—would espouse something terribly unpopular like government ownership of land they'll just question your sanity, but pocket a candy bar and they'll have you arrested. If I do either one, it would be just the reverse. We have limits, of course. The first and most powerful enforcement is gossip and scorn. They're the sap and sinew of a small town.*

"half a bubble off plumb": a slang term among carpenters, meaning "not quite straight or even"; in this sense meaning "not quite normal."

"sap and sinew": the life and strength, in this case, of a small town.

When she gets up to ready the kitchen for lunch, I ask whether she or the Emma Chase has ever been scorned, and she says, *You'd be more likely to hear that than I would.*

Now, late afternoon, October 1988: the painted coffee cup still 18 steams on the window, and stalwart Emma Chase looks over the stacked chairs and onto Broadway, and the dank odor of an old and unused building slips between the locked twin doors. The café has been closed for nearly a year, and there's nothing more than a hope of somebody reopening it, although everyone is tired of coffee in Styrofoam cups and factory cookies in the Senior Citizens' Center a few doors down. Linda Woody has gone to Washington as a NOW lobbyist, and Linda Thurston is sixty miles up the road at Kansas State University, an assistant professor in rural special education. The café is for sale, and she's asking eight thousand dollars less than she paid for it, in spite of its becoming known as one of the best small-town eateries in the state, in spite of a Kansas Citian's offer to underwrite the franchising of Emma Chase Cafés.

I've just returned from lunch with her in the student union, 19 where she said, *Standing in front of that big Wolf stove I kept remembering my degree and how useless it was becoming with every fried egg. I'm forty-three, and I'm ten years behind my colleagues. I worked long hours at the café, and my feet hurt all the time, and I got arthritis in my hands, and finally I realized I didn't want to work that hard day after day and still not earn enough money to send my son to college. Every other businessperson on Broadway has at least one additional source of income—the furniture dealer runs a funeral parlor, the owners of the two dress shops have their husbands' incomes, the filling station man has another in Strong City. The Emma Chase would support one frugal person, but it wouldn't even do that without weekend city people. Tourists coming to see the Hills, bicycle clubs— they kept us alive after we earned a name around the state by being special. But there were local folks who never came in, and I'd ask them what it would take to get them inside, and they'd say, "We let the kids decide where we're going to eat out, and they choose Mc-Donald's." How does a box of toys in the Emma Chase compete against television commercials? And there's something else: good home-cooking*

"let me see men again as people instead of the enemy": In paragraph 8, Thurston began to wonder who the enemy was; she found herself fighting a battle of abstractions.

"silage": fodder (coarse food for livestock) preserved through fermentation in a silo, which is a typically cylindrical structure located near a barn.

POSSIBLE ANSWERS

Meaning and Purpose

1. Depending on the age of the student, the definition of *old* varies. Nevertheless, this question often elicits a personalized response that makes the student aware of her or his neighborhood. Answers, of course, will vary.

2. Least Heat-Moon gets into the body of the excerpt in an unusual way. His first paragraph gives us the impression that the focus will be on the café itself, and the woman for whom it is named, not on the owner. Not until we read on, do we discover that Emma is fictional, a character invented by Thurston, who does not take center stage until the third paragraph.

3. Thurston is a strong person, a woman of high ethical and moral standards who will not compromise her deeper values. Throughout these two paragraphs, she clearly explains herself in relation to politics and activism. Yet it is important to note that she herself is aware that although she is accepted, "the café isn't a hardware store or a transmission shop"; she is accepted as a woman doing woman's work.

4. Choosing a name for the café was a spontaneous act, just as Linda Thurston is a spontaneous person. When she decides to act, she acts. The paragraph illustrates Thurston's marketing skills as well. Soon after she and her twin invent Emma Chase, the whole county becomes convinced that Emma did indeed live near Elmdale.

5. Getting back to one's "roots" carries with it the idea that returning to one's former home, concrete and predictable, will aid a person in discovering who she is and what she stands for. Thurston has battled the bureaucracy for a long time. She has become tired and needs to be renewed psychologically. What better place to do so than in her old hometown?

is common in the county. Franchise food is the novelty, especially when it's twenty miles away. What our café offered, city people wanted, but they also wanted clean floors, and the cowboys were afraid to come in and get the floor dirty.

I asked, was it a loss, and she said, *I lost some money and something professionally because I never found time to write, but I realized my fantasy, and I was at home for the last two years of my father's life. And I got to live again according to the dictates of rainfall and the price of cattle and grain and the outbreaks of chicken pox. I was part of a community rebuilding its café, and working with those helpers let me see men again as people instead of the enemy. It meant something for my son to go to school with children of neighbors I went to school with. And—I think I can say this—because of the café, I see my femaleness differently: now I think feminism means being connected with other people, not just with other feminists.* 20

She was quiet for some time, and then she said, *There were losses, no question, but there was only one real failure: we never did get the farmers to eat alfalfa sprouts. They know silage when they see it. Maybe we should have tried it with gravy.* 21

Meaning and Purpose

1. Is there an old café, hair salon, automobile repair shop, women's club or men's club, or the like in your area? Have you ever passed by and looked inside? Can you describe it? Do you think that the place will disappear one day because it has "gone out of style"?

2. As you read the first paragraph, did you think that the piece would be about a café? If so, what made you think so? If not, how do you believe you might have been misled?

3. What does Thurston's extended statement in paragraphs 13 and 14 tell you about her?

4. Reread paragraph 3. What is important about how the Emma Chase Café got its name?

Strategy

1. Depending on how closely students read it, the major impression in paragraph 18 could be that which signifies failure or loss. Students are free to select the words and phrases that they believe lend themselves to their own impression. Some of the more common selections are "stacked chairs," "dank odor," "locked twin doors," "closed," "tired," and "for sale."

2. The first paragraph of the excerpt describes the men's table and the women's table, both carryovers from an earlier time. The portrait of Emma Chase, described in the middle of the first paragraph, goes back more than one hundred years. The second paragraph describes an event in 1889; former President Reagan is mentioned in paragraph 4, which strengthens the description of Thurston's political stance, and the excerpt itself is the descriptive history of four years in the life of Linda Thurston and the Emma Chase Café.

3. Most students agree that Linda Thurston paid a reasonable price for living out her fantasy. Thurston went home to be close to the land, to discover more about herself, and she accomplished what she had set out to do. She lived a builder's life, building her café while rebuilding herself psychically. As a result of her experience, she has come to redefine feminism to her own satisfaction. The humorous ending shows that she was not at all unhappy with her experience at the Emma Chase Café.

4. Paragraph 7 functions as a descriptive break between the present and the past. It shows a glimpse of Thurston at work in the café, quick, humane, and thoughtful. In paragraph 6, Thurston is telling Least Heat-Moon how her friends feel. Paragraph 8 describes recent past events that brought her back to Chase County. The author interrupts with paragraph 7, to remind the reader that he and Thurston are in a working café as they talk.

5. Chase County is a single-source economy with a single religion. Christianity fulfills the people's moral needs, and cattle their economic ones, which for them are all that is necessary for the good life.

5. In paragraph 9, what does the clause *the Hills could heal* mean, as far as Linda Thurston is concerned?

Strategy

1. What major impression does William Least Heat-Moon create in paragraph 18? What words and phrases strengthen that impression?

2. How does William Least Heat-Moon use description to show that history is an important feature of this excerpt?

3. Is the conclusion appropriate to this essay? Do the last two paragraphs in some way point out that Linda Thurston had done the right thing by opening the café in the first place? Or was the whole enterprise a waste of time? Explain your response.

4. Paragraph 7 is a one-sentence paragraph. Why is it separated from the longer paragraphs that come before it and that follow it? What does the paragraph tell you about Linda Thurston?

5. What does the clause in paragraph 12, "where beef stands second only to Christianity," tell you about Chase County, Kansas?

Style

1. Read the definition of *tone* in the Glossary. What are five adjectives you can use to describe the tone of this piece of writing?

2. The author of this piece begins it by talking about himself, about his activities. Based on his limited description of himself, what do you know about the author?

3. The slogan in paragraph 4 reads, "THE ROOSTER CROWS BUT THE HEN DELIVERS." What does that slogan mean as it is used in the paragraph?

4. Paragraph 11 includes the suggestions that several people have given as a possible name for the café. What do those names tell you about some of the people who live in Chase County?

5. In paragraph 19, how does the subjective description of the

Style

1. Given the enormous choice available to students, the answers will vary. Some of the adjectives that have been used include "depressing," "reportorial," "calm," "cool-headed," "detached," and "curious." Students should shun such catch-all words as "interesting," "nice," and "good."

2. The author is not businesslike: He sits in the cafe as a customer, not as the energetic, inquiring reporter. He is patient, waiting for the sun to pass across his notebook. He has an eye for detail, as in his description of the portrait of Emma Chase. He listens carefully, hearing and recording the voice from the kitchen. He knows something of history, with his mentioning Salmon P. Chase, Lincoln, and the Emancipation Proclamation.

3. This slogan is often used by Thurston to rebut a sexist comment. It means, roughly, that while men do all the talking, women do all the work.

4. The "Clean Stove Café" is a practical name; the "Double L" is cute; the "Quarthouse" is a play on words; the "Soup and Psychological Services" is insightful. In many ways, the people who live in Chase County resemble the people who live anywhere else. Some are practical, some like cute-sounding names, some have fun with words, some are insightful, and so forth.

5. In paragraph 19, the café is described objectively, but not concretely, in terms of how it affected Thurston, of how Thurston worked with it and worked with herself. The café is described as making her tired and giving her arthritis. The café can support only one person, provided that person lives for the café. Thurston knows that the cafe is not for her. Even though it earned a reputation throughout the state, she was no longer interested in living up to the cafe's reputation. She is her own woman. Subjectively, she knows that the Emma Chase Café served its purpose for her when she needed to get back to the hills. That time has passed, and so has her needing the café.

Emma Chase Café relate to the objective description of Linda Thurston? (For a discussion of subjective and objective description, see p. 127.)

Writing Tasks

1. Linda Thurston opened the Emma Chase Café so that she could live out her fantasy. She had a dream, and she acted because of her dream. What is your dream, one of your compelling beliefs? Describe what you would most like to do to test whether what you believe is worth believing in.

2. Where one lives or where one grew up powerfully affects a person's sense of security. Linda Thurston, from Kansas, believed that the "hills could heal." Imagine that something profoundly sad happened to you. Describe where you would go for "healing" and why you would go there.

3. This essay in part describes history, real and imaginary. Emma Chase is a fictional person, but other historical characters mentioned in the essay were real. Describe a "historical character." Invent the character the same way that Emma Chase was invented, and give reasons why your character is personally important to you.

Call it "optional fright": All of us at one time or another have voluntarily frightened ourselves—in short, we have dipped into our childhood from time to time. But few of us have been as affected by rides as Peter Schjeldahl by his adventure on Cyclone. Or at least few of us have bothered to tell how we have been affected.

Often, instructors introduce this essay with a reminiscence about deliberately becoming involved in a frightening situation, just for the thrill. One instructor described her first parachute jump, and how it determined her to jump and jump again. Another instructor shouted at a police officer, when he was ten, just to see if he could outrun the law. (He couldn't.)

Such quick descriptions may relax the class enough so that some want to volunteer their own memorable events. Stimulate descriptions with questions: When did it happen? How did you look? Why did you do it, *really*? How did your stomach feel? Did you have friendly witnesses? Were you with others?

❦ Peter Schjeldahl ❦

Peter Schjeldahl was born in North Dakota in 1942. He has published several collections of poetry, including White Country *(1968),* An Adventure of the Thought Police *(1971), and* Dreams *(1973), and in 1964 he cofounded the poetry magazine,* Mother. *He has also been an art critic for* Art News *and for the* Village Voice. *His book* Samaras Pastels *was published by the Denver Art Museum in 1981.*

Cyclone!
Rising to the Fall

This short essay, first published in Harper's in 1988, is written with a poet's eye for detail. Telling comparisons add to this vivid description of riding a famous roller coaster at Coney Island. Schjeldahl describes the sheer fun of the experience, gives each section of the track a name, and takes the reader for a ride that turns out to be as memorable as the one he took.

As you read Schjeldahl, notice how he includes physical detail but focuses on his impressions and perceptions throughout the essay.

MARGINAL NOTES

Loosely defined, a cyclone—from the Greek *kykloein*, "to circle around; to whirl"—is a windstorm with a violently whirling movement: a tornado or a hurricane.

A play on "art for art's sake": art is its own excuse for being.

The Cyclone is a wooden roller coaster.

The Cyclone is on Brooklyn's Coney Island, a peninsula at the southwest end of Long Island.

The Cyclone is art, sex, God, the greatest. It is the most fun you can have without risking bad ethics. I rode the Cyclone seven times one afternoon last summer, and I am here to tell everybody that it is fun for fun's sake, the pure abstract heart of the human capacity for getting a kick out of anything. Yes, it may be anguishing initially. (I promise to tell the truth.) Terrifying, even, the first time or two the train is hauled upward with groans and creaks and with you in it. At the top then—where there is sudden strange quiet but for the fluttering of two tattered flags, and you have a poignantly brief view of Brooklyn, and of ships far out on the Atlantic—you may feel very lonely and that you have made a serious mistake, cursing yourself in the last gleam of the re-

1

The outline enclosing the words or thoughts of a character in a cartoon.

Anticipatory behavior once allowed people to avoid danger before disaster. We have now "evolved" into placing ourselves into a position of imaginary danger for the sake of fun.

The force pulling a thing outward when it is rotating rapidly around a center.

"articulated": A play on words: "having parts connected by joints," as in roller-coaster construction; also, "made of distinct syllables or words," as in poetic constructions.

An oxymoron, yoking two contradictory words. The word *nostalgia* refers to longing for something far away or long ago, not ordinarily associated with *instantaneous.*

Turkish, *qismet,* from the arabic *qismah,* akin to *qasama,* "to divide," alluding to philosophical differences between free will and determinism.

In Turkey, the title of rank or honor formerly placed after the name of a high civil or military official.

Endorphins: chemical substances produced in the brain that act as opiates producing analgesia, absence of a normal sense of pain. The "rush" is a momentary feeling of euphoria, exaggerated high spirits.

That is, pushes you both together in such a way that you feel you have become physically attached, joined like Siamese twins.

flective consciousness you are about, abruptly, to leave up there between the flags like an abandoned thought-balloon. To keep yourself company by screaming may help, and no one is noticing: try it. After a couple of rides, panic abates, and after four or five you aren't even frightened, exactly, but *stimulated,* blissed, sent. The squirt of adrenaline you will never cease to have at the top as the train lumbers, wobbling slightly, into the plunge, finally fuels just happy wonderment because you can't, and never will, *believe* what is going to happen.

Every roller coaster has that first, immense drop. In practical terms, it provides the oomph for the entire ride, which is of course impelled by nothing but ecologically sound gravity, momentum, and the odd slingshot of centrifugal force. The coaster is basically an ornate means of falling and a poem about physics in parts of stanzas, with jokes. The special quality of the Cyclone is how different, how *articulated,* all the components of its poem are, the whole of which lasts a minute and thirty-some seconds—exactly the right length, composed of distinct and perfect moments. By my fifth ride, my heart was leaping at the onset of each segment as at the approach of a dear old friend, and melting with instantaneous nostalgia for each at its finish. 2

I think every part of the Cyclone should have a name, the better to be recalled and accurately esteemed. In my mind, the big drop is Kismet—fate, destiny. I can't think of what to call the second, a mystery drop commenced in a jiffy after we have been whipped around, but good, coming out of Kismet. (Someday soon I will devote particular attention to the huge and violent but elusive second drop.) I do know that the third drop's name can only be Pasha. It is so round and generous, rich and powerful, looking like a killer going in but then actually like a crash landing in feathers that allows, for the first time in the ride, an instant for luxuriating in one's endorphin rush. . . . 3

Rolling up out of Pasha, we enter the part of the Cyclone that won't quit laughing. First there's the whoop of a whipping hairpin curve, which, if someone is sitting with you, Siamese-twins you. (Having tried different cars in different company, I prefer being 4

"Irene": An ironic name for this sharp drop. In classical mythology, the Horae are the goddesses of the seasons, of cyclical death and rebirth. Usually three, they are Dikē (justice), Eunomia (order), and Irēnē (peace).

"banal": Dull or stale; commonplace.

In Belgium, the scene of Napoleon's final defeat, Waterloo refers to any loosely defined disaster.

Aversion training: applying or showing frightening or disturbing situations or objects to a person, to ease phobias by gradually increasing familiarity with those objects or situations. The author wants to learn how to flee "Irene types," rather than to learn how to tolerate them.

The author relives his passage to maturity at every pass through this part of Cyclone.

Part of the author's infatuation with Cyclone is its age. Wear and tear over the years have produced a unique roller coaster, on which no two rides are exactly the same.

alone at the very front—call me a classicist.) The ensuing dips, humps, dives, and shimmies that roar, chortle, cackle, and snort continue just long enough to suggest that they may go on forever—as worrisome as the thought, when you're laughing hard, that maybe you can never stop—and then it's hello, Irene. Why do I think Irene is the name of the very sharp drop, not deep but savage, that wipes the grin off the laughing part of the Cyclone? (Special about it is a crosspiece, low over the track at the bottom, that you swear is going to fetch you square in the eyebrows.) Irene is always the name—or kind of name, slightly unusual but banal—of the ordinary-seeming girl whom a young man may pursue idly, in a bored time, and then *wham!* fall horribly in love with, blasted in love with this person he never bothered to even particularly look at and now it's too late, she's his universe, Waterloo, *personal* Kismet. This is one good reason I can think of for growing older: learning an aversion reflex for girls named something like Irene. In this smallish but vicious, sobering drop, abstract shapes of my own youthful romantic sorrows do not fail to flash before my inner eye . . . but then, with a jarring zoom up and around, I am once more grown-up, wised-up me, and the rest of the ride is rejoicing.

The Cyclone differs from other roller coasters in being (a) a   5
work of art and (b) old, and not only old but odd-looking, decrepit, rusting in its metal parts and peeling in its more numerous wooden parts, filthy throughout and jammed into a wire (Cyclone!) fence abutting cracked sidewalks of the Third World sinkhole that Coney Island is, intoxicatingly. Nor is it to be denied or concealed that the Cyclone, unlike newer coasters, tends to run *rough,* though each ride is unique and some are inexplicably velvety. One time the vibration, with the wheels shrieking and the cars threatening to explode with strain, made me think, "This is *no fun at all!*" It was an awful moment, with a sickening sense of betrayal and icy-fingered doubt: was my love malign?

That was my worst ride, which left me with a painfully yanked   6
muscle in my shoulder, but I am glad to say it wasn't my last. I got back on like a thrown cowboy and discovered that the secret of handling the rough rides is indeed like riding a horse, at trot

The author learns at Coney Island what the cowboy learns in Wyoming. One prevents fear by facing that which could cause fear.

"upholstered": Again, the very age of Cyclone provides some of its grandest thrills.

In entertainment-business jargon, a gaffer is the head electrician on a movie or television set. "Gaffer's tape" is electrical tape, known to stick to almost anything, often used for quick non-electrical repairs that are usually temporary.

Partly because of television, many celebrities are now famous merely for being well known; they are swift and showy, like Cyclone's Celebrity. The term *afflatus* refers to an artist's or poet's powerful impulse or inspiration. "Nirvana": In Buddhism, state of perfect blessedness achieved when individual existence ends and the soul is absorbed into the supreme spirit, after desires and passions are extinguished.

"diminuendo": In music, a gradual decrease in loudness or intensity.

The author wrote earlier of an "endorphin rush." Here, quite soon after the ride, the "rush" is still upon him, affecting his perspective, making the ride worthwhile all over again.

or gallop—not tensing against it, as I had, but posting and rolling. It's all in the thighs and rear end, as I especially realized when—what the hell—I joined pimpled teenagers in the arms-raised *no hands!* trick. I should mention that a heavy, cushioned restraining bar locks down snugly into your lap and is very reassuring, although, like everything upholstered in the cars, it may be cracked or slashed and leaking tufts of stuffing from under swatches of gray gaffer's tape. One thing consistently disquieting is how, under stress, a car's wooden sides may *give* a bit. I wish they wouldn't do that, or that my imagination were less vivid. If a side did happen to fail on a curve, one would depart like toothpaste from a stomped-on tube.

I was proud of braving the *no hands!* posture—as trusting in the restraining bar as a devout child in his heavenly Father—particularly the first time I did it, while emerging from the slinging return that succeeds Irene into the long, long careen that bottoms out at absolute ground level a few feet from the fence where pedestrians invariably gather to watch, transfixed. I call this swift, showy glide Celebrity: the ride's almost over, and afflatus swells the chest. But going *no hands!* soon feels as cheap and callow as it looks, blocking with vulgar self-centeredness the wahoo-glimmering-away-of-personality-in-compulsive-Nirvana that is the Cyclone's essence. A righteous ride is hands on, though lightly, like grace. The payoff is intimacy in the sweet diminuendo, the jiggling and chuckling smart little bumps and dandling dips that brings us to a quick, pillowy deceleration in the shed, smelling of dirty machine oil, where we began and will begin again. It is a warm debriefing, this last part: "Wasn't that *great?*" it says. "Want to go again?"

Of course, I do, but first there is the final stage of absorption, when you squeeze out (it's easy to bang a knee then, so watch it) to stand wobbly but weightless, euphoric, and then to enjoy the sensation of walking as if it were a neat thing you had just invented. Out on the sidewalk, the object of curious gazes, you see that they see that you see them, earthlings, in a diminishing perspective, through the wrong end of the telescope of your plea-

POSSIBLE ANSWERS

Meaning and Purpose

1. Most students will think at least some of Schjeldahl's descriptions are successful. The first paragraph has such expressions as "anguishing initially," "terrifying, even," "screaming may help," "the squirt of adrenaline," and "into the plunge," which describe most people's experiences on roller coasters.

2. Some students may know this roller coaster by name. For some, "I rode the Cyclone" may give it away, or "the train is hauled upward."

3. The dominant impression is that riding the Cyclone is exhilarating and scary—unadulterated fun. Schjeldahl says you are *stimulated, blissed, sent* (1).

4. "Fun for fun's sake" is a play on "art for art's sake"; that is, art—or fun—is its own excuse for being.

5. This sentence refers to nirvana, the Buddhist state of selfless blessedness and union with the supreme spirit, and the blocking of this state by the conscious effort of riding *no hands!* The bliss of riding the Cyclone is exaggerated in a humorous way.

Strategy

1. The impressions of feelings are dominant in these passages: "The squirt of adrenaline you will never cease to have at the top . . . what is going to happen" (1); "By my fifth ride, my heart was leaping at the onset of each segment . . . at its finish" (2); and "Out on the sidewalk, the object of curious gazes . . . pitying" (8).

2. The first two paragraphs describe the Cyclone as the author sees it; paragraph 3 begins the discussion of the Cyclone's parts, and Schjeldahl names the first and third parts; paragraph 4 names the fourth part; paragraphs 5 and 6 describe the roughness of the ride; paragraph 7 calls the last part Celebrity; and the last paragraph ends the ride out on the sidewalk. Schjeldahl has so much to say about the Cyclone that dividing the ride into parts and naming them organizes his description in a manageable way and helps readers experience the ride—and all it means to him—with him.

3. In paragraph 4, Schjeldahl has just talked

sure, and your heart is pitying. You nod, smiling, to convey that yes, they should ride, and no, they won't regret it.

Meaning and Purpose

1. Schjeldahl intends to re-create the experience of riding a roller coaster—the Cyclone at Coney Island, New York. Is his description successful for you? Why or why not?

2. Schjeldahl doesn't mention the name roller coaster until paragraph 2. When did you know that he was describing a roller coaster?

3. What dominant impression of riding the Cyclone does Schjeldahl's description leave you with?

4. What does "fun for fun's sake" in paragraph 1 signify?

5. In paragraph 7, what does Schjeldahl mean by "blocking with vulgar self-centeredness the wahoo-glimmering-away-of-personality-in-convulsive-Nirvana that is the Cyclone's essence"?

Strategy

1. How does Schjeldahl use impressions or perceptions to convey the feeling of riding the Cyclone? Give examples of passages that convey feelings.

2. Outline briefly the structure Schjeldahl uses to organize his descriptions. What is the overall effect of structuring the essay as he does?

3. A digression is material, unrelated or distantly related to the subject, which is inserted into a work. Paragraphs 5 and 6 make up a digression from the subject of naming the parts of the ride. Why do you think Schjeldahl digresses here? Does the digression fit? Is it effective?

about youthful romance, then being "once more grown up" after a "jarring zoom up and around." The jarring suggests roughness, which he describes in the digression, and growing up out of youth ties in with the Cyclone's being "old" (5). These are the transitions into a discussion of the effect of old age on the Cyclone. The digression fits here also because it comes right before the description of the ride's end.

4. Schjeldahl embellishes his descriptions to match his enthusiasm and pleasure in riding the Cyclone. The embellishment is necessary to convey Schjeldahl's excitement, thrill, and awe.

Style

1. In paragraph 2, Schjeldahl compares the Cyclone to a "poem about physics." This metaphor fits because he holds the Cyclone up as a work of art and says it is "the right length, composed." A poem suggests something carefully constructed, beautiful beyond the ordinary. In paragraph 6 the cyclone is like a bucking bronco, and Schjeldahl like a cowboy riding it. This description is appropriate to the discussion of how rough the ride is.

2. This phrase is ironic because, after nearly risking his life on a ride, Schjeldahl cautions about a little thing like a banged knee.

3. "Instantaneous nostalgia" is an oxymoron, an expression joining two contradictory terms. The effect is exaggerated humor about how eagerly Schjeldahl anticipates each part of the ride. "Siamese-twins you" means that, if two people are in the seat, they are pushed together so forcefully that they feel physically attached. "Waterloo" is the scene in Belgium of Napoleon's final defeat, and now the word can refer to any disaster. "Gaffer's tape" is electrical tape used for temporary repairs by a gaffer, the head electrician on a movie or television set. "Earthlings" refers to people who have not ridden the Cyclone; those who have ridden it see them as if through the eyes of aliens.

4. The final paragraph has words that summarize Schjeldahl's feelings about riding the Cyclone. The tone here is of elation, otherworldliness, satisfaction—as it is throughout the essay.

4. "Embellish" means to enhance, or to add ornamental details, to create a desired impression. Do you think Schjeldahl embellishes his descriptions of the Cyclone? If so, give examples. Does the embellishment make the essay better? How?

Style

1. Identify the metaphors in paragraphs 2 and 6 and explain why they are appropriate or inappropriate.

2. Why is the phrase "it's easy to bang a knee," in paragraph 8, ironic?

3. Explain these words and phrases as they are used in the essay: *instantaneous nostalgia* (2); *Siamese-twins you* (4); *Waterloo* (4); *gaffer's tape* (6); *earthlings* (8).

4. Do you agree that the final paragraph captures Schjeldahl's attitude toward riding the Cyclone and embodies the tone of the whole essay? If so, how does the final paragraph do these things?

Writing Tasks

1. Write a descriptive passage about an exhilarating ride you've had—perhaps a carnival ride, a ski or toboggan run, or a motorcycle sprint—whatever you feel lends itself to a description similar to Schjeldahl's. Describe the experience in detail while trying to create a dominant impression. Be generous with figures of speech, such as simile or metaphor.

2. In a descriptive paragraph about a place, focus on the order in spatial arrangement and describe your subject from near to far, right to left, center outward, top to bottom, and so on, as you want your reader's eyes to see the place.

Woman Brushing Her Hair

Before children speak, they see. A child looks and recognizes before it can form words. At an early age we learn to respond to visual experience and interpret it. A smiling or scowling face, a closed or open hand, an erect or slumped body—all are gestures that invite our interpretation.

As we move through life, our interpretations of visual experiences become more complex. A young man walking down the street might go unnoticed. But add spiked hair, a leather coat, and torn jeans held up by a chain belt. Put a safety pin through one earlobe and thread an earring in his pierced nose, and this visual experience catches our attention. We examine the details of the young man's attire and perhaps draw conclusions about his character, lifestyle, personal values, or musical taste.

Photographs, unlike spontaneous visual experience, arrange details for a viewer. They are not, as is often assumed, a realistic record of an experience, but an arranged and reproduced moment of experience. Whenever we look at a photograph we are being guided by the hand that held the camera. And whenever we look at a photograph we are being invited to respond to the image—to interpret it.

At first glance, "Woman Brushing Her Hair" seems to be a snapshot that captures a spontaneous moment in this woman's day. But on closer examination, the image seems to be carefully arranged, the hand of the photographer reaching to pull a response from the viewer.

With description as a dominant method of development, complete one of the following writing tasks. Before beginning your essay, reread "Description: Capturing Sensory Details" at the beginning of this chapter to familiarize yourself with the conventions of effective descriptive writing.

1. Write a "fly-on-the-wall" description, one that strictly reports the arrangement and content of "Woman Brushing Her Hair." After studying the contents of the photograph, decide on how you wish to arrange your description. Through your essay, be sure to follow the arrangement consistently.

2. Use "Woman Brushing Her Hair" as the basis of an *objective* description that creates a dominant impression of this woman's life. Like any writer, or photographer for that matter, you must select details, gestures, objects, arrangements that help generate the dominant impression you wish to create. Remember, your task is not to describe everything in the photo, but to use material from the photo for your purpose.

3. Use "Woman Brushing Her Hair" as the basis of a *subjective* description that creates a dominant impression of this woman's life. You, as in assignment 1, must select material from the photo that leads readers to a single impression, but because you are approaching the photograph subjectively, you may color the details with your feelings.

4. Select a photograph that engages your interest. Title the photograph, and then using it as the basis of your description, complete one of the writing tasks just outlined. Be sure to include the photograph as part of your final draft.

❦ Additional Writing Tasks ❦

Description

1. Recall a spot you visited when younger, not far from your home. It should be a place you remember well but not one you visit constantly. Once you have selected the spot, draw upon your strength of recollection: visualize yourself in this place, seeing the physical features, hearing the sounds, and smelling the odors and aromas. Jot down your memories. What details do you recall, and in what order of importance? Record your memories just as the place was at that time in your life. How would you tell what you saw if you were describing the scene for a stranger? Which details would create images in this stranger's mind? Try to write this part of the description from a child's perspective.

   Once you have described the place as you recall it, write a description of how the place appears now, after years have passed. This part of the description should be done from an adult's perspective. Perhaps the place has not held up under time's pressure. Perhaps your view of it has changed. Perhaps you colored this place with romantic illusions.

   Once the second rough description is completed, begin the first draft. Develop a structure that shifts between past and present, revealing both the child's and the adult's attitude.

2. Select several photographs that represent milestones in your life. Describe them as if you were a reporter relating the events that are taking place in the photo. Keep your description objective but vivid. Or, if you wish, use several magazine ads as the basis for a description. Here, too, describe the events in the advertisement objectively, merely reporting the image you see on the page, not interpreting it.

3. Describe an animal you have encountered, perhaps a wild animal such as a coyote, wolf, deer, bear, or whale. Begin with a description of the animal from folklore, which will probably require a visit to the library. Then follow with a description of the animal as you experienced it. Seek a connection between the two elements in this description.

4. Do something slightly out of the ordinary and describe the ex-

perience. Perhaps you will climb a tree and sit among the branches. Maybe you will sit in a closed closet for half an hour. You might roller skate, stand on your head, dance a waltz, lie on the grass and stare at the clouds—the possibilities are endless. Once you have had the experience, describe it in detail.

5. Select a physical event and describe it in detail: the fog rolling through the woods or city streets; a storm gathering in the distance and sweeping toward you; a cloudburst; wind roaring through the trees and rattling the windows; an earthquake. In your description capture a sense of motion, sound, and smell, as well as visual detail.

6. Describe people at work in various settings:
    A supermarket
    A fast-food restaurant
    A newsstand
    A factory
    A car wash
    A pizza parlor
In your description create a dominant impression.

5

Examples

Illustrating Ideas

The Method

Examples bring the vague and abstract down to earth. They clarify the historian's lectures. They make concrete the philosopher's abstractions. They electrify the politician's arguments. By using examples effectively you will not only help your readers understand your point, but you will also improve your chances of holding their attention because vivid, concrete examples can make your writing more interesting to read.

Examples are much used, even in everyday conversation. If someone claims that advertisers use fear of rejection to manipulate consumers, you might say, "Show me."

Examples such as these would follow: "What about those mouthwash commercials? One actually shows a salesman rejected because he has bad breath. And then after a quick rinse, Presto! he makes the sale, and the customer drives away smiling. And what about the commercial that shows a young female banker passed over for a promotion? A wiser, older colleague whispers in her ear. In the next scene she is scrubbing her head with the advertiser's shampoo, and the commercial closes with the smiling banker now managing her own department."

The speaker is using examples to clarify the general observation that advertisers use fear of rejection to manipulate consumers into buying their products. Writers use examples with the same intent—to illustrate a generalization; that is, to select one thing from many to represent the *whole*. In fact, the word *example* derives from the Latin *exemplum,* which refers to "one thing selected from the many." Examples used to represent ideas are essential to clear communication because they give readers something concrete to visualize. It might be difficult for a reader to understand what social critic Jack Solomon means by this statement:

No matter how you look at it, in the scant space of some forty years, television has revolutionized our lives. First introduced as a novelty alternative to radio, television has rapidly evolved into the most profound invention of the age. Nothing is immune from its influence.

For the sake of clarity, Solomon immediately provides several examples to illustrate his idea for the reader:

> Politicians play for the cameras, and so do international terrorists. Physicians call news conferences, and judges host courtroom dramas. Television, through its hyping of the Olympic Games, has transformed sport into politics and politics into sport, treating everything from presidential elections to military conflicts as prime-time entertainment. What is not televised is hardly thought of at all in a world in which television creates reality as much as it records.

These examples add clarity to Solomon's statement. Without them the reader would have only a vague understanding of Solomon's point in this paragraph, which would amount to a slip in communication.

Strategies

Professional writers use three kinds of examples—specific, typical, and hypothetical—to support their ideas. They can be used in any combination and are often mixed within one paragraph.

Specific Examples

Specific examples capture an experience, event, incident, or fact. Banesh Hoffman, in "My Friend, Albert Einstein," uses a specific example (an **anecdote**) to support the general comment that the essence of Einstein's personality was simplicity.

> He was one of the greatest scientists the world has ever known, yet if I had to convey the essence of Albert Einstein

in a single word, I would choose *simplicity*. Perhaps an anecdote will help. Once, caught in a downpour, he took off his
hat and held it under his coat. Asked why, he explained,
with admirable logic, that the rain would damage the hat,
but his hair would be none the worse for its wetting. This
knack for going instinctively to the heart of the matter was
the secret of his major scientific discoveries.

Hoffman selects this specific example with a clear purpose in
mind. He wants to make concrete the generalization in the topic
sentence. The example is vivid and interesting, capturing Einstein's essence.

Hoffman's specific example illustrating Einstein's simplicity
is a short narrative, but writers often shape examples in other
ways. Sometimes the writer will use several specific examples in
one paragraph. A series of brief examples might function like
verbal snapshots, freezing in time several events or experiences.
In this paragraph, naturalist Jane van Lawick-Goodall uses seven
short visual examples to illustrate social behavior among the chimpanzees she studied in Tanzania.

> While many details of their [the chimpanzees'] social
> behavior were hidden from me by the foliage, I did get
> occasional fascinating glimpses. I saw one female, newly
> arrived in a group, hurry up to a big male and hold her
> hand toward him. Almost regally he reached out, clasped
> her hand in his, drew it toward him, and kissed it with his
> lips. I saw two adult males embrace each other in greeting.
> I saw youngsters having wild games through treetops, chas-
> ing around after each other or jumping again and again, one
> after the other, from a branch to a springy bough below. I
> watched small infants dangling happily by themselves for
> minutes on end, patting at their toes with one hand, rotating
> gently from side to side. Once two tiny infants pulled on
> opposite ends of a twig in a gentle tug-of-war. Often during
> the heat of midday or after a long spell of feeding, I saw
> two or more adults grooming each other, carefully looking
> through the hair of their companions.

Sometimes writers will create a *list* or a *catalogue* of specific examples to illustrate their observations. In this paragraph from *The Distant Mirror,* historian Barbara Tuchman catalogues how people in fourteenth-century England might imagine the distant places they had heard of but never seen.

> Faraway lands, however—India, Persia, and beyond—were seen through a gauze of fabulous fairy tales revealing an occasional nugget of reality: forests so high they touch the clouds, horned pygmies who move in herds and grow old in seven years, brahmins who kill themselves on funeral pyres, men with dogs' heads and six toes, "cyclopeans" with only one eye and one foot who move as fast as the wind, the "monoceros" which can be caught only when it sleeps in the lap of a virgin, Amazons whose tears are of silver, panthers who practice the caesarean operation with their own claws, trees whose leaves supply wool, snakes 300 feet long, snakes with precious stones for eyes, snakes who so love music that for prudence they stop up one ear with their tail.

Tuchman's and Goodall's paragraphs also illustrate another point: examples can come from various sources. Tuchman finds her specific examples by researching historical documents; Goodall gets hers by observing chimpanzees in their natural habitat. Both writers use their examples for the same purpose, however: to illustrate a general observation.

Typical Examples

In contrast to specific examples, writers compose **typical examples** by generalizing from many experiences, events, incidents, or facts. Consider this paragraph from Jonathan Kozol's essay "The Human Cost of an Illiterate Society." Kozol uses a typical example to develop the point that illiterates, people who cannot read, lead a precarious existence, even when they are in the care of professionals trained to provide for their health. As you read Kozol's paragraph, keep in mind that this typical example represents the experience of many people, not that of one specific person.

> Illiterates live, in more than literal ways, an uninsured existence. They cannot understand written details on a health insurance form. They cannot read the waivers that they sign preceding surgical procedures. Several women I have known in Boston have entered a slum hospital with the intention of obtaining a tubal ligation and have emerged a few days later after having been subjected to a hysterectomy. Unaware of their rights, incognizant of jargon, intimidated by the unfamiliar air of fear and atmosphere of ether that so many of us find oppressive in the confines even of the most attractive and expensive medical facilities, they have signed their names to documents they could not read and which nobody, in the hectic situation that prevails so often in those overcrowded hospitals that serve the urban poor, had even bothered to explain.

Kozol begins with a general statement that establishes the dangers illiterate patients face. He follows with two sentences of background: illiterate patients cannot understand insurance forms or the legal documents that give away their rights during surgery. He then supports his general statement with an extended typical example, thus illustrating, even dramatizing, the result of being unable to read: several illiterate Boston women signed papers permitting hysterectomies when they wanted tubal ligations.

Typical examples, as Kozol's illustrates, are composites of many experiences. They are not rooted in specific times but compiled after many observations over an extended period. In the next paragraph cultural anthropologist Edward T. Hall uses typical examples developed after extended observation to illustrate how people react when their sense of space is violated:

> People are very sensitive to any intrusion into their spatial bubble. If someone stands too close to you, your first

instinct is to back up. If that's not possible, you lean away and pull yourself in, tensing your muscles. If an intruder doesn't respond to these body signals, you may then try to protect yourself, using a briefcase, umbrella, or raincoat. Women—especially when traveling alone—often plant their pocketbook in such a way that no one can get very close to them. As a last resort, you may move to another spot and position yourself behind a desk or a chair that provides screening. Everyone tries to adjust the space around himself in a way that's comfortable for him; most often, he does this unconsciously.

Hypothetical Examples

Sometimes writers create **hypothetical examples** from their imagination. Hypothetical examples are similar to typical examples, usually composed from bits and pieces of experience or information. Often a writer will use a hypothetical example where something concrete is needed to tie down an abstraction and no *actual* example is available. In the opening paragraph of *The White Album*, essayist and novelist Joan Didion uses hypothetical examples to illustrate why stories are important in life.

> We *tell* ourselves stories in order to live. The princess is caged in a consulate. The man with candy will lead the children to the sea. The naked woman on the ledge outside the window on the sixteenth floor is a victim of *accidie,* or the naked woman is an exhibitionist, and it would be "interesting" to know which. We *tell* ourselves that it makes some difference whether the naked woman is about to commit a mortal sin or is about to register a political protest or is about to be, the Aristophanic view, snatched back to the human condition by the fireman in priest's clothing just visible in the window behind her, the one smiling at the telephoto lens. We *look* for the sermon in the suicide, for the social or moral lesson in the murder of five. We *interpret* what we see, select the most workable of the multiple choices. We *live* entirely, especially if we are writers, by the imposition

of a narrative line upon disparate images, by the "ideas" with which we have learned to freeze the shifting phantasmagoria which is our actual experience.

Didion has clearly drawn these brief examples from her imagination, yet they are effective because they make her observation more concrete. With these conjectures, she hopes to stir her readers' interest by appealing to typical experiences they might have encountered in fairy tales and newspapers, the mysterious experiences for which many seek explanations.

Mixing Examples

When studying professional writing, you'll notice that writers use different strategies to develop their examples. You'll find specific, typical, and hypothetical examples mixed, and you'll notice that sometimes examples illustrating one point will be presented in several paragraphs. In this passage from *No House Calls,* Peter Gott, a practicing physician and medical columnist, develops his point in several paragraphs and mixes examples with explanation to reveal the scientific facts behind the commercial claims of mouthwash and disinfectant companies.

> With people's increasing knowledge about bacteria, it was inevitable that some companies would, with success, try to play upon the fear that we have all developed about "bacterial infection." For instance, Listerine and Lysol are currently being advertised to produce "clean breath" and a clean environment, respectively, as a result of their bacteria-killing properties. While it is true that these compounds do, in fact, kill bacteria, the consumer would do well to demand more precision in evaluating their claims.
>
> As an example, the mouth contains billions of harmless bacteria. Some forms of bad breath are caused by bacterial decomposition of food between teeth. Listerine—and many other mouthwashes—will kill millions of bacteria on contact, but only a tiny proportion of the *total.* Furthermore,

as soon as the Listerine has been spit out, billions of bacteria are reintroduced into the mouth during breathing and eating. So while the consumer's mouth will feel "fresh," in fact the bacterial count rapidly rises to "pretreatment" levels; essentially, nothing has been accomplished.

Lysol spray when applied to surfaces will kill some bacteria, but most of these are nonpathogens and would do us no harm anyway. Bacteria that cause venereal disease die quickly outside the body and would be unlikely to reside on public toilet seats long enough for the spray to make any difference. The Lysol spray will scent the air, however, and that seems to be the important consideration. Somehow, if we don't see or smell the germs, we assume they're all gone. The room must be safe. The evil has been repelled. We can take a shower.

Peter Gott's passage establishes an important principle to keep in mind: every writer, whether a professional writer or a student writer, must develop an eye for examples. The most effective way we know of developing that eye is to read critically; that is, read as a writer reads. Study how professional writers shape their examples. Study how their examples relate to their generalizations. And study the kinds of examples they develop.

Examples in College Writing

Examples are so effective in clarifying an idea that you will probably use them in every college essay you write. The following passage is from an essay written for a course on law and society. Rick Yocum, the student writer, illustrates how fans menace not only the "rich and famous" but also community leaders. In these three paragraphs, a significant part of the essay's discussion, Yocum uses varied examples to support his observations.

Yocum opens this
passage by clearly

When increased public attention is placed
on the lives of celebrities, disturbed fans often

stating his general observation.

He develops the paragraph with specific examples that remind readers of past attacks by fans on celebrities.

become dangerous menaces. For example, in 1980 Mark Chapman, a disturbed fan, murdered the former Beatle John Lennon; in 1981 John W. Hinckley Jr. stalked actress Jodie Foster before he tried to kill President Reagan; in 1988 a woman falsely claimed to be talk-show-host David Letterman's wife and kept trying to move into his home; in 1989 a delusional fan murdered Rebecca Schaeffer, star of the television series "My Sister Sam."

He opens the second paragraph by rephrasing his general observation and supporting it with one extended specific example.

Even more menacing were a fan's delusions involving actress Theresa Saldana. The man had traveled from Scotland under the belief that the two of them shared a common destiny and had to be "united." When he finally met the actress, he attacked her with a knife. She survived, and he was arrested and jailed. Even in prison his delusions continued. When he was about to be paroled, Saldana objected and prosecutors kept him in custody by filing new charges that he had threatened her from jail.

He opens this paragraph by shifting focus from "the rich and famous" to local leaders. With an extended hypothetical example he gives the reader an impression of how a typical case might develop.

People need not be among the very famous to be a target of such delusions. Typically, they could be local elected officials, such as county supervisors, council members, or aldermen. They could be teachers, community activists, or prominent business people. A typical case might develop as follows: Mr. Smith meets a well-known female attorney over a business matter. Although the meeting concentrates on his business concerns, Mr. Smith decides that she has fallen in love with him and he is in love with her. To recognize her love and declare his, he besieges her with telephone calls, love letters, and flowers. She is stunned, of course, and denies any interest in Mr. Smith, finally filing harassment charges with the police. He inter-

prets her reactions as a "test of love." He soon
leaves his wife and abandons his business to
pursue the lawyer. When she continues to
rebuff his advances, he sends threatening letters and demands to see her. The next step
is difficult to predict: he could become violent,
or he could be committed to psychiatric care.
From any angle, the situation is menacing.

· · ·

Yocum has carefully selected and mixed his examples to represent
his general observation—a series of brief examples that catalogue
recent assaults by fans on celebrities, an extended example about
a highly dramatic attack, and an extended hypothetical example
that illustrates a typical situation a local celebrity might face. He
has met one of his primary obligations as a writer: his examples
clearly represent his general observation. These examples also take
away any confusion a reader might have about his meaning and
they add interest to his essay. Why does Yocum use a hypothetical
example instead of a victim's actual experience as he does with
celebrities? If you think about the subject, you will realize that
fewer assaults on local leaders than on celebrities are recorded.
Yocum must therefore create a hypothetical example from reports
to nail down his general observation. Yocum's use of examples is
very effective: they will probably convince the reader that he
knows what he's talking about.

As you read the essays in this section, you will see that there
is no one way of developing examples. Sometimes a writer will
use a single extended example. At other times, a writer will combine short and extended examples, specific and typical examples,
and include personal observations and background information.

Sometimes examples will serve as the dominant pattern of
development, but, like narration and description, examples also
function in essays with other dominant patterns, such as comparison and contrast, cause and effect, classification, and argumentation. Always, however, writers use examples with one
fundamental purpose in mind: *to make the general more specific
and the abstract more concrete.*

This brief essay can be used to illustrate the difference between deductive and inductive arrangement of material. Writers frequently use examples to illustrate a thesis already stated (deductive); Thomas inverts that sequence to present examples first and their meaning later (inductive). Class discussion might consider how this arrangement suits Thomas's purpose. He asks us to consider death from a somewhat different angle, and his inductive arrangement seemingly allows us to witness his thinking. His method leads to speculative conclusions rather than certain ones and creates a meditative tone attractive to most readers.

❦ Lewis Thomas ❦

Lewis Thomas, born in 1913, studied at Princeton University and Harvard Medical School. He has had a distinguished career as research pathologist, medical doctor, biologist, professor, and writer, but is best known for his collections of essays, many of which first appeared in The New England Journal of Medicine. *He has been a professor of pathology and medicine at the Cornell University Medical School and has served as both president and chief executive officer of the Memorial Sloan-Kettering Cancer Center in New York City. His first collection,* Notes of a Biology Watcher: The Lives of a Cell *(1975), won the National Book Award and was followed by* More Notes of a Biology Watcher: The Medusa and the Snail *(1979).*

On Natural Death

In this short essay from The Medusa and the Snail, *Lewis Thomas invites the reader to consider a new way of thinking about death. His examples are taken from his own observations and from medical research, from the professional realm as well as the personal, from the extraordinary and the mundane.*

   Keep in mind the essay's title, "On Natural Death," as you read. Apply the title to each paragraph to determine exactly how convincing Thomas's contentions about death are.

MARGINAL NOTES

Students will probably see how ironically associating books on dying with how-to books sets up the subtle humor in the last sentence of the paragraph. His point in the essay is that dying is a "natural" phenomenon. His including sex manuals (designed to instruct us in another natural activity) in his list of how-to books helps sharpen the irony.

There are so many new books about dying that there are now special shelves set aside for them in bookshops, along with the health-diet and home-repair paperbacks and the sex manuals. Some of them are so packed with detailed information and step-by-step instructions for performing the function that you'd think this was a new sort of skill which all of us are now required to learn. The strongest impression the casual reader gets, leafing through, is that proper dying has become an extraordinary, even an exotic experience, something only the specially trained get to do.

1

Thomas points out that we consider deaths of people to be "special" but deaths in nature "natural," part of a recycling. You might ask your students if nature has "special" deaths. Remind them that we have pet cemeteries, which suggest that we value some animals more than others.

A specific example. Thomas's elm tree was "taken" in two senses. "Taken" is a euphemism for "died," and in the literal sense the tree was "carted off." This might be a good time to ask students to think of other expressions we use to describe death, such as "passed away" and "moved on." Ask why we don't simply say "They died," when we talk about people we knew.

A typical example comparing the death of an animal to that of a tree. Because the mouse, unlike the tree, has pain receptors, it must feel pain before it dies (but maybe not *just* before it dies, as the author explains in paragraph 6). The death of an animal seems horrid, compared to that of a tree. This comparison prepares us for later discussion of human deaths.

Thomas uses clinical words to explain the mouse's absence of pain. He elevates (or reduces) the immediate pain before death to a scientific description. This cold, clinical analysis lacks emotional appeal. Then Thomas shifts abruptly to the mouse, who would "shrug" if he could, bringing us back to the warmth of emotion. Your students might want to give some thought to this question: If we knew absolutely that we were going to die, would we "shrug" if we could?

Also, you could be led to believe that we are the only creatures capable of the awareness of death, that when all the rest of nature is being cycled through dying, one generation after another, it is a different kind of process, done automatically and trivially, more "natural," as we say.   2

An elm in our backyard caught the blight this summer and dropped stone dead, leafless, almost overnight. One weekend it was a normal-looking elm, maybe a little bare in spots but nothing alarming, and the next weekend it was gone, passed over, departed, taken. Taken is right, for the tree surgeon came by yesterday with his crew of young helpers and their cherry picker, and took it down branch by branch and carted it off in the back of a red truck, everyone singing.   3

The dying of a field mouse, at the jaws of an amiable household cat, is a spectacle I have beheld many times. It used to make me wince. Early in life I gave up throwing sticks at the cat to make him drop the mouse, because the dropped mouse regularly went ahead and died anyway, but I always shouted unaffections at the cat to let him know the sort of animal he had become. Nature, I thought, was an abomination.   4

Recently I've done some thinking about that mouse, and I wonder if his dying is necessarily all that different from the passing of our elm. The main difference, if there is one, would be in the matter of pain. I do not believe that an elm tree has pain receptors, and even so, the blight seems to me a relatively painless way to go even if there were nerve endings in a tree, which there are not. But the mouse dangling tail-down from the teeth of a gray cat is something else again, with pain beyond bearing, you'd think, all over his small body.   5

There are now some plausible reasons for thinking it is not like that at all, and you can make up an entirely different story about the mouse and his dying if you like. At the instant of being trapped and penetrated by teeth, peptide hormones are released by cells in the hypothalamus and the pituitary gland; instantly these substances, called endorphins, are attached to the surface of other cells responsible for pain perception; the hormones have the pharmacologic properties of opium; there is no pain. Thus it   6 is that the mouse seems always to dangle so languidly from the jaws, lies there so quietly when dropped, dies of his injuries without a struggle. If a mouse could shrug, he'd shrug.

I do not know if this is true or not, nor do I know how to   7
prove it if it is true. Maybe if you could get in there quickly enough and administer naloxone, a specific morphine antagonist, you could turn off the endorphins and observe the restoration of pain, but this is not something I would care to do or see. I think I will leave it there, as a good guess about the dying of a cat-chewed mouse, perhaps about dying in general.

Montaigne had a hunch about dying, based on his own close   8
call in a riding accident. He was so badly injured as to be believed dead by his companions, and was carried home with lamentations, "all bloody, stained all over with the blood I had thrown up." He remembers the entire episode, despite having been "dead, for two full hours," with wonderment:

A specific example. Montaigne's view of death connects with the speculation about the final peacefulness of the mouse's death (6). Inspired by the Latin classics, especially Plutarch, Montaigne's essays reflect his skeptical spirit.

It seemed to me that my life was hanging only by the tip of my lips. I closed my eyes in order, it seemed to me, to help push it out, and took pleasure in growing languid and letting myself go. It was an idea that was only floating on the surface of my soul, as delicate and feeble as all the rest, but in truth not only free from distress but mingled with that sweet feeling that people have who have let themselves slide into sleep. I believe that this is the same state in which people find themselves whom we see fainting in the agony of death, and I maintain that we pity them without cause. . . . In order to get used to the idea of death, I find there is nothing like coming close to it.

Later, in another essay, Montaigne returns to it:

If you know not how to die, never trouble yourself: Nature will in a moment fully and sufficiently instruct you; she will exactly do that business for you; take you no care for it.

Thomas talks about "the early days of the invasion." Some students need to be told that Thomas refers to an action during World War II, and that "MPs" means "military police." This paragraph brings us to Thomas's personal credibility: he witnessed deaths that share the natural features of the mouse's death in paragraphs 4 and 5. In a sense, the MPs "shrugged."

In his conclusion, Thomas expresses admiration for nature's way of handling death. He no longer sees it as an abomination, as he mentions in paragraph 4, but as an "indispensable part of living," handled efficiently.

9
The worst accident I've ever seen was on Okinawa, in the early days of the invasion, when a jeep ran into a troop carrier and was crushed nearly flat. Inside were two young MPs, trapped in bent steel, both mortally hurt, with only their hands and shoulders visible. We had a conversation while people with the right tools were prying them free. Sorry about the accident, they said. No, they said, they felt fine. Is everyone else okay, one of them said. Well, the other one said, no hurry now. And then they died.

10
Pain is useful for avoidance, for getting away when there's time to get away, but when it is end game, and no way back, pain is likely to be turned off, and the mechanisms for this are wonderfully precise and quick. If I had to design an ecosystem in which creatures had to live off each other and in which dying was an indispensable part of living, I could not think of a better way to manage.

POSSIBLE ANSWERS

Meaning and Purpose

1. The reader discovers the topic of the essay in sentence 1, paragraph 3, suddenly, as the elm dies almost overnight. This sudden shift leads the reader into the topic of "natural death," also mentioned in the title of the work.
2. Thomas describes the sophisticated—and rather beautiful—mechanism that shuts down pain; it sets in naturally when a creature is mortally injured. He therefore suggests that the natural process of death is not trivial but something to be admired, even to be in awe of.
3. He uses the specific examples of a tree stricken with blight, a mouse caught in a cat's jaws, and soldiers crushed in a jeep. These are all individual events or experiences. Thomas does say that he doesn't know if his "story" about the mouse's dying without pain is true. This story part of the example has hypothetical elements.

Meaning and Purpose

1. The first paragraph may make readers think they are going to read an essay about "books on dying." What is the topic of the essay, and where does it first appear?
2. In the second paragraph, Thomas suggests that most of us think the deaths of things or creatures other than human beings are "natural," or trivial. How does Thomas use the example of a mouse's death to turn that notion around? Is nature necessarily trivial?
3. What kind or kinds of examples does Thomas use—specific, typical, hypothetical, or a combination of these—to support his ideas? Explain.
4. What does Thomas tell you that is important for you to know about death? Do you agree with him?
5. The author quotes Montaigne, who says elsewhere, "Let us give Nature a chance; she knows her business better than we do." How is this quotation important to the essay?

4. Students might respond by saying something about how important it is to know that dying is natural, even painless. Some may mention that they had never before thought about the actual experience of dying, but only about the prelude and the aftermath.

5. This quotation is important because the essayist deals with the knowledge that nature knows how to handle death. This mildly sarcastic quotation says much the same thing.

Strategy

1. Everyone sings to show that life itself goes on, oblivious to the natural death of an elm tree. It is "natural" to sing while one works. The dead elm tree is now a thing to be removed, a job.

2. Thomas begins with the lesser life form to emphasize his point that "natural"—and all the sophistication it implies—is not necessarily trivial. By the time we read about the soldiers' deaths, we can easily apply Thomas's thesis and see the connection death makes among all living things.

3. This light humor, mostly in the first paragraph and in the author's way of describing his relationship with the cat in paragraph 4, helps hold the reader's interest in a potentially morbid subject. This touch generates interest in a topic that readers often avoid.

4. In this personal essay that deals with a universal topic the author uses "I" throughout, comments personally on death, and concludes with another personal reference. Students might comment on his various uses of the first person.

Style

1. The word *amiable* suggests the connotative qualities that constitute friendliness. Cats are not by nature overly friendly, but they have natural "amiable" qualities that make people like them. The word *beheld* suggests the regal quality often associated with feline demeanor. *Spectacle* connotes drama, consistent with the many small dramas witnessed by the author.

Strategy

1. In the last sentence of paragraph 3, why does everyone sing?
2. Why do you think Thomas devotes four paragraphs to his thoughts about details in the mouse's death, and only one to the soldiers' deaths? How does the former example set you up for the latter?
3. Despite the topic, this essay has some humor. How is this humor appropriate to the essay?
4. Would you call this a "personal" essay? Which specific sentences in the essay support your answer?

Style

1. Reread the first sentence in paragraph 4. The author uses the word "amiable" instead of "friendly," "spectacle" instead of "sight," and "beheld" instead of "seen." How are these words more appropriate than their synonyms? Look up the words in a good dictionary before you answer this question.
2. The first sentence in paragraph 8 is written in an informal style. Reread the sentence and then tell how a reader would know that it is informal.
3. The final paragraph includes the chess expression "end game," which means "the final stage of a game, usually after the exchange of queens and the serious reduction of forces." How is this phrase appropriate to the paragraph and to the essay?

Writing Tasks

1. Your views on death may be strengthened or changed by this essay, even if only a little. In an essay, discuss your views on death and then tell how Thomas's essay has strengthened those views or changed them. If you believe that death is "normal" to

2. "Had a hunch" and "close call" are trite phrases inappropriate to a formal sentence.

3. "End game" compares the finality of death to the end of a chess game.

all things, including human beings, what do you mean by "normal"? If you believe that human beings somehow die differently, what do you think makes their deaths different from those of other creatures?

2. Think of something—an experience, a situation—which at first appears unpleasant or distressing, but which actually has redeeming or beneficial features. Write an essay exploring these ideas and use examples to support your statements. Decide whether to use specific, typical, or hypothetical examples, or a mixture.

One entrance into this essay is to have your students describe situations in which the subjects of their conversations and the language they use vary. That is, what do they talk about when they are with friends of the same sex? Friends of both sexes? What do they talk about when with people they don't know well? With their co-workers? With their parents? Does their language change with the subject matter? How? Point out to them that when they give examples, particularly examples that entail some narrative, they are following the format that Tan uses in her essay.

❦ Amy Tan ❦

Amy Tan was born in Oakland, California, in 1952, two and a half years after her parents emigrated to the United States from China. Her parents expected her to become a neurosurgeon, but instead she became a consultant to programs for disabled children and then a free-lance writer. She visited China for the first time in 1987 and felt an instant cultural identity with her parents' homeland. Her first novel, The Joy Luck Club *(1989), spent several weeks on American bestseller lists and earned much critical acclaim. It sensitively explores the relationships between young Chinese-American women and their immigrant mothers. Her second novel,* The Kitchen God's Wife *(1991), further explores this theme.*

Mother Tongue

In the following essay, first published in Threepenny Review, *Tan describes how her use of English changes according to the needs of the circumstance and moment. During her exploration of language she also manages to paint an affectionate portrait of her mother and the relationship she has with her.*

Tan uses example after example to demonstrate her points. Notice how specific those examples are, how they aptly illustrate her generalizations, and how they lend interest to what she says.

At the outset, Tan establishes that what follows will not be a scientific examination of language. Indeed, her evidence will be anecdotal and, therefore, inappropriate for scientific discourse. She does, however, establish her authority over her subject matter in the second paragraph since she is a professional writer and a lifelong lover of language.

Tan begins with a story that introduces us to one of her "Englishes," standard English.

I am not a scholar of English or literature. I cannot give you much more than personal opinions on the English language and its variations in this country or others. 1

I am a writer. And by that definition, I am someone who has always loved language. I am fascinated by language in daily life. I spend a great deal of my time thinking about the power of language—the way it can evoke an emotion, a visual image, a complex idea, or a simple truth. Language is the tool of my trade. And I use them all—all the Englishes I grew up with. 2

Recently, I was made keenly aware of the different Englishes 3

I do use. I was giving a talk to a large group of people, the same talk I had already given to half a dozen other groups. The nature of the talk was about my writing, my life, and my book, *The Joy Luck Club*. The talk was going along well enough, until I remembered one major difference that made the whole tale sound wrong. My mother was in the room. And it was perhaps the first time she had heard me give a lengthy speech, using the kind of English I have never used with her. I was saying things like, "The intersection of memory upon imagination" and "There is an aspect of my fiction that relates to thus-and-thus"—a speech filled with carefully wrought grammatical phrases, burdened, it suddenly seemed to me, with nominalized forms, past perfect tenses, conditional phrases, all the forms of standard English that I had learned in school and through books, the forms of English I did not use at home with my mother.

She now tells another story to introduce us to her family language of intimacy that will be her primary focus.

Just last week, I was walking down the street with my mother, and I again found myself conscious of the English I was using, the English I do use with her. We were talking about the price of new and used furniture and I heard myself saying this: "Not waste money that way." My husband was with us as well, and he didn't notice any switch in my English. And then I realized why. It's because over the twenty years we've been together I've often used that same kind of English with him, and sometimes he even uses it with me. It has become our language of intimacy, a different sort of English that relates to family talk, the language I grew up with.

Here Tan summarizes her mother's story that she will then quote verbatim in paragraph 6.

So you'll have some idea of what this family talk I heard sounds like, I'll quote what my mother said during a recent conversation which I videotaped and then transcribed. During this conversation, my mother was talking about a political gangster in Shanghai who had the same last name as her family's, Du, and how the gangster in his early years wanted to be adopted by her family, which was rich by comparison. Later, the gangster became more powerful, far richer than my mother's family, and one day showed up at my mother's wedding to pay his respects. Here's what she said in part:

"Du Yusong having business like fruit stand. Like off the street kind. He is Du like Du Zong—but not Tsung-ming Island people. The local people call putong, the river east side, he belong to that side local people. That man want to ask Du Zong father take him in like become own family. Du Zong father wasn't look down on him, but didn't take seriously, until that man big like become a mafia. Now important person, very hard to inviting him. Chinese way, came only to show respect, don't stay for dinner. Respect for making big celebration, he shows up. Mean gives lots of respect. Chinese custom. Chinese social life that way. If too important won't have to stay too long. He come to my wedding. I didn't see, I heard it. I gone to boy's side, they have YMCA dinner. Chinese age I was nineteen."

You should know that my mother's expressive command of 7 English belies how much she actually understands. She reads the *Forbes* report, listens to *Wall Street Week,* converses daily with her stockbroker, reads all of Shirley MacLaine's books with ease—all kinds of things I can't begin to understand. Yet some of my friends tell me they understand 50 percent of what my mother says. Some say they understand 80 to 90 percent. Some say they understand none of it, as if she were speaking pure Chinese. But to me, my mother's English is perfectly clear, perfectly natural. It's my mother tongue. Her language, as I hear it, is vivid, direct, full of observation and imagery. That was the language that helped shape the way I saw things, expressed things, made sense of the world.

The body of the essay, which begins here, is an extended examination of her mother's "limited" English and the effects it has had on her, Tan.

Lately, I've been giving more thought to the kind of English 8 my mother speaks. Like others, I have described it to people as "broken" or "fractured" English. But I wince when I say that. It has always bothered me that I can think of no way to describe it other than "broken," as if it were damaged and needed to be fixed, as if it lacked a certain wholeness and soundness. I've heard other terms used, "limited English," for example. But they seem just as bad, as if everything is limited, including people's perceptions of the limited English speaker.

The conclusion of paragraph 8 leads to Tan's consideration of the various ways her mother's language had limited both of them.

I know this for a fact, because when I was growing up, my 9 mother's "limited" English limited *my* perception of her. I was ashamed of her English. I believed that her English reflected the quality of what she had to say. That is, because she expressed them imperfectly her thoughts were imperfect. And I had plenty of empirical evidence to support me: the fact that people in department stores, at banks, and at restaurants did not take her seriously, did not give her good service, pretended not to understand her, or even acted as if they did not hear her.

Tan uses general examples to demonstrate why her perceptions of her mother were limited.

My mother has long realized the limitations of her English as well, When I was fifteen, she used to have me call people on the phone to pretend I was she. In this guise, I was forced to ask for information or even to complain and yell at people who had been rude to her. One time it was a call to her stockbroker in New York. She had cashed out her small portfolio and it just so happened we were going to go to New York the next week, our very first trip outside California. I had to get on the phone and say in an adolescent voice that was not very convincing, "This is Mrs. Tan."   10

Paragraphs 10–13 constitute a humorous extended anecdote that demonstrates her mother's recognition of her own language limitations.

And my mother was standing in the back whispering loudly, "Why he don't send me check, already two weeks late. So mad he lie to me, losing me money."   11

And then I said in perfect English, "Yes, I'm getting rather concerned. You had agreed to send the check two weeks ago, but it hasn't arrived."   12

Then she began to talk more loudly. "What he want, I come to New York tell him front of his boss, you cheating me?" And I was trying to calm her down, make her be quiet, while telling the stockbroker, "I can't tolerate any more excuses. If I don't receive the check immediately, I am going to have to speak to your manager when I'm in New York next week." And sure enough, the following week there we were in front of this astonished stockbroker, and I was sitting there red-faced and quiet, and my mother, the real Mrs. Tan, was shouting at his boss in her impeccable broken English.   13

Another anecdote, this time a more serious one, further illustrates her mother's acute awareness of her limitations.

CAT (computerized axial tomography) scan: a method for diagnosing disorders of the brain,

We used a similar routine just five days ago, for a situation that was far less humorous. My mother had gone to the hospital for an appointment, to find out about a benign brain tumor a CAT scan had revealed a month ago. She said she had spoken very good English, her best English, no mistakes. Still, she said,   14

lung, liver, spleen, and other soft tissue using a computerized combination of many X-ray photographs taken by a special instrument that displays computerized cross-sectional images of the body.

Paragraphs 15–17 concentrate on the ways Tan herself was limited.

the hospital did not apologize when they said they had lost the CAT scan and she had come for nothing. She said they did not seem to have any sympathy when she told them she was anxious to know the exact diagnosis, since her husband and son had both died of brain tumors. She said they would not give her any more information until the next time and she would have to make another appointment for that. So she said she would not leave until the doctor called her daughter. She wouldn't budge. And when the doctor finally called her daughter, me, who spoke in perfect English—lo and behold—we had assurances the CAT scan would be found, promises that a conference call on Monday would be held, and apologies for any suffering my mother had gone through for a most regrettable mistake.

I think my mother's English almost had an effect on limiting my possibilities in life as well. Sociologists and linguists probably will tell you that a person's developing language skills are more influenced by peers. But I do think that the language spoken in the family, especially in immigrant families which are more insular, plays a large role in shaping the language of the child. And I believe that is affected my results on achievement tests, IQ tests, and the SAT. While my English skills were never judged as poor, compared to math, English could not be considered my strong suit. In grade school I did moderately well, getting perhaps B's, sometimes B-pluses, in English and scoring perhaps in the sixtieth or seventieth percentile on achievement tests. But those scores were not good enough to override the opinion that my true abilities lay in math and science, because in those areas I achieved A's and scored in the ninetieth percentile or higher. 15

This was understandable. Math is precise; there is only one correct answer. Whereas, for me at least, the answers on English tests were always a judgment call, a matter of opinion and personal experience. Those tests were constructed around items like fill-in-the-blank sentence completion, such as, "Even though Tom was _____, Mary thought he was _____." And the correct answer always seemed to be the most bland combinations of thoughts, for example, "Even though Tom was shy, Mary thought he was charming," with the grammatical structure "even though" 16 limiting the correct answer to some sort of semantic opposites, so you wouldn't get answers like, "Even though Tom was foolish, Mary thought he was ridiculous." Well, according to my mother, there were very few limitations as to what Tom could have been and what Mary might have thought of him. So I never did well on tests like that.

The same was true with word analogies, pairs of words in   17
which you were supposed to find some sort of logical, semantic relationship—for example, "*Sunset* is to *nightfall* as _____ is to _____." And here you would be presented with a list of four possible pairs, one of which showed the same kind of relationship: *red* is to *stoplight, bus* is to *arrival, chills* is to *fever, yawn* is to *boring.* Well, I could never think that way. I knew what the tests were asking, but I could not block out of my mind the images already created by the first pair, "*sunset* is to *nightfall*"—and I would see a burst of colors against a darkening sky, the moon rising, the lowering of a curtain of stars. And all the other pairs of words—red, bus, stoplight, boring—just threw up a mass of confusing images, making it impossible for me to sort out something as logical as saying: "A sunset precedes nightfall" is the same as "a chill precedes a fever." The only way I would have gotten that answer right would have been to imagine an associative situation, for example, my being disobedient and staying out past sunset, catching a chill at night, which turns into feverish pneumonia as punishment, which indeed did happen to me.

In the first paragraph of this concluding section, Tan considers the possibility that the personal limitations she described in the previous three paragraphs can be extended to other Asian Americans.

I have been thinking about all this lately, about my mother's   18
English, about achievement tests. Because lately I've been asked, as a writer, why there are not more Asian Americans represented in American literature. Why are there few Asian Americans enrolled in creative writing programs? Why do so many Chinese students go into engineering? Well, these are broad sociological questions I can't begin to answer. But I have noticed in surveys—in fact, just last week—that Asian students, as a whole, always do significantly better on math achievement tests than in English. And this makes me think that there are other Asian-American students whose English spoken in the home might also be de-

Tan now contracts her focus to herself—how she became a writer and the writing of her first novel, *The Joy Luck Club.*

scribed as "broken" or "limited." And perhaps they also have teachers who are steering them away from writing and into math and science, which is what happened to me.

Fortunately, I happen to be rebellious in nature and enjoy the challenge of disproving assumptions made about me. I became an English major my first year in college, after being enrolled as pre-med. I started writing nonfiction as a freelancer the week after I was told by my former boss that writing was my worst skill and I should hone my talents toward account management. 19

But it wasn't until 1985 that I finally began to write fiction. And at first I wrote using what I thought to be wittily crafted sentences, sentences that would finally prove I had mastery over the English language. Here's an example from the first draft of a story that later made its way into *The Joy Luck Club,* but without this line: "That was my mental quandary in its nascent state." A terrible line, which I can barely pronounce. 20

After concentrating on limitations, Tan ends with a near paean to her mother, a respect and love that has been implicit in all of her anecdotes.

Fortunately, for reasons I won't get into today, I later decided I should envision a reader for the stories I would write. And the reader I decided upon was my mother, because these were stories about mothers. So with this reader in mind—and in fact she did read my early drafts—I began to write stories using all the Englishes I grew up with: the English I spoke to my mother, which for lack of a better term might be described as "simple"; the English she used with me, which for lack of a better term might be described as "broken"; my translation of her Chinese, which could certainly be described as "watered down"; and what I imagined to be her translation of her Chinese if she could speak in perfect English, her internal language, and for that I sought to preserve the essence, but neither an English nor a Chinese structure. I wanted to capture what language ability tests can never reveal: her intent, her passion, her imagery, the rhythms of her speech and the nature of her thoughts. 21

Appropriately, Tan's mother becomes her most telling critic.

Apart from what any critic had to say about my writing, I knew I had succeeded where it counted when my mother finished reading my book and gave me her verdict: "So easy to read." 22

POSSIBLE ANSWERS

Meaning and Purpose

1. Tan states her thesis in the last sentence of the second paragraph.

2. Tan's mother exhibits a keen understanding of language by reading *Forbes*, listening to *Wall Street Week*, conversing with her stockbroker, and reading Shirley MacLaine's books—the last a tongue-in-cheek example (7). She also understands how her own English limits her and has a firm grasp of the predicaments which that inability puts her in. Tan gives two examples of this understanding. The first is the humorous story about her stockbroker (10–13), the second a serious anecdote about the results of a CAT scan (14).

3. As a girl Tan was embarrassed by her mother's English, thinking her defective language reflected defective thinking. This embarrassment severely limited Tan's perception of her mother (9).

4. Tan believes that the language spoken by the family, especially insular immigrant families, shapes the language of the child more than sociologists and linguists think. She thus was a higher achiever in math than she was in English (15) and conjectures this influence may account for the paucity of Asian-American writers (18).

Strategy

1. A narrative essay usually has a single story line. Tan's anecdotes are individual stories that illustrate individual points.

2. Tan's examples are always specific, written in concrete language, and are often humorous, or poignant, or both.

3. Tan divides her essay into three parts. The first section (1–7) introduces the reader to the idea that she uses several "Englishes" and describes in detail her "family" English. The second section (8–17) is more reflective and examines the ways her mother's English have

Meaning and Purpose

1. What is Tan's thesis? Where does she state it?
2. Tan asserts that her mother's lack of command of standard English ". . . belies how much she actually understands" (7). How is this so?
3. Explain how her mother's "limited" English limited Tan's perception of her.
4. Explain how her mother's lack of English skills nearly limited some of the author's life possibilities.

Strategy

1. Tan uses anecdotes to illustrate her points, yet this is not a narrative essay. Why?
2. How effectively do Tan's examples illustrate her points?
3. Why does Tan distinctly break her essay at the end of paragraph 8 and again at the end of paragraph 17?

Style

1. In paragraph 7 Tan says that some of her friends claim to understand little of her mother's speech, while some others claim to understand none of it. Translate the transcription of her mother's language in paragraph 6. Can it be accurately described as an "expressive command of English" (7)?
2. How many "Englishes" does Tan speak?
3. Tan says she eliminated the line "That was my mental quandary in its nascent state" from her novel *The Joy Luck Club* and labels the line "terrible." Why?
4. If necessary, look up the following in a good dictionary: *wrought, nominalized* (3); *transcribed* (5); *belies* (7); *empirical* (9); *guise* (10); *impeccable* (13); *benign* (14); *insular* (15); *semantic* (16); *quandary, nascent* (19).

been limiting. The final section (18–21) describes why she became a writer and how she writes. The three sections serve as the essay's introduction, body, and conclusion.

Style

1. Most students will be able to decipher the gist of the story, and many may recognize it as colorful and perceptive. Tan's childhood assessment that this stumbling English reflected defective thinking was certainly faulty.

2. Tan's "Englishes" can be placed in two categories: the English she grew up with: "simple" English, "broken" English, "watered down" English (20); standard English that she ". . . had learned in school and through books . . ." (2).

3. The line is awkward, the diction pretentious. As an exercise you might have your students translate the line into plain English. "That was the beginning of my uncertainty," is a possibility.

4. *Wrought*: worked; *nominalized*: to have converted another part of speech into a noun, as in changing the adjective *lowly* to *the lowly,* or to have converted an underlying clause into a noun phrase, as in changing *he drinks* to *his drinking; transcribed*: made a written copy; *belies*: shows to be false, contradicts; *empirical*: derived from or guided by experience; *guise*: general external appearance; *impeccable*: faultless; *benign*: not malignant; *insular*: detached, isolated; *semantic*: arising from the different meanings of words; *quandary*: a state of perplexity or uncertainty; *nascent*: beginning to exist or develop.

Writing Tasks

1. Using Amy Tan's essay as a model, write an essay in which you examine the various Englishes you use. What do you talk about when you speak with friends of the same sex? Of the opposite sex? With both sexes? With your co-workers? With your parents? How does your language change? Make sure your examples are many and specific.

2. If you work in a job that has specialized jargon, or if you play a sport or participate in any social activity that has its own slang, write an essay in which you categorize and explain that language.

❧ Phyllis Rose ❧

*Phyllis Rose was born in 1926 in New Jersey and attended Connecticut College, Duke University, and the University of Wisconsin, where she earned her Ph.D. in English. She has been a professor of English at the University of Hawaii and a member of the board of several Hawaiian councils for the arts and humanities. She has published two works of biography—*Woman of Letters: A Life of Virginia Woolf *and* Parallel Lives: Five Victorian Marriages—*and a collection of essays,* Writing of Women. *She wrote the "Hers" column for* The New York Times *for ten weeks and has contributed to numerous national publications, including* The Atlantic, Vogue, *and* The Nation. *She is an English professor at Wesleyan University.*

Tools of Torture

In this work, first published in The Atlantic *in 1968, Phyllis Rose takes an uncompromising look at the social and psychological sources of and rationalizations for torture. She uses specific examples from an exhibit in Paris of torture instruments to draw conclusions about the relation of pleasure to pain.*

Determine, as precisely as you can, the answers to these questions: Why are there so many torture devices? Why were they invented in the first place? What are the justifications for institutionalized torture? What is the relation of pleasure to pain?

In a gallery off the rue Dauphine, near the *parfumerie* where I get my massage, I happened upon an exhibit of medieval torture instruments. It made me think that pain must be as great a challenge to the human imagination as pleasure. Otherwise there's no accounting for the number of torture instruments. One would be quite enough. The simple pincer, let's say, which rips out flesh. Or the head crusher, which breaks first your tooth sockets, then your skull. But in addition I saw tongs, thumbscrews, a rack, a ladder, ropes and pulleys, a grill, a garrote, a Spanish horse, a

The Inquisition was a Roman Catholic ecclesiastical tribunal instituted by Pope Innocent III in the thirteenth century to suppress heresy and punish heretics. The inquisitor's chair was one of the tortures devised to further this end, as were most of the other devices described in the essay. That is the reasoning behind the claim in paragraph 6 that human torture has been instituted, condoned, and "vetted" hand in hand by church and state.

Judas cradle, an iron maiden, a cage, a gag, a strappado, a stretching table, a saw, a wheel, a twisting stork, an inquisitor's chair, a breast breaker, and a scourge. You don't need complicated machinery to cause incredible pain. If you want to saw your victim down the middle, for example, all you need is a slightly bigger than usual saw. If you hold the victim upside down so the blood stays in his head, hold his legs apart, and start sawing at the groin, you can get as far as the navel before he loses consciousness.

Even in the Middle Ages, before electricity, there were many things you could do to torment a person. You could tie him up in an iron belt that held the arms and legs up to the chest and left no point of rest, so that all his muscles went into spasm within minutes and he was driven mad within hours. This was the twisting stork, a benign-looking object. You could stretch him out backward over a thin piece of wood so that his whole body weight rested on his spine, which pressed against the sharp wood. Then you could stop up his nostrils and force water into his stomach through his mouth. Then, if you wanted to finish him off, you and your helper could jump on his stomach, causing internal hemorrhage. This torture was called the rack. If you wanted to burn someone to death without hearing him scream, you could use a tongue lock, a metal rod between the jaw and collarbone that prevented him from opening his mouth. You could put a person in a chair with spikes on the seat and arms, tie him down against the spikes, and beat him, so that every time he flinched from the beating he drove his own flesh deeper onto the spikes. This was the inquisitor's chair. If you wanted to make it worse, you could heat the spikes. You could suspend a person over a pointed wooden pyramid and whenever he started to fall asleep, you could drop him onto the point. If you were Ippolito Marsili, the inventor of this torture, known as the Judas cradle, you could tell yourself you had invented something humane, a torture that worked without burning flesh or breaking bones. For the torture here was supposed to be sleep deprivation.

The secret of torture, like the secret of French cuisine, is that nothing is unthinkable. The human body is like a foodstuff, to be grilled, pounded, filleted. Every opening exists to be stuffed, all flesh to be carved off the bone. You take an ordinary wheel, a heavy wooden wheel with spokes. You lay the victim on the ground with blocks of wood at strategic points under his shoulders, legs, and arms. You use the wheel to break every bone in his body. Next you tie his body onto the wheel. With all its bones broken, it will be pliable. However, the victim will not be dead. If you want to kill him, you hoist the wheel aloft on the end of a pole and leave him to starve. Who would have thought to do this with a man and a wheel? But, then, who would have thought to take the disgusting snail, force it to render its ooze, stuff it in its own shell with garlic butter, bake it, and eat it?

Not long ago I had a facial—only in part because I thought I needed one. It was research into the nature and function of pleasure. In a dark booth at the back of the beauty salon, the aesthetician put me on a table and applied a series of ointments to my face, some cool, some warmed. After a while she put something into my hand, cold and metallic. "Don't be afraid, madame," she said. "It is an electrode. It will not hurt you. The other end is attached to two metal cylinders, which I roll over your face. They break down the electricity barrier on your skin and allow the moisturizers to penetrate deeply." I didn't believe this hocus-pocus. I didn't believe in the electricity barrier or in the ability of these rollers to break it down. But it all felt very good. The cold metal on my face was a pleasant change from the soft warmth of the aesthetician's fingers. Still, since Algeria it's hard to hear the word "electrode" without fear. So when she left me for a few minutes with a moist, refreshing cheesecloth over my face, I thought, What if the goal of her expertise had been pain, not moisture? What if the electrodes had been electrodes in the Algerian sense? What if the cheesecloth mask were dipped in acid?

In Paris, where the body is so pampered, torture seems particularly sinister, not because it's hard to understand but because—as the dark side of sensuality—it seems so easy. Beauty care is among the glories of Paris. *Soins esthétiques* include makeup, facials, massages (both relaxing and reducing), depilations (partial

The French colonized Algeria in 1830. The native Muslim Algerians, like all conquered peoples, continually smarted under foreign rule and finally rebelled, attaining independence in 1962. In the last convulsions of the revolution, the French tortured Algerians with electrodes and other devices to elicit information. Having ruled Algeria for so long, the French involved in the atrocities considered their acts both patriotic and necessary.

and complete), manicures, pedicures, and tanning, in addition to the usual run of *soins* for the hair: cutting, brushing, setting, waving, styling, blowing, coloring, and streaking. In Paris the state of your skin, hair, and nerves is taken seriously, and there is little of the puritanical thinking that tries to persuade us that beauty comes from within. Nor do the French think, as Americans do, that beauty should be offhand and low-maintenance. Spending time and money on *soins esthétiques* is appropriate and necessary, not self-indulgent. Should that loving attention to the body turn malevolent, you have torture. You have the procedure—the aesthetic, as it were—of torture, the explanation for the rich diversity of torture instruments, but you do not have the cause.

After explaining why so many instruments of torture are to be found, the author proposes to move to the even more important question of why they were invented in the first place.

Historically torture has been a tool of legal systems, used to get information needed for a trial or, more directly, to determine guilt or innocence. In the Middle Ages confession was considered the best of all proofs, and torture was the way to produce a confession. In other words, torture didn't come into existence to give vent to human sadism. It is not always private and perverse but sometimes social and institutional, vetted by the government and, of course, the Church. (There have been few bigger fans of torture than Christianity and Islam.) Righteousness, as much as viciousness, produces torture. There aren't squads of sadists beating down the doors to the torture chambers begging for jobs. Rather, as a recent book on torture by Edward Peters says, the institution of torture creates sadists: the weight of a culture, Peters suggests, is necessary to recruit torturers. You have to convince people that they are working for a great goal in order to get them to overcome their repugnance to the task of causing physical pain to another person. Usually the great goal is the preservation of society, and the victim is presented to the torturer as being in some way out to destroy it. 6

Milgram's experiments reinforce the idea that sadists are not responsible for institutionalized human cruelty. On the contrary, ordinary peo-

From another point of view, what's horrifying is how easily you can persuade someone that he is working for the common good. Perhaps the most appalling psychological experiment of modern times, by Stanley Milgram, showed that ordinary, decent people in New Haven, Connecticut, could be brought to the point of inflicting (as they thought) severe electric shocks on other 7

ple can be convinced that the pain they inflict is for some higher cause, this time for scientific learning. Milgram also cites Hannah Arendt's 1963 book, *Eichmann in Jerusalem.* She contends that the prosecution's assertion that the Nazi Eichmann was a sadist monster, responsible for the murder of thousands of Jews, was wrong. Rather, she claims, he came closer to being a dull bureaucrat who simply sat at his desk and followed orders (Stanley Milgram, *Obedience to Authority,* 1974).

Jeremy Bentham (1748–1832) was an English philosopher who promoted utilitarianism, the ethical doctrine that asserted actions are right or good in proportion to their usefulness or as they tend to promote happiness. The doctrine claimed that the end and criterion of public action is the greatest happiness of the greatest number. Thus, human happiness becomes the one and only measure of right and wrong.

Marie Antoinette (1755–1793), queen of France, was the wife of Louis XVI, whom she married when she was fifteen. As daughter of Maria Theresa of Austria, she sought Austria's aid against French revolutionaries. In 1791 she counseled Louis to flee from France, an attempt that ended in their imprisonment. They were regarded as traitors and Marie Antoinette was guillotined on October 16, 1793. Her personal charm, her naive ignorance of practical life, her extravagance, and her frank and courageous honesty contributed to her unpopularity both at court and with the French masses. When she was told that a revolution was threatening because the people had no bread, she is said to have replied, "Let them eat cake."

people in obedience to an authority and in pursuit of a goal, the advancement of knowledge, of which they approved. Milgram used—some would say abused—the prestige of science and the university to make his point, but his point is chilling nonetheless. We can cluck over torture, but the evidence at least suggests that with intelligent handling most of us could be brought to do it ourselves.

In the Middle Ages, Milgram's experiment would have had 8 no point. It would have shocked no one that people were capable of cruelty in the interest of something they believed in. That was as it should be. Only recently in the history of human thought has the avoidance of cruelty moved to the forefront of ethics. "Putting cruelty first," as Judith Shklar says in *Ordinary Vices,* is comparatively new. The belief that the "pursuit of happiness" is one of man's inalienable rights, the idea that "cruel and unusual punishment" is an evil in itself, the Benthamite notion that behavior should be guided by what will produce the greatest happiness for the greatest number—all these principles are only two centuries old. They were born with the eighteenth-century democratic revolutions. And in two hundred years they have not been universally accepted. Wherever people believe strongly in some cause, they will justify torture—not just the Nazis, but the French in Algeria.

Many people who wouldn't hurt a fly have annexed to fashion 9 the imagery of torture—the thongs and spikes and metal studs— hence reducing it to the frivolous and transitory. Because torture has been in the mainstream and not on the margins of history, nothing could be healthier. For torture to be merely kinky would be a big advance. Exhibitions like the one I saw in Paris, which presented itself as educational, may be guilty of pandering to the tastes they deplore. Solemnity may be the wrong tone. If taking one's goals too seriously is the danger, the best discouragement of torture may be a radical hedonism that denies that any goal is worth the means, that refuses to allow the nobly abstract to seduce us from the sweetness of the concrete. Give people a good croissant and a good cup of coffee in the morning. Give them an occasional facial and a plate of escargots. Marie Antoinette picked a bad moment to say "Let them eat cake," but I've often thought she was on the right track.

All of which brings me back to Paris, for Paris exists in the imagination of much of the world as the capital of pleasure—of fun, food, art, folly, seduction, gallantry, and beauty. Paris is civilization's reminder to itself that nothing leads you less wrong than your awareness of your own pleasure and a genial desire to spread it around. In that sense the myth of Paris constitutes a moral touchstone, standing for the selfish frivolity that helps keep priorities straight.

10

Meaning and Purpose

1. What is the thesis of the essay and where is it explicitly stated?
2. Rose gives a long list of garish torture devices in the first paragraph. What do you think her purpose is in using examples in this way? Do you feel that they overwhelm and discourage the reader, or hook the reader?
3. In paragraph 3, the author says "The secret of torture, like the secret of French cuisine, is that nothing is unthinkable." How is this statement both a compliment and a condemnation?
4. According to the author, what is the primary cause of human torture? What does this idea imply about social values and human nature? What examples does the author give to demonstrate that those social and psychological tendencies are still with us?
5. In the last two paragraphs the author argues that hedonistic, selfish frivolity is just the thing to keep our moral priorities straight. Why?

Strategy

1. The author says in the opening sentence of paragraph 2 that even before electricity many ways had been devised to torture a person. Why does the author bring in the idea of electricity?

5. Because allegiance to abstract ideals leads people to torture, its precise opposite, the absolute pursuit of sensual pleasure, is torture's natural antidote (9).

Strategy

1. Electricity vastly expands the potential for human torture, but even without it the fertility of the human imagination applied to torture is impressive.

2. One specific example is Milgram's experiment (7). It supports the topic (first) sentence of paragraph 1 and is concrete: it actually happened. In one typical example, Rose describes how a person might have been tortured on the wheel (3). The example is effective because it suggests that this torture was used many times on nameless, and helpless, victims.

3. Paragraph 7 is focused on the Milgram experiments. Rose reminds us that cruelty was accepted before the enlightenment; thus, Milgram's experiments would have been meaningless at that time (8). Recent history suggests, however, that the enlightenment's ideals have not really taken hold. She considers the possibility that cruelty may have drifted to the margins of society, leading to her conclusion that radical hedonism may be the cure for abstract idealism (9).

4. Some readers might consider the graphic examples an assault on the senses. Rose does not back away from her topic and make torture seem less terrible than it is or was. This honest tone gives her argument strength and her voice as a writer credibility.

Style

1. Because one of Rose's themes is that the French have a unique talent for creating ways to give "loving attention to the body," it is appropriate to use the French rather than English word in order to capture the French flavor. *Parfumerie* means perfume store (the author gets her massage in one). *Soins esthétiques* means beauty care.

2. The final paragraph sums up Rose's belief

2. Can you point out one specific and one typical example in the essay? How effective is each?

3. Reread paragraphs 7, 8, and 9. Describe the focus of each paragraph and the logic of moving from one to the other.

4. In informative (some might say academic) essays like this one, writers use examples "to make the general more specific and the abstract more concrete" (chapter introduction [page 191]). What effect overall does Rose accomplish with her graphic examples of torture? Read as a writer and assess how her examples affect tone and the reader's senses.

Style

1. Two French expressions go untranslated: *parfumerie* (1) and *soins esthétiques* (5). Presumably, the author thinks their meanings should be evident from the context. Are they? What effect is created by leaving the words in the original French?

2. In the final paragraph, Rose generalizes when she uses Paris as *the* example of a place of pleasure, a "moral touchstone." How does this general paragraph, following as it does many paragraphs of specific and even graphic examples and facts, serve to close the essay?

3. Explain how the expression "puritanical thinking" is used in paragraph 5.

4. If necessary, check a dictionary for the meaning of these words: *benign* (1); *aesthetician* (4); *malevolent* (5); *vetted* (6); *inalienable* (8); *transitory* (9); *touchstone* (10).

Writing Tasks

1. In "Tools of Torture," Rose uses an event in her life to generate a thesis. Can you think of an event or incident in your life that you can expand into an essay? Make the essay informative, developing your thesis with specific, concrete examples; you may have to do some research.

that Paris can be considered the "capital of pleasure." She has already given specific examples (4, 5). Ending the essay with her thoughts on the pleasures of modern Paris is a neat connection to her having begun with thoughts on the opposite sensation (pain) in medieval Paris.

3. Because the Puritans shunned the flesh, the idea that beauty radiates from the inner self must be puritanical. The French, according to the author, will have none of that thinking.

4. *benign:* showing or expressive of gentleness or kindness; *aesthetician:* a person who is versed in aesthetics, the branch of philosophy dealing with such notions as the beautiful, the ugly, the sublime, and the comic as applicable to the fine arts; *malevolent:* evil, harmful, injurious; *vetted:* to have appraised, verified, or checked for accuracy, authenticity, validity, and so on; *inalienable:* not transferable to another or capable of being repudiated; *transitory:* not lasting, enduring, permanent, or eternal; *touchstone:* a test or criterion for the quality of a thing.

2. In a few paragraphs, write about a typical example of something—that is, a composite. You might write about a typical day at the beach, a typical American traveler overseas, a typical pet, a typical birthday, and so on.

Teaching Suggestions

Postman is provocative, though easy to understand. His remarks about the show-business mentality in politics, religion, education, and news programs should elicit strong responses from students. Some will think he exaggerates. Others will be eager to provide additional examples. A good beginning is a discussion of student responses to the overall message.

Don't miss the opportunity to discuss the strategies Postman employs to keep the reader interested and to present his challenging views as reasonable.

❦ Neil Postman ❦

Neil Postman has written widely on education, often examining how language relates to education and calling for radical reform in the field. His books include Crazy Talk, Stupid Talk: How We Defeat Ourselves by the Way We Talk and What to Do about It *(1976),* Teaching as a Conserving Activity *(1980),* The Disappearance of Childhood *(1982), and* Amusing Ourselves to Death: Public Discourses in the Age of Show Business *(1985). He is also coauthor of several books on educational reform, including* Linguistics: A Revolution in Teaching *(1966) and* Teaching as a Subversive Activity *(1969). He was born in 1931 and has been a professor of media ecology at New York University. His articles have appeared in major periodicals, including* The Atlantic *and* The Nation.

Future Shlock

In "Future Shlock," from his Conscientious Objections: Stirring up Trouble about Language, Technology and Education *(1988), Postman uses a string of examples—from politics, religion, film, and literature—to illustrate the dangers of eroding intelligence in a society hooked on entertainment. He mentions in particular the danger of television, which presents everything, from news reports to religion, as entertainment.*

Keep Postman's contention that "We will become . . . a people amused into stupidity" in mind while you read the essay and his claim that such serious subjects as news broadcasting, politics, and religion have been reduced in this country to mere entertainment.

Marginal Notes

The first three sentences plunge us directly into the subject. If you assign this essay as outside reading, it might be useful to read these sentences aloud in class first and ask if students are inclined to agree or disagree at first thought.

Human intelligence is among the most fragile things in nature. It doesn't take much to distract it, suppress it, or even annihilate it. In this century, we have had some lethal examples of how easily and quickly intelligence can be defeated by any one of its several nemeses: ignorance, superstition, moral fervor, cruelty, cowardice, neglect. In the late 1920s, for example, Germany was, 1

215

The long example of Germany prior to World War II may need amplification, briefly identifying the men listed:

Albert Einstein (1879–1955). Physicist; theory of relativity. Nobel Prize, 1921. Became United States citizen in 1940.

Sigmund Freud (1856–1939). Founder of modern psychoanalysis.

Thomas Mann (1875–1955). Novelist and critic. Nobel Prize, 1929. Came to United States in 1937.

Stefan Zweig (1881–1942). Austrian dramatist, critic, novelist.

Konrad Lorenz (born 1903). Ethologist. Nobel Prize, 1973.

Werner Heisenberg (1901–1976). Physicist. Nobel Prize, 1932.

Martin Heidegger (1889–1976). Philosopher and writer.

Gerhardt Hauptmann (1862–1946). Dramatist, novelist, poet. Nobel Prize, 1912.

Marcel Proust (1871–1922). French novelist.

André Gide (1869–1951). French novelist, poet, critic. Nobel Prize, 1947.

Emile Zola (1840–1902). French novelist.

Jack London (1876–1916). United States novelist and short-story writer.

Upton Sinclair (1878–1968). United States novelist.

The paragraph ends with an emphatic clincher sentence. Postman often uses this device to drive a point home or to look ahead to the next paragraph. See 2–4, 11, 14, 15, 19, and 24.

Having evoked the memory of pre–World War II Germany, an easy-to-accept example, Postman challenges his readers by saying that a similar erosion of intelligence could happen in the United States. This contrast between America's past and Postman's perception of its present condition gives his readers a measure of how much he feels has been lost.

by any measure, the most literate, cultured nation in the world. Its legendary seats of learning attracted scholars from every corner. Its philosophers, social critics, and scientists were of the first rank; its humane traditions an inspiration to less favored nations. But by the mid-1930s—that is, in less than ten years—this cathedral of human reason had been transformed into a cesspool of barbaric irrationality. Many of the most intelligent products of German culture were forced to flee—for example, Einstein, Freud, Karl Jaspers, Thomas Mann, and Stefan Zweig. Even worse, those who remained were either forced to submit their minds to the sovereignty of primitive superstition, or—worse still—willingly did so: Konrad Lorenz, Werner Heisenberg, Martin Heidegger, Gerhardt Hauptmann. On May 10, 1933, a huge bonfire was kindled in Berlin and the books of Marcel Proust, André Gide, Emile Zola, Jack London, Upton Sinclair, and a hundred others were committed to the flames, amid shouts of idiot delight. By 1936, Joseph Paul Goebbels, Germany's Minister of Propaganda, was issuing a proclamation which began with the following words: "Because this year has not brought an improvement in art criticism, I forbid once and for all the continuance of art criticism in its past form, effective as of today." By 1936, there was no one left in Germany who had the brains or courage to object.

Exactly why the Germans banished intelligence is a vast and largely unanswered question. I have never been persuaded that the desperate economic depression that afflicted Germany in the 1920s adequately explains what happened. To quote Aristotle: Men do not become tyrants in order to keep warm. Neither do they become stupid—at least not *that* stupid. But the matter need not trouble us here. I offer the German case only as the most striking example of the fragility of human intelligence. My focus here is the United States in our own time, and I wish to worry you about the rapid erosion of our own intelligence. If you are confident that such a thing cannot happen, your confidence is misplaced, I believe, but it is understandable.

After all, the United States is one of the few countries in the world founded by intellectuals—men of wide learning, of extraordinary rhetorical powers, of deep faith in reason. And al-

2

3

The Land Grant Act of 1862 was a federal-government act that financed the establishment of state colleges.

Henry Steele Commager (born 1902). United States historian and author.

Shlock—of inferior quality, cheap, junk (also spelled *schlock*).

The first sentence is a fairly direct statement of Postman's thesis. (A fuller statement is at the end of paragraph 11.)

For readers who are saying to themselves that the United States is different from Germany, Postman accepts the objection, but argues that similar methodology is not necessary. He picks up this contrast later in discussing Orwell's *1984* and Huxley's *Brave New World*.

Have students comment on the effectiveness of the three sentences that begin with "a culture" and the shock value of the word "stupidity" in the last sentence.

though we have had our moods of anti-intellectualism, few people have been more generous in support of intelligence and learning than Americans. It was the United States that initiated the experiment in mass education that is, even today, the envy of the world. It was America's churches that laid the foundation of our admirable system of higher education; it was the Land-Grant Act of 1862 that made possible our great state universities; and it is to America that scholars and writers have fled when freedom of the intellect became impossible in their own nations. This is why the great historian of American civilization Henry Steele Commager called America "the Empire of Reason." But Commager was referring to the United States of the eighteenth and nineteenth centuries. What term he would use for America today, I cannot say. Yet he has observed, as others have, a change, a precipitous decline in our valuation of intelligence, in our uses of language, in the disciplines of logic and reason, in our capacity to attend to complexity. Perhaps he would agree with me that the Empire of Reason is, in fact, gone, and that the most apt term for America today is the Empire of Shlock.

In any case, this is what I wish to call to your notice: the 4 frightening displacement of serious, intelligent public discourse in American culture by the imagery and triviality of what may be called show business. I do not see the decline of intelligent discourse in America leading to the barbarisms that flourished in Germany, of course. No scholars, I believe, will ever need to flee America. There will be no bonfires to burn books. And I cannot imagine any proclamations forbidding once and for all art criticism, or any other kind of criticism. But this is not a cause for complacency, let alone celebration. A culture does not have to force scholars to flee to render them impotent. A culture does not have to burn books to assure that they will not be read. And a culture does not need a Minister of Propaganda issuing proclamations to silence criticism. There are other ways to achieve stupidity, and it appears that, as in so many other things, there is a distinctly American way.

To explain what I am getting at, I find it helpful to refer to 5 two films, which taken together embody the main lines of my argument. The first film is of recent vintage and is called *The Gods Must Be Crazy*. It is about a tribal people who live in the Kalahari Desert plains of southern Africa, and what happens to their culture when it is invaded by an empty Coca-Cola bottle tossed from the window of a small plane passing overhead. The bottle lands in the middle of the village and is construed by these gentle people to be a gift from the gods, for they not only have never seen a bottle before but have never seen glass either. The people are almost immediately charmed by the gift, and not only because of its novelty. The bottle, it turns out, has multiple uses, chief among them the intriguing music it makes when one blows into it.

But gradually a change takes place in the tribe. The bottle   6
becomes an irresistible preoccupation. Looking at it, holding it, thinking of things to do with it displace other activities once thought essential. But more than this, the Coke bottle is the only thing these people have ever seen of which there is only one of its kind. And so those who do not have it try to get it from the one who does. And the one who does refuses to give it up. Jealousy, greed, and even violence enter the scene, and come very close to destroying the harmony that has characterized their culture for a thousand years. The people begin to love their bottle more than they love themselves, and are saved only when the leader of the tribe, convinced that the gods must be crazy, returns the bottle to the gods by throwing it off the top of a mountain.

The film is great fun and it is also wise, mainly because it is   7
about a subject as relevant to people in Chicago or Los Angeles or New York as it is to those of the Kalahari Desert. It raises two questions of extreme importance to our situation: How does a culture change when new technologies are introduced to it? And is it always desirable for a culture to accommodate itself to the demands of new technologies? The leader of the Kalahari tribe is forced to confront these questions in a way that Americans have refused to do. And because his vision is not obstructed by a belief in what Americans call "technological progress," he is able with minimal discomfort to decide that the songs of the Coke bottle

are not so alluring that they are worth admitting envy, egotism, and greed to a serene culture.

The second movie example illustrates a different point: We are in danger of so trivializing dignified, serious, and important aspects of life that they will become mere entertainment.

The second film relevant to my argument was made in 1967. It is Mel Brooks's first film, *The Producers. The Producers* is a rather raucous comedy that has at its center a painful joke: An unscrupulous theatrical producer has figured out that it is relatively easy to turn a buck by producing a play that fails. All one has to do is induce dozens of backers to invest in the play by promising them exorbitant percentages of its profits. When the play fails, there being no profits to disperse, the producer walks away with thousands of dollars that can never be claimed. Of course, the central problem he must solve is to make sure that his play is a disastrous failure. And so he hits upon an excellent idea: he will take the most tragic and grotesque story of our century—the rise of Adolf Hitler—and make it into a musical.

Because the producer is only a crook and not a fool, he assumes that the stupidity of making a musical on this theme will be immediately grasped by audiences and that they will leave the theater in dumbfounded rage. So he calls his play *Springtime for Hitler,* which is also the name of its most important song. The song begins with the words:

> Springtime for Hitler and Germany;
> Winter for Poland and France.

The melody is catchy, and when the song is sung it is accompanied by a happy chorus line. (One must understand, of course, that *Springtime for Hitler* is no spoof of Hitler, as was, for example, Charlie Chaplin's *The Great Dictator.* The play is instead a kind of denial of Hitler in song and dance; as if to say, it was all in fun.)

The ending of the movie is predictable. The audience loves the play and leaves the theater humming *Springtime for Hitler.* The musical becomes a great hit. The producer ends up in jail, his joke having turned back on him. But Brooks's point is that the joke is on us. Although the film was made years before a movie actor became President of the United States, Brooks was making a kind of prophecy about that—namely, that the producers of American culture will increasingly turn our history, politics, religion, commerce, and education into forms of entertainment, and that we will become as a result a trivial people, incapable of coping with complexity, ambiguity, uncertainty, perhaps even reality. We will become, in a phrase, a people amused into stupidity.

For those readers who are not inclined to take Mel Brooks as seriously as I do, let me remind you that the prophecy I attribute here to Brooks was, in fact, made many years before by a more formidable social critic than he. I refer to Aldous Huxley, who wrote *Brave New World* at the time that the modern monuments to intellectual stupidity were taking shape: Nazism in Germany, fascism in Italy, communism in Russia. But Huxley was not concerned in his book with such naked and crude forms of intellectual suicide. He saw beyond them, and mostly, I must add, he saw America. To be more specific, he foresaw that the greatest threat to the intelligence and humane creativity of our culture would not come from Big Brother and Ministries of Propaganda, or gulags and concentration camps. He prophesied, if I may put it this way, that there is tyranny lurking in a Coca-Cola bottle; that we could be ruined not by what we fear and hate but by what we welcome and love, by what we construe to be a gift from the gods. 12

And in case anyone missed his point in 1932, Huxley wrote *Brave New World Revisited* twenty years later. By then, George Orwell's *1984* had been published, and it was inevitable that Huxley would compare Orwell's book with his own. The difference, he said, is that in Orwell's book people are controlled by inflicting pain. In *Brave New World,* they are controlled by inflicting pleasure. 13

The Coke bottle that has fallen in our midst is a corporation of dazzling technologies whose forms turn all serious public business into a kind of *Springtime for Hitler* musical. Television is the principal instrument of this disaster, in part because it is the medium Americans most dearly love, and in part because it has become the command center of our culture. Americans turn to television not only for their light entertainment but for their news, 14

Aldous Huxley (1894–1963). English novelist and critic.

"Big Brother" (the television image in Orwell's *1984*), "Ministries of Propaganda," "gulags," and "concentration camps" represent the tyranny of force.

The Coca-Cola bottle is used as a symbol of new technologies.

George Orwell [Eric Blair] (1903–1950). English novelist and essayist.

Paragraph 14 marks the culmination of Postman's interpretation of the current situation. His examples thus far have pointed to the insufficiently examined power of show business (particularly, but not exclusively, television) to trivialize serious discourse.

their weather, their politics, their religion, their history—all of which may be said to be their serious entertainment. The light entertainment is not the problem. The least dangerous things on television are its junk. What I am talking about is television's preemption of our culture's most serious business. It would be merely banal to say that television presents us with entertaining subject matter. It is quite another thing to say that on television all subject matter is presented as entertaining. And that is how television brings ruin to any intelligent understanding of public affairs.

Beginning with paragraph 15, Postman turns to examples of this trivialization in politics, religion, education, news, and history in the next six paragraphs. This section will probably stimulate most discussion. Some students will undoubtedly be delighted with Postman's examples and want to add some of their own. Others may feel that he overstates his position and succumbs to the very disease he warns us of. With the following examples he attempts to show the scope of the influence:

Geraldine Ferraro (born 1935). First woman vice-presidential nominee, 1984.

William Miller (born 1914). Republican candidate for vice president in 1964.

Sam Ervin (1896–1985). U.S. Senator, chairman of Senate Watergate investigation committee.

George McGovern (born 1922). Democratic presidential candidate, 1972.

Ralph Nader (born 1934). Consumer advocate, lawyer, writer.

Ed Koch (born 1924). Former mayor of New York City, 1977–1989.

Jesse Jackson (born 1941). Civil-rights activist, minister, presidential hopeful.

Henry Kissinger (born 1923). Secretary of State, 1973–1977. Nobel Prize, 1973.

Gerald Ford (born 1913). President of United States, 1974–1977.

Tip O'Neill (born 1912). Speaker of the House, 1977–1987.

Michael Dukakis (born 1933). Democratic candidate for president, 1988.

Richard Nixon (born 1913). President of United States, 1969–1974.

Everett Dirksen (1896–1969). U.S. Senator.

15 Political campaigns, for example, are now conducted largely in the form of television commercials. Candidates forgo precision, complexity, substance—in some cases, language itself—for the arts of show business: music, imagery, celebrities, theatrics. Indeed, political figures have become so good at this, and so accustomed to it, that they do television commercials even when they are not campaigning, as, for example, Geraldine Ferraro for Diet Pepsi and former Vice-Presidential candidate William Miller and the late Senator Sam Ervin for American Express. Even worse, political figures appear on variety shows, soap operas, and sitcoms. George McGovern, Ralph Nader, Ed Koch, and Jesse Jackson have all hosted "Saturday Night Live." Henry Kissinger and former President Gerald Ford have done cameo roles on "Dynasty." Tip O'Neill and Governor Michael Dukakis have appeared on "Cheers." Richard Nixon did a short stint on "Laugh-In." The late Senator from Illinois, Everett Dirksen, was on "What's My Line?" a prophetic question if ever there was one. What *is* the line of these people? Or, more precisely, *where* is the line that one ought to be able to draw between politics and entertainment? I would suggest that television has annihilated it.

16 It is significant, I think, that although our [then] current President, a former Hollywood movie actor, rarely speaks accurately and never precisely, he is known as the Great Communicator; his telegenic charm appears to be his major asset, and that seems to be quite good enough in an entertainment-oriented politics. But lest you think his election to two terms is a mere aberration, I must remind you that, as I write [1988], Charlton

Heston is being mentioned as a possible candidate for the Republican nomination in 1988. Should this happen, what alternative would the Democrats have but to nominate Gregory Peck? Two idols of the silver screen going one on one. Could even the fertile imagination of Mel Brooks have foreseen this? Heston giving us intimations of Moses as he accepts the nomination; Peck recreating the courage of his biblical David as he accepts the challenge of running against a modern Goliath. Heston going on the stump as Michelangelo; Peck countering with Douglas MacArthur. Heston accusing Peck of insanity because of *The Boys from Brazil*. Peck replying with the charge that Heston blew the world up in *Return to Planet of the Apes*. *Springtime for Hitler* could be closer than you think.

Jonathan Edwards (1703–1758). Clergyman and theologian.
Charles Finney (1792–1875). Clergyman and educator.
George Whitefield (1714–1770). Methodist revivalist.
Jimmy Swaggart (born 1935). Television evangelist.
Jim Bakker (born 1948). Former television evangelist.
Jerry Falwell (born 1933). Television evangelist.

But politics is only one arena in which serious language has 17 been displaced by the arts of show business. We have all seen how religion is packaged on television, as a kind of Las Vegas stage show, devoid of ritual, sacrality, and tradition. Today's electronic preachers are in no way like America's evangelicals of the past. Men like Jonathan Edwards, Charles Finney, and George Whitefield were preachers of theological depth, authentic learning, and great expository power. Electronic preachers such as Jimmy Swaggart, Jim Bakker, and Jerry Falwell are merely performers who exploit television's visual power and their own charisma for the greater glory of themselves.

We have also seen "Sesame Street" and other educational 18 shows in which the demands of entertainment take precedence over the rigors of learning. And we well know how American businessmen, working under the assumption that potential customers require amusement rather than facts, use music, dance, comedy, cartoons, and celebrities to sell their products.

Even our daily news, which for most Americans means tele- 19 vision news, is packaged as a kind of show, featuring handsome news readers, exciting music, and dynamic film footage. Most especially, film footage. When there is no film footage, there is no story. Stranger still, commercials may appear anywhere in a news story—before, after, or in the middle. This reduces all events to trivialities, sources of public entertainment and little more.

After all, how serious can a bombing in Lebanon be if it is shown to us prefaced by a happy United Airlines commercial and summarized by a Calvin Klein jeans commercial? Indeed, television newscasters have added to our grammar a new part of speech—what may be called the "Now . . . this" conjunction, a conjunction that does not connect two things, but disconnects them. When newscasters say, "Now . . . this," they mean to indicate that what you have just heard or seen has no relevance to what you are about to hear or see. There is no murder so brutal, no political blunder so costly, no bombing so devastating that it cannot be erased from our minds by a newscaster saying, "Now . . . this." He means that you have thought long enough on the matter (let us say, for forty seconds) and you must now give your attention to a commercial. Such a situation is not "the news." It is merely a daily version of *Springtime for Hitler,* and in my opinion accounts for the fact that Americans are among the most ill-informed people in the world. To be sure, we know *of* many things; but we know *about* very little.

To provide some verification of this, I conducted a survey a 20 few years back on the subject of the Iranian hostage crisis. I chose this subject because it was alluded to on television *every day for more than a year.* I did not ask my subjects for their opinions about the hostage situation. I am not interested in opinion polls; I am interested in knowledge polls. The questions I asked were simple and did not require deep knowledge. For example, Where is Iran? What language do the Iranians speak? Where did the Shah come from? What religion do the Iranians practice, and what are its basic tenets? What does "Ayatollah" mean? I found that almost everybody knew practically nothing about Iran. And those who did know something said they had learned it from *Newsweek* or *Time* or *The New York Times.* Television, in other words, is not the great information machine. It is the great disinformation machine. A most nerve-wracking confirmation of this came some time ago during an interview with the producer and the writer of the TV mini-series *Peter the Great.* Defending the historical inaccuracies in the drama—which included a fabricated meeting between Peter and Sir Isaac Newton—the producer said

How do your students take to the accusation leveled here against all of us?

Similar "polls" appear regularly in the press. Students may want to discuss others they have heard about, or question how accurate they are and what conclusions they justify.

Ayatollah: a highly advanced scholar of Islamic law and religion (Shi'ite title).

Peter the Great (1672–1725). Peter I, czar of Russia, 1682–1725.

Sir Isaac Newton (1642–1727). English philosopher and mathematician. Formulated the law of gravitation.

that no one would watch a dry, historically faithful biography. The writer added that it is better for audiences to learn something that is untrue, if it is entertaining, than not to learn anything at all. And just to put some icing on the cake, the actor who played Peter, Maximilian Schell, remarked that he does not believe in historical truth and therefore sees no reason to pursue it.

I do not mean to say that the trivialization of American public discourse is all accomplished on television. Rather, television is the paradigm for all our attempts at public communication. It conditions our minds to apprehend the world through fragmented pictures and forces other media to orient themselves in that direction. You know the standard question we put to people who have difficulty understanding even simple language: we ask them impatiently, "Do I have to draw a picture for you?" Well, it appears that, like it or not, our culture will draw pictures for us, will explain the world to us in pictures. As a medium for conducting public business, language had receded in importance; it has been moved to the periphery of culture and has been replaced at the center by the entertaining visual image. 21

Please understand that I am making no criticism of the visual arts in general. That criticism is made by God, not by me. You will remember that in His Second Commandment, God explicitly states that "Thou shalt not make unto thee any graven image, nor any likeness of anything that is in Heaven above, or that is in the earth beneath, or the waters beneath the earth." I have always felt that God was taking a rather extreme position on this, as is His way. As for myself, I am arguing from the standpoint of a symbolic relativist. Forms of communication are neither good nor bad in themselves. They become good or bad depending on their relationship to other symbols and on the functions they are made to serve within a social order. When a culture becomes overloaded with pictures; when logic and rhetoric lose their binding authority; when historical truth becomes irrelevant; when the spoken or written word is distrusted or makes demands on our attention that we are incapable of giving; when our politics, history, education, religion, public information, and commerce are expressed 22

In three paragraphs (21, 22, 23), Postman tells us he is not blaming television alone, nor is he attacking the visual arts or entertainment in themselves.

largely in visual imagery rather than words, then a culture is in serious jeopardy.

Neither do I make a complaint against entertainment. As an old song has it, life is not a highway strewn with flowers. The sight of a few blossoms here and there may make our journey a trifle more endurable. But in America, the least amusing people are our professional entertainers. In our present situation, our preachers, entrepreneurs, politicians, teachers, and journalists are committed to entertaining us through media that do not lend themselves to serious, complex discourse. But these producers of our culture are not to be blamed. They, like the rest of us, believe in the supremacy of technological progress. It has never occurred to us that the gods might be crazy. And even if it did, there is no mountaintop from which we can return what is dangerous to us.

We would do well to keep in mind that there are two ways in which the spirit of a culture may be degraded. In the first— the Orwellian—culture becomes a prison. This was the way of the Nazis, and it appears to be the way of the Russians. In the second—the Huxleyan—culture becomes a burlesque. This appears to be the way of the Americans. What Huxley teaches is that in the Age of Advanced Technology, spiritual devastation is more likely to come from an enemy with a smiling countenance than from one whose face exudes suspicion and hate. In the Huxleyan prophecy, Big Brother does not watch us, by his choice; we watch him, by ours. When a culture becomes distracted by trivia; when political and social life are redefined as a perpetual round of entertainments; when public conversation becomes a form of baby talk; when a people become, in short, an audience and their public business a vaudeville act, then—Huxley argued— a nation finds itself at risk and culture-death is a clear possibility. I agree.

23

24

In paragraph 23, he restates his belief that "entertainment" has permeated the serious aspects of our culture and reminds us, using the words "the gods must be crazy," about the message of that film: The effects of new technology must be examined carefully.

In the concluding paragraph he reminds us again that America seems to have chosen the Huxleyan rather than the Orwellian road.

Postman offers no specific way out of the situation he describes. In fact, paragraph 23 ends with a discouraging note: "there is no mountaintop from which we can return what is dangerous to us."

POSSIBLE ANSWERS

Meaning and Purpose

1. Postman's purpose is to warn us about the "rapid erosion of our own intelligence" as a result of the trivialization of serious matters: politics, education, religion, and news. He simply informs us; he does not offer solutions. The last sentences in paragraphs 22–24 discourage hope. Students should be able to support their opinions about whether or not the purpose succeeds. **2.** Paragraph 11 includes the statement that seems most nearly complete.
3. *The Gods Must Be Crazy* example shows that new technologies profoundly affect cultures, and they should be examined and discarded if necessary. *The Producers* example shows how serious matters can be trivialized.
4. The Reagan example is fairly well explained, and Postman shows that Reagan's style is "good enough in an entertainment-oriented politics." (Some students may disagree with Postman's opinion of Reagan; encourage discussion.) *Sesame Street* is mentioned briefly and criticized for placing learning second to entertainment. Postman does not offer support for this opinion, so that the example does not demonstrate his meaning as clearly as the other does. (Some students may have watched *Sesame Street* as children and may have an opinion different from Postman's.) Encourage them to evaluate other examples for their contributions to meaning.
5. Perhaps only a few students will agree with Postman completely. Some may feel he exaggerates; others will strongly resist his intensely critical message.

Strategy

1. This sentence—"We will become, in a phrase, a people amused into stupidity"—summarizes the lengthy sentence preceding it and provides shock value with the word "stupidity."

"And that is how television brings ruin.

Meaning and Purpose

1. The purpose of an essay is like a goal that the writer sets. The writer has to keep the reader reminded of the purpose and pointed in the right direction. What do you think Postman's purpose is in "Future Shlock," and does he achieve it? How does he do so, and if he doesn't, why does he fail?
2. Postman states his general thesis in a number of ways. Paragraphs 2, 3, 4, 11, and 12 have sentences that sound like thesis statements. Reread these paragraphs and find the statement that you think best summarizes the essay as a whole.
3. What is the main point in *The Gods Must Be Crazy* example? In *The Producers* example?
4. Choose any two examples (such as, Reagan as an example of the blurred distinction between politics and entertainment [6]; Sesame Street as an example of the needs of entertainment overriding the "rigors of learning" [18]), and discuss whether or not these choices help elucidate Postman's meaning. Are they effective in their immediate contexts?
5. How convincing is Postman? Does his view of our culture coincide with yours? In what ways? Do you disagree with portions of his argument?

Strategy

1. Postman often ends paragraphs with strong statements. See paragraphs 1, 2, and 3. Find other strong statements that end paragraphs and discuss the purpose they serve.
2. Why does Postman begin with a pre-World War II German example in an essay about the United States? Why does he turn away from the example without examining its causes?
3. Whom do you think Postman had in mind as his audience when he wrote "Future Shlock"? What kind of reader does he appeal to? Do you think he wants to provoke readers with his criticisms of television and American culture and intelligence? Discuss.
4. Trace the use of examples in the essay. Are they specific or

. . ." The uncompromising harshness of "ruin" conveys the seriousness of his charge in the preceding sentence (14).

"I would suggest that television has annihilated it." The word *annihilated* means total erasure of the line, thus conveying Postman's contention that politics has become entertainment (15).

"To be sure, we know *of* many things; but we know *about* very little." The parallelism used here to contrast *of* and *about* creates a memorable phrasing, reinforcing his point that television news is not really educating people (19).

"I agree." Coming after a long (sixty-word) sentence developed with parallel structure, the punchiness of this two-word sentence is emphatic (24).

2. Germany is, first, a notorious example of unexplained "madness." Therefore, it is easy for a reader to accept the example and the conclusion. When he moves in the next paragraph to the United States example, the reader has already, at least in part, accepted his credibility.

3. Postman appeals to an intelligent, aware audience that can understand many of his historical references, or know how to look them up. Yet he probably knows that some of his readers get most of their information from television, even though he criticizes this habit. He surely intends to be provocative and make readers think and perhaps reevaluate.

4. In the first half of the essay (through paragraph 13), he uses specific, extended examples: Germany, the United States, *The Gods Must Be Crazy, The Producers,* and *Brave New World,* as well as a brief mention of *1984.*

In the second half of the essay the examples are brief and both specific and typical (see paragraph 19 for a good illustration), though he gives one extended example of a hypothetical Heston versus Peck political campaign.

Style

1. *Cathedral* may be loosely applied to any large church. The connotation here is of spiritual authority, suggesting dedication, piety, learning,

typical? extended or brief? Are different types of examples put to different uses?

Style

1. In Postman's opening example, Germany, he says, "this cathedral of human reason had been transformed into a cesspool of barbaric irrationality." Comment on the effectiveness of this metaphor, especially the words "cathedral," "cesspool," and "barbaric."

2. The Coca-Cola bottle so vital to Postman's discussion of *The Gods Must Be Crazy* is used as a metaphor for what? Comment on the connection between these statements and the original metaphor:

    ". . . there is tyranny lurking in a Coca-Cola bottle" (12).

    ". . . we could be ruined . . . by what we welcome and love" (12).

    "The Coke bottle that has fallen in our midst is a corporation of dazzling technologies" (14).

    "Television . . . is the medium Americans most dearly love" (14).

3. If necessary, check a dictionary for the meaning of these words: *shlock; nemeses* (1); *rhetorical; precipitous* (3); *preemption* (14); *banal* (14); *intimations* (16); *sacrality* (17); *Ayatollah* (20); *paradigm* (21); *countenance* (24).

Writing Tasks

1. In paragraph 1, Postman says, "In this century, we have had some lethal examples of how easily and quickly intelligence can be defeated by any one of its several nemeses: ignorance, superstition, moral fervor, cruelty, cowardice, neglect." Have you ever seen these forces at work in your studies or in your own experience? Consider your own behavior, your friends' behavior, the workings of your city or community, national or international

reverence, love, aspiration—the best human qualities.

A *cesspool* is a drainage hole for sewage. It brings to mind filth, foul smells, disease, and waste.

Barbarian originally meant anyone who belonged to a group outside one's own culture, and *barbaric* denoted such a person's behavior, whatever it might be. Now the word commonly indicates lack of learning, lack of restraint, wild, uneducated, uncivilized, and uncultured—a person living without reasonable values and behaviors.

The metaphor moves from the lofty to the debased and characterizes the change as a retreat to less than civilized behavior.

2. The Coca-Cola bottle is a metaphor for new technologies. The quotations, in turn, mean a new technology can become tyrannical, recall the bottle's effect on the tribe, connect television with the Coke bottle, and restate the original metaphor.

3. *Shlock:* shoddy; *nemeses* (plural of nemesis): a powerful rival, one who inflicts destruction; *rhetorical:* use of words for persuasion; *precipitous:* steep; *preemption:* acquisition or appropriation of something beforehand; *banal:* predictable, trite; *intimations:* declarations; *sacrality:* religious rites; *Ayatollah:* Islamic scholar of high rank; *paradigm:* a model; *countenance:* appearance.

affairs, your college, your clubs and organizations. Write an essay about one of these forces as you have seen it at work in one or more situations. Develop your essay with either typical or specific examples.

2. Postman argues that "serious matters of public concern" have been turned into entertainment. Write an essay in which you agree or disagree with his view in relation to one serious matter of public concern. Use one or more specific, extended examples to support your assertions.

❦ Alleen Pace Nilsen ❦

Alleen Pace Nilsen was born in 1936 and attended Brigham Young University as an undergraduate and American University as a masters student. She received her doctorate from the University of Iowa, where she studied linguistic sexism in children's literature. She is coauthor, with her husband, of two books: Pronunciation Contrasts in English *(1971) and* Semantic Theory: A Linguistic Perspective *(1975). Continuing her work in linguistic sexism and children's literature, she has coedited a book of essays,* Sexism and Language *(1977), and a textbook,* Literature for Today's Young Adults *(1980). Currently she is a professor of English and assistant vice president for academic affairs at Arizona State University.*

Sexism in English:
A 1990s Update

In an essay written in the early 1970s, Nilsen examined the sexist biases inherent in numerous words of the English language. The article was published as part of a series sponsored by the Modern Language Association's Commission on the Status of Women. Nilsen wrote this following essay, in which she looks at how language use has changed since then, and adds new examples to her old list. "A 1990s Update" first appeared in Language Awareness, *a composition anthology.*

Nilsen establishes a powerful case on how our current use of language still promotes sexual stereotypes. Watch for those places where she thinks our language may be changing to help remedy those stereotypes.

Twenty years ago I embarked on a study of the sexism inherent in American English. I had just returned to Ann Arbor, Michigan, after living for two years (1967–69) in Kabul, Afghanistan, where I had begun to look critically at the role society assigned to women. The Afghan version of the *chaderi* prescribed for Moslem women was particularly confining. Few women at-

1

tended the American-built Kabul University where my husband was teaching linguistics because there were no women's dormitories, which meant that the only females who could attend were those whose families happened to live in the capital city. Afghan jokes and folklore were blatantly sexist, for example this proverb, "If you see an old man, sit down and take a lesson; if you see an old woman, throw a stone."

Nilsen compares the roles of Afghan women with those of American women, particularly those in Kabul. She gives examples of how women are treated in Kabul, which open her eyes to the ways in which women in general are treated.

But it wasn't only the native culture that made me question women's roles; it was also the American community. Nearly six hundred Americans lived in Kabul, mostly supported by U.S. taxpayers. The single women were career secretaries, school teachers, or nurses. The three women who had jobs comparable to the American men's jobs were textbook editors with the assignment of developing reading books in Dari (Afghan Persian) for young children. They worked at the Ministry of Education, a large building in the center of the city. There were no women's restrooms, so during their two-year assignment whenever they needed to go to the bathroom they had to walk across the street and down the block to the Kabul Hotel.

Removed from their own culture, the American women in Kabul take up ways of life that are unusual for them. Nilsen gives examples of how the American women's activities in Kabul changed her way of thinking about women's roles in general.

The rest of the American women were like myself—wives and mothers whose husbands were either career diplomats, employees of USAID, or college professors who had been recruited to work on various contract teams including an education team from Teachers College, Columbia University and an agricultural team from the University of Wyoming. These were the women who were most influential in changing my way of thinking. We were suddenly bereft of our traditional roles; some of us became alcoholics; others got very good at bridge, while others searched desperately for ways to contribute either to our families or to the Afghans. The local economy provided few jobs for women and certainly none for foreigners; we were isolated from former friends and the social goals we had grown up with. Most of us had three servants (they worked for $1.00 a day) because the cook refused to wash dishes and the dishwasher refused to water the lawn or sweep the sidewalks—it was their form of unionization. Occasionally, someone would try to get along without servants, but it was impossible because the houses were huge and we didn't have

2

3

Notice the hint of imitation here. The American man seems to be imitating what he sees as a facet of Afghan culture. He takes "valuable" time out from his "important work"—an hour a week—to listen to his wife's complaints. The rhetorical question that concludes this paragraph is meant to reflect sarcastically the man's inflated view of his job.

the mechanical aids we had at home. Drinking water had to be brought from the deep well at the American Embassy, and kerosene and wood stoves had to be stocked and lit. The servants were all males, the highest-paid one being the cook who could usually speak some English. Our days revolved around supervising these servants. One woman's husband got so tired of hearing her complain about such annoyances as the *bacha* (the housekeeper) stealing kerosene and needles and batteries, and about the cook putting chili powder instead of paprika on the deviled eggs, and about the gardener subcontracting his work and expecting her to pay all his friends that he scheduled an hour a week for listening to complaints. The rest of the time he wanted to keep his mind clear to focus on his important work with his Afghan counterparts and with the president of the university and the Minister of Education. What he was doing in this country was going to make a difference! In the great eternal scheme of things, of what possible importance could be his wife's trivial troubles with the servants?

Nilsen decides to take up academic involvement in the feminist movement, rather than an overtly political part. Not being ready for a revolution, she instead decides to study the ways in which language affects people's attitudes.

These were the thoughts in my mind when we finished our contract and returned in the fall of 1969 to the University of Michigan in Ann Arbor. I was surprised to find that many other women were also questioning the expectations that they had grown up with. In the spring of 1970, a women's conference was announced. I hired a babysitter and attended, but I returned home more troubled than ever. Now that I knew housework was worth only a dollar a day, I couldn't take it seriously, but I wasn't angry in the same way these women were. Their militancy frightened me. Since I wasn't ready for a revolution, I decided I would have my own feminist movement. I would study the English language and see what it could tell me about sexism. I started reading a desk dictionary and making notecards on every entry that seemed to tell something about male and female. I soon had a dog-eared dictionary, along with a collection of notecards filling two shoe boxes.

4

Ironically, I started reading the dictionary because I wanted to avoid getting involved in social issues, but what happened was that my notecards brought me right back to looking at society.

5

Language and society are as intertwined as a chicken and an egg. The language that a culture uses is telltale evidence of the values and beliefs of that culture. And because there is a lag in how fast a language changes—new words can easily be introduced, but it takes a long time for old words and usages to disappear—a careful look at English will reveal the attitudes that our ancestors held and that we as a culture are therefore predisposed to hold. My notecards revealed three main points. Friends have offered the opinion that I didn't need to read the dictionary to learn such obvious facts. Nevertheless, it was interesting to have linguistic evidence of sociological observations.

Briefly, the "Whorfian hypothesis" (after Benjamin Lee Whorf) says that the language a culture uses determines its perceptions of the world. The popularity of this view has waned because we seem to have no way to prove that different groups of languages reflect different thought processes. Nilsen is not dealing with *language* linguistically defined, however; she is dealing with words and how those words can tell us something about ourselves, which is part of the semantic component of language.

Women Are Sexy; Men Are Successful

First, in American culture a woman is valued for the attractiveness and sexiness of her body, while a man is valued for his physical strength and accomplishments. A woman is sexy. A man is successful.   6

A persuasive piece of evidence supporting this view are the eponyms—words that have come from someone's name—found in English. I had a two-and-a-half-inch stack of cards taken from men's names, but less than a half-inch stack from women's names, and most of those came from Greek mythology. In the words that came into American English since we separated from Britain, there are many eponyms based on the names of famous American men: bartlett pear, boysenberry, diesel engine, franklin stove, ferris wheel, gattling gun, mason jar, sideburns, sousaphone, schick test, and winchester rifle. The only common eponyms taken from American women's names are *Alice blue* (after Alice Roosevelt Longworth), *bloomers* (after Amelia Jenks Bloomer), and *Mae West jacket* (after the buxom actress). Two out of the three feminine eponyms relate closely to a woman's physical anatomy, while the masculine eponyms (except for *sideburns* after General Burnsides) have nothing to do with the namesake's body, but instead honor the man for an accomplishment of some kind.   7

The writer offers general arguments based on examination of the evidence, then moves from general arguments to particular examples that support those arguments. "A women is sexy" is a general argument, as is "A man is successful." Nilsen sets out to prove both general arguments by offering the wealth of examples that she found to support them.

Although in Greek mythology women played a bigger role than they did in the biblical stories of the Judeo-Christian cultures   8 and so the names of goddesses are accepted parts of the language in such place names as Pomona from the goddess of fruit and Athens from Athena and in such common words as *cereal* from Ceres, *psychology* from Psyche, and *arachnoid* from Arachne, the same tendency to think of women in relation to sexuality is seen in the eponyms *aphrodisiac* from Aphrodite, the Greek name for the goddess of love and beauty, and *venereal disease,* from Venus, the Roman name for Aphrodite.

Another interesting word from Greek mythology is *Amazon.* According to Greek folk etymology, the *a* means "without" as in *atypical,* or *amoral* while *mazon* comes from *mazos,* meaning *breast* as still seen in *mastectomy.* In the Greek legend, Amazon women cut off their right breasts so that they could better shoot their bows. Apparently, the storytellers had a feeling that for women to play the active, "masculine" role that the Amazons adopted for themselves, they had to trade in part of their femininity.   9

Moving from examples in Greek mythology to examples in American regional English, Nilsen shows that our own language is stocked with examples to prove her argument that "Women are sexy."

This preoccupation with women's breasts is not limited to ancient stories. As a volunteer for the University of Wisconsin's *Dictionary of American Regional English (DARE),* I read a western trapper's diary from the 1830s. I was to make notes of any unusual usages or language patterns. My most interesting finding was that he referred to a range of mountains as *The Teats,* a metaphor based on the similarity between the shapes of the mountains and women's breasts. Because today we use the French wording, *The Grand Tetons,* the metaphor isn't as obvious, but I wrote to the map-makers and found the following listings: *Nippletop* and *Little Nipple Top* near Mt. Marcy in the Adirondacks, *Nipple Mountain* in Archuleta County, Colorado, *Nipple Peak* in Coke County, Texas, *Nipple Butte* in Pennington, South Dakota, *Squaw Peak* in Placer County, California (and many other locations), *Maiden's Peak* and *Squaw Tit* (they're the same mountain) in the Cascade Range in Oregon, *Mary's Nipple* near Salt Lake City, Utah, and *Jane Russell Peaks* near Stark, New Hampshire.   10

Except for the movie star Jane Russell, the women being referred to are anonymous—it's only a sexual part of their body that is mentioned. When topographical features are named after men, it's probably not going to be to draw attention to a sexual   11 part of their bodies but instead to honor individuals for an accomplishment. For example, no one thinks of a part of the male body when hearing a reference to Pike's Peak, Colorado, or Jackson Hole, Wyoming.

Going back to what I learned from my dictionary cards, I was surprised to realize how many pairs of words we have in which the feminine word has acquired sexual connotations while the masculine word retains a serious businesslike aura. For example, a *callboy* is the person who calls actors when it is time for them to go on stage, but a *callgirl* is a prostitute. Compare *sir* and *madam*. *Sir* is a term of respect while *madam* has acquired the specialized meaning of a brothel manager. Something similar has happened to *master* and *mistress*. Would you rather have a painting by *an old master* or *an old mistress*?

It's because the word *woman* had sexual connotations, as in "She's his woman," that people began avoiding its use, hence such terminology as *ladies' room, lady of the house,* and *girls' school* or *school for young ladies.* Feminists, who ask that people use the term *woman* rather than *girl* or *lady,* are rejecting the idea that *woman* is primarily a sexual term. They have been at least partially successful in that today *woman* is commonly used to communicate gender without intending implications about sexuality.

I found two hundred pairs of words with masculine and feminine forms, e.g., *heir–heiress, hero–heroine, steward–stewardess, usher–usherette,* etc. In nearly all such pairs, the masculine word is considered the base with some kind of a feminine suffix being added. The masculine form is the one from which compounds are made, e.g., from *king–queen* comes *kingdom* but not *queendom,* from *sportsman–sportslady* comes *sportsmanship* but not *sportsladyship*. There is one—and only one—semantic area in which the masculine word is not the base or more powerful word. This is in the area dealing with sex and marriage. When someone refers to a *virgin,* a listener will probably think of a female unless the speaker specifies *male* or uses a masculine pronoun. The same is true for *prostitute*.

In relation to marriage, there is much linguistic evidence showing that weddings are more important to women than to

12

13

14

15

This is a good time to remind students that *connotation* refers to the meaning "surrounding" a term or word. They may have a friend who is "mildly obese" (a positive connotation) though someone they do not particularly like is "fat" (a negative connotation).

In this paragraph, she discusses some words historically, showing how they change (or are changed) in meaning as time passes. Students are interested to learn that the best source in which to study how words change meaning is the *Oxford English Dictionary*.

First cited from evidence in the twelfth century, Middle English *grom* means "young man" or "boy." The Middle English *guma*, "man," is the original suffix in "bridegroom." The "bride and groom" are talked about in that order, just as many people still begin speeches with "Ladies and Gentlemen."

The *widow's peak* is the point formed by hair that grows down in the middle of a forehead. At one time it was believed to signal early widowhood. A *widow's walk* is a roof platform built on some New England coastal homes, so that one could observe ships at sea.

In the relatively few years since Nilsen's first in-depth study of words and sexism, cultural ideas have helped to change the connotations of some words. Notice that every time Nilsen offers a general argument, she follows it with examples that show her argument's worth.

As words have changed, so also have customs and attitudes. Younger students often do not realize how many changes have occurred in such a short time, resulting in comparatively diminished sexist attitudes.

men. A woman cherishes the wedding and is considered a bride for a whole year, but a man is referred to as a groom only on the day of the wedding. The word *bride* appears in *bridal attendant, bridal gown, bridesmaid, bridal shower,* and even *bridegroom. Groom* comes from the Middle English *grom,* meaning "man," and in this sense is seldom used outside of a wedding. With most pairs of male/female words, people habitually put the masculine word first—*Mr. and Mrs., his and hers, boys and girls, men and women, kings and queens, brothers and sisters, guys and dolls,* and *host and hostess*—but it is the *bride and groom* who are talked about, not the *groom and bride.*

16   The importance of marriage to a woman is also shown by the fact that when a marriage ends in death, the woman gets the title of *widow.* A man gets the derived title of *widower.* This term is not used in other phrases or contexts, but *widow* is seen in *widowhood, widow's peak,* and *widow's walk.* A *widow* in a card game is an extra hand of cards, while in typesetting it is an extra line of type.

17   How changing cultural ideas bring changes to language is clearly visible in this semantic area. The feminist movement has caused the differences between the sexes to be downplayed, and since I did my dictionary study two decades ago, the word *singles* has largely replaced such sex-specific and value-laden terms as *bachelor, old maid, spinster, divorcee, widow,* and *widower.* And in 1970 I wrote that when a man is called *a professional* he is thought to be a doctor or a lawyer, but when people hear a woman referred to as *a professional* they are likely to think of a prostitute. That's not as true today because so many women have become doctors and lawyers that it's no longer incongruous to think of women in those professional roles.

18   Another change that has taken place is in wedding announcements. They used to be sent out from the bride's parents and did not even give the name of the groom's parents. Today, most couples choose to list either all or none of the parents' names. Also it is now much more likely that both the bride and groom's picture will be in the newspaper, while a decade ago only the bride's picture was published on the "Women's" or the "Society"

page. Even the traditional wording of the wedding ceremony is being changed. Many officials now pronounce the couple "husband and wife" instead of the old "man and wife," and they ask the bride if she promises "to love, honor, and cherish," instead of "to love, honor, and obey."

Women Are Passive; Men Are Active

The transition from the preceding subtopic is structurally smooth, moving from the wedding-ceremony examples to roles in general, considered historically and currently.

The wording of the wedding ceremony also relates to the second point that my cards showed, which is that women are expected to play a passive or weak role while men play an active or strong role. In the traditional ceremony, the official asks, "Who gives the bride away?" and the father answers, "I do." Some fathers answer, "Her mother and I do," but that doesn't solve the problem inherent in the question. The idea that a bride is something to be handed over from one man to another bothers people because it goes back to the days when a man's servants, his children and his wife were all considered to be his property. They were known by his name because they belonged to him and he was responsible for their actions and their debts. [19]

"grammar": In some regions of the country, the verb form *to wed* has been replaced by the nonsexist verb form *to marry*. That is, a woman can "marry" a man, and a man can "marry" a woman.

The grammar used in talking or writing about weddings as well as other sexual relationships shows the expectation of men playing the active role. Men *wed* women while women *become* brides of men. A man *possesses* a woman; he *deflowers* her; he *performs;* he *scores;* he *takes away* her virginity. Although a woman can *seduce* a man, she cannot offer him her virginity. When talking about virginity, the only way to make the woman the actor in the sentence is to say that "She lost her virginity," but people lose things by accident rather than by purposeful actions, and so she's only the grammatical, not the real-life, actor. [20]

Ms. first came into use in the 1950s as a title before a woman's surname when her marital status was unknown or irrelevant. In the early 1970s, the women's movement encouraged *Ms.*, reasoning that if *Mr.* does not indicate a man's marital status, then we have no reason to indicate a woman's marital status.

The reason that women tried to bring the term *Ms.* into the language to replace *Miss* and *Mrs.* relates to this point. Married women resented being identified only under their husband's names. For example, when Susan Glascoe did something newsworthy, she would be identified in the newspaper only as Mrs. John Glascoe. The dictionary cards showed what appeared to be an attitude on the part of editors that it was almost indecent to let [21] a respectable woman's name march unaccompanied across the pages of a dictionary. Women were listed with male names whether or not the male contributed to the woman's reason for being in the dictionary or in his own right was as famous as the woman. For example, Charlotte Brontë was identified as Mrs. Arthur B. Nicholls, Amelia Earhart as Mrs. George Palmer Putnam, Helen Hayes as Mrs. Charles MacArthur, Jenny Lind as Mme. Otto Goldschmit, Cornelia Otis Skinner as the daughter of Otis Skinner, Harriet Beecher Stowe as the sister of Henry Ward Beecher, and Edith Sitwell as the sister of Osbert and Sacheverell. A very small number of women got into the dictionary without the benefit of a masculine escort. They were rebels and crusaders: temperance leaders Frances Elizabeth Caroline Willard and Carry Nation, women's rights leaders Carrie Chapman Catt and Elizabeth Cady Stanton, birth control educator Margaret Sanger, religious leader Mary Baker Eddy, and slaves Harriet Tubman and Phyllis Wheatley.

Mrs., first recorded in the seventeenth century, was originally synonymous with *Miss.*; both were abbreviations for *mistress*.

Etiquette books used to teach that if a woman had *Mrs.* in front of her name then the husband's name should follow because *Mrs.* is an abbreviated form of *Mistress* and a woman couldn't be a mistress of herself. As with many arguments about "correct" language usage, this isn't very logical because *Miss* is also an abbreviation of *Mistress.* Feminists hoped to simplify matters by introducing *Ms.* as an alternative to both *Mrs.* and *Miss,* but what happened is that *Ms.* largely replaced *Miss* to become a catch-all business title for women. Many married women still prefer the title *Mrs.,* and some resent being addressed with the term *Ms.* As one frustrated newspaper reporter complained, "Before I can write about a woman, I have to know not only her marital status but also her political philosophy." The result of such complications may contribute to the demise of titles which are already being ignored by many computer programmers who find it more efficient to simply use names; for example in a business letter: "Dear Joan Garcia," instead of "Dear Mrs. Joan Garcia," "Dear Ms. Garcia," or "Dear Mrs. Louis Garcia."   22

From her earlier examples, the writer forecasts how titles will be handled in the near future. They might well disappear.

The titles given to royalty provide an example of how males can be disadvantaged by the assumption that they are always to   23

Traced from its Germanic roots, *king* probably means in its basic sense "head of a kin" or "son of noble kin." The word *queen* comes from the Gothic *qens,* "woman." The husband of a queen who rules in her own right is the *prince consort,* to distinguish him from other princes of the royal family.

Some would suggest that the names *Ruby, Jewel,* and *Pearl* connote wealth, and the great worth that parents place on their daughters.

This paragraph illustrates inductive reasoning: The writer moves from a series of examples to her conclusion, that the gender line is dimming.

play the more powerful role. In British royalty, when a male holds a title, his wife is automatically given the feminine equivalent. But the reverse is not true. For example, a *count* is a high political officer with a *countess* being his wife. The same is true for a *duke* and a *duchess* and a *king* and a *queen*. But when a female holds the royal title, the man she marries does not automatically acquire the matching title. For example, Queen Elizabeth's husband has the title of *prince* rather than *king,* but if Prince Charles should become king while he is still married to Lady or Princess Diana, she will be known as the queen. The reasoning appears to be that since masculine words are stronger, they are reserved for true heirs and withheld from males coming into the royal family by marriage. If Prince Phillip were called *King Phillip,* it would be much easier for British subjects to forget where the true power lies.

The names that people give their children show the hopes 24 and dreams they have for them, and when we look at the differences between male and female names in a culture we can see the cumulative expectations of that culture. In our culture girls often have names taken from small, aesthetically pleasing items, e.g., *Ruby, Jewel,* and *Pearl*. *Esther* and *Stella* mean "star." *Ada* means "ornament," and *Vanessa* means "butterfly." Boys are more likely to be given names with meanings of power and strength, e.g., *Neil* means "champion," *Martin* is from Mars, the god of war, *Raymond* means "wise protection," *Harold* means "chief of the army," *Ira* means "vigilant," *Rex* means "king," and *Richard* means "strong king."

We see similar differences in food metaphors. Food is a passive 25 substance just sitting there waiting to be eaten. Many people have recognized this and so no longer feel comfortable describing women as "delectable morsels." However, when I was a teenager, it was considered a compliment to refer to a girl (we didn't call anyone a *woman* until she was middle-aged) as *a cute tomato, a peach, a dish, a cookie, honey, sugar,* or *sweetie-pie*. When being affectionate, women will occasionally call a man *honey* or *sweetie,* but in general, food metaphors are used much less often with men than with women. If a man is called *a fruit,* his masculinity is being questioned. But it's perfectly acceptable to use a food metaphor if the food is heavier and more substantive than that used for women. For example, pinup pictures of women have long been known as *cheesecake*, but when Burt Reynolds posed for a nude centerfold, the picture was immediately dubbed *beefcake*, c.f. *a hunk of meat*. That such sexual references to men have come into the general language is another reflection of how society is beginning to lessen the differences between their attitudes toward men and women.

Students occasionally point out that in their experience, boys refer to girls as "wallflowers" and the like, but girls do not apply these descriptions to other girls. What are your students' observations?

Something similar to the *fruit* metaphor happens with references to plants. We insult a man by calling him *a pansy*, but it wasn't considered particularly insulting to talk about a girl being a *wallflower*, a *clinging vine*, or a *shrinking violet*, or to give girls such names as *Ivy, Rose, Lily, Iris, Daisy, Camellia, Heather,* and *Flora*. A plant metaphor can be used with a man if the plant is big and strong, for example Andrew Jackson's nickname of *Old Hickory*. Also, the phrases *blooming idiots* and *budding geniuses* can be used with either sex, but notice how they are based on the most active thing a plant can do which is to bloom or bud.

26

A metaphor is an implied analogy that suggestively identifies one object with another, here particular animals with particular people, depending on their sex and on their actions and personal characteristics.

Animal metaphors also illustrate the different expectations for males and females. Men are referred to as *studs, bucks,* and *wolves* while women are referred to with such metaphors as *kitten, bunny, beaver, bird, chick,* and *lamb*. In the 1950s we said that boys went *tomcatting*, but today it's just *catting around* and both boys and girls do it. When the term *foxy,* meaning that someone was sexy, first became popular, it was used only for girls, but now someone of either sex can be described as *a fox*. Some animal metaphors that are used predominantly with men have negative connotations based on the size and/or strength of the animals, e.g., *beast, bullheaded, jackass, rat, loanshark,* and *vulture*. Negative metaphors used with women are based on smaller animals, e.g., *social butterfly, mousy, catty,* and *vixen*. The feminine terms connote action, but not the same kind of large-scale action as with the masculine terms.

27

Connotation refers to the meanings or implications "surrounding" a word, as distinguished from *denotation,* which refers to the lexical definition of a word.

Women Are Connected with Negative Connotations, Men with Positive Connotations

The final point that my notecards illustrated was how many positive connotations are associated with the concept of mascu-

28

line, while there are either trivial or negative connotations connected with the corresponding feminine concept. An example from the animal metaphors makes a good illustration. The word *shrew* taken from the name of a small but especially vicious animal was defined in my dictionary as "an ill-tempered scolding woman," but the word *shrewd* taken from the same root was defined as "marked by clever, discerning awareness" and was illustrated with the phrase "a shrewd businessman."

Early in life, children are conditioned to the superiority of the masculine role. As child psychologists point out, little girls have much more freedom to experiment with sex roles than do little boys. If a little girl acts like a *tomboy,* most parents have mixed feelings, being at least partially proud. But if their little boy acts like a *sissy* (derived from *sister*), they call a psychologist. It's perfectly acceptable for a little girl to sleep in the crib that was purchased for her brother, to wear his hand-me-down jeans and shirts, and to ride the bicycle that he has outgrown. But few parents would put a boy baby in a white and gold crib decorated with frills and lace, and virtually no parents would have their little boy wear his sister's hand-me-down dresses, nor would they have their son ride a girl's pink bicycle with a flower-bedecked basket. The proper names given to girls and boys show this same attitude. Girls can have "boy" names—*Cris, Craig, Jo, Kelly, Shawn, Teri, Toni,* and *Sam*—but it doesn't work the other way around. A couple of generations ago, *Beverley, Frances, Hazel, Marion,* and *Shirley* were common boys' names. As parents gave these names to more and more girls, they fell into disuse for males, and some older men who have these names prefer to go by their initials or by such abbreviated forms as *Haze* or *Shirl.*

When a little girl is told to *be a lady,* she is being told to sit with her knees together and to be quiet and dainty. But when a little boy is told to *be a man,* he is being told to be noble, strong, and virtuous—to have all the qualities that the speaker looks on as desirable. The concept of manliness has such positive connotations that it used to be a compliment to call someone a *he-man,* to say that he was doubly a man. Today many people are more ambivalent about this term and respond to it much as they

29

30

We rarely examine masculine names, feminine names, and crossover names, all at the same time. The class might consider names other than those in this paragraph, such as Sydney, Jamie, Sandy, Wendy, and Merle, and nicknames, such as Curly, Red, Happy, Shorty, and Smiley. Which in the preceding list are absolutely masculine names, according to your class? Which are absolutely feminine names?

Students are interested to learn that the Latin *vir*, "man," is akin to the Old English *wer*, the "man" in *werewolf*.

do to the word *macho*. But calling someone a *manly man* or a *virile man* is nearly always meant as a compliment. *Virile* comes from the Indo-European *vir* meaning "man," which is also the basis of *virtuous*. Contrast the positive connotations of both *virile* and *virtuous* with the negative connotations of *hysterical*. The Greeks took this latter word from their name for *uterus* (as still seen in *hysterectomy*). They thought that women were the only ones who experienced uncontrolled emotional outbursts and so the condition must have something to do with a part of the body that only women have.

Differences between positive male and negative female con- 31 notations can be seen in several pairs of words which differ denotatively only in the matter of sex. *Bachelor* as compared to *spinster* or *old maid* has such positive connotations that women try to adopt them by using the term *bachelor-girl* or *bachelorette*. *Old maid* is so negative that it's the basis for metaphors: pretentious and fussy old men are called *old maids*, as are the leftover kernels of unpopped popcorn and the last card in a popular children's game.

The word *patron*, from Latin *patronus*, "legal protector or advocate," is derived from *pater*, "father." The word *matron* is from Latin *mater*, "mother."

Patron and *matron* (Middle English for *father* and *mother*) have 32 such different levels of prestige that women try to borrow the more positive masculine connotations with the word *patroness*, literally "female father." Such a peculiar term came about because of the high prestige attached to *patron* in such phrases as *a patron of the arts* or *a patron saint*. *Matron* is more apt to be used in talking about a woman in charge of a jail or a public restroom.

Here, point out that in the armed services, a registered nurse is a commissioned officer, but a corpsman or a medic is an enlisted person.

When men are doing jobs that women often do, we apparently 33 try to pay the men extra by giving them fancy titles; for example, a male cook is more likely to be called a *chef*, while a male seamstress will get the title of *tailor*. The armed forces have a special problem in that they recruit under such slogans as "The Marine Corps Builds Men!" and "Join the Army! Become a Man." Once the recruits are enlisted, they find themselves doing much of the work that has been traditionally thought of as "woman's work." The solution to getting the work done and not insulting anyone's masculinity was to change the titles as shown below:

waitress ⟶ orderly
nurse ⟶ medic or corpsman
secretary ⟶ clerk-typist
assistant ⟶ adjutant
dishwasher or kitchen helper ⟶ KP (kitchen police)

Compare *brave* and *squaw.* Early settlers in America truly   34
admired Indian men and hence named them with a word that
carried connotations of youth, vigor, and courage. But they used
the Algonquin's name for "woman," and over the years it developed almost opposite connotations to those of *brave. Wizard* and
witch contrast almost as much. The masculine *wizard* implies skill
and wisdom combined with magic, while the feminine *witch* implies evil intentions combined with magic. Part of the unattrac-
tiveness of both *witch* and *squaw* is that they have been used so
often to refer to old women, something with which our culture
is particularly uncomfortable, just as the Afghans were. Imagine
my surprise when I ran across the phrases *grandfatherly advice*
and *old wives' tales* and realized that the underlying implication
is the same as the Afghan proverb about old men being worth
listening to while old women talk only foolishness.

Other terms which show how negatively we view old women   35
as compared to young women are *old nag* as compared to *filly,*
old crow or *old bat* as compared to *bird,* and being *catty* as compared to being *kittenish.* There is no matching set of metaphors
for men. The chicken metaphor tells the whole story of a woman's
life. In her youth she is a *chick.* Then she marries and begins
feathering her nest. Soon she begins feeling *cooped up,* so she goes
to *hen parties* where she *cackles* with her friends. Then she has
her *brood,* begins to *henpeck* her husband, and finally turns into
an old biddy.

I embarked on my study of the dictionary not with the in-   36
tention of prescribing language change but simply to see what
the language would tell me about sexism. Nevertheless I have
been both surprised and pleased as I've watched the changes that
have occurred over the past two decades. I'm one of those linguists

---

Students are interested to learn that *warlock* refers to the male equivalent of *witch.* Also, some
students have pointed out that colloquially, *wizard* can refer to anyone who does something
quite well, as in the sentence, "Shirley is a math
wizard."

Nilsen comes full circle here, mentioning that
the Afghan proverb and some English phrases
share some features.

A filly is a young female horse. Interestingly, in
horse-racing jargon, a "maiden" is *any* horse that
has never won a race.

In some American-English dialects, "old dog"
refers to an old man, and "young whelp," albeit
redundant, refers to a young man.

A biddy is a chicken and, by extension, a fussy
old woman.

who believes that new language customs will cause a new generation of speakers to grow up with different expectations. This is why I'm happy about people's efforts to use inclusive language, to say *he or she* or *they* when speaking about individuals whose names they do not know. I'm glad that leading publishers have developed guidelines to help writers use language that is fair to both sexes, and I'm glad that most newspapers and magazines list women by their own names instead of only by their husbands' names and that educated and thoughtful people no longer begin their business letters with "Dear Sir" or "Gentlemen," but instead use a memo form or begin with such salutations as "Dear Colleagues," "Dear Reader," or "Dear Committee Members." I'm also glad that such words as *poetess, authoress, conductress,* and *aviatrix* now sound quaint and old fashioned and that *chairman* is giving way to *chair* or *head, mailman* to *mail carrier, clergyman* to *clergy,* and *stewardess* to *flight attendant.* I was also pleased when the National Oceanic and Atmospheric Administration bowed to feminist complaints and in the late '70s began to alternate men's and women's names for hurricanes. However, I wasn't so pleased to discover that the change did not immediately erase sexist thoughts from everyone's mind as shown by a headline about Hurricane David in a 1979 New York tabloid, "David Rapes Virgin Islands." More recently a similar metaphor appeared in a headline in the *Arizona Republic* about Hurricane Charlie: "Charlie Quits Carolinas, Flirts with Virginia."

Nilsen ends her essay positively, pointing out that our language is changing for the better, socially and politically. And she reminds us that our speaking and writing determine our way of viewing our world.

What these incidents show is that sexism is not something existing independently in American English or in the particular dictionary that I happened to read. Rather, it exists in people's minds. Language is like an x-ray in providing visible evidence of invisible thoughts. The best thing about people being interested in and discussing sexist language is that as they make conscious decisions about what pronouns they will use, what jokes they will tell or laugh at, how they will write their names, or how they will begin their letters, they are forced to think about the underlying issue of sexism. This is good, because as a problem that begins in people's assumptions and expectations, it's a problem

37

that will be solved only when a great many people have given it a great deal of thought.

Meaning and Purpose

1. Encourage students to examine their own experiences with sexism in language and compare those experiences with some of Nilsen's information.

2. The author argues for examining the words that we use to describe the genders so that we may see what we mean when we use them. She argues against using any words that demean people, especially women. Several sentences could be cited, including the "for" sentence, "I'm one of those linguists who believes that new language customs will cause a new generation of speakers to grow up with different expectations" (36); and the "against" sentence, the last in paragraph 28.

3. Nilsen's main point is stated in paragraph 5, when she says, "The language that a culture uses is telltale evidence of the values and beliefs of that culture." Each of the sections has a main point, or thesis, which is a more specific example of the main thesis. The first sentence in each section is the main point of that section.

4. These experiences are included because they pushed the author into awareness of how another culture treated its females, and made her question sexism in our own culture.

5. Some students will be overwhelmed with the examples. Others will say they are necessary to show the reader just what Nilsen means, and will not feel overwhelmed because each example is brief.

Meaning and Purpose

1. What is your first response to Nilsen's essay? Are you aware of sexist language? Explain.
2. An argument is a reason or reasons stated for or against something. What is the author arguing for? What is she arguing against? Find one sentence from the essay that shows each position.
3. Where does Nilsen state her purpose in this essay? What is her point in each of the three sections, and how are these points related to the thesis?
4. The first three paragraphs tell about Nilsen's experiences in another culture. Why are those experiences included in this essay?
5. Nilsen fills her essay with examples of words and phrases that support her assertions about language. As a reader, how do you react to her using so many examples? Do you feel overwhelmed with information, or does she need the many examples to make her meaning clear?

Strategy

1. Does Nilsen use specific, typical, or hypothetical examples? How effective is her choice?
2. Paragraph 33 lists examples of the differences in job descriptions between the jobs women hold in civilian life and those men hold in the armed services. What role do you believe Nilsen thinks the language of these examples has in people's attitudes toward the jobs?

Strategy

1. Nilsen's examples are specific—they are all words and their meanings and connotations. Her study requires specific examples to support her assertions about sexism in language.

2. Nilsen suggests that the language fools no one but is necessary for image. She refers to the military job titles as "fancy titles."

3. Nilsen ends with some examples of how language is changing to eliminate sexism. In her final paragraph she refines her thesis to say, "[Sexism] exists in people's minds. Language is like an x-ray in providing visible evidence of invisible thoughts." She uses this paragraph to express her opinion that people will begin thinking consciously about the language they use. This positive statement somewhat balances all the examples of sexism still in force that she has given in the essay.

Style

1. Nilsen is calm and informative. She intends to expose sexism in language for what it is without being militantly feminist. One example of this tone is the sentence, "When topographical features are named after men, it's probably not going to be to draw attention to a sexual part of their bodies but instead to honor individuals for an accomplishment" (11).

2. The reading pace is fast because each example is short and gives way quickly to the next. Readers have one interesting bit of information to read after another.

3. The three sections set off the three large areas in which Nilsen found sexist language. These sections are necessary for clarity and readability in an essay that is so long and full of facts. They help guide the reading.

3. How does Nilsen use her final paragraph in the structure of the essay?

Style

1. How do you characterize this essayist's tone? Is she angry? Is she informative? Is she calm? Is the tone neutral? Show evidence of Nilsen's tone from the essay.

2. How does her use of many short examples affect the pace of the essay, or your way of reading it?

3. Why does Nilsen use subtitles and divide her essay into sections? How effective are the subtitles?

Writing Tasks

1. What is your opinion of the way in which women are portrayed in sitcoms? In an essay, develop a thesis and use specific examples of television shows to support it. (You could also write this essay about the way in which men are portrayed in sitcoms.)

2. In a few paragraphs for each person, draw two hypothetical examples—one male and one female—illustrating the abstractions of masculinity and femininity.

Style Is the Man

What is style? If we say a certain person has style, what exactly do we mean? Is it behavior? Clothing? Speech? Posture? Grooming? All of these? Some other things? Does everyone have style or only a few?

Style may be hard to define precisely, but we know it when we see it, right? And most people would undoubtedly agree that the young man in the photograph "Style Is the Man" has it.

Style communicates. Before interacting with a person we form impressions based on some elements at least of his or her personal style. We may be able to trace this impression to very specific things, or we may say we just have a feeling but are unable to specify particulars. A style may be created consciously and purposefully (perhaps to deceive) or it may simply grow out of the true values and accumulated experiences of the individual.

After reviewing "Examples: Illustrating Ideas" at the beginning of this chapter, complete one of the following writing tasks.

1. Using specific examples from the photograph as your method of development, write a paper that characterizes the style portrayed by the young man. Begin with a short physical description of the man leading to a generalization about his style and the attitude and values it communicates to you. Then examine various items and aspects of his appearance and discuss each as a specific example which led you to your interpretation of his message.

2. Write a paper combining typical and specific examples. Find three photographs of humans, each showing a different sense of style. These need not be as dramatic as the style illustrated in "Style Is the Man," though they may be. As in number 1, begin with a short description of the three photographs leading to a generalization about each style and what it communicates to you. In the discussion section of your paper, point to specific examples in each photograph that support your generalization and then relate typical examples of the expected behavior, dress, and attitudes of a member of each style group. Include the photographs when you submit your final draft.

❦ Additional Writing Tasks ❦

Examples

1. Write an essay on one of the general statements listed here or on a general statement you compose. Throughout your essay use examples to illustrate your main idea or thesis. Your discussion should include a mixture of typical and specific examples. Remember: you are not bound by any of these statements; you may rewrite them to reflect your interests, or you may compose your own.

   a. People must assume responsibility for their actions.
   b. Success comes from 5 percent talent and 95 percent hard work.
   c. Vandals control the night in local neighborhoods.
   d. Teenagers can learn both positive and negative lessons about economic survival from part-time jobs.
   e. Graffiti scrawled on walls throughout the city carry psychological messages about human behavior.
   f. Books I have read have taught me a great deal about life.
   g. Bumper stickers reveal a person's values.
   h. Public obscenity is objectionable.
   i. Life in the fast lane leads to head-on collisions.

2. Write a full essay related to one of these situations. Be sure examples serve as the dominant essay pattern of development.

   a. Some contemporary political figures have demonstrated courage in office. Using examples from recent history, write an essay illustrating how important political courage is.
   b. Society seems to require more and more cooperation among individuals and groups to function effectively. Write an essay illustrating how cooperation is needed for success.
   c. Although society seems to require more and more cooperation among individuals and groups, the values of the "rugged individualist" are still required for success. Write an essay illustrating how much "rugged individualism" helps in becoming successful.

d. Often the better moments in life go unnoticed. Recollect some of your better moments and write an essay making use of them to illustrate what they have taught you.

e. Magazine advertisers attempt to entice customers to buy products not by high quality but by associating the products with selected "life-styles." Write an essay illustrating that some magazine advertisements encourage consumers to buy products for the wrong reasons.

3. Read this paragraph from Jack Solomon's *The Signs of Our Time,* in which he generally concentrates on the messages that clothing communicates in American society.

> The complexity of the dress code in America, the astonishing range of styles that are available to us in our choice of clothing designs, directly reflects the cultural diversity of our country. Americans are differentiated by ethnic, regional, religious, and racial differences that are all expressed in the clothing they wear. Age differences, political differences, class differences, and differences in personal taste further divide us into finer and finer sub-cultures that maintain, and even assert, their sense of distinct identity through their characteristic clothing. From the severe black suits of the Amish to the safety-pinned T-shirts and chains of punk culture, Americans tell one another who they are through the articles of their dress.

> Write an essay, with examples as the dominant method of development, illustrating Solomon's general observation that "Americans tell one another who they are through the articles of their dress."

6

Comparison and Contrast
Presenting Similarities and Differences

The Method

In conversation we often hear comments that could lead to **comparison and contrast**:

"I eat vegetables, fruits, grains, nuts, and dairy products. It is a lot healthier than a diet that includes red meat, fowl, and even fish."

"Strip away the rhetoric and compare their economic platforms; you will see few differences between Republicans and Democrats."

"The effects of marijuana are no more harmful than those of alcohol. In fact they may be less harmful."

No doubt in class discussions, at family gatherings, or during arguments at the local pizza parlor you have heard similar comments. How such comparisons are developed in conversation probably depends on the group's mood and analytical talent. Nevertheless, a fundamental principle is at work: We all make decisions by comparing and contrasting our options.

To compare is to point out similarities; to contrast is to point out differences. Poems and song lyrics are often similar in some ways: both often rhyme; they are constructed on rhythmic patterns; sometimes they repeat key lines. They also have one major difference: poems are written to be spoken; songs are written to be sung to music. Presenting similarities and differences is a common technique not only in conversation but also in all forms of writing, including essays, research papers, reports, and examinations.

Commonly, writers include informal comparisons that are merely incidental to the dominant essay pattern. Often such brief comparisons are implied rather than fully developed, merely suggesting a comparison. This paragraph opens an essay explaining the causes directing new trends in city planning.

In southern California, historically known for its suburban sprawl, city planning seems to have come full circle. Using the concept of the traditional village, planners are designing new urban villages that feature a main street and a mix of stores, offices, town halls, and parks. They are trying to re-create the traditional village by designing neighborhoods where thousands of residents can live and work, where they can walk to shopping and stroll to places of entertainment.

The writer, Jack Scott, does not intend to compare traditional with contemporary city design; he alludes to traditional design merely to place his reader in familiar territory.

When writers use comparison and contrast as a dominant essay pattern, they explore their subjects in detail, applying several principles to guide the composition. To sharpen your critical eye and read as a writer reads, be aware of these general principles.

Strategies

Professional writers know they need a basis for the comparison: any subjects they choose to compare must belong to the same general category. If the subjects do not belong to that category, the writers have no logical reason to enumerate the similarities and differences. Usually, but not always, the general categories are obvious. For such a discussion, consider hammerhead sharks, great white sharks, chimpanzees, and dolphins.

Comparing and contrasting a hammerhead with a great white shark is clearly logical because although they are similar, they differ in several distinctive ways. But to compare and contrast a chimpanzee to a great white shark is clearly illogical. Yes, they belong to a category we might call "living creatures," but do you see any other basis for a comparison? The chimpanzee is a mammal, the great white shark a fish. One lives on land, the other in the sea. One is a hunter, the other a forager. To compare and contrast them just would not make much sense.

To compare and contrast a dolphin and a great white shark, however, does make sense. Even though the dolphin is a mammal, it is a marine mammal. The dolphin and the great white shark are also shaped roughly alike, but with significant differences. Perhaps most important, both the dolphin and the great white shark are significant in sea lore. In fact, Hollywood films featuring a dolphin and a great white shark have been box-office hits, as in *Flipper* and *Jaws*.

What about comparing a dolphin and a chimpanzee? Although they are not obvious selections, both are categorized as mammals. A writer might ask if their both being mammals makes them subjects worth comparing and contrasting. What else do they have in common? Close examination reveals that scientists are studying communication patterns of both chimpanzees and dolphins. Perhaps they are in the limited category of animals that communicate with human beings. Taking up this similarity, a writer might explore the possibility of comparing chimpanzees and dolphins.

Now we must consider an exception to the principle that subjects should belong to the same general category if they are to be logically compared. This figurative comparison is called **analogy.** Writers use analogy to explain something difficult to understand by describing it as if it were something familiar. A writer might choose to explain life by comparing it with a river, watching a situation comedy with taking a narcotic, or being in love with riding a roller coaster. Writers of analogy are interested only in using one subject to explain another; they are not out to explain the major similarities and differences of both subjects equally as they would be when writing a typical comparison-and-contrast passage.

In this following paragraph, humorist James Thurber develops an analogy by comparing his editor Harold Ross to a skilled auto mechanic.

> Having a manuscript under Ross's scrutiny was like putting your car in the hands of a skilled mechanic, not an automotive engineer with a bachelor of science degree, but a guy who knows what makes a motor go, and sputter, and wheeze, and sometimes come to a dead stop; a man with

an ear for the faintest body squeak as well as the loudest engine rattle. When you first gazed, appalled, upon an uncorrected proof of one of your stories or articles, each margin had a thicket of queries and complaints—one writer got a hundred and forty-four on one profile. It was as though you beheld the works of your car spread all over the garage floor, and the job of getting the thing together again and making it work seemed impossible. Then you realized that Ross was trying to make your Model T or old Stutz Bearcat into a Cadillac or Rolls-Royce. He was at work with the tools of his unflagging perfectionism, and, after an exchange of growls or snarls, you set to work to join him in his enterprise.

Clearly, Thurber has stuck to the principle of analogy: he uses the familiar work of an auto mechanic to explain the unfamiliar work of a magazine editor.

Professional writers are always wary of confusing their readers. As you study comparison-and-contrast essays, notice how writers immediately orient their readers by informing them that a comparison and contrast follows.

Read the opening paragraph in Russell Baker's "From Song to Sound: Elvis and Bing." Baker quickly establishes that he will compare two eras and the popular singers who represent them.

> The grieving for Elvis Presley and the commercial exploitation of his death were still not ended when we heard of Bing Crosby's death the other day. Here is a generational puzzle. Those of an age to mourn Elvis must marvel that their elders could really have cared about Bing, just as the Crosby generation a few weeks ago wondered what all the to-do was about when Elvis died.

Baker's opening paragraph gives a clear idea that the essay is headed into comparison and contrast. Most professional writers do likewise, thus keeping their readers on the track.

Professional writers also use clear—and we stress that word—stylistic techniques to keep their readers from becoming confused.

Sometimes they use parallel structure to balance the similarities and differences of their subjects. They also use such transitional words and phrases as *on the one hand, on the other hand, in contrast, like,* and *unlike,* words with which they delineate similarities and differences.

In a paragraph from an essay contrasting crows and ravens, Barry Lopez applies both transitional phrases and parallel structures.

> The raven is larger than the crow and has a beard of black feathers at his throat. He is careful to kill only what he needs. Crows, on the other hand, will search out the great horned owl, kick and punch him awake, and then for roosting too close to their nests, they will kill him. They will come out of the sky on a fat, hot afternoon and slam into the head of a dozing rabbit and go away laughing. They will tear out a whole row of planted corn and eat only a few kernels. They will defecate on scarecrows and go home and sleep with 200,000 of their friends in an atmosphere of congratulation. Again, it is only a game; this should not be taken to mean that they are evil.

In his paragraph Lopez concentrates primarily on the crow's destructive behavior, contrasting it sharply to the raven in the two sentences describing that black bird. Usually, writers will develop both subjects in more detail. They generally employ one of two organizational strategies when comparing and contrasting: **subject-by-subject** development or **point-by-point** development.

Subject-by-Subject Development

Developing a subject-by-subject comparison is quite simple: all the details of one side of the comparison or contrast are presented first, followed by all the details of the other side. Anthropologist Edward T. Hall uses subject-by-subject development to contrast Arab and American attitudes in a paragraph from *The Hidden Dimension.*

Another silent source of friction between Americans and Arabs is in an area that Americans treat very informally—the manners and rights of the road. In general, in the United States we tend to defer to the vehicle that is bigger, more powerful, faster, and heavily laden. While a pedestrian walking along a road may feel annoyed he will not think it unusual to step aside for a fast-moving automobile. He knows that because he is moving he does not have the right to the space around him that he has when he is standing still. It appears that the reverse is true with the Arabs who apparently *take on rights to space as they move*. For someone else to move into a space an Arab is also moving into is a violation of his rights. It is infuriating to an Arab to have someone else cut in front of him on the highway. It is the American's cavalier treatment of moving space that makes the Arab call him aggressive and pushy.

Hall contrasts these subjects in one paragraph, but sometimes a writer will divide the subjects into separate contrasting paragraphs, as Noel Perrin does in these two discussion paragraphs from his essay "The Two Faces of Vermont."

On the one hand, it's to the interest of everyone in the tourist trade to keep Vermont (their motels, ski resorts, chambers of commerce, etc., excepted) as old-fashioned as possible. After all, it's weathered red barns with shingle roofs the tourists want to photograph, not concrete-block barns with sheet aluminum on top. Ideally, from the tourist point of view, there should be a man and two boys inside, milking by hand, not a lot of milking machinery pumping directly into a bulk tank. Out back, someone should be turning a grindstone to sharpen an ax—making a last stand, so to speak, against the chainsaw.

On the other hand, the average farmer can hardly wait to modernize. He wants a bulk tank, a couple of arc lights, an automated silo, and a new aluminum roof. Or in a sense he wants these things. Actually, he may like last-stand farming as well as any tourist does, but he can't make a living at it. In my town it's often said that a generation ago a man could raise and educate three children on fifteen cows and still put a little money in the bank. Now his son can just barely keep going with 40 cows. With fifteen cows, hand-milking was possible, and conceivably even economic; with 40 you need all the machinery you can get. But the tourists don't want to hear it clank.

Point-by-Point Development

Subject-by-subject development is effective for an essay of a few paragraphs, but when an essay is longer the reader may lose track of the information about the first subject while reading about the second. The point-by-point development solves this short-coming by alternately presenting each point under consideration. Alison Lurie, in a paragraph from *The Language of Clothes,* uses the point-by-point method to compare and contrast boys' and girls' clothes.

In early childhood girls' and boys' clothes are often identical in cut and fabric, as if in recognition of the fact that their bodies are much alike. But the T-shirts, pull-on slacks and zip jackets intended for boys are usually made in darker colors (especially forest green, navy, red and brown) and printed with designs involving sports, transportation and cute wild animals. Girls' clothes are made in paler colors (especially pink, yellow and green) and decorated with flowers and cute domestic animals. The suggestion is that the boy will play vigorously and travel over long distances; the girl will stay home and nurture plants and small mammals. Alternatively, these designs may symbolize their wearers: the boy is a cuddly bear or a smiling tiger, the girl a flower or a kitten. There is also a tendency for boys' clothes to be fullest at the shoulders and girls' at the hips, anticipating their adult figures. Boys' and men's garments also emphasize the shoulders with horizontal stripes, epaulets or yokes of contrasting color. Girls' and women's garments emphasize the hips and rear through the strategic placement of gathers and trimmings.

Lurie's strategy is quite simple. She organizes the discussion around three points: the different colors in girls' and boys' clothes; the different designs that decorate them; and the different cut. She presents the details point by point, carefully balancing one with the other.

Comparison and Contrast in College Writing

When you compare the similarities and differences of two subjects, carefully follow the principles that govern this pattern: be sure to select subjects from the same general category (unless, of course, you are developing an analogy); be especially careful to guide your reader through a comparison with stylistic techniques such as overt transitions and parallel structure; and select the appropriate structural strategies, whether block method, point-by-point method, or a combination.

You must also consider your purpose in using comparison. Generally, in college writing, you will compare the similarities and differences of your subjects for one of two reasons: to describe two subjects in order to clarify them or to evaluate two subjects in order to determine which is better. For either comparison, you must consider the outstanding features of each subject, and when the purpose is evaluation, you must carefully delineate both positive and negative aspects of the subjects.

For an assignment in American literature, Jim Cartozian compares and contrasts Ernest Hemingway and William Faulkner. In this four-paragraph passage from his essay, Cartozian develops his subjects by using both subject-by-subject and point-by-point development. He even develops an analogy.

Opening establishes Hemingway and Faulkner as the subjects.

If Ernest Hemingway and William Faulkner were to attend the same party, both would command attention for different reasons. Hemingway was a big bear of a man, seemed gregarious, and liked to hold the center of attention. He was handsome, and some have said he prided himself on being a lady's man. Faulkner was slight of build, soft-spoken, and tended to be reclusive. He would not seek the attention Hemingway seemed to thrive on, but would probably find a mantel to lean on. Speaking in a gentle, lilting voice, he would tell a story about the rural South while holding the attention of everyone within earshot.

Subject-by-subject development contrasts the physical and social differences between the subjects.

No modern American writers have gained as much worldwide critical recognition as Ernest Hemingway and William Faulkner, and no two could be more different. Both did win the coveted Nobel Prize for literature, but when the mild-mannered Faulkner won first, Hemingway is said to have lost his temper and then sulked. Both were publishing at a young age, but Hemingway attracted popular attention early in his career while Faulkner worked in near obscurity. Hemingway became America's first modern literary media star. Magazines featured spreads of his war exploits, his African safaris, and his bullfighting adventures. Faulkner, in contrast, was never a media celebrity. Instead, he seemed to embody the lifestyle of small-town Southern gentry, spending most of his quiet life in Oxford, Mississippi. Hemingway's novels and stories were often set in exotic locales like France, Spain, and Cuba; Faulkner set his works in the South, in the mythical Yoknapatawpha County. Each dealt with very different visions: Hemingway's work displays psychologically wounded characters struggling to establish a personal code of values in an absurd world. Faulkner's work displays characters who are victims of history, suffering because of the sins of their ancestors,

Point-by-point is more effective than subject-by-subject development here because similarities and differences are so numerous.

the men who wrenched the land from Native Americans and enslaved Native Africans. In 1961 Hemingway died violently by his own hand; in 1962 Faulkner died peacefully.

Whatever quality made such different men successful novelists is difficult to identify. No doubt their success came from determination and hard work, for both men were dedicated craftsmen. But another quality—inspiration—must be figured into the equation. Inspiration that comes from pursuing the creative process is perhaps similar to the spiritual insight that comes from participating in a mystical practice. A mystical practice, such as meditation, is usually performed daily in psychological isolation. Most successful novelists pursue their creative inspiration by isolating themselves, too. Faulkner and Hemingway were no different. Both created special spaces to write in. When Faulkner wrote he isolated himself in an upstairs bedroom located in the family house. Although Hemingway was more nomadic than Faulkner, he still created a "space apart" to write in no matter where he was living, the most famous one in a tower at his Cuban hacienda.

Final paragraphs develop an analogy exploring similarities in both writers' ways of working. As in paragraph 1, subject-by-subject development is used.

Too often spiritual insight and creative inspiration are thought to arrive like a bolt of lightning. But mystics claim insight comes from the relentless pursuit of routines. As writers, Faulkner and Hemingway ritualistically pursued their routines. Hemingway would rise at first light and spend the morning writing with a hand-sharpened pencil while standing at a high desk or bookcase top. Faulkner would also rise early, but he would sit at a desk and plunk away at an old typewriter. The routines seldom varied, but perhaps it was routine pursued with the fervor of a mystic that generated their inspiration and led to their recognition.

In Cartozian's passage the principles of comparison and contrast are clearly at work. Hemingway and Faulkner are both members of the same logical category of critically acclaimed American writers, and so Cartozian had no trouble selecting his subjects. In the opening sentences he establishes that the two writers will be his subjects, thus preparing his reader for comparison and contrast. Finally, he combines organizational strategies. In the opening paragraphs Cartozian contrasts Hemingway's and Faulkner's physical and social characteristics with subject-by-subject development. In paragraph 2, he presents both similarities and differences with point-by-point development. In the last two paragraphs he stresses the novelists' similarities by concentrating on their work habits with analogy. Cartozian's purpose is also clear: he is not judging these authors, he is clarifying who they are and what they achieved; consequently, he carefully balances his points.

The most effective way to develop skill in comparison and contrast is to study the professionals. Analyze their choices. Ask yourself why one writer chooses point-by-point development over subject-by-subject development for a passage. Notice how another mixes the two types of development. Study the kinds of transitional techniques they use. This kind of careful reading—that is, reading with a critical eye—will prepare you to write your own comparisons.

You might want to start by discussing how some current civil conflicts (Lebanon, Northern Ireland, and El Salvador, perhaps) resemble our Civil War and how they differ. Outlining these similarities and differences can lead to discussion of the essay's structure: the first three paragraphs as introduction; paragraphs 4–6 describing the attributes of Robert E. Lee and the society he represented; paragraphs 7–9 describing Ulysses S. Grant and the values he represented; paragraphs 10 and 11 paired against each other; point-by-point contrast in paragraph 12; paragraph 13 a transition moving from contrast to comparison; and paragraphs 14, 15, and 16 showing the similarities of the two men, moving from the least important to the most important.

From there you might ask students to evaluate the contrary social ideals the two men represented.

❦ Bruce Catton ❦

Bruce Catton (pronounced Cayton) was one of those rare historians who could bring the past to life. Born in Michigan in 1899, he grew up hearing Civil War stories from the many Civil War veterans in his small midwestern town. After attending Oberlin College he was a reporter for newspapers in Boston and Cleveland, served as director of information for government agencies in Washington, D.C., and finally accepted a position as full-time editor and writer for American Heritage *magazine, which he kept until his death in 1978. Considered one of the foremost authorities on the American Civil War era, he published many books on the subject. The most popular of those books is* A Stillness at Appomattox *(1953), which won both the Pulitzer Prize for history and, in 1954, the National Book Award.*

Grant and Lee:
A Study in Contrasts

In this essay, first published in The American Story, *an anthology of essays by noted historians, Catton describes the similarities and differences in style and character between the opposing Civil War generals. It was their coming together and their ability to put aside their extreme differences that marked the end of the war and a turning point in American history.*

Catton claims in this essay that Ulysses S. Grant and Robert E. Lee represent two different American cultures. Make sure while you read, then, to distinguish the various facets of their personalities as well as the differences of the two societies they personified.

MARGINAL NOTES

The contrast between the closing of "a great chapter in American history" taking place in "the parlor of a modest house" emphasizes the enormity of the occasion.

When Ulysses S. Grant and Robert E. Lee met in the parlor of a modest house at Appomattox Court House, Virginia, on April 9, 1865, to work out the terms for the surrender of Lee's Army of Northern Virginia, a great chapter in American life came to a close, and a great new chapter began.

After students have looked up *poignant,* you might discuss why it is such a fitting word here, why it is better than *teary, sad,* or *touching,* for instance.

Not only does this sentence serve as the essay's thesis, but it also has a metaphor that emphasizes the strength of the two men's personalities and characters and the power of the two societies they represented; that is, they were "two conflicting currents" so powerful that when they met the "collision" was "final." Paragraph 4 leads to a discussion of Lee and the society and ideal he represented. It also is a kind of mini-thesis that controls the essay's next section (5, 6).

It was the Virginia tidewater where the very first permanent English settlers landed and founded Jamestown, well before the *Mayflower* (1620). Ironically, in fact, the *Mayflower* was headed there but veered off course and landed at Plymouth instead. These first settlers brought with them medieval English ideals (chivalry and all the aristocratic and ritualistic courtesies that went with it, including idealization of women) and a feudal social structure, described in the rest of the paragraph.

The implication here seems to be that as the war wore on to an end and it became more and more apparent that the Confederacy itself would fall, the Confederate soldier found it psychologically necessary to personify his ideals in a living man. Lee, thus ironically, became a symbol, an abstraction.

These men were bringing the Civil War to its virtual finish. 2
To be sure, other armies had yet to surrender, and for a few days the fugitive Confederate government would struggle desperately and vainly, trying to find some way to go on living now that its chief support was gone. But in effect it was all over when Grant and Lee signed the papers. And the little room where they wrote out the terms was the scene of one of the poignant, dramatic contrasts in American history.

They were two strong men, these oddly different generals, 3
and they represented the strengths of two conflicting currents that, through them, had come to final collision.

Back of Robert E. Lee was the notion that the old aristocratic 4
concept might somehow survive and be dominant in American life.

Lee was tidewater Virginia, and in his background were family, culture, and tradition . . . the age of chivalry transplanted to 5
a New World which was making its own legends and its own myths. He embodied a way of life that had come down through the age of knighthood and the English country squire. America was a land that was beginning all over again, dedicated to nothing much more complicated than the rather hazy belief that all men had equal rights and should have an equal chance in the world. In such a land Lee stood for the feeling that it was somehow of advantage to human society to have a pronounced inequality in the social structure. There should be a leisure class, backed by ownership of land; in turn, society itself should be keyed to the land as the chief source of wealth and influence. It would bring forth (according to this ideal) a class of men with a strong sense of obligation to the community; men who lived not to gain advantage for themselves, but to meet the solemn obligations which had been laid on them by the very fact that they were privileged. From them the country would get its leadership; to them it could look for the higher values—of thought, of conduct, of personal deportment—to give it strength and virtue.

Lee embodied the noblest elements of this aristocratic ideal. 6
Through him, the landed nobility justified itself. For four years, the Southern states had fought a desperate war to uphold the

ideals for which Lee stood. In the end, it almost seemed as if the Confederacy fought for Lee; as if he himself was the Confederacy . . . the best thing that the way of life for which the Confederacy stood could ever have to offer. He had passed into legend before Appomattox. Thousands of tired, underfed, poorly clothed Confederate soldiers, long since past the simple enthusiasm of the early days of the struggle, somehow considered Lee the symbol of everything for which they had been willing to die. But they could not quite put this feeling into words. If the Lost Cause, sanctified by so much heroism and so many deaths, had a living justification, its justification was General Lee.

The first sentence in paragraph 7, the topic sentence, immediately draws the distinctions between Lee and Grant. Grant, a product of the frontier rather than the settled and aristocratic East Coast, differed from Lee in everything. The rest of the paragraph lists some primary differences.

Grant, the son of a tanner on the Western frontier, was everything Lee was not. He had come up the hard way and embodied nothing in particular except the eternal toughness and sinewy fiber of the men who grew up beyond the mountains. He was one of a body of men who owed reverence and obeisance to no one, who were self-reliant to a fault, who cared hardly anything for the past but who had a sharp eye for the future.   7

These frontier men were the precise opposites of the tidewater aristocrats. Back of them, in the great surge that had taken people over the Alleghenies and into the opening Western country, there was a deep, implicit dissatisfaction with a past that had settled into grooves. They stood for democracy, not from any reasoned conclusion about the proper ordering of human society, but simply because they had grown up in the middle of democracy and knew how it worked. Their society might have privileges, but they would be privileges each man had won for himself. Forms and patterns meant nothing. No man was born to anything, except perhaps to a chance to show how far he could rise. Life was competition.   8

Yet along with this feeling had come a deep sense of belonging to a national community. The Westerner who developed a farm, opened a shop, or set up in business as a trader could hope to prosper only as his own community prospered—and his community ran from the Atlantic to the Pacific and from Canada down to Mexico. If the land was settled, with towns and highways and accessible markets, he could better himself. He saw his fate   9 in terms of the nation's own destiny. As its horizons expanded, so did his. He had, in other words, an acute dollars-and-cents stake in the continued growth and development of his country.

And that, perhaps, is where the contrast between Grant and Lee becomes most striking. The Virginia aristocrat, inevitably, saw himself in relation to his own region. He lived in a static society which could endure almost anything except change. Instinctively, his first loyalty would go to the locality in which that society existed. He would fight to the limit of endurance to defend it, because in defending it he was defending everything that gave his own life its deepest meaning. 10

Whereas Lee's commitment to community was local and insular, Grant's was national and even expansionist.

The Westerner, on the other hand, would fight with an equal tenacity for the broader concept of society. He fought so because everything he lived by was tied to growth, expansion, and a constantly widening horizon. What he lived by would survive or fall with the nation itself. He could not possibly stand by unmoved in the face of an attempt to destroy the Union. He would combat it with everything he had, because he could only see it as an effort to cut the ground out from under his feet. 11

So Grant and Lee were in complete contrast, representing two diametrically opposed elements in American life. Grant was the modern man emerging; beyond him, ready to come on the stage, was the great age of steel and machinery, of crowded cities and a restless burgeoning vitality. Lee might have ridden down from the old age of chivalry, lance in hand, silken banner fluttering over his head. Each man was the perfect champion of his cause, drawing both his strengths and his weaknesses from the people he led. 12

Paragraph 13 serves as a transition, carrying the reader from the differences between the two men to a comparison of their likenesses.

Yet it was not all contrast, after all. Different as they were—in background, in personality, in underlying aspiration—these two great soldiers had much in common. Under everything else, they were marvelous fighters. Furthermore, their fighting qualities were really very much alike. 13

The topic sentence cites their first similarity and is followed by examples.

Each man had, to begin with, the great virtue of utter tenacity and fidelity. Grant fought his way down the Mississippi Valley in spite of acute personal discouragement and profound military handicaps. Lee hung on in the trenches at Petersburg after hope 14

After citing the qualities that made them great warriors, Catton points out that their greatest virtue was their ability to be men of peace after the fighting was over.

Catton's phrasing of the last two sentences recalls that of the thesis sentence in paragraph 3, thus bringing the essay to a satisfying close.

POSSIBLE ANSWERS

Meaning and Purpose

1. Recall some of the economic and social differences between the North and South that Catton cites as the cause of the United States Civil War. Lead students to discuss in detail the major differences between the Civil War and modern conflicts in other regions. Currently, civil strife exists in Yugoslavia and seems endless in Afghanistan and Northern Ireland.

2. In paragraph 5, Catton describes a social system in which privilege was based on land ownership, inspiring a strong sense of obligation to the community. Lee, embodying "the noblest elements of this aristocratic ideal" (6), became a symbol of that ideal for the soldiers who had been willing to die to preserve it.

3. Throughout history, wars have been fought for emotional attachment to ideals rather than intellectual understanding of realities. Ask students for examples of this tendency (the Crusades, Vietnam). Even poor southerners saw Lee as a hero who could save the integrity of the southern way of life. The romance in backing such a cause was stronger, for many, than the fear of deprivation and death.

4. Grant represented a society with great hope for the future and disregard for the past. He stood for democracy, with privilege based on what a man did for himself, not on landed birthright (8).

5. Both Lee and Grant had virtues that made them great soldiers, such as "tenacity," "fidelity," and the "ability to think" (14, 15). Greatest among these virtues was their ability to become men

itself had died. In each man there was an indomitable quality . . . the born fighter's refusal to give up as long as he can still remain on his feet and lift his two fists.

Daring and resourcefulness they had, too: the ability to think faster and move faster than the enemy. These were the qualities which gave Lee the dazzling campaigns of Second Manassas and Chancellorsville and won Vicksburg for Grant.   15

Lastly, and perhaps greatest of all, there was the ability, at the end, to turn quickly from war to peace once the fighting was over. Out of the way these two men behaved at Appomattox came the possibility of a peace of reconciliation. It was a possibility not wholly realized, in the years to come, but which did, in the end, help the two sections to become one nation again . . . after a war whose bitterness might have seemed to make such a reunion wholly impossible. No part of either man's life became him more than the part he played in their brief meeting in the McLean house at Appomattox. Their behavior there put all succeeding generations of Americans in their debt. Two great Americans, Grant and Lee—very different, yet under everything very much alike. Their encounter at Appomattox was one of the great moments of American history.   16

Meaning and Purpose

1. The essay begins with a brief description of the negotiations at Appomattox that led to the end of the Civil War. Can you think of any countries today so torn by civil strife and bitterness that reunion and reconciliation seem difficult or nearly impossible? What are the differences between their condition now and that of the United States at the time of the Civil War?

2. Describe the social structure of the Confederacy that Lee defended. The author claims that Lee was also a symbol of that social order (6). In what way was he such a symbol?

3. In paragraph 5, Catton states, "Lee stood for the feeling that it

of peace after the war (16). Their pivotal difference was the kind of society each represented: Grant stood for a modern, expanding one; Lee an established, stagnant one.

6. The expression "tidewater Virginia" refers to the tidal flats, up to the Piedmont Plateau, where all the rivers met. Here grew the quintessential southern plantations where slavery began, and where the Virginia aristocracy was founded.

Strategy

1. The first three paragraphs form the introduction, which ends with the thesis (3); the next paragraph begins the body of the essay with a discussion of Lee. The rest of the essay is structured as a comparison and contrast; the introduction is not. In the introduction, Catton gives background facts about the meeting between the two generals at the close of the Civil War, and sets the basis for comparison.

2. The first and second sentences tell us that Lee and Grant, "these men" (the transition from the preceding paragraph), have brought the war to a virtual end, the key word being *virtual*. The third confirms that the war is essentially over, and the fourth, which concludes the paragraph, points forward to the body of the essay, the contrasts between the two men and the societies they represented.

3. Catton uses paragraph 13 as a transition from contrasting the differences between the two men to comparing their likenesses.

4. The first sentence in each paragraph uses a clear transition that tightly connects it with the preceding paragraph, thus giving the entire essay solid coherence.

5. Catton uses the subject-by-subject method in paragraphs 4 to 11. Paragraph 12 begins point-by-point comparison of similarities between the two men until the conclusion in paragraph 16. The subject-by-subject structure gives, uninterrupted, all the background on each man that Catton needs to make his point-by-point comparisons in the second half.

was somehow of advantage to human society to have a pronounced inequality in the social structure." Apparently, one underclass in that society consisted of the "Thousands of tired, underfed, poorly clothed Confederate soldiers, long since past the simple enthusiasm of the early days of the struggle," but who, nonetheless, "somehow considered Lee the symbol of everything for which they had been willing to die" (6). Discuss the apparent contradictions in this situation.

4. Describe the social structure that Grant represented.

5. How were the two men the same? What was their most important similarity? What was their key difference?

6. What is the meaning of "tidewater Virginia" (5), and what is its significance in this essay?

Strategy

1. Identify the introduction in Catton's essay and state his thesis. How do you know where the introduction ends? How does the information in the introduction differ from that in the rest of the essay; in other words, what characterizes Catton's introductory remarks?

2. Paragraph 2 consists of four sentences. Describe the function of each.

3. What new rhetorical technique does Catton begin to apply in paragraph 13?

4. Examine the first sentence in each paragraph. What transitional devices does the author use in each? What effect do these devices have?

5. Study Catton's method or methods of comparison and contrast in the essay. Does he use the subject-by-subject method, the point-by-point method, or a combination of the two? Discuss the effectiveness of his rhetorical structure.

Style

1. The metaphor suggests that the unfolding history of the United States is a story—a narrative that could be written and read—and that the close of the Civil War is a natural ending to one chapter and beginning of another. The metaphor is effective because Catton goes on to tell the "story" of Lee and Grant.

2. Lee, as a knight in shining armor, may represent a lost cause and a social ideal that has been bypassed by history, but to interpret such a description satirically would miss the tone of the essay, which is entirely laudatory.

3. *Virtual:* being in effect, though not actually or expressly; *poignant:* keenly distressing to the feelings; *chivalry:* the medieval institution and principles of knighthood, the ideal qualities of which include courage, generosity, and courtesy; *legends:* nonhistorical or unverifiable stories handed down by tradition from earlier times and popularly accepted as historic; *myths:* stories or beliefs that are attempts to explain basic truths; *embodied:* given a concrete form; *deportment:* demeanor, conduct, behavior; *obeisance:* a movement of the body expressing deep respect or deferential courtesy, as before a superior; *static:* pertaining to or characterized by a fixed or stationary condition; *tenacity:* holding fast; *fidelity:* loyalty; *indomitable:* unable to be subdued or overcome.

4. Ending the essay in the same place as it began brings it full circle and reconnects the reader to the situation described in the first paragraph. This technique is structurally satisfying because in the body of the essay Catton has given background on and expanded the meaning of the scene in the Court House.

5. Though Lee and Grant represent two entirely different social ideals, Catton admires them both. Both were, in their own ways, admirable. Even when the author contrasts them, he always does so on positive terms. When comparing them, he speaks only of virtues: tenacity and faithfulness (14); daring, resourcefulness, and the ability to think quickly (15); and, ultimately, the capacity to be men of peace (16).

Style

1. In paragraph 1, Catton uses a metaphor comparing the negotiations to end the Civil War to a concluding chapter in the larger book of American life. How effective is that metaphor? What are its implications?

2. In paragraph 12, the author says that "Lee might have ridden down from the old age of chivalry, lance in hand, silken banner fluttering over his head." What effect does this language have? Is it satirical?

3. Check the dictionary for the meaning of these words: *virtual, poignant, chivalry, legends, myths, embodied, deportment, obeisance, static, tenacity, fidelity, indomitable.*

4. In the final paragraph, Catton brings the reader back to the setting he describes in the opening paragraph. What is the stylistic effect of this technique?

5. What is Catton's attitude toward Lee and Grant? How is this attitude shown?

Writing Tasks

1. Write an essay in which you compare and contrast two historical or literary characters who represent two ways of life or value systems. The structure of your essay should include an introduction in which you set the scene for the two people you will discuss; that is, put them in the same category or on the same basis. Choose the subject-by-subject method, point-by-point method, or a combination to set up your comparison and contrast. Pay attention to transitions. Conclude your essay by bringing the two characters together again.

2. Write a brief dialogue between the two characters you chose for the assignment above, or any other two people you want to compare and contrast. Put them in a scene and let their conversation illustrate clearly the differences and similarities between them. You might enjoy presenting this exercise as a dramatic reading with fellow students.

Students know unfortunately little about the history of American Indians and their cultures, including their myths. Few realize how the American Indians were treated, especially in the nineteenth century, by the American government. Also, not many people know that the following states have names whose roots are in American Indian languages: Alabama, Arizona, Arkansas, Connecticut, Illinois, Iowa, Kansas, Kentucky, Massachusetts, Michigan, Minnesota, Mississippi, Missouri, Nebraska, North and South Dakota, Ohio, Oklahoma, Tennessee, Texas, Wisconsin, and Wyoming. Ask your students what kind of information they have about American Indians, and ask them where they found that information. Then encourage them to compare the information they already have with the information contained in this essay.

MARGINAL NOTES

The New Age movement involves people who, generally speaking, are actively interested in protecting the environment, in seeking a personal spiritual awakening, and in looking for meaning and happiness within themselves. They strive for compassionate living, and they see their lives as spiritual journeys. Although mindful of Zen, Taoism, and other non-European philosophies, people of the New Age movement do not favor any particular religion or philosophy.

Feminists are those who espouse feminism, advocating political, social, and all other rights of women equal to those of men.

❦ Andy Smith ❦

A member of the Cherokee tribe, Ms. Andy Smith co-founded Women of All Red Nations (WARN), which is based in Chicago, Illinois. An American Indian feminist, she is also involved in the movement against sexual assaults. Two of her more recent articles appeared in the feminist journal Off Our Backs: *"Journeys in Peacemaking: The Eighth Evangelical Women's Caucus Conference" (Jan. 1989), and "Beyond the Pow-Wow" (July 1989).*

For All Those Who Were Indian in a Former Life

This essay compares and contrasts feminists, "feminists" (which Smith defines internally), and American Indians—in terms of beliefs and attitudes. The author makes apparent those ideas about how we treat Indians, which most people not thought of, if for no other reason than that American Indians are often overlooked as people, while ironically they are accepted for their beliefs.

A number of movies have dealt with the relationships between American Indians and European Americans, including Dances with Wolves, The Great Scout and Cathouse Thursday, Running Brave, Hondo and the Apaches, *and* War Drum. *Perhaps you have seen one or two of these movies or others that portray relationships between Indians and European Americans. As you read this essay, ask yourself whether the movie versions of American Indians agree or disagree with the thoughts presented here.*

The New Age movement has sparked a new interest in Native American traditional spirituality among European American women who claim to be feminists. Indian spirituality, with its respect for nature and the interconnectedness of all things, is often presented as the panacea for all individual and global problems. Not surprisingly, many white "feminists" see the opportunity

Sweat lodges locate ceremonies conducted to cleanse the body, heart, mind, and spirit.

The sacred pipe has two parts: the bowl and the stem. The bowl usually represents the Earth Mother, and the stem represents the male powers. When the bowl and stem are joined together, the pipe becomes sacred.

Genocide is the systematic, planned annihilation of a racial, political, or cultural group.

Evangelical Christianity emphasizes the teaching and authority of the Scriptures, especially the New Testament, as opposed to the institutional authority of the church itself. It stresses that salvation is achieved by personal communion to faith in the atonement of Christ.

An insidious motive is an impulse or action that seems harmless, but which in fact could have grave effects.

to make a great profit from this new craze. They sell sweat lodges or sacred pipe ceremonies, which promise to bring individual and global healing. Or they sell books and records that supposedly describe Indian traditional practices so that you, too, can be Indian.

On the surface, it may appear that this new craze is based on a respect for Indian spirituality. In fact, however, the New Age movement is part of a very old story of white racism and genocide against the Indian people. The "Indian ways" that these white, New Age "feminists" are practicing have little grounding in reality.

True spiritual leaders do not make a profit from their teachings, whether it is through selling books, workshops, sweat lodges, or otherwise. Spiritual leaders teach the people because it is their responsibility to pass what they have learned from their elders to the younger generations. They do not charge for their services.

Furthermore, the idea that an Indian medicine woman would instruct a white woman to preach the "true path" of Indian spirituality sounds more reminiscent of evangelical Christianity than traditional Indian spirituality. Indian religions are community-based, not proselytizing religions. For this reason, there is no *one* Indian religion, as many New Agers would have you believe. Indian spiritual practices reflect the needs of a particular community. Indians do not generally believe that their way is "the" way and, consequently, they have no desire to tell outsiders about their practices. Also, considering how many Indians there are who do not know the traditions, a medicine woman would be more likely to look into her own culture and find what is liberating in it.

However, some white women seem determined *not* to look into *their* own cultures for sources of strength. This is puzzling, since pre-Christian European cultures contain many of the same elements these women are ostensibly looking for in Native American cultures. This phenomenon leads me to suspect that there is a more insidious motive for latching onto Indian spirituality.

When white "feminists" see how white people have historically oppressed others and how they are coming very close to destroying the earth, they often want to disassociate themselves from their whiteness. They do this by opting to "become Indian."

In this way, they can escape responsibility and accountability for white racism.

Of course, white "feminists" want to become only partly Indian. They do not want to be a part of our struggles for survival against genocide, and they do not want to fight for treaty rights or an end to substance abuse or sterilization abuse. They do not want to do anything that would tarnish their romanticized notions of what it means to be Indian.

Moreover, they want to become Indian without holding themselves accountable to Indian communities. If they did, they would have to listen to Indians telling them to stop carrying around sacred pipes, stop doing their own sweat lodges, and stop appropriating our spiritual practices. Rather, these New Agers see Indians as romanticized gurus who exist only to meet their consumerist needs. Consequently, they do not understand our struggles for survival, and thus they can have no genuine understanding of Indian spiritual practices.

While New Agers may think that they are escaping white racism by becoming "Indian," they are in fact continuing the same genocidal practices of their forebears. The one thing that has maintained the survival of Indian people through 500 years of colonialism has been the spiritual bonds that keep us together. When the colonizers saw the strength of our spirituality, they tried to destroy Indian religions by making them illegal. They forced Indian children into missionary schools and cut their tongues if they spoke their Native languages. Sundances were made illegal; Indian participation in the Ghost Dance precipitated the Wounded Knee massacre. The colonizers recognized that it was our spirituality that maintained our spirit of resistance and sense of community. Even today, Indians do not have religious freedom: the Supreme Court recently ruled that the First Amendment does not guarantee our right to use peyote in sacred ceremonies.

Many white New Agers are continuing this practice of destroying Indian spirituality. They have the privilege and power to make themselves heard at the expense of Native Americans and they trivialize Native American practices so that these practices lose their spiritual force. Our voices are silenced, and conse-

---

Romanticized notions are fanciful, untrue, or impractical.

Sun-dances are religious ceremonies associated with the sun, practiced by North American Indians of the Plains having various symbolic rites.

The Ghost Dance is an attempt to establish communication with the dead; it is a dance especially associated with various messianic western American Indian communities in the late nineteenth century.

Wounded Knee, a village in South Dakota, was the site of a massacre of about 300 Oglala Sioux Indians on December 29, 1890.

The First Amendment reads, in part, "Congress shall make no law respecting an establishment of religion, or prohibiting the free exercise thereof."

Peyote is a hallucinatory drug derived from mescal, a spineless, globe-shaped cactus that is also the source of mescaline, a drug that produces abnormal mental states.

"morass of consumerist spirituality": A *morass* is soggy ground, a bog or a marsh. "Consumerist spirituality" is an oxymoron, a figure of speech in which contradictory terms are combined.

"our burden to service the white women's needs": Compare with lines from "The White Man's Burden" (1899) by Rudyard Kipling (1865–1936): "Take up the White Man's burden/ Send forth the best ye breed—/ Go, bind your sons to exile/ To serve your captives' need."

Depo-Provera is a trade name for medroxyprogesterone acetate, a chemical agent that has the effect of progesterone, a steroid hormone. It is used in birth control pills.

"treaty rights": For example, as far back as 1830, during Andrew Jackson's presidency, American Indians who lived east of the Mississippi River, including the Choctaw, Chickasaw, Creek, and Cherokee Nations, were told that they must give up their ancient ancestral lands in what is now mainly Mississippi, Alabama, and Georgia, and move to the wide-open spaces of the western Great Plains. Congress wrote this policy into law, and scores of treaties were negotiated with the Indians. However, within fifteen years, as settlers migrated west, the pacts turned out to be mere scraps of paper. The "permanent frontier" lasted about fifteen years.

quently, the younger generation of Indians who are trying to find their way back to the Old Ways become hopelessly lost in this morass of consumerist spirituality.

These practices also promote the subordination of Indian 11
women to European American women. We are told that we are "greedy" not to share our spirituality. Apparently it is our burden to service white women's needs rather than to spend time organizing within our own communities. Their perceived need for warm and fuzzy mysticism takes precedence over our need to survive.

The New Age movement completely trivializes the oppression 12
we as Indian women face: Indian women are suddenly no longer the women who are forcibly sterilized and tested with such unsafe drugs as Depo-Provera; we are no longer the women who generally live below the poverty level and face an average 75 percent unemployment rate. No, we're cool and spiritual.

This trivialization of our oppression is compounded by the 13
fact that nowadays anyone can be Indian if she or he wants to. All that is required is that one be Indian in a former life, or take part in a sweat lodge, or be mentored by a "medicine woman," or read a how-to book.

Since according to this theory, anyone can now be an "Indian," 14
then the term "Indians" no longer refers to those who have survived 500 years of colonization and genocide. This furthers the goals of white supremacists to abrogate treaty rights and take away what little we have left. When everyone becomes "Indian," then it is easy to lose sight of the specificity of oppression faced by those who are Indian in *this* life.

The most disturbing aspect about these racist practices is that 15
some of them are promoted in the name of feminism. Sometimes it seems that I can't open a feminist periodical without seeing ads promoting white "feminist" businesses—with little medicine wheel designs. I can't seem to go to a feminist conference without the only Indian presenter being the woman who begins the conference with a ceremony. Participants then feel so "spiritual" after this opening that they fail to notice the absence of Indian women at the rest of the conference or the fact that there will be nobody discussing pressing issues in Native American communities.

If European Americans are going to act in solidarity with their   16
Indian sisters, they must take a stand against Indian spiritual
abuse. Feminist book and record stores should stop advertising
such rip-off products. Many have claimed that Indians are not
respecting "freedom of speech" by demanding that whites stop
exploiting Indian spirituality. But promotion of this material is
destroying freedom of speech for Native Americans, by ensuring
that our own voices will never be heard. (Feminists have already
made choices about what they will promote. I haven't seen many
books by right-wing, fundamentalist women sold in feminist
bookstores.) The issue is not censorship; the issue is racism.
Feminists must make a choice: to respect Indian political and
spiritual autonomy or to promote materials that are fundamentally
racist under the guise of "freedom of speech."

Respecting the integrity of Native people and their spirituality   17
does not mean that there can never be cross-cultural sharing.
However, such sharing should take place in a way that is respectful
to Indian people. The way to be respectful is for non-Indians to
become involved in our political struggles and to develop an
ongoing relationship with Indian *communities* based on trust and
mutual respect. When this happens, Indian people may invite a
non-Indian to take part in a ceremony—but it will be on Indian
terms.

I hesitate to say even this much about cross-cultural sharing,   18
however, because many white people take this to mean that they
can join in our struggles solely for the purpose of being invited
to ceremonies. If this does not occur, they feel that Indians have
somehow unfairly withheld spiritual teachings from them. We
are expected to pay the price in spiritual exploitation in order to
gain allies in our political struggles.

In fact, however, we are not obligated to teach anyone about   19
our spirituality. It is our choice if we want to share with people
we think will be respectful.

It is also important for non-Indians to build relationships   20
with Indian communities rather than with specific individuals.
Many non-Indians express their confusion about knowing who
is and who is not a legitimate spiritual teacher. The only way for

non-Indians to know who are legitimate teachers is if they know who the *community* respects as *its* spiritual leaders. This is a process that takes time.

Unfortunately, many do not want to take this time in their quest for instant spirituality. And alas, racism and profit-making seem to get in the way of solidarity between women.   21

Our spirituality is not for sale.   22

POSSIBLE ANSWERS

Meaning and Purpose

1. According to paragraphs 5 and 6, they want to distance themselves from that part of history which makes white people the source of oppression and the destroyers of the earth.

2. "The" way refers to the way of becoming spiritual. By putting the word inside quotation marks, Smith implies that some people, but not Indians, believe that only one way exists to become spiritual, that there is only one path: "The" path. Students often have strong beliefs that affect the answer to the second question.

3. This question brings forth many interesting answers, including one which argues that a person adopted into an Indian tribe might become a member of that tribe, but the choice is ultimately up to the tribe whether to accept the adoption. Students usually maintain that anyone can become a politician, as opposed to becoming an Indian, merely by registering his or her candidacy for office.

4. Smith hesitates about "cross-cultural sharing" because she fears that white people might take the sharing lightly, not unlike their being invited to join a local country club. If white people do not discover that merely joining in ceremonies is no guarantee of finding "the" way, then they might become disillusioned, feeling cheated. Students ordinarily discuss the strengths and weaknesses of such sharing in terms of relative strengths or of relative dilutions, either pointing out that such sharing can strengthen

Meaning and Purpose

1. According to the essay, why do some white women choose not to look into their own cultures for sources of strength?
2. Paragraph 4 says, "Indians do not generally believe that their way is 'the' way. . . ." What is meant in this sentence by "the" way? Do you know of another "way"?
3. In your opinion, is it true that "anyone can be an Indian if he or she wants to," as stated in paragraph 13? How does that statement compare and contrast with the statement "Anyone can be a politician if she or he wants to"?
4. Why is Smith hesitant to suggest "cross-cultural sharing" in paragraph 18? In your own words, point out what the advantages and disadvantages of cross-cultural sharing might be.
5. After we read this essay, we begin to understand its title. What group of people does Smith refer to in the title "For All Those Who Were Indian in a Former Life"? What groups of people is she comparing and contrasting to that group in the body of her essay?

Strategy

1. How do paragraphs 2 and 19 differ in terms of affecting their readers emotionally?
2. How does Smith's analogy between Indian spirituality and evan-

both groups or can weaken both groups if the sharing is not carried out in depth.

5. The title of the essay mocks those New Age believers who embrace a form of transmigration, holding that a soul passes after death into another body. In the body of her essay, Smith compares and contrasts them with ordinary white people, particularly feminists, and with American Indians.

Strategy

1. Paragraph 2 shocks its readers by claiming that the New Age movement, instead of being concerned with personal betterment, personal happiness, and personal spirituality among other admirable goals, promotes racism and the annihilation of American Indians. Paragraph 19 awakens its readers by bluntly informing them that whether to impart the American Indians' spiritual knowledge will remain the decision of American Indians.

2. The analogy in paragraph 4 serves as a reminder that white Europeans have their own culture, which includes the spirituality embedded in religion. Paragraph 5 moves from that reminder to a brief consideration of the preludes to European culture and its religion, in effect saying that white Europeans should be drawing from their own spiritual past, not the spiritual past of American Indians.

3. Paragraph 16 offers the alternative to current practices. It calls for true equality among all feminists as an urgently needed substitute for the racism and the blithe attitudes toward American Indian spirituality that Smith claims "feminists" embrace.

4. "Of course," which as a transitional phrase usually means "certainly" or "without doubt," is used here cynically to help intensify the point that white "feminists" want the best of American Indian spiritual practices, but they do not want to become Indians in any profound sense. In fact, "feminists" are uncertain; "feminists" do have doubt.

gelical Christianity in paragraph 4 prepare the reader for paragraph 5?

3. What function does paragraph 16 serve?

4. Why does Smith begin paragraph 7 with "Of course"? What is the importance of that transitional phrase to the rest of the paragraph?

Style

1. How does the last sentence of the essay compare with the first sentence of the essay in terms of tone? (For a definition of *tone*, see the Glossary.)

2. How can you tell that the word *sell* in the first paragraph is used sarcastically?

3. In paragraph 11, what is the "warm and fuzzy mysticism"?

4. Why are the words *community* and *communities* mentioned several times in this essay? To what do they refer?

5. In the first paragraph of this essay, the word *feminists* appears without quotation marks (feminists) and then later in the paragraph, the word appears inside quotation marks ("feminists"). Why does Smith sometimes put this word inside quotation marks and sometimes not?

Writing Tasks

1. Compare and contrast a movie or a television show's "Indians" with the American Indians that this essay portrays. How do the fictional Indians compare with the Indians discussed here? If the movie or program that you watched did not contain anything about what Indians believe or about other facets of their culture, why do you think those things were excluded?

2. This essay mentions "cross-cultural" sharing. In a brief essay, explain which of your beliefs you would like to share with a

Style

1. The first sentence is a calm informative introduction to the essay; the final sentence is a cold direct termination.

2. What is being "sold" in the first paragraph is precisely that which can never be bought: sweat lodges, sacred pipe ceremonies, and books and records that tell a person how to become an Indian. Without being deeply involved in the religious part of the culture, the paraphernalia of a culture has no value, monetary or otherwise.

3. The "warm and fuzzy mysticism" is Smith's description of the "feminist's" ideas of Indian beliefs. This phrase is also oxymoronic, a figure of speech combining contradictory terms, used sarcastically here to describe the apparent attitude of these women toward what is of high spirituality in American Indian cultures.

4. The words *community* and *communities* are used throughout the essay to refer to American Indians. The words are used again and again to emphasize the point that Indians, unlike European Americans, have a close familiarity with one another's spirituality. As it is used here, the word *community* means "a social group or class with a culture of kindred interests."

5. Smith puts the word *feminists* between quotation marks when she means those women who, consciously or not, separate themselves from other groups of women, American Indians in this case. She uses the word without the quotation marks when she means all women thoughtfully involved in the feminist movement.

person from an American Indian tribe and what you would hope to learn from a member of that tribe.

3. Since you have been in college, you have met several people whose cultural beliefs differ from your own. Discuss your beliefs freely with your new acquaintances and then write a short essay comparing and contrasting your cultural beliefs with theirs.

TEACHING SUGGESTIONS

You might begin by asking your students for whom English is their second language, or who come from a bilingual household, to compare their experiences with language to those of Rodriguez. Ask native speakers to relate their experiences with languages other than English. Were there situations for both groups that made them feel discomfort or frustration? From that discussion you might lead the students to a consideration of some of the elements of the essay's construction: the point-by-point development of paragraphs 2 and 3, for instance, and the subject-by-subject development of 7 and 8. You might want to teach the essay in conjunction with the other Rodriguez essay, "Los Pobres," or with Maya Angelou's "Finishing School" or Harry Mark Petrakis's "Barba Nikos."

❦ Richard Rodriguez ❦

Richard Rodriguez was born in San Francisco in 1944 to Mexican-American parents who spoke only Spanish at home. Rodriguez nonetheless mastered the English language and went on to study at Stanford, Columbia, and the University of California at Berkeley, where he earned a Ph.D. in English literature. He also received a Fulbright fellowship to study English literature in London. In spite of several offers to teach, Rodriguez made writing and journalism his profession. In The Hunger of Memory *(1982), a collection of autobiographical essays, he examines the American educational system from the point of view of an immigrant who has gone all the way through it, and he strongly opposes bilingual education.*

Los Otros, Mis Hermanos

This exerpt from Richard Rodriguez's autobiography, The Hunger of Memory, *portrays one of the conflicts he felt growing up as a Hispanic in an Anglo culture. He concentrates here on his youthful sensitivity to language and how he identified his Spanish-speaking world with the comfort and security of family and the English-speaking world that surrounded him as alien and threatening.*

In the essay Rodriguez explains the different ways that language formed his identity. While you read, imagine as vividly as you can how he perceived people, and his relationship to them, in the way that they spoke. Notice the various ways he isolated in his mind the Spanish-speaking world from the English.

MARGINAL NOTES

All of the opening images set Rodriguez, his family, and his house apart from his neighbors: the size of the family, the color of the house, the animals.

I grew up in a house where the only regular guests were my relations. For one day, enormous families of relatives would visit and there would be so many people that the noise and the bodies would spill out to the backyard and front porch. Then, for weeks, no one came by. (It was usually a salesman who rang the doorbell.) Our house stood apart. A gaudy yellow in a row of white bungalows. We were the people with the noisy dog. The people who

278

In the opening two paragraphs Rodriguez uses both parallel structure and clear transitions (as discussed on p. 256) to keep his contrasts clear. The phrases "In public" (sentence 1) and "At home" (sentence 3) are participial phrases that begin their respective sentences and clearly distinguish the subject of each. The opening prepositional phrase of the second paragraph's opening sentence connects the time of the paragraph with that in the opening paragraph and thus serves as a transition. The compound sentence is balanced by the semicolon, with thesis (hearing) in the first part and antithesis (replying) in the second.

Paragraphs 4, 5, 6, and the first half of 7 concentrate on the child's lack of ability to speak and understand English.

raised pigeons and chickens. We were the foreigners on the block. A few neighbors smiled and waved. We waved back. But no one in the family knew the names of the old couple who lived next door; until I was seven years old, I did not know the names of the kids who lived across the street.

In public, my father and mother spoke a hesitant, accented, not always grammatical English. And they would have to strain—their bodies tense—to catch the sense of what was rapidly said by *los gringos*. At home they spoke Spanish. The language of their Mexican past sounded in counterpoint to the English of public society. The words would come quickly, with ease. Conveyed through those sounds was the pleasing, soothing, consoling reminder of being at home. 2

During those years when I was first conscious of hearing, my mother and father addressed me only in Spanish; in Spanish I learned to reply. By contrast, English *(inglés),* rarely heard in the house, was the language I came to associate with *gringos.* I learned my first words of English overhearing my parents speak to strangers. At five years of age, I knew just enough English for my mother to trust me on errands to stores one block away. No more. 3

I was a listening child, careful to hear the very different sounds of Spanish and English. Wide-eyed with hearing, I'd listen to sounds more than words. First, there were English *(gringo)* sounds. So many words were still unknown that when the butcher or the lady at the drugstore said something to me, exotic polysyllabic sounds would bloom in the midst of their sentences. Often, the speech of people in public seemed to me very loud, booming with confidence. The man behind the counter would literally ask, "What can I do for you?" But by being so firm and so clear, the sound of his voice said that he was a *gringo;* he belonged in public society. 4

I would also hear then the high nasal notes of middle-class American speech. The air stirred with sound. Sometimes, even now, when I have been traveling abroad for several weeks, I will hear what I heard as a boy. In hotel lobbies or airports, in Turkey or Brazil, some Americans will pass, and suddenly I will hear it again—the high sound of American voices. For a few seconds I 5 will hear it with pleasure, for it is now the sound of *my* society—a reminder of home. But inevitably—already on the flight headed for home—the sound fades with repetition. I will be unable to hear it anymore.

When I was a boy, things were different. The accent of *los gringos* was never pleasing nor was it hard to hear. Crowds at Safeway or at bus stops would be noisy with sound. And I would be forced to edge away from the chirping chatter above me.

I was unable to hear my own sounds, but I knew very well that I spoke English poorly. My words could not stretch far enough to form complete thoughts. And the words I did speak I didn't know well enough to make into distinct sounds. (Listeners would usually lower their heads, better to hear what I was trying to say.) But it was one thing for *me* to speak English with difficulty. It was more troubling for me to hear my parents speak in public; their high-whining vowels and guttural consonants; their sentences that got stuck with 'eh' and 'ah' sounds; the confused syntax; the hesitant rhythm of sounds so different from the way *gringos* spoke. I'd notice, moreover, that my parents' voices were softer than those of *gringos* we'd meet.

I am tempted now to say that none of this mattered. In adulthood I am embarrassed by childhood fears. And, in a way, it didn't matter very much that my parents could not speak English with ease. Their linguistic difficulties had no serious consequences. My mother and father made themselves understood at the county hospital clinic and at government offices. And yet, in another way, it mattered very much—it was unsettling to hear my parents struggle with English. Hearing them, I'd grow nervous, my clutching trust in their protection and power weakened.

There were many times like the night at a brightly lit gasoline station (a blaring white memory) when I stood uneasily, hearing my father. He was talking to a teenaged attendant. I do not recall what they were saying, but I cannot forget the sounds my father made as he spoke. At one point his words slid together to form one word—sounds as confused as the threads of blue and green oil in the puddle next to my shoes. His voice rushed through

6

7

8

9

"But" in the middle of the paragraph is an emphatic transition that brings the reader's attention from the child's language difficulties to his parents' and the consequent change of attitude he has.

The first half of the paragraph shows how his parents' language problems didn't really matter when he looks at the situation from an adult perspective. But after the transitional "And yet . . ." he shows how their language struggles meant something significant to him as a child.

Here Rodriguez uses a general example to illustrate how the power of English and his parents' difficulties in dealing with it caused him to lose confidence in them.

what he had left to say. And, toward the end, reached falsetto notes, appealing to his listener's understanding. I looked away to the lights of passing automobiles. I tried not to hear anymore. But I heard only too well the calm, easy tones in the attendant's reply. Shortly afterward, walking toward home with my father, I shivered when he put his hand on my shoulder. The very first chance that I got, I evaded his grasp and ran on ahead into the dark, skipping with feigned boyish exuberance.

These next two paragraphs concentrate on the comforts he found in his family's language, *Español*. For him his family becomes extended to anyone who speaks Spanish. Paragraph 10 begins with the oppositional transition "But," and the two paragraphs contrast with the preceding three.

But then there was Spanish. *Español:* my family's language. *Español:* the language that seemed to me a private language. I'd hear strangers on the radio and in the Mexican Catholic church across town speaking in Spanish, but I couldn't really believe that Spanish was a public language, like English. Spanish speakers, rather, seemed related to me, for I sensed that we shared—through our language—the experience of feeling apart from *los gringos*. It was thus a ghetto Spanish that I heard and I spoke. Like those whose lives are bound by a barrio, I was reminded by Spanish of my separateness from *los otros, los gringos* in power. But more intensely than for most barrio children—because I did not live in a barrio—Spanish seemed to me the language of home. (Most days it was only at home that I'd hear it.) It became the language of joyful return.

A family member would say something to me and I would feel myself specially recognized. My parents would say something to me and I would feel embraced by the sounds of their words. Those sounds said: *I am speaking with ease in Spanish. I am addressing you in words I never use with los gringos. I recognize you as someone special, close, like no one outside. You belong with us. In the family.*

(*Ricardo.*)

Because his private and public worlds remained so separate, Rodriguez believes his psychological development was retarded.

At the age of five, six, well past the time when most other children no longer easily notice the difference between sounds uttered at home and words spoken in public, I had a different experience. I lived in a world magically compounded of sounds. I remained a child longer than most; I lingered too long, poised at the edge of language—often frightened by the sounds of *los gringos,* delighted by the sounds of Spanish at home. I shared with my family a language that was startlingly different from that used in the great city around us.

For me there were none of the gradations between public and private society so normal to a maturing child. Outside the house was public society; inside the house was private. Just opening or closing the screen door behind me was an important experience. I'd rarely leave home all alone or without reluctance. Walking down the sidewalk, under the canopy of tall trees, I'd warily notice the—suddenly—silent neighborhood kids who stood warily watching me. Nervously, I'd arrive at the grocery store to hear there the sounds of the *gringo*—foreign to me—reminding me that in this world so big, I was a foreigner. But then I'd return. Walking back toward our house, climbing the steps from the sidewalk, when the front door was open in summer, I'd hear voices beyond the screen door talking in Spanish. For a second or two, I'd stay, linger there, listening. Smiling, I'd hear my mother call out, saying in Spanish (words): "Is that you, Richard?" All the while her sounds would assure me: *You are home now; come closer; inside. With us.*

"*Sí,*" I'd reply.

Once more inside the house I would resume (assume) my place in the family. The sounds would dim, grow harder to hear. Once more at home, I would grow less aware of that fact. It required, however, no more than the blurt of the doorbell to alert me to listen to sounds all over again. The house would turn instantly still while my mother went to the door. I'd hear her hard English sounds. I'd wait to hear her voice return to soft-sounding Spanish, which assured me, as surely as did the clicking tongue of the lock on the door, that the stranger was gone.

Plainly, it is not healthy to hear such sounds so often. It is not healthy to distinguish public words from private sounds so easily. I remained cloistered by sounds, timid and shy in public, too dependent on voices at home. And yet it needs to be emphasized: I was an extremely happy child at home. I remember many nights when my father would come back from work, and I'd hear him call out to my mother in Spanish, sounding relieved.

14

15

16

17

While the final two paragraphs are full of the comforting images of home, family, and native language, he makes the negative moral judgment that such extended separation of public and private language is not healthy (first sentence, paragraph 17).

In Spanish, he'd sound light and free notes he never could manage in English. Some nights I'd jump up just at hearing his voice. With *mis hermanos* I would come running into the room where he was with my mother. Our laughing (so deep was the pleasure!) became screaming. Like others who know the pain of public alienation, we transformed the knowledge of our public separateness and made it consoling—the reminder of intimacy. Excited, we joined our voices in a celebration of sounds. *We are speaking now the way we never speak out in public. We are alone—together,* voices sounded, surrounded to tell me. Some nights, no one seemed willing to loosen the hold sounds had on us. At dinner, we invented new words. (Ours sounded Spanish, but made sense only to us.) We pieced together new words by taking, say, an English verb and giving it Spanish endings. My mother's instructions at bedtime would be lacquered with mock-urgent tones. Or a word like *si* would become, in several notes, able to convey added measures of feeling. Tongues explored the edges of words, especially the fat vowels. And we happily sounded that military drum roll, the twirling roar of the Spanish *r.* Family language: my family's sounds. The voices of my parents and sisters and brother. Their voices insisting: *You belong here. We are family members. Related. Special to one another. Listen!* Voices singing and sighing, rising, straining, then surging, teeming with pleasure that burst syllables into fragments of laughter. At times it seemed there was steady quiet only when, from another room, the rustling whispers of my parents faded and I moved closer to sleep.

Meaning and Purpose

1. What are Rodriguez's childhood feelings about Spanish and English? Use examples from the essay to illustrate your answer.
2. In paragraph 7 the author says he felt differently about his own inability to speak fluent English and his parents' inability to do so. Why does he feel so differently? How strong are his feelings? Explain.

POSSIBLE ANSWERS

Meaning and Purpose

1. Spanish, for the youthful Rodriguez, is the language of home and family. In all of the examples he gives, he associates Spanish with the comfort and protection of home, a safe oasis that protects him from the surrounding and alien world of *los gringos.* English, the language of the public world that surrounds him, he finds threatening. Both he and his parents struggle to understand and speak English, but they must do so just to function in the Anglo world in which they live. Even the sounds of English he finds alien and grating: "The accent of *los gringos* was never pleasing nor was it hard to hear" (6). So Spanish, the language of home and protection, becomes an escape from the frightening and alien public world of English. "It [Spanish] became the language of joyful return" (10).

2. As a child Rodriguez views his own insecurity and fear as natural. His security lies with his parents. So when he sees them stumble in their attempts to speak English in the public world, his insecurity is heightened and he is, in a sense, embarrassed. He recognizes the surety of the native English speakers, compared to his parents, in their voices' volume: "I'd notice, moreover, that my parents' voices were softer than those of *gringos* we'd meet" (7).

3. As an adult Rodriguez recognizes that his parents' English language insufficiencies made no practical difference in either his or their lives. They could handle the language well enough to manage everyday problems. But as a child his trust in their authority diminished because he perceived his own security was threatened by their English language deficiencies in the public world.

4. For the native English speaker, the language of family and the language of the other, "public" world are the same, so the two worlds become connected early. For the non-native speaker, like Rodriguez, his Spanish-speaking home becomes a refuge from the ubiquitous English-speaking world outside of his home and the larger Spanish-speaking community that he considers family. He therefore remains psychologically dependent on his family longer than would a native speaker.

Strategy

1. The first paragraph introduces the reader to the general contrast between his home and family and the outside world represented by a salesman and his neighbors. He then focuses in on the differences in his perceptions of Spanish and English in the second paragraph with point-by-point development.

2. The illustration contrasts Rodriguez's attitudes toward English as an adult to when he was a child. Now, when he is abroad, English stands out because it is different from the language that predominates in the area, just as English stood out when he was a Spanish-speaking child in an English-speaking world. But he finds hearing English in such a context comforting now because English makes up his world. The

3. Rodriguez says in paragraph 8 that his parents' difficulties with English didn't matter in some ways but did in others. Explain this.

4. "I remained a child longer than most . . ." says the author in paragraph 13. What does he mean by this? What does he consider the characteristics of childhood? How did language affect his slow development?

Strategy

1. Where and how does the author make clear what he intends to compare and contrast?
2. Paragraph 5 is an example. What function does it serve?
3. Paragraph 9 is also an example. What is its function?
4. Paragraph 15 consists of a short, single sentence. Why does Rodriguez separate it from the preceding paragraph?

Style

1. Examine the essay closely and point out some places where Rodriguez uses point-by-point development and where he uses subject-by-subject development. Why do you think he chose those methods when and where he did?
2. Rodriguez uses Spanish words and phrases to demonstrate "private" language. Are the meanings clear in context? What effect do they create even if you are unable to translate them?
3. What does the word *gringo* mean? What are its connotations? How does the author want the word to affect you? Explain.

Writing Tasks

1. If English is not your first language, write an essay in which you compare aspects of your native culture to those of American

entire paragraph, except for the transitional opening two sentences, contrasts with the preceding paragraph.

3. The example illustrates Rodriguez's last point in the preceding paragraph: When he heard his parents struggle with English, his ". . . trust in their protection and power weakened."

4. Rodriguez emphasizes the sentence by making it a separate paragraph. It dramatizes the boy's relief in returning home from the threatening world of *los gringos* with an emphatic affirmation.

Style

1. The author uses point-by-point development (see pp. 258–259) to quickly emphasize the differences between his two childhood worlds. He uses subject-by-subject development (pp. 256–258) in two different ways. In the first, he contrasts individual paragraphs. The stumbling and insecure English of his parents and himself described in paragraph 7, for instance, is contrasted against the confidence of native English speakers in paragraphs 3 and 4. He also uses subject-by-subject development within paragraphs, as when he contrasts the two different ways he felt about his parents' English insufficiencies (7).

2. The sense of the Spanish words, if not all of their precise meanings, should be clear to any reader. Almost all students will know the meaning of *los gringos*, though they may be unclear about the phrase's connotations. Rodriguez translates *inglés* for us in paragraph 3. They may not know the exact meaning of *los otros* (the others), but it is clearly associated with "my separateness" and "*los gringos*" that precedes and follows it (10). It is clear, too, in paragraph 17 that *mis hermanos* (my brothers) refers to his siblings.

3. *Gringo* means foreigner, especially one of U.S. or English descent, and is usually used disparagingly. But the pejorative connotation seems muted in this piece, since the boy views his surrounding world of *los gringos* as threatening rather than hostile.

culture. If you are a native American but have encountered foreign cultures, compare some aspects of those cultures to your own. What were things you liked or disliked? Why?

2. Think about where you grew up. Did the place, the people, and your family affect the way you learned to think of yourself? How? Write an essay in which you enumerate and describe those things that formed your sense of identity.

Some students have already traveled abroad, most of them probably to European countries. Others plan to travel abroad. If anyone in your class has been to Europe, especially to France, now is a good time to ask that person to discuss her or his cultural experiences with the rest of the class. Some students have friends in this country who came from other countries, and they have visited those friends' homes. Ask them to talk about the differences between their own homes and their friends' homes. If you have visited a European country, tell your class about your own cultural experiences. Many students assume that they are culturally related to Europeans, when in fact they might be only historically related to Europeans. Now is a good time to discuss the difference between a person's being historically related to another country and being culturally aware of another country. For example, some of your students might have French surnames; in itself, that does not make them French.

The first two paragraphs, both anecdotal, foreshadow the overall structure of the rest of the essay. Carroll compares the comments of the naive American anthropologist with the comments of her French mother to show at the very beginning that people quickly condemn actions which do not accord with their own cultural ways. The last line of the second paragraph brings the contrast into Carroll's own home. Structurally, the rest of the essay for the most part follows each cultural-anthropological statement with an anecdote that illustrates that statement.

❧ Raymonde Carroll ❧

Raymonde Carroll, an anthropologist born in Tunisia, was educated in France and in the United States. She has done fieldwork in both countries. She also did fieldwork for three years on Nukuoro, a Polynesian atoll in Micronesia, which resulted in her book Nukuoro Stories *(1980). The essay "Intercultural Misunderstandings: Crossing the Threshold" comes from her book* Cultural Misunderstandings: The French-American Experience *(1988), translated by Carol Volk from its French edition,* Évidences invisibles *(1987). Professor Carroll, married to an American anthropologist, teaches in the Department of Romance Languages at Ohio's Oberlin College.*

Intercultural Misunderstandings:
Crossing the Threshold

In this essay, Raymonde Carroll compares and contrasts French houses and American houses as places where American culture and French culture differ—to attempt, as she says elsewhere, "to identify the context in which cultural misunderstandings can arise."

Note how Carroll uses anecdotes, which are short accounts of interesting or humorous incidents, to help illustrate the comparisons and contrasts between the French and the Americans in how they treat one another and expect to be treated in their homes.

Several years ago, an American anthropologist returning from France, where he had spent the summer on his way back from Africa, told me that what had really struck him was the distrustfulness of the French, who always kept their shutters closed. Just the idea of shutters . . . They made the streets particularly gloomy, as if the villages were uninhabited, or as if people were spying on you from behind them. (This anthropologist did not do research in France.)

When my mother came to visit me in the United States, she

liked the style of American houses, the way they stood separate from each other, the big lawns, the architectural diversity, the space. One day, we were quietly seated in the living room when she suddenly became aware of the large bay window and, visibly shocked, said to me, "My goodness, you live in the street!" And I understood exactly what she was feeling. It took me years to get used to "living in the street." And when I stroll around my neighborhood in the evening, I am still somewhat surprised at being able to see right into each home. People read, watch television, throw parties, eat dinner, do the dishes, or whatever without closing their drapes, and they are apparently not the least bit bothered by the possibility of a stranger's eyes peering into their lives. And even today, I'm the one who always closes the drapes in our home, much to the amusement of my American husband.

Note the quiet humor in the personification of lawns, as if they had established their own cultural differences.

The lawns surrounding American houses display this same refusal to separate the street and the house. In certain American cities the sidewalk itself disappears, the lawn ends where the street begins, and the owner of the house is responsible for its upkeep (as he or she would be for the upkeep of the sidewalk). Space substitutes for walls, railings, or fences, which are sometimes replaced by bushes or trees. But the cutoff point is not clearly defined. Thus, in spring and summer, it is common to see passing strollers sit awhile on your lawn to rest, without, however, going beyond an implicit limit. Backyards and gardens blend into each other in certain small American cities, but more often they are separated by low hedges, across which neighbors exchange produce from their gardens or simply chat. According to an old American tradition, when a family moves into a neighborhood the neighbors immediately come to welcome them, bringing hot coffee and cakes. I benefited from this type of welcome in two different cities, each with over one hundred thousand inhabitants. (I'm speaking here about moving into houses, not apartments.) 3

This passage objectively points out an American cultural peculiarity to a French reader. Recall that this essay was first published in France.

We can therefore understand an American's surprise when faced with the walls, gates, shutters, and drawn curtains that "protect" French houses, as well as the uneasiness of a French person before these "open" American houses. But these differences 4 do not really cause any problems. It is inside the house that blunders or misunderstandings have a greater chance of arising.

Here begins the first of several well-wrought anecdotes that serve to clarify cultural distinctions for general readers.

Dick and Jill are invited to dinner at Pierre and Jeanne's. The conversation becomes lively during cocktails. Pierre speaks enthusiastically about a book he thinks would interest Dick a great deal. He has it in fact, and goes to look for it in his study. He is taken aback, as he heads toward the room, when he realizes that Dick is following him. Jeanne goes to the kitchen to check if something is burning. She is just as taken aback when she sees Jill walk in right behind her. Jill offers to help. "No, no thank you, everything is ready . . . ." Or at the end of the meal, Jill gets up to clear the table and carries the dishes into the kitchen, or else Dick offers to do the dishes. Pierre and Jeanne protest; if they are unfamiliar with American habits, they might very well consider Jill and Dick to be "intrusive" or "inconsiderate," or they might be "ashamed" that Dick or Jill has seen the rooms "in a terrible mess." ("But what could I do? I wasn't expecting him to follow me all over the house, I didn't know how to stop him.") In fact, it would have sufficed to say "I'll be back in a minute" for Dick not to have gotten up, for him not to have felt obliged to accompany Pierre because Pierre was going out of his way for him.

French people are often surprised when, the first time they enter an American home, their hosts show them around the house, and they interpret this as "showing off." Without excluding this possibility, it is important to understand that an American considers this an attempt to make you "feel at home" by immediately giving you an opportunity to orient yourself, so to speak. Thus, instead of taking your coat when you arrive at a party, the host will show you in which bedroom and on what floor "the coats go." This, among other things, allows you to check your hair, or whatever you like, in the bathroom mirror next door. And if the party is a success, it will spill over into every room on the ground floor, with a definite preference for the kitchen. Guests serve themselves at the bar set up for the occasion (unless the party is more "formal"), help themselves to beer from the refrigerator—

in short, they try hard to do as much as they can by themselves so as not to "bother" their host, who also has a right to have fun. This means that the cupboards and drawers are likely to be opened and closed freely, which would give French people the sense that they were being "intruded upon" or that their guests had "been all over the place."

These few examples, and there are many others, already show how different the relationship to the home is in these two cultures. 7

The preceding series of examples comprises strong evidence for Carroll's comment here. Throughout this essay, we can see the scientific bent of the writer's mind. First, she amasses information, and then she objectively comments on it, pulling it together into an anthropological statement concerning culture.

A French informant told me that he had never entered the kitchen at his grandmother's house, where he ate lunch once a week, until she became very old and less mobile and resigned herself to sending him to get things from the kitchen during meals. While the division between public and private is clearly marked outside the house by its division from the street, thanks to the walls, gates, and drawn curtains mentioned earlier, it is not so clearly marked inside the French home. But the dividing line, though implicit, exists just the same. 8

Note the difference between explicit dividing lines and implicit dividing lines in French culture.

One can, in fact, determine the degree of intimacy between two people if one knows to which rooms one person has access in the other's house. The unknown person, the stranger, stays at the door. The next step consists in access to the foyer, then to the living room, then to the dining room (and, if need be, to the toilet). Many visitors will never go any further. A child's friends may have access to the room of that child, as well as to the kitchen for something to drink or for a snack, if they are regular guests in the house. The bathroom, which is separate from the toilet, is off-limits and is reserved for those who could be invited to spend the night. The refrigerator, the closets and the drawers are rarely accessible, except to those considered to be true "intimates" of the house. The room that remains sacred is the parents' bedroom. Of course we are talking about a house that has all these rooms, but space is not the significant factor in this context. Rather, it is the way in which this space is opened, or not opened, to all those who are not part of the "immediate" family (comprised of the parents and children). Thus, if my father-in-law or mother-in-law, or even my father or mother, lives under my roof, that does not automatically give him or her access to my bedroom. 9

In French culture, intimacy is interrelated with social access: Where one is allowed to go in a home determines the rapport of that person with the members of the household.

Another anecdote that has great appeal to lay readers, who would be put off by other techniques, scientifically cast, of explaining cultural misunderstandings.

On the contrary. "Well brought up" French people know all this. But one can easily imagine the misunderstandings that can arise when Americans are invited to French homes or when they live (as students) with French families for a period of time.

Similarly, there are misunderstandings in the reverse direction, which may seem surprising given the "relaxed" attitude with which Americans receive guests. A French writer, whose name I will not mention, wrote a book explaining Americans to the French. He enthusiastically tells us that when the lady of the house receives you wearing curlers, it is precisely to make you relax and "feel at home." No problem up to that point. The writer, grateful and admiring, describes the comfort of the room reserved for him, mentions the small touches like letter paper and stamps on the desk. Then the maid (rather a rare character, except in certain social spheres) asks him if he is going to dine with his hosts, and what he would like for dinner. The first evening, he tells us, he goes down to eat with his hosts. Then the second evening, because of the "relaxed" attitude and "kindness" of his hosts, and because he has a great deal of work to do, he decides to eat dinner in his room and "orders a steak and french fries from the maid." 10

If the writer in question actually did this, his hosts undoubtedly respected his wishes. But it is also more than likely that they attributed his request to "the well-known arrogance" of the French, or at least that they were deeply shocked by the "vulgarity" of this French person, whom, nevertheless, they would never think of enlightening as to his "monstrous" blunder. (The two questions he was asked probably mean "Are you planning to go out for dinner?" and "We'll do our best to please you," or something of that nature.) An unfortunate misunderstanding crowns the best of intentions in this case: the writer-character comes off as a boor, whereas it is his enthusiasm for American hospitality (as he understands it) that makes him unknowingly behave in an impolite fashion. 11

Compare Carroll's explanation of how one is "introduced" to an American home with the preceding explanation by the unnamed French writer.

The misunderstanding is easy to comprehend. Indeed, when you are a house guest in an American home, your hosts immediately show you your room, the "bathroom" (which includes the toilet), the place where towels are kept (or where you can get 12 new ones, if there are already some in your room), the kitchen, including everything you need to make a cup of coffee or tea if you wake up in the middle of the night, and, finally, the refrigerator. At the same time, they invite you to "make yourself at home" and to "help yourself to anything you want." It is therefore possible that one's enthusiasm for "so much openness" might leave one with the impression of having all the advantages of a hotel at home, and that this would result in one's taking the invitation not to stand on ceremony literally. It is, in fact, almost impossible, without cultural analysis, to know where the line is drawn, a line which remains completely implicit. All the Americans to whom I told this story were shocked by the blunder, surprised that such a mistake was possible. One need only, however, carry the logic beyond the invisible line to make such an error.

An American student who spent a year living with a French family told me that an uncomfortable situation had developed toward the end of her stay, that there had been a kind of estrangement, for reasons which she did not understand. After she answered all kinds of questions from me, we reconstructed the misunderstanding as follows. At the beginning of her stay, as she did not yet know the family, she spent a good deal of time chatting with the mother and children on returning from school, before going to work in her room. Since she didn't feel quite comfortable yet, she kept the door to her room open. Much later, when she thought that she had become "a member of the family" and really felt at home, she (unconsciously) began acting exactly as she did at home. That is, on returning from school, she simply said hello and went directly to her room to work, automatically closing one door. It was at this point that the family, who must have felt she was rejecting them without understanding why, began to treat her with greater distance, "like a foreigner." Only after our discussion did she realize that what was for her a kind of compliment to the family (they made her feel at home) was on the contrary an insult (undeserved, and therefore all the more baffling) to the family, who had treated her as one of them.

Another student, this time one who lived in a small hotel

13

14

"cultural analysis": Carroll gives her working definition of cultural analysis in the introduction to her book *Cultural Misunderstandings: The French-American Experience,* from which this essay is taken: "Very plainly, I see cultural analysis as a means of perceiving as 'normal' things which initially seem 'bizarre' or 'strange' among people of a culture different from one's own."

In the social sciences, *acceptance-rejection* often denotes a continuum of openness and closedness by a person or group toward experiences, individuals, or groups. Neither of the terms is meaningful alone; where a degree of rejection is noted, a degree of acceptance is implied, and vice versa, except in rare cases.

which had been transformed into a residence for foreign students, told me of an unpleasant experience which she didn't understand. This story, once again, involves a door. One Saturday morning, as neither she nor her roommate had classes, they told the cleaning woman that they would make their beds themselves because they wanted to sleep late. The cleaning woman, according to them, left looking very angry. The following Saturday, in order to assure that they would not be awakened, they put a "do not disturb" sign on the outer doorknob. This in no way stopped the cleaning woman, who knocked and entered. The two young women didn't stop her, because "the only other solution, which is very difficult for Americans, would have been to tell her to leave." What shocked them most of all was that the cleaning woman knocked and entered almost simultaneously, without giving them a chance to answer. What they considered to be an inviolable space, a room with a closed door, was simply invaded, as if by right. The student who told me of this experience summarized the source of the misunderstanding in this way: "In France, people knock on the door to announce that they are entering, whereas in the United States, it is to ask for permission to enter (for which one must wait) or to make certain the room is empty." I myself remember that, after having spent several years in the United States, I was shocked when a new colleague, who had just arrived from France, knocked and "barged into" my office. Everyone else waited for a "come in," including French people who had been living in the United States for a longer period of time.

"inviolable space": Space protected by custom or law from trespass or abuse.

A young American, who was boarding with a family in the sixteenth arrondissement in Paris, began, he says, to "behave like a member of the family" until the day when, to his great disappointment, the mother told him that she had rented him the room for purely economic reasons and not to establish a quasi-familial relationship with him. He could not understand how one could have someone in one's home and at one's table and at the same time treat that person "like a stranger." In an equivalent case in the United States, a family who rents a room to a student gives

15

"arrondissement": An administrative district in Paris and in some other large French cities.

"quasi-familial relationship": The prefix *quasi* is a combining form meaning "resembling" or "having some, but not all, of the features of."

him access to the kitchen ("kitchen privileges") but not to the dining table without a special invitation. A permanent invitation to share the family meals calls for "member of the family" behavior, which undoubtedly explains why the "pension" system does not exist nowadays in most places.

A French student in the United States explained to another French woman, in my presence, that she had moved into a room she liked very much and which an American professor, known for his fine cooking, rented to her. When the woman asked if she ate with the professor's family, the student protested, with both an amused and indignant air, "Oh, no! He made it clear that meals were not part of the deal, and that I shouldn't feel tempted, no matter what kinds of smells emanated from the kitchen. . . . He promised to invite me to dinner. . . . I can't wait." The dividing line had been clearly indicated in this particular case—a rare occurrence. But this clarification did not seem to have prevented the French student from feeling somewhat ruffled, so difficult it is to get used to the assumptions of others. It is all the more difficult for a French person to understand this attitude, since "everyone knows" that Americans invite "people they meet on the street" to dinner, "warmly" open their homes to people they hardly know, easily lend their houses to friends so that friends of their friends, whom they don't know, can use it in their absence. The nonexistence of the boarding system can be explained by the fact that an American will easily put his possessions and himself at your disposal if you are his guest but will not agree to "sell" you his services right inside his home, to give you the rights of a "paying customer" over him and over his freedom. In the French family, everyone usually eats dinner together. The meal must therefore be prepared in any case, and one more person at the table doesn't make much difference. In the American family, on the other hand, it is possible for each family member to eat dinner separately on certain evenings, when it is most convenient for her or him, because schedules are often difficult to coordinate. Having a boarder and owing him or her a meal every day would demand more of the "parents" than the children do themselves.

The next two paragraphs show that what one perceives about the exteriors of the French houses and the American houses is true of their interiors, and by extension, their cultures.

It is now clear that French and American houses differ not only on the exterior. Their differences are in fact reproduced, but less visibly, inside the house. The distinct separation between the inside and the outside in French culture anticipates the barriers to be crossed once inside. Access to different rooms denotes the path toward intimacy, so to speak, and corresponds to the visible/invisible division. What I mean is that the rooms which are "off limits" are closed and hidden from the eyes of those who have not been specifically admitted. By the same token, someone who stands close to a window, perfectly visible from the street, should adopt an "outside" form of behavior, even though he is separated from the outside by the window.   17

On the other hand, the American house is as open to strangers as it is visible from the street. In the evening, lit up on a dark street, it even attracts attention. If this does not seem to bother an American, it is because such openness in no way encroaches on his privacy, which he defines by setting up the barriers of his choice—by closing the door to his room, by surrounding himself by huge lawns or thick trees, by refusing all boarders, or simply by stopping you on your way to a room by saying "I'd rather you didn't see the mess," or "I'll be right back." Fences, walls, and high hedges give him the impression of being closed in and seem to deprive him of the spectacle of the street, the forest, or the beach bordering his house. And he will consider as an invasion of his privacy any intrusion made without his knowledge or against his wishes (electronic surveillance, of course, but also a door opened without waiting for permission, and the like). An American colleague does not enter your office without being invited: he or she remains on the threshold, even if the door is wide open. If your window is near the street, passersby will make it their business "not to see you," and if by chance your gazes meet through the window, they will smile or make a friendly gesture as if to say that they were looking into your house "by accident."   18

Here, Carroll reasons from the physical evidence to its cultural conclusions. In France, the guest

If I take the logic of the preceding analysis to its limit, I obtain two literally inverse situations. In French culture, the person who   19

already knows the spatial limits of the owner's home, which depend on the guest's social relationship to the owner. In America, the owner of the home sets those spatial limits, and they may change from time to time depending on circumstances.

POSSIBLE ANSWERS

Meaning and Purpose

1. Carroll compares and contrasts French and American homes to give evidence supporting the larger perception that the French and Americans are not nearly so culturally alike as ordinary people might assume. By confining her comments to the similarities and differences between how the French and how the Americans deal with things domestic, Carroll connects with her audience: They all can identify with homes, and by extension they can reason that if attitudes differ so greatly among the French and Americans when it comes to the home, then they undoubtedly differ greatly in other ways.
2. Americans, or people from any other culture for that matter, assume that what is culturally presumed acceptable for them must be culturally presumed acceptable for others as well. Therefore, they are surprised at "anomalies." If American houses are not completely protected, then why should French houses be so? Carroll notes in the first paragraph of the essay that the

enters my house is responsible for knowing the rules, for remaining within the spatial limits that our relationship authorizes. (Thus I must be wary of a stranger who would invite me to skip some steps, to penetrate the depths of his house immediately.) I therefore have no defense against guests who feel "at ease" in my home, like Americans who follow me into the kitchen. In American culture, on the other hand, I am the one who is responsible for indicating the limits beyond which a person entering my house must not venture. What is troubling for French people is that these limits can change according to my mood. Here is an example: Tom (American) is putting up the parents of his wife (French), who are vacationing in the United States. On certain evenings, Tom is "charming" and sociable, whereas on others he comes home from work, barely says hello, takes a beer from the refrigerator ("without even offering them one"), sinks into his chair, and reads the paper. In this case, Tom, for personal reasons which, according to American culture, he need not explain, is indicating that he does not want his "space," his privacy, to be invaded. It is very probable that Tom would behave in exactly the same way in the absence of his in-laws, that his desire for solitude has nothing to do with them. But the in-laws, not knowing how to interpret this message, are hurt and do not understand why Tom "has them at his home, only to treat them this way."

As we can see, hardly have we crossed the threshold when the intercultural misunderstandings begin. We can easily imagine that these won't be the last.

20

Meaning and Purpose

1. The author of this essay compares and contrasts French and American homes to comment on a much larger perception. What is the more important perception that is being culturally compared and contrasted in this essay, and why does she confine her comments to homes?

anthropologist who found the French so distrustful had not done research in France. He therefore unconsciously compared what he saw in France with what he knew to be acceptable in America.

3. The French writer had totally misinterpreted the evidence that he had accumulated by being a guest in an American home. Carroll has no reason to ridicule him; instead, she uses his conclusions as part of an anecdote to clarify her own point: Our interpretation of evidence should be based more on cultural analysis than on our own cultural background.

4. The anecdote is especially appropriate because it focuses on the misunderstandings that can result from only one circumstance, whether a door inside a house remains opened or closed. The anecdote illustrates how the French and the Americans can arrive at quite different culturally based conclusions, even from such evidence as a simple decision to leave a door open or to leave a door closed.

5. Paraphrases will differ, of course, but they should show that students know that in French culture, the guest is responsible for knowing how to act, and in American culture, the host is responsible for setting limits for the guest's actions.

Strategy

1. Paragraphs 15 and 16 clearly compare and contrast two related incidents. In both paragraphs, a student from one country was a foreigner rooming in a house in another country. In both paragraphs, an incident occurred that was misinterpreted by the guest and the host. And in both paragraphs, Carroll comments on the incident as further evidence for saying that invisible cultural lines exist both in France and America.

2. The author discusses her husband and her mother to establish her credibility, to show the reader that not only is she herself French and still intimately exposed to French culture, but also she is married to an American and therefore intimately exposed daily to American culture.

2. Why would an American be surprised to see that French houses are completely protected from the "outside world"?
3. In paragraphs 10 and 11, why does the author of this essay refrain from mentioning the name of the French writer who "wrote a book explaining Americans to the French"?
4. The author of this essay has thoroughly researched the differences between American and French customs. Why is the anecdote in paragraph 13 especially appropriate to illustrate one of those differences? What is the difference that the anecdote illustrates?
5. In your own words, paraphrase the contrast in paragraph 19 between how people who enter French houses should act and how people who enter American houses should act.

Strategy

1. Why do paragraphs 15 and 16 belong together?
2. Why is it important that the author discuss her husband and her mother early in this essay?
3. In paragraph 5, what does the term *taken aback* mean? Why is it a good term to describe Pierre's reaction?
4. What is the function of paragraph 7?
5. How would you describe the tone in paragraph 17?

Style

1. To whom does *we* refer, in the final paragraph of the essay? Why does the author use *we* instead of the more formal pronoun *one,* which is often used in scholarly analyses?
2. In paragraph 15, what does the word *arrondissement* mean?
3. Why are lawns personified in the first sentence of paragraph 3? (See *personification* in the Glossary.)
4. What does the phrase *inviolable space* mean, in paragraph 14?

3. The term *taken aback* means "to be startled," and is ordinarily used to describe social bewilderment. Pierre was bewildered at the apparent breach of etiquette that Dick committed by his following Pierre to the study without being directly invited to do so.

4. This one-sentence paragraph (7) concludes the first part of the essay, which compares and contrasts attitudes among two cultures. The next paragraph (8) shows how people of the same culture can be compared and contrasted.

5. The first half of the paragraph (17) has a scientific, objective tone, one which summarizes its preceding information much as an anthropologist would be expected to write, using the formality of the discipline. The sentence that begins with "What I mean is . . ." shifts to a more informal tone, as if the author is trying to explain, using a warmly common vocabulary, what she had just noted in more academic terms.

Style

1. The word *we* refers to both the author and to her audience. She has taken the audience into her confidence, as she shows them by using this pronoun. It is as if she were ending a speech, warmly and directly addressing her audience.

2. The word *arrondissement* has two definitions. It can refer to the largest administrative division of a French department, comprising a number of cantons, or territorial districts. As it is used in this essay, however, it means an administrative district of a large city.

3. Personification is often used to express wry humor. Personifying the lawns is Carroll's way of noting that even American lawns are, well, American in their refusal to function as barriers.

4. An *inviolable space* is any space that is safe from intrusion or transgression, without permission. (The inviolable space mentioned here is not so much legally inviolable as it is culturally "considered to be an inviolable space" by an American girl and her roommate.)

5. The word *ruffled* in this context means to be flustered or disturbed. (The word comes from Middle English *ruffelen,* "to scratch.")

5. In paragraph 16, a French student is described as "feeling somewhat ruffled." What does *ruffled* mean in this context?

Writing Tasks

1. If you have visited a foreign country, compare and contrast some of the customs you observed there with similar customs here. For example, you might want to compare and contrast customs of dating, eating, tipping, drinking, vacations, traveling, clothing, or entertainment.

2. One of your friends may be new to this country or be the child of parents who are from another country. While visiting your friend's home, notice the decorations on the walls, the furniture and its placement, the way you are greeted by your friend's parents, the area around your friend's house, and so forth. Then write a paper comparing and contrasting your friend's house with your house, paying particular attention to the differences that you believe result from your friend's culture or from her or his parents' culture.

3. Carefully reread this essay, paying particular attention to the remarks that Carroll makes about American culture and American homes. Then write a paper comparing and contrasting point by point what the author said about American culture and American homes with what you think about your home and your culture.

This essay extends an analogy, like tentacles, into several allied topics, but the body of the analogy remains clear. Our modern battles are usually no more important, though just as exciting to an objective observer, as the battle of the ants. Students occasionally need reminding that each recent generation has had a war: World War II in the 1940s, the Korean War in the 1950s, the Vietnam War in the late 1960s and early 1970s. What about the 1980s and the new 1990s? For openers, we have Desert Storm.

Thoreau's ants mirror the actions of two peoples at war. Thoreau's ants are fighting for a principle, the author remarks sarcastically. No war, at least according to propaganda, was ever fought except for a principle. But some of the principles are as trivial as that which caused the Trojan War, the kidnaping of one person.

Students like to brainstorm principles. List several words on the chalk board and then discuss whether those words in fact name principles. Truth? Honesty? Art? Ethics? The discussion invariably leads to analogies, for students will use analogies to explain their thinking about each "principle."

MARGINAL NOTES

Thoreau, a legendary master of diction, using words precisely, did not "see" the ants; he "observed" them. The analogy between ants and soldiers becomes obvious in description in sentence 1: the ants are not "fighting"; they are "fiercely contending." This strategy of *personification,* writing about something as if it were human, permeates the essay.

The chips are left over from Thoreau's chopping wood. A *duellum* is a duel; a *bellum* is a war. The "races" of ants remind us that Thoreau's America was militantly divided over slavery, and Thoreau was strongly against it.

❦ Henry David Thoreau ❦

When he was twenty-eight years old, Henry David Thoreau built a cabin in the woods by Walden Pond, Massachusetts, and lived there alone for two years. His best-known book, Walden *(1854), is about that experience. Born in nearby Concord, Massachusetts, in 1817, Thoreau was educated at Harvard University and was influenced by the American essayist, poet, and philosopher Ralph Waldo Emerson, who was also a close friend. Thoreau believed in the citizens' duty to act on their conscience and once spent a night in jail for refusing to pay a poll tax on the grounds that he objected to United States involvement in war with Mexico. In his famed essay, "Civil Disobedience" (1849), he outlines his philosophy of passive resistance and has often been cited in support of the American civil-rights movement.*

The Battle of the Ants

In this extended analogy from Walden, *Thoreau compares a battle between red ants and black ants that he witnessed on his woodpile, to the wars men have waged all through history. While elevating the ants by comparing them to men, Thoreau diminishes the glory of human wars by comparing them to battles among insects.*

By using an analogy that compares ant wars to human wars, Thoreau satirizes the brutality and ultimate futility of war. Take notice of all the various aspects of war making he satirizes.

One day when I went out to my wood-pile, or rather my pile of stumps, I observed two large ants, the one red, the other much larger, nearly half an inch long, and black, fiercely contending with one another. Having once got hold they never let go, but struggled and wrestled and rolled on the chips incessantly. Looking farther, I was surprised to find that the chips were covered with such combatants, that it was not a *duellum,* but a *bellum,* a war between two races of ants, the red always pitted against the black, and frequently two red ants to one black. The legions of

The Myrmidons were ants, changed into warriors by Zeus, supreme deity of the ancient Greeks. They accompanied Achilles to the Trojan War.

The soldier ants "fast locked in each other's embraces" remind students that lovers, not warriors, are usually so described. The next sentence heightens that ironic comparison by moving us from lovers' to warriors' language.

The writer's almost microscopic view of ants in battle alludes to the notion that all wars are petty and that nature itself carries on benignly.

Notice Thoreau's euphemism here, substituting inoffensive words for some that could be distasteful. Contrasts with the brutal reality of "tore off his legs."

A Roman motto, *aut vincere aut mori*, literally "either to conquer or to die," intended to inspire soldiers going into battle.

Notice the personification, the human qualities of the red ant.

The mothers of Sparta, an ancient Greek city-state, told their sons, "Return with your shield or [carried] upon it," literally, "Win or die trying."

Achilles was a Greek hero in the Trojan Wars; Patroclus was his friend slain in those wars. From Homer's *Iliad*.

these Myrmidons covered all the hills and vales in my wood-yard, and the ground was already strewn with the dead and dying, both red and black. It was the only battle which I have ever witnessed, the only battle-field I ever trod while the battle was raging; internecine war; the red republicans on the one hand, and the black imperialists on the other. On every side they were engaged in deadly combat, yet without any noise that I could hear, and human soldiers never fought so resolutely. I watched a couple that were fast locked in each other's embraces, in a little sunny valley amid the chips, now at noonday prepared to fight till the sun went down, or life went out. The smaller red champion had fastened himself like a vise to his adversary's front, and through all the tumblings on that field never for an instant ceased to gnaw at one of his feelers near the root, having already caused the other to go by the board; while the stronger black one dashed him from side to side, and, as I saw on looking nearer, had already divested him of several of his members. They fought with more pertinacity than bulldogs. Neither manifested the least disposition to retreat. It was evident that their battle-cry was "Conquer or die." In the meanwhile there came along a single red ant on the hillside of this valley, evidently full of excitement, who either had dispatched his foe, or had not yet taken part in the battle; probably the latter, for he had lost none of his limbs; whose mother had charged him to return with his shield or upon it. Or perchance he was some Achilles, who had nourished his wrath apart, and had now come to avenge or rescue his Patroclus. He saw this unequal combat from afar—for the blacks were nearly twice the size of the red—he drew near with rapid pace till he stood on his guard within half an inch of the combatants; then, watching his opportunity, he sprang upon the black warrior, and commenced his operations near the root of his right foreleg, leaving the foe to select among his own members; and so there were three united for life, as if a new kind of attraction had been invented which put all other locks and cements to shame. I should not have wondered by this time to find that they had their respective musical bands stationed on some eminent chip, and playing their national airs the while, to excite the slow and cheer

The writer's internal transition, moving the reader from ant wars to human wars, reinforcing the analogy.

Two bloody battles won in the early 1800s by Napoleon's armies.

The Battle of Concord Bridge, 1775, involved few soldiers (including "Davis and Hosmer") but became famous in American history.

A reference to the Boston Tea Party, December 16, 1773, when the colonists defied the English crown. The British won the battle of Bunker Hill, fought in June 1775, but suffered enormous casualties. Notice how this battle compares with those won with great loss of men by Napoleon's armies.

Notice the calm, objective curiosity here, contrasted with the furious life-and-death battle being studied. The description that follows depicts graphically and minutely the thirty-minute struggle.

A home for old soldiers, in Paris, and the actual tomb of Napoleon I, as well.

the dying combatants. I was myself excited somewhat even as if they had been men. The more you think of it, the less the difference. And certainly there is not the fight recorded in Concord history, at least, if in the history of America, that will bear a moment's comparison with this, whether for the numbers engaged in it, or for the patriotism and heroism displayed. For numbers and for carnage it was an Austerlitz or Dresden. Concord Fight! Two killed on the patriots' side, and Luther Blanchard wounded! Why here every ant was a Buttrick—"Fire! for God's sake fire!"— and thousands shared the fate of Davis and Hosmer. There was not one hireling there. I have no doubt that it was a principle they fought for, as much as our ancestors, and not to avoid a three-penny tax on their tea; and the results of this battle will be as important and memorable to those whom it concerns as those of the battle of Bunker Hill, at least.

I took up the chip on which the three I have particularly described were struggling, carried it into my house, and placed it under a tumbler on my window-sill, in order to see the issue. Holding a microscope to the first-mentioned red ant, I saw that, though he was assiduously gnawing at the near foreleg of his enemy, having severed his remaining feeler, his own breast was all torn away, exposing what vitals he had there to the jaws of the black warrior, whose breastplate was apparently too thick for him to pierce; and the dark carbuncles of the sufferer's eyes shone with ferocity such as war only could excite. They struggled half an hour longer under the tumbler, and when I looked again the black soldier had severed the heads of his foes from their bodies, and the still living heads were hanging on either side of him like ghastly trophies at his saddle-bow, still apparently as firmly fastened as ever, and he was endeavoring with feeble struggles, being without feelers, and with only the remnant of a leg, and I know not how many other wounds, to divest himself of them, which at length, after half an hour more, he accomplished. I raised the glass, and he went off over the window-sill in that crippled state. Whether he finally survived that combat, and spent the remainder of his days in some Hôtel des Invalides, I do not know; but I thought that his industry would not be worth much thereafter. I never learned which party was victorious, nor the cause of the war, but I felt for the rest of that day as if I had my feelings excited and harrowed by witnessing the struggle, the ferocity and carnage, of a human battle before my door.

Kirby and Spence tell us that the battles of ants have long been celebrated and the date of them recorded, though they say that Huber is the only modern author who appears to have witnessed them. "Aeneas Sylvius," say they, "after giving a very circumstantial account of one contested with great obstinacy by a great and small species on the trunk of a pear tree," adds that " 'this action was fought in the pontificate of Eugenius the Fourth, in the presence of Nicholas Pistoriensis, an eminent lawyer, who related the whole history of the battle with the greatest fidelity.' A similar engagement between great and small ants is recorded by Olaus Magnus, in which the small ones, being victorious, are said to have buried the bodies of their own soldiers, but left those of their giant enemies a prey to the birds. This event happened previous to the expulsion of the tyrant Christian the Second from Sweden." The battle which I witnessed took place in the Presidency of Polk, five years before the passage of Webster's Fugitive-Slave Bill.

Kirby, Spence, and Huber were three leading specialists in the study of insects.

(1383–1447) Pope from 1431 to 1447.

(1490–1558) Swedish Roman Catholic ecclesiastic and historian who wrote a Swedish history that was long accepted in Europe as authoritative.

(1481–1559) called "The Cruel." King of Denmark and Norway, 1513–1523. Showed extreme cruelty against the Swedes, massacring their nobility (1520). Imprisoned for life in 1532.

James Knox Polk (1795–1849) was eleventh president of the United States (1845–1849). Thoreau published his first book, *A Week on the Concord and Merrimac Rivers*, in 1849.

The Fugitive-Slave Bill required that slaves who escaped to the North be captured and returned to their owners in the South.

POSSIBLE ANSWERS

Meaning and Purpose

1. Encourage students to explore first their personal responses to Thoreau's essay. Ask them to be specific in connecting their responses to statements or ideas in the essay.

2. Thoreau considered war a far from noble pursuit, beneath human dignity, to be fought by ants if fought at all. This extended analogy between ants and soldiers is evidence of this opinion, as are his numerous and satiric examples of wars fought throughout history.

3. Thoreau buries his thesis statements well into the first paragraph: "I was myself excited somewhat even as if they had been men. The more you think of it, the less the difference." The next sentence might also be considered part of his main point.

Meaning and Purpose

1. Have you ever stopped to observe and perhaps become fascinated by small things in nature? Explain. What in Thoreau's essay reminds you of your own experience?

2. What was Thoreau's opinion of war? Use evidence from the essay for your answer.

3. Can you find a statement or statements of Thoreau's main point, or thesis?

4. Thoreau mentions Greek heroes, great historical battles, a pope, and a president of the United States. What is his purpose in these widely different references?

4. Thoreau's commentary is timeless. With mockery, he raises the battle of the ants to such "heights" as comparing it to an ancient Greek war and a patriotic American war. Of course, he is mocking our seeing wars as glorious, serving his purpose (satire), and extending his analogy.

5. Thoreau wrote mostly for an educated male readership. Most who could then read were well-educated men, many holding authority in government or church. Thoreau used this essay to mock the very thing most learned men admired, and to point out to them the folly in their thinking.

6. Thoreau extends the analogy through history by showing that such battles have been noteworthy for centuries. With great mocking, Thoreau raises the battle of the ants to the level of recorded human history and compares it to other ant battles celebrated in writing. He ends the extended analogy by poking fun at academic historians, whose style he mocks here.

Strategy

1. Ants and men in this essay share cruelty, tenacity, courage, bravery, and other qualities associated with combat.

2. The comparison is between soldiers and ants. He has been personifying ants and talking about them as if they were men. He realizes that he is as excited as if they were human and that the ant–human differences are less than he thought. Of course Thoreau is making fun here.

3. The analogy is between a wounded ant and a wounded soldier who spends his days in a home for old soldiers, trying to keep the glory of the war alive. Of course, the analogy is factually weak, but it is ironic.

4. Satire is a literary technique or style that combines humor and wit with a critical attitude for the purpose of improving human institutions or actions. The satirist pokes fun not so much to tear down as to inspire remodeling of the subject being satirized. Jonathan Swift's famous "A Modest Proposal" is a good example of satire to place alongside Thoreau's essay.

5. Think of the time in which Thoreau lived. What audience do you think he is addressing?
6. Although the last paragraph in the essay seems to drift into other topics, in fact, it serves an important purpose. What is that purpose?

Strategy

1. The body of this essay is an extended analogy that parallels some activities of ants and men. What are two qualities that ants and men share in this essay? Give examples from specific sentences.
2. Midway through the first paragraph, Thoreau says, "The more you think of it, the less the difference." What is he comparing? What "difference" is he talking about?
3. Toward the end of paragraph 2, Thoreau wonders whether a crippled ant survived to spend the rest of his days "in some Hôtel des Invalides." What is the analogy here?
4. Thoreau makes generous use of satire as a strategy in his analogy. What is satire and how is it effective here?
5. Overall, how effective do you judge Thoreau's extended analogy is in comparing human battles with those of ants? Without this analogy, how might Thoreau have talked about the folly of war, and do you think his message would have been as forceful?

Style

1. Early in the essay, Thoreau says that he witnessed an "internecine war." Define that kind of war.
2. The first paragraph in the essay includes "Concord Fight!" and "Two killed on the patriots' side, and Luther Blanchard wounded!" Where do these kinds of exclamations often appear? Who might Luther Blanchard be?
3. The second paragraph in the essay includes this description: "the dark carbuncles of the sufferer's eyes shone with ferocity such

5. Students should evaluate Thoreau's use of satire on his subject. Without the analogy's mockery, Thoreau might have written a more formal, pedantic, or sermonlike treatise on war and principles and how thinly they disguise petty human squabbles. Such a hypothetical essay probably would have been boring by comparison, not as attention-getting, amusing, or successful in making his points.

Style

1. An internecine war is mutually destructive, full of slaughter, with enormous casualties on both sides. It is a "no-win" war.
2. These kinds of exclamations appear in newspaper headlines. Luther Blanchard, in the headline's context, is an American who fought at Concord.
3. This could have been a factual description of a man-soldier, but not an ant-soldier. Ants do not have the eyes described here, or the kind of body that permits a carbuncle. By analogy, however, it is a realistic description imaginatively comparing ant with man.
4. *Pertinacity* means "the quality of holding firmly to a belief or purpose," and "the quality of being hard to get rid of, physically." The first meaning compares ants with men, the second with bulldogs.

as war only could excite." Is this description realistic, or is it factual? Support your answer with your own opinions.
4. Thoreau says that the soldier-ants "fought with more pertinacity than bulldogs." Look up *pertinacity*. The word has at least two meanings. Which meaning compares ants with men? Which meaning compares ants with bulldogs?

Writing Tasks

1. In the essay, Thoreau says, "I have no doubt that it was a principle they fought for, as much as our ancestors. . . ." Can you think of a principle many people believe in that you feel is not worth fighting or working for? Write an essay in which you use an analogy and compare that principle to something familiar to readers in order to show why it is not worth the struggle.
2. There are other analogies for war besides the battle of the ants. Finish the statement "War is like . . . ," listing three things to compare war to. Write a few paragraphs of analogy for each comparison you choose.

❧ Responding to Photographs ❧
Comparison and Contrast

The New Warriors

For general purposes, think of photography as having two main uses: to record private experiences and to record public experiences. A photograph of private experience—a snapshot of a family outing, a portrait of a father, a candid photo of a child—is appreciated within a private context by those who have some direct connection with the recorded event or person.

A photograph that records public experience usually has nothing directly to do with us, its viewers, but nevertheless we bring meaning to it based on our experiences.

Both private and public photographs can evoke infinite associations from the viewer's own experience. But most public photographs have a second dimension. They create social or political associations that many people share. Often they suggest discontinuity in our common social experience. As an organizing principle, photographers create discontinuity through juxtaposition—that is, they oppose contrasting elements in their photographs.

Select one of the following writing assignments to explore the use of contrasting elements in photographs. Before you begin, reread "Comparison and Contrast: Presenting Similarities and Differences" at the beginning of this chapter to review strategies for developing contrasts.

1. "The New Warriors" is a public photograph that ironically explores the ideas on which the United States is predicated. By referring to details in "The New Warriors," examine its contrasting elements and determine what social or political message it embodies. Remember you must select details from the photograph to support your contention, presenting them to readers as if they have not seen the image.

2. Select a private photograph from your or your family's collection. Be sure to find one that embodies contrasting elements. In a brief essay, examine the contrasting elements in the photograph. Keep in mind that since your readers have not been part of your family history, you must supply background information to create a context for the photograph.

❦ Additional Writing Tasks ❦

Comparison and Contrast

1. Using comparison and contrast as the dominant pattern, write an essay on one of these tasks or one you compose for yourself. Keep in mind that you may modify any of the tasks to fit your interests.

    a. At the library find two advertisements for the same product, one published in the 1950s and one published within the last year. Write an essay presenting the similarities and differences in these advertisements.

    b. Select two fairy tales that have similar patterns and characters, such as children journeying into a forest, an encounter with death, the appearance of a mysterious creature, a magical transformation. Identify at least three significant elements the tales have in common and three significant elements that are different. Write an essay comparing and contrasting the similarities and differences in these two tales.

    c. Collect several advertisements for two brands of the same product type that direct their advertising campaigns toward men and women, such as Marlboro cigarettes (men) and Virginia Slims (women). After examining the advertisements, write an essay comparing and contrasting how these advertisements appeal to male consumers and how they appeal to female consumers.

    d. Accurately and fairly, compare and contrast the arguments on both sides of a controversial issue, such as abortion, capital punishment, pornography, or gun control.

    e. Most people hold important social or political beliefs that are opposed by people close to them. Select a belief you hold and in an essay contrast your attitude to the opposing attitude of one of your parents, a brother, a sister, or a close friend.

    f. Select two classes you have attended, two jobs you have held, or two vacations you have taken. Write a comparison-and-contrast essay discussing the similarities and differences of your subjects.

g. Compare and contrast a past experience with a current experience. You might compare how you once viewed a holiday, such as Thanksgiving, Christmas, or Chanukah, with your view of it today. Or you might compare how you once viewed a special place, such as a vacation site, a fun zone, or even your bedroom, with your current view.

h. Compare and contrast how two people from different cultures, economic situations, or age groups might perceive the same experience.

i. Select two public figures with opposing views on one controversial issue. After familiarizing yourself with their positions, write an essay contrasting their attitudes.

j. Select two campus groups that hold opposing social values. In an essay, compare and contrast their views and behavior.

2. Write an essay with comparison and contrast as the dominant pattern on one of these general subjects or on a subject of your own choice. By the end of your essay, the reader should know why you prefer one thing to the other.

a. two people who embrace different life-styles
b. a national news program and a local news program
c. two methods for losing weight
d. female and male consumers
e. children's games yesterday and today
f. two characters from film or fiction
g. a film created from a novel
h. watching a movie on television and watching it in the cinema
i. coverage of a news event by television and by a newspaper
j. two classic films: horror, western, mystery, or romance

3. Read this quotation from social critic Morton Hunt:

> The record of man's inhumanity to man is horrifying, when one compiles it—enslavement, castration, torture, rape, mass slaughter in war after war. But who has compiled the record of man's kindness to man—the trillions of acts of gentleness and goodness, the helping hands, smiles, shared meals, kisses, gifts, healings, rescues? If we were no more than murderous predators, with a freakish lack of inhibition against slaughtering our own species, we would

have been at a terrible competitive disadvantage compared with other animals; if this were the central truth of our nature, we would scarcely have survived, multiplied and become the dominant species on earth. Man does have an aggressive instinct, but it is not naturally or inevitably directed to killing his own kind. He is a beast and perhaps at times the cruelest beast of all—but sometimes he is also the kindest beast of all. He is not all good and not perfectible, but he is not all bad and not wholly unchangeable or unimprovable. That is the only basis on which one can hope for him; but it is enough.

Hunt stresses humanity's dual nature. Write an essay with comparison and contrast as the dominant pattern that makes Hunt's general observation specific.

7

Cause and Effect

Identifying Reasons and Results

The Method

When you explain why something happened or the consequences of that happening, you are engaged in an intellectual activity that seems to be at the core of human curiosity—that is, the search for **causes and effects.**

In their simplest form cause-and-effect relationships appear as a series of escalating events, one triggering another like a chain reaction. Consider the children's song in which a woman swallows a fly. The lively fly causes her to swallow a spider to catch the fly. She then swallows a bird to catch the spider; then a cat to catch the bird; then a dog to catch the cat; then a goat; then a cow; and finally, a horse. The effect? She dies, of course.

In a more complex form, cause and effect is often at work in thrillers and mysteries. A wealthy politician falls dead during a banquet. He had been in excellent health. There seems to be no clear cause of death. Could he have been murdered in some mysterious way? The question triggers the appearance of a supersleuth who begins the investigation. The detective discovers clues, each of which reveals a new suspect. After an exhaustive exploration of the many reasons suspects had for wanting the victim dead, the murderer is unmasked, the mysterious murder method explained, and the dark reasons for the murder revealed.

Of course, mystery fans aren't consciously seeking cause or effect patterns. They're probably trying to beat the writer at his or her own game by figuring out "Whodunit?" before the final scene. But that question is not much different from, What caused it?

If you think of causes as **reasons** and effects as **results**, you might better understand cause-and-effect patterns. Like a detective you can begin with questions: Why did something happen? What are the consequences of something's happening? When you answer the Why, you are giving reasons; that is, causes. When you answer the What, you are giving results; that is, effects. Professional writers observe this distinction when exploring the causes or effects behind any event. Generally, the distinction keeps them on the track.

Consider this question: "Why did the women's liberation movement bloom in the 1960s?" The question would lead a writer to seek reasons—that is, causes.

But the question, "What were the consequences of the women's liberation movement on college campuses during the 1970s?" would lead a writer to seek results—that is, effects.

And the compound question, "Why did the women's liberation movement falter in the 1980s, and what will be the consequences in the 1990s?" would lead a writer to explain the reasons and the results—that is, both causes and effects.

Strategies

When you begin analyzing the cause or effect relationships in a complex subject, you may feel somewhat like a detective unraveling a mystery. You must be prepared for the false starts and deceptive clues that will send you down the wrong path, but don't lose heart: you can learn by studying professional writers, who often approach cause-and-effect analysis from several angles, depending on the characteristics of their subjects. First, they may narrow their effort by concentrating only on the causes. Second, they may concentrate only on the effects. And third, they may choose to concentrate on both causes and effects. If you understand cause-and-effect development patterns and apply your knowledge critically as you read, you'll soon master the technique of analyzing cause-and-effect relationships in your own writing.

Identifying Causes

When effects are clear, writers will concentrate on causes. In 1948, Harry Truman upset Thomas Dewey, Governor of New York, for the presidency. Dewey was predicted to win by a landslide. In fact, one newspaper prematurely printed headlines announcing Dewey's victory. The political pundits were wrong: Truman won. A writer who asked, "Why did Truman win?" would not have to establish the result (Truman's victory), but he or she would concentrate on the reasons—that is, the causes—behind Truman's victory. Did his "underdog" image generate sympathy among voters? Did a last-minute whistlestop campaign through America's heartland swing the election his way? Was it a well-oiled Democratic machine that kept the party faithful in line? These and other causes would have to be explored in any analysis of the election.

In *Redoing America,* Robert Faltermayer discusses the interwoven character of American cities. In the following paragraph, Faltermayer concentrates on causes. He opens with the common assumption that the automobile has had a destructive effect on the "close-knit fabric" of cities. He then presents the reasons for this phenomenon:

> The close knit fabric was blown apart by the automobile, and by the postwar middle-class exodus to suburbia which the mass-ownership of automobiles made possible. The automobile itself was not to blame for this development, nor was the desire for suburban living, which is obviously a genuine aspiration of many Americans. The fault lay in our failure, right up to the present time, to fashion new policies to minimize the disruptive effects of the automobile revolution. We have failed not only to tame the automobile itself, but to overhaul a property-tax system that tends to foster automotive-age sprawl and to institute coordinated planning in the politically fragmented suburbs that have caught the brunt of the postwar building boom.

In the opening sentence Faltermayer establishes a relationship between automobiles and the changing character of cities and sprawling suburbs. In the next sentence he refines his focus by dismissing two possible causes, the automobile itself and the desire for suburban living. In the remainder of the paragraph he explains what he believes to be the true cause, the failure to fashion public policies that would have controlled the automobile and the building boom.

Identifying Effects

When writers select subjects with very clear causes, they will then concentrate on effects. For instance, drug merchants are expanding their operations into rural communities. Crack houses are springing up in small towns where drugs had previously been scarce. This fact has been substantiated by law-enforcement agencies across the nation. A writer who asked, "What are the consequences of increased drug use in rural communities?" would spend very little time establishing the existence of increased drug activity in small-town America because it is widely known. He or she would, however, concentrate on the effects this trend might have on rural communities. What, for instance, are the consequences for families? What will be the effects on undertrained and underbudgeted law-enforcement agencies, on social services, and on schools?

In this paragraph from *Anatomy of an Illness,* Norman Cousins uses this pattern. He quickly establishes the cause, a hypothetical injury, and then concentrates on exploring effects of pain suppressants on injured professional athletes.

Professional athletes are sometimes severely disadvantaged by trainers whose job it is to keep them in action. The more famous the athlete, the greater the risk that he or she may be subjected to extreme medical measures when injury strikes. The star baseball pitcher whose arm is sore because of a torn muscle or tissue damage may need sustained rest more than anything else. But this team is battling for a place in the World Series; so the trainer or team doctor, called upon to work his magic, reaches for a strong dose of butazolidine or other powerful pain suppressants. Presto, the pain disappears! The pitcher takes his place on the mound and does superbly. That could be the last game, however, in which he is able to throw the ball with full strength. The drugs didn't repair the torn muscle or cause the damaged tissue to heal. What they did was to mask the pain, enabling the pitcher to throw hard, further damaging the torn muscle. Little wonder that so many star athletes are cut down in their prime, more the victims of overzealous treatment of their injuries than of the injuries themselves.

Cousins opens by establishing the direction the paragraph will take. He then states the cause of the effects that will follow—a hypothetical injury to a star baseball pitcher's throwing arm. Next, he develops the effects of the injury—under pressure to win, a trainer or team doctor prescribes a pain killer; the pitcher plays as if he had no injury; and the ultimate effect, a career cut short, not by injury but by the mistreatment of injury.

Identifying Causes and Effects

Writers are always cautious about assuming that readers know the causes or effects of an event, especially when exploring a complex subject that is not part of common knowledge. When such a subject is discussed, they usually explain both causes and effects. Often they will alternate causes and effects in one paragraph.

Victor C. Cline uses this pattern in a paragraph from "How TV Violence Damages Your Children."

Much of the research that has led to the conclusion that TV and movie violence could cause aggressive behavior in some children has stemmed from the work in the area of imitative learning or modeling which, reduced to its simplest expression, might be termed "monkey see, monkey do." Research by Stanford psychologist Albert Bandura has shown that even brief exposure to novel aggressive behavior on a *one-time basis* can be repeated in free play by as high as 88 percent of the young chidren seeing it on TV. Dr. Bandura also demonstrated that even a single viewing of a novel aggressive act could be recalled and produced by children six months later, without any intervening exposure. Earlier studies have estimated that the average child between the ages of 5 and 15 will witness, during this 10-year period, the violent destruction of more than 13,400 fellow humans. This means that through several hours of TV-watching, a child may see more violence than the average adult experiences in a lifetime. Killing is as common as taking a walk, a gun more natural than an umbrella. Children are thus taught to take pride in force and violence and to feel ashamed of ordinary sympathy.

Cline's first sentence establishes that children learn aggressive behavior from television through modeling, or, as Cline phrases it, "monkey see, monkey do." In the second sentence he presents his first cause and first effect—even *brief exposure* to aggressive behavior (cause) can lead to children's repeating it in free play (effect). In the third sentence, he presents the second cause and its effect—a *single viewing* of an aggressive act (cause) can be recalled by children six months later (effect). The next three sentences detail the violence a typical child might see over ten years, thus establishing a very dramatic cause. In his final sentence, Cline states the ultimate effect: television teaches children to take pride in violence and to be ashamed of sympathy.

Rather than alternate causes and effects in individual paragraphs, writers will sometimes divide them into separate paragraphs. The following two paragraphs are from Frank Trippett's humorous essay, "The Great American Cooling Machine." In the first paragraph, Trippett establishes that air conditioning has been overlooked as a major cause for change in American society. In the second paragraph he presents three effects of air conditioning on society.

Neither scholars nor pop sociologists have really got around to charting and diagnosing all the changes brought about by air conditioning. Professional observers have for years been preoccupied with the social implications of the automobile and television. Mere glancing analysis suggests that the car and TV, in their most decisive influences on

American habits, have been powerfully aided and abetted by air conditioning. The car may have created all those shopping centers in the boondocks, but only air conditioning has made them attractive to mass clienteles. Similarly, the artificial cooling of the living room undoubtedly helped turn the typical American into a year-round TV addict. Without air conditioning, how many viewers would endure re-runs (or even Johnny Carson) on one of those pestilential summer nights that used to send people out to collapse on the lawn or to sleep on the roof?

Many of the side effects of air conditioning are far from being fully pinned down. It is a reasonable suspicion, though, that controlled climate, by inducing Congress to stay in Washington longer than it used to during the swelter season, thus presumably passing more laws, has contributed to bloated government. One can only speculate that the advent of the supercooled bedroom may be linked to the carnal adventurism associated with the mid-century sexual revolution. Surely it is a fact—if restaurant complaints about raised thermostats are to be believed—that air conditioning induces at least expense-account diners to eat and drink more; if so, it must be credited with adding to the national fat problem.

Identifying Immediate and Ultimate Causes

Careful writers usually distinguish between immediate and ultimate causes; that is, those which are most apparent and those which underlie them. In the example above, Trippett, in his humorous way, presents the ultimate effects of air conditioning: bloated government, the sexual revolution, and the national fat problem. The depth to which a writer analyzes causes or effects depends upon the subject and the purpose. Exploring the ultimate causes or effects requires more effort than getting to the immediate ones because a writer must establish a foundation for the analysis.

In *The Seasons of a Man's Life,* Daniel J. Levenson studies the psychological development of men. In these two paragraphs, after establishing a solid foundation for his conclusions, he presents the ultimate effects of middle age on a man's relationships with young adults.

> At around 40 a man is deeply involved in the Young/Old polarity. This developmental process has a powerful effect upon his relationships with his offspring and with young adults generally. When his own aging weighs heavily upon him, their exuberant vitality is more likely to arouse his envy and resentment than his delight and forbearance. He may be preoccupied with grievances against his own parents for damage, real or imagined, that they have inflicted upon him at different ages. These preoccupations make him less appreciative of the (often similar) grievances his offspring direct toward him.
>
> If he feels he has lost or betrayed his own early Dream, he may find it hard to give his wholehearted support and blessing to the Dreams of young adults. When his offspring show signs of failure or confusion in pursuing their adult goals, he is afraid that their lives will turn out as badly as his own. Yet, when they do well, he may resent their success. Anxiety and guilt may undermine his efforts to be helpful and lead him instead to be nagging and vindictive.

Levenson's analysis probes deeply into the nagging relationship some middle-aged men might have with young adults. He exposes the ultimate cause and its effects—anxiety over aging, failure, and competition.

In this paragraph from *The Faces of the Enemy*, Sam Keen explores the ultimate cause of war, not the politicians who start wars or the generals who carry them out, but the "good people" who allow their leaders to act out community neuroses by waging war.

> The major responsibility for war lies not with villains and evil men but with reasonably good citizens. Any depth understanding of the social function of war leads to the conclusion that it was the "good" Germans who created the

social ecology that nurtured the Nazis. Lincoln said, "War is much too important to be left to the generals." But the psychological truth is much more disturbing. The generals are the (largely unconscious) agents of a (largely unconscious) civilian population. The good people send out armies as symbolic representatives to act out their repressed shadows, denied hostilities, unspoken cruelties, unacceptable greed, unimagined lust for revenge against punitive parents and authorities, uncivil sexual sadism, denied animality, in a purifying blood ritual that confirms their claim to goodness before the approving eyes of history or God. Warfare is the political equivalent of the individual process of seeking "vindictive triumph," which Karen Horney described as the essence of neurosis.

Writers keep two cautions in mind when exploring cause-and-effect relationships; be aware of them. First, writers avoid confusing process patterns with cause-and-effect patterns. The analysis of a process usually stems from a question of How? not Why? or What? *How* did Ronald Reagan get elected to the presidency? sends a writer into process analysis. *Why* was Ronald Reagan elected to the presidency? sends a writer into an examination of the causes—that is, the reasons. *What* were the consequences of Ronald Reagan's presidency? sends a writer to examine the effects—that is, the results.

Second, they avoid the *post hoc, ergo propter hoc* fallacy; that is, "after this, therefore because of this" or "false-cause," fallacy. Writers commit this fallacy (argument from a false inference) by jumping to conclusions based on insufficient information. That former president Ronald Reagan was elected when the electorate's average life expectancy was increasing does not mean an older voting population will elect older presidents.

In a variation of the false-cause fallacy, an event is identified as triggering a series of events in a cause-and-effect chain reaction, or *causal chain*. This kind of reasoning was at work in the arguments of politicians who supported the United States military action in Vietnam during the 1960s and 1970s. They maintained that if North Vietnam was successful in its efforts to take over South Vietnam, then the nearby Southeast Asian countries would soon be taken over by Communist regimes one at a time, like a file of falling dominoes triggered by the first domino toppling into the second. History, of course, has shown that these events did not happen. But keep in mind that causes of complicated events are seldom simple or obvious, and that predicting the future with cause-and-effect reasoning is a chancy business.

Cause and Effect in College Writing

Essays exploring causes or effects are common assignments in academic writing. In history you might be asked to discuss the causes of racial discrimination following the Civil War. In economics you might be asked to explain the international effects of the massive United States budget deficit. In psychology you might be asked to discuss the causes of clinical depression and its effects on personality. When responding to a cause-and-effect question, decide if you need to explore both causes and effects, or simply causes *or* effects. Also be sure to select the most important causes or effects to emphasize; weigh them carefully to avoid becoming mired in the obvious and trivial.

The next paragraphs are part of a student essay responding to an assignment in mass communications: Discuss the influence of television on politics. The writer, Nancy Pringle, decided to concentrate on the influence of television and related technology in totalitarian countries, specifically the Communist-controlled East European countries that gained independence during 1989. These three paragraphs begin her essay.

Pringle's opening announces cause and effect. Both Orwell and Huxley are pertinent to

George Orwell's <u>1984</u> and Aldous Huxley's <u>Brave New World</u>, both anti-utopian novels, warn of the effect communication technology might have on society. Orwell

her point: they repre-
sent general views
of the ways in which
governments might
use television to control
their people.

warns that governments might use it to control society by inflicting pain; Huxley warns that governments might use it to control society by stimulating pleasure. The ultimate effect would be the same: Dictators would stay in power by controlling history's most powerful medium—television. Recent events, however, seem to prove both authors wrong. Television and related technology, rather than being a tool of repression, seems to be a tool of liberation.

She presents the effect
of television entertain-
ment and news: they
provided information
and stimulated
discontent.

In Europe's communist-bloc countries, television fueled the 1989 desire for liberty. Although Communist governments controlled their own broadcast systems, their citizens still had access to western entertainment programs and films. These programs indirectly showed that West Europeans had more freedom and were more affluent than East Europeans, all of which inspired discontent. Moreover, many Soviet-bloc countries saw news broadcasts that spilled over from neighboring countries. East Berliners would watch West German news broadcasts. Communist-controlled Hungarians watched Austrian news broadcasts. People throughout the Soviet Union, East Germany, and Czechoslovakia watched liberalized Polish news broadcasts. Nightly reports of political victories against Communist governments filled the airwaves. Soon a domino effect began: victories in Poland inspired Hungarians, Hungarian victories inspired East Germans, and the East Germans inspired the Czechoslovaks.

Here she presents a
series of causes and
effects.

Pringle shifts to related
technology—video cam-
eras and playback sys-
tems—presenting their
effects.

Inexpensive video cameras and playback systems also dramatically affected liberation politics. Solidarity, the workers union that spearheaded the Polish revolution, spread its message with crude "homemovies" reproduced by the thousands and played in homes throughout Poland. The message was quite simple—there is an alternative to Communist-party rule—and had the effect of keeping the freedom movement alive. In Czechoslovakia, when the government-controlled television stations suppressed reports of uprisings put down by government troops, students used video cameras to film the events, copied the cassettes, and distributed them throughout the country, thus revealing to an entire nation the secret actions of its repressive government.

In the first sentence, Pringle indicates that she will be seeking effects. Clearly the cause, the reason for the discussion—television and related technology—is pervasive in the West, and so she does not need to establish its existence. Then, referring to the works of two internationally known novelists, she points out that television's influence might not be what many people expected. In the second paragraph, she concentrates on the specific effects: television stimulated the desire for liberty in Soviet-bloc countries by showing that westerners had more freedom and wealth and by reporting the gains made in other Communist-controlled countries, thus creating a domino effect. In the third paragraph, Pringle turns to the effects of video cameras and playback systems. Their use kept an alternative point of view alive in Poland and captured events the government wanted to suppress in Czechoslovakia. Throughout the passage Pringle keeps her eye on the task by effectively discussing the effects of television on totalitarian governments.

TEACHING SUGGESTIONS

One way to introduce students to the ideas of this essay is to ask, "What responsibilities go with material wealth?" The answers will be mixed, many students saying that materially wealthy people should care for the homeless and the hungry, others saying that the affluent have few responsibilities beyond caring for themselves and their own families. The follow-up question is, "Does material wealth cause a restriction of one's freedom?" Usually, students reply, "No," almost in unison.

But wait! Many materially wealthy people must wear specific kinds of clothing; otherwise, they will risk being outcasts from their own society. How about cars? Don't materially wealthy people have to drive expected makes and models? What about friends? Can materially wealthy people afford to have poor friends? What about bodyguards? Security gates? Special places in which to live?

After students see that one effect of material wealth is lack of social freedom, they are better able to grasp the points made in Forster's essay.

MARGINAL NOTES

The British have been in India since 1600. India became independent in 1947, after many years of strife. Forster's *A Passage to India* chronicles life among the British in India before its independence. Mention the British and American English differences: Many American dialects have "woods" for *wood,* and Americans spell *cheque* "check." Notice the simple cause-and-effect statement in the first paragraph. Forster's check allows him to buy the wood. The interjection "blast it" is Forster's momentary opinion of the public footpath in his wood. The paragraph's last sentence introduces the psychological cause-and-effect topic of the essay.

❦ E. M. Forster ❦

Edward Morgan Forster was born in London in 1879 and attended King's College, Cambridge, where he studied classics and history and developed a strong interest in foreign cultures. From a family of bankers, he had no interest in business, and after finishing his education traveled to India, Greece, and Italy. He later settled in London to pursue a career as a writer. His travels in India (in 1912 and again in 1921) inspired his best-known novel, A Passage to India (1924). His other books include the novels, A Room with a View (1908) and Howard's End (1910), two collections of essays, and a collection of short stories. Forster died in 1970.

My Wood

This selection is from Forster's Abinger Harvest *(1936), a collection of essays. He opens with a reference to his novel* A Passage to India, *and uses his experience in buying a piece of land to examine the effects of property ownership. He distinguishes between the unavoidable materialism of "life on earth" and the problematic desire for ownership.*

We usually associate wealth with freedom. In reading this essay, be alert to the ways Forster turns the common perception around to show how property ownership actually restricts freedom.

A few years ago I wrote a book which dealt in part with the difficulties of the English in India. Feeling that they would have had no difficulties in India themselves, the Americans read the book freely. The more they read it the better it made them feel, and a cheque to the author was the result. I bought a wood with the cheque. It is not a large wood—it contains scarcely any trees, and it is intersected, blast it, by a public footpath. Still, it is the first property that I have owned, so it is right that other people should participate in my shame, and should ask themselves, in accents that will vary in horror, this very important question:

322

What is the effect of property upon the character? Don't let's touch economics; the effect of private ownership upon the community as a whole is another question—a more important question, perhaps, but another one. Let's keep to psychology. If you own things, what's their effect on you? What's the effect on me of my wood?

In the first place, it makes me feel heavy. Property does have this effect. Property produces men of weight, and it was a man of weight who failed to get into the Kingdom of Heaven. He was not wicked, that unfortunate millionaire in the parable, he was only stout; he stuck out in front, not to mention behind, and as he wedged himself this way and that in the crystalline entrance and bruised his well-fed flanks, he saw beneath him a comparatively slim camel passing through the eye of a needle and being woven into the robe of God. The Gospels all through couple stoutness and slowness. They point out what is perfectly obvious, yet seldom realized: that if you have a lot of things you cannot move about a lot, that furniture requires dusting, dusters require servants, servants require insurance stamps, and the whole tangle of them makes you think twice before you accept an invitation to dinner or go for a bathe in the Jordan. Sometimes the Gospels proceed further and say with Tolstoy that property is sinful; they approach the difficult ground of asceticism here, where I cannot follow them. But as to the immediate effects of property on people, they just show straightforward logic. It produces men of weight. Men of weight cannot, by definition, move like the lightning from the East unto the West, and the ascent of a fourteen-stone bishop into a pulpit is thus the exact antithesis of the coming of the Son of Man. My wood makes me feel heavy.

In the second place, it makes me feel it ought to be larger.

The other day I heard a twig snap in it. I was annoyed at first, for I thought that someone was blackberrying, and depreciating the value of the undergrowth. On coming nearer, I saw it was not a man who had trodden on the twig and snapped it, but a bird, and I felt pleased. My bird. The bird was not equally pleased. Ignoring the relation between us, it took fright as soon as it saw the shape of my face, and flew straight over the boundary

See New Testament, Matthew 19:24: "It is easier for a camel to go through the eye of a needle, than for a rich man to enter into the kingdom of God." Forster follows that verse with a coupling of the religious and secular cause-and-effect possibilities. Leo Tolstoy (1828–1910), social and moral philosopher and Russian mystic, wrote *War and Peace* (1865–1869), among other great works. He emancipated his serfs in 1861. *Stone*: a unit of weight in Great Britain equal to 14 pounds. The stout bishop weighs 196 pounds.

The first and last lines of the paragraph end with the same four words, for effective emphasis: "makes me feel heavy." Forster, too, feels stout.

"In the second place" is the clearest kind of transition, as the author moves from the psychological effect of weight, caused by owning his property, to that of size. The property Forster acquired has caused him to want more.

"The other day" begins Forster's example displaying how the psychological effect of wanting more property has caused him to view his surroundings—greedily. King Ahab in the Old

Testament, the seventh king of Israel (c. 875–853 **B.C.**), greatly expanded his territories, especially by marrying Jezebel, daughter of the king of Sidon. In Herman Melville's *Moby-Dick*, Captain Ahab's obsession was to find and kill the white whale, at whatever cost. Forster discusses his growing obsession for getting more land. Canute II of Denmark (994?–1035), subject of many legends, conquered England and was chosen king in 1017 by the witan, the king's council of Anglo-Saxons. Alexander the Great (356–323 B.C.), said to have wept after he had no more worlds to conquer, directed enormously successful campaigns in Greece, Persia, northern India, Syria, and Egypt, among others. Sirius, the Dog Star, is the brightest star in the constellation Canis Major. Forster's imaginary domain is boundless, a cause of sadness when he compares it with his real, limited domain. The bird reminds us of nature's "definition" of property. We "own" only ourselves.

Owning property causes us to want to change it, to make it clearly ours. This psychology of ownership—nothing really belongs to us until we change it, pseudo-creatively—deeply bothers Forster. We want to mold our property into an extension of our personality, but without a creative motive. Shakespeare's Sonnet 129 begins, "The expense of spirit in a waste of shame / Is lust in action. . . ." The "internal defect" is our inability to accept ourselves as we are, just as we are unable to accept our property for what it is. As Forster uses *carnal,* the word relates to the body as the seat of physical appetites, without intellectual or moral influence. Our life on earth should be carnal and material, yet managed by the intellect and morality. Ironically, however, our desire for ownership manages our intellect and morality. Dante Alighieri (1265–1321) wrote *The Divine Comedy*.

hedge into a field, the property of Mrs. Henessy, where it sat down with a loud squawk. It had become Mrs. Henessy's bird. Something seemed grossly amiss here, something that would not have occurred had the wood been larger. I could not afford to buy Mrs. Henessy out, I dared not murder her, and limitations of this sort beset me on every side. Ahab did not want that vineyard—he only needed it to round off his property, preparatory to plotting a new curve—and all the land around my wood has become necessary to me in order to round off the wood. A boundary protects. But—poor little thing—the boundary ought in its turn to be protected. Noises on the edge of it. Children throw stones. A little more, and then a little more, until we reach the sea. Happy Canute! Happier Alexander! And after all, why should even the world be the limit of possession? A rocket containing a Union Jack, will, it is hoped, be shortly fired at the moon. Mars. Sirius. Beyond which . . . But these immensities ended by saddening me. I could not suppose that my wood was the destined nucleus of universal dominion—it is so very small and contains no mineral wealth beyond the blackberries. Nor was I comforted when Mrs. Henessy's bird took alarm for the second time and flew clean away from us all, under the belief that it belonged to itself.

In the third place, property makes its owner feel that he ought to do something to it. Yet he isn't sure what. A restlessness comes over him, a vague sense that he has a personality to express— the same sense which, without any vagueness, leads the artist to an act of creation. Sometimes I think I will cut down such trees as remain in the wood, at other times I want to fill up the gaps between them with new trees. Both impulses are pretentious and empty. They are not honest movements towards money-making or beauty. They spring from a foolish desire to express myself and from an inability to enjoy what I have got. Creation, property, enjoyment form a sinister trinity in the human mind. Creation and enjoyment are both very, very good, yet they are often unattainable without a material basis, and at such moments property pushes itself in as a substitute, saying, "Accept me instead—I'm good enough for all three." It is not enough. It is, as Shakespeare said of lust, "The expense of spirit in a waste of shame": it is "Before, a joy proposed; behind, a dream." Yet we don't know how to shun it. It is forced on us by our economic system as the alternative to starvation. It is also forced on us by an internal defect in the soul, by the feeling that in property may lie the germs of self-development and of exquisite or heroic deeds. Our life on earth is, and ought to be, material and carnal. But we have not yet learned to manage our materialism and carnality properly; they are still entangled with the desire for ownership, where (in the words of Dante) "Possession is one with loss."

Forster's homely transition detaches us from his deeply philosophical paragraph.

And this brings us to our fourth and final point: the blackberries.

Blackberries are not plentiful in this meagre grove, but they are easily seen from the public footpath which traverses it, and all too easily gathered. Foxgloves, too—people will pull up the foxgloves, and ladies of an educational tendency even grub for toadstools to show them on the Monday in class. Other ladies, less educated, roll down the bracken in the arms of their gentlemen friends. There is paper, there are tins. Pray, does my wood belong to me or doesn't it? And, if it does, should I not own it best by allowing no one else to walk there? There is a wood near Lyme Regis, also cursed by a public footpath, where the owner has not hesitated on this point. He had built high stone walls each side of the path, and has spanned it by bridges, so that the public circulate like termites when he gorges on the blackberries unseen. He really does own his wood, this able chap. Dives in Hell did pretty well, but the gulf dividing him from Lazarus could be traversed by vision, and nothing traverses it here. And perhaps I shall come to this in time. I shall wall in and fence out until I really taste the sweets of property. Enormously stout, endlessly avaricious, pseudo-creative, intensely selfish, I shall weave upon my forehead the quadruple crown of possession until those nasty Bolshies come and take it off again and thrust me aside into the outer darkness.

The natural products of Forster's wood attract people. Foxgloves have long spikes of thimble-like flowers. A medicine made from their leaves (digitalis) is used as a heart stimulant. Bracken are large, coarse, weedy ferns. All the public activity causes Forster to question the definition of ownership. Does the owner own the property, or does the property own the owner? For Dives, see the parable of the selfish rich man, Luke 16:19–31; Lazarus is the poor diseased man in the same parable.

To make his "quadruple crown of possession," Forster weaves together the four subtopics in this essay: worldly wealth, greed, false creativity, and selfishness. "[N]asty Bolshies": Bolsheviks are Communists or, loosely used, any radicals.

6

7

Meaning and Purpose

1. Forster intends to explore the questions he poses in the first paragraph: "What is the effect of property upon the character?" and "What's the effect on me of my wood?" These two sentences are his thesis in question form; he is asserting that ownership *does* affect a person.
2. Encourage students to share their stories about things they have owned and done something to. Be sure they account for clear causes and effects, such as "I painted an American flag on my leather jacket because I want people to know that I am patriotic."
3. Students are free to select their own allusions. Occasionally reading and discussing the better papers in class is an exercise that helps students realize this essay's depth.
4. The author's freedom is restricted by his imagined obligations to himself and his possession, which stem from his owning the wood in the first place. Now that he has the wood, he feels obliged to enlarge it, improve it, and protect it.
5. The interjection "blast it" sums up his opinion of the wood's being publicly and easily accessible by the footpath. This is the first clue that Forster will feel possessive about his wood.

Strategy

1. Forster gives the cause in paragraph 1: the acquiring of money that enabled him to buy the wood. In subsequent paragraphs, he develops one effect at a time. This structure is effective because it is clear and makes his reasoning easy to follow. Giving one long paragraph to each effect allows him to single it out and explore it in depth.
2. The statement quoted is an example of a causal chain, or a series of things, one triggering the next, in chronological order. This technique here exaggerates Forster's point that owning property is heavy or cumbersome. He imagines that ownership will cause slowness, having things "you

Meaning and Purpose

1. What is Forster's purpose in "My Wood," and where does he most clearly state it?
2. In paragraph 5, he says "property makes its owner feel that he ought to do something to it." What do you own that you have done something to, just because you owned it? A pair of shoes? a jacket? a car? Briefly describe the ways in which you changed it and your reasons for changing it.
3. An allusion often refers to a historical or literary figure, event, or object. Choose one allusion from this essay and learn more about it. If you chose "Canute," you might look it up in an unabridged dictionary, an encyclopedia, or other reference works. Select an allusion other than "Canute" and describe it briefly.
4. In paragraph 2, Forster says that owning many things restricts one's freedom. How does owning the wood restrict the author's freedom?
5. The first paragraph includes the words "blast it." Why does the author use that interjection?

Strategy

1. Study the cause-and-effect structure of the essay. Does Forster alternate cause and effect in each paragraph, or develop them one at a time in separate paragraphs? Explain the effectiveness of the structure.
2. In the middle of paragraph 2 is the statement, "if you have a lot of things you cannot move about a lot, that furniture requires dusting, dusters require servants, servants require insurance stamps, and the whole tangle of them makes you think twice before you accept an invitation to dinner or go for a bathe in the Jordan." What is the cause-and-effect structure of this sentence called, and how is it used here?
3. The last paragraph in this essay says that the owner of a wood near Lyme Regis "really does own his wood." What caused that ownership? What is the effect of that kind of ownership?

cannot move about," until you'd better think twice before you "bathe in the Jordan." Forster is using humor to stress one danger of ownership.

3. The ownership was caused by the high stone walls that the owner built on both sides of the path. The effect is that those walls have imprisoned the owner.

4. The fourth and final point is selfishness. Forster means that blackberries lure people in until he is tempted to "wall in and fence out . . . property. [acts that are] Enormously . . . selfish" (7).

Style

1. The ladies are probably elementary school teachers, and the author thinks little of them for "grubbing" in his wood just to show the children toadstools.

2. Forster extends his need to enlarge the boundary of his wood all the way to the sea to keep out noise and children. This exaggeration stresses his point that once he is an owner, his greed will know no bounds.

3. These two paragraphs are transitions from discussion of one effect to the next. They are clear statements of Forster's chronology in presenting his points. And they are stylistically effective because they are short and rather abrupt between two long paragraphs. They catch attention and bring the reader back on track.

4. In paragraph 6, he says that the fourth and final point in the essay is blackberries. But it is not. What is the fourth and final point, and why does the author tell us it is blackberries?

Style

1. What is the occupation of the "ladies of an educational tendency," in paragraph 7, and why do you think the author describes them as he does?

2. In paragraph 4, the author says, "A little more, and then a little more, until we reach the sea." What is the author describing in this sentence?

3. Look at paragraphs 3 and 6. Why do you think each has only one sentence?

Writing Tasks

1. The American writer Henry David Thoreau said, "A man is rich in proportion to the number of things which he can afford to let alone." E. M. Forster's essay "My Wood" has much in common with Thoreau's statement. In your paper, consider being rich a cause and discuss what you think are some of its effects. Develop each effect in a paragraph.

2. Here is a list of causes. Write about one effect of each. Develop at least one causal chain.

   Teenager watching MTV
   Landfill overflowing
   Apple trees blossoming
   Car breaking down in the fast lane during rush hour

❦ Gerald Early ❦

A teacher of English and Afro-American studies at Washington University in St. Louis, Gerald Early began his career writing weekly columns for his college newspaper, The Daily Pennsylvanian. *His work has appeared in* The Best American Essays *of 1988 and 1991. In the introduction to a collection of his essays,* Tuxedo Junction: Essays on American Culture *(1989), Early credits Amiri Baraka's (Le Roi Jones's)* Home: Social Essays *(1966) as the book that created his desire to be an essayist.*

Baby, Take a Bow

In this selection from Tuxedo Junction, *Gerald Early ponders the significance of the selection of Vanessa Williams as the first black Miss America and considers the role Miss America plays in our culture. He speculates on possible effects of Williams's selection on black people, white people, and the Miss America pageant itself.*

Although the essay is a serious one, notice the gentle humor Early uses to establish a warm relationship with his readers.

Rich relations give crusts of bread and such.

—Billie Holiday, "God Bless the Child"

For the benefit of those who never knew
I'm a Miss America! How do you do!
I won a prize in '44 and of course all this is through with;
And I have a great big silver loving cup that I don't know
      what to do with.

I'm Miss America . . . so what?
They had me posing like I wouldn't
And they photographed me where they shouldn't,

328

But it's nice to be Miss America, it makes life so trés gai,
Now if I could only find a way to eat three times a day.

—sung by Miss Venus Ramey, Miss America of 1944,
in her nightclub act after her inauspicious reign

Dolgin's is the sort of store that reveals just what retailing will be like everywhere in America's future, a future that will show that expansion is reduction, after all; Dolgin's shelves tell the story of the slouch toward a cunning yet bland anonymity that has made the old style of crass salesmanship through the frenzied pitch outmoded. It is stores like Dolgin's that Sears wants to imitate, creating an ambience like an American consumer's fantasyland where customers buy items about which they know very little because through some sort of subliminal hearsay they were informed that the product was good or needed. American retailing nowadays does not seem condensed so much as it seems compressed; every huge retailing outlet must sell everything from blank tape cassettes to baby food, and the workers are no longer interested in selling anything; they merely "ring you out." One is left almost eerily to the mercies of one's own impulses. It was pleasant to think that at one time a store such as Dolgin's thought the customer needed the services of an informed, trained salesperson; but customers no longer have needs that must be accommodated, simply urges that must be appeased. Shopping, to a large extent, is a tawdry sort of therapy; one can push a cart up and down the aisles of any store now, not just supermarkets, and commune with the self while half believing that America is still a land of plenty. This mass shopping habit, so similar to the vision of retailing in Edward Bellamy's 1888 futuristic novel *Looking Backward,* is simply the intensified loneliness of the herd instinct of popular culture; the alienation we experience these days is not from the strange but from the familiar.

It was at Dolgin's that our new Miss America made her first— and probably only—appearance in St. Louis, giving away autographed snapshots of herself with anyone who cared to be in a picture with her. In fact, the event was advertised as "Have your photograph taken with Miss America." I suppose it was fitting

Edward Bellamy's (1850–1898) *Looking Backward* presented a method of economic organization, socialistic in nature, that would guarantee material equality for all citizens.

This paragraph may seem superfluous at first, but is really integral: Miss America is another "consumer item" and consumers fulfill individual needs through their contact with her.

"another product" ties this paragraph to the preceding one.

that she should be appearing at Dolgin's; she was, in some sense, another product that everyone should certainly be familiar with. There were no introductions made when she appeared before huge crowds waiting to see her and she said little or nothing to the people who came, one by one, to have their picture taken with her. Words were superfluous for someone who seemed to be more of an emanation from the Godhead than a human being. She smiled beautifully and constantly in a way that was completely expressionless. Her smile was not devoid of meaning; it resonated a rather genteel mocking quality that heightened its bored de-tachment. I especially liked how she stood on the ambiguous edge of being a tragic mulatto and a conjure woman, on the edge of absolute love and absolute power; for, at that moment, sitting in that store, she was the most loved and most suspect woman in America. She was loved as all Miss Americas are loved; she was, after all, no different from her predecessors: a sweet girl with ambition and a more than ardent belief that anyone in America can make it by working hard enough. She was the most suspect woman in America because she is black and, as such, is as in-scrutable a symbol of American womanhood as one could hope to find. In other words, some blacks don't trust her motives and some whites don't trust her abilities. Yet she became, for those people in Dolgin's, America's version of a princess without a realm or, to put it more precisely, with a limitless realm since it was the entire fantasy of American popular culture. Doubtless, Dolgin's never had so many black folk pass through its portals or, at least, so many black folk pass through who had absolutely no intention of buying anything. There were young black men with fancy cameras, young black women with little sons and daughters dressed in their Sunday best, older black women who giggled with ex-citement every time they saw Miss America smile. It was as if they had all come to pay homage to some great person instead of merely having a picture taken with a young woman of twenty who had done nothing more notable than win a contest, which, I suppose, was more an act of chance than anything else. Yet these black people, who had come out in frightful rush-hour traffic in a tremendous autumnal rainstorm, must have felt that it was an act of destiny that this girl was crowned Miss America.

Two brief mentions of causes (reasons) for being
"most loved" and "most suspect."

This paragraph examines the fantasy aspects of
Miss America.

Paragraphs 3–8 illustrate the triumphant enthusiasm and humor of these black people who are also in the grip of the fantasy.

"This is history, man," said one young black man to another. "I would've come through a hurricane to meet *this* Miss America. They sure ain't gonna pick another black woman to be Miss America no time soon." 3

"That ain't no lie," replied the other. "White folks might be sorry they picked this one before the year is over." 4

"She sure is pretty," said a grandmotherly-looking black woman. "I never thought they'd pick a black girl to be Miss America during my lifetime." 5

"Hey, white folks gonna think we taking over," said another young black man. "First, we get a black mayor in Chicago, then we get the Martin Luther King holiday, and now we got Miss America. The man who run Dolgin's figure the only time he see this many niggers in his store is if he was giving away watermelons or Cadillacs." 6

People standing nearby laughed at the last remark. 7

"That's just it," said a young black woman. "They're not use to *black* people coming out to see Miss America." 8

And indeed that young woman spoke truer than she knew. In the past, I would imagine that the few black people who bothered to see Miss America when she made a public appearance were motivated only by the most disinterested sort of curiosity, a curiosity approaching the immaculate objectivity of the scientist: for, of course, a white woman as Miss America was merely an object for conversation, not veneration. For the first time, black people can now be motivated to see Miss America for the same reason that whites would crowd stores like Dolgin's to see her in the past: out of admiration, that sort of public love that, in the instance of black Americans, is so dammed up because they have so few public figures they can love so unconditionally and totally because nothing more is expected of them than that they look beautiful and act in some remotely "cultured," polished way. To be sure, a good many black people will seek excuses to hate our new Miss America, but a much greater number will love her obsessively. 9

There were many white folk standing and waiting as well, and while some probably came out of curiosity, most seemed to esteem truly and deeply our new Miss America. One blond woman, 10 looking as though she had just escaped a dull office and a duller job, was positively flushed with the electricity of the moment. A mother had her son rehearse these lines to say to Miss America when he would finally meet her: "I think you're very beautiful and I'm glad you're Miss America." Another woman had her young daughter, perhaps ten or twelve, wearing a blue dress, patent leather pumps, stockings, a tiara, and a banner draped across the shoulder that proclaimed "Miniature Miss." This youngster, possibly a future Miss America, certainly a future contestant in somebody's beauty contest, was the only person to curtsy before Miss America as if she were meeting the Queen of England. I heard a thirtyish white man speaking to a young black fellow: "I just had to come and get a picture of Miss America. I think this is wonderful. My wife won't believe that I saw Miss America unless I get a picture. I think this is wonderful. I can't believe it." I think that Miss America must have been gratified and grateful that so many whites were there, not so much because she sought their approval but because she sought their acceptance. Their presence might assure that her reign would not be a separate but equal one. The importance of this cannot be overstated, for she has probably unconsciously conceived her symbolic stature as a force to fuse, if only momentarily, our divided culture. Since her black skin, by virtue of the historic burden it carries, brings the element of "social relevance" to the dazzling idiocy of beauty contests, our new Miss America must be aware that she can do more with the title than any white woman ever could, that she can greatly enhance the symbolic yet antique meaning of young womanhood in this culture simply because she is black. She has effectively done two things: she has encouraged blacks to participate in this fairly sterile cultural rite of passage; she has revitalized white interest in the contest by forcing them to see the title in a new and probably more deeply appreciative light. For whites who relish the idea of a black woman as Miss America, she simply serves the artless assumption that America is truly a land without racism, a land of equal opportunity at last. After all, so goes the reasoning from these quarters, twenty-five years ago, if Dolgin's existed in St. Louis, blacks probably could not shop there; they

---

"separate but equal": an allusion to the phrase used to justify separate schools for black and white children prior to the Supreme Court decision in Brown vs. Board of Education (1954) in which Chief Justice wrote, Earl Warren "The doctrine of 'separate but equal' has no place. Separate educational facilities are inherently unequal." An earlier use of the phrase, from which it may have been borrowed by segregationists, occurs in the Declaration of Independence: "When . . . it becomes necessary for one people . . . to assume . . . separate and equal station. . . ."

The presence of so many whites at the photo signing indicates another possible effect of her winning the crown.

A summary statement of two possible effects of having a black Miss America.

The effect on whites may be divided into two further effects (results) depending on a white's attitude toward race.

certainly could not work there. Now a young black woman as Miss America is signing autographs in such a store. Racial progress moves apace. Whites who detest the fact that a black woman is Miss America will simply campaign all the harder to make sure that such a lapse does not occur again. For more whites than one might care to imagine, the Miss America crown and the heavy-weight title in prizefighting are the flimsy supports for the idea of racial superiority along sexual lines.

The last time a woman who was chosen Miss America was even slightly enmeshed in a similar welter of social and cultural complexities was in 1945, when Bess Myerson, another Miss New York, became the first Jew to win the pageant. Admittedly, only *Life* magazine (of all the publications that ran stories on Myerson during her reign) briefly mentioned her religion; it was never an issue of public discussion because it was never an object of publicity. Yet with the ending of the Second World War—a war fought, in large part, against the absolute nihilism of pathological racism—and with the holocaust and the subject of war trials still fresh on everyone's mind, the selection of a Jew by the Miss America judges strikes one as being, at least, self-consciously but subtly profound or momentous; it was a contrived but important effort to legitimize the contest. Since the 1945 contest was the first in which scholarships were given away, it was essential that the winner also have some real talent. Myerson had already received her B.A. degree in music from Hunter College when she entered the pageant, and during the talent segment she played Gershwin on the flute and Grieg on the piano. There was little doubt that she was not only the most skilled contestant for *that* year, but probably the most gifted entrant in the entire history of the pageant. As *The New York Times* stated in an article printed the day after she won: "The only reason she entered the contest in the first place was . . . the lure of a $5,000 scholarship that would enable her to continue for another four years her twelve-year study of music." Myerson was not simply another pretty face; she changed the entire nature of the contest from being a gross flesh show to being, of all things, a scholarship competition. Vanessa Williams is seen by the people who run the Miss America

11

Early shifts to an earlier example of a Miss America from a minority group.

Early speculates that just as the selection of the talented Meyerson legitimized the contest and therefore allowed a return to the selection of mediocrities, the selection of the first black Miss America may allow a comfortable return to the selection of white contestants.

contest as another possible legitimizing force. The selection of Myerson did not change the fundamental spirit or intention of the contest; nor did her winning enhance the general caliber of the average contestant who came after her. Myerson simply eased the way for the contest to return to its fantasy, pop-culture preoccupations and continue to select gentile mediocrities. Williams will most likely serve the same ends; the judges can, with a cleaner conscience, return to selecting white women almost exclusively. None of this is exactly sinister; it is, in fact, the bald, guileless stupidity and pointlessness of it all that galls one more than anything.

I stood in line for nearly an hour, along with my wife and two small daughters, waiting to be photographed with Miss America. I might not have gone through all of this had my children been boys, but I knew I simply had to have my daughters in a photograph with the first black Miss America. They would, at least, find it amusing to see the picture when they were older and they might even think it "significant." The photograph turned out to be less than I hoped for. My four-year-old, who would have infinitely preferred having her photograph taken with Michael Jackson, was a bit confused by it all. My two-year-old was completely terrified of the crowd; she never even faced the camera when the picture was taken. So the picture shows a smiling, demure, quite lovely Miss America with a blue and black suit, light brown hair, and green eyes as bright and brilliant as slightly moistened, clear glass beads; a young father smiling slightly with his two children on his knees—one faintly nonplussed and greatly surprised, the other faintly annoyed and greatly distressed. I suppose I am the most humorous figure in the photograph, looking like nothing so much as a candidate for Father of the Year. Miss America probably felt a bit of sympathy for the valiant young father and his uncooperative children—but not half as much as I felt for her, traveling to all the stores like Dolgin's all over the country, signing autographs by the hundreds of thousands, surrounded by more guards than the president, seeing the worst of America as a grotesque phantasmagoria of shopping malls, hotels, and airports. As she sat there in Dolgin's, smiling benignly as

12

each person stepped forward to have his or her picture taken, I could not help but think of her as a courtesan receiving her clients with graceful indifference. All of this was surely immaculate enough; no one was allowed to touch her. But that seems only to have intensified the perversity of the service she was providing; for to maintain the purity of her presence, the public was, in some way, being reminded that it could only defile her, if it had its druthers. And perhaps we would have, since nothing brings out American bloodthirstiness more boldly than the victimization of the innocent.

Early deepens the significance of the essay by presenting an ultimate cause of our fascination with Miss America.

We are secretly driven slightly mad by the fact that Miss America is sweet and wholesome because it reveals our tremendous preoccupation with our own vehemently stated innocence. Miss America is sweet and wholesome because she symbolizes our deep neurotic obsession with chastity (which is really the only quality that makes a young girl truly sweet and wholesome and *desirable* in our culture). Watching our new Miss America with her beautiful, overly made-up face and perfectly manicured hands, I thought of the direct counterpart to the question that was posed to James Baldwin, as he relates in his description of his conversion experience in *The Fire Next Time:* Whose little girl are you? And because Vanessa Williams's eyes answered dutifully to each person who came forward and silently posed the question: "Why, yours of course," it occurred to me that the ease with which the answer was given belied the sincerity of the response entirely. The Miss America role is tough work; one must have the beauty and charm of a princess, the elegant fortitude of a courtesan, and the cheap hustle of a tease. She is not America's dream girl, she is America's sick fantasy of girlhood and innocence.

He ends with a personal scene in his own family.

As we were leaving the store with our photographs and our two rather relieved children, my wife turned to me and said, "Wouldn't it be something if one of our girls became Miss America twenty years from now? This photograph would be sought by all the papers: 'New Miss America photographed as child with first black Miss America.'"

"Yes," I said, "that would be something."

Although in one very obvious way it is very wonderful now

that black mothers can tell their young daughters, "Yes, my darling, you too can become Miss America," one wonders what might be the larger psychic costs demanded by this bit of acculturation. Despite the fact that I do not wish my daughters to grow up desiring to be Miss America, I take a strange pleasure in knowing that that contest can no longer terrorize them; and this pleasure is worth the psychic costs and dislocations, whatever they might be. After all, black folk knew for a long time before Henry James discovered the fact that it is a complex fate to be an American.

Postscript: In July 1984, shortly before this essay was published, 17
Vanessa Williams became the first Miss America to be stripped of her crown, when *Penthouse* magazine published sexually provocative photos of Williams taken a few years before she became Miss America. Her replacement, Suzette Charles, Miss New Jersey, became the second black woman to become Miss America, which means that blacks are, on the whole, doing better than Jews in this business, as Bess Myerson remains the only Jew to have won the contest. Or perhaps blacks are doing worse, as some have perversely joked that it takes two light-skinned black women to equal the reign of one white woman.

Meaning and Purpose

1. What is Early's thesis? Does he state it directly?
2. According to Early, what role does Miss America play in American culture?
3. What effect does the selection of a black Miss America have on black people?
4. What effect does the selection of a black Miss America have on white people?
5. In paragraph 13, Early discusses ultimate causes for the popularity of the Miss America contest. Do you agree? From your

---

The humor of the postscript pulls us back to a more mundane perception of the whole Miss America phenomenon.

Possible Answers

Meaning and Purpose

1. Early's thesis is multifaceted and not stated directly at any one point. He is examining possibilities rather than defending a position. Among the conclusions that might be drawn from his essay: (1) the selection of a black Miss America might broaden the meaning of the title or it might be just a temporary "crust of bread"; (2) Miss America is a product, like any other at Dolgin's; (3) Blacks no longer need to be "terrorized" by the contest, but there may be psychic costs; and (4) Miss America is our "sick fantasy of girlhood and innocence."
2. The winner serves as an object of public love (2) as well as a symbol of "our deep neurotic obsession with chastity" (13).
3. Though the author warns (9) that some blacks will hate her, at least for those at Dolgin's her selection brings a sense of triumph, of winning something previously denied. This sense of triumph is most clearly revealed in the quoted

conversations of paragraphs 3–8. Even the author, who has a more detached view throughout the essay, takes pleasure in the selection, though he is extremely cautious about its real significance (16).

4. For those at Dolgin's she is easily accepted and her selection is seen as a hope for the healing of racial tensions. This hope is best seen in the rehearsed lines of a small boy, ". . . and I'm glad you're Miss America" (10), a gesture of harmony his mother would probably not have had him recite to a white Miss America. Early reminds us, though, that some whites detest the selection (10) and others, he hints, will accept it as a momentary gesture allowing a return to the selection of white winners (11).

5. This question calls for personal responses and answers will vary.

Strategy

1. Both quotations relate to points Early makes later in the essay. "Crusts of bread" relates to his conjecture that having chosen a black Miss America, the judges can, in good conscience, return to many years of selecting white women (11). The song from Venus Ramey's nightclub act suggests that a Miss America's fame is brief and that she is used for some symbolic public purpose and then discarded. Ask students the name of the most recent Miss America or how many Miss Americas they can recall. See also paragraphs 2 and 13.

2. Phrases describing the store are echoed in the description of Miss America in paragraph 2 and beyond. For example: "bland anonymity" is echoed in "completely expressionless smile" and "no different from her predecessors"; "subliminal hearsay" sells products. "No introductions" are given Miss America and "words were superfluous." Students will doubtless find other examples here and in other paragraphs.

3. These bits of conversation reveal the good-natured enthusiasm of the black people who have come to see Miss America and reflect their sense of a victory in a never-ending contest with white people.

own familiarity with the contest, can you provide evidence to support or deny his assertion?

Strategy

1. How does each of the two quotations that precede the essay relate to the essay as a whole?
2. Although the essay is about a personal appearance of the first black Miss America, Early begins with a long paragraph describing Dolgin's department store and American stores in general. How does this description tie in with the rest of the essay?
3. Why does Early include the conversation quotations in paragraphs 3–8?
4. Why does Early include the long paragraph (10) describing the behavior of the white people who have also come to see Miss America?
5. Early uses comparison when he relates the example of Bess Meyerson, the first Jewish Miss America. What does her example have to do with Vanessa Williams?

Style

1. Early says, "American retailing nowadays does not seem condensed so much as it seems compressed." What is the difference between *condensed* and *compressed?*
2. This essay is obviously written by a well-educated, thoughtful person, and yet the tone is anything but "ivory tower." Examine paragraph 2 for examples of formal and informal phrasing. What effect does the combination of both have on your attitude as a reader?
3. How would you describe the tone of the essay's postscript? Does its tone have an effect on your perception of the meaning of the essay?
4. If necessary look up the following words in a dictionary: *ambience*

4. This paragraph shows she is accepted with equal enthusiasm by whites and allows Early to comment that some see this as "racial progress." He cautions at the end of the paragraph, though, that not all whites share this attitude.

5. Both Meyerson and Williams, while seeming to broaden and elevate the process of selecting a Miss America, may actually share a common fate—to be used as excuses to return to the selection of gentile mediocrities (in Meyerson's case) and to white women (in Williams's case).

Style

1. Although roughly synonymous in most contexts, here *condensed* means "reduced" and *compressed* means "forced into less space." As Early states, retail outlets tend to sell everything, adding merchandise even when unable to add space. Perhaps the only thing that has been reduced is the service.

2. Different readers may take different stands on the effect of this inclusion of formal and informal phrasing, but most will probably agree that it humanizes the writer and gives the essay a warmth that could be absent in an essay of similar content by a less skillful writer. Formal: "words were superfluous"; "an emanation from the Godhead"; "resonated a rather genteel mocking"; "as inscrutable a symbol." Informal: "snapshots"; "conjure woman"; "don't trust"; "black folk"; "giggled."

3. In the latter half of the postscript, the tone turns amusingly cynical, in effect ridiculing any too profound concern for the significance of having a black Miss America.

4. *ambience*: the atmosphere of a particular setting; *emanation*: to originate from a particular source; *inscrutable*: difficult to understand; enigmatic; *veneration*: to regard with great respect; *gentile*: non-Jewish; *guileless*: without deceit; *nonplussed*: perplexed; bewildered; *phantasmagoria*: a changing *scene made up of* many elements; dreamlike images; *acculturation*: adapting to a new culture or becoming used to new behaviors.

(1); *emanation, inscrutable* (2); *veneration* (9); *gentile, guileless* (11); *nonplussed, phantasmagoria* (12); *acculturation* (16).

Writing Tasks

1. Write a paper exploring the effects some popular entertainment celebrity has had on a portion of the American people. You might consider someone like Bart Simpson, Madonna, Oprah Winfrey, Bruce Springsteen, Roseanne (Barr) Arnold, Eddie Murphy, Priscilla Presley, Tom Cruise, Paula Abdul.

2. People the world over are becoming increasingly concerned about environmental problems: the ozone layer, the greenhouse effect, pollution of waterways, the disappearing rain forest, and so on. Select one environmental problem and write an essay explaining why it has become a problem. Include both immediate and ultimate causes.

Four distinct but complementary approaches
may prove profitable in teaching this brief but
provocative essay. First, discuss differences and
effects of inductive versus deductive methods.
Many writers state the thesis first and follow
with examples to demonstrate its validity. Miller
begins by vividly describing an actual experience and then lists examples that are more and
more hypothetical until he reaches his speculative conclusion.

Second, Miller deals with cause and effect.
The "severing of the human connection" in each
example is immediately caused by "chiselers."
He then speculates about the ultimate cause. Are
people incorrigibly dishonest? But people behave as they are expected to, and we have a
different ultimate cause: our collective paranoia,
which causes us to overreact to the chiselers,
creating more chiselers, who force us to react
even more.

Thirdly, even the most speculative examples are rooted in the most concrete language.
Linguistic analysis of each paragraph easily
demonstrates that concrete language is more effective than vague and abstract words. Miller
offers us no abstractions (1). He precedes the
more abstract "thievery" and "violence" with a
list of vivid things to demonstrate meaning (6).
Instead of reflecting on an abstract, vague "future," he says we are on a dark and descending
road.

Finally, discussing Miller's ideas could
prove provocative. His conclusion is pessimistic:
he admits to intellectual understanding of the
problem, but cannot accept it emotionally. Students will take sides; show that they must accumulate evidence, facts, to convince someone
that their reactions are valid.

MARGINAL NOTES

Miller uses a striking turn of phrase ("these
days of expensive gas and cut-rate ethics") to
describe his attitude toward the social situation
that has created the atrocity he describes in paragraph 1.

❧ H. Bruce Miller ❧

*Bruce Miller was born in New Jersey in 1946 and studied at Princeton
University. He received his master's degree in journalism from Columbia
University, after which he began his journalistic career at the* Tren-
tonian *in Trenton, New Jersey. He has also worked at* Newsday *in
Los Angeles and the* San Jose Mercury News, *where he was first an
editorial writer for several years and then a columnist. He is currently
managing editor of the* Bulletin *in Bend, Oregon.*

Severing the Human Connection

In this short essay from the San Jose Mercury News *(August 4, 1981),
Miller laments the widespread distrust in American society. Beginning
by describing a specific result of this self-protective distrust, the pay-
before-you-pump gas station, he gradually moves toward a consideration of possible causes.*

*The humorous exaggeration Miller uses makes this essay enjoyable
to read. As you do, look for hints that Miller, in spite of the humor,
wants you to take his message seriously.*

Went down to the local self-serve gas station the other morn- [1]
ing to fill up. The sullen cashier was sitting inside a dark, glassed-
in, burglar-proof, bullet-proof, probably grenade-proof cubicle
covered with cheerful notices. "No Checks." "No Credit." "No
Bills Over $50 Accepted." "Cashier Has No Small Change." And
the biggest one of all: "Pay Before Pumping Gas." A gleaming steel
box slid out of the wall and gaped open. I dropped in a $20 bill.
"Going to fill 'er up with no-lead on Number 6," I said. The
cashier nodded. The steel box swallowed my money and retracted
into the cubicle. I walked back to the car to pump the gas, trying
not to slink or skulk. I felt like I ought to be wearing striped
overalls with a number on the breast pocket.

The pay-before-you-pump gas station (those in the trade call   2
it a "pre-pay") is a response to a real problem in these days of
expensive gas and cut-rate ethics: people who fill their tanks and
then tear out of the station without paying. Those in the business
call them "drive-offs." The head of one area gasoline dealers'
association says drive-offs cost some dealers $500 to $600 a month.
With a profit margin of only about a nickel a gallon, a dealer has
to sell a lot of gallons to make up that kind of loss. The police
aren't much help. Even if the attendant manages to get a license
plate number and description of the car, the cops have better
things to do than tracking down a guy who stole $15 worth of
gas. So the dealers adopt the pre-pay system.

Intellectually, I understand all of this, yet I am angry and   3
resentful. Emotionally I cannot accept the situation. I understand
the dealers' position, I understand the cops' position. But I cannot
understand why I should be made to feel like John Dillinger every
time I buy a tank of gasoline. It's the same story everywhere. You
go to a department store and try to pay for a $10.99 item with
a check and you have to pull out a driver's license, two or three
credit cards and a character reference from the pope—and then
stand around for 15 minutes to get the manager's approval. Try
to pay with a credit card and you have to wait while the cashier phones the central computer bank to make sure you're not a
deadbeat or the Son of Sam or something. It's not that we don't
trust you, they smile. It's just that we have to protect ourselves.

Right. We all have to protect ourselves these days. Little old   4
ladies with attack dogs and Mace and 12-gauges, shopkeepers
with closed-circuit TVs and electronic sensors to nab shoplifters,
survivalists storing up ammo and dehydrated foods in hope of
riding out Armageddon, gas station owners with pay-before-you-
pump signs and impenetrable cashiers' cages—all protecting
themselves. From what? From each other. It strikes me that we
are expending so much time, energy and anguish on protecting
ourselves that we are depleting our stock of mental and emotional
capital for living. It also strikes me that the harder we try to
protect ourselves, the less we succeed. With all the home burglar
alarms and guard dogs and heavy armament, the crime rate keeps

---

This is the only place in the essay where Miller actually uses facts.

The topic sentence has a strong transition ("I understand all of this") and creates the organizational pattern for the paragraph, comparison and contrast: his intellectual understanding of the situation and his emotional inability to accept it.

John Dillinger (1902–1934) was an American bank robber and murderer.

David Berkowitz was arrested in 1977 for a 1976–1977 series of murders with satanic overtones in New York City. He often left notes with his victims calling himself Son of Sam.

Armageddon was the name given in "The Revelation of St. John the Divine" (Rev. 16:16) to the site of the last great battle between good and evil before the Day of Judgment; hence, any great final struggle or conflict.

Our efforts to protect ourselves have not had the desired effect. Crime keeps going on.

going up. With all the electronic surveillance devices, the shop-lifters' take keeps climbing. The gas chiselers haven't figured out a way to beat the pre-pay system yet, but they will.

Is it that the people are simply incorrigibly dishonest, that   5
the glue of integrity and mutual respect that holds society together is finally dissolving? I don't know, but I suspect that if something like this really is going on, our collective paranoia contributes to the process. People, after all, tend to behave pretty much the way other people expect them to behave. If the prevailing assumption of a society is that people are honest, by and large they will be honest. If the prevailing assumption is that people are crooks, more and more of them will be crooks.

What kind of message does a kid get from an environment   6
where uniformed guards stand at the entrance of every store, where every piece of merchandise has an anti-shoplifting tag stapled to it, where every house has a burglar alarm and a .38, where the gas station cashiers huddle in glass cages and pass your change out through a metal chute? What can he conclude but that thievery and violence are normal, common, expected behaviors?

A society which assumes its members are honest is humane,   7
comfortable, habitable. A society which treats everyone like a criminal becomes harsh, unfeeling, punitive, paranoid. The human connection is severed; fear of detection and punishment becomes the only deterrent to crime, and it's a very ineffective one. Somehow, sometime—I don't know when, but it was within my lifetime—we changed from the first type of society to the second. Maybe it's too late to go back again, but the road we are now on is a dark and descending one.

Meaning and Purpose

1. What is Miller's thesis and where is it stated? What does his title mean and how does it relate to his thesis?

Miller begins the paragraph with a question that he will answer in the last two sentences of the same paragraph. The "glue" mentioned here that he claims holds society together connects with the title and the clause in the concluding paragraph that "The human connection is severed. . . ." An affirmative answer to these questions would suggest the ultimate causes of our perceived need for protection. Neither accepting nor rejecting these causes, Miller says that if the answer is "yes" the cause is even closer to the ultimate: our collective paranoia.

POSSIBLE ANSWERS

Meaning and Purpose

1. Miller states his thesis at the end of the essay, that sometime during his life we have changed from "A society which assumes its members are honest and humane" to one that "treats everyone like a criminal. . . ." In the opening paragraph he vividly describes a commonplace in our society that insulates us from one another and, for Miller, is emblematic of a society that has become "harsh, unfeeling, punitive, paranoid" (7). The "glue of integrity and mutual respect" that has held our society together has dissolved (5) so that now "The human connection is severed . . ." (7).
2. The prepay gas station is an effect, and Miller draws out the description in cold details to stress the inhumanity of it. The cause behind such a gas station is a world in which people feel they have to protect themselves and treat everyone like criminals.
3. Miller shows that ordinary people can be made to feel like criminals in their everyday business transactions (1, 3). The more we do to protect ourselves against crime, the more crime is created (4). If that hypothesis can be borne out by fact, then so can the opposite.
4. Miller implies that a society forcing many citizens to feel guilty is innately inhumane (3). Encourage students to differentiate cause from effect in the experiences.

5. In each case, the author has been made to feel that he is under suspicion, potentially criminal. Logically, the two men must be examples of criminals.

Strategy

1. Miller generally gives whole paragraphs to either causes or effects. Paragraphs 1 and 2 are effects. He explains how these effects of a paranoid society make him feel (3). Cause dominates paragraph 4, about how people protect themselves; the effect is not less crime but more inhumanity. He gives possible causes that can result in prepay gas stations (5, 6). In the last paragraph Miller states what he thinks is the final effect: we will behave as we expect each other to behave.

2. The topic sentence states why the absurd and inhumane incident in paragraph 1 can occur. He explains why the incident is not an anomaly, and why it has, in fact, become typical. The author understands the problem and establishes his authority to fight it.

3. That little old ladies are protecting themselves is an immediate effect of society's paranoia about self-protection. Other immediate effects are in paragraph 4, and prepay gas stations in the first part of the essay. By contrast, ultimate effects are that more and more people will be crooks (5), that kids will believe "thievery and violence are normal" (6), and that society will become "harsh, unfeeling, punitive, paranoid" (7).

4. Miller successfully portrays himself as a victim of society's attempts to make him feel guilty and criminal (paragraph 3 makes this feeling clearest). He gives examples of alienation from human interchange that readers probably have in their own experience, the effects caused by the need for self-protection. He gives no strong evidence that all this change occurred in Miller's lifetime; that is just his perception. The effect on the reader of Miller's pessimism might be awareness of the situation that could lead to the reader's taking some action to turn the situation around. "Maybe it's too late" in the last paragraph could be taken as a challenge.

2. Is the "pre-pay" gas station described in the first paragraph a cause or an effect? Explain.

3. Reread the last two sentences of paragraph 5. Do you feel that the author's conclusion is valid? Why or why not? How well does the author prepare us for that conclusion?

4. Have you had experiences that made you feel as Miller does in paragraph 3? What do you think might be the causes of the situations you describe in your experiences?

5. In paragraph 3, the author mentions John Dillinger and Son of Sam. Even if you do not know who they were, what conclusions can you draw about them by examining the context in which they are mentioned?

Strategy

1. How does Miller develop his cause-and-effect strategy, by alternating each in the same paragraph, or by exploring each in separate paragraphs? Give examples.

2. Critique paragraph 2 for its structure and function in the essay.

3. Would you say that "little old ladies with attack dogs and Mace and 12-gauges" (4) are an immediate or ultimate effect? Give reasons for your answer.

4. In the last paragraph, Miller claims that during his lifetime, society changed from being humane to being inhumane. He ends pessimistically. What do you think is the effect on the reader of his bleak pronouncements? Does he present enough evidence for his conclusions?

Style

1. Examine paragraph 1, sentence by sentence, paying close attention to the author's use of concrete language. How does each sentence work stylistically? What tone is created by this language?

2. After describing situations in which he is made to feel guilty for

Style

1. The paragraph is a marvel of vivid concrete language that grabs the reader and creates the essay's pervading tone of shocked disbelief and disenchantment.

In sentence 1 he uses informal language that creates the normalcy of the situation, with the author going down to the "local self-serve" station one morning to "fill up."

The tone suddenly changes with the "sullen cashier" sitting in a dark cubicle entirely cut off and protected from the outside world (2). The cashier is further cut off by the "cheerful notices" plastered on his cubicle.

The notices are made emphatic by their capitalization (3).

The "gleaming steel box" further separates human being from human being while it becomes an inhuman mouth that "gaped" (4) for money (5).

The common—and cryptic—language between narrator and attendant. The physical setup of the station discourages either from acknowledging the other's humanity (6, 7).

That inhuman steel mouth "swallowed" the author's money and immediately "retracted into the cubicle," emphasizing separation (8).

"Slink" is to move in a furtive abject manner, as from fear, cowardice, or shame, and "skulk" is to move in a stealthy way (9). The author walks back to his car "trying" not to walk in these ways. Miller feels like a convict in the last sentence.

2. Miller has prepared us for the disdainful tone of paragraph 4 by the examples he cites in paragraph 3. If we are continually scrutinized and made to feel guilty, the last two sentences in paragraph 4 sound not only hypocritical but dishonest. Opening the next paragraph with "Right," therefore, he creates a tone of sarcastic disbelief. This sarcasm is then confirmed by the absurd list that follows.

3. Miller asks the reader these questions directly. His tone is despairing, yet pleading, as if he wants his readers to say no to the first question, agree with him on the last—and then do something about the condition. Questions usually draw the reader into direct participation in the dialogue.

transacting everyday business in paragraph 3, the author concludes that he is told: " 'It's not that we don't trust you,' they smile. 'It's just that we have to protect ourselves.' " What tone does he create by beginning the next paragraph with the word "Right"?

3. Miller asks questions in paragraphs 5 and 6. How do these questions work stylistically? Are they effective?

Writing Tasks

1. In a short essay, explain either the causes or effects of one of the following. Decide how far back to go for ultimate causes or effects.

   Pass-fail grading policy

   Installation of front-seat air bags in all cars

   Proliferation of McDonald's restaurants worldwide

   A serious disagreement with your parents or roommate

   Popularity of a rock group or singer

   Benefit concerts by artists

   The need for doctors to have malpractice insurance

2. Consider your own attitudes about the ways in which people treat each other in our society. Assuming your attitudes can be considered effects, what are the causes of your attitudes? Explore these causes in an essay in which you first give concrete evidence of your attitudes.

Many, if not most, of your students will have had first-hand and extensive mall experience. They can testify to the validity of Kowinski's observations, therefore, from immediate, first-hand knowledge—not always from an unbiased or critical perspective, perhaps, but from an extensive background nonetheless. Starting off by asking students to respond to the first two paragraphs can serve several purposes in getting them to evaluate the essay critically. First, because they will have personal knowledge, they will, we're sure, be able to add specific examples to the two that Kowinski gives in paragraph 1. This activity, logically enough, leads to an evaluation of his typical examples in paragraph 2. In turn, this examination could turn into a discussion of the author's strategy in the first three paragraphs to convince the reader of the importance of thinking about what spending so much time in the mall does to teenagers. Most students will probably agree with Kowinski's early observations. Many, no doubt, will object to his later, critical commentary. The question could then be asked: If his early factual observations seem on target, how does he go wrong in evaluating this behavior later on? No doubt some students will remain adamant in their uncritical acceptance of the behavior Kowinski describes. Others may start looking more objectively at his evaluation.

❦ William Severini Kowinski ❦

William Kowinski grew up in Pennsylvania and attended Knox College in Illinois. He spent one semester at the University of Iowa studying fiction and poetry writing. His writing career, however, has been in nonfiction. To research his book, The Malling of America *(1985), Kowinski visited malls all over both the United States and Canada. He has been a writer and editor for the* Boston Phoenix *and for* Newsworks *of Washington, D.C., and his articles have appeared in* Esquire, The New York Times, *and the* New York Times Magazine.

Kids in the Mall:
Growing Up Controlled

Many American children grow up almost entirely in the controlled environments of home, school, and "the mall." What are the effects, Kowinski asks, of "growing up controlled"? The essay is from his book, The Malling of America: An Inside Look at the Great Consumer Paradise *(1985).*

As you read Kowinski's essay, be alert to how he moves from causes to effects. Pay particular attention to how he passes judgments on some of his effects.

Butch heaved himself up and loomed over the group. 1
"Like it was different for me," he piped. "My folks used to drop me off at the shopping mall every morning and leave me all day. It was like a big free baby-sitter, you know? One night they never came back for me. Maybe they moved away. Maybe there's some kind of a Bureau of Missing Parents I could check with."

—Richard Peck
Secrets of the Shopping Mall,
a novel for teenagers

344

From his sister at Swarthmore, I'd heard about a kid in Florida whose mother picked him up after school every day, drove him straight to the mall, and left him there until it closed—all at his insistence. I'd heard about a boy in Washington who, when his family moved from one suburb to another, pedaled his bicycle five miles every day to get back to his old mall, where he once belonged.

These stories aren't unusual. The mall is a common experience for the majority of American youth; they have probably been going there all their lives. Some ran within their first large open space, saw their first fountain, bought their first toy, and read their first book in a mall. They may have smoked their first cigarette or first joint or turned them down, had their first kiss or lost their virginity in the mall parking lot. Teenagers in America now spend more time in the mall than anywhere else but home and school. Mostly it is their choice, but some of that mall time is put in as the result of two-paycheck and single-parent households, and the lack of other viable alternatives. But are these kids being harmed by the mall?

I wondered first of all what difference it makes for adolescents to experience so many important moments in the mall. They are, after all, at play in the fields of its little world and they learn its ways; they adapt to it and make it adapt to them. It's here that these kids get their street sense, only it's mall sense. They are learning the ways of a large-scale artificial environment: its subtleties and flexibilities, its particular pleasures and resonances, and the attitudes it fosters.

The presence of so many teenagers for so much time was not something mall developers planned on. In fact, it came as a big surprise. But kids became a fact of mall life very early, and the International Council of Shopping Centers found it necessary to commission a study, which they published along with a guide to mall managers on how to handle the teenage incursion.

The study found that "teenagers in suburban centers are bored and come to the shopping centers mainly as a place to go. Teenagers in suburban centers spent more time fighting, drinking,

The first sentence serves as a transition and leads into the description of typical teenage mall activities. The examples are arranged chronologically to show typical stages in teenage development. The question at the end of the paragraph tells us that a cause-and-effect discussion will follow.

"Street sense" connotes hard-won practical knowledge; "mall sense" connotes a knowledge that is somehow separated and protected from the real world.

Paragraphs 5, 6, and 7 are grouped to show how mall developers were originally unprepared for the incursion by teenagers, how they then studied the phenomenon, and how, finally, the malls became finishing schools for kids who had already been indoctrinated into the consumer ethic.

littering and walking than did their urban counterparts, but presented fewer overall problems." The report observed that "adolescents congregated in groups of two to four and predominantly at locations selected by them rather than management." This probably had something to do with the decision to install game arcades, which allow management to channel these restless adolescents into naturally contained areas away from major traffic points of adult shoppers.

The guide concluded that mall management should tolerate and even encourage the teenage presence because, in the words of the report, "The vast majority support the same set of values as does shopping center management." *The same set of values* means simply that mall kids are already preprogrammed to be consumers and that the mall can put the finishing touches to them as hard-core, lifelong shoppers just like everybody else. That, after all, is what the mall is about. So it shouldn't be surprising that in spending a lot of time there, adolescents find little that challenges the assumption that the goal of life is to make money and buy products, or that just about everything else in life is to be used to serve those ends.

Growing up in a high-consumption society already adds inestimable pressure to kids' lives. Clothes consciousness has invaded the grade schools, and popularity is linked with having the best, newest clothes in the currently acceptable styles. Even what they read has been affected. "Miss [Nancy] Drew wasn't obsessed with her wardrobe," noted *The Wall Street Journal,* "but today the mystery in teen fiction for girls is what outfit the heroine will wear next." Shopping has become a survival skill and there is certainly no better place to learn it than the mall, where its importance is powerfully reinforced and certainly never questioned.

Kowinski cites authority to demonstrate that the seemingly benevolent mall of the preceding paragraph can actually be psychologically damaging.

The mall as a university of suburban materialism, where Valley Girls and Boys from coast to coast are educated in consumption, has its other lessons in this era of change in family life and sexual mores and their economic and social ramifications. The plethora of products in the mall, plus the pressure on teens to buy them, may contribute to the phenomenon that psychologist David Elkind calls "the hurried child": kids who are exposed to too much

7

8

9

of the adult world too quickly, and must respond with a sophistication that belies their still-tender emotional development. Certainly the adult products marketed for children—form-fitting designer jeans, sexy tops for preteen girls—add to the social pressure to look like an adult, along with the home-grown need to understand adult finances (why mothers must work) and adult emotions (when parents divorce).

Kids spend so much time at the mall partly because their parents allow it and even encourage it. The mall is safe, it doesn't seem to harbor any unsavory activities, and there is adult supervision; it is, after all, a controlled environment. So the temptation, especially for working parents, is to let the mall be their babysitter. At least the kids aren't watching TV. But the mall's role as a surrogate mother may be more extensive and more profound.   10

Karen Lansky, a writer living in Los Angeles, has looked into the subject and she told me some of her conclusions about the effects on its teenaged denizens of the mall's controlled and controlling environment. "Structure is the dominant idea, since true 'mall rats' lack just that in their home lives," she said, "and adolescents about to make the big leap into growing up crave more structure than our modern society cares to acknowledge." Karen pointed out some of the elements malls supply that kids used to get from their families, like warmth (Strawberry Shortcake dolls and similar cute and cuddly merchandise), old-fashioned mothering ("We do it all for you," the fast-food slogan), and even home cooking (the "homemade" treats at the food court).   11

In this paragraph real psychological growth that involves active acceptance of responsibility is contrasted with the mall's promotion of passive consumption. This passivity is further emphasized in the opening sentence of the next paragraph.

The problem in all this, as Karen Lansky sees it, is that while families nurture children by encouraging growth through the assumption of responsibility and then by letting them rest in the bosom of the family from the rigors of growing up, the mall as a structural mother encourages passivity and consumption, as long as the kid doesn't make trouble. Therefore all they learn about becoming adults is how to act and how to consume.   12

Kids are in the mall not only in the passive role of shoppers— they also work there, especially as fast-food outlets infiltrate the mall's enclosure. There they learn how to hold a job and take responsibility, but still within the same value context. When *CBS*   13

Reports went to Oak Park Mall in suburban Kansas City, Kansas, to tape part of their hour-long consideration of malls, "After the Dream Comes True," they interviewed a teenaged girl who worked in a fast-food outlet there. In a sequence that didn't make the final program, she described the major goal of her present life, which was to perfect the curl on top of the ice-cream cones that were her store's specialty. If she could do that, she would be moved from the lowly soft-drink dispenser to the more prestigious ice-cream division, the curl on top of the status ladder at her restaurant. These are the achievements that are important at the mall.

The meaninglessness of teenage mall employment in the preceding paragraph is assaulted a second time by citing academic authority.

Other benefits of such jobs may also be overrated, according to Laurence D. Steinberg of the University of California at Irvine's social ecology department, who did a study on teenage employment. Their jobs, he found, are generally simple, mindlessly repetitive and boring. They don't really learn anything, and the jobs don't head anywhere. Teenagers also work primarily with other teenagers; even their supervisors are often just a little older than they are. "Kids need to spend time with adults," Steinberg told me. "Although they get benefits from peer relationships, without parents and other adults it's a one-sided socialization. They hang out with each other, have age-segregated jobs, and watch TV." 14

Because the author has already established that mall teenagers have been conditioned as consumers before they ever became mall denizens and have now completed their consumer higher education, the likelihood is slight that they will ever assimilate this list of deeper values.

Perhaps much of this is not so terrible or even so terribly different. Now that they have so much more to contend with in their lives, adolescents probably need more time to spend with other adolescents without adult impositions, just to sort things out. Though it is more concentrated in the mall (and therefore perhaps a clearer target), the value system there is really the dominant one of the whole society. Attitudes about curiosity, initiative, self-expression, empathy, and disinterested learning aren't necessarily made in the mall; they are mirrored there, perhaps a bit more intensely—as through a glass brightly. 15

A sad irony colors this entire paragraph. Though the mall has objects with educational value, they will never be bought or used by mall children. And though older people with stories are there— knowledge used to be handed down from the old to the young in stories—the stories will not be heard. Instead, teenagers will just watch the "passing show."

Besides, the mall is not without its educational opportunities. There are bookstores, where there is at least a short shelf of classics at great prices, and other books from which it is possible to learn more than how to do sit-ups. There are tools, from hammers to VCRs, and products, from clothes to records, that can help the 16 young find and express themselves. There are older people with stories, and places to be alone or to talk one-on-one with a kindred spirit. And there is always the passing show.

The mall itself may very well be an education about the future. I was struck with the realization, as early as my first forays into Greengate, that the mall is only one of a number of enclosed and controlled environments that are part of the lives of today's young. The mall is just an extension, say, of those large suburban schools—only there's Karmelkorn instead of chem lab, the ice rink instead of the gym: It's high school without the impertinence of classes. 17

Growing up, moving from home to school to the mall—from enclosure to enclosure, transported in cars—is a curiously continuous process, without much in the way of contrast or contact with unenclosed reality. Places must tend to blur into one another. But whatever differences and dangers there are in this, the skills these adolescents are learning may turn out to be useful in their later lives. For we seem to be moving inexorably into an age of preplanned and regulated environments, and this is the world they will inherit. 18

Still, it might be better if they had more of a choice. One teenaged girl confessed to *CBS Reports* that she sometimes felt she was missing something by hanging out at the mall so much. "But I'm here," she said, "and this is what I have." 19

Possible Answers

Meaning and Purpose

1. Most students will probably have experiences to relate about shopping malls. Encourage them to compare their experiences with the situations Kowinski talks about.

2. Kowinski asks, "Are these kids being harmed by the mall?" (3). His thesis is the last sentence in paragraph 4. The thesis does not completely answer the question because he has yet to explore the values of the mall environment and the extent of their effects on kids.

Meaning and Purpose

1. What has been your experience in malls? What is your response to Kowinski's essay? Do you agree or disagree with him? Do you identify with the situations he describes?

2. What primary questions does the author attempt to answer in the essay? What is the thesis and where is it stated?

3. What negative effects does growing up in the mall have on children? Are there any positive effects?

3. Kowinski points out all through the essay that mall life hones to a fine edge kids' already accepted false assumptions that life's primary goal is to buy and consume (7). Probably the most damaging effect the mall has on our kids is serving as a surrogate nurturing mother and family (10–12). All the mall's positive effects are described ironically.

4. Teenagers themselves would probably have their eyes opened by some of the facts Kowinski presents. But certainly the parents of mall teenagers would benefit most from reading this article. The information, the language, and the authorities cited suggest that adults are the target audience.

5. Kowinski's values can be determined by simply inverting the values he finds disconcerting—in his title, in his discussion of consumerism, and particularly in his description of the mall serving as a surrogate family (10–12). More explicitly, he lists attitudes he finds valuable that are not made in the mall: "curiosity, initiative, self-expression, empathy, and disinterested learning" (15).

Strategy

1. Kowinski cites two specific examples, both tinged with dark humor, of kids who live at malls (2). He switches to typical examples to show how many children have gone through typical milestones of development at the mall (3). He speculates about all that important experience happening in an artificial environment and states his thesis in the final sentence (4).

2. The immediate cause is the "plethora of products in the mall, plus the pressure on teens to buy them." The effect from this cause is both immediate and ultimate—"the hurried child"—who must grow up too fast. This child learns how to shop in the short term, but in the longer term, he or she is pressured to look like an adult and to understand adult finances and emotions.

3. Superficially the two examples seem contradictory, but they are almost totally unlike. First, children are pressured to act in adult ways sexually and emotionally far beyond their own emotional development. Second, children just beginning to face responsibilities in the public work force need adult models on which to base their own behavior.

4. Whom is Kowinski addressing in this essay? Who should hear his message?

5. Can a careful reading of the essay establish the author's values? What are they? Where are these attitudes evident?

Strategy

1. Paragraphs 2–4 serve as the essay's introduction. How does each function independently? How do they fit together to form the larger unit?

2. Does Kowinski talk about immediate or ultimate causes and effects in paragraph 9? Explain.

3. Compare paragraphs 9 and 14. In paragraph 9, Kowinski describes "the hurried child syndrome," the negative effect on a child who is too quickly exposed to the adult world and must respond with a sophistication still beyond him or her. In paragraph 14, discussing how teenagers who work in malls work mostly with other teenagers, Kowinski cites an authority who claims kids need more time in their work with adults. Do you see a contradiction here?

4. A related cause-and-effect structure is visible in paragraphs 10–12. What is it and how does it work?

5. Study the structure of paragraph 18. How does it contribute to the essayist's main purpose of showing how stultifying and controlling malls are for teenagers?

Style

1. Comment on the effects of the final sentence in paragraph 13 on the rest of the paragraph. What does it say about the mall experience as a whole?

2. What is Kowinski's attitude toward his subject? Where is this attitude manifest?

3. If necessary, look up the meanings of these words: *resonances*

4. The cause of kids' spending time in the mall is that parents allow or encourage it (10). Kids' spending time at the mall becomes a cause of the mall's role of surrogate parent, which is the effect, but then this role itself becomes a cause (11) of structure being imposed on kids and elements of family life. Because kids crave structure and family life, they are drawn to cuddly merchandise and "home cooking." These elements in turn are causes, and their effects are that kids embrace passivity and consumerism. The whole progression is a causal chain.

5. Paragraph 18 is divided into two parts. The first two sentences describe how frighteningly insulated a child's mall existence is and how, therefore, every place becomes the same place. The next two sentences project that this is actually a good preparation for the future they face. In the first part, Kowinski looks back at the essay and encapsulates the experience he has just described, and in the second he looks forward to an ominous future.

Style

1. After describing how a teenage girl's major ambition was to learn how to put the perfect swirl on an ice-cream cone in order to gain a promotion in the company she worked for, and then to call that "achievement," makes a mockery of the emptiness and vapidity of the entire mall experience. Compare that to the achievement of "attitudes" (15).

2. Kowinski seems sympathetic toward his subject. He both acknowledges and understands the problem of teenagers in malls (first sentence in 4, 8, and 10). Still, he sees the dangers and hopes for a better choice for teenagers (7, first sentence, 19).

3. *Resonances:* the states or qualities of resounding or echoing; *incursion:* a hostile entrance into or invasion of a place or territory, especially a hostile one; *plethora:* overabundance, excess; *denizens:* inhabitants, residents; *impertinence:* unmannerly intrusion or presumption, insolence; *inexorably:* unyieldingly, unalterably.

(4), *inclusion* (5), *plethora* (9), *denizens* (11), *impertinence* (17), *inexorably* (18).

Writing Tasks

1. Kowinski takes a rather dim view of what happens to kids when they "grow up" in a mall. Write an essay in which you either show that mall experiences do not have such dire consequences, or agree with Kowinski. Either way, draw from your own experience or that of those you know. Be sure to discuss immediate and ultimate causes and effects, either alternately in the same paragraphs, or in separate paragraphs.

2. Think of a place, other than a mall, where you spent a lot of time during your teenage years—a hangout of some sort. What do you think some of the immediate and ultimate effects were and are from your having spent time there? Answer this question in a short essay. Be specific.

Students rarely talk publicly about their anxieties. This is a good time to encourage them to become open about the subject. Begin the discussion by taking a poll. Write a vertical list on the board of the usual subjects that students take as part of their general education requirements: English, history, psychology, math, and so forth. Then ask for a show of hands that indicate how many students are anxious at one time or another about each of these disciplines. Record the number of responses according to gender. For example, how many women in your class are anxious about history? How many men? How many women in your class are anxious about math? How many men? Ask your students what, in their opinion, causes such anxieties. Is it the discipline itself? The way it is taught? The way it is perceived according to how "useful" it might be? Point out that everyone who has graduated from college had, at one time or another, some anxiety about some course. You might even want to mention a course that you had in college, your anxiety about the course, and what effect the anxiety had on your grade or on your attitude about the course. After you have shown that anxiety is a part of everyone's college life, then introduce this essay by noting that Tobias and other scholars deeply involve themselves in the study of anxieties, and are producing more and more information about the subject that will help both students and teachers, now and in the future.

Note the word *If,* which introduces two conditions. Other factors could cause math anxiety (or any other kind of academic anxiety). Tobias wants to put those aside for the purpose of this essay.

❦ Sheila Tobias ❦

One of the founding members of the National Organization for Women (NOW), Sheila Tobias was born in 1935 in Brooklyn, New York. She received her undergraduate education at Radcliffe College and earned her M.A. in history from Columbia University. She has taught at the City University of New York and at Vanderbilt University. The following selection is from her book Overcoming Math Anxiety *(1978).*

Who's Afraid of Math, and Why?

In this essay, Sheila Tobias discusses the causes and effects of math anxiety, especially among women. She discusses the several factors that may be responsible for why comparatively few women enter disciplines that require a strong background in mathematics.

Every college student at one time or another experiences anxiety about a course, whether it be a history course, an English course, a math course, or some other course. As you read this essay, find the remarks the author makes about anxiety and its causes that apply to you.

The first thing people remember about failing at math is that it felt like sudden death. Whether the incident occurred while learning "word problems" in sixth grade, coping with equations in high school, or first confronting calculus and statistics in college, failure came suddenly and in a very frightening way. An idea or a new operation was not just difficult, it was impossible! And, instead of asking questions or taking the lesson slowly, most people remember having had the feeling that they would never go any further in mathematics. If we assume that the curriculum was reasonable, and that the new idea was but the next in a series of learnable concepts, the feeling of utter defeat was simply not rational; yet "math anxious" college students and adults have revealed that no matter how much the teacher reassured them, they could not overcome that feeling.

A common myth about the nature of mathematical ability holds that one either has or does not have a mathematical mind. Mathematical imagination and an intuitive grasp of mathematical principles may well be needed to do advanced research, but why should people who can do college-level work in other subjects not be able to do college-level math as well? Rates of learning may vary. Competency under time pressure may differ. Certainly low self-esteem will get in the way. But where is the evidence that a student needs a "mathematical mind" in order to succeed at learning math?

Consider the effects of this mythology. Since only a few people are supposed to have this mathematical mind, part of what makes us so passive in the face of our difficulties in learning mathematics is that we suspect all the while we may not be one of "them," and we spend our time waiting to find out when our nonmathematical minds will be exposed. Since our limit will eventually be reached, we see no point in being methodical or in attending to detail. We are grateful when we survive fractions, word problems, or geometry. If that certain moment of failure hasn't struck yet, it is only temporarily postponed.

Parents, especially parents of girls, often expect their children to be nonmathematical. Parents are either poor at math and had their own sudden-death experiences, or, if math came easily for them, they do not know how it feels to be slow. In either case, they unwittingly foster the idea that a mathematical mind is something one either has or does not have.

Mathematics and Sex

Although fear of math is not a purely female phenomenon, girls tend to drop out of math sooner than boys, and adult women experience an aversion to math and math-related activities that is akin to anxiety. A 1972 survey of the amount of high school

Myth as used here means "fallacy."

The second rhetorical question is a strategical device to lead the reader into the next paragraph.

Note how Tobias deliberately introduces the tension needed to link her reader to her prose.

Here is the first indication that the article will focus on math anxiety among girls.

Not having taken high school math has long-term effects, beginning in one's college years.

mathematics taken by incoming freshmen at Berkeley revealed that while 57 percent of the boys had taken four years of high school math, only 8 percent of the girls had had the same amount of preparation. Without four years of high school math, students at Berkeley, and at most other colleges and universities, are ineligible for the calculus sequence, unlikely to attempt chemistry or physics, and inadequately prepared for statistics and economics.

Unable to elect these entry-level courses, the remaining 92 percent of the girls will be limited, presumably, to the career choices that are considered feminine: the humanities, guidance and counseling, elementary school teaching, foreign languages, and the fine arts.   6

Boys and girls may be born alike with respect to math, but certain sex differences in performance emerge early according to several respected studies, and these differences remain through adulthood. They are: 7

1. Girls compute better than boys (elementary school and on).
2. Boys solve word problems better than girls (from age thirteen on).
3. Boys take more math than girls (from age sixteen on).
4. Girls learn to hate math sooner and possibly for different reasons.

Why the differences in performance? One reason is the amount of math learned and used at play. Another may be the difference in male-female maturation. If girls do better than boys at all elementary school tasks, then they may compute better for no other reason than that arithmetic is part of the elementary school curriculum. As boys and girls grow older, girls become, under pressure, academically less competitive. Thus, the falling off of girls' math performance between ages ten and fifteen may be because: 8

This list offers possible causes of the facts in the list above.

1. Math gets harder in each successive year and requires more work and commitment.

2. Both boys and girls are pressured, beginning at age ten, not to excel in areas designated by society to be outside their sex-role domains.

3. Thus girls have a good excuse to avoid the painful struggle with math; boys don't.

Such a model may explain girls' lower achievement in math   9
overall, but why should girls even younger than ten have difficulty in problem-solving? In her review of the research on sex differences, psychologist Eleanor Maccoby noted that girls are generally more conforming, more suggestible, and more dependent upon the opinion of others than boys (all learned, not innate, behaviors). Being so, they may not be as willing to take risks or to think for themselves, two behaviors that are necessary in solving problems. Indeed, in one test of third-graders, girls were found to be not nearly as willing to estimate, to make judgments about "possible right answers," or to work with systems they had never seen before. Their very success at doing what is expected of them up to that time seems to get in the way of their doing something new.

If readiness to do word problems, to take one example, is as   10
much a function of readiness to take risks as it is of "reasoning ability," then mathematics performance certainly requires more than memory, computation, and reasoning. The differences in math performance between boys and girls—no matter how consistently those differences show up—cannot be attributed simply to differences in innate ability.

Still, if one were to ask the victims themselves, they would   11
probably disagree: they would say their problems with math have to do with the way they are "wired." They feel they are somehow missing something—one ability or several—that other people have. Although women want to believe they are not mentally inferior to men, many fear that, where math is concerned, they really are. Thus, we have to consider seriously whether mathematical ability has a biological basis, not only because a number of researchers believe this to be so, but because a number of victims agree with them.

Marginal notes:

An additional possible cause: Girls may not be risk takers.

Tobias rejects "innate ability" as the explanation for differences in math performance.

This transitional paragraph indicates why Tobias must, nevertheless, examine biological arguments.

The Arguments from Biology

Tobias explains the difficulty of testing the truth of the biological argument.

The search for some biological basis for math ability or disability is fraught with logical and experimental difficulties. Since not all math underachievers are women, and not all women are mathematics-avoidant, poor performance in math is unlikely to be due to some genetic or hormonal difference between the sexes. Moreover, no amount of research so far has unearthed a "mathematical competency" in some tangible, measurable substance in the body. Since "masculinity" cannot be injected into women to test whether or not it improves their mathematics, the theories that attribute such ability to genes or hormones must depend for their proof on circumstantial evidence. So long as about 7 percent of the Ph.D.'s in mathematics are earned by women, we have to conclude either that these women have genes, hormones, and brain organization different from those of the rest of us, or that certain positive experiences in their lives have largely undone the negative fact that they are female, or both.

12

Chromosomes, the DNA-containing linear bodies of the cell nuclei of plants and animals, determine and transmit hereditary characteristics.

Genetically, the only difference between males and females (albeit a significant and pervasive one) is the presence of two chromosomes designated X in every female cell. Normal males exhibit an X-Y combination. Because some kinds of mental retardation are associated with sex-chromosomal anomalies, a number of researchers have sought a converse linkage between specific abilities and the presence or absence of the second X. But the linkage between genetics and mathematics is not supported by conclusive evidence.

13

Androgen is a hormone that develops and maintains masculine characteristics; estrogen is any of several hormones that regulate certain female reproductive functions and maintain female secondary sex characteristics.

Since intensified hormonal activity commences at adolescence, a time during which girls seem to lose interest in mathematics, much more has been made of the unequal amounts in females and males of the sex-linked hormones androgen and estrogen. Biological researchers have linked estrogen—the female hormone—with "simple repetitive tasks," and androgen—the male hormone—with "complex restructuring tasks." The assumption here is not only that such specific talents are biologically based (probably undemonstrable) but also that one cannot be good at *both* repetitive and restructuring kinds of assignments.

14

Sex Roles and Mathematics Competence

The fact that many girls tend to lose interest in math at the   15
age they reach puberty (junior high school) suggests that puberty
might in some sense cause girls to fall behind in math. Several
explanations come to mind: the influence of hormones, more
intensified sex-role socialization, or some extracurricular learning
experience exclusive to boys of that age.

One group of seventh-graders in a private school in New   16
England gave a clue as to what children themselves think about
all of this. When asked why girls do as well as boys in math until
the sixth grade, while sixth-grade boys do better from that point
on, the girls responded: "Oh, that's easy. After sixth grade, we
have to do real math." The answer to why "real math" should be
considered to be "for boys" and not "for girls" can be found not
in the realm of biology but only in the realm of ideology of sex
differences.

In this context, *ideology* refers to the current body of culturally accepted ideas that reflect the social needs and aspirations of girls as a group and of boys as a group.

Parents, peers, and teachers forgive a girl when she does badly   17
in math at school, encouraging her to do well in other subjects
instead. " 'There, there,' my mother used to say when I failed at
math," one woman says. "But I got a talking-to when I did badly
in French." Lynn Fox, who directs a program for mathematically
gifted junior high boys and girls on the campus of Johns Hopkins
University, has trouble recruiting girls and keeping them in her
program. Some parents prevent their daughters from participating
altogether for fear that excellence in math will make them too
different. The girls themselves are often reluctant to continue with
mathematics, Fox reports, because they fear social ostracism.

Where do these associations come from?   18

Note the connotative differences between "mathematician" and "writer," which might also reflect "ideology" as the word is used in paragraph 16.

The association of masculinity with mathematics sometimes   19
extends from the discipline to those who practice it. Students,
asked on a questionnaire what characteristics they associate with
a mathematician (as contrasted with a "writer"), selected terms
such as rational, cautious, wise, and responsible. The writer, on
the other hand, in addition to being seen as individualistic and
independent, was also described as warm, interested in people,
and altogether more compatible with a feminine ideal.

"psychological conditioning": If "learning" and "conditioning" are assumed to be synonymous, then anything acquired through social or cultural experience must have been "conditioned." This moderately loose usage has been adopted by some as a basis for refuting the argument that social behavior is instinctive. These girls "learned" that the "feminine ideal" and achieving in mathematics are somehow socially or culturally incompatible.

Barbie is the trademark for a brand of doll representing a slim, pretty young woman, especially one with blond hair, blue eyes, and fair skin. In slang, the term refers to a young woman perceived as monotonously attractive and empty-headed.

Paragraphs 21–24 contrast the play of girls and boys as a possible cause of math performance differences.

As a result of this psychological conditioning, a young woman 20 may consider math and math-related fields to be inimical to femininity. In an interesting study of West German teenagers, Erika Schildkamp-Kuendiger found that girls who identified themselves with the feminine ideal underachieved in mathematics, that is, did less well than would have been expected of them based on general intelligence and performance in other subjects.

Street Mathematics: Things, Motion, Scores

Not all the skills that are necessary for learning mathematics 21 are learned in school. Measuring, computing, and manipulating objects that have dimensions and dynamic properties of their own are part of the everyday life of children. Children who miss out on these experiences may not be well primed for math in school.

Feminists have complained for a long time that playing with 22 dolls is one way of convincing impressionable little girls that they may only be mothers or housewives—or, as in the case of the Barbie doll, "pinup girls"—when they grow up. But doll-playing may have even more serious consequences for little girls than that. Do girls find out about gravity and distance and shapes and sizes playing with dolls? Probably not.

A curious boy, if his parents are tolerant, will have taken apart 23 a number of household and play objects by the time he is ten, and, if his parents are lucky, he may even have put them back together again. In all of this he is learning things that will be useful in physics and math. Taking parts out that have to go back in requires some examination of form. Building something that stays up or at least stays put for some time involves working with structure.

Sports is another source of math-related concepts for children 24 which tends to favor boys. Getting to first base on a not very well hit grounder is a lesson in time, speed, and distance. Intercepting a football thrown through the air requires some rapid intuitive eye calculations based on the ball's direction, speed, and trajectory. Since physics is partly concerned with velocities, trajectories, and collisions of objects, much of the math taught to prepare a student for physics deals with relationships and formulas that can be used to express motion and acceleration.

What, then, can we conclude about mathematics and sex? If math anxiety is in part the result of math avoidance, why not require girls to take as much math as they can possibly master? If being the only girl in "trig" is the reason so many women drop math at the end of high school, why not provide psychological counseling and support for those young women who wish to go on? Since ability in mathematics is considered by many to be unfeminine, perhaps fear of success, more than any bodily or mental dysfunction, may interfere with girls' ability to learn math. 25

Final paragraph summarizes possible causes of math anxiety in females and the second and third questions present possible solutions to the problem.

POSSIBLE ANSWERS

Meaning and Purpose

1. Girls do not excel in math because of an ideological guilt by association; society associates math competence with masculine characteristics including the biological association of androgen with "complex restructuring tasks" (14). Girls are "psychologically conditioned" (19) to associate math with qualities that are "unfeminine."

2. The essay makes by implication the even more important point that ideology, nurtured by peer pressures and parental ones, can prevent women from reaching their academic potentials.

3. It is difficult to determine a biological cause, since it is true that not all women are poor at math, just as not all men are good at math. No clear-cut biological cause already exists that can be shown conclusively to prove a biological effect.

4. Answers vary depending on how students marshal their evidence. It can be shown that the essay's audience includes parents, female students, curriculum developers—anyone interested in improving the social and academic lot of women.

5. These paragraphs show how students themselves view math from the standpoint of peer grouping. "Mathematician" suggests connotations associated with masculine characteristics; "Writer" suggests connotations associated with feminine characteristics. The effect of these associations is to "teach" students that women should not become mathematicians.

Meaning and Purpose

1. In the essay, what does Tobias say is the main reason that girls do not excel in math?
2. Is the essay only about what causes math anxiety, or is the author talking about an even more important topic in terms of cause and effect? What might be that more important topic?
3. According to the essay, why is it difficult to determine a biological cause for one's inability to do math well?
4. In your opinion, who is the primary audience for this essay, and what evidence do you have for choosing that audience?
5. Reread paragraphs 19 and 20. What possible cause-and-effect relationship is being discussed in those paragraphs?

Strategy

1. What does Tobias mean by the phrase "fear of success," in the last paragraph of the essay?
2. Who are the "victims" mentioned in paragraph 11? Why are they called "victims"?

Strategy

1. Ironically, "fear of success" in mathematics reflects fear of failure at being feminine. Tobias makes the point throughout the essay that women are ideologically habituated to associate success in math with possible rejection as a person.

2. The victims are those who, for one external reason or another, do not do well in math. They are called victims because they have been victimized by a society that resists associating women with mathematicians.

3. Tobias brings up these two hormones to show, in paragraph 14, that while biologists have linked hormones with causing the abilities to perform certain tasks, it probably cannot be demonstrated that the effects of those hormones are mutually exclusive. The author here attempts to refute the arguments from biology for the level of one's mathematical ability.

4. The woman demonstrates autobiographically that society ideologically accepts women who excel at a foreign language, but merely accommodates women who excel at math.

5. The sort of "social ostracism" meant here is that of a girl's being excluded or ostracized from her peer group because of the ability to do math well, which students consider to be a male's specialty.

Style

1. We can describe the tone in this essay by using a number of adjectives, most of them centering on friendly objectivity. Some of the adjectives and phrases used to describe the tone have been impartial," "fair," "explanatory," "purposeful," "scientific in a sociological sense," "argumentative yet concerned," and "journalistic."

2. The term *mathematical mind* refers to the fallacy of some people's believing that others have a "natural" intuitive grasp of things mathematical; some people are "born mathematicians."

3. As used in this essay, the term *mythology* means "unexamined claims," akin to the words "error," "flaw," and "inaccuracy."

3. Why does Tobias bring up androgen and estrogen?

4. In paragraph 17, a woman said that she "got a talking-to" when she did poorly in French, but that if she did poorly in math, she was forgiven. What is the significance of that woman's statement?

5. Paragraph 17 notes that girls often hesitate to continue to study mathematics, fearing social ostracism. What sort of "social ostracism" do you think is meant here?

Style

1. How would you describe the *tone* of this essay? What do you suppose causes the author to adopt that tone? (See the Glossary for a definition of *tone*.)

2. What is meant by the term *mathematical mind* in the second paragraph?

3. Look up the word *mythology* in a college-level dictionary. Which definition best describes how Tobias uses the term in this essay?

4. The last paragraph of the essay contains four sentences. The first three of them are questions. Why do you think Tobias ended this essay with these three questions?

5. Look up the word *feminist*. Was this essay written from a feminist point of view? How can you tell?

Writing Tasks

1. At one time or another, all of us have experienced some kind of academic anxiety, be it math anxiety, English-composition anxiety, test-taking anxiety, or some other kind of anxiety. Write a cause-and-effect essay pointing out an anxiety that you once had (or now have). What are the causes for that anxiety? What are the effects of that anxiety?

2. Write an autobiographical essay in which you look back at a successful or embarrassing incident in your childhood. What

4. Tobias uses these three questions to nudge the reader into a thoughtfully involved frame of mind. The questions are not rhetorical in the sense that the author herself answers them immediately. They are audience-based, in the sense that Tobias wants her audience to ponder them. **5.** The word *feminist* describes a person who believes that women and men should be equal socially, economically, and politically. Tobias points out the causes of math anxiety among women to show that the effect gives rise to inequality, thus demonstrating that Tobias is writing from the standpoint of endorsing equality—the feminist standpoint.

caused the success or embarrassment? What were the effects of that incident on you personally?

3. Recall a college or high school course that you once took and enjoyed, and from which you learned something academically important. What features of the class caused you to enjoy taking it? What were the effects of your having learned something academically important from it?

❧ *Responding to Photographs* ❧

Cause and Effect

A Woman

Noted author Sharon Curtin has criticized American attitudes toward those who are growing old. In the following quotation, she expresses her own feeling about aging and projects those feelings to others:

> I am afraid to grow old—we're all afraid. In fact, the fear of growing old is so great that every aged person is an insult and a threat to society. They remind us of our own death, that our body won't always remain smooth and responsive, but will someday betray us by aging, wrinkling, faltering, failing. The ideal way to age would be to grow slowly invisible, gradually disappearing, without causing worry or discomfort to the young. In some ways that does happen. Sitting in a small park across from a nursing home one day, I noticed that the young mothers and their children gathered

on one side, and the old people from the home on the other. Whenever a youngster would run over to the "wrong" side, chasing a ball or just trying to cover all the available space, the old people would lean forward and smile. But before any communication could be established, the mother would come over, murmuring embarrassed apologies, and take her child to the "young" side.

Curtin's reflections on aging find a haunting expression in "A Woman," which features an older woman with a photograph of herself when young. Drawing on Curtin's observations and elements in the photograph, compose an essay with cause and/ or effect as the dominant development pattern. Before starting your project, review "Cause and Effect: Identifying Reasons and Results" at the beginning of the chapter; then select one of the following writing tasks as the basis for your essay.

1. Begin with the assertion that aging is the subject of "A Woman." Review Curtin's reflection on aging and also study the photograph, allowing its imagery to work on your imagination. Identify an emotion the photograph creates. Then relate the reasons the photograph has this effect.

2. Imagine you are a psychologist who shares Curtin's belief about growing old in our society. The young woman in "A Woman" is your client. She is beautiful, and because of her beauty, she has a deep fear of growing old. She asks you what you believe the physical and social effects of growing old will be for her. You decide to be blunt and state your feelings as directly as possible, but you decide to do so in writing. First you describe her current beauty and relate the effects of her beauty on others. Then you describe her as she will appear fifty years in the future and what will result from growing old. You then give her positive advice on how to deal with the aging process, and then you predict the effects the advice will have on her twilight years if she follows it.

❦ *Additional Writing Tasks* ❦
Cause and Effect

1. Using cause and effect (or one of the two alone) as the dominant development pattern, write an essay explaining something that interests you. These general questions are offered as ways to get you started. Revise them in any way that reflects your interests and then in a well-developed essay answer them, using the principles of cause and effect or one of the two.
   a. Why do works by some artists, filmmakers, poets, or novelists affect you?
   b. Why do people need "idols," such as singers, athletes, actors, and politicians?
   c. Why does a television series—police drama, situation comedy, talk show—succeed?
   d. What are the effects of music lyrics that some political activists believe are obscene and condone violence?
   e. What are the effects of stand-up comedians who deliver monologues that critics claim are racist and sexist?
   f. Why are stories that repeat familiar formulas successful?
   g. Is common sense an effective way to solve complex problems?
   h. Is routine the great deadener or do we need it to organize experience?
   i. Is homelessness a "real" problem in America?
   j. Can government solve the national-deficit problem by printing more money?
   k. Should children be seen and not heard?
   l. What results can you expect from an education?
   m. Is deceit self-destructive?
   n. Should children be made to feel guilty as a way of controlling teenage recklessness?
   o. Why should a dieter avoid eating foods high in fat?
   p. What causes stress and what are its temporary and lasting effects?
   q. What are the effects of a mental illness?

    r.   Why does the destruction of symbols such as the American flag enrage some people?

    s.   What would happen if everyone were given the college degree of his or her choice without completing course work?

2.   Discuss one of these subjects in an essay using cause and effect (or one of the two) as the dominant pattern.

    a.   Violence has always been a major element in action-oriented entertainment, from Flash Gordon to Indiana Jones. In recent years, however, action-oriented children's television cartoons, such as "G.I. Joe" and "Rambo," have become stripped of story line of any value and of characterization. The shows present unrelenting karate chopping and related mayhem and "us versus them" worlds with little or no complexity. Currently, some experts and a growing number of parents are beginning to worry about the possible harmful effects these shows might have upon children. In a cause-and-effect (or cause or effect alone) essay, explain the influence of action-oriented cartoons on children.

    b.   David A. Goslin, Ph.D., of the American Institute for Research in Washington, D.C., which conducts behavioral and social-science research, claims, "Choices do not make life easier; they make it more difficult, for all of us. As social scientists, we know that with an increase in choices, people tend to become more anxious."

        In your experience, is Dr. Goslin's comment valid? Write a cause-and-effect (or cause or effect alone) essay discussing his point of view. You might keep in mind that Americans can choose from more than 25,000 items shelved in their supermarkets. They can tune in more than fifty television channels. They can buy more than 11,000 magazines or periodicals. They are solicited by tens of thousands of special-interest groups. Some call this opportunity "freedom of choice," but social critics and experts are beginning to believe that the marketplace may have outsmarted itself by creating all these choices.

    c.   In *The Tyranny of Malice,* Joseph H. Berke explains that "Envy is a state of exquisite tension, torment, and ill will provoked by an overwhelming sense of inferiority, impotence, and worthlessness. It begins in the eye of the beholder and is so painful to the mind that the envious person will go to almost any lengths to diminish, if not destroy, whatever or whoever may have aroused it." Basing a cause-and-effect (or cause or effect alone) essay on personal observation, discuss the sources of envy and how it might affect behavior.

d.   "Think globally, act locally" was the rallying cry of environmental activism in the 1960s. This advice is as appropriate now as it was then. Just as the Greenpeace movement started more than two decades ago not with governments but at the grass roots, so today it is individuals who must occupy the front lines in protecting the environment. In a cause-and-effect (or cause or effect alone) essay discuss individual or local-government actions that have resulted from environmental activism.

e.   In "The Slaughterer," a short story by Isaac Bashevis Singer, Yoineh Meir wanted to be a rabbi. Instead, the religious authorities in his community made him the ritual slaughterer. Obediently, Meir learned the laws of slaughter as found in religious texts and followed the command of authority.

"Barely three months had passed since Yoineh Meir had become a slaughterer," Singer wrote, "but the time seemed to stretch endlessly. He felt as though he were immersed in blood and lymph. His ears were beset by the squawking of hens, the crowing of roosters, the gobbling of geese, the lowing of oxen, the mooing and bleating of calves and goats; wings fluttered, claws tapped on the floor. The bodies refused to know any justification or excuse—every body resisted in its own fashion, tried to escape, and seemed to argue with the Creator to its last breath."

Yoineh Meir's life ended in madness: "The killing of every beast, great or small, caused him as much pain as though he were cutting his own throat. Of all the punishments that could have been visited upon him, slaughtering was the worst."

Although Yoineh Meir is an extreme example, many people are forced to follow the dictates of authority against their better judgment. In an essay describe a situation in which authority has been used to pressure an individual into action that seems contrary to his or her nature and discuss the related causes and effects.

8

Process Analysis
Explaining Step by Step

The Method

Are you, like many readers, fascinated by how things work? Are you attracted to writing that explains how to organize your life and time? You might want to understand how the stock market works or how Colombian drug producers smuggle cocaine into the United States. Perhaps your interests have to do with the mind—you might want to learn how psychotherapy works. Authors of essays or books explaining how things work use **process analysis**: they help us to better understand something by breaking it down into its components.

In some ways process analysis comes close to narration and cause-and-effect analysis by attending to a sequence of related events. Narration, however, is meant to tell a story, and cause-and-effect analysis deals with the reasons for and results of an event or experience. In process analysis a writer examines the way in which something works. In short, narration concentrates on *what* happened; cause and effect, on *why* it happened; and process analysis, on *how* it happened.

Strategies

Careful writers distinguish between two kinds of process analysis: **directive** and **informative**. Directive process analysis explains *how to* do something. Directive process analysis is usually a practical kind of writing based on the assumption that someone will follow the directions to complete a task. Informative process analysis emphasizes *how* something works rather than *how to* do something. Informative process analysis might explain how the brain functions, how gravity holds human beings to the face of the earth, or how food is grown, processed, and merchandised, but an informative process analysis will not offer directions for completing a task.

Directive Process Analysis

Directive process analysis can range from brief instructions on a soup-can label to a complicated plan for putting an astronaut on another planet. Keep in mind that directive process analysis has one clear purpose: to guide a reader to a predetermined goal by breaking down the steps required to get there. Consider this paragraph from Tom Cuthbertson's *Anybody's Bike Book,* setting out simple directions for checking bike tire pressure.

> There's a great *curb-edge test* you can do to make sure your tires are inflated just right. Rest the wheel on the edge of a curb or stair so the bike sticks out into the street or path, perpendicular to the curb or stair edge. Get the wheel so you can push down on it at about a 45 degree angle from above the bike. Push hard on the handlebars or seat, depending on which wheel you're testing. The curb should flare the tire a bit but shouldn't push right through the tire and clunk against the rim. You want the tire to have a little give when you ride over chuckholes and rocks, in other words, but you don't want it so soft that you bottom out. If you are a hot-shot who wants tires so hard that they don't have any give, you'll have to stick to riding on cleanswept Velodrome tracks, or watch very carefully for little sharp objects on the road. Or you'll have to get used to that sudden riding-on-the-rim feeling that follows the blowout of an overblown tire.

Cuthbertson's paragraph illustrates several characteristics of directive process analysis. First, he clearly establishes his purpose: to explain how to test bike tires for proper inflation. Second, he breaks the process down into simple steps and explains the final result: "The curb should flare the tire . . . ." Third, Cuthbertson addresses his reader directly by using the second person pronoun *you,* a practice that many writers adopt in directive process analysis: "There's a great curb-edge test *you* can do to make sure *your* tires are inflated just right." A fourth frequent characteristic of directive process analysis alerts the reader to possible mistakes and their consequences. Notice that Cuthbertson states the consequences of overinflated bike tires.

Now consider this passage from *The New York Times Complete Manual of Home Repair*. Bernard Gladstone gives directions for building a fire. Notice that Gladstone's passage embodies most of the common characteristics of process analysis, but he chooses not to address the reader as "you." Instead he writes in the more impersonal passive voice, which seems to create a distance between the reader and the subject.

> Though "experts" differ as to the best technique to follow when building a fire, one generally accepted method consists of first laying a generous amount of crumpled newspaper on the hearth between the andirons. Kindling wood is then spread generously over this layer of newspaper and one of the thickest logs is placed across the back of the andirons. This should be as close to the back of the fireplace as possible, but not quite touching it. A second log is then placed an inch or so in front of this, and a few additional sticks of kindling are laid across these two. A third log is then placed on top to form a sort of pyramid with air space between all logs so that flames can lick freely up between them.
>
> A mistake frequently made is in building the fire too far forward so that the rear wall of the fireplace does not get properly heated. A heated back wall helps increase the draft and tends to suck smoke and flames rearward with less chance of sparks or smoke spurting out into the room.
>
> Another common mistake often made by the inexperienced firetender is to try to build a fire with only one or two logs, instead of using at least three. A single log is difficult to ignite properly, and even two logs do not provide an efficient bed with adequate fuel-burning capacity.
>
> Use of too many logs, on the other hand, is also a common fault and can prove hazardous. Building too big a fire can create more smoke and draft than the chimney can safely handle, increasing the possibility of sparks or smoke

being thrown out into the room. For best results, the home-owner should start with three medium-size logs as described above, then add additional logs as needed if the fire is to be kept burning.

Like Cuthbertson, Gladstone opens by clearly stating his purpose; that is, to explain the steps necessary to build a fire in a fireplace. He then follows with a series of steps—six in all—that are clearly written and easy to follow. After devoting a paragraph to directions for building a fire, he presents three common mistakes people make when building a fire, and their consequences, with one brief paragraph devoted to each mistake. Although Gladstone's directions for building a fire are longer than Cuthbertson's for testing air pressure in a bike tire, both follow the same general pattern. They begin with a clear statement of purpose, then present the steps necessary to complete the process, and, as is often done in directive process analysis, they identify the common mistakes people make when following the procedure.

Informative Process Analysis

Instead of guiding a reader through a series of directions to complete a task as directive process analysis does, informative process analysis explains how something happens or how it works. In this paragraph from Caroline Sutton's *How Do They Do That?* she explains how stripes are put into striped toothpaste.

Although it's intriguing to imagine the peppermint stripes neatly wound inside the tube, actually stripes don't go into the paste until it's on its way out. A small hollow tube, with slots running lengthwise, extends from the neck of the tooth-paste tube back into the interior a short distance. When the toothpaste tube is filled, red paste—the striping material—is inserted first, thus filling the conical area around the hollow tube at the front. (It must not, however, reach beyond the point to which the hollow tube extends into the tooth-paste tube.) The remainder of the dispenser is filled with the familiar white stuff. When you squeeze the toothpaste tube, pressure is applied to the white paste, which in turn presses on the red paste at the head of the tube. The red then passes through the slots and onto the white, which is moving through the inserted tube—and which emerges with five red stripes.

Sutton doesn't expect any of her readers to make a tube of striped toothpaste, but she does answer a common question, one that might have aroused your curiosity, too, "How do they get the stripes into the tube?"

An informative process analysis is usually arranged in chronological order and makes careful use of transitional techniques to guide a reader through the process. Sometimes the procedure is quite simple and easily organized in a step-by-step sequence. Often, however, the process is complex, such as a chemical reaction or human digestion, and challenges a writer's organizational skills, especially when the writer wishes to interrupt the explanation to add additional information or description.

For example, John McPhee in *Oranges* devotes a paragraph to describing the process oranges undergo when made into concentrated juice. As you read McPhee's paragraph, notice that he interrupts to bring in related information—first, to explain that oranges culled from the crop were once dumped in fields and eaten by cattle, thus accounting for the orangeade flavor of Florida milk; and second, to describe two kinds of juicing machines. Even though McPhee interrupts the process, he still guides the reader's attention with clear transitional techniques, especially phrases that create a sense of movement, such as, "As the fruit starts to move . . . ," "Moving up a conveyor belt . . . ," "When an orange tumbles in . . . ," and, finally, "As the jaws crush the out side . . . ."

As the fruit starts to move along a concentrate plant's assembly line, it is first culled. In what some citrus people remember as "the old fresh-fruit days," before the Second World War, about forty per cent of all oranges grown in Florida were eliminated at packinghouses and dumped in fields. Florida milk tasted like orangeade. Now, with the exception of the split and rotten fruit, all of Florida's orange crop is used. Moving up a conveyor belt, oranges are scrubbed with detergent before they roll on into juicing machines. There are several kinds of juicing machines, and they are something to see. One is called the Brown Seven Hundred. Seven hundred oranges a minute go into it and are split and reamed on the same kind of rosettes that are in the centers of ordinary kitchen reamers. The rinds that come pelting out the bottom are integral halves, just like the rinds of oranges squeezed in a kitchen. Another machine is the Food Machinery Corporation's FMC In-line Extractor. It has a shining row of aluminum jaws, upper and lower, with shining aluminum teeth. When an orange tumbles in, the upper jaw comes crunching down on it while at the same time the orange is penetrated from below by a perforated steel tube. As the jaws crush the outside, the juice goes through the perforations in the tube and down into the plumbing of the concentrate plant. All in a second, the juice has been removed and the rind has been crushed and shredded beyond recognition.

Some processes defy chronological explanation because they take place simultaneously. Here a writer must present the material in parallel stages, as McPhee does in the last three sentences of his paragraph when he describes juicing, clearly indicating with transitional markings that two or more interlocked events are taking place at once.

In a paragraph from in "The Spider and the Wasp," zoologist Alexander Petrunkevitch presents the procedure a female *Pepsis* wasp follows when paralyzing a tarantula before burying it with a wasp egg attached to its belly. The challenge Petrunkevitch faced was to show both the wasp's and the spider's simultaneous behavior.

> When the grave is finished, the wasp returns to the tarantula to complete her ghastly enterprise. First, she feels it all over once more with her antennae. Then her behavior

becomes more aggressive. She bends her abdomen, pro-
truding her sting, and searches for the soft membrane at the
point where the spider's legs join its body—the only spot
where she can penetrate the horny skeleton. From time to
time, as the exasperated spider slowly shifts ground, the
wasp turns on her back and slides along with the aid of her
wings, trying to get under the tarantula for a shot at the
vital spot. During all this maneuvering, which can last for
several minutes, the tarantula makes no move to save itself.
Finally the wasp corners it against some obstruction and
grasps one of its legs in her powerful jaws. Now at last the
harassed spider tries a desperate but vain defense. The two
contestants roll over and over on the ground. It is a terrifying
sight and the outcome is always the same. The wasp finally
manages to thrust her sting into the soft spot and holds it
there for a few seconds while she pumps in the poison.
Almost immediately the tarantula falls paralyzed on its back.
Its legs stop twitching; its heart stops beating. Yet it is not
dead, as is shown by the fact that if taken from the wasp it
can be restored to some sensitivity by being kept in a moist
chamber for several months.

Often the success of a process-analysis essay rests on clear
information about the reader. The writer must estimate how much
knowledge about the process the reader may already have and
how much additional information must be included in the essay.
If the writer's guess is wildly inaccurate, then he or she will include
either too much information, which may send the reader into a
fit of yawning, or too little, which may send the reader into an
intellectual fog bank.

Process Analysis in College Writing

In the sciences and social sciences, process analysis is an
important pattern of development. In laboratory sciences you will
often use directive process analysis to write reports that com-

municate the procedure in an experiment or research project. Courses such as geology, biology, cultural anthropology, and social psychology concentrate on such processes as the formation of mountains, photosynthesis, initiation ceremonies, and socialization. In courses such as these, informative process analysis comes with the territory.

The following six paragraphs are part of an extended essay written for an introduction to psychology course. John Barton, a psychology major, chose to write about new techniques used in psychotherapy. After reviewing traditional therapeutic techniques in three paragraphs, he turns to a recent technique, "photoanalysis."

Barton establishes photo-analysis as his topic. He points out it might save time in therapy.

Although some critics of psychotherapy claim the field is slow to change, some new techniques are developing. One is photoanalysis. No doubt you have heard that "A photograph is worth a thousand words." Well, photoanalysists would agree, but with a slight revision, "A family photo album is worth a thousand words." For example, a person might be aware that he has difficulty showing affection and expressing himself. After a session with a photoanalyst, usually a certified psychiatrist or psychologist, he could become aware that the difficulty is rooted in his family history. Instead of spending hours verbally exploring his family relationships, a client working with a photoanalyst would examine a family photo album where the patterns of restraint might be documented in photographs.

This paragraph clearly indicates Barton will use process analysis, and he begins by stating the importance of using a group of photographs.

Besides being trained as a therapist, a photoanalyst should also be sensitive to visual images and the nonverbal expression they embody. But analyzing photographs to uncover family themes is not simple. The analyst should use group photographs taken over a number of years. A single photograph may whet curiosity but is no more helpful in unearthing patterns of family relationship than a crystal ball.

"The process might begin . . ." reminds the reader that Barton is using process analysis and also that the procedures are not rigid. Throughout these three paragraphs, notice how he works in additional information. His intent is not to "train" someone to analyze photographs but to give an "impression" of what is involved in the process.

The process might begin by spreading the photographs on a table. Then the analyst will study the faces to determine the general "tone" of the relationships. Are the subjects looking at each other or at the camera? Are their expressions happy? Or severe? Or angry? Often a child's first impression of the world comes from parents. Their expressions, captured in a series of photographs, may reveal their general perceptions.

Next, the analyst will study the body language of family members. Do they stand rigidly or are they relaxed, at ease? Do they seem to interact with each other or do they seem emotionally isolated from each other? Are they touching? Perhaps one has an arm around another's shoulder or a hand on another's leg. Is the hand open or clenched?

Finally, the analyst will also examine family members' proximity to each other. If they are close enough to rub elbows, they probably enjoy a warm relationship. If they put distance between themselves to avoid touching, they may shun intimacy with each other. What if males and females are clearly separated? Does this distance suggest that men and women play traditional roles within the family? An analyst will notice who takes the dominant place in the photographs. Mother? Father? A grandparent? Perhaps the children. Whoever takes a dominant place in a series of photographs probably takes the dominant role at home as well. A parent who consistently gravitates toward one child in photographs might play favorites in family relationships. A person who always chooses to stand at the outside of the group might feel like an outsider.

Barton ends with an indirect warning and one more detail related to interpretation.

Throughout a photoanalysis session, the analyst should avoid narrow interpretations of the photographs, but should offer observations for the client's response. After all, the client is the one with the direct experience and therefore should have the last word in interpreting any photograph. The photoanalyst must, however, point out that a friendly smile might be masking the tension revealed by a clenched fist half hidden in a lap.

Barton's strategy is very effective. Rather than simply defining photoanalysis, he describes the general process while clearly indicating what photoanalysis involves. The opening paragraph provides a brief transition from the preceding paragraphs and introduces photoanalysis as the subject. Here Barton also shows the benefits of photoanalysis. In the next paragraph, he clearly indicates he will be using process analysis and clarifies what an analyst needs to get started. The next three paragraphs describe the process. Because an analyst would use neither a chronological nor a step-by-step procedure in photoanalysis, Barton merely suggests the chronological order to give his paragraphs structure while working additional information into his text along the way. Finally, Barton ends with a bit of advice: an analyst should avoid narrowly interpreting a photograph but instead should allow a client's responses to guide the procedure.

To some members of the class, 1950 designates a time in the dark ages. To help students make historical connections between then and now, occasionally teachers mention a few facts about the 1950s: In 1950, World War II had been over for only five years. Harry S Truman was president of the United States. George VI was king of England. Josef Stalin was still heading Russia. The Korean War ("police action") was fought from 1950 to 1953. And the contraceptive pill was not developed until 1955. (By the end of 1961, 500,000 American women were on "the pill.")

A good way to engender discussion is to ask both male and female students how long the process of dressing for a date takes them. As a follow-up question, you might want to ask if the procedure takes longer for a blind date than for a date already known. For that matter, do we "dress for" a date now, or do we mostly dress for ourselves? One way to fire the discussion is to ask a question like this: Would you favor returning to the dress code of 1950? Why or why not?

MARGINAL NOTES

The author not only sets the stage, but she also comments on cultural affairs in 1950. A single woman over twenty should be worried about being unmarried. Being single means not being grown up. A woman cannot call a man for a date. She must signal that she is a "nice girl."

Culturally significant in 1950, each item of clothing carries its own signal, which she hopes will be received properly by the man.

❦ Joan Gould ❦

Joan Gould was born in 1927 in New York City and attended Bryn Mawr College. She has written a juvenile novel and the "Hers" column in The New York Times, *and has contributed to major magazines such as* Esquire, Life, Sports Illustrated, *and* McCall's. *Many of her essays are very personal explorations of the experience of being a wife, a mother, a mother-in-law, and an adult daughter of an aging mother. Her book* Spirals: A Woman's Journey Through Family Life *(1988) is a collection of those essays.*

Binding Decisions

This essay was first printed in Memories *magazine in 1989. The author describes an event from her past, the ritual of getting ready for a blind date in 1950, which she uses to reveal social attitudes about women and men, marriage, and relationships at that time. The essay invites us to wonder how much attitudes like these have changed since then.*

This process comprises a set of steps, with a description of each step. As you read, separate the steps from their descriptions to find out exactly how many steps Joan Gould took to get ready for her date.

I'm out of the bathtub. I'm ready to get dressed for my date tonight, which is a blind date, serious business in this year of 1950 for any girl who's over 20 and still single. I'm 22. No matter how much money I may earn in my job, I'll never be allowed to have an apartment of my own; I'll never pay an electric bill or buy a bedspread or spend a night away from home without my parents; in fact, I'll never be a grown-up so long as I remain single. 1

How shall I dress? I want to look sexy enough to attract this unknown man, so that he'll call and ask me for another date next week. (Needless to say, I won't call him, even if my life depends on it.) On the other hand, I don't want to hide the fact that I'm what's known as a Nice Girl, addicted to Peter Pan collars and 2 velvet hats and white gloves, which means that I'm good wife material, and also makes it clear that he'll get nothing more than a goodnight kiss from me tonight.

And so I dress carefully. Every single item that I put on not only is complicated in itself but carries an even more complicated message.

My girdle comes first. Here's the badge, the bind, the bondage of womanhood. Here's the itch of it. This is the garment that tells me I'm not a little girl anymore, who wears only underpants, but neither am I middle-aged like my mother, who wears a real corset with bones that dig into her diaphragm and leave cruel sores there. I can get away with either a panty girdle or a two-way stretch, both of which are made of Lastex with a panel of stiff satin over the abdomen. The basic difference is that a panty girdle, unlike a two-way stretch, covers the crotch, which was considered a shocking—indeed obscene—idea when first introduced. Victorian women were obliged to wear half a dozen petticoats at a time to be respectable, but never, never would they put on anything that slipped between their thighs, like a pair of pants.

But why should I be bothering with this sausage casing when I weigh a grand total of a hundred and two pounds?

I bother because being thin has nothing to do with it. A girdle is a symbolic garment, and unless I want to be regarded as a child or a slut I have to put it on. When I go out with girlfriends in the daytime I may choose to be more comfortable in only a garter belt, a device with four long, wiggly elastics that dangle down my thighs like hungry snakes lunging at my stockings. When I'm with a boy, however, it would be unthinkable—it would be downright indecent—to let him see my rear end jiggle or let him notice that it has two halves. (All males are called "boys," no matter what their age, so long as they're single.) My backside is supposed to be molded in a rigid piece that divides into two legs, like a walking clothespin.

Besides, if I don't wear a girdle every day, the older girls warn me, I'm going to "spread." Spreading is somehow related to letting my flesh hang loose, which is in turn related to the idea of the "loose" woman, and none of us wants to be considered loose. A

The process begins: step 1. Notice that each step is descriptively, personally, and culturally explained. These paragraphs hold a wealth of information beyond the description of girdles. The cultural process described here reflects the lock-step 1950s thinking in Gould's element of society. Gould fits her process to the symbolism required by each social situation because such modifications are expected by her mother and her friends, who themselves are bound to the same symbol-laden process. Gould finally compromises, but not to the point of innovation. Betty Friedan says about the generation following Gould's, in *The Feminine Mystique* (1963), "When she stopped conforming to the conventional picture of femininity, she finally began to enjoy being a woman" (chapter 14).

3

4

5

6

7

man doesn't buy a cow if he can get milk for free, our mothers tell us in dire tones. We don't point out that we're not cows, and we don't fight against girdles, which apparently do a good job of discouraging wandering hands, since most of the single girls I know are virgins.

But which girdle should I wear? If I pick the panty girdle, I'll need 10 minutes' advance notice before going to the toilet. If I wear the two-way stretch, it will ride up and form a sausage around my waist. Either way, my flesh will be marked with welts and stripes when, at that delirious moment in my bedroom, I can strip off my clothes and scratch and scratch.

I pick the two-way stretch but, born compromiser that I am, put underpants over it.

Next comes the bra. I don't dare look at myself in the mirror as I put it on. This is the era of the pinup girl, the heyday of Lana Turner and Betty Grable, when breasts bubble and froth over the rims of C-cups and a flat chest is considered about as exciting as flat champagne. Not until Twiggy appears on the scene in the 1960's will thinness become acceptable in a girl, much less desirable—but how am I supposed to survive until then? The answer is the garment I've just put on, the confession of my disgrace—a padded bra. If I wear a strapless gown, I pin foam-rubber bust pads, which are known as "falsies," in place. Occasionally one of these breaks loose during a particularly ardent conga or mambo and rises above my dress like the rim of the sun peering over a hilltop.

At least the bra won't show under my silk slip. Silk is expensive, of course, and no male will see my underwear unless he marries me or I'm carried off to a hospital emergency room—but then, as all the mothers warn us, accidents do happen.

Stockings next. During World War II, just as I became old enough to wear them, our wonderful new nylons were snatched away from us in order to make parachutes for what was known as the "war effort." What were we girls supposed to do—go out on a date in socks, like little children? If there weren't any stockings around, we'd have to create them. And so we bought bottles of makeup base and painted stockings on our legs and drew seams

Lana Turner and Betty Grable, voluptuous American movie stars and pinup girls during World War II, predated Twiggy, the British model thin almost to emaciation, by more than twenty years. The padded bra was first advertised in nineteenth-century Paris. The first modern bra was designed and made by socialite Mary Phelps Jacobs, in 1913. Notice the mother's warning. Some things never change.

Nylon stockings were again available in 1950. Gould reminisces about "stockings" during World War II. The Du Pont chemical company had invented nylon in 1938 and sent spools of nylon to selected hosiery manufacturers in 1940. Chosen stores received nylon stockings only if they agreed not to sell them before May 15, 1940, "Nylon Day"; riots nearly broke out as women all over the United States rushed hosiery departments. By the end of 1940, 36 million pairs of nylons had been sold—only because no more could be had.

up the back with eyebrow pencils, which was undoubtedly the last time my seams were ever straight.

My dress, oddly enough, is easy to choose. For a woman of my years, a skirt-and-sweater is out of the question on a date. The dress mustn't be too high-style or expensive, however, or else the young man will think that I'm spoiled, a fatal defect in a girl who might otherwise qualify as good wife material. Never mind that I earned the money to buy my own clothes; I still have to show that it won't cost much to support me once we marry and I quit my job. For the same reason, wherever we go—which is always at his expense, of course—I'll insist that we travel by bus or subway, never by taxi. If he invites me out to dinner (which doesn't happen often, because of cost, and never on a first date), I'll eat a sandwich at home before I leave, to make sure I won't be tempted to order an appetizer or dessert in the restaurant. 13

Shoes. I'd like to wear my fashionable new ones, with their ankle straps crisscrossing in back and fastening above the ankle bone, but they have 3½-inch heels, and I have no idea if I'll tower over this unknown man. If I choose low heels, on the other hand, he may think that I'm condescending. I pick the high heels but hide a low-heeled pair in the hall closet, just in case. Blind dates have their special hazards. 14

I still have to put on my makeup, which includes lots of lipstick, loose face power and an eyebrow pencil to extend my brow line, but no eye shadow, much less liner. I also have to do my hair, which is set with heavy lotion and rollers in the beauty parlor every week. (At night I sleep in a cotton mesh hairnet that I tie around my head, in order to preserve the set for at least a week.) 15

Speeding up the pace, I rush to equip my pocketbook with a monogrammed handkerchief and some "mad money," including several nickels for phone calls or a bus, obligatory for a blind date. I run to my glove drawer and hunt up a pair in white kid, since he's invited me to a concert. I won't need a hat. He'll wear one, of course. 16

The doorbell rings. I dab Shalimar on a tuft of cotton, which I tuck inside my bra; I check my stocking seams and move toward 17

Notice how Gould embodies her times. Although the man is obliged socially to pay for everything on the date, Gould is obliged to do all that society expects from a woman who "needs" to marry.

Her process of dressing for the occasion is consciously based on 1950s social requirements for a date.

Tell the class about this 1770 legislation in the British Parliament: "That women of whatever age, rank, or profession, whether virgins, maids, or widows, who shall seduce or betray into matrimony, by scents, paints, cosmetic washes, artificial teeth, [or] false hair, shall incur the penalty of the law as against witchcraft, and that the marriage shall stand null and void." The bill was defeated.

Her process of getting ready for the date is almost complete. In this entire essay, Gould has mentioned only two requirements for her blind date: that he pay all expenses incurred on the date and that he wear a hat, as befits the occasion.

Shalimar: A popular scent by Guerlain, developed in 1925. Its name is from Sanskrit, meaning "temple of love." Notice that the process is completed with the opening of the door. Her blind date, oblivious to her careful preparations for the evening, concentrates on himself and his cold. She wears Shalimar; he carries Kleenex.

the door. For an instant, my hand rests on the knob, while I wonder what sort of person is breathing out there, only inches away from me but still unrevealed, unexplored. And then I open the door, and I see his face and hear his voice, because he's already in mid-sentence. As a matter of fact, he's in mid-story, as if it's inconceivable that anyone could be less than fascinated with what he's saying, which happens to be true, or as if he's my husband already and has waited all day, or maybe all his life, to tell me about what happened to him that afternoon.

A box of Kleenex is tucked under his arm, because he has a cold, and he lays the box down on the hall table with the assurance of the rightful prince stepping into his kingdom at last. This one I'll marry or I'll marry no one, I say to myself an hour later.   18

Three dates—which means three weeks—later, he proposes. "Wait. I have to tell you something first," I declare in distress. He waits. I'm in turmoil. I'm risking everything on candor, and candor isn't a virtue in which I've had much practice. I've never said anything like this out loud before. "You have a right to know," I announced. "I wear a padded bra."   19

He says he imagines he can handle that.   20

We were married three months later. I wonder, if he hadn't proposed so promptly, how much longer it would have been before he discovered my secret for himself.   21

All the planning and process itself lead to the man's proposing, after the proper length of time has passed, of course. Before she gives him her answer, she injects candor, in a sense revealing part of the process.

The process works! Notice the element of small mystery in the last line.

POSSIBLE ANSWERS

Meaning and Purpose

1. Gould devotes several paragraphs to the subject of girdles (4–9). The "Binding" of the title relates first to what girdles do to the body (sentence 2, paragraph 4). A bra, which Gould describes choosing, is also binding. Dressing for a date in 1950 bound young women to a rigid set of behaviors and values. The word "Decisions" in the title is ironic because young women then were not free to choose not to follow the rules of dating, courtship, and marriage; they could make only decisions that were ultimately insig-

Meaning and Purpose

1. What significance does the title have for you after you read the essay?

2. In paragraph 6, Gould says that the girdle is a "symbolic garment." We still have symbolic garments. What is one of them? How is it symbolic?

3. The author makes sure that she "won't be tempted to order an appetizer or dessert" if she is invited by a date to eat in a restaurant (13). Why?

nificant and superficial, such as which girdle to wear.

2. Students may choose any symbolic garment, including white wedding gown, veil, necktie, vest, and hat. Their reasoning provides the key to judging the answer to this question.

3. She might want to show that she is "naturally" frugal, or she might want to keep down her date's expenses. Either way, she will be more appealing as a wife.

4. We know from Gould's mention of Twiggy in the 1960s (10) that Gould is looking back from more than a decade in the future of 1950. Her article captures a particular social etiquette in a particular time and intimates the values of the whole decade. This period-piece article can be useful for comparison with any current dating preparations and social values.

5. The conga originated in Latin America; the mambo in Cuba; both are energetic dances quite popular in the 1950s. *Ardent* means "warm or intense in feeling; passionate." The author feared becoming too intense during either dance, and therefore forgetful.

Strategy

1. Three of the steps are: choosing a girdle (9); putting on a padded bra (10); and "Stockings next" (12).

2. In describing her choice of a girdle, Gould begins with "My girdle comes first" (4). From here through 7, she digresses about girdles that older women wear, girdles that Victorian women wore, the girdle as a symbolic garment (6), and the consequences of not wearing a girdle (7). Gould then resumes the chronology of dressing (8).

3. Gould does not spare details about dressing for a date, or other relevant facts. She assumes her readers may be younger than herself, may not have first-hand experience with the procedure she describes, and may know little about dating and women's clothes in the 1950s. On the other hand, readers who were dating in the 1950s might be amused and carried back by her details. The information thus is not necessarily too much for an audience of Gould's peers.

4. The young man seems nervous, intent on talking to himself, and not attentive to his date.

4. What is Gould's purpose in writing about the procedure of getting ready for a blind date in 1950? From what perspective is she writing?

5. In paragraph 10, she talks about what could happen during "an ardent conga or mambo." To what do *conga* and *mambo* refer? Why is *ardent* an appropriately descriptive word?

Strategy

1. The process in this essay can be broken into specific steps. What are three of those steps?

2. Gould often interrupts the chronology of her process of dressing for a date to give explanations and related information. Where is one example of this strategy, and how does it work in the essay?

3. From the kind and detail of information in this essay, what decision would you say Gould has made about the knowledge her audience has of her subject?

4. The blind date is in "mid-story" as the author opens the door. What does this strategy of description tell you about the mental attitude of the blind date?

Style

1. The process described in this essay was carried out forty or so years ago. Why is the essay written in the present tense?

2. What is Gould's attitude toward the procedure she must go through for a date? Point out specific language that illustrates her attitude.

3. Why is the word *delirious* so appropriate, as it is used in paragraph 8?

4. How does the word *candor* in paragraph 19 serve as an ironic comment on the entire process of dressing for a blind date in the 1950s?

Style

1. Written in present tense, the essay has a tone of immediacy, of excitement. The author is reliving her own past. This tone fits the essay's process—of dressing symbolically and appropriately, with anxiety, for a blind date who later becomes the author's husband.

2. Gould, even at the time of the date, is less than pleased with the rigmarole she has to go through. But her perspective from a future time also shows that she considered the ritual false and unnecessary, even humorous. Some language that illustrates her attitude: paragraph 4, "Here's the itch of it"; paragraph 5, "sausage casing"; paragraph 6, "like a walking clothespin"; and paragraph 10, "rises above my dress like the rim of the sun peering over a hilltop." Ask students for other examples.

3. The word *delirious* means, among other definitions, "wildly excited." The author is ecstatic because she can now "scratch and scratch," and be relieved of the binding girdle.

4. The word *candor* refers to "sharp honesty or frankness in expressing oneself." The author's candor serves as counterpoint to the masquerade imposed by society on her choice of clothing—particularly, here, the padded bra. Custom restricted her from using candor until now.

Writing Tasks

1. The title is quite important to this essay. The expression "binding decisions" means at least two things. Using the material in this essay, write a paper exploring two meanings of "binding decisions": as the expression describes the process in this essay, and as the expression defines the reason the author carries out that process.

2. How do you dress for a date, or for some other occasion? Write a brief essay chronicling the steps in the process. If it is relevant, give background information that places your process in a larger social context.

❦ Don Lago ❦

Don Lago, has written for the Bulletin of Atomic Scientists, Science Digest, *and* Cosmic Search *magazine. In 1981 Lago received the* Cosmic Search *magazine award for young writers. Apparently fascinated by the mysterious, Lago writes about the future, space exploration, and the search for intelligent life beyond earth.*

Symbols of Mankind

From Science Digest, *March 1981, Lago's essay describes in a few paragraphs the development of written communication throughout human history. By greatly simplifying this historical process, the author leads us to consider how advanced technology has brought us full circle, back to "new beginnings."*

As Lago discusses the process of writing, going from lines in the sand to interstellar communication, notice how much detailed information he manages to compress into such a short work.

1 Many thousands of years ago, a man quietly resting on a log reached down and picked up a stick and with it began scratching upon the sand at his feet. He moved the stick slowly back and forth and up and down, carefully guiding it through curves and straight lines. He gazed upon what he had made, and a gentle satisfaction lighted his face.

2 Other people noticed this man drawing on the sand. They gazed upon the figures he had made, and though they at once recognized the shapes of familiar things such as fish or birds or humans, they took a bit longer to realize what the man had meant to say by arranging these familiar shapes in this particular way. Understanding what he had done, they nodded or smiled in recognition.

3 This small band of humans didn't realize what they were

387

Lago now explains what he has just described and the enormous consequences to the human race with the invention of writing.

To emphasize the vast potential of writing, Lago contrasts it with memory and speech.

Now Lago focuses on early written language and compares pictographs with the more sophisticated ideograms.

After a simple transition ("The next leap occurred"), Lago describes the next development of writing by comparing syllabic and alphabetic systems.

Human knowledge exploded with the development of new technologies, but those technologies could not have been born without written language.

Technology has progressed so far that we must now go back to pictographs in order to attempt to communicate with other intelligences in space.

beginning. The images these people left in the sand would soon be swept away by the wind, but their new idea would slowly grow until it had remade the human species. These people had discovered writing.

Writing, early people would learn, could contain much more information than human memory could and contain it more accurately. It could carry thoughts much farther than mere sounds could—farther in distance and in time. Profound thoughts born in a single mind could spread and endure. 4

The first written messages were simply pictures relating familiar objects in some meaningful way—pictographs. Yet there were no images for much that was important in human life. What, for instance, was the image for sorrow or bravery? So from pictographs humans developed ideograms to represent more abstract ideas. An eye flowing with tears could represent sorrow, and a man with the head of a lion might be bravery. 5

The next leap occurred when the figures became independent of things or ideas and came to stand for spoken sounds. Written figures were free to lose all resemblance to actual objects. Some societies developed syllabic systems of writing in which several hundred signs corresponded to several hundred spoken sounds. Others discovered the much simpler alphabetic system, in which a handful of signs represented the basic sounds the human voice can make. 6

At first, ideas flowed only slightly faster when written than they had through speech. But as technologies evolved, humans embodied their thoughts in new ways: through the printing press, in Morse code, in electromagnetic waves bouncing through the atmosphere and in the binary language of computers. 7

Today, when the Earth is covered with a swarming interchange of ideas, we are even trying to send our thoughts beyond our planet to other minds in the Universe. Our first efforts at sending our thoughts beyond Earth have taken a very ancient form: pictographs. The first message, on plaques aboard Pioneer spacecraft launched in 1972 and 1973, featured a simple line drawing of two humans, one male and one female, the male holding up his hand in greeting. Behind them was an outline of the Pioneer 8 spacecraft, from which the size of the humans could be judged. The plaque also included the "address" of the two human figures: a picture of the solar system, with a spacecraft emerging from the third planet. Most scientists believe that when other civilizations attempt to communicate with us they too will use pictures.

All the accomplishments since humans first scribbled in the sand have led us back to where we began. Written language only works when two individuals know what the symbols mean. We can only return to the simplest form of symbol available and work from there. In interstellar communication, we are at the same stage our ancestors were when they used sticks to trace a few simple images in the sand. 9

We still hold their sticks in our hands and draw pictures with them. But the stick is no longer made of wood; over the ages that piece of wood has been transformed into a massive radio telescope. And we no longer scratch on sand; now we write our thoughts onto the emptiness of space itself. 10

POSSIBLE ANSWERS

Meaning and Purpose

1. "Mankind" in the title encompasses all the possibilities that the word connotes, including abilities to write, to communicate, to feel, and to share ideas. Lago means that symbolic systems of communication are unique to humanity on this planet.

2. First, by writing, man could store more information than could human memory, and could store it more accurately. Thoughts could be disseminated more widely in time and distance. By writing, the thoughts of one man "could spread and endure" (4). Thus grew knowledge and communication so that new technologies could be developed to even further expand human knowledge (7). Now, "The Earth is covered with a swarming interchange of ideas," and we are attempting to send our thoughts beyond earth (8).

Meaning and Purpose

1. Why do you think Lago titles his essay "Symbols of Mankind" and not "Symbols of Communication"?

2. In paragraph 3, Lago says that the original invention of writing "would slowly grow until it had remade the human species." What does he mean by that? In what ways have people changed because of writing?

3. What function of writing is intimated in paragraph 2?

4. What process has writing gone through, according to Lago? Why do we have to go back to rather primitive pictographs in our attempt at interstellar communication?

3. Writing is a means of communication and thus is directed to an audience.

4. First, people drew pictures of things—pictographs—which could depict only concrete things. In order to depict emotions and abstractions, ideograms were developed (5). Then, written figures became independent of things and ideas and came to represent spoken sounds. Two such basic systems evolved: syllabic systems, in which hundreds of figures corresponded to hundreds of spoken sounds; and alphabetic systems, in which just a few figures represented the basic sounds of the human voice (6). These systems can work only when both writer and reader understand what the written symbols mean. In attempting to communicate with extraterrestrials, therefore, we must return to universal pictographs.

Strategy

1. Probably the most difficult thing for students to recognize about a process essay is that it is organized around paragraphs that are, or should be, tightly organized units, that the essay is not "this happened, and this happened, and then this happened." Lago's essay is short enough that you can examine each paragraph to demonstrate this principle.

2. Lago switches to first person plural in paragraph 8 when, after tracing the history of writing, he comes to the present, "today." By using "we" he includes all humanity in the current endeavor to "send our thoughts beyond our planet to other minds in the Universe."

3. Beginning with the solitary man making designs with a stick in the sand as a cause, a series of effects, causes, and effects follows in subsequent paragraphs. Finally, the cause of our returning to primitive pictographs is our desire to reach beyond earth to other life, and our belief that pictographs are a universal language. The structure is a causal chain.

4. Lago follows the progression from pictographs to alphabets to binary notation—and back to pictographs. But the use of pictographs at the end is of course much more sophisticated than

Strategy

1. Lago traces the development of writing from its hypothetical discovery to the present. Examine each paragraph as an organizational unit that helps demonstrate that progression. What function does each paragraph serve?

2. Where does the author switch from third person to first person plural? What is the reason for this switch?

3. Sometimes process analysis is closely related to cause and effect. How could the structure of this essay be analyzed as a cause-and-effect analysis?

4. As a process analysis, the structure of Lago's essay appears to be circular because it comes back to pictographs at the end. Explain how this circular process works in the essay.

Style

1. Examine the use of punctuation in paragraph 10. Why does Lago link clauses with semicolons rather than make them separate sentences?

2. Compare Lago's use of detail in paragraphs 2 and 8. Why would he choose to use more detail in one than the other?

3. What do you think are Lago's feelings about his subject—the tone of the essay? Point to language that shows this tone.

Writing Tasks

1. Using Lago's essay as a model, write an informative process-analysis essay in which you inform your audience about a process that falls within your expert knowledge, such as how your team came to win the championship. Your essay should cover the problems and situations your readers might encounter with a process that is new to them.

their first use because interstellar probes carry their message into deep space. Irony lies in the contrast between this technology and the form of communication it carries. With a new species the process begins again.

Style

1. The first sentence in paragraph 10, the topic sentence, indicates that we write now very much as our ancestors did. The next two sentences contrast the past with the present, balancing the two in each sentence by using semicolons, thereby connecting them and giving equal weight to each.

2. Paragraph 2 has enough detail to make it vivid. But the situation is hypothetical and Lago includes just enough detail to make the scene plausible. Paragraph 8, on the other hand, is a present-day reality, and the extensive detail here both transmits important information and gives the passage immediacy.

3. Lago is direct and informative, yet he seems to be in awe thinking of how writing began, and how it evolved: "He gazed upon what he had made, and a gentle satisfaction lighted his face" (1); "Profound thoughts born in a single mind could spread and endure" (4); and "now we write our thoughts onto the emptiness of space itself" (10).

2. Choose something about which you know how to give instructions, such as putting up a tent or raising golden retrievers. Write a short, directive process-analysis essay in which you guide your readers toward a goal, step by step.

In this essay the writer imaginatively discovers the writing process, engaging it by using her notes as a source of invention (accumulating information). Then she moves to drafting and revising, which for her requires an active imagination and memory, including "what some would call lies." She leaves out mention of the edited version, trusting that the essay readers hold in their hands will show that such a thing is possible.

You might want to discuss briefly the writing process, focusing on poetic license as it is used when writing drafts, according to this essay. Some students who have heard the expression "poetic license" seem to believe that it means "to write in any way you want because it's *your* writing."

"Poetic license" connotes departing from that which is acceptable as normal, but the departure must have its own defense. Didion uses "lies" in drafts of her essays, but her defense is that such a strategy gives her the creative latitude necessary to produce another kind of truth, universally interesting truth. Didion uses her notes to trigger her creative imagination.

You might want to have students bring to class and discuss an editorial or a story from the sports page of a newspaper, examining word choice. Do athletic teams "kill," "slaughter," "roll over," or "stomp" their opponents? Or do they merely "win"?

Marginal Notes

The essay begins *in medias res*, "in the midst of things." Didion opens the story in the middle of an action and then adds information with flashbacks and other devices. *crêpe-de-Chine*: soft, crinkly fabric, usually silk.

The process of keeping a notebook has shaped Didion's life by helping her recollect general incidents. Her memory is jogged here, and the audience receives an anecdote replete with detail.

❦ Joan Didion ❦

A Californian by birth, educated at the University of California at Berkeley, descended from pioneers, Joan Didion has written extensively about contemporary life in the western United States. From 1956 to 1963 she was an associate feature editor at Vogue *magazine, and during that time published widely in prominent national magazines. Her first book of essays,* Slouching Towards Bethlehem *(1968), compiles many of those early essays and focuses on America in the 1960s, particularly San Francisco. She has written four novels, including* Play It as It Lays *(1970) and* Book of Common Prayer *(1977), and collaborated with her husband on several screenplays. Her latest book of essays is* After Henry *(1992). She is known for her incisive reflections and unique vision of American lifestyles.*

On Keeping a Notebook

In this essay from Slouching Towards Bethlehem, *Joan Didion explains the purpose and importance, for her, of keeping a notebook. Though her analysis is primarily informational, it might also be considered directional for readers who are inclined to keep notebooks. She offers the process as a way for the writer to "keep in touch" with the people he or she "used to be."*

As you read this essay, look for ways that Didion distinguishes between the factual steps and the psychological steps involved in keeping a diary.

" 'That woman Estelle,' " the note reads, " 'is partly the reason why George Sharp and I are separated today.' *Dirty crêpe-de-Chine wrapper, hotel bar, Wilmington RR, 9:45 A.M. August Monday morning.*" 1

Since the note is in my notebook, it presumably has some meaning to me. I study it for a long while. At first I have only the most general notion of what I was doing on an August Monday morning in the bar of the hotel across from the Pennsylvania 2

Railroad station in Wilmington, Delaware (waiting for a train? missing one? 1960? 1961? why Wilmington?), but I do remember being there. The woman in the dirty crêpe-de-Chine wrapper had come down from her room for a beer, and the bartender had heard before the reason why George Sharp and she were separated today. "Sure," he said, and went on mopping the floor. "You told me." At the other end of the bar is a girl. She is talking, pointedly, not to the man beside her but to a cat lying in the triangle of sunlight cast through the open door. She is wearing a plaid silk dress from Peck & Peck, and the hem is coming down.

She develops the psychological details of the incident, expanding the note into a developing story. The 1960s New York stock character in the story represents Didion's imaginatively working out the details in her note.

Here is what it is: the girl has been on the Eastern Shore, and now she is going back to the city, leaving the man beside her, and all she can see ahead are the viscous summer sidewalks and the 3 A.M. long-distance calls that will make her lie awake and then sleep drugged through all the steaming mornings left in August (1960? 1961?). Because she must go directly from the train to lunch in New York, she wishes that she had a safety pin for the hem of the plaid silk dress, and she also wishes that she could forget about the hem and the lunch and stay in the cool bar that smells of disinfectant and malt and make friends with the woman in the crêpe-de-Chine wrapper. She is afflicted by a little self-pity, and she wants to compare Estelles. That is what that was all about.

The process is cyclic. The author reads one of her notes and then develops the note into a detailed fictional account. Then she moves to question herself about having written the note in the first place. Or about keeping a notebook, for that matter, which she justifies as being compulsive, growing from an impulse unique to some people.

Why did I write it down? In order to remember, of course, but exactly what was it I wanted to remember? How much of it actually happened? Did any of it? Why do I keep a notebook at all? It is easy to deceive oneself on all those scores. The impulse to write things down is a peculiarly compulsive one, inexplicable to those who do not share it, useful only accidentally, only secondarily, in the way that any compulsion tries to justify itself. I suppose that it begins or does not begin in the cradle. Although I have felt compelled to write things down since I was five years old, I doubt that my daughter ever will, for she is a singularly blessed and accepting child, delighted with life exactly as life presents itself to her, unafraid to go to sleep and unafraid to wake up. Keepers of private notebooks are a different breed altogether,

The cyclic process moves autobiographically, giving the author a chance to remark that she did not progress gradually through life. Instead, she went through stages, a concept that permits Didion to examine her five-year-old self as if that person were now external.

Didion's notebook, not factually accurate, nevertheless provides a psychological record of her experiences. The process of keeping the notebook holds her life together, but not necessarily in the austere, orderly way that would come from her keeping a record of each day's events.

The author's cyclic process of keeping and using a notebook, her way of recording experiences and then remembering them, grows from her imagination. Unlike the newspaper journalist or the keeper of a diary, Didion does not simply record experiences. She filters her experiences however she wishes. But when she looks back at what she has done to those experiences—adding a fictitious cracked crab to a lunch, for example—she remembers the details of their reality.

lonely and resistant rearrangers of things, anxious malcontents, children afflicted apparently at birth with some presentiment of loss.

My first notebook was a Big Five tablet, given to me by my mother with the sensible suggestion that I stop whining and learn to amuse myself by writing down my thoughts. She returned the tablet to me a few years ago; the first entry is an account of a woman who believed herself to be freezing to death in the Arctic night, only to find, when day broke, that she had stumbled onto the Sahara Desert, where she would die of the heat before lunch. I have no idea what turn of a five-year-old's mind could have prompted so insistently "ironic" and exotic a story, but it does reveal a certain predilection for the extreme which has dogged me into adult life; perhaps if I were analytically inclined I would find it a truer story than any I might have told about Donald Johnson's birthday party or the day my cousin Brenda put Kitty Litter in the aquarium.

So the point of my keeping a notebook has never been, nor is it now, to have an accurate factual record of what I have been doing or thinking. That would be a different impulse entirely, an instinct for reality which I sometimes envy but do not possess. At no point have I ever been able successfully to keep a diary; my approach to daily life ranges from the grossly negligent to the merely absent, and on those few occasions when I have tried dutifully to record a day's events, boredom has so overcome me that the results are mysterious at best. What is this business about "shopping, typing piece, dinner with E, depressed"? Shopping for what? Type what piece? Who is E? Was this "E" depressed, or was I depressed? Who cares?

In fact I have abandoned altogether that kind of pointless entry; instead I tell what some would call lies. "That's simply not true," the members of my family frequently tell me when they come up against my memory of a shared event. "The party was not for you, the spider was *not* a black widow, *it wasn't that way at all*." Very likely they are right, for not only have I always had trouble distinguishing between what happened and what merely

5

6

7

might have happened, but I remain unconvinced that the distinction, for my purposes, matters. The cracked crab that I recall having for lunch the day my father came home from Detroit in 1945 must certainly be embroidery, worked into the day's pattern to lend verisimilitude; I was ten years old and would not now remember the cracked crab. The day's events did not turn on cracked crab. And yet it is precisely that fictitious crab that makes me see the afternoon all over again, a home movie run all too often, the father bearing gifts, the child weeping, an exercise in family love and guilt. Or that is what it was to me. Similarly, perhaps it never did snow that August in Vermont; perhaps there never were flurries in the night wind, and maybe no one else felt the ground hardening and summer already dead even as we pretended to bask in it, but that was how it felt to me; and it might as well have snowed, could have snowed, did snow.

How it felt to me: that is getting closer to the truth about a [8] notebook. I sometimes delude myself about why I keep a notebook, imagine that some thrifty virtue derives from preserving everything observed. See enough and write it down, I tell myself and then some morning when the world seems drained of wonder, some day when I am only going through the motions of doing what I am supposed to do, which is write—on that bankrupt morning I will simply open my notebook and there it will be, a forgotten account with accumulated interest, paid passage back to the world out there: dialogue overheard in hotels and elevators and at the hatcheck counter in Pavillon (one middle-aged man shows his hat check to another and says, "That's my old football number"); impressions of Bettina Aptheker and Benjamin Sonnenberg and Teddy ("Mr. Acapulco") Stauffer; careful *aperçus* about tennis bums and failed fashion models and Greek shipping heiresses, one of whom taught me a significant lesson (a lesson I could have learned from F. Scott Fitzgerald, but perhaps we all must meet the very rich for ourselves) by asking, when I arrived to interview her in her orchid-filled sitting room on the second day of a paralyzing New York blizzard, whether it was snowing outside.

I imagine, in other words, that the notebook is about other [9]

Didion's notebook causes her to remember Didion, rather than the events around her. She sees events, she writes them down colored by her own reactions to them or their effects on her, and she later processes them, adding her own details. Life processes life.

The cyclic process is explained here. The ostensible reason for her keeping a notebook is to have detailed descriptions of people, places, and events, so that on days when the imagination will not boil forth, Didion can summon the remembrances of things past from her notebook and then write.

Aperçus: quick insights or surveys.

F. Scott Fitzgerald (1896–1940) chronicled the extraordinary lives of wealthy Americans, especially in *The Great Gatsby* (1925).

But no. The notebook does not collect other people and events so much as it gathers Didion's reactions *to* other people and events. The notebook tells Didion about how she was, among the events, not about how the events were, with her looking, describing, and recording them.

Didion herself is the "unmentioned girl in the plaid silk dress."

How we act and how we think while we act parallel the notions of appearance versus reality. Here, the reality is what Didion constructs from her notebook, fragments expanded by her imagination into newly minted events, giving old reality a new meaning and life of its own, a fiction.

The author begins by admitting the obvious, that we are taught a particular way to affect behavior. But in the notebook of our minds we behave in quite another way, directed by "the implacable 'I'."

Pensées: reflections or thoughts.

If the maker has difficulty with the meaning, even then the meaning remains. Everything in Didion's notebook either is later expanded in her imagination or is a point on her mental compass to remind her where she was or where she is. Nothing is useless that remains in her notebook.

people. But of course it is not. I have no real business with what one stranger said to another at the hatcheck counter in Pavillon; in fact I suspect that the line "That's my old football number" touched not my own imagination at all, but merely some memory of something once read, probably "The Eighty-Yard Run." Nor is my concern with a woman in a dirty crêpe-de-Chine wrapper in a Wilmington bar. My stake is always, of course, in the unmentioned girl in the plaid silk dress. *Remember what it was to be me:* that is always the point.

It is a difficult point to admit. We are brought up in the ethic 10 that others, any others, all others, are by definition more interesting than ourselves; taught to be diffident, just this side of self-effacing. ("You're the least important person in the room and don't forget it," Jessica Mitford's governess would hiss in her ear on the advent of any social occasion; I copied that into my notebook because it is only recently that I have been able to enter a room without hearing some such phrase in my inner ear.) Only the very young and the very old may recount their dreams at breakfast, dwell upon self, interrupt with memories of beach picnics and favorite Liberty lawn dresses and the rainbow trout in a creek near Colorado Springs. The rest of us are expected, rightly, to affect absorption in other people's favorite dresses, other people's trout.

And so we do. But our notebooks give us away, for however 11 dutifully we record what we see around us, the common denominator of all we see is always, transparently, shamelessly, the implacable "I". We are not talking here about the kind of notebook that is patently for public consumption, a structural conceit for binding together a series of graceful *pensées;* we are talking about something private, about bits of the mind's string too short to use, an indiscriminate and erratic assemblage with meaning only for its maker.

And sometimes even the maker has difficulty with the mean- 12 ing. There does not seem to be, for example, any point in my knowing for the rest of my life that, during 1964, 720 tons of soot fell on every square mile of New York City, yet there it is in my notebook, labeled "FACT." Nor do I really need to remember

Ambrose Bierce (1842–1914?): American journalist and short-story writer best known for *Devil's Dictionary* (1906), in which he defined *achievement,* for example, as "the death of endeavor and the birth of disgust."

Leland Stanford (1824–1893): Capitalist and politician. Governor of California (1861–1863). Promoted and financed Central Pacific Railroad, western link in transcontinental line. United States Senator (1885–1893). Founded Stanford University.

Ambergris: a gray waxy substance from the intestinal canal of sperm whales. It used to be the basis for the most expensive perfume extracts until a substitute was synthesized.

The Wall Street stock-market crash of 1929.

James Riddle Hoffa (1913–1975?): President of the International Brotherhood of Teamsters (1957–1971). Murder suspected—involved with gangsters; body never found.

Syndicate: A nationwide network of criminals.

that Ambrose Bierce liked to spell Leland Stanford's name "£eland $tanford" or that "smart women almost always wear black in Cuba," a fashion hint without much potential for practical application. And does not the relevance of these notes seem marginal at best?:

> In the basement of the Inyo County Courthouse in Independence, California, sign pinned to a mandarin coat: "This MANDARIN COAT was often worn by Mrs. Minnie S. Brooks when giving lectures on her TEAPOT COLLECTION."

> Redhead getting out of car in front of Beverly Wilshire Hotel, chinchilla stole, Vuitton bags with tags reading:
> MRS LOU FOX
> HOTEL SAHARA
> VEGAS

Well, perhaps not entirely marginal. As a matter of fact, Mrs. Minnie S. Brooks and her MANDARIN COAT pull me back into my own childhood, for although I never knew Mrs. Brooks and did not visit Inyo County until I was thirty, I grew up in just such a world, in houses cluttered with Indian relics and bits of gold ore and ambergris and the souvenirs my Aunt Mercy Farnsworth brought back from the Orient. It is a long way from that world to Mrs. Lou Fox's world where we all live now, and is it not just as well to remember that? Might not Mrs. Minnie S. Brooks help me to remember what I am? Might not Mrs. Lou Fox help me to remember what I am not?

But sometimes the point is harder to discern. What exactly did I have in mind when I noted down that it cost the father of someone I know $650 a month to light the place on the Hudson in which he lived before the Crash? What use was I planning to make of this line by Jimmy Hoffa: "I may have my faults, but being wrong ain't one of them"? And although I think it interesting to know where the girls who travel with the Syndicate have their hair done when they find themselves on the West Coast, will I

John O'Hara (1905–1970): Journalist, realistic novelist—*Appointment in Samarra* (1934), *Butterfield 8* (1935), and *Pal Joey* (1940).

Titanic: A British luxury liner, supposedly unsinkable, which sank after hitting an iceberg in the North Atlantic on her maiden voyage in April 1912, with a loss of 1,517 lives.

The first exemplar paragraph. The woman who wanted to go back to Paris and the checkout clerk both have their stories, which Didion duly records. Later, upon reflection, she sees how those women's stories are, in themselves, not important. What matters is how those stories have affected Didion. Her aspirations mirror part of each woman's life.

Didion's keeping this kind of notebook amounts to the psychological process of recording her individuality as she moves from one phase in her life to the next. The value of this process is that it reminds Didion of herself as that self has evolved over the years. Rereading the notes that bring imaginatively to mind the former selves helps to contain the former selves.

ever make suitable use of it? Might I not be better off just passing it on to John O'Hara? What is a recipe for sauerkraut doing in my notebook? What kind of magpie keeps this notebook? *"He was born the night the* Titanic *went down."* That seems a nice enough line, and I even recall who said it, but is it not really a better line in life than it could ever be in fiction?

But of course that is exactly it: not that I should ever use the line, but that I should remember the woman who said it and the afternoon I heard it. We were on her terrace by the sea, and we were finishing the wine left from lunch, trying to get what sun there was, a California winter sun. The woman whose husband was born the night the *Titanic* went down wanted to rent her house, wanted to go back to her children in Paris. I remember wishing that I could afford the house, which cost $1,000 a month. "Someday you will," she said lazily. "Someday it all comes." There in the sun on her terrace it seemed easy to believe in someday but later I had a low-grade afternoon hangover and ran over a black snake on the way to the supermarket and was flooded with inexplicable fear when I heard the checkout clerk explaining to the man ahead of me why she was finally divorcing her husband. "He left me no choice," she said over and over as she punched the register. "He has a little seven-month-old baby by her, he left me no choice." I would like to believe that my dread then was for the human condition, but of course it was for me, because I wanted a baby and did not then have one and because I wanted to own the house that cost $1,000 a month to rent and because I had a hangover. 14

It all comes back. Perhaps it is difficult to see the value in having one's self back in that kind of mood, but I do see it; I think we are well advised to keep on nodding terms with the people we used to be, whether we find them attractive company or not. Otherwise they turn up unannounced and surprise us, come hammering on the mind's door at 4 A.M. of a bad night and demand to know who deserted them, who betrayed them, who is going to make amends. We forget all too soon the things we thought we could never forget. We forget the loves and the betrayals alike, forget what we whispered and what we screamed, 15 forget who we were. I have already lost touch with a couple of people I used to be; one of them, a seventeen-year-old, presents little threat, although it would be of some interest to me to know again what it feels like to sit on a river levee drinking vodka-and-orange-juice and listening to Les Paul and Mary Ford and their echoes sing "How High the Moon" on the car radio. (You see I still have the scenes, but I no longer perceive myself among those present, no longer could even improvise the dialogue.) The other one, a twenty-three-year-old, bothers me more. She was always a good deal of trouble, and I suspect she will reappear when I least want to see her, skirts too long, shy to the point of aggravation, always the injured party, full of recriminations and little hurts and stories I do not want to hear again, at once saddening me and angering me with her vulnerability and ignorance, an apparition all the more insistent for being so long banished.

It is a good idea, then, to keep in touch and I suppose that keeping in touch is what notebooks are all about. And we are all on our own when it comes to keeping those lines open to ourselves: your notebooks will never help me, nor mine you. *"So what's new in the whiskey business?"* What could that possibly mean to you? To me it means a blonde in a Pucci bathing suit sitting with a couple of fat men by the pool at the Beverly Hills Hotel. Another man approaches, and they all regard one another in silence for a while. "So what's new in the whiskey business?" one of the fat men finally says by way of welcome, and the blonde stands up, arches one foot and dips it in the pool, looking all the while at the cabana where Baby Pignatari is talking on the telephone. That is all there is to that, except that several years later I saw the blonde coming out of Saks Fifth Avenue in New York with her California complexion and a voluminous mink coat. In the harsh wind that day she looked old and irrevocably tired to me, and even the skins in the mink coat were not worked the way they were doing them that year, not the way she would have wanted them done, and there is the point of the story. For a while after that I did not like to look in the mirror, and my eyes would skim the newspapers and pick out only the deaths, the cancer victims, the premature coronaries, the suicides, and I stopped

16

The second exemplar paragraph. Baby Pignatari was a leader in the Syndicate. Our notebooks are for ourselves. The anecdote about the blonde reminds Didion heavily of how time affects other people's looks and fortunes, so strongly that she begins to avoid evidence of how time affects her.

Writing about the process of keeping her notebook benefits Didion: "It all comes back." She wrote a passage that amounts to an extended notebook entry about the process of keeping a notebook, which in turn led her to remember details of events entered in the original notebook. The process is complete.

POSSIBLE ANSWERS

Meaning and Purpose

1. A diary is an "actual factual record" of what one has been doing. A notebook tells "what some would call lies," as stated in paragraph 7.
2. Students will have varied experiences in keeping journals or notebooks. You might want to discuss what the words *notebook* and *journal* mean to students. They should compare their experiences with some that Didion relates.
3. Didion is talking about the writing process, intuitively. Students need to learn about their own writing process so that they can better understand and control it and so become better writers.
4. Our notebooks give us away to ourselves, the "implacable 'I' ".
5. These statements show Didion's main point: "I tell what some would call lies" (7); "*How it felt to me*: that is getting closer to the truth about a notebook" (8); "*Remember what it was to be me*: that is always the point" (9); "But our notebooks give us away . . . the implacable 'I' " (11); "I suppose that keeping in touch is what notebooks are all about" (16). All these statements are about the self, keeping in touch with the process of who we have been so that we can better understand ourselves in the present.

Strategy

1. The opening is immediate and puts the reader right in Didion's notebook, as if the curtain opens and we see her standing there reading. She doesn't bother with providing a context for what she is saying until paragraph 4. By then the reader is hooked by the details of the little scene

riding the Lexington Avenue IRT because I noticed for the first time that all the strangers I had seen for years—the man with the seeing-eye dog, the spinster who read the classified pages every day, the fat girl who always got off with me at Grand Central—looked older than they once had.

It all comes back. Even that recipe for sauerkraut: even that brings it back. I was on Fire Island when I first made sauerkraut, and it was raining, and we drank a lot of bourbon and ate the sauerkraut and went to bed at ten, and I listened to the rain and the Atlantic and felt safe. I made the sauerkraut again last night and it did not make me feel any safer, but that is, as they say, another story. 17

Meaning and Purpose

1. After reading this essay, you know that a diary and a notebook differ. What is one big difference?
2. Do you keep a notebook or journal? If so, how does your method of writing in it, and the use you make of it, compare to Didion's?
3. What is one process the author discusses, and why does any writer need to become familiar with it?
4. In a line in paragraph 11, Didion says, "Our notebooks give us away." To whom do they give us away?
5. Several statements in the essay could be taken as versions of Didion's main point. What are some of them, and how are they related to one another?

Strategy

1. The essay begins in the middle of an action—Didion is reading a note she wrote in her notebook. Then, before she gives a

in the hotel bar. Didion then backs away from this scene and talks about having written the note. A lengthy explanatory opening about her subject would surely not be as effective.

2. The little stories about the notes tie together the progression of Didion's main points. She expands the context of the notes to lead herself to realize what she is really doing: remembering, and thereby keeping an account of herself. Paragraph 7 is a good example of this act when she talks about the cracked crab that "makes me see the afternoon all over again . . . that is what it [the incident] was to me." And then in paragraph 8 she solidifies this insight with, "*How it felt to me:* that is getting closer to the truth about a notebook."

3. Didion does in a sense bring the essay full circle by explaining the note about the sauerkraut recipe. But she has also gained insight here by going through the process of the notebook. "It all comes back" (17)—the notebook is about bringing the past back, remembering who she was. And when she makes the sauerkraut "again last night," she suggests there is another story, one that perhaps won't be understood until she can look back later at what she recorded in her notebook.

Style

1. Didion's language is informal and conversational, as if she is thinking out loud. She is sharing something quite personal in her notebooks. The transition from paragraphs 7 to 8 shows this thinking-aloud voice. She is conjecturing here about the truth of one of her notes, and then she comes suddenly to a realization—"*How it felt to me*"—in paragraph 8.

2. An "Estelle" is whoever or whatever triggers a feeling of self-pity. It could be "the other woman" as it is for the woman in the crêpe-de-chine wrapper, or any other reminder of an injustice.

3. Students' answers will vary. They might include references to a suntan, sunstreaked hair—whatever else they believe the stereotype includes.

4. A predilection is a preconceived liking, a partiality. A "predilection for the extreme" describes a person who sees or imagines the exotic or extreme in a situation. This is Didion talking about herself as a writer.

context for the note, she talks about it and embellishes it. Why do you think she begins in this way?

2. In the structure of her essay, how does Didion make use of the little stories behind the brief notes she has written in her notebook?

3. Didion ends her essay with the story of the recipe for sauerkraut, another note expanded into an anecdote. Is she ending in the middle again, as she began? Discuss the effectiveness of the ending.

Style

1. What is Didion's tone in this essay—her attitude toward her subject?

2. In paragraph 3, the writer says she "wants to compare Estelles," using the noun metaphorically. What is an "Estelle"?

3. "California complexion," in paragraph 16, is an example of stereotyping. In your opinion, what is "California complexion"?

4. In paragraph 5, Didion mentions that she has a "predilection for the extreme." Explain this phrase.

Writing Tasks

1. Describe one of your dreams and discuss what it reveals about you, just as Didion discusses what her notebook reveals about her.

2. Didion describes a process linked to the creative imagination. Her notes themselves are not so important as what those notes suggest to her, imaginatively. Using a similar procedure, choose three related personal items. Write an informative process analysis in which you describe these items briefly, and then discuss what they mean emotionally to you.

The essay can be approached in a variety of ways. You can treat it, of course, as a fine example of informative process analysis (see pp. 373–376). In the first ten paragraphs, Murray details the skills writers must develop and the problems they must overcome in order to revise their manuscripts. He then details chronologically the process professional writers go through to improve their texts. But you might want to ignore analyzing the essay's form, or combine that analysis with a lesson on revision. The essay could serve as your very first lesson in revision or as a follow-up lesson after the students have completed a paper or two. If this is the case, have them take a paper they have completed earlier and now revise it again following the Murray process step by step. The changes may prove instructive.

❦ Donald M. Murray ❦

Donald M. Murray was born in 1924 in Boston. He has had a long and distinguished career as a writer and teacher. Murray has published fiction, nonfiction, and poetry, served as an editor of Time *magazine, and won the Pulitzer Prize for editorial writing in 1959. Currently he is a professor of English at the University of New Hampshire, Durham. His teaching career and the textbooks he has published on how to write—*A Writer Teaches Writing, Write to Learn, *and* Read to Write—*have established him as one of America's most influential teachers of writing. He sees the writing teacher as a coach and is convinced that a student must want to learn and be willing to exert much effort in order to write well.*

The Maker's Eye:
Revising Your Own Manuscripts

Originally published in The Writer, *this essay demonstrates the process professional writers go through to revise their manuscripts. Murray distinguishes the differences in attitudes that student writers and professional writers take to the revising process and cites other professional writers to argue for the essential importance of meticulous revision.*

As you read, note any differences between the methods you use to revise a paper and the methods the professional writer uses. Jot down advice you might find helpful in improving your own writing.

When students complete a first draft, they consider the job of writing done—and their teachers too often agree. When professional writers complete a first draft, they usually feel that they

1

MARGINAL NOTES

Peter F. Drucker (born 1909) was born in Vienna and emigrated to the United States in 1937. He has taught in several U.S. universities and authored books on business, technology, and society. He has contributed articles to *Harper's*, the *Wall Street Journal*, the *New York Times*, and *Public Interest*.

Ray Bradbury (born 1920), an American science fiction writer, is known for his fantastic tales that combine acute social criticism with fanciful science fiction. He is best known for his short story collections *The Martian Chronicles* (1950), *Dandelion Wine* (1957), and *I Sing the Body Electric!* (1969). He also wrote screenplays and plays as well as the novels *Farhenheit 451* (1953) and *Something Wicked This Way Comes* (1962).

Nancy Hale (1908–1988), born in Boston, was a painter, journalist, and author. She published nineteen volumes of fiction, biography, memoirs, and many short stories documenting changing upper-class American manners. She was the first woman reporter for the *New York Times*.

John Ciardi (1916–1985) was an American poet, teacher, and critic. He was poetry editor of the *Saturday Review* for many years and wrote numerous essays on the art of reading and enjoying poetry. He published many volumes of his own poetry and made a notable translation of Dante's *Inferno* into idiomatic English to recall Dante's use of the vernacular.

are at the start of the writing process. When a draft is completed, the job of writing can begin.

That difference in attitude is the difference between amateur and professional, inexperience and experience, journeyman and craftsman. Peter F. Drucker, the prolific business writer, calls his first draft "the zero draft"—after that he can start counting. Most writers share the feeling that the first draft, and all of those which follow, are opportunities to discover what they have to say and how best they can say it.

To produce a progression of drafts, each of which says more and says it more clearly, the writer has to develop a special kind of reading skill. In school we are taught to decode what appears on the page as finished writing. Writers, however, face a different category of possibility and responsibility when they read their own drafts. To them the words on the page are never finished. Each can be changed and rearranged, can set off a chain reaction of confusion or clarified meaning. This is a different kind of reading, which is possibly more difficult and certainly more exciting.

Writers must learn to be their own best enemy. They must accept the criticism of others and be suspicious of it; they must accept the praise of others and be even more suspicious of it. Writers cannot depend on others. They must detach themselves from their own pages so that they can apply both their caring and their craft to their own work.

Such detachment is not easy. Science fiction writer Ray Bradbury supposedly puts each manuscript away for a year to the day and then rereads it as a stranger. Not many writers have the discipline or the time to do this. We must read when our judgment may be at its worst, when we are close to the euphoric moment of creation.

Then the writer, counsels novelist Nancy Hale, "should be critical of everything that seems to him most delightful in his style. He should excise what he most admires, because he wouldn't thus admire it if he weren't . . . in a sense protecting it from criticism." John Ciardi, the poet, adds, "The last act of the writing must be to become one's own reader. It is, I suppose, a schizophrenic process, to begin passionately and to end critically, to begin hot and to end cold; and, more important, to be passion-hot and critic-cold at the same time."

Most people think that the principal problem is that writers are too proud of what they have written. Actually, a greater problem for most professional writers is one shared by the majority of students. They are overly critical, think everything is dreadful, tear up page after page, never complete a draft, see the task as hopeless.

The writer must learn to read critically but constructively, to cut what is bad, to reveal what is good. Eleanor Estes, the children's book author, explains: "The writer must survey his work critically, coolly, as though he were a stranger to it. He must be willing to prune, expertly and hard-heartedly. At the end of each revision, a manuscript may look . . . worked over, torn apart, pinned together, added to, deleted from, words changed and words changed back. Yet the book must maintain its original freshness and spontaneity."

Most readers underestimate the amount of rewriting it usually takes to produce spontaneous reading. This is a great disadvantage to the student writer, who sees only a finished product and never watches the craftsman who takes the necessary step back, studies the work carefully, returns to the task, steps back, returns, steps back, again and again. Anthony Burgess, one of the most prolific writers in the English-speaking world, admits, "I might revise a page twenty times." Ronald Dahl, the popular children's writer, states, "By the time I'm nearing the end of a story, the first part will have been reread and altered and corrected at least 150 times. . . . Good writing is essentially rewriting. I am positive of this."

Rewriting isn't virtuous. It isn't something that ought to be done. It is simply something that most writers find they have to do to discover what they have to say and how to say it. It is a condition of the writer's life.

There are, however, a few writers who do little formal rewriting, primarily because they have the capacity and experience

---

Eleanor Estes (1906–1988), born in New Haven, Connecticut, was a prolific children's author. She is best known for her earliest work, family stories based on her own childhood.

Anthony Burgess (born 1917) is an English novelist and critic. A prolific, versatile, and comic writer, Burgess has an extraordinary facility with language, a talent he admired in James Joyce, the subject of one of his works, *Joysprick: An Introduction to the Language of James Joyce* (1973). Probably the best known of his many novels is *A Clockwork Orange* (1962), in which he envisions a future state terrorized by teenage gangs who speak Nadsat, a language created by Burgess from British and American slang, and Russian.

Roald Dahl (1916–1990) was a Welsh-born fiction and screen writer. He is best known for his macabre short fiction and children's books, the latter including *Charlie and the Chocolate Factory* and *Chitty Chitty Bang Bang*, both later adapted to film. He also wrote the script for the James Bond movie, *You Only Live Twice*.

Murray here, in a single paragraph, disposes of the minority of professional writers who do not meticulously revise draft by draft. Notice that although their methods may be untypical, they nonetheless include extensive revision.

to create and review a large number of invisible drafts in their minds before they approach the page. And some writers slowly produce finished pages, performing all the tasks of revision simultaneously, page by page, rather than draft by draft. But it is still possible to see the sequence followed by most writers most of the time in rereading their own work.

12   Most writers scan their drafts first, reading as quickly as possible to catch the larger problems of subject and form, then move in closer and closer as they read and write, reread and rewrite.

13   The first thing writers look for in their drafts is *information.* They know that a good piece of writing is built from specific, accurate, and interesting information. The writer must have an abundance of information from which to construct a readable piece of writing.

14   Next writers look for *meaning* in the information. The specifics must build a pattern of significance. Each piece of specific information must carry the reader toward meaning.

15   Writers reading their own drafts are aware of *audience.* They put themselves in the reader's situation and make sure that they deliver information which a reader wants to know or needs to know in a manner which is easily digested. Writers try to be sure that they anticipate and answer the questions a critical reader will ask when reading the piece of writing.

16   Writers make sure that the *form* is appropriate to the subject and the audience. Form, or genre, is the vehicle which carries meaning to the reader, but form cannot be selected until the writer has adequate information to discover its significance and an audience which needs or wants that meaning.

17   Once writers are sure the form is appropriate, they must then look at the *structure,* the order of what they have written. Good writing is built on a solid framework of logic, argument, narrative, or motivation which runs through the entire piece of writing and holds it together. This is the time when many writers find it most effective to outline as a way of visualizing the hidden spine by which the piece of writing is supported.

Here Murray uses an analogy, comparing a piece of writing structure to a body's supporting spine.

18   The element on which writers may spend a majority of their

He uses another analogy here, comparing the amount of information needed to make a point both satisfying and convincing to the amount of garlic needed to make a salad just right. Garlic lovers know there is no such thing as too much garlic.

time is *development*. Each section of a piece of writing must be adequately developed. It must give readers enough information so that they are satisfied. How much information is enough? That's as difficult as asking how much garlic belongs in a salad. It must be done to taste, but most beginning writers underdevelop, underestimating the reader's hunger for information.

As writers solve development problems, they often have to consider questions of *dimension*. There must be a pleasing and effective proportion among all the parts of the piece of writing. There is a continual process of subtracting and adding to keep the piece of writing in balance. 19

Finally, writers have to listen to their own voices. *Voice* is the force which drives a piece of writing forward. It is an expression of the writer's authority and concern. It is what is between the words on the page, what glues the piece of writing together. A good piece of writing is always marked by a consistent, individual voice. 20

Few student writers recognize the importance of such minute scrutiny for a writer to create precisely the effect he wants. Even the space between type must contribute to clarity.

As writers read and reread, write and rewrite, they move closer and closer to the page until they are doing line-by-line editing. Writers read their own pages with infinite care. Each sentence, each line, each clause, each phrase, each word, each mark of punctuation, each section of white space between the type has to contribute to the clarification of meaning. 21

Slowly the writer moves from word to word, looking through language to see the subject. As a word is changed, cut, or added, as a construction is rearranged, all the words used before that moment and all those that follow that moment must be considered and reconsidered. 22

Writers often read aloud at this stage of the editing process, muttering or whispering to themselves, calling on the ear's experience with language. Does this sound right—or that? Writers edit, shifting back and forth from eye to page to ear to page. I find I must do this careful editing in short runs, no more than fifteen or twenty minutes at a stretch, or I become too kind with myself. I begin to see what I hope is on the page, not what actually is on the page. 23

Here Murray repeats an idea he stated in paragraph 2: Writers don't know what they think until they actually write about it. The concept is almost totally alien to most student writers.

This sounds tedious if you haven't done it, but actually it is fun. Making something right is immensely satisfying, for writers 24 begin to learn what they are writing about by writing. Language leads them to meaning, and there is the joy of discovery, of understanding, of making meaning clear as the writer employs the technical skills of language.

Words have double meanings, even triple and quadruple meanings. Each word has its own potential for connotation and denotation. And when writers rub one word against the other, they are often rewarded with a sudden insight, an unexpected clarification.

The maker's eye moves back and forth from word to phrase to sentence to paragraph to sentence to phrase to word. The maker's eye sees the need for variety and balance, for a firmer structure, for a more appropriate form. It peers into the interior of the paragraph, looking for coherence, unity, and emphasis, which make meaning clear.

I learned something about this process when my first bifocals were prescribed. I had ordered a larger section of the reading portion of the glass because of my work, but even so, I could not contain my eyes within this new limit of vision. And I still find myself taking off my glasses and bending my nose towards the page, for my eyes unconsciously flick back and forth across the page, back to another page, forward to still another, as I try to see each evolving line in relation to every other line.

When does this process end? Most writers agree with the great Russian writer Tolstoy, who said, "I scarcely ever reread my published writings, if by chance I come across a page, it always strikes me: all this must be rewritten; this is how I should have written it."

The maker's eye is never satisfied, for each word has the potential to ignite new meaning. This article has been twice written all the way through the writing process, and it was published four years ago. Now it is to be republished in a book. The editors make a few small suggestions, and then I read it with my maker's eye. Now it has been re-edited, re-revised, re-read, re-re-edited, for each piece of writing to the writer is full of potential and alternatives.

A piece of writing is never finished. It is delivered to a deadline, torn out of the typewriter on demand, sent off with a sense

---

This paragraph is used to illustrate how the preceding contention is true.

Count Leo Tolstoy (1828–1910) was a Russian novelist and moral philosopher. Best known for his novels, Tolstoy also wrote short stories, plays, and essays. Together with another great nineteenth-century Russian novelist, Fyodor Dostoyevsky, Tolstoy, according to many literary critics, made the realistic novel a literary genre that ranks in importance with classical Greek tragedy and Elizabethan drama. *War and Peace* and *Anna Karenina* are probably his two greatest works.

POSSIBLE ANSWERS

Meaning and Purpose

1. Many students might object to Murray's claim that student writers consider their first draft their final draft (1), especially if they do any revision at all. But most will certainly agree that the extensive revision a professional writer does goes far beyond their efforts. Both student writers and professionals share the problem of being overcritical of their work (7).

2. "Normal" readers read what they believe to be a finished piece of writing. Writers, on the other hand, read their own drafts with the possibility of change always in their consciousness (3).

3. Writers must accept both the praise and criticism of others and be suspicious of both at the same time. They must remain detached from their own work in order to work on it objectively (4).

4. It might be worthwhile here to lead the students through these eight elements of writing to make sure they genuinely understand what Murray means by them.

5. Information does not exist for its own sake, but is structured for a purpose, leading the reader to an understanding, a meaning.

6. All of the information in this essay leads the reader to the understanding that for a writer a piece of writing is never complete. It can always be reworked to make it more effective.

Strategy

1. The thesis is stated in the opening paragraph: For a professional writer a draft is just the beginning of writing. Murray restates the thesis, in somewhat different form, in paragraph 10.

2. Ostensibly, Murray is writing an informative process analysis, showing ". . . the sequence followed by most writers most of the time in rereading their own work" (11). But the information is so explicit that it could certainly be used as a guide for revision. If followed, it would be directive process analysis.

of accomplishment and shame and pride and frustration. If only there were a couple more days, time for just another run at it, perhaps then . . .

Meaning and Purpose

1. According to Murray, what are the differences in the ways that professional writers and student writers view their first drafts? Do his observations ring true? Do both types of writers share any common problems?

2. What two kinds of reading skills does the author distinguish? How does the writer's reading skill differ from that of the normal reader's?

3. What does Murray mean when he says, "Writers must learn to be their own best enemy"? Explain.

4. In paragraphs 13–30, Murray takes the reader chronologically through each of the elements that a writer must consider to revise a manuscript. Describe the ways a writer must consider each of these elements.

5. Murray distinguishes between "information" and "meaning." Explain the difference between the two.

6. Explain Murray's contention that "A piece of writing is never finished" (30).

Strategy

1. What is the essay's thesis? Where is it stated?

2. Is the essay an example of directive or informative process analysis (see pp. 371–376)? Explain.

3. Murray cites other writers in his description of the revision process. Why?

3. Murray quotes other authors to give authority to his contention that the biggest part of writing is rewriting.

4. This is another version of the story told about a writer who, when asked what he thought about a subject replied, "How should I know? I haven't written about it yet." This points up the idea that writing forces the writer to make connections about things that he could never make without going through the writing process, an idea that most beginning writers have a hard time understanding.

5. Murray first establishes the importance of the process for effective writing. He distinguishes between the attitudes of professional and amateur writers, explains how writers must read with a different eye than readers who don't write, establishes a common problem shared by amateurs and professionals, and cites several writers as to not only the importance, but the necessity, of revision. Only then does he describe the typical process itself.

Style

1. In these three paragraphs Murray personalizes the revision process to make it more real for the reader. Before this he was speaking in typical terms, and now he shows how he personally applies some of the elements of the process. We think the anecdote of paragraph 27 is particularly effective.

2. Since the thrust of the entire essay is that professional writers feel a near compulsion to revise and tinker with their work continually, it is wholly appropriate for the essay to end without ending.

3. *Journeyman*: a person who has served an apprenticeship at a trade or handicraft and is certified to work at it assisting or under another person; *prolific*: highly productive; *euphoric*: being in a state of happiness, confidence, or well-being; *schizophrenic*: a state characterized by the coexistence of contradictory or incompatible elements; *connotation*: the associated or secondary meaning of a word; *denotation*: the explicit or direct meaning of a word as distinguished by the ideas or meanings associated with it or suggested by it.

4. Explain the author's seemingly odd statement that " . . . most writers share the feeling that the first draft, and all of those which follow, are opportunities to discover what they have to say . . ." (2).

5. Murray doesn't actually begin a description of the professional writer's revision process until paragraph 12. What is the purpose of such a long introduction?

Style

1. Murray changes from the third person ("writer," "writers," "the maker") to the first person ("I") in paragraphs 23, 27, and 29. What effect does he create by this change of person?

2. Why does Murray end the essay in mid-sentence?

3. If necessary, use a dictionary to determine the meanings of these words: *journeyman, prolific* (2); *euphoric* (5); *schizophrenic* (6); *connotation, denotation* (25).

Writing Tasks

1. Write an essay in which you detail the way you revise an essay. Explain, in the process, why this method may work for you better than the method explained by Murray.

2. If you use a computer to write, explain the advantages of revising on a computer.

3. Write an essay in which you explain to the reader a process that you do regularly and well. Without being moralistic, demonstrate how this might actually benefit the reader.

TEACHING SUGGESTIONS

You might begin with a discussion of how Viorst describes heroines to represent different stages in her own maturation. What is interesting about an essay explaining the forces that shaped her life? What is not? This subject could lead into a discussion of heroes and heroines that your students have found attractive, and why they found them so. Which come from books? Are films and television now a greater source of influence?

❧ Judith Viorst ❧

Born in Newark, New Jersey, Judith Viorst is a graduate of Rutgers University and has been a regular columnist and contributing editor at Redbook *magazine since 1968. In 1970 she wrote a series of poetic monologues for a CBS special entitled "Annie: The Women in the Life of a Man," for which she received an Emmy award. She has written children's books, both fiction and nonfiction, and several volumes of light verse, including* It's Hard to Be Hip Over Thirty and Other Tragedies of Married Life *(1968) and* How Did I Get to be Forty and Other Atrocities *(1976). Her book* Necessary Losses: The Loves, Illusions, Dependencies and Impossible Expectations That All of Us Have to Give Up in Order to Grow *(1986), reached the top of* The New York Times *bestseller list.*

How Books Helped Shape My Life

First published in Redbook, *this essay analyzes the ways in which literary heroines influenced the author's life. Using examples from the books of her childhood through those she read as a young woman, Viorst describes a process of growing awareness through literature.*

As you read Viorst's essay, see if you can recall fictional characters that have had an influence on your own thinking.

MARGINAL NOTES

Viorst states her thesis in its most typical position, the last sentence in paragraph 1.

In books I've read since I was young I've searched for heroines who could serve as ideals, as models, as possibilities—some reflecting the secret self that dwelled inside me, others pointing to whole new ways that a woman (if only she dared!) might try to be. The person that I am today was shaped by Nancy Drew; by Jo March, Jane Eyre and Heathcliff's soul mate Cathy; and by other fictional females whose attractiveness or character or audacity for a time were the standards by which I measured myself. 1

I return to some of these books to see if I still understand the powerful hold that these heroines once had on me. I still understand. 2

410

A series of Nancy Drew mystery novels was published under the name of Carolyn Keene. A television series based on the novels was broadcast in the 1970s.

Consider teen-aged Nancy Drew—beautiful, blond-haired, blue-eyed girl detective—who had the most terrific life that I as a ten-year-old could ever imagine. Motherless (in other words, quite free of maternal controls), she lived with her handsome indulgent lawyer father in a large brick house set back from the street with a winding tree-lined driveway on the outside and a faithful, nonintrusive housekeeper Hannah cooking yummy meals on the inside. She also had a boy friend, a convertible, nice clothes and two close girl friends—not as perfect as she, but then it seemed to me that no one could possibly be as perfect as Nancy Drew, who in dozens and dozens of books (*The Hidden Staircase, The Whispering Statue, The Clue in the Diary, The Clue of the Tapping Heels*) was resourceful and brave and intelligent as she went around solving mysteries left and right, while remaining kind to the elderly and invariably polite and absolutely completely delightfully feminine.

I mean, what else *was* there?

I soon found out what else when I encountered the four March sisters of *Little Women,* a sentimental, old-fashioned book about girls growing up in Civil War time in New England. About spoiled, vain, pretty Amy. And sickly, saintly Beth. And womanly, decent Meg. And about—most important of all—gawky, bookworm Jo. Dear Jo, who wasn't as flawless as the golden Nancy Drew but who showed me that girls like her—like *us*—could be heroines. Even if we weren't much to look at. Even if we were clumsy and socially gauche. And even if the transition into young womanhood often appeared to our dubious eye to be difficult and scary and even unwelcome.

Little Women is a widely read story by Louisa May Alcott (1832–1888). The heroine is Jo March, the tomboyish and literary member of the family, who retires to the attic when "genius burns." Meg, her older, pretty sister, marries a young tutor, John Brooke. Gentle, music-loving Beth dies young. The fashionable and artistic Amy finally marries Laurie, a high-spirited boy who had long been Jo's boon companion, but who failed to persuade her to marry him. Jo herself becomes the wife of a kindly old German professor, Mr. Bhaer.

Jo got stains on her dress and laughed when she shouldn't and lost her temper and didn't display tact or patience or restraint. Jo brought a touch of irreverence to the cultural constraints of the world she lived in. And yet her instincts were good and her heart was pure and her headstrong ways led always to virtue. And furthermore Jo—as I yearned to be—was a writer!

In the book the years go by, Beth dies, Meg and Amy marry and Jo—her fierce heart somewhat tamed—is alone. " 'An old maid, that's what I'm to be. A literary spinster, with a pen for a spouse, a family of stories for children, and twenty years hence a morsel of fame, perhaps!' . . . Jo sighed, as if the prospect was not inviting."

This worried young reader concurred—not inviting at all! 8

And so I was happy to read of Jo's nice suitor, Mr. Bhaer, not 9
handsome or rich or young or important or witty, but possessed of kindness and dignity and enough intelligence to understand that even a girl who wasn't especially pretty, who had no dazzling charms and who wanted to write might make a wonderful wife. And a wonderful mother. And live happily ever after.

What a relief! 10

What Jo and Nancy shared was active participation in life— 11
they went out and *did;* they weren't simply done to—and they taught and promised me (at a time when mommies stayed home and there was no Women's Movement) that a girl could go out and do and still get a man. Jo added the notion that brusque, ungainly girls could go out and do and still get a man. And Jane of *Jane Eyre,* whose author once said, "I will show you a heroine as small and as plain as myself," added the further idea that such women were able to "feel just as men feel" and were capable of being just as passionate.

Orphaned Jane, a governess at stately Thornfield Hall, was a 12
no-nonsense lady, cool and self-contained, whose lonely, painful childhood had ingrained in her an impressive firmness of character, an unwillingness to charm or curry favor and a sense of herself as the equal of any man. Said Jane to Mr. Rochester, the brooding, haughty, haunted master of Thornfield: "Do you think I am an automaton?—a machine without feelings? Do you think, because I am poor, obscure, plain, and little, I am soulless and heartless? You think wrong!—I have as much soul as you, and full as much heart!"

I loved it that such hot fires burned inside so plain a Jane. I 13
loved her for her unabashed intensity. And I loved her for being so pure that when she learned of Mr. Rochester's lunatic wife, she sacrificed romance for honor and left him immediately.

For I think it's important to note that Nancy and Jo and Jane, 14
despite their independence, were basically as good as girls can

Charlotte Brontë (1816–1855) struggled with several literary works and finally published *Jane Eyre,* which achieved spectacular success.

be: honest, generous, kind, sincere, reliable, respectable, possessed of absolute integrity. They didn't defy convention. They didn't challenge the rules. They did what was right, although it might cause them pain. And their virtue was always rewarded—look at Jane, rich and married at last to her Mr. Rochester. Oh, how I identified with Jane!

Emily Brontë (1818–1848), younger sister of Charlotte, wrote the passionate and mystically intense novel *Wuthering Heights*. Wuthering Heights is the Yorkshire moorland estate where the story takes place. The adjective *wuthering* is a Yorkshire word referring to turbulent weather, and so the place and the weather reflect the psychological turbulence of the story.

But then I read *Wuthering Heights,* a novel of soul-consuming love on the Yorkshire moors, and Catherine Earnshaw totally captured me. And she captured me, not in spite of her dangerous, dark and violent spirit, but *because* of it.   15

Cathy was as wild as the moors. She lied and connived and deceived. She was insolent, selfish, manipulative and cruel. And by marrying meek, weak Edgar instead of Heathcliff, her destiny, she betrayed a love she described in throbbing, unforgettable prose as . . . elemental: 16

"My love for Heathcliff resembles the eternal rocks beneath— a source of little visible delight, but necessary. Nelly, I *am* Heathcliff—he's always, always in my mind—not as a pleasure, any more than I am always a pleasure to myself—but as my own being. . . ."   17

Now who, at the age of 16, could resist such quivering intensity? Who would settle for less than elemental? Must we untamed creatures of passion—I'd muse as I lay awake in my red flannel nightie—submit ourselves to conventional morality? Or could I actually choose not to be a good girl?   18

The Sun Also Rises is a novel by Ernest Hemingway (1899–1961). Considered by many critics to be his finest work, it deals with the "lost generation" of Americans who fought in France during World War I and then expatriated themselves from the America of Calvin Coolidge. The story is told by Jake Barnes, rendered impotent by a war wound. Lady Brett Ashley, who is divorcing her husband, is in love with him. These two go to Spain with a group that includes Michael Campbell, whom Brett plans to marry; Bill Gorton, a friend of Jake; a Greek nobleman; and Robert Cohn, an American-Jewish writer. Brett has an affair with Romero, a bullfighter whom the others respect for his grace and control in the face of danger; she eventually leaves him and returns to Michael. At the end, nothing has really changed in life for any of the characters, which is exactly the point of the novel: for these disillusioned people, life can have no direction, no point toward which to develop.

Cathy Earnshaw told me that I could. And so did lost Lady Brett, of *The Sun Also Rises.*   19

Brett Ashley was to me, at 18, free, modern, woman incarnate, and she dangled alluring new concepts before my eyes: 20

The value of style: "She wore a slipover jersey sweater and a tweed skirt, and her hair was brushed back like a boy's. She started all that."   21

The glamour of having a dark and tortured past: "Finally, when he got really bad, he used to tell her he'd kill her. . . . She hasn't had an absolutely happy life."   22

The excitement of nonconformity: "I've always done just what I wanted."   23

The importance of (understated) grace under pressure: "Brett was rather good. She's always rather good." 24

And the thrill of unrepressed sexuality: "Brett's had affairs with men before. She tells me all about everything." 25

Brett married lovelessly and drank too much and drifted too much and had an irresponsible fling with a bullfighter. But she also had class—and her own morality. She set her bullfighter free—"I'd have lived with him if I hadn't seen it was bad for him." And even though she was broke, she lied and "told him I had scads of it. . . . I couldn't take his money, you know." 26

Brett's wasn't the kind of morality that my mother was teaching me in suburban New Jersey. But maybe I wasn't meant for suburban life. Maybe—I would muse as I carefully lined my eyes with blue liner—maybe I'm meant for something more . . . emancipated. 27

I carried Brett's image with me when, after college, I lived for a while in Greenwich Village, in New York. But I couldn't achieve her desperate gallantry. And it struck me that Brett was too lonely and sad, and that Cathy had died too young (and that Scarlett O'Hara got Tara but lost her Rhett), and that maybe I ought to forget about unconventionality if the price was going to be so painfully high. Although I enjoyed my Village fling, I had no wish to live anguishedly ever after. I needed a heroine who, like me, wanted just a small taste of the wild before settling down into happy domesticity. 28

I found her in *War and Peace*. Her name was Natasha. 29

Natasha, the leading lady of this epic of Russian society during Napoleon's time, was "poetic . . . charming . . . overflowing with life," an enchanting girl whose sweet eagerness and passionate impulsivity were tempered by historic and private tragedies. Betrothed to the handsome and excellent Prince Andrew, she fell in love with a heel named Anatole, and when she was warned that this foolish and dangerous passion would lead to her ruin, "I'll go to my ruin . . . ," she said, "as soon as possible." 30

It ended badly with Anatole. Natasha tried suicide. Prince Andrew died. Natasha turned pale, thin, subdued. But unlike Brett and Cathy, her breach with convention was mended and, 31

Scarlett O'Hara is the heroine of *Gone with the Wind,* a historical novel by Margaret Mitchell (1900–1949). She is a fiery southern belle, whose love for Ashley Wilkes is frustrated when he marries gentle Melanie Hamilton. After being widowed twice, Scarlett marries Rhett Butler, who proves more than a match for her. The novel also depicts, from a southern viewpoint, the tumult and suffering caused by the War between the States and Reconstruction.

War and Peace, a novel by Count Leo Tolstoy (1828–1910), is considered the author's masterwork. The story covers roughly the years between 1805 and 1820, centering on the invasion of Russia by Napoleon's army in 1812 and the Russian resistance to the invader. More than 500 characters, all completely and individually rendered, throng the pages of the novel. Every social level from Napoleon himself to the peasant Platon Karatayen, is represented. Interwoven with the story of the war are narrations on the lives of several main characters, especially those of Natasha Rostova, Prince Andrei Balkonski, and Pierre Bezukhov. These people are shown as they progress from youthful uncertainties and searchings toward more mature understanding of life. Natasha exemplifies the instinctual approach to life that Tolstoy was later to preach as the way to true happiness. She is one of the most successful characters in the book and perhaps ranks as Tolstoy's greatest achievement in character creation. Everything from her girlish excitement at her first ball through her experiences of first love and her final role as wife and mother are depicted with perfect skill.

at long last, she married Pierre—a decent, substantial, loving man, the kind of man all our mothers want us to marry.

In marriage Natasha grew stouter and "the old fire very rarely kindled in her face now." She became an exemplary mother, an ideal wife. "She felt that her unity with her husband was maintained not by the poetic feelings that had attracted him to her but by something else—indefinite but firm as the bond between her own body and soul." 32

It sounded—if not elemental and doomed—awfully nice. 33

I identified with Natasha when, the following year, I married and left Greenwich Village. I too was ready for domesticity. And yet . . . her husband and children became "the subject which wholly engrossed Natasha's attention." She had lost herself—and I didn't want to lose me. What I needed next was a heroine who could reconcile all the warring wants of my nature—for fire and quiet, independence and oneness, ambition and love, and marriage and family. 34

But such reconciling heroines, in novels and real life, may not yet exist. 35

Nevertheless Natasha and Jane and Jo, Cathy, Nancy and Brett—each spoke to my heart and stirred me powerfully. On my journey to young womanhood I was fortunate to have them as my companions. They were, they will always remain, a part of me. 36

Meaning and Purpose

1. What books have shaped your life so far? Name at least three and describe their heroes and heroines. Can you associate these books with specific times in your life, as Viorst does with hers?

2. What is Viorst's main point in her essay, and where does she state it?

3. Who were Viorst's heroines, and what does she find attractive about each? Why does she put them in the order she chooses?

vividly and psychologically real than those in history. Good novelists are able to imaginatively penetrate the human psyche.

5. In paragraph 28, Viorst describes a darker side to a few of her heroines and says, "I had no wish to live anguishedly [as they did]." She ends her essay by acknowledging that "such reconciling heroines [whom she now longs for], in novels and real life, may not yet exist" (35).

Strategy

1. Viorst can talk about her heroines in first person only because they are peculiar to her and were important at specific times in her life. She can't speak so for anyone else. But the general appeal of this first-person strategy is that readers are free to fill in their own heroes and heroines and make a similar list for themselves. The more specific writing is, the more universal its appeal.

2. In this informative process analysis, Viorst begins chronologically with Nancy Drew and ends five heroines later with Natasha of *War and Peace*. Viorst talks about how each one influenced her at the time she read them, and also relates what was important then in her own life. She makes clear her identification with each heroine (last sentence, 14; 27). Viorst paces her chronology with an explanation of each heroine's character, often with quotations from the novels, and with summaries of her fascination with the heroine. Within the order in which she read the books is Viorst's own chronology, from age ten to being "ready for domesticity" (34).

3. Each of these paragraphs serves as a transition, carrying the reader gracefully from one heroine to the next. Paragraph 2 is a transition from thesis to body of the essay.

Style

1. Viorst is looking back as a grown woman on her childhood (2). She has insight into her own maturation that she couldn't have had as a girl. Paragraph 18 illustrates this viewpoint. Viorst's attitude is fond and affectionate—and understanding—toward her fascination with girlhood

4. Why do you think Viorst chose heroines from works of fiction rather than from real life?
5. Do Viorst's heroines always have a positive, uplifting effect on her? Explain.

Strategy

1. Viorst uses first person throughout her essay and does not address the reader directly. How does this strategy draw readers into her analysis?
2. How does Viorst organize her essay? How is the process structured?
3. Viorst uses some one- and two-sentence paragraphs (2, 4, 8, 10, 15, 19, 29, 33, 35). How does each of these function in the essay?

Style

1. From what perspective does Viorst discuss her heroines, and what is her attitude toward them and toward their influence on her? Support your answers with statements from the essay.
2. Viorst often uses dashes in her sentences. What effect do they create?
3. How does Viorst use sentence fragments? Are they effective? Why or why not?
4. If necessary, check a dictionary for the meanings of these words: *gawky, gauche* (5); *brusque* (11); *curry favor* (12); *unabashed* (13); *incarnate* (20).

Writing Tasks

1. Using Viorst's essay as a model, write an informative process analysis showing how a series of events, situations, or people helped you grow up.

heroines (sentence 1, paragraph 11), and she says, "I was fortunate to have had them as my companions" (last paragraph).

2. Dashes set off sentence elements from each other sharply and usually emphasize them. Viorst uses the dash to set off an appositive (sentence 1, paragraph 1), to set off a parenthetical element that is abrupt (sentence 1, paragraph 3), and to mark a sudden break in thought (sentence 3, paragraph 3).

3. Viorst uses fragments for emphasis and sometimes informality. With fragments she can avoid colorless or repetitious noun or verb phrases. In context, these fragments (often called "minor sentences") are clear and complete, but they are grammatically incomplete (they do not have an independent noun phrase plus verb-phrase core). Viorst's most extensive use of fragments for rhetorical purposes is in 5. The first group of minor sentences sets off each of the main characters in *Little Women*. The second group isolates characteristics that the author and fictional characters Jo and Nancy Drew have in common.

Many students are not ready to use fragments stylistically and should stick to complete sentences.

4. *Gawky:* awkward, ungainly, clumsy; *gauche:* lacking social grace, sensitivity; *brusque:* abrupt in manner, blunt, rough; *curry favor:* to seek to advance oneself by flattery or fawning; *unabashed:* unashamed; *incarnate:* embodied in flesh.

2. When Judith Viorst was a preteenager, girls read Nancy Drew and boys read the Hardy boys. What did you read when you were ten to twelve years old, and how did those books and characters reflect your values? How were they a standard of measure for you?

❦ *Responding to Photographs* ❦

Process Analysis

Untitled

For some writers the act of writing can be so painful they go to remarkable lengths to postpone the labor. They travel to the farthest stationery store for the "right" pencil, the one with the exact texture of lead that works best with the amount of pressure they apply to the paper. When they return, they may discover that they are short of the right kind of paper—you know, the yellow pads with the blue lines. Again back to the stationery store. Home once again, all those new pencils must be sharpened to a fine, a very, very fine, point.

What's the solution to this kind of procrastination?

There probably isn't one, for writing is a deeply personal process, one that is full of mystery. Probably no two people go about it exactly the same way. We all use devices to get ourselves started and to keep ourselves at the task. Nevertheless, something must get written. We must get the images and thoughts out of our heads, translate them to words, and put them on paper. Then, of course, a new process begins—the revision process.

Clearly, the untitled photograph here captures a moment in the writing process. For this essay, you are to explore the writing process by completing one of the following writing tasks. Before beginning the task reread "Process Analysis: Explaining Step by Step" at the beginning of the chapter, to remind yourself of process analysis strategies.

1. Create an appropriate title for the untitled photograph. Then describe its content as capturing part of the writing process. In your essay, account for all the elements in the photograph that relate to the writing process—manuscript, pencils, coffee, calendar, stapler, glasses, desk or table, even the writer's posture.

2. Document your own writing process with photographs of its various stages. Then use the photographs to compose a "photo-essay" that concentrates on your own writing process. Use at least five photographs, each one capturing a stage in the process, and explain to your readers what the photographs signify. Keep in mind that writing is a highly personal process, so be sure your photographs and essay embody your personal writing quirks.

❧ Additional Writing Tasks ❧

Process Analysis

1. Develop one of these subjects (or one you create for yourself) through *directive process analysis*. Explain the process one step at a time and be sure to provide your reader with enough detail to make each step clear.

   a. how to prepare a vegetable garden
   b. how to live without an automobile
   c. how to domesticate a wild creature, such as a falcon or rabbit
   d. how to get rid of pests without using poisons
   e. how to prepare for an acting role
   f. how to prepare a canvas for paint
   g. how to show appreciation to others
   h. how to toss a Frisbee, football, baseball, and so on
   i. how to skateboard, roller blade, roller skate
   j. how to bluff at poker
   k. how to survive Muzak
   l. how to complain effectively
   m. how to overcome shyness
   n. how to write an effective essay
   o. how to take effective notes
   p. how to outsmart a video game
   q. how to survive a natural disaster, such as an earthquake or tornado
   r. how to meditate in a crowded setting
   s. how to ride a roller coaster
   t. how to attend a concert
   u. how to run for local elected office
   v. how to win others to your point of view
   w. how to buy a used motorcycle or car

2. Develop one of these subjects (or one you create for yourself) through *informative process analysis*. Remember that this technique does not explain "how to" do something; it explains how something happens—it informs, often using narrative and descriptive techniques.

a. how psychoanalysis works
b. how secret codes are broken
c. how to read detective, espionage, or suspense fiction
d. how to learn from past experience
e. how a stroke damages the brain
f. how Alzheimer's disease develops
g. how dreams work
h. how intuition works
i. how to taste wine
j. how to create a frightening film scene
k. how to create suspense
l. how to collect art, rare books, or something else
m. how to detect lies
n. how to overcome guilt
o. how to change community thinking
p. how to live as an outsider
q. how to become an insider
r. how an idea becomes accepted
s. how voodoo works

9

Classification and Division

Establishing Categories

The Method

Have you ever played Twenty Questions, a parlor game in which one participant selects a person, place, or thing and the other participants try to guess it? The participants have twenty yes-or-no questions to find the answer. To discover that answer is a difficult task—unless you understand the principles of **classification.**

The game usually begins with a series of questions that divide the world into three roughly drawn categories: animal, vegetable, or mineral. Once the correct category is determined—"animal," for our purposes—the interrogation begins, the participants moving logically from category to category.

"Does it live in water?" a questioner might ask. A sensible question, for the earth is easily divided into land and water.

"No," the person with the secret responds. But "No" means the animal lives on land, keeping in mind that birds may fly but may also nest on land. The process of elimination continues.

"Does it have two legs?" Another logical question, because animals can be classified by locomotion.

"No."

"Four legs?" The pace of questions quickens.

"No."

Aha! the questioner has it, "Is this creature an insect?"

"Nope!" Oops . . . must be a snake, right? But what snake? The only two large categories are venomous and nonvenomous. If the answer is venomous, the questions will take one direction, "Does it have rattles?" If the answer is nonvenomous, the questions will move in another direction, "Does it kill by coiling around and crushing its prey?" And so on, until the secret is revealed or twenty questions are exhausted.

To classify is to divide a large subject into components and sort them into categories with common characteristics, a principle that clearly guides the search in any round of Twenty Questions. Classification is so pervasive that it must be fundamental to the human way of perceiving and understanding experience. Few things, no matter how significant or insignificant, seem to escape classification. Think how chaotic your campus library would be without a clear classification system. Your supermarket trips are probably organized by the manager's way of classifying products—first the vegetables, on to dairy products, rush to meats, march to canned goods, stalled at the register. Television shows, books, actors, restaurants, fun-zone rides—the possibilities for classification are endless because of our desire to understand and organize experience.

Keep in mind, too, that most subjects can be classified in a number of ways, depending on the purpose and who's doing the classifying. Consider the subject *college students*. For statistical purposes, a registrar might classify college students by age, sex, major, grade-point average, or region. An art teacher might classify students by their talent: painters, sculptors, ceramicists, illustrators, and print makers. A political-science teacher might classify the same students by their politics: reactionary, conservative, liberal, or radical. Much of this kind of classification is done informally, but in writing, a classification system should be complete and follow consistent principles.

Writers using classification as a pattern of development begin by carefully analyzing their subject—that is, by breaking it into components. They look for qualities that some components share and that others don't share. Using the qualities they've identified, they create categories. They then sort through the various components to group them in the appropriate category. They are careful to be logical, sorting and grouping the parts in a consistent manner. They also keep in mind that their categories must be complete. It would not be complete if they divided voters into Republicans and Democrats, because some voters are registered in the Peace and Freedom and Libertarian parties, among others. But if a writer's subject is limited to elected senators, then the categories might indeed be Republicans and Democrats, because no other party is represented in the Senate. Writers also make sure their categories do not overlap. To classify a group of congresswomen as Republicans, Democrats, and politicians would not make much sense because all are politicians.

Professional writers distinguish between the terms *division* and *classification,* yet these categories are intellectual companions in the classification procedure. Writers begin by first *dividing* a subject into manageable categories. They then *classify* the components of the subject according to the shared qualities. Consider the subject *movies,* which can be broken down into such categories as mystery, romance, horror, musical, comedy, western, and war. This step is division. Once the categories are established, a writer might evaluate several films, and sort them according to the qualities of each category. This step is classification. Remember, division breaks one subject into categories; classification groups the parts of the subject into the categories. Although this distinction may be important for understanding the intellectual procedure of classification, it is less important in reaching the result, a system that shows the relationship between parts of a subject.

The simplest form of classification is **two-part**, often called **binary**, classification. This pattern divides a subject in two, usually into positive and negative categories, such as vegetarians and nonvegetarians; smokers and nonsmokers; television viewers and non–television viewers; deaf people and hearing people; or runners and nonrunners. But two-part classification is usually inexact and skirts the edge of comparison and contrast. Most classification systems, therefore, have at least three categories.

Strategies

Careful writers arrange their classifications in a straightforward division, usually in blocks and according to the order that seems most appropriate. Each block is a subclass and will usually be identified by a name or phrase to keep the reader on track. In the following paragraph, anthropologist Ruth Benedict divides the ceremonial societies of the Zuni. She clearly identifies each society—the priestly societies, the masked-god societies, and the medicine societies—before describing them.

This ceremonial life that preoccupies Zuni attention is organized like a series of interlocking wheels. The priesthoods have their sacred objects, their retreats, their dances, their prayers; and their year-long program is annually initiated by the great winter solstice ceremony that makes use of all the different groups and sacred things and focuses all their functions. The tribal masked-god society has similar possessions and calendric observances, and these culminate in the great winter tribal masked god ceremony, the Shalkado. In like fashion the medicine societies, with their special relation to curing, function throughout the year and have their annual culminating ceremony for tribal health. These three major cults of Zuni ceremonial life are not mutually exclusive. A man may be, and often is, for the greater part of his life, a member of all three. They each give him sacred possessions "to live by" and demand of him exacting ceremonial knowledge.

Writers use one of two strategies to identify their categories. They either use ready-made categories or they create their own. In the next classification passage, from *Blood and Money,* Thomas Thompson uses subclasses to present his view of the personal characteristics that describe surgeons.

Among those who train students to become doctors, it is said that surgeons find their niche in accordance with their personal characteristics. The orthopedic surgeon is medicine's carpenter—up to his elbows in plaster of Paris— and tradition holds that he is a gruff, slapdash sort of man whose labor is in a very physical area of healing. Away from the hospital, the orthopedists are often hunters, boaters, outdoorsmen.

The neurosurgeon, classically, does not get too involved with his patients. Or, for that matter, with anybody. They are cool men, blunted, rarely gregarious.

Heart surgeons are thundering egotists, star performers in a dazzling operating theater packed with assistants, nurses, paramedics, and a battery of futuristic equipment which could seemingly lift the room into outer space. These are men who relish drama, who live life on the edge of the precipice.

And the plastic surgeon? He is, by nature, a man of art, and temperament, and sensitivity. "We are the artists who deal in beauty lost, or beauty that never was," said one plastic man at a national convention. "Our stitches are hidden, and so are our emotions."

Because Thompson is working with established categories, part of his task is to make his material fresh. Most readers know the professional qualities of surgeons, and so Thompson creates a sense of the person holding the scalpel by including descriptive details of each type's dominant personality trait.

In the next paragraph, Larry McMurtry uses established categories in a slightly different way. He classifies beer bars in the city of Houston according to their location: East side, West side, and North side.

The poor have beer-bars, hundreds of them, seldom fancy but reliably dim and cool. Most of them are equipped with jukeboxes, shuffleboards, jars of pig's feet and talkative drunks. There are lots of bar burlesques, where from 3 P.M. on girls gyrate at one's elbow with varying degrees of grace. On the East side there are a fair number of open-air bars— those who like to watch the traffic can sit, drink Pearl, observe the wrecks, and listen to "Hello, Vietnam" on the juke box. Louisiana is just down the road, and a lot of the men wear Cajun sideburns and leave their shirttails out. On the West side cowboys are common. Members of the cross-continental hitch-hiking set congregate on Franklin Street, at places like The Breaking Point Lounge. Symbolic *latinos* slip over to the Last Concert on the North side; or, if they are especially bold, go all the way to McCarty Street, where one can view the most extraordinary example of Mexican saloon-and-whorehouse architecture north of the border.

McMurtry opens with a general description of Houston beer bars: They are dim and cool with jukeboxes, shuffleboards, jars of pig's feet, and drunks—a watering hole for blue-collar men. After rendering the general qualities of these bars, McMurtry presents the geographic categories, each with a brief description that characterizes it.

Writers often classify a subject that has no ready-made categories. They must, therefore, create their own categories and the labels that identify them. In this paragraph from "Here Is New York," E. B. White divides the population of New York into three categories according to a person's relation to the city.

> There are roughly three New Yorks. There is, first, the New York of the man or woman who was born here, who takes the city for granted and accepts its size and its turbulence as natural and inevitable. Second, there is the New York of the commuter—the city that is devoured by locusts each day and spat out each night. Third, there is the New York of the quest of something. Of these three trembling cities the greatest is the last—the city of final destination, the city that is a goal. It is this third city that accounts for New York's high-strung disposition, its poetical deportment, its dedication to the arts, and its incomparable achievements. Commuters give the city its tidal restlessness; natives give it solidarity and continuity; but the settlers give it passion. And whether it is a farmer arriving from Italy to set up a small grocery store in a slum, or a young girl arriving from a small town in Mississippi to escape the indignity of being observed by her neighbors, or a boy arriving from the Corn Belt with a manuscript in his suitcase and a pain in his heart, it makes no difference: each embraces New York with the intense excitement of first love, each absorbs New York with the fresh eyes of an adventurer, each generates heat and light to dwarf the Consolidated Edison Company.

Commuters, natives, and settlers, these are White's three categories. He uses each category to present characteristics of New York City. The commuter gives the city a sense of restlessness;

the native gives it solidarity; and the settler, the category he stresses, gives it passion.

Classification in College Writing

The physical sciences, social sciences, humanities, all make use of classification. In fact, you can expect to use the classification pattern across the academic curriculum. For example, Mark Freeman was assigned an informal classification paper in cultural anthropology. The subject was *leisure time*. His task was to observe people pursuing a leisure activity or hobby. Freeman narrowed his subject to offbeat hobbies and concentrated on comic-book collectors, a hobby he has pursued for years. He begins his essay with this classification paragraph that establishes the categories and the general characteristics of the collectors who comprise them.

Freeman opens with a sentence that identifies his subject—comic-book collectors. He follows with a generalized physical description of collectors.

To keep his reader on track, Freeman lists the categories he'll use to group collectors.

Freeman devotes most of the paragraph to grouping collectors into one of the categories according to their motivation for collecting.

One fascinating off-beat hobbyist is the comic book collector. Usually male, pale, wearing glasses, bushy-haired and disheveled, collectors can be found rummaging through pile after pile of unsorted, second-hand comics in magazine marts across the country. Comic book collectors, the serious ones, seem to fall into four major groups: Antiquarians, Mercenaries, Idolators, and Compulsive Completers. The Antiquarian cares only for age value; subject matter is of no concern. He is looking for a 1933 <u>Funnies on Parade</u> from the days when men were men and comics were comics. To the Mercenary, value is all-important. Certain numbers and titles ring a bell in his cash-register brain and start him furtively checking through a half dozen price sheets. A pristine first edition of <u>Action Comics</u> (value $4,000) would

Notice that the categories are arranged in blocks.

suit him just fine. The Idolator could not care less about age or value. He is looking for favorites: <u>Sheena,</u> a <u>Flash Gordon,</u> or an <u>Incredible Hulk.</u> Hiding in the corner, reading those he cannot afford to buy, the Idolator will be the last one out of the mart at night and the first one back in the morning. The most frustrated collector is the Compulsive Completer. He will examine and reject thousands of comics in his search for a badly needed <u>Felix the Cat</u> to complete a year's set or the one <u>Howdy Doody</u> missing from his

He closes with a clincher that identifies a trait all collectors share.

collection. But no matter what the reason for collecting, these hobbyists share a common trait: They love the thrill of the hunt.

Because no ready-made categories are available, Freeman creates his own—Antiquarians, Mercenaries, Idolators, and Compulsive Completers—and groups them according to their motivation for collecting. He arranges this paragraph in a common classification structure, opening with a general description of collectors, then listing the categories he'll group them in. Next, he discusses each category in detail, identifying the characteristics of the collector who falls into each group.

❦ Alison Lurie ❦

*Born in Chicago in 1926, Alison Lurie graduated from Radcliffe College.
As a fiction writer, she has often been compared to Jane Austen, both
for her style and for her subject matter, which has often been a particular
segment of American society—that of the wealthy and educated. Since
publication of her first novel,* Love and Friendship, *in 1962, she has
published seven more, the latest of which is* The Truth about Lorin
Jones *(1988). She received a Pulitzer Prize for her novel* Foreign
Affairs *(1984). She has also published three children's books and a
nonfiction book on the social history of clothes.*

American Regional Costume

In this excerpt from her book The Language of Clothes *(1981), Lurie
classifies American styles of dress by region, and the people of those
regions by the clothes they wear. She traces the historical influences of
climate, landscape, economy, and life-style on various regional "costumes."*

*While reading this essay, pay careful attention to the ways that
Lurie carefully describes each regional costume so that the classifications
of dress do not overlap.*

Even today, when the American landscape is becoming more 1
and more homogeneous, there is really no such thing as an all-
American style of dress. A shopping center in Maine may superficially resemble one in Georgia or California, but the shoppers
in it will look different, because the diverse histories of these
states have left their mark on costume.

Regional dress in the United States, as in Britain, can best be 2
observed at large national meetings where factors such as occupation and income are held relatively constant. At these meetings
regional differences stand out clearly, and can be checked by
looking at the name tags Americans conventionally wear to conventions. Five distinct styles can be distinguished: (1) Old New

432

England, (2) Deep South, (3) Middle American, (4) Wild West and (5) Far West or Californian. In border areas, outfits usually combine regional styles.

Americans who do not travel much within their own country often misinterpret the styles of other regions. Natives of the Eastern states, for instance, may misread Far Western clothing as indicating greater casualness—or greater sexual availability—than is actually present. The laid-back-looking Los Angeles executive in his open-chested sport shirt and sandals may have his eye on the main chance to an extent that will shock his Eastern colleague. The reverse error can also occur: a Southern Californian may discover with surprise that the sober-hued, buttoned-up New Englander he or she has just met is bored with business and longing to get drunk or hop into bed.

3

Northeast and Southeast:
Puritans and Planters

The drab, severe costumes of the Puritan settlers of New England, and their suspicion of color and ornament as snares of the devil, have left their mark on the present-day clothes of New Englanders. At any large meeting people from this part of the country will be dressed in darker hues—notably black, gray and navy—often with touches of white that recall the starched collars and cuffs of Puritan costume. Fabrics will be plainer (though heavier and sometimes more expensive) and styles simpler, with less waste of material: skirts and lapels and trimmings will be narrower. More of the men will also wear suits and shoes made in England (or designed to look as if they had been made in England). The law of camouflage also operates in New England, where gray skies and dark rectangular urban landscapes are not unknown.

4

The distinctive dress of the Deep South is based on a climate that did not demand heavy clothing and an economy that for years exempted middle- and upper-class whites from all manual labor and made washing and ironing cheap. Today the planter's white suits and fondness for fine linen and his wife's and daugh-

5

She now explains how styles can be misinterpreted by someone alien to a region. This confusion bolsters her contention that dress styles reflect history, geography, and climate rather than social mores or personal morals.

Here Lurie begins the paragraph with its topic sentence and then cites examples to establish its validity.

She again begins with a topic sentence and proceeds with examples. Now, though, the often elaborate dress of the Deep South is contrasted with the severer dress of New England described in the preceding paragraph.

ters' elaborate and fragile gowns survive in modern form. At our imaginary national meeting the male southerners will wear lighter-colored suits—pale grays and beiges—and a certain dandyism will be apparent, expressing itself in French cuffs, more expensive ties, silkier materials and wider pin stripes. The women's clothes will be more flowery, with a tendency toward bows, ruffles, lace and embroidery. If they are white, they will probably be as white as possible; a pale complexion is still the sign of a Southern lady, and female sun tans are unfashionable except on tourists.

Midwest and Wild West: Pioneers and Cowboys

The American Midwest and Great Plains states were settled by men and women who had to do their own work and prided themselves on it. They chose sturdy, practical clothes that did not show the dirt, washed and wore well and needed little ironing, made of gingham and linsey-woolsey and canvas. From these clothes descends the contemporary costume of Middle Americans. This style is visible to everyone on national television, where it is worn by most news announcers, politicians, talk-show hosts and actors in commercials for kitchen products. A slightly dowdier version appears in the Sears and Montgomery Ward catalogues. But even when expensive, Middle American fashion is apt to lag behind fashion as it is currently understood back East; it is also usually more sporty and casual. The pioneer regard for physical activity and exercise is still strong in this part of the country, and as a result the Midwesterners at our convention will look healthier and more athletic—and also somewhat beefier—than their colleagues from the cold, damp Northeast and the hot, humid South. Their suits will tend toward the tans and browns of plowed cornfields rather than the grays of Eastern skies. More of them will wear white or white-on-white shirts, and their striped or foulard ties will be brighter and patterned on a larger scale than those purchased in sober New York and Boston.

The traditional Western costume, of course, was that of the cowboy on the range. Perhaps because of the isolation of those

6

7

Lurie uses the first two sentences to introduce her next classification, midwestern dress, and to lead to her topic sentence, the third. After describing midwestern dress, she compares it to dress in New England and the South to even more clearly distinguish it.

She now describes dress in the Wild West and claims that the language as well as the dress of the Wild Westerners reflects a ranching background.

wide-open spaces, this is the style which has been least influenced by those of other regions. At any national convention the Wild Westerners will be the easiest to identify. For one thing, they are apt to be taller—either genetically or with the help of boots. Some may appear in full Western costume, the sartorial equivalent of a "he-went-thataway" drawl; but even the more conservative will betray, or rather proclaim, their regional loyalty through their dress, just as in conversation they will from time to time use a ranching metaphor, or call you "pal" or "pardner." A man in otherwise conventional business uniform will wear what look like cowboy boots, or a hat with an enlarged brim and crown. Women, too, are apt to wear boots, and their jackets and skirts may have a Western cut, especially when viewed from the rear. Some may wear red or navy-blue bandanna-print shirts or dresses, or an actual cotton-print bandanna knotted round their necks.

The Far West:
Adventurers and Beach Boys

First Lurie gives a brief historical background on California's development and then shows how the present reflects the past.

The men and women who settled the Far West were a mixed and rather raffish lot. Restlessness, the wish for excitement, the hope of a fortune in gold and sometimes a need to escape the law led them to undertake the long and dangerous journey over mountains and deserts, or by sea round Cape Horn. In more than one sense they were adventurers, and often desperadoes—desperate people. California was a territory where no one would ask about your past, where unconventionality of character and behavior was easily accepted. Even today when, as the country song puts it, "all the gold in California is in a bank in the middle of Beverly Hills in somebody else's name," the place has the reputation of an El Dorado. Men and women willing to risk everything on long odds in the hope of a big hit, or eager to put legal, financial and personal foul-ups behind them, often go west.

8

El Dorado was a legendary treasure city in South America sought by early Spanish explorers. By extension, then, it is any place promising great wealth.

Present-day California styles are still in many ways those of adventurers and eccentrics. Whatever the current fashion, the California version will be more extreme, more various and—possibly because of the influence of the large Spanish-American

9

population—much more colorful. Clothes tend to fit more tightly than is considered proper elsewhere, and to expose more flesh: an inability to button the shirt above the diaphragm is common in both sexes. Virtuous working-class housewives may wear outfits that in any other part of the country would identify them as medium-priced whores; reputable business and professional men may dress in a manner which would lose them most of their clients back east and attract the attention of the Bureau of Internal Revenue if not of the police.

Southern Californians, and many other natives of what is now called the Sun Belt (an imaginary strip of land stretching across the bottom of the United States from Florida to Santa Barbara, but excluding most of the Old South), can also be identified by their year-round sun tans, which by middle age have often given the skin the look of old if expensive and well-oiled leather. The men may also wear the getup known as Sun Belt Cool: a pale beige suit, open-collared shirt (often in a darker shade than the suit), cream-colored loafers and aviator sunglasses. The female version of the look is similar, except that the shoes will be high-heeled sandals.

10

Regional Disguise:
Sunbelt Puritans and Urban Cowboys

Some long-time inhabitants of California and the other sartorially distinct regions of the United States refuse to wear the styles characteristic of that area. In this case the message is clear: they are unhappy in that locale and/or do not want anyone to attribute to them the traits associated with it. Such persons, if depressed, may adopt a vague and anonymous mode of dress; if in good spirits they may wear the costume of some other region in order to proclaim their sympathy with it. In terms of speech, what we have then is not a regional accent, but the conscious adoption of a dialect by an outsider.

11

In the urban centers of the West and Far West bankers and financial experts of both sexes sometimes adopt an Eastern manner of speech and a Wall Street appearance in order to suggest

12

To emphasize the sometimes outlandish Californian dress, Lurie shows how that dress might be interpreted in other parts of the country.

Lurie now connects southern Californians with others in the Sun Belt and gives two more examples that distinguish them from those of other regions.

In the last section of the essay, Lurie explains why some people who live in a region refuse to dress typically and why some styles are popular in all regions. She begins by giving some general examples of people who choose to dress outside the norm.

She now offers specific examples.

reliability and tradition. And today in Southern California there are professors who speak with Bostonian accents, spend their days in the library stacks, avoid the beach and dress in clothes that would occasion no comment in Harvard Yard. New arrivals to the area sometimes take these men and women for visiting Eastern lecturers, and are surprised to learn that they have lived in Southern California for thirty or forty years, or have even been born there.

Lurie introduces two other factors that influence the popularity of a regional style and offers examples from the past.

13 The popularity of the various regional styles of American costume, like that of the various national styles, is also related to economic and political factors. Some years ago modes often originated in the Far West and the word "California" on a garment was thought to be an allurement. Today, with power and population growth shifting to the Southwestern oil-producing states, Wild West styles—particularly those of Texas—are in vogue. This fashion, of course, is not new. For many years men who have never been nearer to a cow than the local steakhouse have worn Western costume to signify that they are independent, tough and reliable. In a story by Flannery O'Connor, for instance, the sinister traveling salesman is described as wearing "a broad-brimmed stiff gray hat of the kind used by businessmen who would like to look like cowboys"—but, it is implied, seldom succeed in doing so.

She concludes with an explanation of the current popularity of western costume and gives present-day examples.

14 The current popularity of Western costume has been increased by the turn away from foreign modes that has accompanied the recent right-wing shift in United States politics. In all countries periods of isolationism and a belligerently ostrichlike stance toward the rest of the world have usually been reflected in a rejection of international modes in favor of national styles, often those of the past. Today in America the cowboy look is high fashion, and even in New York City the streets are full of a variety of Wild West types. Some are dressed in old-fashioned, well-worn Western gear; others in the newer, brighter and sleeker outfits of modern ranchers, while a few wear spangled, neon-hued Electric Cowboy and Cowgirl costumes of the type most often seen on Texas country-rock musicians.

POSSIBLE ANSWERS

Meaning and Purpose

1. Encourage students to examine their own ideas about what regional American dress is, as well as where those ideas come from and what attitudes they might reflect.

2. Attendees of national meetings generally come from similar occupational and economic backgrounds. Their dress would vary not because of social and economic status, but because of the regions they come from (3).

3. Lurie's thesis is that Americans have five distinct kinds of dress, as she states (2).

4. Regional styles are determined by the region's history and climate and do not reflect moral attitudes. Someone from outside a region may misinterpret the dress of that region by reading moral values into the style of dress (3).

5. She claims that history, local interests, geography, and climate account for the differences in regional dress styles.

6. The current popularity of western costume reflects recent far-right politics and isolationism and a turning away from foreign modes (14).

Strategy

1. Lurie's organizational scheme follows the historical development of the United States from the Northeast to the South, the Midwest to the Southwest, and, finally, to the Far West.

2. Lurie's first two subheadings pair adjacent regions, and the two style categories under each are markedly different. The Far West gets its own subheading because it is traditionally big and bold enough to stand alone. California is usually set apart from other regions.

3. To clearly distinguish the "sturdy and practical" dress of the midwesterner, Lurie compares this style to that of both the New Englander and the southerner (6). She emphasizes the often outlandish California styles by showing how such dress would be interpreted in other parts of the country, particularly the more formally attired Northeast (9).

Meaning and Purpose

1. If you were to classify American regional dress, would you choose Lurie's categories? Why or why not? If not, what would your categories be?
2. Why does Lurie claim that large, national meetings are best for observing regional dress?
3. What is Lurie's main point, and where does she state it?
4. Why is it possible to misinterpret the dress styles of different regions?
5. How does Lurie explain the differences in dress from region to region?
6. How does Lurie account for the current popularity of western costume? Do you agree with her?

Strategy

1. What scheme does Lurie use to organize her categories?
2. In paragraph 2, Lurie lists five categories of style of dress, but only three subheadings cover those five categories. Why do you suppose she puts the first two and the second two together, and gives the Far West its own subheading?
3. Lurie adds to classification and division other rhetorical strategies to support her categories. Look again at paragraphs 4 and 5, and paragraph 8 and paragraph 9. What strategies does she use in these places?
4. Lurie quotes a country song in paragraph 8 and the short-story writer and novelist Flannery O'Connor in paragraph 13. What is the purpose of these quotations?

Style

1. Lurie often juxtaposes formal sociological and anthropological language with the language of casual conversation and slang.

4. The quotations show that the kinds of dress she describes are reflected in popular and literary culture. These facts bolster the validity of her thesis.

Style

1. Some examples: "homogeneous" (1), "factors such as occupation and income are held relatively constant" (2), "laid-back-looking" and "hop into bed" (3). The casual language gives the impression that she's talking about real people.

2. Lurie makes no explicit judgments, but some of her descriptive language sounds opinionated or stereotypical.

3. *Homogeneous:* composed of parts or elements that are all of the same kind; *superficially:* externally or outwardly; *Puritan:* a member of a group of Protestants that arose in the sixteenth century within the Church of England, demanding simpler doctrine and worship and stricter religious discipline; many Puritans migrated to New England; *dandyism:* excessive attention to clothes and appearance; *gingham:* yarn-dyed, plain-weave cotton fabric, usually striped or checked; *linsey-woolsey:* a coarse fabric woven from linen warp, or sometimes cotton and coarse wool filling; *dowdier:* to be dowdy is to be out of style, drab, old-fashioned, untidy; *foulard:* a soft, lightweight silk, rayon, or cotton of plain or twill weave with printed design; *sartorial:* of or pertaining to clothing or style or manner of dress; *raffish:* mildly or sometimes engagingly disreputable or nonconformist; *allurement:* fascination, charm; *isolationism:* the policy or doctrine of isolating one's country from the affairs of other nations by declining to enter alliances, foreign economic commitments, international agreements, and so on; *belligerently:* warlike, aggressively hostile.

What are some examples of this mixture? What is the effect of such juxtapositions?

2. In her categories and descriptions, is Lurie making any judgments about regional dress, or is she neutral? Support your answer with language from the essay.

3. If necessary, check a dictionary for the meanings of these expressions: *homogeneous, superficially* (1); *Puritan* (4); *dandyism* (5); *gingham, linsey-woolsey, dowdier, foulard* (6); *sartorial* (7); *raffish* (8); *allurement* (13); *isolationism, belligerently* (14).

Writing Tasks

1. Analyze the styles of dress popular on your campus. Create four or five style categories and use as many specific examples as you can. In a classification-and-division essay, establish clearly the basis for your classifications.

2. Examine the ways in which popular entertainment—movies, television, rock music, and rock-music stars—affects dress, speech, or hair style. Write a classification essay in which you show how these influences have produced the styles you describe.

The essay could be used for discussing both childrearing and learning. The students' own backgrounds will undoubtedly determine their attitudes toward each of the kinds of discipline Holt describes, especially that of Superior Force. Encourage students to give specific examples to back up their opinions, demonstrating that specifics are always needed to be convincing.

❦ John Holt ❦

John Holt is the author of, among other famous books, How Children Fail *(1964) and* How Children Learn *(1967). He was born in 1923 and studied at Yale University. His fourteen years of experience in elementary and high-school teaching led him to some radical and controversial conclusions about the ineffectiveness of the American educational system. In many of his books he addresses this problem and offers alternative methods for helping children learn. He was a visiting lecturer at Harvard University and the University of California at Berkeley. After 1969 he devoted himself primarily to writing, lecturing, social activism, and playing the cello, which he took up at age forty. He founded, edited, and published* Growing Without Schooling, *a magazine by and for families who choose to teach their children at home. He died in 1985.*

Three Kinds of Discipline

This tightly organized short essay offers a general prescription for the use of discipline by classifying it in three categories. Here and in the book where this passage first appeared, Freedom and Beyond *(1972), Holt argues that, in order to learn, children need to be left alone as much as they need to be disciplined.*

As you read Holt's essay, think of your own childhood and compare the ways that you were disciplined with how Holt would like to see children disciplined.

MARGINAL NOTES

Holt begins with examples that immediately illustrate the Discipline of Nature.

A child, in growing up, may meet and learn from three different kinds of disciplines. The first and most important is what we might call the Discipline of Nature or of Reality. When he is trying to do something real, if he does the wrong thing or doesn't do the right one, he doesn't get the result he wants. If he doesn't pile one block right on top of another, or tries to build on a slanting surface, his tower falls down. If he hits the wrong key, he hears the wrong note. If he doesn't hit the nail squarely on the head, it bends, and he has to pull it out and start with another. If he doesn't measure properly what he is trying to build, it won't open, close, fit, stand up, fly, float, whistle, or do whatever he wants it to do. If he closes his eyes when he swings, he doesn't hit the ball. A child meets this kind of discipline every time he tries to *do* something, which is why it is so important in school to give children more chances to do things, instead of just reading or listening to someone talk (or pretending to). This discipline is a good teacher. The learner never has to wait long for his answer; it usually comes quickly, often instantly. Also it is clear, and very often points toward the needed correction; from what happened he can not only see that what he did was wrong, but also why, and what he needs to do instead. Finally, and most important, the giver of the answer, call it Nature, is impersonal, impartial, and indifferent. She does not give opinions, or make judgments: she cannot be wheedled, bullied, or fooled; she does not get angry or disappointed; she does not praise or blame; she does not remember past failures or hold grudges; with her one always gets a fresh start, this time is the one that counts.

He then shows why this kind of discipline is important in schools: it is a good teacher.

After explaining the Discipline of Culture, Holt gives examples to show that it works in the real world.

The next discipline we might call the Discipline of Culture, of Society, of What People Really Do. Man is a social, a cultural animal. Children sense around them this culture, this network of agreements, customs, habits, and rules binding the adults together. They want to understand it and be a part of it. They watch very carefully what people around them are doing and want to do the same. They want to do right, unless they become convinced they can't do right. Thus children rarely misbehave seriously in church, but sit as quietly as they can. The example of all those grownups is contagious. Some mysterious ritual is going on, and children, who like rituals, want to be part of it. In the same way, the little children that I see at concerts or operas, though they may fidget a little, or perhaps take a nap now and then, rarely make any disturbance. With all those grownups sitting there, neither moving nor talking, it is the most natural thing in the world to imitate them. Children who live among adults who are habitually courteous to each other, and to them, will soon learn to be courteous. Children who live surrounded by people who speak a certain way will speak that way, however much we may try to tell them that speaking that way is bad or wrong.

The third discipline is the one most people mean when they speak of discipline—the Discipline of Superior Force, of sergeant to private, of "you do what I tell you or I'll make you wish you had." There is bound to be some of this in a child's life. Living as we do surrounded by things that can hurt children, or that children can hurt, we cannot avoid it. We can't afford to let a small child find out from experience the danger of playing in a busy street, or of fooling with the pots on the top of a stove, or of eating up the pills in the medicine cabinet. So, along with other precautions, we say to him, "Don't play in the street, or touch things on the stove, or go into the medicine cabinet, or I'll punish you." Between him and the danger too great for him to imagine we put a lesser danger, but one he can imagine and maybe therefore wants to avoid. He can have no idea of what it would be like to be hit by a car, but he can imagine being shouted at, or spanked, or sent to his room. He avoids these substitutes for the greater danger until he can understand it and avoid it for its own sake. But we ought to use this discipline only when it is necessary to protect the life, health, safety, or well-being of people or other living creatures, or to prevent destruction of things that people care about. We ought not to assume too long, as we usually do, that a child cannot understand the real nature of the danger from which we want to protect him. The sooner he avoids the danger, not to escape our punishment, but as a matter of good sense, the better. He can learn that faster than we think. In Mexico, for example, where people drive their cars with a good deal of spirit, I saw many children no older than five or four walking unattended on the streets. They understood about cars, they knew what to do. A child whose life is full of the threat and fear of punishment is locked into babyhood. There is no way for him to grow up, to learn to take responsibility for his life and acts. Most important of all, we should not assume that having to yield to the threat of our superior force is good for the child's character. It is never good for *anyone's* character. To bow to superior force makes us feel impotent and cowardly for not having had the

Holt begins the paragraph using the same format as the last, a brief explanation of the Discipline of Superior Force followed by examples.

He now cautions that this kind of discipline should be used sparingly and goes on to explain why.

3

strength or courage to resist. Worse, it makes us resentful and vengeful. We can hardly wait to make someone pay for our humiliation, yield to us as we were once made to yield. No, if we cannot always avoid using the discipline of Superior Force, we should at least use it as seldom as we can.

With an extended example of ballet training Holt illustrates how all three disciplines often overlap.

There are places where all three disciplines overlap. Any very demanding human activity combines in it the disciplines of Superior Force, of Culture, and of Nature. The novice will be told, "Do it this way, never mind asking why, just do it that way, that is the way we always do it." But it probably *is* just the way they always do it, and usually for the very good reason that it is a way that has been found to work. Think, for example, of ballet training. The student in a class is told to do this exercise, or that; to stand so; to do this or that with his head, arms, shoulders, abdomen, hips, legs, feet. He is constantly corrected. There is no argument. But behind these seemingly autocratic demands by the teacher lie many decades of custom and tradition, and behind that, the necessities of dancing itself. You cannot make the moves of classical ballet unless over many years you have acquired, and renewed every day, the needed strength and suppleness in scores of muscles and joints. Nor can you do the difficult motions, making them look easy, unless you have learned hundreds of easier ones first. Dance teachers may not always agree on all the details of teaching these strengths and skills. But no novice could learn them all by himself. You could not go for a night or two to watch the ballet and then, without any other knowledge at all, teach yourself how to do it. In the same way, you would be unlikely to learn any complicated and difficult human activity without drawing heavily on the experience of those who know it better. But the point is that the authority of these experts or teachers stems from, grows out of their greater competence and experience, the fact that what they do *works,* not the fact that they happen to be the teacher and as such have the power to kick a student out of the class. And the further point is that children are always and everywhere attracted to that competence, and ready and eager to submit themselves to a discipline that grows out of it. We hear constantly that children will never do anything unless compelled to by bribes or threats. But in their private lives, or in extracurricular activities in school, in sports, music, drama, art, running a newspaper, and so on, they often submit themselves willingly and wholeheartedly to very intense disciplines, simply because they want to learn to do a given thing well. Our Little-Napoleon football coaches, of whom we have too many and hear far too much, blind us to the fact that millions of children work hard every year getting better at sports and games without coaches barking and yelling at them.

POSSIBLE ANSWERS

Meaning and Purpose

1. Holt means that children will "meet and learn" from discipline. His first sentence is his thesis. He goes into detail about three kinds of discipline and how children may learn best from them.

2. Give students time to talk about discipline they have observed and their opinions about it. Encourage them to compare their observations to some of Holt's descriptions.

3. Students will have their own opinions about this statement. Holt's point is that children usually imitate the adults around them and that example is the best teacher. He says, "They watch very carefully what people around them are doing and want to do the same" (2). The evidence he offers is general and perhaps idealistic, but his argument is effective.

4. He believes children are basically good and easily trained, and also that they will naturally strive for the best. The penultimate sentence in the essay illustrates this attitude.

Strategy

1. Holt's classification system has to do with the kinds of things in the world outside the self that he thinks impose discipline on children. He chooses nature, culture, and force as three large

Meaning and Purpose

1. What does Holt set out to say in this essay?
2. What methods of discipline have you seen in practice, and how effective do you think they are?
3. Do you agree with the statement, "Thus children rarely misbehave seriously in church, but sit as quietly as they can" (2). Does Holt make a good case for the truth of the statement? Why or why not?
4. What is Holt's attitude toward children? Where is this attitude evident in the essay?

Strategy

1. Holt divides discipline into three kinds. What is the basis for this division, and why does he identify only three kinds?
2. Does paragraph 4 describe a fourth kind of discipline? If so, does this category cause an imbalance in the essay's structure (Holt announces only three categories in the beginning)? Why or why not?
3. How does Holt make use of examples in this essay?

areas of influence. Another social scientist might choose three other categories, or more than three. Holt's categories result from his own observations and opinions.

2. Paragraph 4 describes where his categories overlap. He doesn't say this is a fourth category, but rather sums up the three and brings them together. In practice, his kinds of discipline don't always occur in isolation. The essay is not imbalanced but balanced by this last paragraph, tied up neatly and brought to an end.

3. Each paragraph contains a series of brief, typical examples illustrating Holt's general statements.

Style

1. The names are capitalized because they are formal labels of each division.

2. Holt appreciates the value of all three kinds of discipline while trusting the child to grow naturally without excessive adult interference. He is clearly advocating an approach to teaching in its broadest sense: allow the child to learn from hands-on experiences; provide good examples for the child to imitate; and protect the child from danger, but do not underestimate his or her ability to understand its real nature.

3. *Wheedled*: to have endeavored to influence a person by smooth, flattering, or beguiling words or acts; *contagious*: tending to spread from person to person; *fidget*: to move about restlessly, nervously, or impatiently; *impotent*: lacking power or ability; *novice*: a person who is new to the circumstances in which he is placed; *autocratic*: tyrannical, despotic, domineering; *suppleness*: the condition of being flexible, pliant.

Style

1. Why do you think Holt capitalizes the names of the kinds of discipline he classifies?

2. What is Holt's attitude toward his subject? Is he neutral about it or is he advocating something? How do you know?

3. If necessary, look up the meaning of these words: *wheedled* (1); *contagious, fidget* (2); *impotent* (3); *novice, autocratic, suppleness* (4).

Writing Tasks

1. Write an essay in which you classify parents according to the kinds of discipline they use with their children. Speak from first-hand knowledge, and take Holt as a model for using specific examples.

2. Write an essay in which you classify students. You might want to use elementary, high-school, or college students, or you might show how each kind of student behaves at each of the three levels of education. Make sure you use typical examples and then demonstrate them in real life with specific examples.

Excepting a few who may have had a sociology or social anthropology course, students do not often encounter the social-scientific methods of classification used by Morris. Some say that humankind is not to be treated like other animals. But what of athletes? We classify them like tools—according to their uses, not their intrinsic worth as people. Tribal, family, and personal territories are often thought of as occupying the whole planet, a thought decried by ecologists.

Territory carries responsibility. Do we protect the territory that we display as ours? Or do we ruin it as part of our displaying that it is ours?

While Morris examines territorial behavior, it enlivens the class discussion to add the concept of responsibility to that behavior. Explore the question of whether we should protect for ourselves what is ours alone or whether we should keep our territory in trust. If we keep it in trust, how far are we willing to go to protect it? As far as war? War destroys territory. Are we willing to be constantly vigilant politically to protect territory? And from whom are we protecting it?

❦ Desmond Morris ❦

Born in England in 1928, Desmond Morris studied at Birmingham University and Oxford University. After receiving his doctorate from Oxford, he was a researcher in the zoology department there for a short time. He later worked for several years at the Zoological Society of London, first as curator of mammals and later as director of the society's television and film department. He has also been director of London's Institute of Contemporary Arts, and in 1950 had a one-man show in which he exhibited his own paintings. He is best known, however, as writer of popular—if sometimes controversial—books on human behavior, including The Naked Ape *(1967) and* The Human Zoo *(1969).*

Territorial Behavior

This essay is from Morris's book Manwatching *(1974), another of his works on human behavior. He supports his premise that human beings are "remarkably territorial animals" by classifying and describing three kinds of human territory, each of which induces its own form of territorial behavior.*

As you read this essay, pay close attention to how Morris uses metaphors and similes to help the reader understand each classification.

MARGINAL NOTES

Morris begins by dividing human territory into three classifications. Before he expands those classifications, he discusses their sociology. First, he describes the penalties for violating the territories of others. Next, he discusses briefly the healthy reasons for having "owned space." Then he tells how we mark our territories.

A territory is a defended space. In the broadest sense, there are three kinds of human territory: tribal, family and personal. 1

It is rare for people to be driven to physical fighting in defense of these "owned" spaces, but fight they will, if pushed to the limit. The invading army encroaching on national territory, the gang moving into a rival district, the trespasser climbing into an orchard, the burglar breaking into a house, the bully pushing to the front of a queue, the driver trying to steal a parking space, all of these intruders are liable to be met with resistance varying from the vigorous to the savagely violent. Even if the law is on 2 the side of the intruder, the urge to protect a territory may be so strong that otherwise peaceful citizens abandon all their usual controls and inhibitions. Attempts to evict families from their homes, no matter how socially valid the reasons, can lead to siege conditions reminiscent of the defense of a medieval fortress.

The fact that these upheavals are so rare is a measure of the success of Territorial Signals as a system of dispute prevention. It is sometimes cynically stated that "all property is theft," but in reality it is the opposite. Property, as owned space which is *displayed* as owned space, is a special kind of sharing system which reduces fighting much more than it causes it. Man is a cooperative species, but he is also competitive, and his struggle for dominance has to be structured in some way if chaos is to be avoided. The establishment of territorial rights is one such structure. It limits dominance geographically. I am dominant in my territory and you are dominant in yours. In other words, dominance is shared out spatially, and we all have some. Even if I am weak and unintelligent and you can dominate me when we meet on neutral ground, I can still enjoy a thoroughly dominant role as soon as I retreat to my private base. Be it ever so humble, there is no place like a home territory.

Of course, I can still be intimidated by a particularly dominant individual who enters my home base, but his encroachment will be dangerous for him and he will think twice about it, because he will know that here my urge to resist will be dramatically magnified and my usual subservience banished. Insulted at the heart of my own territory, I may easily explode into battle—either symbolic or real—with a result that may be damaging to both of us.

In order for this to work, each territory has to be plainly advertised as such. Just as a dog cocks its leg to deposit its personal scent on the trees in its locality, so the human animal cocks its leg symbolically all over his home base. But because we are predominantly visual animals we employ mostly visual signals, and it is worth asking how we do this at the three levels: tribal, family and personal.

First: the Tribal Territory. We evolved as tribal animals, living

Returning to the first of his classifications, Morris develops it by the strategy of cyclic expansion. That is, he starts at the center, the small group, and expands outward, each circle of expansion larger: The tribe's home base expands, finally, to become the capital city of a nation.

The nation itself, fixed by borders, holds so many people that individuals begin to lose their tribal identity. They compensate by forming subgroups, social tribes, to gain a sense of belonging, which includes the territorial signals such social tribes agree to use.

in comparatively small groups, probably of less than a hundred, and we existed like that for millions of years. It is our basic social unit, a group in which everyone knows everyone else. Essentially, the tribal territory consisted of a home base surrounded by extended hunting grounds. Any neighbouring tribe intruding on our social space would be repelled and driven away. As these early tribes swelled into agricultural super-tribes, and eventually into industrial nations, their territorial defence systems became increasingly elaborate. The tiny, ancient home base of the hunting tribe became the great capital city, the primitive war-paint became the flags, emblems, uniforms and regalia of the specialized military, and the war-chants became national anthems, marching songs and bugle calls. Territorial boundary-lines hardened into fixed borders, often conspicuously patrolled and punctuated with defensive structures—forts and lookout posts, check-points and great walls, and, today, customs barriers.

Today each nation flies its own flag, a symbolic embodiment of its territorial status. But patriotism is not enough. The ancient tribal hunter lurking inside each citizen finds himself unsatisfied by membership of such a vast conglomeration of individuals, most of whom are totally unknown to him personally. He does his best to feel that he shares a common territorial defence with them all, but the scale of the operation has become inhuman. It is hard to feel a sense of belonging with a tribe of fifty million or more. His answer is to form sub-groups, nearer to his ancient pattern, smaller and more personally known to him—the local club, the teenage gang, the union, the specialist society, the sports association, the political party, the college fraternity, the social clique, the protest group, and the rest. Rare indeed is the individual who does not belong to at least one of these splinter groups, and take from it a sense of tribal allegiance and brotherhood. Typical of all these groups is the development of Territorial Signals—badges, costumes, headquarters, banners, slogans, and all the other displays of group identity. This is where the action is, in terms of tribal territorialism, and only when a major war breaks out does the emphasis shift upwards to the higher group level of the nation.

Each of these modern pseudo-tribes sets up its own special

kind of home base. In extreme cases non-members are totally excluded, in others they are allowed in as visitors with limited rights and under a control system of special rules. In many ways they are like miniature nations, with their own flags and emblems and their own border guards. The exclusive club has its own "customs barrier": the doorman who checks your "passport" (your membership card) and prevents strangers from passing in unchallenged. There is a government: the club committee; and often special displays of the tribal elders: the photographs or portraits of previous officials on the walls. At the heart of the specialized territories there is a powerful feeling of security and importance, a sense of shared defence against the outside world. Much of the club chatter, both serious and joking, directs itself against the rottenness of everything outside the club boundaries—in that "other world" beyond the protected portals.

In social organizations which embody a strong class system, such as military units and large business concerns, there are many territorial rules, often unspoken, which interfere with the official hierarchy. High-status individuals, such as officers or managers, could in theory enter any of the regions occupied by the lower levels in the peck order, but they limit this power in a striking way. An officer seldom enters a sergeant's mess or a barrack room unless it is for a formal inspection. He respects those regions as alien territories even though he has the power to go there by virtue of his dominant role. And in businesses, part of the appeal of unions, over and above their obvious functions, is that with their officials, headquarters and meetings they add a sense of territorial power for the staff workers. It is almost as if each military organization and business concern consists of two warring tribes: the officers versus the other ranks, and the management versus the workers. Each has its special home base within the system, and the territorial defence pattern thrusts itself into what, on the surface, is a pure social hierarchy. Negotiations between managements and unions are tribal battles fought out over the neutral ground of a boardroom table, and are as much concerned with territorial display as they are with resolving problems of wages and conditions. Indeed, if one side gives in too quickly

Notice that this classification is as cyclic as the strategy Morris uses to describe it. As the tribe expands, members of the tribe circle back to making efforts to form a subgroup, keeping their own membership small enough to be comfortably identifiable.

and accepts the other's demands, the victors feel strangely cheated and deeply suspicious that it may be a trick. What they are missing is the protracted sequence of ritual and counter-ritual that keeps alive their group territorial identity.

Likewise, many of the hostile displays of sports fans and teenage gangs are primarily concerned with displaying their group image to rival fan-clubs and gangs. Except in rare cases, they do not attack one another's headquarters, drive out the occupants, and reduce them to a submissive, subordinate condition. It is enough to have scuffles on the borderlands between the two rival territories. This is particularly clear at football matches, where the fan-club headquarters becomes temporarily shifted from the club-house to a section of the stands, and where minor fighting breaks out at the unofficial boundary line between the massed groups of rival supporters. Newspaper reports play up the few accidents and injuries which do occur on such occasions, but when these are studied in relation to the total numbers of displaying fans involved it is clear that the serious incidents represent only a tiny fraction of the overall group behaviour. For every actual punch or kick there are a thousand war-cries, war-dances, chants and gestures. 10

Second: the Family Territory. Essentially, the family is a breeding unit and the family territory is a breeding ground. At the centre of this space, there is the nest—the bedroom—where, tucked up in bed, we feel at our most territorially secure. In a typical house the bedroom is upstairs, where a safe nest should be. This puts it farther away from the entrance hall, the area where contact is made, intermittently, with the outside world. The less private reception rooms, where intruders are allowed access, are the next line of defence. Beyond them, outside the walls of the building, there is often a symbolic remnant of the ancient feeding grounds—a garden. Its symbolism often extends to the plants and animals it contains, which cease to be nutritional and become merely decorative—flowers and pets. But like a true territorial space it has a conspicuously displayed boundary-line, the garden fence, wall, or railings. Often no more than a token barrier, this is the outer territorial demarcation, separating the 11

Moving down as they read, from the tribe classification to the family classification, students are occasionally shocked to see the family defined as a "breeding unit" and the family's territory as a "breeding ground." They might be reminded that Morris is not being cavalier with the family unit; instead, he is using the neutral terminology of the social scientist.

Morris's "typical house" is typical for the author's area, but houses differ in this country, according to cost and location. Because his house can be described as "ideal Victorian," students from other kinds of homes might need to be reminded that he is using a model here to represent reality, not to define it.

private world of the family from the public world beyond. To cross it puts any visitor or intruder at an immediate disadvantage. As he crosses the threshold, his dominance wanes, slightly but unmistakably. He is entering an area where he senses that he must ask permission to do simple things that he would consider a right elsewhere. Without lifting a finger, the territorial owners exert their dominance. This is done by all the hundreds of small ownership "markers" they have deposited on their family territory: the ornaments, the "possessed" objects positioned in the rooms and on the walls; the furnishings, the furniture, the colours, the patterns, all owner-chosen and all making this particular home base unique to them.

It is one of the tragedies of modern architecture that there 12 has been a standardization of these vital territorial living-units. One of the most important aspects of a home is that it should be similar to other homes only in a general way, and that in detail it should have many differences, making it a *particular* home. Unfortunately, it is cheaper to build a row of houses, or a block of flats, so that all the family living-units are identical, but the territorial urge rebels against this trend and house-owners struggle as best they can to make their mark on their mass-produced properties. They do this with garden-design, with front-door colours, with curtain patterns, with wallpaper and all the other decorative elements that together create a unique and different family environment. Only when they have completed this nest-building do they feel truly "at home" and secure.

When they venture forth as a family unit they repeat the 13 process in a minor way. On a day-trip to the seaside, they load the car with personal belongings and it becomes their temporary, portable territory. Arriving at the beach they stake out a small territorial claim, marking it with rugs, towels, baskets and other belongings to which they can return from their seaboard wanderings. Even if they all leave it at once to bathe, it retains a characteristic territorial quality and other family groups arriving will recognize this by setting up their own "home" bases at a respectful distance. Only when the whole beach has filled up with these marked spaces will newcomers start to position themselves

Morris's comments on modern architecture can deeply affect students, particularly if they live in apartments, condominiums, or in some older tracts of homes that were built quickly and identically. Teachers often break here, to discuss with their students the ways in which we mark our property as our own, with plants, paint, lawns, fences, pets, trees, and so on. A stimulating question is: "How much do we mark our territory as being comfortably ours before we begin to mark it as a warning to others not to trespass?" It is one thing to build a white picket fence around our house, quite another to build a six-foot chain-link fence, for example.

So also with temporary territory: Here is a good place to discuss the worth of Morris's comments. Does it really happen as he describes it? Do we stake out territory in the mountains, at the park, the river, the lake, or near the ocean? What happens when our territory is violated? Does it make a difference what kind of people violate our territory? If an old woman and an old man sit quite near our territory, do we feel differently than we would if a teenage boy and girl violated our territory?

in such a way that the inter-base distance becomes reduced. Forced to pitch between several existing beach territories they will feel a momentary sensation of intrusion, and the established "owners" will feel a similar sensation of invasion, even though they are not being directly inconvenienced.

The same territorial scene is being played out in parks and fields and on riverbanks, wherever family groups gather in their clustered units. But if rivalry for spaces creates mild feelings of hostility, it is true to say that, without the territorial system of sharing and space-limited dominance, there would be chaotic disorder. 14

The third classification, the personal space, brings us to the subject many students call the "rights" of the individual. They should notice that Morris is not talking about rights; he is precisely describing the results of socioscientific observations. Determining where we sit and how we protect our personal space is the cultural manifestation of our tribe's territorial habits.

Third: the Personal Space. If a man enters a waiting-room and sits at one end of a long row of empty chairs, it is possible to predict where the next man to enter will seat himself. He will not sit next to the first man, nor will he sit at the far end, right away from him. He will choose a position about halfway between these two points. The next man to enter will take the largest gap left, and sit roughly in the middle of that, and so on, until eventually the latest newcomer will be forced to select a seat that places him right next to one of the already seated men. Similar patterns can be observed in cinemas, public urinals, aeroplanes, trains and buses. This is a reflection of the fact that we all carry with us, everywhere we go, a portable territory called a Personal Space. If people move inside this space, we feel threatened. If they keep too far outside it, we feel rejected. The result is a subtle series of spatial adjustments, usually operating quite unconsciously and producing ideal compromises as far as this is possible. If a situation becomes too crowded, then we adjust our reactions accordingly and allow our personal space to shrink. Jammed into an elevator, a rush-hour compartment, or a packed room, we give up altogether and allow body-to-body contact, but when we relinquish our Personal Space in this way, we adopt certain special techniques. In essence, what we do is to convert these other bodies into "nonpersons." We studiously ignore them, and they us. We try not to face them if we can possibly avoid it. We wipe all expressiveness from our faces, letting them go blank. We may look up at the ceiling or down at the floor, and we reduce body 15 movements to a minimum. Packed together like sardines in a tin, we stand dumbly still, sending out as few social signals as possible.

Even if the crowding is less severe, we still tend to cut down   16
our social interactions in the presence of large numbers. Careful observations of children in play groups revealed that if they are high density groupings there is less social interaction between the individual children, even though there is theoretically more opportunity for such contacts. At the same time, the high-density groups show a higher frequency of aggressive and destructive behaviour patterns in their play. Personal Space—"elbow room"— is a vital commodity for the human animal, and one that cannot be ignored without risking serious trouble.

Of course, we all enjoy the excitement of being in a crowd,   17
and this reaction cannot be ignored. But there are crowds and crowds. It is pleasant enough to be in a "spectator crowd," but not so appealing to find yourself in the middle of a rush-hour crush. The difference between the two is that the spectator crowd is all facing in the same direction and concentrating on a distant point of interest. Attending a theatre, there are twinges of rising hostility towards the stranger who sits down immediately in front of you or the one who squeezes into the seat next to you. The shared armrest can become a polite, but distinct, territorial boundary-dispute region. However, as soon as the show begins, these invasions of Personal Space are forgotten and the attention is focused beyond the small space where the crowding is taking place. Now, each member of the audience feels himself spatially related, not to his cramped neighbours, but to the actor on the stage, and this distance is, if anything, too great. In the rush-hour crowd, by contrast, each member of the pushing throng is competing with his neighbours all the time. There is no escape to a spacial relation with a distant actor, only the pushing, shoving bodies all around.

Those of us who have to spend a great deal of time in crowded   18
conditions become gradually better able to adjust, but no one can ever become completely immune to invasions of Personal Space. This is because they remain forever associated with either powerful hostile or equally powerful loving feelings. All through our

The higher the density, the less we socially interact. This behavior surprises students until they test its validity by observation. Notice the differences between "crowds and crowds": the spectator crowd has a special, collective goal. The rush-hour crowd has diverse goals, a fact that might lead to disputes.

Students are often interested in discussing this observation as it might be applied to driving their cars. Is rush-hour traffic more frenetic because the drivers are focusing on diverse goals? On freeways, expressways, thoroughfares, and toll roads, why does it seem that cars travel in packs, like crowds?

Adjusting to crowds takes a combination of practice, patience, and observation.

childhood we will have been held to be loved and held to be hurt, and anyone who invades our Personal Space when we are adults is, in effect, threatening to extend his behaviour into one of these two highly charged areas of human interaction. Even if his motives are clearly neither hostile nor sexual, we still find it hard to suppress our reactions to his close approach. Unfortunately, different countries have different ideas about exactly how close is close. It is easy enough to test your own "space reaction": when you are talking to someone in the street or in any open space, reach out with your arm and see where the nearest point on his body comes. If you hail from western Europe, you will find that he is at roughly fingertip distance from you. In other words, as you reach out, your fingertips will just about make contact with his shoulder. If you come from eastern Europe you will find you are standing at "wrist distance." If you come from the Mediterranean region you will find that you are much closer to your companion, at little more than "elbow distance."

Trouble begins when a member of one of these cultures meets and talks to one from another. Say a British diplomat meets an Italian or an Arab diplomat at an embassy function. They start talking in a friendly way, but soon the fingertips man begins to feel uneasy. Without knowing quite why, he starts to back away gently from his companion. The companion edges forward again. Each tries in this way to set up a Personal Space relationship that suits his own background. But it is impossible to do. Every time the Mediterranean diplomat advances to a distance that feels comfortable for him, the British diplomat feels threatened. Every time the Briton moves back, the other feels rejected. Attempts to adjust this situation often lead to a talking pair shifting slowly across a room, and many an embassy reception is dotted with western-European fingertip-distance men pinned against the walls by eager elbow-distance men. Until such differences are fully understood, and allowances made, these minor differences in "body territories" will continue to act as an alienation factor which may interfere in a subtle way with diplomatic harmony and other forms of international transaction.   19

If there are distance problems when engaged in conversation,   20

Morris is discussing *proxemics* here, both sociologically and linguistically. Sociologically, proxemics describes human spatial requirements and the effects of population density on behavior. Linguistically, proxemics describes how far apart people in conversation stand, depending on their degree of intimacy.

Students from Latin America usually stand closer to each other when talking than students from western Europe. You might want to ask your students to observe proxemics in practice throughout the campus or at their jobs.

Libraries are sometimes crowded. Workers often are assigned carrels. Students often share apartments with roommates. They all "cocoon," carving out their own privacy in one way or another.

Morris thoroughly discusses by example each part of this classification. Students are often eager to investigate some of these examples. Do your students have their own territories, favorite chairs in the library or favorite tables in the cafeteria? Do they have favorite parking places that they feel territorially belong to them? How do they react when that territory is "invaded"?

then there are clearly going to be even bigger difficulties where people must work privately in a shared space. Close proximity of others, pressing against the invisible boundaries of our personal body-territory, makes it difficult to concentrate on non-social matters. Flatmates, students sharing a study, sailors in the cramped quarters of a ship, and office staff in crowded workplaces, all have to face this problem. They solve it by "cocooning." They use a variety of devices to shut themselves off from the others present. The best possible cocoon, of course, is a small private room—a den, a private office, a study or a studio—which physically obscures the presence of other nearby territory-owners. This is the ideal situation for non-social work, but the space-sharers cannot enjoy this luxury. Their cocooning must be symbolic. They may, in certain cases, be able to erect small physical barriers, such as screens and partitions, which give substance to their invisible Personal Space boundaries, but when this cannot be done, other means must be sought. One of these is the "favoured object." Each space-sharer develops a preference, repeatedly expressed until it becomes a fixed pattern, for a particular chair, or table, or alcove. Others come to respect this, and friction is reduced. This system is often formally arranged (this is my desk, that is yours), but even where it is not, favoured places soon develop. Professor Smith has a favourite chair in the library. It is not formally his, but he always uses it and others avoid it. Seats around a mess-room table, or a board-room table, become almost personal property for specific individuals. Even in the home, father has his favourite chair for reading the newspaper or watching television. Another device is the blinkers-posture. Just as a horse that overreacts to other horses and the distractions of the noisy racecourse is given a pair of blinkers to shield its eyes, so people studying privately in a public place put on pseudo-blinkers in the form of shielding hands. Resting their elbows on the table, they sit with their hands screening their eyes from the scene on either side.

A third method of reinforcing the body-territory is to use personal markers. Books, papers and other personal belongings are scattered around the favoured site to render it more privately

You might want to discuss with students the various methods they use to let others know they have already claimed a space. Do they use the "favored object," the "personal marker," or the "reservation effect"? With what success? Do they have other peaceful ways of claiming their own territory?

Morris points out that we hear about the exceptions to territorial respect, that most of us respect the other person's "territory," be it the temporary space of a library chair or the more lasting space of a home.

Time permitting, you might want to ask your students whether their city or neighborhood is running out of space that each person or household can call its own. If space is becoming scarce, then you might want to discuss ways of redefining territory or creating respect for territory so that we can keep strife from getting out of hand.

owned in the eyes of companions. Spreading out one's belongings is a well-known trick in public-transport situations, where a traveller tries to give the impression that seats next to him are taken. In many contexts carefully arranged personal markers can act as an effective territorial display, even in the absence of the territory owner. Experiments in a library revealed that placing a pile of magazines on the table in one seating position successfully reserved that place for an average of 77 minutes. If a sports-jacket was added, draped over the chair, then the "reservation effect" lasted for over two hours.

In these ways, we strengthen the defences of our Personal   22
Spaces, keeping out intruders with the minimum of open hostility. As with all territorial behaviour, the object is to defend space with signals rather than with fists and at all three levels—the tribal, the family and the personal—it is a remarkably efficient system of space-sharing. It does not always seem so, because newspapers and newscasts inevitably magnify the exceptions and dwell on those cases where the signals have failed and wars have broken out, gangs have fought, neighbouring families have feuded, or colleagues have clashed, but for every territorial signal that has failed, there are millions of others that have not. They do not rate a mention in the news, but they nevertheless constitute a dominant feature of human society—the society of a remarkably territorial animal.

POSSIBLE ANSWERS

Meaning and Purpose

1. Morris's main point is that we are territorial animals, and territory by definition must be defended. The thesis is implicit in a general way in the very first sentence. The third sentence in paragraph 3 is the thesis, and the last sentence in paragraph 5 narrows the thesis.

Meaning and Purpose

1. What is the main point Morris makes in this essay? Does it have a thesis statement?
2. Can you tell from the title what kind of essay this will be?
3. In paragraph 11, the author says, "we feel at our most territorially secure" in our bedroom. Does this statement apply to you? Where is another place in which you feel quite "territorially secure"?

2. The title is neutral-sounding and could signal an academic and informative essay (which this is), or the title could be ironic or humorous, depending on the content of the essay. In other words, the title isn't much help in knowing the content of the essay absolutely before reading it.

3. A number of students mention the bathroom! Some include their place of work (the backroom or storage areas), and others specify attics, basements, garages, and the like.

4. We form subgroups (7) in our large tribal territories to feel a sense of belonging. We choose a "splinter group" to identify with, such as a union or political party.

5. Because so many homes look alike, people have more difficulty displaying theirs as a particular home in an attempt to feel secure and "at home" (12).

6. Morris's words are the neutral terminology of social science.

Strategy

1. Morris discusses the sociology of the three categories of territory, including the penalties for violating someone else's territory, and the reasons for having "owned space" (3). The first five paragraphs give background and definitions so that readers know Morris's basis for classification.

2. The strategy of development is a kind of cyclic expansion. Morris starts with the small group at the center, expands it outward to hunting grounds, and eventually the home base becomes the capital city. When nations become too big for people to feel personal belonging, people circle back to form small groups that they can belong to.

3. Morris talks about the distances at which people stand from each other in conversation and labels three categories: fingertip, wrist, and elbow distance (18). He also discusses how people in crowded places stake out personal space. He calls the strategy "cocooning" (20), and names three kinds: small private office or studio, favored object such as a chair or alcove, and personal markers such as books or jackets. All these subdivisions help organize and order Morris's information so that it is clear and understandable to readers.

4. What does Morris say we do in our large tribal territory to feel a sense of belonging?

5. Why is it "one of the tragedies of modern architecture" that so many new homes look alike?

6. In paragraph 11, Morris calls the family and its territory a "breeding unit" and "breeding ground." What does he mean by these expressions? Is he being sarcastic or judgmental?

Strategy

1. Morris begins his categories of territories in paragraph 6. How does he use the first five paragraphs?

2. What strategy does Morris use to develop the classification of "Tribal Territory"?

3. In the personal-space category, Morris has some subcategories. What are they, and how do they work in the structure of this category?

4. In paragraph 4, Morris mentions a "home base." If Morris had wanted, he could have classified several kinds of home bases. In your opinion, what are two kinds of home bases?

Style

1. How would you describe the tone of this essay? Where is the tone evident?

2. What is a "pseudo-tribe"?

3. Judging from the tone and style of this essay, whom do you think Morris has in mind for his audience?

Writing Tasks

1. Classify your "tribe's territory." How does your neighborhood, town, city, parish, county, or other easily identifiable political

4. A home base can be one of a number of areas, depending on the student's perspective. It could be a play area, a favored street corner, one side of a fence, or a car.

Style

1. The tone is formal and academic, and people are labeled clinically—this is a social-science essay. Almost any sentence demonstrates this tone, such as the first in paragraph 3: "The fact that these upheavals are so rare is a measure of the success of Territorial Signals as a system of dispute prevention."
2. A "pseudo-tribe" is a modern imitation of the historical tribes mentioned earlier in the essay (8). The prefix *pseudo* means "fictitious, pretending, or falsely seeming."
3. Morris's audience probably consists of readers who have read academic writing before, for he doesn't talk down to them. But they are not necessarily social scientists. His language is understandable and readable for lay readers, and he is careful to define his terms in context.

territory differ from others in its display? How do its looks make it different? How do its people make it different? How does its economy make it different? In what other ways does classifying your territory show that it is different from other territories in the same class?

2. Personal space is becoming more and more difficult to enjoy. What is your own definition of "personal space"? How do you separate and protect your space? How do you handle intruders into your space? How would you instruct elementary-school children who tell you they would like to learn how to have more personal space?

This essay runs counter to the accepted (and unexamined) notions held by some students about our society; therefore, while discussing the essay, many instructors like to ask their students if indeed we have class distinctions in our country. Is it true, as the critic Mary Colum said, that "The only difference between the rich and other people is that the rich have more money"? Encourage students to explore their notions of ethics, where *ethics* refers to standards of conduct and moral judgment. For example, do people treat each other as equals, regardless of economic, social, or academic status? Ask your students whether standards of conduct, in their opinion, would change according to a person's class, as defined by Fussell. Question your students about whether they have ever witnessed others being treated in a certain way or others treating people a certain way, depending on how people looked or how they dressed.

❦ Paul Fussell ❦

Paul Fussell, born in 1924, earned his Ph.D. at Harvard and taught English at Connecticut College and at Rutgers. An infantry officer in World War II, he received the Bronze Star for bravery and was wounded twice. He is well known for his studies in eighteenth-century British literature and for his Poetic Meter and Poetic Form (1965; rev. 1979). His book The Great War and Modern Memory, a study of World War I and its literature, won the National Book Award. A contributing editor for Harper's and The New Republic, he is the Donald T. Regan Professor of English at the University of Pennsylvania.

Notes on Class

This essay deals with a subject rarely discussed but often acknowledged: the classification of American society into distinct and recognizable segments. Fussell bases his analysis on such factors as income, actions, and appearances—but most of all on his personal perceptions.

As you read this essay, you might enjoy trying to place your friends, acquaintances, and relatives into one or more of the essay's social classes.

Fussell quickly sets a tone of mild sarcasm by equating an earlier view of sex with a more modern view of social class, as dirty little secrets. "Dr. Kinsey" is, of course, Alfred Charles Kinsey (1894–1956), the U.S. zoologist who studied human sexual behavior. He co-authored *Sexual Behavior in the Human Male* (1948), and *Sexual Behavior in the Human Female* (1953), each offending a large segment of society forty years or so ago. Note the assertion that a person born into one class finds it "virtually impossible" to break out of that class.

If the dirty little secret used to be sex, now it is the facts about social class. No subject today is more likely to offend. Over thirty years ago Dr. Kinsey generated considerable alarm by disclosing that despite appearances one-quarter of the male population had enjoyed at least one homosexual orgasm. A similar alarm can be occasioned today by asserting that despite the much-discussed mechanism of "social mobility" and the constant redistribution of income in this country, it is virtually impossible to break out of the social class in which one has been nurtured. Bad news for the ambitious as well as the bogus, but there it is. 1

Defining class is difficult, as sociologists and anthropologists 2 have learned. The more data we feed into the machines, the less likely it is that significant formulations will emerge. What follows here is based not on interviews, questionnaires, or any kind of quantitative technique but on perhaps a more trustworthy method—perception. Theory may inform us that there are three classes in America, high, middle, and low. Perception will tell us that there are at least nine, which I would designate and arrange like this:

Fussell points out that he is using "perception" to classify, instead of the more usual techniques practiced by social scientists. The word *perception* as used here refers to using the senses and relying on intuition. The "Class X" list, while humorous, also puts individuals into a class, making that class easily distinguishable.

Top Out-of-Sight
Upper
Upper Middle

Middle
High-Proletarian
Mid-Proletarian
Low-Proletarian

Destitute
Bottom Out-of-Sight

In addition, there is a floating class with no permanent location in this hierarchy. We can call it Class X. It consists of well-to-do hippies, "artists," "writers" (who write nothing), floating bohemians, politicians out of office, disgraced athletic coaches, residers abroad, rock stars, "celebrities," and the shrewder sort of spies.

Here, after a one-sentence argument against a more traditional method of classification, Fussell begins in earnest to classify while keeping his witty tone—as in the anecdote of the Boston ladies. Inherited money is the main characteristic that sets apart the Top Out-of-Sight Class from all others.

The quasi-official division of the population into three economic classes called high-, middle-, and low-income groups rather misses the point, because as a class indicator the amount of money is not as important as the source. Important distinctions at both the top and bottom of the class scale arise less from degree of affluence than from the people or institutions to whom one is beholden for support. For example, the main thing distinguishing the top three classes from each other is the amount of money inherited in relation to the amount currently earned. The Top Out-of-Sight Class (Rockefellers, du Ponts, Mellons, Fords, Whitneys) lives on inherited capital entirely. Its money is like the hats

3

of the Boston ladies who, asked where they got them, answer, "Oh, we *have* our hats." No one whose money, no matter how ample, comes from his own work, like film stars, can be a member of the Top Out-of-Sights, even if the size of his income and the extravagance of his expenditure permit him temporary social access to it.

Since we expect extremes to meet, we are not surprised to find the very lowest class, Bottom Out-of-Sight, similar to the highest in one crucial respect: It is given its money and kept sort of afloat not by its own efforts but by the welfare machinery or the prison system. Members of the Top Out-of-Sight Class sometimes earn some money, as directors or board members of philanthropic or even profitable enterprises, but the amount earned is laughable in relation to the amount already possessed. Membership in the Top Out-of-Sight Class depends on the ability to flourish without working at all, and it is this that suggests a curious brotherhood between those at the top and the bottom of the scale.

It is this also that distinguishes the Upper Class from its betters. It lives on both inherited money and a salary from attractive, if usually slight, work, without which, even if it could survive and even flourish, it would feel bored and a little ashamed. The next class down, the Upper Middle, may possess virtually as much as the two above it. The difference is that it has earned most of it, in law, medicine, oil, real-estate, or even the more honorific forms of trade. The Upper Middles are afflicted with a bourgeois sense of shame, a conviction that to live on the earnings of others, even forebears, is not entirely nice.

The Out-of-Sight Classes at top and bottom have something else in common: They are literally all but invisible (hence their name). The facades of Top Out-of-Sight houses are never seen from the street, and such residences (like Rockefeller's upstate New York premises) are often hidden away deep in the hills, safe from envy and its ultimate attendants, confiscatory taxation and finally expropriation. The Bottom Out-of-Sight Class is equally invisible. When not hidden away in institutions or claustrated in monasteries, lamaseries, or communes, it is hiding from creditors,

Fussell connects the very top with the very bottom, pointing out their ironic common features.

Note that the Upper Middles are *afflicted* with a bourgeois sense of shame, as if that sense of shame were somehow a disease.

Another characteristic that the Top Out-of-Sight Class and the Bottom Out-of-Sight Class hold in common: Both are nearly invisible. Yet both greatly affect the economy, each in its way. In this paragraph, *claustrated* means "to be secluded or closed off"; *lamaseries* are monasteries of lamas, priests or monks in Lamaism, a form of Buddhism characterized by elaborate ritual and a strong hierarchal organization. The White House is Fussell's strongest example of one's residence being the measure of one's class.

deceived bail-bondsmen, and merchants intent on repossessing cars and furniture. (This class is visible briefly in one place, in the spring on the streets of New York City, but after this ritual yearly show of itself it disappears again.) When you pass a house with a would-be impressive façade addressing the street, you know it is occupied by a mere member of the Upper or Upper Middle Class. The White House is an example. Its residents, even on those occasions when they are Kennedys, can never be classified as Top Out-of-Sight but only Upper Class. The house is simply too conspicuous, and temporary residence there usually constitutes a come-down for most of its occupants. It is a hopelessly Upper- or Upper-Middle-Class place.

Another feature of both Top and Bottom Out-of-Sight Classes 7 is their anxiety to keep their names out of the papers, and this too suggests that socially the President is always rather vulgar. All the classes in between Top and Bottom Out-of-Sight slaver for personal publicity (monograms on shirts, inscribing one's name on lawn-mowers and power tools, etc.), and it is this lust to be known almost as much as income that distinguishes them from their Top and Bottom neighbors. The High- and Mid-Prole Classes can be recognized immediately by their pride in advertising their physical presence, a way of saying, "Look! We pay our bills and have a known place in the community, and you can find us there any time." Thus hypertrophied house numbers on the front, or house numbers written "Two Hundred Five" ("Two Hundred and Five" is worse) instead of 205, or flamboyant house or family names blazoned on façades, like "The Willows" or "The Polnickis."

(If you go behind the façade into the house itself, you will 8 find a fairly trustworthy class indicator in the kind of wood visible there. The top three classes invariably go in for hardwoods for doors and panelling; the Middle and High-Prole Classes, pine, either plain or "knotty." The knotty-pine "den" is an absolute stigma of the Middle Class, one never to be overcome or disguised by temporarily affected higher usages. Below knotty pine there is plywood.)

Façade study is a badly neglected anthropological field. As 9 we work down from the (largely white-painted) bank-like façades

Again, the Top and Bottom Out-of-Sight Classes are compared, the comparison leading to an off-hand comment about the President, who strives to keep his name in the public eye. Presidential candidates, who often present a program for helping the quite poor, also often receive large contributions from the quite rich. Note the transition: Compared to the Top and Bottom Classes, the High- and Mid-Prole Classes advertise themselves proudly. *Hypertrophied* means "abnormally enlarged"; it is usually used in a medical description.

Enclosed entirely in parentheses, this witty aside further illustrates the differences between the classes and moves the reader into the paragraph that follows, which concerns façades.

Note the tongue-in-cheek introductory sentence, followed by the humorous ranking, in descending order, of seven classes of façades.

of the Upper and Upper Middle Classes, we encounter such Middle and Prole conventions as these, which I rank in order of social status:

Middle	1.	A potted tree on either side of the front door, and the more pointy and symmetrical the better.
	2.	A large rectangular picture-window in a split-level "ranch" house, displaying a table-lamp between two side curtains. The cellophane on the lampshade must be visibly inviolate.
	3.	Two chairs, usually metal with pipe arms, disposed on the front porch as a "conversation group," in stubborn defiance of the traffic thundering past.
High-Prole	4.	Religious shrines in the garden, which if small and understated, are slightly higher class than
Mid-Prole	5.	Plaster gnomes and flamingoes, and blue or lavender shiny spheres supported by fluted cast-concrete pedestals.
Low-Prole	6.	Defunct truck tires painted white and enclosing flower beds. (Auto tires are a grade higher.)
	7.	Flower-bed designs worked in dead light bulbs or the butts of disused beer bottles.

The last part of the paragraph accounts for those classes left out of the seven ranks listed in the "façade study."

Continuing with his short "anthropological study of façades," Fussell points out that materials which are natural and products which are difficult to maintain both signify class.

Sophie Portnoy is the mother of the main character in *Portnoy's Complaint* (1969), a humorous novel by Philip Roth.

The Preppy Handbook (1980) amusingly described how students and former students of private preparatory schools looked, dressed, and acted.

Dacron, a trademark, denotes a brand of polyester textile fiber that is strong, wrinkle-resistant, and inexpensive.

The Destitute have no façades to decorate, and of course the Bottom Out-of-Sights, being invisible, have none either, although both these classes can occasionally help others decorate theirs—painting tires white on an hourly basis, for example, or even watering and fertilizing the potted trees of the Middle Class. Class X also does not decorate its façades, hoping to stay loose and unidentifiable, ready to re-locate and shape-change the moment it sees that its cover has been penetrated.

In this list of façade conventions an important principle emerges. Organic materials have higher status than metal or plastic. We should take warning from Sophie Portnoy's aluminum venetian blinds, which are also lower than wood because the slats are curved, as if "improved," instead of classically flat. The same principle applies, as *The Preppy Handbook* has shown so effectively, to clothing fabrics, which must be cotton or wool, never Dacron

10

Fussell moves from a consideration of expenses to a consideration of supervision, associating status with how or whether one is supervised. He points out that titles imply class, but they in fact do not define class. Note the comment Fussell makes about a tenured professor; Fussell himself is a tenured professor.

Constraints, insecurities, habits, attitudes—these are more important than money when classifying groups of people.

camp refers to something that is amusing to the sophisticated because it is so unconsciously artless or self-consciously artificial. For example, a plastic statue of a horse with a light socket coming out of its mouth and a lampshade covering its head, is "camp."

"Shakespeare series": Fussell does not equate the Upper Middle Class with educated taste. Note the irony of structure: The paragraph begins with the Top Out-of-Sight Class, who watches no television programs but who pays people to watch them, and ends with the Bottom Out-of-Sights, who watch television programs but have no choice about which television programs to watch.

or anything of that prole kind. In the same way, yachts with wood hulls, because they must be repaired or replaced (at high cost) more often, are classier than yachts with fiberglass hulls, no matter how shrewdly merchandised. Plastic hulls are cheaper and more practical, which is precisely why they lack class.

As we move down the scale, income of course decreases, but 11 income is less important to class than other seldom-invoked measurements: for example, the degree to which one's work is supervised by an omnipresent immediate superior. The more free from supervision, the higher the class, which is why a dentist ranks higher than a mechanic working under a foreman in a large auto shop, even if he makes considerably more money than the dentist. The two trades may be thought equally dirty: It is the dentist's freedom from supervision that helps confer class upon him. Likewise, a high-school teacher obliged to file weekly "lesson plans" with a principal or "curriculum co-ordinator" thereby occupies a class position lower than a tenured professor, who reports to no one, even though the high-school teacher may be richer, smarter, and nicer. (Supervisors and Inspectors are titles that go with public schools, post offices, and police departments: The student of class will need to know no more.) It is largely because they must report that even the highest members of the naval and military services lack social status: They all have designated supervisors—even the Chairman of the Joint Chiefs of Staff has to report to the President.

Class is thus defined less by bare income than by constraints 12 and insecurities. It is defined also by habits and attitudes. Take television watching. The Top Out-of-Sight Class doesn't watch at all. It owns the companies and pays others to monitor the thing. It is also entirely devoid of intellectual or even emotional curiosity: It *has* its ideas the way it has its money. The Upper Class does look at television but it prefers Camp offerings, like the films of Jean Harlow or Jon Hall. The Upper Middle Class regards TV as vulgar except for the highminded emissions of National Educational Television, which it watches avidly, especially when, like the Shakespeare series, they are the most incompetently directed and boring. Upper Middles make a point of forbidding children to watch more than an hour a day and worry a lot about violence in society and sugar in cereal. The Middle-Class watches, preferring the more "beautiful" kinds of non-body-contact sports like tennis or gymnastics or figure-skating (the music is a redeeming feature here). With High-, Mid-, and Low-Proles we find heavy viewing of the soaps in the daytime and rugged body-contact sports (football, hockey, boxing) in the evening. The lower one is located in the Prole classes the more likely one is to watch "Bowling for Dollars" and "Wonder Woman" and "The Hulk" and when choosing a game show to prefer "Joker's Wild" to "The Family Feud," whose jokes are sometimes incomprehensible. Destitutes and Bottom Out-of-Sights have in common a problem involving choice. Destitutes usually "own" about three color sets, and the problem is which three programs to run at once. Bottom Out-of-Sights exercise no choice at all, the decisions being made for them by correctional or institutional personnel.

The time when the evening meal is consumed defines class 13 better than, say, the presence or absence on the table of ketchup bottles and ashtrays shaped like little toilets enjoining the diners to "Put Your Butts Here." Destitutes and Bottom Out-of-Sights eat dinner at 5:30, for the Prole staff on which they depend must clean up and be out roller-skating or bowling early in the evening. Thus Proles eat at 6:00 or 6:30. The Middles eat at 7:00, the Upper Middles at 7:30 or, if very ambitious, at 8:00. The Uppers and Top Out-of-Sights dine at 8:30 or 9:00 or even later, after nightly protracted "cocktail" sessions lasting usually around two hours. Sometimes they forget to eat at all.

Similarly, the physical appearance of the various classes de- 14 fines them fairly accurately. Among the top four classes thin is good, and the bottom two classes appear to ape this usage, although down there thin is seldom a matter of choice. It is the three Prole classes that tend to fat, partly as a result of their use of convenience foods and plenty of beer. These are the classes too where anxiety about slipping down a rung causes nervous overeating, resulting in fat that can be rationalized as advertising the security of steady wages and the ability to "eat out" often. Even "Going Out for Breakfast" is not unthinkable for Proles, if we are to believe that they respond to the McDonald's TV ads as

Time helps to define class to the extent that the later one eats—or whether one is in any condition to eat at all—the higher one's class.

Note the allusion to altitude in the phrase "down there" and the allusion to classes as being on a ladder, in the phrase "down a rung." This paragraph, which targets a person's weight as a measure of class, directly equates thinness with status, and then comes to an aesthetic observation, albeit humorous, that the Proles seem to flaunt their obesity.

they're supposed to. A recent magazine ad for a diet book aimed at Proles stigmatizes a number of erroneous assumptions about body weight, proclaiming with some inelegance that "They're all a crock." Among such vulgar errors is the proposition that "All Social Classes Are Equally Overweight." This the ad rejects by noting quite accurately:

> Your weight is an advertisement of your social standing. A century ago, corpulence was a sign of success. But no more. Today it is the badge of the lower-middle-class, where obesity is *four times* more prevalent than it is among the upper-middle and middle classes.

It is not just four times more prevalent. It is at least four times more visible, as any observer can testify who has witnessed Prole women perambulating shopping malls in their bright, very tight jersey trousers. Not just obesity but the flaunting of obesity is the Prole sign, as if the object were to give maximum aesthetic offense to the higher classes and thus achieve a form of revenge.

Among the top three classes, plaster casts are worn as the equivalent in status to clothing; they represent a sort of stylishness. Medical bills mean little, just as the cost of clothes means little. Not so with the other classes, however.

Another physical feature with powerful class meaning is the 15 wearing of plaster casts on legs and ankles by members of the top three classes. These casts, a sort of white badge of honor, betoken stylish mishaps with frivolous but costly toys like horses, skis, snowmobiles, and mopeds. They signify a high level of conspicuous waste in a social world where questions of unpayable medical bills or missed working days do not apply. But in the matter of clothes, the Top Out-of-Sight is different from both Upper and Upper Middle Classes. It prefers to appear in new clothes, whereas the class just below it prefers old clothes. Likewise, all three Prole classes make much of new garments, with the highest possible polyester content. The question does not arise in the same form with Destitutes and Bottom Out-of-Sights. They wear used clothes, the thrift shop and prison supply room serving as their Bonwit's and Korvette's.

The piece comes full circle, back to paragraph 3. It returns to the opinion that income, how income originates, what one buys and displays with that income, how one acts based on in-

This American class system is very hard for foreigners to 16 master, partly because most foreigners imagine that since America was founded by the British it must retain something of British

come, and the freedom from pettiness that a significant income brings—these are the major factors that distinguish classes in America. These classificatory gradations show why the American class system differs from the British class system. The British system depends on absolute distinctions between one class and another, based on clearly defined prohibitions.

Vincenzo Bellini (1801–1835): an Italian composer who composed melodic operas including *Il Pirata* (1827) and *Norma* (1831).

W(ystan) H(ugh) Auden (1907–1973): an English-born American poet.

institutions. But our class system is more subtle than the British, more a matter of gradations than of blunt divisions, like the binary distinction between a gentleman and a cad. This seems to lack plausibility here. One seldom encounters in the United States the sort of absolute prohibitions which (half-comically, to be sure) one is asked to believe define the gentleman in England. Like these:

> *A gentleman never wears brown shoes in the city, or*
> *A gentleman never wears a green suit, or*
> *A gentleman never has soup at lunch, or*
> *A gentleman never uses a comb, or*
> *A gentleman never smells of anything but tar, or*
> *"No gentleman can fail to admire Bellini."*
>
> W. H. Auden

In America it seems to matter much less the way you present yourself—green, brown, neat, sloppy, scented—than what your backing is—that is, where your money comes from. What the upper orders display here is no special uniform but the kind of psychological security they derive from knowing that others recognize their freedom from petty anxieties and trivial prohibitions.

POSSIBLE ANSWERS

Meaning and Purpose

1. When students agree with this statement, they usually support their answers by giving evidence from the essay and from their personal knowledge of people they know. When students disagree with this statement, they usually support their answers by asserting that in a free country people can work their way into any class except the highest, where money is inherited rather than earned outright.

2. See paragraphs 6 and 7: The Top and Bottom Out-of-Sight Classes are both "all but invisible." They also strive to retain anonymity. Each class, in it own way, hides. The Top hides from the general public; the Bottom hides from those to whom they owe money.

Meaning and Purpose

1. In the first paragraph, Fussell says, "it is virtually impossible to break out of the social class in which one has been nurtured," yet we call ours a "mobile society." Do you agree with Fussell's statement? If so, why? If not, why not?

2. What do the Bottom Out-of-Sight and the Top Out-of-Sight Classes have in common?

3. In paragraph 9, Fussell makes the statement, "Façade study is a badly neglected anthropological field," yet anthropologists do not have a field called "façade study." Why do you suppose Fussell makes that statement?

3. The purpose of this tongue-in-cheek statement is to add humorous credibility to the essay. Fussell is reinforcing his earlier statement that perception—in this instance, personally passing judgments on façades—is perhaps a more trustworthy way to define classes than is scientific data.

4. This phrase's purpose is to illustrate the trivial attitudes that the top three classes have about their accidents. Other classes have serious on-the-job accidents; these classes injure themselves while at play, and their casts are rarely dirtied. The "honor" is the result of having played hard, not the result of having worked hard.

5. Students' opinions of what is petty and what is trivial will depend on their own backgrounds. Ordinarily, their answers are personal and include such anxieties and problems as worrying about paying for health care, about paying for college, about earning money, about avoiding emotional and physical pain, and about providing for their futures.

Strategy

1. Many subjects today, such as fraud in government, obscenity on television, and senseless killings, are more likely to offend than facts about social class. Fussell makes this statement precisely because it so obviously does not offend; instead, it functions as a strategy to "hook" readers, to make them curious enough to read on, to see why Fussell himself believes the subject is offensive.

2. In science and in mathematics, "X" traditionally stands for an unknown quantity or a variable. Fussell shows here that not every class is clearly delineated in a classification system based in part on perception. Class X comprises a mobile group of people who enter and exit a class, "with no permanent location in this hierarchy" (2), never remaining one place long enough to assume a stable identity. Therefore, they represent a group variable, as a social scientist might say.

3. Fussell wants to establish that different classes can have seemingly common features. The mechanic gets dirty from working on vehicles; the dentist gets dirty from working on patients. To that extent, they are equal. What separates them

4. In paragraph 15, why are plaster casts called "a sort of white badge of honor"?

5. The last paragraph of this essay says that the "upper orders" are free from "petty anxieties and trivial problems." In your opinion, what are some of those petty anxieties and trivial problems?

Strategy

1. Why does Fussell make the unusually strong statement in the first paragraph that "No subject today is more likely to offend" than facts about social class?

2. Why does Fussell call one of the classes "Class X"? Why not name the class, as he did with the other classes?

3. Paragraph 11 says that a mechanic and a dentist engage in trades that are "equally dirty." Why does Fussell choose that particular phrase?

4. Paragraph 12 makes the point that certain classes watch certain television shows. What do the names of some of the television shows suggest to you?

5. Why does the essay include the six lines of poetry in paragraph 16?

Style

1. "Oh, we *have* our hats," say the Boston ladies in paragraph 3. What attitude or tone are the ladies conveying in that comment?

2. In paragraph 8, what do *claustrated* and *lamaseries* mean?

3. In paragraph 14, Fussell makes an ironic comment about being thin. What is that comment?

4. Look up the word *vulgar* in a college-level dictionary. Why do you suppose Fussell says in paragraph 7 that "the President is always rather vulgar"?

5. In paragraph 8, why is the word *den* set off in quotation marks?

is that the dentist has no supervisor, while the mechanic does. Thus, according to Fussell, the mechanic belongs to a class lower than the dentist's.

4. The answers will vary depending on the student's familiarity with each of the television shows. Fussell is writing to a broad audience. To make his point clearly, he relies here on the ability of that audience to equate his class distinctions with television show distinctions already familiar to his audience.

5. Those six lines of poetry illustrate what Fussell means when he talks of the "absolute prohibitions" that define an English gentleman. This illustration helps the reader to see how Fussell's classification differs so greatly from that in another country.

Style

1. The Boston ladies take their hats and their status for granted, to the extent that they appear oblivious to the marketplace. With its stress on *have,* the sentence implies that the hats have always existed; the tone is condescending to the point of unconscious snobbery.

2. *Claustrated* means to be secluded or closed off. The word comes from the Latin *claustrum,* "a bolt, or a place shut in." *Lamaseries* are monasteries of lamas, who themselves are priests or monks in Lamaism. Lamaism, a form of Buddhism, has elaborate rituals and a strong hierarchal organization. (The word *lama,* from the Tibetan *blama,* means "a chief" or "a high priest.")

3. The ironic comment is that the top four classes are starved by choice, but the bottom two classes are starved by circumstance.

4. The word *vulgar* refers to that which is common to the mass of people in general, suggesting a lack of culture, taste, and sensitivity. The word is from the Latin *vulgaris,* "the common people." According to paragraph 7, the President is a bit vulgar because, unlike the Top and Bottom Out-of-Sight Classes, he keeps his name *in* the papers as much as he can, mainly because he must appeal to the common people.

5. The word *den* is set off in quotation marks because it is a word used in a special way by Fussell's Middle Class. It refers to any room that the Middle Class wants to call a "den," to mean a small cozy room where one can be alone to read, work, and so forth.

Writing Tasks

1. Classify several of your friends using a light, humorous tone. Invent and label your own categories, and make sure that your categories do not overlap.

2. Choose one of Fussell's classes, and show why or why not the class is a legitimate one, based on your perceptions of how people should be classified.

3. Watch a current episode of a popular dramatic television show, such as *Murder, She Wrote; Murphy Brown; In the Heat of the Night; L.A. Law; The Commish;* or *Matlock.* Classify three characters other than the main ones who appear weekly, in terms of how they react to other characters, how they dress, and how they treat those around them.

Most of us, including students, have probably not thought much about the value of secrecy nor the necessity for it, so much of what Bok says provides us with a new way of looking at the subject. After the essay has been read, urge students to relate Bok's analysis to their personal experiences. Another avenue of approach might be to show that what Bok calls secrecy we often call privacy. Along this line, direct students' attention to Bok's discussion of protecting property through secrecy (19, 20). This section relates to current concerns over the "right to privacy": Who, if anyone, has the right to know the results of another person's tests for drugs or the AIDS virus?

Following such a discussion, you might profitably turn to an examination of the construction of the essay. Point out that like all good classification systems, Bok's grows from the material itself: her own observation and understanding of human behavior. The four classes are not imposed; they describe what she has seen and learned. Also point out that Bok frequently illustrates her ideas with specific, typical, and hypothetical examples.

Born in Stockholm in 1934 and educated in Europe and the United States, Sissela Bok holds a Ph.D. in philosophy from Harvard University. She has taught philosophy and ethics at several colleges and universities, including Harvard, and has published numerous articles on ethical issues as well as several books, notably Lying: Moral Choice in Public and Private *(1978) and* Secrets: On the Ethics of Concealment and Revelation *(1983), from which the following excerpt has been taken.*

The Need for Secrecy

Secrecy, as Bok suggests, is usually considered a negative word. We often assume that the keeper of a secret has something to hide, some guilt or crafty plan that for the general welfare should be revealed. But her analysis reveals the positive side of secrecy. She argues that secrecy is essential for our mental health and well-being and that without it humans would be "unable to exercise choices about their lives." She then classifies four elements of human autonomy and explains why secrecy is needed to protect "what we are, what we intend, what we do, and what we own."

As you read Bok's discussion of each of her classes, try to relate her examples to examples from your own experience.

Bok announces the subject, secrecy, at once and compares it to fire to pique readers' interest, but she makes no direct thesis statement until the end of the essay.

Secrecy is as indispensable to human beings as fire, and as greatly feared. Both enhance and protect life, yet both can stifle, lay waste, spread out of all control. Both may be used to guard intimacy or to invade it, to nurture or to consume. And each can be turned against itself; barriers of secrecy are set up to guard against secret plots and surreptitious prying, just as fire is used to fight fire.   1

We must keep in mind this conflicted, ambivalent experience of secrecy as we study it in its many guises, and seek standards   2

She directly states her intent to discuss the need for secrecy first.

Orwell's famous novel about political tyranny first appeared in 1949, a product of a post–World War II disillusionment.

Paragraphs 3–6 explore why humans *need* secrecy.

for dealing with it. But because secrecy is so often negatively defined and viewed as primarily immature, guilty, conspiratorial, or downright pathological, I shall first discuss the need for the protection it affords.

Consider how, in George Orwell's *1984,* Winston Smith tried to preserve one last expression of independence from the Thought-police. He had decided to begin a diary, even though he knew he thereby risked death or at least twenty-five years in a forced-labor camp. He placed himself in an alcove in his living room where the telescreen could not see him, and began to write. When he found himself writing DOWN WITH BIG BROTHER over and over, he panicked and was tempted to give up.

> He did not do so, however, because he knew that it was useless. Whether he wrote DOWN WITH BIG BROTHER, or whether he refrained from writing it, made no difference. Whether he went on with the diary, or whether he did not go on with it, made no difference. The Thought-police would get him just the same. He had committed—would still have committed, even if he had not set pen to paper—the essential crime that contained all others in itself. Thought-crime, they called it. Thoughtcrime was not a thing that could be concealed forever. You might dodge successfully for a while, even for years, but sooner or later they were bound to get to you.

Subjected to near-complete surveillance, Winston Smith was willing to risk death rather than to forgo the chance to set down his thoughts in secret. To the extent that he retained some secrecy for his views, he had a chance to elude the Thought-police. Though aware that "sooner or later they were bound to get to you," he did not know that he was under surreptitious observation even as he prepared to write—that his most secret undertaking was itself secretly spied upon.

The example from *1984* has prepared us for the shift to a more general discussion that equates secrecy with power.

Conflicts over secrecy—between state and citizen, as in this case, or parent and child, or in journalism or business or law—are conflicts over power: the power that comes through controlling the flow of information. To be able to hold back some information about oneself or to channel it and thus influence how one is seen by others gives power; so does the capacity to penetrate similar defenses and strategies when used by others. True, power requires not only knowledge but the capacity to put knowledge to use; but without the knowledge, there is no chance to exercise power. To have no capacity for secrecy is to be out of control over how others see one; it leaves one open to coercion. To have no insight into what others conceal is to lack power as well. Those who are unable or unwilling ever to look beneath the surface, to question motives, to doubt what is spoken, are condemned to live their lives in ignorance, just as those who are unable to keep secrets of their own must live theirs defenseless.

Control over secrecy provides a safety valve for individuals   5
in the midst of communal life—some influence over transactions between the world of personal experience and the world shared with others. With no control over such exchanges, human beings would be unable to exercise choice about their lives. To restrain some secrets and to allow others freer play; to keep some hidden and to let others be known; to offer knowledge to some but not to all comers; to give and receive confidences and to guess at far more: these efforts at control permeate all human contact.

Those who lose all control over these relations cannot flourish   6
in either the personal or the shared world, nor retain their sanity. If experience in the shared world becomes too overwhelming, the sense of identity suffers. Psychosis has been described as the breaking down of the delineation between the self and the outside world: the person going mad "flows out onto the world as through a broken dam." Conversely, experience limited to the inside world stunts the individual: at best it may lead to the aching self-exploration evoked by Nietzsche. "I am solitude become man— That no word ever reached me forced me to reach myself. . . ."

The claims in defense of some control over secrecy and open-   7
ness invoke four different, though in practice inseparable, elements of human autonomy: identity, plans, action, and property. They concern protection of what we are, what we intend, what we do, and what we own.

A good example of parallel structure.

Bok argues that those who lose all control over relations with others will lose their sanity.

Friedrich Wilhelm Nietzsche (1844–1900). German philosopher.

This paragraph divides human autonomy into four elements, labels them, and adds a phrase of explanation for each to reinforce our understanding.

Paragraphs 8–13 discuss the need for secrecy to protect identity.

The first of these claims holds that some control over secrecy and openness is needed in order to protect identity: the sense of what we identify ourselves as, through, and with. Such control may be needed to guard solitude, privacy, intimacy, and friendship. It protects vulnerable beliefs or feelings, inwardness, and the sense of being set apart: of having or belonging to regions not fully penetrable to scrutiny, including those of memory and dream; of being someone who is more, has become more, has more possibilities for the future than can ever meet the eyes of observers. Secrecy guards, therefore, not merely isolated secrets about the self but access to the underlying experience *of* secrecy.

Human beings can be subjected to every scrutiny, and reveal much about themselves; but they can never be entirely understood, simultaneously exposed from every perspective, completely transparent either to themselves or to other persons. They are not only unique but unfathomable. The experience of such uniqueness and depth underlies self-respect and what social theorists have called the sense of "the sacredness of the self." This sense also draws on group, familial, and societal experience of intimacy and sacredness, and may attach to individual as well as to collective identity. The growing stress in the last centuries on human dignity and on rights such as the right to privacy echoes it in secular and individualized language.

Without perceiving some sacredness in human identity, individuals are out of touch with the depth they might feel in themselves and respond to in others. Given such a sense, however, certain intrusions are felt as violations—a few even as desecrations. It is in order to guard against such encroachments that we recoil from those who would tap our telephones, read our letters, bug our rooms: no matter how little we have to hide, no matter how benevolent their intentions, we take such intrusions to be demeaning.

Not only does control over secrecy and openness preserve central aspects of identity; it also guards their *changes,* their growth or decay, their progress or backsliding, their sharing and transformation of every kind. Here as elsewhere, while secrecy can be destructive, some of it is indispensable in human lives. Birth,

8

9

10

11

sexual intimacy, death, mourning, experiences of conversion or of efforts to transcend the purely personal are often surrounded by special protections, and with rituals that combine secrecy and openness in set proportions.

Consider, for example, the role of secrecy, probing, and revelation with respect to pregnancy. In most cultures its workings have been thought mysterious, miraculous, at times terrifying. Like other experiences in which human boundaries are uncertain or shifting, pregnancy often increases vulnerability and the need for secrecy. Merely conjectured at first and pondered in secret by women, then perhaps revealed to a few, it is destined to unfold and to become known to many more. It is a period of heightened inwardness, awe, and joy for many women, giving them a sense of mattering in part because they have a secret to keep or to reveal. At times these feelings are overwhelmed by fear and anxiety—concerning the future of the baby, perhaps, or of the pregnant mother herself once her condition becomes known. 12

A work that illuminates such conflicts over secrecy in pregnancy is *The Confessions of Lady Nijō,* written in fourteenth-century Japan. When still a child, Lady Nijō was forced to become the concubine of a retired emperor. She had several babies not fathered by him. Her book tells of the stratagems required each time to conceal her pregnant state, and to give birth in secret to a baby she could never hope to rear but had to turn over to others; it recounts her despair over this fate, her fear lest the emperor should learn she was the mother of a baby not his own, and her repeated attempts to escape her life at court to travel and write poetry as a Buddhist nun. Like Lady Nijō, women in many other cultures have had to conceal their condition, fearful that it be noticed, and afraid of the gossip, the loss of face if they were unmarried, perhaps the dismissal from work once concealment was no longer possible. 13

The second and third claims to control over secrecy presuppose the first. Given the need to guard identity, they invoke, in addition, the need for such control in order to protect plans and actions. 14

Choice is future-oriented, and never fully expressed in present 15

Towazu-gatari, Lady Nijō's remarkably frank diary, covers the years 1271–1306. The oldest known copy, dating from the seventeenth century, is in the Imperial Household Library in Tokyo. One good English translation, by Wilfrid Whitehouse and Eizo Yanagisawa, uses the title *Lady Nijō's Own Story* The Candid Diary of a 13th Century *Japanese Imperial Concubine* (1974).

A short transition to the next point.

Paragraphs 15–18 discuss the next two elements of autonomy together.

action. It requires what is most distinctive about human reasoning: intention—the capacity to envisage and to compare future possibilities, to make estimates, sometimes to take indirect routes to a goal or to wait. What is fragile, unpopular, perhaps threatened, such as Winston Smith's plan to express his views freely in his diary, seeks additional layers of secrecy. To the extent that it is possible to strip people of their capacity for secrecy about their intentions and their actions, their lives become more transparent and predictable; they can then the more easily be subjected to pressure and defeated.

Secrecy for plans is needed, not only to protect their formulation but also to develop them, perhaps to change them, at times to executive them, even to give them up. Imagine, for example, the pointlessness of the game of chess without secrecy on the part of the players. Secrecy guards projects that require creativity and prolonged work: the tentative and the fragile, unfinished tasks, probes and bargaining of all kinds. An elopement or a peace initiative may be foiled if prematurely suspected; a symphony, a scientific experiment, or an invention falters if exposed too soon. In speaking of creativity, Carlyle stressed the need for silence and secrecy, calling them "the element in which great things fashion themselves together." 16

Thomas Carlyle (1795–1881). English critic, historian, and essayist. A leading thinker of his day, Carlyle stressed the importance of individual morality, duty, and action as a counterbalance to the mass movements and social turbulence of his day.

Joint undertakings as well as personal ones may require secrecy for the sharing and working out of certain plans and for cooperative action. Lack of secrecy would, for instance, thwart many negotiations, in which all plans cannot easily be revealed from the outset. Once projects are safely under way, however, large portions of secrecy are often given up voluntarily, or dispelled with a flourish. Surprises are sprung and jokes explained. The result of the jury trial can be announced, the statue unveiled, the secretly negotiated treaty submitted for ratification, the desire to marry proclaimed. Here again, what is at issue is not secrecy alone, but rather the control over secrecy and openness. Many projects need both gestation and emergence, both confinement and publicity. Still others, such as certain fantasies and daydreams and hopes, may be too ephemeral or intimate, at times too discreditable, ever to see the light of day. 17

Secrecy about plans and their execution, therefore, allows unpredictability and surprise. These are often feared; yet without them human existence would not only be unfree but also monotonous and stifling. Secrecy heightens the value of revelations; it is essential for arousing suspense, whether through stories told, surprises prepared, or waiting times imposed. It can lend the joy of concentration and solemnity to the smallest matters. Secrecy may also lower intensity and provide relief, so that when a revelation is finally made—as after the death of those most intimately connected with events described in an author's private diaries—the anguish of exposure is lessened. In all these ways, secrecy is the carrier of texture and variety. Without it, and without the suspense and wit and unexpectedness it allows, communication would be oppressively dull—lifeless in its own right.

Paragraphs 19–20 discuss property, the fourth element, and link it back to identity, the first element.

The fourth claim to control over secrecy concerns property. At its root, it is closely linked to identity, in that people take some secrets, such as hidden love letters, to *belong* to them more than to others, to be *proper to* them. We link such secrets with our identity, and resist intrusions into them. But the claim to own secrets about oneself is often far-fetched. Thus the school-bus driver who has a severe heart condition cannot rightfully claim to *own* this medical information, even though it concerns him intimately. Even when outsiders have less need to share the information than in such a case, the question who owns a secret may be hard to answer. Should one include only those "about whom" it is a secret, those who claim a right to decide whether or not to disclose it, or all who know it?

In addition to such questions of owning secrets, secrecy is invoked to protect what one owns. We take for granted the legitimacy of hiding silver from burglars and personal documents from snoopers and busybodies. Here, too, the link to identity is close, as is that to plans and their execution. For had we no belongings whatsoever, our identity and our capacity to plan would themselves be threatened, and in turn survival itself. As H. L. A. Hart points out, life depends on the respect for at least "some minimal form of the institution of property (though not necessarily individual property) and the distinctive kind of rule

H(erbert) L(ionel) A(dolphus) Hart (born 1907). A former professor of jurisprudence at Oxford University, Hart has made major contributions to twentieth-century philosophy of law. One of his major works is *Law, Liberty, and Morality* (1963).

which requires respect for it." At the most basic level, if crops are to be grown, land must be secure from indiscriminate entry, and food must be safe from being taken by others.

The four claims to control over secrecy and openness to pro- 21 tect identity, plans, actions, and property are not always persuasive. They may be stretched much too far, or abused in many ways. No matter how often these claims fail to convince, however, I shall assume that they do hold for certain fundamental human needs. Some capacity for keeping secrets and for choosing when to reveal them, and some access to the underlying experience of secrecy and depth, are indispensable for an enduring sense of identity, for the ability to plan and to act, and for essential belongings. With no control over secrecy and openness, human beings could not remain either sane or free.

The thesis statement is in the last two sentences of the essay.

POSSIBLE ANSWERS

Meaning and Purpose

1. The last two sentences of the essay contain the most direct statement of the thesis.

2. The more fundamental conflict is the one over the power to control the flow of information (4).

3. The four elements are identity, plans, action, and property (7). Bok says the four are inseparable in practice, and in fact she discusses two of them, plans and action, together. She also says that the fourth, property, is closely linked to the first, identity.

4. Identity: See paragraphs 8–13. Secrecy guards the uniqueness of each individual. Without the sense of uniqueness, there can be no self-respect. Plans and actions: See paragraphs 15–18. If our plans (intentions) cannot be kept secret, we become more vulnerable to control by others. Secrecy also allows for surprises. Without it, Bok says, life would be monotonous and stifling. Property: See paragraphs 19–20. Secrecy is necessary to protect property, many items of which are closely linked to identity and our freedom to make plans.

5. Loss of sanity (6, 21).

Meaning and Purpose

1. What is the thesis of Bok's essay? Is it stated directly? Where?
2. According to Bok, what is the more fundamental conflict beneath conflicts over secrecy?
3. What are the four elements of human autonomy that Bok says require secrecy? How are the four related to each other?
4. Explain briefly why secrecy is important for each element according to Bok.
5. In Bok's view, what are the consequences of an individual's loss of control over his or her own secrets?

Strategy

1. Bok uses many examples to illustrate her analysis. Find at least one specific example, one typical example, and one hypothetical example.

Strategy

1. Specific examples: Winston Smith in *1984* (3) and Lady Nijō (13); typical example: pregnancy (12); hypothetical example: bus driver (19). In addition brief hypothetical examples abound in her lists. See, for example, paragraphs 10 and 16–19.

2. Narration: paragraph 3; comparison and contrast: paragraph 1; cause and effect: paragraphs 4–6, 17, and 18.

3. The second sentence makes the abstract terms easier to understand.

4. Judgments may vary, but the analogy strikes us as being quite successful. It is brief, imaginative, not belabored, and captures the dual nature of secrecy Bok explores—it can protect and it can harm.

Style

1. Such examples, from series of single words to more complicated structures, abound. We hope someone mentions the last sentences of paragraphs 5, 7, 10, and 13. Other good examples appear in paragraphs 2, 9, 11, 12, 15–19, and 21.

2. The phrase refers to that unknowable unique aspect of each person which we feel must not be violated nor fully revealed lest it be dissipated. In paragraph 6, Bok defines psychosis as the loss of the distinction between this self and the outside world, and in paragraph 21, she again asserts that secrecy is essential for sanity.

3. *Surreptitious*: secret and stealthy; *ambivalent*: having two conflicting thoughts about a person or an idea; *coercion*: to force to act or think in a particular manner; *delineation*: draw accurately. The sense here is to make an accurate distinction between the self and the outside world. *unfathomable*: not understandable; *gestation*: a time of development.

2. Bok also uses a variety of other rhetorical strategies. Locate examples of narration, comparison and contrast, and cause and effect.

3. The four elements of human autonomy are listed in the first sentence of paragraph 7. What is the function of the second sentence in that paragraph?

4. The essay begins with an analogy. Comment on its effectiveness as a strategy to interest a potential reader. (See "analogy," pp. 657–658.)

Style

1. Three of the four sentences in paragraph 8 are built on parallel structure, a technique that adds power and emphasis to a statement. Read the paragraph aloud several times and then find other effective examples of parallel structure in this essay.

2. What does the phrase "sacredness of the self" in paragraph 9 mean? How does sacredness relate to Bok's discussion of psychosis in paragraph 6 and to the last sentence of paragraph 21?

3. If necessary look up the meaning of these words: *surreptitious* (1); *ambivalent* (2); *coercion* (4); *delineation* (6); *unfathomable* (9); *gestation* (17).

Writing Tasks

1. President Harry Truman said, "Secrecy and a free democratic government don't mix," and yet we all know that our government sometimes keeps secrets. To what extent and in what circumstances is government secrecy acceptable? Write a classification paper considering the kinds (classes) of situations in which government secrecy is acceptable, perhaps even necessary, or write a paper presenting those kinds of situations in which it is unacceptable and dangerous. Use examples to illustrate your ideas.

2. Without revealing any secrets that would jeopardize the "sacredness" of your self, write a paper on secrets that classifies the secrets you keep. You do not need to use examples for this paper; instead, concentrate on describing the nature of each different class. Be sure to have at least three classes.

Veterans Day

Humans are social beings. We form groups and subgroups for a variety of purposes—social, economic, vocational, political.

Some of these groups are informal and temporary: a study group for the final exam, a tour group to a vacation spot, an ad hoc committee to support a municipal bond issue. Others are more formal and longer lasting, binding together the common interests of large numbers of people across geographic and generational lines. Why do we join groups? What do we expect our membership in the group to accomplish for us or for others? Do groups provide us with a sense of identity? Of self-worth? Undoubtedly the reasons vary from one individual to another.

The picture, "Veterans Day," shows two members of a veterans' group posing in uniform with an American flag unobtrusively in the background. Their stance, legs apart and feet planted firmly, gives a solidity to their figures, which is tempered by the warmth of their smiles. They look content, happy, proud. Clearly, each has found some satisfaction in belonging to this organization.

We might wonder, though, if the satisfaction of membership, or the reason for joining this organization, is the same for the woman as for the man. Wearing their uniforms and standing in the noonday sun, they represent the values of the veterans' organization. But as individuals their motivations for being here are personal, a product of their own backgrounds and experiences.

After reviewing "Classification and Division: Establishing Categories" at the beginning of the chapter, complete one of the following writing tasks.

1. Write a division paper that considers the woman and the man in the photograph separately. Describe the physical appearance of each. For each, determine what you believe are possible motivations for joining the armed services and, later, a veterans' organization. What do you imagine the service experience of each was like? What would the veterans' organization represent to each? What satisfactions would each receive from membership? One caution: Since there are only the two figures prominent in the picture, this will be a binary division. Don't slip into comparison and contrast, but profile the woman and the man separately.

2. Write a classification paper that presents categories of people of similar age: children, youth, young adults, older adults, seniors. Find at least five photographs of people of one age group in social situations. Describe the people in each photograph as representatives of a category of their age group. Discuss the characteristics of each category. Include the pictures when submitting your final draft.

❦ Additional Writing Tasks ❦
Classification and Division

1. Choose one of the following subjects and write an essay using division as the dominant pattern. Describe each component in some detail, distinguishing it from the other components. Keep your readers in mind by guiding them carefully from component to component.
   a. A musical performance
   b. A board game, like chess, Monopoly, Risk, or Clue
   c. The human mind
   d. A ceremonial event, like a wedding, funeral, campaign rally, banquet, religious service
   e. A week at a teenage vacation spot
   f. A novel
   g. A police drama, situation comedy, or national news broadcast
   h. Your monthly income
   i. Bargaining in a foreign marketplace
   j. A meal in an expensive restaurant
2. Write an essay using classification as the dominant development method. Sort one of the following subjects into categories. Be sure the basis for your classification is clear. To direct your readers' attention, make up names for each category.
   a. The books, records, and/or video tapes you own
   b. Unusual sports, like "earth games" or other sports seldom televised or reported in newspapers
   c. Talk-show hosts
   d. War toys, family-oriented toys, or intellectual toys
   e. People who like to hunt game
   f. Lies
   g. Ways to read a novel or poem
   h. Ways to watch a horror movie
   i. Kinds of photography
   j. Attitudes revealed by bumper stickers
   k. Trends in dating, marriage, or divorce
   l. Kinds of terror
   m. Responses to a dramatic national or international event

n. New ways to learn
o. Kinds of good luck
p. Kinds of bad luck

10

Definition

Limiting Meaning

The Method

Think of how many words you hear in a day. Tens of thousands? Hundreds of thousands? Millions? Spoken words are plentiful. They are easy to produce: just open your mouth, activate your larynx, wag your tongue, and words will take flight. Of course, spoken words are often strung together thoughtlessly. If you have any doubts about this description, just turn your television dial to a talk show and listen to the relentless babble.

But written words are different. They require work. Serious writers select them with care. Some words are so technical that only technically trained readers understand them. Some words are so rarely used that few readers know what they mean. Some have meanings so ambiguous that readers understand them differently. That is why definition is indispensable in writing.

Strategies

Professional writers approach definition in three ways: etymological, or lexical, definition; stipulative definition; and extended definition.

Etymological Definition

An etymological definition is a dictionary definition. It defines a word in a narrow way by specifying its class and its distinguishing characteristics. Consider the word "thriller." A good college dictionary tells you that a thriller is a suspenseful work of fiction—a novel, play, or film—that deals with crime or detection. Sometimes an etymological definition includes synonyms: a "thriller" might be referred to as a "whodunit."

Rather than use a ready-made dictionary definition, writers often expand dictionary information to fit the interests of their audience and requirements that suit their purposes. Consider the dictionary definition of *bird:* "a warm-blooded, two-legged, egg-laying vertebrate with a wishbone, feathers, and wings." Now imagine that a writer wishes to define *bird* for a ten-year-old reader. The definition might read something like this:

> A bird is an animal. It has a backbone, is warm-blooded, and walks on two legs, but a human being does, too. It flies, but insects and bats do, too. It lays eggs, but salamanders, some snakes, and turtles do the same.
>
> What then makes birds different from all other animals? Only birds have feathers and a wishbone.

Stipulative Definition

Sometimes a writer uses a common word extensively in a special or limited way. The writer then usually stipulates the meaning of the word—that is, the writer explains how the word is to be understood as it appears throughout the essay. This explanation creates the *stipulative definition.* In this paragraph from *Amusing Ourselves to Death,* educator and communications critic Neil Postman stipulates the meaning of "conversation."

> I use the word "conversation" metaphorically to refer not only to speech but to all techniques and technologies that permit people of a particular culture to exchange messages. In this sense, all culture is a conversation or, more precisely, a corporation of conversations, conducted in a variety of symbolic modes. Our attention here is on how forms of public discourse regulate and even dictate what kind of content can issue from such forms.

And social critic Don Pierstorff stipulates a meaning for "suits" when examining Michael Levine's *Deep Cover,* an exposé of the Drug Enforcement Administration (DEA).

> Who are the "suits"? They are the men and women who crowd the corridors and sit behind the desks of the Drug

Enforcement Administration. They are government bureaucrats and managers. According to Michael Levine, they are
the people who have no first-hand experience of the drug
war and are unwilling to listen to agents who do. They spend
their days shuffling reports and briefing politicians.

Postman's paragraph stipulates the meaning of "conversation" by
enlarging it to mean all the methods culture uses to communicate.
Pierstorff's paragraph defines the commonly understood word
"suits" by presenting its uncommon slang definition, the way in
which DEA agents use it. Both authors anticipate that their readers
will need to know these special definitions to understand what
they are writing about.

Extended Definitions

Etymological and stipulative definitions usually are concisely
written for the sole purpose of clarification. Extended definitions
are much more detailed and usually employ various patterns of
development to fully explain a word or concept. In this paragraph
from *Hog on Ice,* C. E. Funk defines "white elephant." He uses
examples to establish its class and a brief narration about the
word's origin to differentiate it from others.

That large portrait of your wealthy Aunt Jane, given by
her and which you loathe but do not dare to take down
from your wall; that large bookcase, too costly to discard,
but which you hope will be more in keeping with your
future home; these, and a thousand other like items, are
"white elephants"—costly but useless possessions. The allusion takes us to Siam. In that country it was the traditional
custom for many centuries that a rare albino elephant was,
upon capture, the property of the emperor—who even today
bears the title Lord of the White Elephant—and was thereafter sacred to him. He alone might ride or use such an
animal, and none might be destroyed without his consent.
Because of that latter royal prerogative, it is said that when-

ever it pleased his gracious majesty to bring about the ruin of a courtier who had displeased him, he would present the poor fellow with an elephant from his stables. The cost of feeding and caring for the huge animal that he might neither use nor destroy—a veritable white elephant—gave the term its present meaning.

In this two-paragraph passage from *Alligators in Sewers and Other Urban Legends,* Jan Harold Brunvand defines "urban legend." Brunvand first establishes the class to which "urban legend" belongs and then distinguishes it from other members of the class. His definition goes beyond the etymological category because he develops the expression in greater detail, primarily with brief comparison and contrast and examples.

> Urban legends are realistic stories that are said to have happened recently. Like old legends of lost mines, buried treasure, and ghosts, they usually have an ironic or supernatural twist. They belong to a subclass of folk narratives that (unlike fairy tales) are set in the recent past, involving ordinary human beings rather than extraordinary gods and demigods.
>
> Unlike rumors, which are generally fragmentary or vague reports, legends have a specific narrative quality and tend to attach themselves to different local settings. Although they may explain or incorporate current rumors, legends tend to have a longer life and wider acceptance; rumors flourish and then die out rather quickly. Urban legends circulate by word of mouth, among the "folk" of modern society, but the mass media frequently help to disseminate and validate them. While they vary in particular details from one telling to another, they preserve a central core of traditional themes. In some instances these seemingly fresh stories are merely updatings of classic folklore plots, while other urban legends spring directly from recent conditions and then develop their own traditional patterns in repeated retellings. For example, "The Vanishing Hitchhiker," which describes the disappearance of a rider picked up on a highway, has evolved from

a 19th-century horse-and-buggy legend into modern variants incorporating freeway travel. A story called "Alligators in the Sewers," on the other hand, goes back no further than the 1930s and seems to be a New York City invention. Often, it begins with people who bring pet baby alligators back from Florida and eventually flush them down the drain.

Both Funk's definition of "white elephant" and Brunvand's definition of "urban legend" involve much more than merely looking up the established meanings; nevertheless, they do make use of a common pattern of definition by placing a term in a class and distinguishing it from other members of the class. Funk and Brunvand can use this pattern because the words they define have been in common use for some time. But the strength of an extended definition is to introduce new terms to readers, or, more accurately, to introduce concepts represented by those terms. This kind of extended definition may be highly personal, embodying a writer's values and independent observation.

In this three-paragraph passage from *Zen and the Art of Motorcycle Maintenance,* Robert M. Pirsig defines "mechanic's feel." Clearly, his definition is based on close observation during personal experience.

> The mechanic's feel comes from a deep inner kinesthetic feeling for the elasticity of materials. Some materials, like ceramics, have very little, so that when you thread a porcelain fitting you're very careful not to apply great pressures. Other materials, like steel, have tremendous elasticity, more than rubber, but in a range in which, unless you're working with large mechanical forces, the elasticity isn't apparent.
>
> With nuts and bolts you're in the range of large mechanical forces and you should understand that within these ranges metals are elastic. When you take up a nut there's a point called "fingertight" where there's contact but no takeup of elasticity. Then there's "snug," in which the easy surface elasticity is taken up. Then there's the range called "tight," in which all the elasticity is taken up. The force required to

reach these three points is different for each size of nut and bolt, and different for lubricated bolts and for locknuts. The forces are different for steel and cast iron and brass and aluminum and plastics and ceramics. But a person with mechanic's feel knows when something's tight and stops. A person without it goes right on past and strips the threads or breaks the assembly.

A "mechanic's feel" implies not only an understanding for the elasticity of metal but for its softness. The insides of a motorcycle contain surfaces that are precise in some cases to as little as one ten-thousandth of an inch. If you drop them or get dirt on them or scratch them or bang them with a hammer, they'll lose that precision. It's important to understand that the metal *behind* the surfaces can normally take a great shock and stress but that the surfaces themselves cannot. When handling precision parts that are stuck or difficult to manipulate, a person with mechanic's feel will avoid damaging the surfaces and work with his tools on the nonprecision surfaces of the same part whenever possible. If he must work on the surfaces themselves, he'll always use softer surfaces to work them with. Brass hammers, plastic hammers, wood hammers, rubber hammers and lead hammers are all available for this work. Use them. Vise jaws can be fitted with plastic and copper and lead faces. Use these too. Handle precision parts gently. You'll never be sorry. If you have a tendency to bang things around, take more time and try to develop a little more respect for the accomplishment that a precision part represents.

Pirsig's definition of "mechanic's feel" is unique. Readers have no resource to consult for a commonly accepted definition of an expression like that. Primarily relying on descriptive techniques, Pirsig carefully delineates the qualities of "mechanic's feel," right down to naming the degrees to which someone might tighten down a bolt: "fingertight," "snug," and "tight." Pirsig points out that metal has elasticity, and that someone with "mechanic's feel" must sense that quality or face the consequences—a broken assembly. Pirsig creates a sense of the soft, delicate surfaces of metal and names the tools someone should use when working on them—hammers of many materials varying in softness, as well as vise grips fitted with soft faces. Someone with mechanic's feel is precise; in fact, the need for precision seems to be the message beneath the detail.

Definition in College Writing

Definition is often used as a significant passage in essays with other dominant patterns of development. In the next example, Chris Schneider opens an essay exploring the use of cultural myths in advertising with a definition of "myth," his key term. A thorough definition of "myth" is vital to the success of his essay because its meaning has been enlarged by social critics.

Schneider opens with several cultural myths in question form. He closes by pointing out how the questions reflect "myths" as semiologists use the term.

Do you believe that childhood is a time of innocence separated from the emotions and cares of the adult world? Do you count on science to solve the dangers of fossil fuel shortage, ozone depletion, and toxic pollution? Do you feel that men and women embody a set of opposing psychological and social characteristics; that men, for instance, are rational and women are intuitive? Men are active; women, passive? Men are ambitious; women, nurturing? If you do, then your perceptions have been influenced by common American "myths," as a group of contemporary scholars and social critics known as semiologists would claim.

Schneider illustrates what the term "myth" is commonly understood to mean. But semioticians do not use "myth" in this way.

To most of us, the term "myth" might call to mind marvelous Greek stories of disguised gods cavorting with humans. We might think of heroes wielding swords against dragons or of magicians mesmerizing entire armies.

We might recall the story of Johnny Appleseed planting apple trees across the American landscape or of Rip Van Winkle sleeping for twenty years or of John Henry racing against a steam-powered spike driver. These myths are different from legends because they lack historical background and shade into the supernatural. They are also different from fables because they lack an overt moral intent. Like legends and fables they are stories, imaginative stories, that, according to one popular view, embody cultural patterns. Now semioticians are currently using the term "myth" in a different way.

In the final paragraph, Schneider explains how a semiotician uses "myth," and closes with a sentence that leads the reader into the rest of the paper.

To the semiotician "myth" refers to deeply rooted cultural beliefs, not to ancient stories. These beliefs are held by most members of any given society. Despite whatever evidence there might be to contradict the validity of a myth, semiologists do not judge it as right or wrong. They merely recognize its existence and analyze its social influence. Whether valid or invalid, a myth, therefore, is a psychological and social fact projected onto experience. We never clearly see things as they really are; we only see their reflections of our cultural beliefs. Nowhere is this reflection more pervasive than in advertising.

Schneider's three-paragraph passage is a straightforward extended definition. His strategy is relatively simple. In paragraph 1 he opens with questions to involve the reader before indicating that he will be defining the term "myth" as a group of social critics known as semiologists use it. In paragraph 2, Schneider refers to the way in which most readers would understand the meaning of "myth," which is based on its lexical definition. He concludes the paragraph by indicating that this is not the definition he intends, thus setting up the semiological definition revealed in paragraph 3. Here he explains that for the semiotician a myth is a deeply held cultural belief. As does any successful extended definition, this one goes beyond the dictionary to give the reader broader understanding of the word being defined.

❦ Gretel Ehrlich ❦

About Men

Gretel Ehrlich's essay, from The Solace of Open Spaces, *defines the word "cowboy," but, as the title suggests, her purpose is to challenge some assumptions "about men" in general, not just cowboys in particular. She achieves this intent by describing cowboys as she knows them, dispelling some myths about one of America's favorite stereotypes.*

Keep in mind how cowboys are portrayed on television and in movies, and see how that fictional portrayal compares or differs from Ehrlich's definition of a cowboy.

When I'm in New York but feeling lonely for Wyoming I look for the Marlboro ads in the subway. What I'm aching to see is horseflesh, the glint of a spur, a line of distant mountains, brimming creeks, and a reminder of the ranchers and cowboys I've ridden with for the last eight years. But the men I see in those posters with their stern, humorless looks remind me of no one I know here. In our hellbent earnestness to romanticize the cowboy we've ironically disesteemed his true character. If he's "strong and silent" it's because there's probably no one to talk to. If he "rides away into the sunset" it's because he's been on horseback since four in the morning moving cattle and he's trying, fifteen hours

1

The Chisholm Trail: Named after an American scout, Jesse Chisholm (1806–1868), this cattle trail led north from San Antonio, Texas, to Abilene, Kansas. It was used for about twenty years after the Civil War.

"cultural artifact": As generally used, this expression means an object made by human work, such as a primitive tool or weapon, which illustrates the ideas, customs, skills, or arts of a people during a specific period. Ehrlich suggests that we have defined the real cowboy as a stereotypical one, and then we have used that definition in a part of our culture.

The first half of this paragraph illustrates the figure of speech called *hysteron proteron,* used to describe a passage in which something that should logically come last comes first. According to Ehrlich, Americans have defined a cowboy first, and then fit the cowboy into the definition.

"manliness": Earlier in the essay, Ehrlich said that our society wanted the cowboy to be "the *macho,* trigger-happy man." Notice that she distinguishes between "macho" and "manliness," reserving "macho" for qualities we perceive outwardly, and "manliness" for qualities within a man.

later, to get home to his family. If he's "a rugged individualist" he's also part of a team: ranch work is teamwork and even the glorified open-range cowboys of the 1880s rode up and down the Chisholm Trail in the company of twenty or thirty other riders. Instead of the macho, trigger-happy man our culture has perversely wanted him to be, the cowboy is more apt to be convivial, quirky, and softhearted. To be "tough" on a ranch has nothing to do with conquests and displays of power. More often than not, circumstances—like the colt he's riding or an unexpected blizzard—are overpowering him. It's not toughness but "toughing it out" that counts. In other words, this macho, cultural artifact the cowboy has become is simply a man who possesses resilience, patience, and an instinct for survival. "Cowboys are just like a pile of rocks—everything happens to them. They get climbed on, kicked, rained and snowed on, scuffed up by wind. Their job is 'just to take it,' " one old-timer told me.

A cowboy is someone who loves his work. Since the hours are long—ten to fifteen hours a day—and the pay is $30 he has to. What's required of him is an odd mixture of physical vigor and maternalism. His part of the beef-raising industry is to birth and nurture calves and take care of their mothers. For the most part his work is done on horseback and in a lifetime he sees and comes to know more animals than people. The iconic myth surrounding him is built on American notions of heroism: the index of a man's value as measured in physical courage. Such ideas have perverted manliness into a self-absorbed race for cheap thrills. In a rancher's world, courage has less to do with facing danger than with acting spontaneously—usually on behalf of an animal or another rider. If a cow is stuck in a boghole he throws a loop around her neck, takes his dally (a half hitch around the saddle horn), and pulls her out with horsepower. If a calf is born sick, he may take her home, warm her in front of the kitchen fire, and massage her legs until dawn. One friend, whose favorite horse was trying to swim a lake with hobbles on, dove under water and cut her legs loose with a knife, then swam her to shore, his arm around her neck lifeguard-style, and saved her from drowning. Because these incidents are usually linked to someone or some-

2

"courage": This word's root is the Latin *cor*, "heart." Men of courage act with the heart.

"Jekyll and Hyde": From Robert Louis Stevenson's *The Strange Case of Dr. Jekyll and Mr. Hyde.* The kind, gentle Dr. Jekyll discovers drugs that he can use to transform himself into the mean, vicious Mr. Hyde, and back again.

thing outside himself, the westerner's courage is selfless, a form of compassion.

The physical punishment that goes with cowboying is greatly underplayed. Once fear is dispensed with, the threshold of pain rises to meet the demands of the job. When Jane Fonda asked Robert Redford (in the film *Electric Horseman*) if he was sick as he struggled to his feet one morning, he replied, "No, just bent." For once the movies had it right. The cowboys I was sitting with laughed in agreement. Cowboys are rarely complainers; they show their stoicism by laughing at themselves.

If a rancher or cowboy has been thought of as a "man's man"— laconic, hard-drinking, inscrutable—there's almost no place in which the balancing act between male and female, manliness and femininity, can be more natural. If he's gruff, handsome, and physically fit on the outside, he's androgynous at the core. Ranchers are midwives, hunters, nurturers, providers, and conservationists all at once. What we've interpreted as toughness— weathered skin, calloused hands, a squint in the eye and a growl in the voice—only masks the tenderness inside. "Now don't go telling me these lambs are cute," one rancher warned me the first day I walked into the football-field-sized lambing sheds. The next thing I knew he was holding a black lamb. "Ain't this little rat good-lookin'?"

So many of the men who came to the West were southerners— men looking for work and a new life after the Civil War—that chivalrousness and strict codes of honor were soon thought of as western traits. There were very few women in Wyoming during territorial days, so when they did arrive (some as mail-order brides from places like Philadelphia) there was a stand-offishness between the sexes and a formality that persists now. Ranchers still tip their hats and say, "Howdy, ma'am" instead of shaking hands with me.

Even young cowboys are often evasive with women. It's not that they're Jekyll and Hyde creatures—gentle with animals and rough on women—but rather, that they don't know how to bring their tenderness into the house and lack the vocabulary to express the complexity of what they feel. Dancing wildly all night becomes a metaphor for the explosive emotions pent up inside, and when these are, on occasion, released, they're so battery-charged and potent that one caress of the face or one "I love you" will peal for a long while.

The geographical vastness and the social isolation here make emotional evolution seem impossible. Those contradictions of the heart between respectability, logic, and convention on the one hand, and impulse, passion, and intuition on the other, played out wordlessly against the paradisical beauty of the West, give cowboys a wide-eyed but drawn look. Their lips pucker up, not with kisses but with immutability. They may want to break out, staying up all night with a lover just to talk, but they don't know how and can't imagine what the consequences will be. Those rare occasions when they do bare themselves result in confusion. "I feel as if I'd sprained my heart," one friend told me a month after such a meeting.

My friend Ted Hoagland wrote, "No one is as fragile as a woman but no one is as fragile as a man." For all the women here who use "fragileness" to avoid work or as a sexual ploy, there are men who try to hide theirs, all the while clinging to an adolescent dependency on women to cook their meals, wash their clothes, and keep the ranch house warm in winter. But there is true vulnerability in evidence here. Because these men work with animals, not machines or numbers, because they live outside in landscapes of torrential beauty, because they are confined to a place and a routine embellished with awesome variables, because calves die in the arms that pulled others into life, because they go to the mountains as if on a pilgrimage to find out what makes a herd of elk tick, their strength is also a softness, their toughness, a rare delicacy.

POSSIBLE ANSWERS

Meaning and Purpose

1. Ehrlich's thesis is in the first paragraph: "This macho, cultural artifact the cowboy has become is simply a man who possesses resilience, patience, and an instinct for survival."

2. The title denotes a very broad subject. After reading the essay, however, you see that the word "men" has been placed in Ehrlich's context: they are people who possess both male and female qualities. "There's almost no place in which the balancing act between male and female, manliness and femininity, can be more natural" (4).

3. Many southerners went West because the South was devastated by the Civil War. Others went West to avoid possible capture and incarceration by armies of the North. Still others went simply to seek their fortune in a new land.

4. The word "aching" means "longing" in this sentence. Ehrlich uses a bit of cowboy diction.

5. The expression "emotional evolution" as used in this paragraph refers to our maturing abilities to rank and control our emotions in order of their social acceptance. Most of us learn as we grow that we can control impulse with logic, for example, or passion with convention.

6. The word "torrential," from "torrent," suggests violence, swiftness, that which overwhelms. Wyoming has violent, beautiful storms, swift rivers, and natural beauty that overwhelms its viewers.

Strategy

1. Some features of cowboys mentioned in the essay are being part of a team, softhearted, hardworking, compassionate, childlike, and tender.

2. "About Men" is an extended definition. Ehrlich uses descriptive techniques, covers various characteristics, and gives examples of situations that define "cowboy." Some examples are: "For the most part his work is done on horseback and in a lifetime he sees and comes to know more animals than people" (2); and " 'Now don't go telling me these lambs are cute,' one rancher

Meaning and Purpose

1. What is Ehrlich's thesis, and where does she state it?
2. Comment on the title's significance. Did you understand it differently before you read the essay than after?
3. In paragraph 5, Ehrlich says that many of the men who went West were southerners. Why did so many southerners go West after the Civil War?
4. In paragraph 1, the author says that what she's "aching to see is horseflesh." Why does the author use "aching" in this sentence, and what does "aching" mean here?
5. From information in paragraph 7, write a definition for "emotional evolution."
6. Define "torrential" and tell why you think Ehrlich, in the last paragraph, describes Wyoming's beauty as "torrential."

Strategy

1. Imagine that you must write a concise definition for the word "cowboy." From the essay, list three features which cowboys have in common, and which you think you should include in your definition.
2. Is "About Men" a lexical, stipulative, or extended definition? Give examples from the essay that illustrate which kind it is.
3. You may have seen the Marlboro ads that the author mentions in paragraph 1. Why would a cigarette company advertise a cigarette by showing a cowboy riding a horse near a mountain range that resembles the Wyoming mountains?
4. In paragraph 1, why does Ehrlich define the stereotypical cowboy in the Marlboro ad when that is not the way cowboys really are?

warned me . . . . The next thing I knew he was holding a black lamb. 'Ain't this little rat good-looking?' " (4).

3. Because cigarettes have been proven to be a grave health risk, cigarette companies associate their product with health, nature, youth, and vigor, and either masculinity or femininity.

4. As part of defining the "true character" of a cowboy, Ehrlich first defines the stereotype most people are familiar with. Saying what a cowboy is not helps define what it is.

Style

1. The author is probably talking about the explosive emotions having to do with repressed love and sexuality.

2. The word "peal" refers to the loud ringing of a bell or any prolonged sound, such as laughter or thunder. It has a sense of "echo." The "I love you" need not be repeated because once it has been said, it remains said, as if the listener can still hear its echo.

3. "Androgynous" means that a cowboy has both male and female characteristics. His tough exterior hides an "androgynous core."

Style

1. In paragraph 6, Ehrlich mentions "explosive emotions," but clearly the author is not talking about anger or jealousy. What "explosive emotions" does she probably mean?

2. The last sentence in paragraph 6 says in part that "one 'I love you' will peal for a long while." Why is "peal" used in that sentence?

3. In paragraph 4, Ehrlich says that a cowboy is "androgynous." In fact, an androgynous human being is rare. What does the author mean by that word in this essay?

Writing Tasks

1. Write an extended definition of "cowboy," based on the way in which Hollywood and television portray him. Refer to several specific movies and television roles to give examples for your definition.

2. Imagine that you have just inherited a ranch in Wyoming, so you must hire a few cowboys. Write an extended definition of the kind of cowboys that you want to hire. Your definition will become a job description that appears in the local newspapers.

Modern makers of dictionaries for general use try to remain unbiased when defining words—unlike writers, who often slant their definitions to make a point. Also, modern dictionaries are focused more on individual words than on concepts, and writers—Theroux, in this instance—often define concepts.

Theroux defines *being* a man, not just the word *man*. His definition is active and continuing, culturally determined for the present. To reinforce it, he points out how it affected him and other male writers.

The expressions "being born a male" and "being a man" differ significantly. The first has biological roots; the second has cultural roots. Students enjoy discussing the notion of socially *being*. They respond well to the questions, "What does it mean to you to *be a woman*?" and "What does it mean to you to *be a man*?" The discussion almost always leads to the discovery that social conditions affect social definitions.

The larger question is how we go about changing societal definitions. Teachers usually discuss Theroux's "Being a Man" and Ehrlich's "About Men" together, so that students can see that writers themselves do not always agree on definitions.

Paul Theroux was born in Medford, Massachusetts, in 1941 and attended the University of Massachusetts and Syracuse University. He began a life of extensive world travel by joining the Peace Corps at age twenty-two, spending almost ten years in the organization teaching English in faraway countries such as Malaysia, Uganda, and Singapore. He is a poet and essayist and has published numerous novels, but is best known for his travel writing. The Great Railway Bazaar *(1975),* The Old Patagonian Express *(1979), and most recently his bestseller,* Riding the Iron Rooster *(1988), describe traveling by train through Asia, Central and South America, and China, respectively. He has also published a collection of essays titled* Sunrise with Seamonsters: Travels and Discoveries, 1964–1984 *(1985).*

Being a Man

Theroux defines "being a man" by describing what he considers the prevailing attitudes about what it means to be "manly," attitudes with which he strongly disagrees. Though the essay is personal and subjective, Theroux's opinions are backed by plenty of pertinent examples. The essay originally appeared in The New York Times Magazine *in 1983.*

You will probably strongly agree or strongly disagree with some of Theroux's statements. In the margin, as you read, check the statements with which you most strongly agree and the statements with which you strongly disagree.

"Fetishism": This word denotes a form of mental illness in which one is sexually stimulated at the sight of a shoe, glove, some other article of apparel, or some part of the body. In psychiatry, a fetish is the love object of a person who suffers from fetishism. To the masochist, such objects indicate domination.

There is a pathetic sentence in the chapter "Fetishism" in Dr. Norman Cameron's book *Personality Development and Psychopathology*. It goes, "Fetishists are nearly always men; and their commonest fetish is a woman's shoe." I cannot read that sentence without thinking that it is just one more awful thing about being a man—and perhaps it is an important thing to know about us.   1

I have always disliked being a man. The whole idea of manhood in America is pitiful, in my opinion. This version of mas-   2

Theroux defines with synonyms his version of America's cultural "masculinity": it's a destructive life, socially and emotionally unhealthy.

The female version of this cultural separation of the sexes, femininity, is introduced. Girls are taught how to grow into "proper" women; boys are taught how to grow into "proper" men.

Femininity implies needing men; masculinity celebrates excluding women. The effect is to deny natural bonding with the opposite sex.

At an age when it is natural for a boy to seek the company of a girl, society sends him in the other direction by forcing him to seek the company of other males. As a result, boys mature into men who have been schooled to believe that they should "hang out" together.

culinity is a little like having to wear an ill-fitting coat for one's entire life (by contrast, I imagine femininity to be an oppressive sense of nakedness). Even the expression "Be a man!" strikes me as insulting and abusive. It means: Be stupid, be unfeeling, obedient, soldierly and stop thinking. Man means "manly"—how can one think about men without considering the terrible ambition of manliness? And yet it is part of every man's life. It is a hideous and crippling lie; it not only insists on difference and connives at superiority, it is also by its very nature destructive—emotionally damaging and socially harmful

The youth who is subverted, as most are, into believing in 3 the masculine ideal is effectively separated from women and he spends the rest of his life finding women a riddle and a nuisance. Of course, there is a female version of this male affliction. It begins with mothers encouraging little girls to say (to other adults) "Do you like my new dress?" In a sense, little girls are traditionally urged to please adults with a kind of coquettishness, while boys are enjoined to behave like monkeys towards each other. The nine-year-old coquette proceeds to become womanish in a subtle power game in which she learns to be sexually indispensable, socially decorative and always alert to a man's sense of inadequacy.

Femininity—being lady-like—implies needing a man as witness and seducer; but masculinity celebrates the exclusive company of men. That is why it is so grotesque; and that is also why there is no manliness without inadequacy—because it denies men the natural friendship of women.

It is very hard to imagine any concept of manliness that does 5 not belittle women, and it begins very early. At an age when I wanted to meet girls—let's say the treacherous years of thirteen to sixteen—I was told to take up a sport, get more fresh air, join the Boy Scouts, and I was urged not to read so much. It was the 1950s and if you asked too many questions about sex you were sent to camp—boys' camp, of course: the nightmare. Nothing is more unnatural or prison-like than a boy's camp, but if it were not for them we would have no Elks' Lodges, no pool rooms, no boxing matches, no Marines.

And perhaps no sports as we know them. Everyone is aware 6

Theroux attacks competitive athletes, saying that the preparation, training, and competition in which they engage prepare them only to live physically in society. This kind of "manliness" is "philistine"; that is, smugly narrow, authoritarian, and indifferent to cultural and esthetic values.

When Theroux wrote this essay, Ronald Reagan was president. President Reagan was often photographed wearing clothing that looked as if it had been purchased from L. L. Bean, a mail-order company that specializes in high-quality merchandise such as plaid woolen shirts, canvas jackets, thick parkas, heavy denim pants, waterproof hunting boots—anything one needs to survive with style in the great outdoors.

A consequence of our culture's way of defining stereotyped "manliness" is that this stereotype does not accord with the American definition of male *writer,* and yet the male writer often succumbs to that stereotyped definition. This role playing greatly affected Theroux's early life.

of how few in number are the athletes who behave like gentlemen. Just as high school basketball teaches you how to be a poor loser, the manly attitude towards sports seems to be little more than a recipe for creating bad marriages, social misfits, moral degenerates, sadists, latent rapists and just plain louts. I regard high school sports as a drug far worse than marijuana, and it is the reason that the average tennis champion, say, is a pathetic oaf.

Any objective study would find the quest for manliness essentially right-wing, puritanical, cowardly, neurotic and fueled largely by a fear of women. It is also certainly philistine. There is no book-hater like a Little League coach. But indeed all the creative arts are obnoxious to the manly ideal, because at their best the arts are pursued by uncompetitive and essentially solitary people. It makes it very hard for a creative youngster, for any boy who expresses the desire to be alone seems to be saying that there is something wrong with him.

It ought to be clear by now that I have something of an objection to the way we turn boys into men. It does not surprise me that when the President of the United States has his customary weekend off he dresses like a cowboy—it is both a measure of his insecurity and his willingness to please. In many ways, American culture does little more for a man than prepare him for modeling clothes in the L. L. Bean catalogue. I take this as a personal insult because for many years I found it impossible to admit to myself that I wanted to be a writer. It was my guilty secret, because being a writer was incompatible with being a man.

There are people who might deny this, but that is because the American writer, typically, has been so at pains to prove his manliness that we have come to see literariness and manliness as mingled qualities. But first there was a fear that writing was not a manly profession—indeed, not a profession at all. (The paradox in American letters is that it has always been easier for a woman to write and for a man to be published.) Growing up, I had thought of sports as wasteful and humiliating, and the idea of manliness was a bore. My wanting to become a writer was not a flight from that oppressive role-playing, but I quickly saw that it was at odds with it. Everything in stereotyped manliness goes

7

8

9

Ernest Hemingway (d. 1961), awarded the Nobel Prize in literature (1954), wrote *The Sun Also
Rises* (1926), *For Whom the Bell Tolls* (1940),
and *The Old Man and the Sea* (1952), among
others. He died of a self-inflicted gunshot wound.

Wealth, drinking, hunting, killing—these are the
worst traits of "manliness," according to Theroux.

Nathanael West, a novelist and screen writer
whose best-known work is *The Day of the Locust*
(1940). James Jones (d. 1977) wrote the bestseller *From Here to Eternity* (1951). William
Faulkner (d. 1962), awarded the Nobel Prize in
literature (1949), wrote *As I Lay Dying* (1930),
Absalom, Absalom! (1936), and *The Hamlet*
(1940), among others. Jack Kerouac (d. 1969)
flourished from the mid-1950s to the mid-1960s.
His best-known works are *On the Road* (1957)
and *The Dharma Bums* (1958). Norman Mailer
(b. 1923) probably is best known for *The Naked
and the Dead* (1948) and *The Executioner's Song*
(1979). For the latter he was awarded the Pulitzer Prize in literature. John Irving (b. 1942)
said, "A writer uses what experience he or she
has. It's the translating, though, that makes the
difference." Eric Segal wrote the bestselling *Love
Story* (1970). Joyce Carol Oates (b. 1938) wrote
A Garden of Earthly Delights (1967) and *You
Must Remember This* (1988), among others. Joan
Didion (b. 1934) wrote the acclaimed *Slouching
Towards Bethlehem* (1968), a book of essays.

against the life of the mind. The Hemingway personality is too
tedious to go into here, and in any case his exertions are well-
known, but certainly it was not until this aberrant behavior was
examined by feminists in the 1960s that any male writer dared
question the pugnacity in Hemingway's fiction. All the bullfighting and arm wrestling and elephant shooting diminished Hemingway as a writer, but it is consistent with a prevailing attitude
in American writing: one cannot be a male writer without first
proving that one is a man.

10 It is normal in America for a man to be dismissive or even
somewhat apologetic about being a writer. Various factors make
it easier. There is a heartiness about journalism that makes it
acceptable—journalism is the manliest form of American writing
and, therefore, the profession the most independent-minded
women seek (yes, it is an illusion, but that is my point). Fiction-
writing is equated with a kind of dispirited failure and is only
manly when it produces wealth—money is masculinity. So is
drinking. Being a drunkard is another assertion, if misplaced, of
manliness. The American male writer is traditionally proud of his
heavy drinking. But we are also a very literal-minded people. A
man proves his manhood in America in old-fashioned ways. He
kills lions, like Hemingway; or he hunts ducks, like Nathanael
West; or he makes pronouncements like, "A man should carry
enough knife to defend himself with," as James Jones once said
to a *Life* interviewer. Or he says he can drink you under the table.
But even tiny drunken William Faulkner loved to mount a horse
and go fox hunting, and Jack Kerouac roistered up and down
Manhattan in a lumberjack shirt (and spent every night of *The
Subterraneans* with his mother in Queens). And we are familiar
with the lengths to which Norman Mailer is prepared, in his
endearing way, to prove that he is just as much a monster as the
next man.

11 When the novelist John Irving was revealed as a wrestler,
people took him to be a very serious writer; and even a bubble
reputation like Erich (*Love Story*) Segal's was enhanced by the
news that he ran the marathon in a respectable time. How surprised we would be if Joyce Carol Oates were revealed as a sumo

To strengthen his charge that "manliness" works against a man's being an unapologetic author, Theroux has run the gamut of twentieth-century American authors.

Notice the distinction Theroux draws between "man" and "manly." Being a "man" is biological; being "manly" (acting with "manliness") requires that a man live up to a socially imposed definition, at great personal cost.

POSSIBLE ANSWERS

Meaning and Purpose

1. Being born male is biological; "being a man," in Theroux's meaning, is cultural, learned, imposed.

2. Theroux's audience is certainly other men of his generation, who might agree or disagree with him, feel the cultural stereotype in themselves or not. He also speaks to women, especially mothers of boys, who can do something about the models their sons grow up with. Anyone in our society could appreciate this.

3. This phrase refers to American literature in general, including the learning and knowledge associated with it.

4. The image of the cowboy is a masculine one. People who are insecure about themselves may dress to portray what they would like to be, rather than what they believe they really are.

5. The so-called manly ideal stresses competition and teamwork; the creative arts stress solitude and individuality. Theroux thinks the two roles are incompatible.

6. Possible answers are that athletes have been accused of taking money and favors for attending a school, or that some athletes are allowed to attend a school even if they score low on entrance tests or maintain poor grades.

wrestler or Joan Didion active in pumping iron. "Lives in New York City with her three children" is the typical woman writer's biographical note, for just as the male writer must prove he has achieved a sort of muscular manhood, the woman writer—or rather her publicists—must prove her motherhood.

There would be no point in saying any of this if it were not generally accepted that to be a man is somehow—even now in feminist-influenced America—a privilege. It is on the contrary an unmerciful and punishing burden. Being a man is bad enough; being manly is appalling (in this sense, women's lib has done much more for men than for women). It is the sinister silliness of men's fashions, and a clubby attitude in the arts. It is the subversion of good students. It is the so-called "Dress Code" of the Ritz-Carlton Hotel in Boston, and it is the institutionalized cheating in college sports. It is the most primitive insecurity. 12

And this is also why men often object to feminism but are afraid to explain why: of course women have a justified grievance, but most men believe—and with reason—that their lives are just as bad. 13

Meaning and Purpose

1. In Theroux's essay, is "being a man" different from being born male? How?
2. Whom do you think Theroux imagines his audience to be?
3. In paragraph 9, what is the meaning of "American letters"?
4. Theroux says in paragraph 8 that former President Reagan dressed like a cowboy, and that this was a "measure of his insecurity and his willingness to please." How is dressing like a cowboy a measure of a man's insecurity?
5. All the creative arts are "obnoxious to the manly ideal" (7) according to the author. Why?
6. What do you think is meant by "institutionalized cheating in college sports" (12)?

Strategy

1. This essay can be considered either a stipulative or an extended definition. It is stipulative because Theroux limits the meaning of "being a man" to the context of modern American culture. It is extended because Theroux paints a wide and seemingly all-encompassing picture of what "being a man" means.

2. Theroux has authority to define his term because he is, first, a man himself. He also grew up in the 1950s when much of the cultural pressure he describes influenced boys, and he participated in Boy Scouts, summer camp, and sports. And he is a writer who has experienced the insecurity of being a man in that profession.

3. The word "pugnacity" means being eager and ready to fight, being quarrelsome and combative. Hemingway writes with pugnacity to demonstrate that, though he is a fiction writer, he is also "manly."

4. Theroux describes a "female version of this male affliction" (3) early in the essay, establishing that "being a man" has a counterpart. He links the cultural definition of "manliness" inextricably to femininity when he says "there is no manliness without inadequacy—because it denies men the natural friendship of women" (4). The woman writer "must prove her motherhood" (11) as the male writer must prove his "muscular manhood" (11).

Style

1. Theroux's attitude is in these words, as well as others: "The whole idea of manhood in America is pitiful" (2); "It is a hideous and crippling lie" (2); "It is also by its very nature destructive—emotionally damaging and socially harmful" (2); "It is so grotesque" (4); "being manly is appalling" (12).

2. Let students compare the descriptions in the two essays.

3. *Connives*: cooperates secretly, or conspires; *coquette*: a vain young girl who tries to get men's attention and admiration; *philistine*: crass, and guided by material rather than artistic values; *roistered*: caroused, or engaged in noisy revelry.

Strategy

1. What kind of definition does Theroux write in this essay? Explain.
2. How does Theroux establish his authority for defining what it is to be a man?
3. Define "pugnacity." How does this word in paragraph 9 characterize Hemingway's fiction?
4. Where and how does Theroux bring up for contrast the definition of what it is to be a woman as a help in expressing what it is to be a man?

Style

1. Point out some of Theroux's language that establishes his unhappy and angry attitude toward being a man.
2. Compare Ehrlich's "men" in "About Men" with Theroux's "manly" and "being a man." How does the voice that defines differ in these essays?
3. Define these words: *connives* (2); *coquette* (3); *philistine* (7); *roistered* (10).

Writing Tasks

1. In an essay, define "being a woman" with the same critical eye Theroux uses in his essay. How does our culture define what it is to be a woman?
2. In paragraph 6, Theroux says that "the manly attitude towards sports" can lead to bad marriages and other problems in people's lives. Reread the essay to determine why Theroux made this remark, and then define an attitude toward sports that does not agree with Theroux's definition.

You might take two tacks with this essay. The first is to pursue Harrington's reasoning paragraph by paragraph. His essay is closely reasoned, carefully connecting one point to another. This close-reading approach can help the student appreciate Harrington's impassioned arguments.

From that reading, a discussion on the validity of Harrington's views might ensue. This kind of discussion usually depends on your students' social status. The affluent, conservative student will have less first-hand knowledge of poverty, of course, and can be brought to Harrington's position by capacity for compassion, by second-hand knowledge, and by Harrington's logical persuasiveness. And, of course, a mixed group of students could lead to a lively discussion indeed.

❦ Michael Harrington ❦

Michael Harrington, a leading intellect on the American left, was a political scientist who has written and lectured widely, advocating democratic socialism. He was born in St. Louis in 1928 and studied at the Yale Law School and the University of Chicago. He has been an active and outspoken member of the Socialist Party since the 1950s and more recently served as cochair of the Democratic Socialists of America. His book The Other America: Poverty in the United States *(1962), was instrumental in developing the War on Poverty, a government movement initiated by President Lyndon Johnson in 1964. Harrington has published more than a dozen books, including* The Vast Majority: A Journey to the World's Poor *(1977), which won the National Book Award, and* The New American Poverty *(1984), in which he assesses the War on Poverty. Just recently he died of cancer.*

A Definition of Poverty

Harrington's definition of poverty, excerpted from his very influential The Other America, *is a response to more abstract definitions that avoid the reality of "here and now." As social and economic standards and conditions change through history, the definition of poverty must change accordingly, he claims. Harrington ends by delineating how poverty should be defined.*

Notice how Harrington moves historically, from an older definition, to reasons for arguing against such a definition, and finally to reasons for his contemporary definition of poverty.

Harrington begins with a reason for social inaction that he believes to be absurd.

He shows by examples that current conditions cannot be justified by citing and comparing other times and places.

In the nineteenth century, conservatives in England used to argue against reform on the grounds that the British worker of the time had a longer life expectancy than a medieval nobleman. 1

This is to say that a definition of poverty is, to a considerable extent, a historically conditioned matter. Indeed, if one wanted to play with figures, it would be possible to prove that there are no poor people in the United States, or at least only a few whose 2

507

plight is as desperate as that of masses in Hong Kong. There is starvation in American society, but it is not a pervasive social problem as it is in some of the newly independent nations. There are still Americans who literally die in the streets, but their numbers are comparatively small.

This abstract approach toward poverty in which one compares different centuries or societies has very real consequences. For the nineteenth-century British conservative, it was a way of ignoring the plight of workers who were living under the most inhuman conditions. The twentieth-century conservative would be shocked and appalled in an advanced society if there were widespread conditions like those of the English cities a hundred years ago. Our standards of decency, of what a truly human life requires, change, and they should.

There are two main aspects of this change. First, there are new definitions of what man can achieve, of what a human standard of life should be. In recent times this has been particularly true since technology has consistently broadened man's potential: it has made a longer, healthier, better life possible. Thus, in terms of what is technically possible, we have higher aspirations. Those who suffer levels of life well below those that are possible, even though they live better than medieval knights or Asian peasants, are poor.

Related to this technological advance is the social definition of poverty. The American poor are not poor in Hong Kong or in the sixteenth century: they are poor here and now, in the United States. They are dispossessed in terms of what the rest of the nation enjoys, in terms of what the society could provide if it had the will. They live on the fringe, the margin. They watch the movies and read the magazines of affluent America, and these tell them that they are internal exiles.

To some, this description of the feelings of the poor might seem to be out of place in discussing a definition of poverty. Yet if this book indicates anything about the other America, it is that this sense of exclusion is the source of a pessimism, a defeatism that intensifies the exclusion. To have one bowl of rice in a society where all other people have half a bowl may well be a sign of

---

He first diminishes such arguments by calling them "abstract," removed from the cruel consequences such justifications have in the real world, and then concludes that "standards of decency" must change with time.

Harrington now offers his first definition of poverty.

As his first definition is tied to technological advances, his second involves social standards.

This paragraph and the two preceding deal in one way or another with psychological suffering by the poor in alienation, pessimism, and despair.

achievement and intelligence; it may spur a person to act and to fulfill his human potential. To have five bowls of rice in a society where the majority have a decent, balanced diet is a tragedy.

Harrington concludes this section of the essay by showing that technological and social advances must be made in tandem to avoid human misery.

This point can be put another way in defining poverty. One 7 of the consequences of our new technology is that we have created new needs. There are more people who live longer. Therefore they need more. In short, if there is technological advance without social advance, there is, almost automatically, an increase in human misery, in impoverishment.

And finally, in defining poverty one must also compute the 8 social cost of progress. One of the reasons that the income figures show fewer people today with low incomes than twenty years ago is that more wives are working now, and family income has risen as a result. In 1940, 15 percent of wives were in the labor force; in 1957 the figure was 30 percent. This means that there was more money and, presumably, less poverty.

The next two paragraphs demonstrate that a change some might consider an inroad against poverty (generally higher incomes) may have been bought at too dear a price (the future of our children).

Yet a tremendous growth in the number of working wives is 9 an expensive way to increase income. It will be paid for in terms of the impoverishment of home life, of children who receive less care, love, and supervision. This one fact, for instance, might well play a significant role in the problems of the young in America. It could mean that the next generation, or a part of it, will have to pay the bill for the extra money that was gained. It could mean that we have made an improvement in income statistics at the cost of hurting thousands and hundreds of thousands of children. If a person has more money but achieves this through mortgaging the future, who is to say that he or she is no longer poor?

Harrington's brief, four-paragraph conclusion simplifies and summarizes his definitions of poverty.

It is difficult to take all these imponderables together and to 10 fashion them into a simple definition of poverty in the United States. Yet this analysis should make clear some of the assumptions that underlie the assertions in this book:

Poverty should be defined in terms of those who are denied 11 the minimal levels of health, housing, food, and education that our present stage of scientific knowledge specifies as necessary for life as it is now lived in the United States.

Poverty should be defined psychologically in terms of those 12 whose place in the society is such that they are internal exiles who, almost inevitably, develop attitudes of defeat and pessimism and who are therefore excluded from taking advantage of new opportunities.

Poverty should be defined absolutely, in terms of what man and society could be. As long as America is less than its potential, the nation as a whole is impoverished by that fact. As long as there is the other America, we are, all of us, poorer because of it. 13

Meaning and Purpose

1. Find Harrington's main points about poverty.
2. Harrington claims that "a definition of poverty is, to a considerable extent, a historically conditioned matter" (2). Explain what he means.
3. Harrington says that to compare the poverty of one time to that of another is an "abstract approach toward poverty" (3). Why does he find this approach objectionable?
4. What does Harrington mean in paragraph 8 when he says that "in defining poverty one must also compute the social cost of progress"?
5. In paragraphs 8 and 9, Harrington seems to suggest if women weren't in the work force in such numbers as they are, America's children would have fewer problems. What solutions can you think of for the "impoverishment of home life" other than women's staying at home?
6. Considering all that Harrington said before, explain what he means in the last sentence.

Strategy

1. How does Harrington's argument in the first three paragraphs lead to his definitions of poverty?

POSSIBLE ANSWERS

Meaning and Purpose

1. Harrington's main points are the last three paragraphs.
2. Our perceptions and definitions of poverty are determined by our place in history. The poverty of nineteenth-century England, for instance, would be totally unacceptable now. To argue against social reforms by claiming that the present poor are better off than the poor of another time or place is thus illogical and unacceptable.
3. Comparing the poverty of one historical time to another is purely an intellectual ("abstract") activity that has pernicious consequences in the real world. It allowed nineteenth-century conservatives to ignore inhuman conditions among the poor. And twentieth-century conservatives who would be appalled by the horror of nineteenth-century poverty use the same fallacious reasoning to ignore conditions today (3).
4. Families had higher incomes in 1962 when Harrington published *The Other America* than twenty years earlier because more wives were in the work force. The price of this progress may be that children have less care, love, and supervision. Thus, we may have mortgaged their futures—a high price to pay for "progress" (8, 9).
5. Some students may find Harrington's opinions in these paragraphs sexist. Other solutions would be for men and women to share equally the responsibility for taking care of children, and for companies to provide adequate day-care for children of working parents.
6. Any society that has the wealth to eliminate the horrors of poverty and doesn't is spiritually impoverished.

Strategy

1. Paragraph 1 gives the justification nineteenth-century British conservatives used to avoid change. In paragraph 2, Harrington cites similar arguments and implies their fallaciousness. In paragraph 3, he shows explicitly how these arguments are flawed and concludes that our standards of decency must change with time. **2.** Each of the definitions can be taken as stipulative. In paragraph 5, Harrington stipulates the "social definition of poverty." Each of the last three paragraphs defines a different aspect of poverty: quality of life (11), psychological (12), and moral (13). Together, these stipulative definitions, and all the other points Harrington makes in considering these definitions of poverty (such as "the social cost of progress" in paragraph 8), constitute an extended definition of poverty. **3.** In paragraphs 2–7, Harrington uses the word "this" in the first sentence to clearly refer to ideas just stated. "Finally" indicates (8) that he will make his final point. "Yet" (9) indicates he will now make a distinction from what he has just said. And "all these imponderables" (10) clearly connects the paragraph with all that he has just said.

Style

1. Harrington's tone is formal and controlled, as in these sentences: "Indeed, if one wanted to play with figures . . . United States" (2); "Yet if this book . . . intensifies the exclusion" (6); and "if there is technological advance . . . in impoverishment" (7). The words in these sentences do not convey strong feelings; they sound academic.
2. "Internal exiles" here means that the poor are members of the society, are internal to the society, but they are outcasts because they "are dispossessed . . . had the will" (5).
3. *Pervasive:* spread through all parts of; *dispossessed:* having suffered the loss of expectations, prospects, relationships, and also disinherited, disaffiliated, alienated; *affluent:* having abundant wealth, property, and other material goods; *imponderables:* things that cannot be precisely determined, measured, or evaluated.

2. How would you categorize Harrington's definitions—lexical, stipulative, or extended—and why?
3. What transitions does Harrington use to connect paragraphs 1–10?

Style

1. Analyze the tone of the essay by looking closely at the language and word choices.
2. How does Harrington use the phrase "internal exiles" in paragraph 5?
3. Define these words: *pervasive* (1); *dispossessed, affluent* (5); *imponderables* (10).

Writing Tasks

1. In an essay, develop a definition, or definitions, of wealth. Take social and economic factors into account. Consider offering solutions to the problems of the wealthy.
2. Choose one word, such as "student" or "happiness," and write three kinds of definitions for it—lexical, stipulative, and extended.

TEACHING SUGGESTIONS

Change brings further change, sometimes not entirely foreseen. Shari Miller Sims carefully and expansively defines aggression, assertiveness, and several lesser but contextually important concepts to show that we should interest ourselves in the possible residue of a major change in traditional (or old-fashioned) society. She uses definition as background information. Her thesis—that more women are accepting violence as a means of expression—is primarily developed with examples and by examining cause and effect.

Was the collapse of the Eastern Bloc a global change for the better? Of course. And we have seen better relations between the Soviet republics and the United States. Another change for the better.

But what of the changes that grow from those two alterations in the politics of the planet? Some economists believe that our country will experience strong competition from abroad in the goods and services and manufacturing sectors of our economy. We could have a difficult time of it, all the way down to the personal, financial level.

MARGINAL NOTES

Sims opens her essay with two journalistic anecdotes, designed to get readers' attention at once by engaging them in lightly detailed particulars from interesting events specifically appropriate to her topic.

❦ Shari Miller Sims ❦

Born in New York in 1956, Shari Sims, soon after graduating from Kenyon College, joined the staff at McCall's magazine, where she was an associate editor. She then spent six years as a staff writer and editor for Vogue. She began working for Self magazine in 1987 and is executive editor of Health and Beauty there. She is coauthor, with Lia Schorr, of two beauty books: Lia Schorr's Skin Care Guide for Men (1985) and Seasonal Skin Care (1988). She has also contributed to Working Woman magazine.

Violent Reactions

Domestic violence, reports Sims in an essay from the March 1989 issue of Self, *appears increasingly to be considered an "acceptable" form of communication within families and couples. In her essay she probes the changes in sex roles for possible causes, seeking a new definition for "violence."*

Sims uses psychological and sociological observations to support her definition. As you read this essay, note how she uses the opinions of experts to strengthen her own statements.

A thirty-year-old man moved out of a New York City apartment it had taken him months to find. Nothing unusual, except for the reason: the couple, just about his age, who lived next door. Their fights were getting progressively louder, more intense, and what he'd heard was more than words. The shouting seemed to have escalated into all-out warfare, and lately additional noises—breaking glass, the crash of objects being thrown echoed into his apartment. What was even more disturbing to him was their source: He was convinced it was the woman who was starting the fights, who was screaming the words of abuse and hurling things across the apartment—all aimed at the man. 1

A reporter recently asked a karate champion how she hap- 2

pened to choose her sport. "I tried running and I tried cycling. Then," she paused, "I tried karate. And I discovered how good it felt to hit someone."

The author contrasts the reactive definition—what the word "violence" suggests to American women—with an academic discovery that violence has become socially acceptable, circumstantially, as a form of communication.

When most American women hear the word "violence," they think of criminals armed with knives or guns, or tragic tales of cruelty, psychiatric troubles, alcohol and drug use that lead to headline-making cases of wife or child abuse. But those who study America's social landscape also recognize a more hidden—perhaps even more frightening—side: the emergence of violence as a socially acceptable means of communication, a way of grabbing, or holding on to, power, a way of speaking up for oneself. 3

The paragraph moves from a lexical definition of *violence* to a socially realistic modification of that definition, which includes general examples drawn from life.

In its narrowest sense, violence is defined as an act carried out with the intention of causing physical pain or injury to another. But in real life, severe physical violence is only one extreme of a whole spectrum of aggressive behavior that ranges from "verbal violence"—screaming, shouting, saying vicious, spiteful things—to banging one's fist on the table and slamming doors to actually pushing, hitting, kicking, throwing things at or beating another person. 4

The main topic is introduced in paragraph 5, following the anecdotes and their appropriate definitions, which, combined, form a "hook" introduction, designed to engage readers by piquing their interest.

Wherever one looks—in newspapers, on television, in social- and psychological-science journals—there is evidence that America in the late 1980s is a decidedly aggressive society. What's also showing up in the statistics, but is missing from the headlines: Women, contrary to most of our wishes and stereotypes, may not only be as aggressive as men, they may also, in certain situations, be just as violent. And this violence cuts across barriers of education, race and economic class. 5

The Urge Toward Anger

Paragraph 4 defines *violence* lexically; paragraph 6 defines it as "levels of violence," drawing attention to responsive violence, particularly in human beings, while showing that society has hitherto denied women the reasons for responsive violence.

At the most basic level, violence is an effort to subdue another person, the most extreme sort of control. In the animal kingdom, there is rarely, if ever, random violence; when violence does occur, it's generally in response to a threat, actual or implied, to an animal's family or home. Among people, aggressive impulses also arise in response to threats—to one's power, position, to the possibility that someone else may not follow orders. Women, 6 traditionally, have been thought of as the less aggressive (even nonaggressive) sex. They have also been out of the seats of power and been trained, in a male-dominated society, to deny, rather than express, anger.

An important reason that encourages women to contain the anger that leads to violence is cultural, as shown by psychological studies in the home, where parents, mostly fathers, tell daughters that anger is "not nice."

"Young girls are given the message, incredibly early in life, that it's 'not nice' to get angry," says Jay Lefer, M.D., associate professor of psychiatry at New York Medical College. "Studies in which tape recorders were put in families' homes revealed that as soon as a little girl sounded angry, her parents—and most often the father—would tell her to stop. Ironically, anger that is not expressed, that's bottled up, may be most dangerous, to oneself and to society." 7

Traditional, male-dominated psychology takes one stance; modern psychology accepts other, more inclusive, possibilities, including a girl's accepting the kind of denial that causes her to have profoundly severe psychological difficulties. "alexithymic": From "alexithymia," the inability to verbalize feelings.

Traditional psychological theory has it that men hit out in anger, women hit in. Depression, or melancholia as Freud called it, is thus thought to be the inward turning of aggression—and, again not coincidentally, is also thought to be primarily a woman's problem. Modern psychoanalysts, while acknowledging that some depressed patients do have a great deal of anger, see other possibilities. "A young girl who is taught to deny her feelings, who takes this lesson to heart, can eventually become so good at denial that she becomes alexithymic—which means not being able to put words to one's feelings, to a point at which one stops feeling," says Dr. Lefer. "This is the type of person who can say 'I'm furious' without the slightest hint of heat—or fury—in her voice." 8

In psychoanalytical theory, especially Freudian theory, *suppression* means pushing down painful memories so that they are not available in consciousness. Psychiatrists believe, however, that these memories may persist in some form in the unconscious, occasionally creating psychological havoc.

Suppressing one's emotions, most of us are taught, is the "civilized" way to behave. Expressions such as "keeping a stiff upper lip" or "keeping one's cool" epitomize polite society. But human beings are a passionate species. And in the case of an emotion like anger, suppression may only intensify a feeling. Many mental-health experts believe that a significant amount of violence erupts from pent-up hostility, from anger so tightly bound up that it intensifies to a point at which it bursts out, literally beyond control. 9

A definitive connection links the inability to master a situation and the onset of violent behavior.

"Anger may be the starting point for violence," says Dr. Lefer, "but true physical violence is usually an expression of anger at a much deeper level, of a truly helpless kind of rage. That point at which a person feels helpless is usually when violence occurs— 10 when there's a sense of no longer being able to master a situation. Just about everyone has fantasies of violence—of punching out the guy at the motor vehicle bureau who sends you to the end of yet another line after a two-hour wait, or of hurling your briefcase at the ninth person who tells you 'It's not my job'—but we normally don't act on these fantasies. The norms of civilized behavior just don't allow it."

Verbal Violence: Women as Expert?

The norms of proper behavior do allow women to express 11
their feelings in words—and the angry barb, the rapier-sharp put-down have long been considered women's special province. It also sheds light on how much of what we assume to be natural differences between the sexes often starts with society's molding and controlling of our impulses.

"Most human behavior results from a combination of biolog- 12
ical and societal factors," explains Estelle Ramey, M.D., who is professor emeritus of physiology at Georgetown University School of Medicine in Washington, D.C. "In a historical sense, women, being smaller in structure and musculature than the male of the species, would be more vulnerable to retaliation after physical expressions of anger. So it would be more to a woman's advantage to choose verbal weaponry, an area in which she would safely be on equal footing with a man, over physical force.

"Women have become, in one sense, masters of verbal vio- 13
lence. It's no accident that women are often portrayed in literature as nagging, whining or screaming, or that the expression 'sharp-tongued' is usually applied to a female."

What of the much-touted "testosterone factor" in male aggres- 14
sion? Biological determinism, in this case, has been given far too much credence, argues Dr. Ramey. "It is true that testosterone, when given in abnormally high amounts, can induce aggressive behavior," she says. "A normal, healthy man, though, is not a victim of his hormones, any more than a woman is. Males and females, in fact, both respond to physical threats in the same way, with the release of adrenaline, corticosteroids and other stress

Notice that the author moves from Lefer's "norms of *civilized* behavior" to her own "norms of *proper* behavior," thereafter introducing the notion of society's control over women's behavior.

Structurally and muscularly smaller than most men, most women vent their anger verbally instead of physically. Verbally, women and men are more evenly matched.

Estelle Ramey offers the historical reason that women are often portrayed in literature as being more verbal than physical.

Sims, with the expert's aid, dispenses with the argument that men are more physically violent just because of testosterone.

"corticosteroids": Hormonal steroids, including the sex hormones, of the adrenal cortex.

hormones. While it's true that a woman's hormonal system may need a slightly greater stimulus to elicit the same biochemical level of response, as a practical matter this isn't a big difference. The vast majority of men in civilized cultures don't use physical violence—and women, on the other hand, can be trained to be incredibly ruthless soldiers. The biggest differences come in what boys and girls are taught: Women are sometimes so socialized not to express negative emotions that they are even afraid to hit back when faced with someone else instigating violence."

Sims preserves her definition by strengthening her argument that how girls are taught, their "socialization," determines their responses to violence.

This socialization is confirmed by ground-breaking research   15
into aggressive behavior. In an exhaustive review of fifty psychological studies conducted during the past twenty years, researchers Alice H. Eagly, Ph.D., and Valerie Steffen, Ph.D., concluded that the biggest deterrent to physical aggression for a woman was her concern about the consequences of her actions.

"Research supports the conclusion that women worried about   16
the harm they could cause another person, the guilt or anxiety they would feel themselves, or the danger they would put themselves in by their actions. Interestingly, the studies that conclude that males are much more aggressive than females really apply primarily to children; by the time we're adults, the differences are smaller," notes Dr. Eagly, who is professor of psychology at Purdue University in Indiana.

Mention how the studies confirm that as we mature, we modify our behavior socially.

Power and Physicality

Our views are shaped by our behavior, as that behavior is endorsed by society.

The social roles ascribed to men—the military, sports, the   17
competition of the business world—as well as the superior status of men over women may all help to explain the positive way most men view aggressive behavior. These are spheres, Drs. Eagly and Steffen note, in which the "masculine values" of strength and controlled aggression are especially valued.

These are also spheres into which women have made highly   18
visible, much publicized and encouraged moves within the last two decades. While in the past, women's traditional roles—homemaker, mother, wife—emphasized nurturance and passivity, feminists have put a high value on assertiveness and on challenging

the long-held view of women as "the weaker sex." Adopting masculine roles, sociologists have observed, also has meant for many women endorsing masculine values. "This is a highly charged topic, politically," acknowledges Jackie Macaulay, Ph.D., a former researcher at the University of Wisconsin in Madison who is now a lawyer. "There is just no scientific evidence that women are innately more peaceful than men. If women's nonviolence is a learned behavior, then we have to recognize the possibility that, as we change that learning, we may change women's behavior in ways that aren't all for the better. That's a message feminists don't want to hear."

When socially acceptable learning is changed, behavior is changed in ways that may not have been predicted.

It's also a message that is showing up in subtle and not so 19 subtle ways every day. As women have sought power in the workplace, in relationships and in society at large, they have also sought to claim physical power through fitness and sports. Women in exercise classes, says one observer, rarely seem happier than when doing the punching movements in aerobic dance routines. Fitness marketers seem to have noticed; they're appealing to women with a much more hard-edged approach. In an ad for Nike shoes, triathlete Joanne Ernst talks as tough as the guys: "Just do it," she snaps, staring down her audience.

Recent, socially acceptable learning is reflected in advertising. See also the Virginia Slims cigarette advertisements in magazines, with its slogan directed toward women: "You've come a long way, Baby."

Female wrestlers are now featured weekly on TV, while *People* 20 magazine trumpets the fact that the motorcycle magazine *Harley Women* now has nine thousand female readers. Even radio psychotherapists, normally empathetic, are said to be getting meaner—in a *New York Times* column, West Coast writer Anne Taylor Fleming says they now deliver "karate chops to the soul . . . over the airwaves."

These examples reinforce Sims's exploratory remarks on how changing social attitude will change social behavior.

And women are delivering more than figurative karate chops. 21 Enrollment in martial-arts classes is way up among women all across the country, as are the numbers of women taking boxing classes at once-all-male bastions like Gleason's Gym in New York City. While self-defense is a motive for some, many more are there for the physical challenge. In 1983, when dancer/choreographer Twyla Tharp took lessons at Gleason's in preparation for the ballet *Fait Accompli*, she was an anomaly; today, Gleason's has nearly two hundred women regularly jabbing and feinting and "working out on the bags"—up from two women regulars just five years ago.

More than 100 years ago, Susan B. Anthony said, in a women's suffrage newspaper, "Make [your employers] understand that you are in their service as workers, not as women" (*The Revolution,* October 8, 1868).

Few people would argue that gaining a sense of power in 22 oneself—physically as well as emotionally—isn't a good thing. Or that women's testing themselves against male standards hasn't led to very real benefits for society as a whole. But there may be a fine line between relishing physical power and using it for not so positive ends—and it's a line that, the latest studies suggest, many women in America may be dangerously close to crossing. Recent statistics, for example, suggest that twelve million women in the U.S. own guns—a number that increased 50 percent in the last decade. Even more disturbingly, at a time when the study of family violence is shattering many of our illusions about the sanctity of our homes, research is revealing that on the home front, women's physical aggressiveness may not be the rarity it's assumed to be.

Love and Violence

As used here, *violence* has two meanings: First, it refers to physical force used to injure, damage, or destroy. Second, it refers to unjust or callous use of force or power, as in violating another's rights or sensibilities.

The popular notion of violence is something that happens 23 "out there"—a random shooting in the street, an explosion from afar—but the reality is that "all intimate relationships have a higher propensity to violence than do encounters among strangers or even acquaintances. The sad fact is that the family is the most violent social institution, with the single exception of the army in times of war," says Murray A. Straus, Ph.D., professor of sociology and director, Family Research Laboratory, University of New Hampshire.

Perhaps the most controversial finding of all, says Dr. Straus, 24 is that when it comes to violence against one's spouse, women participate in equal numbers to men. And while three fourths of the violence committed by women against their husbands is in acts of self-defense, one fourth is not. And it is that one fourth that Dr. Straus finds especially worrisome: "It's important to understand that men's greater size and strength means that a man's punch will usually produce more injury and pain than a woman's.

But that doesn't mean that violence by women should be hidden or overlooked. It is part of the hidden violence of American family life."

One reason the data on women's violence hasn't been publicized: fears of misinterpretation of the facts. In 1976, when Dr. Straus announced the results of the first National Survey on Family Violence, the statistics on women's aggression toward their husbands were seized by antifeminist groups in efforts to argue against the need for shelters for battered women. Their claims were that if women were violent, then they didn't need protection against men's violence. Other reports raised false alarms via greatly inflated estimates of the number of battered husbands. In 1985, when the survey was repeated, the number of women aggressors within couples actually increased slightly. But there was no rush to publicize the finding. Experts hesitated to discuss the statistics lest they be used against women.   25

In the last ten years, however, a growing number of studies have come to the same conclusion: An average of one third of unmarried men and women—whether dating, engaged or living together—have been involved in physical aggression with the opposite sex. In studies of couples living together before marriage, Patricia A. Gwaitney-Gibbs, Ph.D., associate professor of sociology at the University of Oregon, found that women were even slightly more likely than men to have thrown something, pushed, grabbed, shoved, slapped, kicked, beaten or punched their living-together partners. "Only in the truly severe areas of assault—beating up, threatening with a knife or gun or actually using a knife or gun—were the men more likely to have inflicted these acts on women," said Dr. Gwaitney-Gibbs.   26

These conclusions are echoed by other researchers. When psychologist K. Daniel O'Leary, Ph.D., of the State University of New York at Stony Brook, and his colleagues studied over two hundred fifty couples during their engagement periods and the first two years of marriage, they found that 44 percent of the women and 31 percent of the men reported pushing, slapping or shoving their partner at least once during the year before   27

Unfortunately, socially derived facts can be used politically, to "prove" whatever a clever manipulator of the language wants to prove.

Notice that Sims carefully includes the results of studies and remarks by specialists. She does not simply make statements about aggression; she lets the experts do that.

These comments deal with *perception,* sensory experience that has meaning or significance. Because of learning, one understands relationships among objects. When learning includes aggression or violence, then aggression or violence is perceived as part of a relationship.

G. H. Mead at the University of Chicago early in this century devised a theory linking society, the development of personality, and communication. Mead's statement is famous: To be able to communicate is to be able to "take the role of the other" toward one's own vocalizations and behavior. Nowadays, some people find it possible to take the role of the other, when the other is a fictitious character in film or on television.

marriage—and that, eighteen months later, the number who pushed, slapped or shoved their spouses were still "at a rate that warrants very serious concern."

"In contrast to cases of serious physical abuse, in which the aim is to truly inflict hurt," says Dr. O'Leary, "much of this violence is seen almost as a means of communication. These couples seem to view physical aggression as a permissible means of expression—a fact our society needs to be very concerned about."   28

In fact, that acceptance of aggressive behavior in general may be the real cause for concern, say experts in the field. While it is true that couples who are younger, poorer and have less education do seem to experience more violence as a group than those who are older, wealthier and more educated, violent relationships exist at all levels of society. It is the observation of violence as a child—along with social class, educational background and being a victim of violence oneself—that is the strongest predictor of becoming a violent adult, claim Dr. Straus and his coauthor, Richard J. Gelles, Ph.D., professor of anthropology and sociology at the University of Rhode Island, in their new book, *Intimate Violence.* The learning experience of being physically punished is most significant, they note, but seeing your mother and father strike one another also teaches a child three lessons: that those we love are those who hit us or are people we can hit; that it is morally right to hit those we love; and that if other means of getting one's way, dealing with stress or expressing oneself don't work, violence is permissible.   29

Thresholds of Aggression

The actions on television shows can be seen as condoning societally centered activities that in fact were not all condoned before those actions were presented on television to a broad spectrum of the population.

This sanctioning of violence can go on not only within the family but in society as well. And for women especially, there seems to have been an explosion of hyperaggressive role models in the seventies and eighties. "On television and in the movies, women certainly seem to be hitting out more," says New York City psychologist Loretta Walder, Ph.D. "In fifties shows like *The Honeymooners,* when Ralph got angry, he yelled, 'Bam! Zoom!' but what did Alice do? She just stood there with her hands on her   30 hips and said 'Ralph.' In the seventies, we started seeing women in gun-toting cop roles, as in *Police Woman* or *Charlie's Angels,* but the level of violence and danger was nothing like the eighties' *Cagney & Lacey.* There are also other messages now, as in *Moonlighting.* Maddie slams her door, David slams his—the door-slamming is one of the show's trademarks, and Maddie and David's means of communication. In the movie *Fatal Attraction,* a clearly psychotic woman tries to kill her lover and the entire American population seemingly can't get enough of the story."

While most experts emphasize that there is no proof that the portrayal or even glorification of violence in the media can actually incite similar actions in the public, many experts do worry that, as with the observation of violence in the family, it can raise a person's "comfort-zone" of physical aggression. 31

Seeing Sigourney Weaver wield a flame-thrower in *Aliens* can't make a woman run out of the movie theater and do something violent. "Human beings are clearly more intelligent than that. But it does add to society's message that violence is appropriate," says Jan Stets, Ph.D., assistant professor of sociology, Washington State University. "There is an attitude toward violence that's built up over time, out of observation and experience, that can increase a person's chances of using violent behavior in a moment of heightened emotion. Just as social learning goes on from one generation to the next within a family, there are messages that are passed on within a culture as well." In some studies, for example, dating couples who were verbally abusive toward each other were more likely to become physically aggressive later on; it was as if their threshold of aggression shifted upward. 32

This paragraph opens with a conditional clause, an "if" clause, indicating that all the facts remain to be sifted and examined.

Sims draws a possible parallel, however: That which has been shown in research into violence done by men may also be shown in research into violence done by women. As used in this paragraph, *vulnerable* means being affected by a specified influence, in this case that of irrationality.

If, in fact, women are being given the message by society that they need to be more and more assertive, to seize control, to be in charge, our society needs to examine where that will take us. Research into violence by men reinforces the notion of physical aggression as a means of control, of getting the other person to do what they wouldn't otherwise do. It also confirms that the most egalitarian of relationships—in society and within a family—are also the least violent. It shouldn't come as a total surprise, then, that women struggling with unresolved issues of intimate 33 relationships and control may be most vulnerable to the powerful and often irrational emotions that can so quickly make verbal violence turn physical.

Meaning and Purpose

1. Seeing a word can cause you to picture elements of its definition. What elements in its definition do you think of when you see the word "violence"?
2. Sims says in paragraph 5 that "Wherever one looks . . . there is evidence that America in the late 1980s is a decidedly aggressive society." In your opinion, what is one current piece of evidence that shows America is a decidedly aggressive society, so far, in the 1990s?
3. What does Sims mean by "seats of power," in paragraph 6?
4. Why have women become, in one sense, "masters of verbal violence"?
5. In your own words, define "concern about the consequences of her actions," in paragraph 15, *based on the comments* in paragraph 16.

Strategy

1. What kind of definition of violence does Sims give in paragraph 4? Why?
2. How does Sims structure her definition of violence, and why? What aspects of the meaning of the word does she include in her definition?
3. In your opinion, what are the differences in the definitions of the expression "civilized behavior," in paragraph 10, and the expression "proper behavior," in paragraph 11?
4. Several examples are included in paragraphs 20 and 21. What do these examples help the author illustrate?

3. "Civilized behavior" is behavior that keeps people living together in relative harmony and that most people in a society understand tacitly. "Proper behavior" is temporary behavior that is fitting, seeming, or right for the occasion.
4. These examples help the author to illustrate how women have become more assertive physically and emotionally by gaining a sense of strength.

Style

1. The journalistic anecdotes in the first two paragraphs are specific and interesting stories that grab readers' attention and ease them into the topic.
2. Sims has obviously done research on her subject. Her tone is academic and factual, and she quotes numerous authorities—as in paragraph 12—to back her assertions.
3. The pronoun *it* refers to "the portrayal or even glorification of violence in the media," earlier in the paragraph.

Style

1. Why do you think Sims begins her essay with two journalistic anecdotes?
2. What gives Sims authority to talk about women and violence? Where do you see this authority in the essay?
3. In paragraph 31, Sims says, "it can raise a person's 'comfort zone' of physical aggression." What does the pronoun *it* refer to in that clause?

Writing Tasks

1. A "working definition" is one that defines a word or a phrase simply, for a specific occasion. Your car may have an "automatic drive," which is the "working definition" for a torque-conversion unit that converts and transfers power from the engine to the drive wheels.
   Select a recent issue of a newsmagazine such as *Time, Newsweek, Insight, U.S. News & World Report,* or *The Economist.* Leaf through the issue, listing all references to violence. Then write a "working definition" of the word *violence,* followed by examples of violence from the newsmagazine that illustrate your definition.
2. Based on the readings in this chapter, write a short essay in which you define a "definition essay." Use the readings as examples, and organize your essay according to what you see as the range of elements in a definition essay.

This essay confronts the current air of discontent that is so pervasive in America life. Many are expressing dissatisfaction with the political parties and with the direction the country is moving. Some are taking politics to the streets instead of the voting booths, and we read of protests, hate crimes, and confrontations full of invective and sometimes violence. Undoubtedly your students have feelings about at least some aspects of the current climate, and this essay may help them to articulate them as well as see them in a larger perspective. Many of Lapham's references to people and events will be unfamiliar to some students. It is hard to say how many of these references must be known in order to understand Lapham's point, but certainly some should be explained. Encourage students, as Lapham does, to be candid in expressing their opinions and emotions. Ask them if they agree with Lapham that honest expression is the first step toward solving these problems. Some may fear that honesty will only fuel the flames. Which position is more in keeping with traditional American values?

Since there is no one definition of "American" in the essay, have your students locate the bits and pieces of a definition that Lapham offers. Can these bits and pieces be put together in one coherent, inclusive statement? With some rewording, we think they can be and encourage you to have your students write a definition based on Lapham's statements in each section.

MARGINAL NOTES

Sir V(ictor) S(awdom) Pritchett (born 1900). British journalist, critic, biographer, and short story writer.

Paragraphs 1–3 describe what to Lapham is a disturbing current social and political attitude: The nation has become divided into social, racial, and ethnic factions.

❦ Lewis H. Lapham ❦

Born in San Francisco in 1935, Lewis Lapham was educated at Yale University and at Cambridge University in England. He has had a long career as a journalist, starting as a reporter for the San Francisco Examiner. *He has also been a reporter for the* New York Herald Tribune *and a writer for the* Saturday Evening Post *and* Life. *He is currently the editor of* Harper's Magazine.

Who and What Is American?

Lapham takes the unusual approach of letting his definition grow implicitly out of a discussion of "false constructions of the American purpose and identity" used by groups and individuals for political purposes. Using the 1992 presidential election as his backdrop, he charges that these false constructions provide those seeking office with much of their rhetoric and ends by urging us to reject these erroneous descriptions of who we are, to "speak plainly about our differences," and to "value what we have in common."

Lapham's essay is presented with great vigor, and it may be too easy to become caught up in the whirlpool of his examples and arguments. As you read his discussion of the false constructions, note the sentences in each section that most clearly present the contradictory view—these constitute his definition of "American."

There may not be an American character, but there is the emotion of being American. It has many resemblances to the emotion of being Russian—that feeling of nostalgia for some undetermined future when man will have improved himself beyond recognition and when all will be well.

—V. S. Pritchett

Were I to believe what I read in the papers, I would find it   1 easy to think that I no longer can identify myself simply as an American. The noun apparently means nothing unless it is dressed up with at least one modifying adjective. As a plain American I have neither voice nor authentic proofs of existence. I acquire a presence only as an old American, a female American, a white American, a rich American, a black American, a gay American, a poor American, a native American, a dead American. The subordination of the noun to the adjectives makes a mockery of both the American premise and the democratic spirit, but it serves the purposes of the politicians as well as the news media, and throughout the rest of this election year I expect the political campaigns to pitch their tents and slogans on the frontiers of race and class. For every benign us, the candidates will find a malignant them; for every neighboring we (no matter how eccentric or small in number), a distant and devouring they. The strategies of division sell newspapers and summon votes, and to the man who would be king (or president or governor) the popular hatred of government matters less than the atmosphere of resentment in which the people fear and distrust one another.

Democratic politics trades in only two markets—the market in expectation and the market in blame. A collapse in the former engenders a boom in the latter. Something goes wrong in the news—a bank swindle of genuinely spectacular size, a series of killings in Milwaukee, another disastrous assessment of the nation's schools—and suddenly the air is loud with questions about the paradox of the American character or the Puritan subtexts of the American soul. The questions arise from every quarter of the political compass—from English professors and political consultants as well as from actors, corporate vice presidents, and advertising salesmen—and the conversation is seldom polite. Too many of the people present no longer can pay the bills, and a stray remark about acid rain or a third-grade textbook can escalate within a matter of minutes into an exchange of insults. Somebody calls Jesse Helms a racist, and somebody else says that he is sick and tired of paying ransom money to a lot of welfare criminals. People drink too much and stay too late, their voices choked with anecdote and rage, their lexicons of historical reference so pas-

Jesse Helms: U.S. senator from North Carolina.

sionately confused that both Jefferson and Lincoln find themselves doing thirty-second commercials for racial quotas, a capital gains tax, and the Persian Gulf War.

The failures in the nation's economy have marked up the prices for obvious villains, and if I had a talent for merchandising I would go into the business of making dolls (black dolls, white dolls, red-necked dolls, feminist dolls, congressional dolls) that each of the candidates could distribute at fundraising events with a supply of color-coordinated pins. Trying out their invective in the pre-season campaigns, the politicians as early as last October were attributing the cause of all our sorrows to any faction, interest, or minority that could excite in its audiences the passions of a beloved prejudice. David Duke in Louisiana denounced the subsidized beggars (i.e., black people) who had robbed the state of its birthright. At a partisan theatrical staged by the Democratic Party in New Hampshire, Senator Tom Harkin reviled the conspiracy of Republican money. President Bush went to Houston, Texas, to point a trembling and petulant finger at the United States Congress. If the country's domestic affairs had been left to him, the President said, everybody would be as prosperous and smug as Senator Phil Gramm, but the liberals in Congress (blind as mollusks and selfish as eels) had wrecked the voyage of boundless opportunity.

The politicians follow the trends, and apparently they have been told by their handlers to practice the arts of the demagogue. Certainly I cannot remember an election year in which the political discourse—among newspaper editorialists and the single-issue lobbies as well as the candidates—relied so unashamedly on pitting rich against poor, black against white, male against female, city against suburb, young against old. Every public event in New York City—whether academic appointment, traffic delay, or homicide—lends itself to both a black and a white interpretation of the news. The arguments in the arenas of cultural opinion echo the same bitter refrain. The ceaseless quarrels about the canon of preferred texts (about Columbus the Bad and Columbus the Good, about the chosen company of the politically correct, about the ice people and the sun people) pick at the scab of the same

3

4

Specific examples to illustrate how political candidates play the politics of blame.

David Duke: Former Grand Wizard of the Ku Klux Klan, a defeated candidate for governor of Louisiana and briefly a candidate for U. S. president in 1992.

Tom Harkin: U.S. senator from Iowa.

Phil Gramm: U.S. senator from Texas.

"politically correct": a popular, but also much derided term for having the proper (acceptable) views (usually liberal) on social and political matters.

According to Leonard Jeffries, a college professor in New York City, Africans are people of the sun and Europeans are people of the ice.

The rhetorical question moves the essay toward definition. If this question is answered, a definition will emerge.

Lapham offers a possible reason for this distrust of each other: With the end of the Cold War, we may be searching for new enemies.

Another rhetorical question further leads the readers' expectation toward a coming definition.

Paragraph 7 answers the previous question in a general way and introduces the idea of "false assumptions." Lapham will argue that, in fact, the opposite of these assumptions is what defines an American.

questions. Who and what is an American? How and where do we find an identity that is something other than a fright mask? When using the collective national pronoun ("we the people" "we happy few," etc.) whom do we invite into the club of the we?

Maybe the confusion is a corollary to the end of the Cold War. The image of the Soviet Union as monolithic evil held in place the image of the United States as monolithic virtue. Break the circuit of energy transferred between negative and positive poles, and the two empires dissolve into the waving of sectional or nationalist flags. Lacking the reassurance of a foreign demon, we search our own neighborhoods for fiends of convincing malevolence and size.

The search is a boon for the bearers of false witness and the builders of prisons. Because it's so easy to dwell on our differences, even a child of nine can write a Sunday newspaper sermon about the centrifugal forces that drive the society apart. The more difficult and urgent questions have to do with the centripetal forces that bind us together. What traits of character or temperament do we hold in common? Why is it that I can meet a black man in a street or a Hispanic woman on a train and imagine that he and I, or she and I, share an allied hope and a joint purpose? That last question is as American as it is rhetorical, and a Belgian would think it the work of a dreaming imbecile.

What we share is a unified field of emotion, but if we mistake the sources of our energy and courage (i.e., if we think that our uniqueness as Americans rests with the adjectives instead of the noun) then we can be rounded up in categories and sold the slogan of the week for the fear of the month. Political campaigns deal in the commodity of votes, and from now until November I expect that all of them will divide the American promise into its lesser but more marketable properties. For reasons of their own convenience, the sponsors of political campaigns (Democratic, environmental, racial, Republican, sexual, or military-industrial) promote more or less the same false constructions of the American purpose and identity. As follows:

That the American achieves visible and specific meaning

5

6

7

8

only by reason of his or her association with the political guilds of race, gender, age, ancestry, or social class.

Cole Porter (1891–1964). American composer of popular music, notably "Night and Day" and "Begin the Beguine."

Lapham's discussion of the first assumption begins with a further, more specific, explanation of the assumption followed by a more lengthy denial of its validity.

This is a technique frequently used in argument papers: Present your opponent's view and then refute it. (See Persuasion and Argument, pp. 545–562.) Lapham will follow this general pattern for each assumption. Each discussion is rich in brief examples.

"divine right of kings": the medieval idea that kings rule by the anointment of God and therefore command unquestioning obedience from their subjects. In England, divine right was brought to an end by the Glorious Revolution in 1688.

John Quincy Adams (1767–1848). Sixth U.S. president; son of the second president, John Adams. Elected to Congress after one term as president, he strongly promoted antislavery views.

John Charles Fremont (1813–1890). American explorer and politician. An antislavery candidate for President in 1856.

The assumption is as elitist as the view that only a woman endowed with an income of $1 million a year can truly appreciate the beauty of money and the music of Cole Porter. Comparable theories of grace encourage the belief that only black people can know or teach black history, that no white man can play jazz piano, that blonds have a better time, and that Jews can't play basketball.   9

America was founded on precisely the opposite premise. We were always about becoming, not being; about the prospects for the future, not about the inheritance of the past. The man who rests his case on his color, like the woman who defines herself as a bright cloud of sensibility beyond the understanding of merely mortal men, makes a claim to special privilege not unlike the divine right of kings. The pretensions might buttress the cathedrals of our self-esteem, but they run counter to the lessons of our history.   10

We are a nation of parvenus, all bound to the hopes of tomorrow, or next week, or next year. John Quincy Adams put it plainly in a letter to a German correspondent in the 1820s who had written on behalf of several prospective émigrés to ask about the requirements for their success in the New World. "They must cast off the European skin, never to resume it," Adams said. "They must look forward to their posterity rather than backward to their ancestors."   11

We were always a mixed and piebald company, even on the seventeenth-century colonial seaboard, and we accepted our racial or cultural differences as the odds that we were obliged to overcome or correct. When John Charles Frémont (a.k.a. The Pathfinder) first descended into California from the East in 1843, he remarked on the polyglot character of the expedition accompanying him south into the San Joaquin Valley: 12

"Our cavalcade made a strange and grotesque appearance, and it was impossible to avoid reflecting upon our position and composition in this remote solitude . . . still forced on south by   13

The Chinook Indians lived on the northern shore of the Columbia River in the northwestern United States.

Daniel Boorstin (born 1914). An historian noted for his trilogy, *The Americans* (1965, 1968, 1973), *A History of the United States* (1980), and *The Discoverers* (1983). He served as librarian of Congress from 1975 to 1987.

a desert on one hand a mountain range on the other; guided by a civilized Indian, attended by two wild ones from the Sierra; a Chinook from the Columbia; and our own mixture of American, French, German—all armed; four or five languages heard at once; above a hundred horses and mules, half-wild; American, Spanish and Indian dresses and equipments intermingled—such was our composition."

The theme of metamorphosis recurs throughout the whole chronicle of American biography. Men and women start out in one place and end up in another, never quite knowing how they got there, perpetually expecting the unexpected, drifting across the ocean or the plains until they lodge against a marriage, a land deal, a public office, or a jail. Speaking to the improvised character of the American experience, Daniel Boorstin, the historian and former Librarian of Congress, also summed up the case against the arithmetic of the political pollsters' zip codes: "No prudent man dared to be too certain of exactly who he was or what he was about; everyone had to be prepared to become someone else. To be ready for such perilous transmigrations was to become an American." 14

That the American people aspire to become more nearly alike. 15

The hope is that of the ad salesman and the prison warden, but it has become depressingly familiar among the managers of political campaigns. Apparently they think that no matter how different the native songs and dances in different parts of the country, all the tribes and factions want the same beads, the same trinkets, the same prizes. As I listen to operatives from Washington talk about their prospects in the Iowa or New Hampshire primary, I understand that they have in mind the figure of a perfect or ideal American whom everybody in the country would wish to resemble if only everybody could afford to dress like the dummies in the windows of Bloomingdale's or Saks Fifth Avenue. The public opinion polls frame questions in the alphabet of name recognitions and standard brands. The simplicity of the results supports 16 the belief that the American citizen or the American family can be construed as a product, and that with only a little more time and little more money for research and development all of us will conform to the preferred images seen in a commercial for Miller beer.

The apologists for the theory of the uniform American success 17 sometimes present the example of Abraham Lincoln, and as I listen to their sentimental after-dinner speeches about the poor country grown to greatness, I often wonder what they would say if they had met the man instead of the statute. Throughout most of his life Lincoln displayed the character of a man destined for failure—a man who drank too much and told too many jokes (most of them in bad taste), who was habitually late for meetings and always borrowing money, who never seized a business opportunity and missed his own wedding.

The spirit of liberty is never far from anarchy, and the ur- 18 American is apt to look a good deal more like one of the contestants on *Let's Make a Deal* (i.e., somebody dressed like Madonna, or Wyatt Earp, or a giant iguana) than any of the yachtsmen standing around on the dock at Kennebunkport. If America is about nothing else, it is about the invention of the self. Because we have little use for history, and because we refuse the comforts of a society established on the blueprint of class privilege, we find ourselves set adrift at birth in an existential void, inheriting nothing except the obligation to construct a plausible self, to build a raft of identity on which (with a few grains of luck and a cheap bank loan) maybe we can float south to Memphis or the imaginary islands of the blessed. We set ourselves the tasks of making and remaking our destinies with whatever lumber we happen to find lying around on the banks of the Snake or Pecos River.

Who else is the American hero if not a wandering pilgrim 19 who goes forth on a perpetual quest? Melville sent Ahab across the world's oceans in search of a fabulous beast; and Thoreau followed the unicorn of his conscience into the silence of the Maine woods. Between them they marked out the trail of American literature as well as the lines of speculation in American real estate. To a greater or a lesser extent, we are all confidence men, actors

Wyatt Berry Stapp Earp (1848–1929). A U.S. frontiersman, gunfighter, and law officer.

Herman Melville (1819–1891). One of America's greatest writers, his best known work is *Moby-Dick,* in which the captain of the whaling ship *Pequod,* the obsessed Ahab, pursues the great white whale.

Henry David Thoreau (1817–1862): American writer. A strong individualist, a fact reflected in his best known works, *On the Duty of Civil Disobedience* (1849) and *Walden* (1854).

playing the characters of our own invention and hoping that the audience—fortunately consisting of impostors as fanciful or synthetic as ourselves—will accept the performance at par value and suspend the judgments or ridicule.

The settled peoples of the earth seldom recognize the American as both a chronic revolutionary and a born pilgrim. The American is always on the way to someplace else (i.e., toward some undetermined future in which all will be well), and when he meets a stranger on the road he begins at once to recite the summary of the story so far—his youth and early sorrows, the sequence of his exits and entrances, his last divorce and his next marriage, the point of his financial departure and the estimated time of his spiritual arrival, the bad news noted and accounted for, the good news still to come. Invariably it is a pilgrim's tale, and the narrator, being American, assumes that he is addressing a fellow pilgrim. He means to exchange notes and compare maps. His newfound companion might be bound toward a completely different dream of Eden (a boat marina in Naples, Florida, instead of a garden in Vermont; a career as a Broadway dancer as opposed to the vice presidency of the Wells Fargo bank), but the destination doesn't matter as much as the common hope of coming safely home to the land of the heart's desire. For the time being, and until something better turns up, we find ourselves embarked on the same voyage, gazing west into the same blue distance. 20

> That the American people share a common code of moral behavior and subscribe to identical theories of the true, the good, and the beautiful 21

Senator Jesse Helms would like to think so, and so would the enforcers of ideological discipline on the vocabulary of the doctrinaire left. The country swarms with people making rules about what we can say or read or study or smoke, and they imagine that we should be grateful for the moral guidelines (market-tested and government-inspected) imposed (for our own good) by a centralized bureau of temporal health and spiritual safety. The would-be reformers of the national character confuse the 22

American sense of equality with the rule of conformity that governs a police state. It isn't that we believe that every American is as perceptive or as accomplished as any other, but we insist on the preservation of a decent and mutual respect across the lines of age, race, gender, and social class. No citizen is allowed to use another citizen as if he or she were a means to an end; no master can treat his servant as if he or she were only a servant; no government can deal with the governed as if they were nothing more than a mob of votes. The American loathing for the arrogant or self-important man follows from the belief that all present have bet their fortunes (some of them bigger than others, and some of them counterfeit or stolen) on the same hypothesis.

An existential premise assumes a self-determining individual accepting full responsibility for his own choices.

The American premise is an existential one, and our moral code is political, its object being to allow for the widest horizons of sight and the broadest range of expression. We protect the other person's liberty in the interest of protecting our own, and our virtues conform to the terms and conditions of an arduous and speculative journey. If we look into even so coarse a mirror as the one held up to us by the situation comedies on prime-time television, we see that we value the companionable virtues—helpfulness, forgiveness, kindliness, and, above all, tolerance. 23

Madame Bovary and Mr. Pickwick: characters in two novels, *Madame Bovary* (1856) by the French novelist Gustave Flaubert and *Pickwick Papers* (serialized 1836–1837) by the English novelist Charles Dickens.

The passenger standing next to me at the rail might be balancing a parrot on his head, but that doesn't mean that he has invented a theory of the self any less implausible than the one I ordered from a department-store catalogue or assembled with the tag lines of a two-year college course on the great books of Western civilization. If the traveler at the port rail can balance a parrot on his head, then I can continue my discussion with Madame Bovary and Mr. Pickwick, and the two gentlemen standing aft of the rum barrels can get on with the business of rigging the price of rifles or barbed wire. The American equation rests on the habit of holding our fellow citizens in thoughtful regard not because they are exceptional (or famous, or beautiful, or rich) but simply because they are our fellow citizens. If we abandon the sense of mutual respect, we abandon the premise as well as the machinery of the American enterprise. 24

That the triumph of America corresponds to its prowess as a nation-state.   25

The pretension serves the purposes of the people who talk   26
about "the national security" and "the vital interest of the American
people" when what they mean is the power and privilege of
government. The oligarchy resident in Washington assumes that
all Americans own the same property instead of taking part in
the same idea, that we share a joint geopolitical program instead
of a common temperament and habit of mind. Even so faithful
a servant of the monied interests as Daniel Webster understood
the distinction: "The public happiness is to be the aggregate of
individuals. Our system begins with the individual man."

Daniel Webster (1792–1852). American orator
and statesman. He was secretary of state under
three presidents: William Henry Harrison, John
Tyler, and Millard Fillmore.

The Constitution was made for the uses of the individual (an   27
implement on the order of a plow, an ax, or a surveyor's plumb
line), and the institutions of American government were meant
to support the liberties of the people, not the ambitions of the
state. Given any ambiguity about the order of priority or precedence, it was the law that had to give way to the citizen's freedom
of thought and action, not the citizen's freedom of thought and
action that had to give way to the law. The Bill of Rights stresses
the distinction in the two final amendments, the ninth ("The
enumeration in the Constitution, of certain rights, shall not be
construed to deny or disparage others retained by the people")
and the tenth ("The powers not delegated to the United States
by the Constitution, nor prohibited by it to the States, are reserved
to the States, respectively, or to the people").

What joins the Americans one to another is not a common   28
nationality, language, race, or ancestry (all of which testify to the
burdens of the past) but rather their complicity in a shared work
of the imagination. My love of country follows from my love of
its freedoms, not from my pride in its fleets or its armies or its
gross national product. Construed as a means and not an end,
the Constitution stands as the premise for a narrative rather than
a plan for an invasion or a monument. The narrative was always
plural. Not one story but many stories.

That it is easy to be an American.   29

I can understand why the politicians like to pretend that   30
America is mostly about going shopping, but I never know why
anybody believes the ad copy. Grant the existential terms and
conditions of the American enterprise (i.e., that we are all bound
to invent ourselves), and the position is both solitary and probably
lost. I know a good many people who would rather be British or
Nigerian or Swiss.

Lately I've been reading the accounts of the nineteenth-cen-   31
tury adventurers and pioneers who traveled west from Missouri
under circumstances almost always adverse. Most of them didn't
find whatever it was they expected to find behind the next range
of mountains or around the next bend in the river. They were
looking for a garden in a country that was mostly desert, and the
record of their passage is largely one of sorrow and failure. Travelers making their way across the Great Plains in the 1850s reported great numbers of dead horses and abandoned wagons on
the trail, the echo of the hopes that so recently preceded them
lingering in an empty chair or in the scent of flowers on a new
grave.

Reading the diaries and letters, especially those of the women   32
in the caravans, I think of the would-be settlers lost in an immense
wilderness, looking into the mirrors of their loneliness and measuring their capacity for self-knowledge against the vastness of the
wide and indifferent sky.

Too often we forget the proofs of our courage. If we wish to   33
live in the state of freedom that allows us to make and think and
build, then we must accustom ourselves to the shadows on the
walls and the wind in trees. The climate of anxiety is the cost of
doing business. Just as a monarchy places far fewer burdens on
its subjects than a democracy places on its citizens, so also bigotry
is easier than tolerance. When something goes wrong with the
currency or the schools, it's always comforting to know that the
faults can be easily found in something as obvious as a color, or
a number, or the sound of a strange language. The multiple
adjectives qualifying the American noun enrich the vocabulary of

In his concluding paragraphs, Lapham argues that a healthy candor in discussing our differences can come about only through recalling the shared values that hold us together and "our talent for assimilation."

James Fenimore Cooper (1789–1851). American novelist. *The American Democrat* (1838) is one of a series of essays Cooper wrote to criticize the behavior of Americans after returning from a seven-year stay in Europe.

blame, and if the election year continues as it has begun I expect that by next summer we will discover that it is not only middle-aged Protestant males who have been making a wreck of the culture but also (operating secretly and sometimes in disguise) adolescent, sallow, Buddhist females.

Among all the American political virtues, candor is probably   34
the one most necessary to the success of our mutual enterprise. Unless we try to tell each other the truth about what we know and think and see (i.e., the story so far as it appears to the travelers on the voyage out) we might as well amuse ourselves (for as long as somebody else allows us to do so) with fairy tales. The vitality of the American democracy always has rested on the capacity of its citizens to speak and think without cant. As long ago as 1838, addressing the topic of *The American Democrat,* James Fenimore Cooper argued that the word "American" was synonymous with the habit of telling the truth: "By candor we are not to understand trifling and uncalled for expositions of truth; but a sentiment that proves a conviction of the necessity of speaking truth, when speaking at all; a contempt for all designing evasions of our real opinions.

"In all the general concerns, the public has a right to be treated   35
with candor. Without this manly and truly republican quality . . . the institutions are converted into a stupendous fraud."

If we indulge ourselves with evasions and the pleasure of   36
telling lies, we speak to our fears and our weaknesses instead of to our courage and our strength. We can speak plainly about our differences only if we know and value what we hold in common. Like the weather and third-rate journalism, bigotry in all its declensions is likely to be with us for a long time (certainly as long as the next hundred years), but unless we can draw distinctions and make jokes about our racial or cultural baggage, the work of our shared imagination must vanish in the mist of lies. The lies might win elections (or sell newspapers and economic theories) but they bind us to the theaters of wish and dream. If I must like or admire a fellow citizen for his or her costume of modifying adjectives (because he or she is black or gay or rich), then I might as well believe that the lost continent of Atlantis will rise next

Atlantis is a legendary island said to have sunk beneath the sea over 10,000 years ago. The search continues.

summer from the sea and that the Japanese will continue to make the payments—now and forever, world without end—on all our mortgages and battleships.

Among all the nations of the earth, America is the one that   37
has come most triumphantly to terms with the mixtures of blood and caste, and maybe it is another of history's ironic jokes that we should wish to repudiate our talent for assimilation at precisely the moment in time when so many other nations in the world (in Africa and Western Europe as well as the Soviet Union) look to the promise of the American example. The jumble of confused or mistaken identities that was the story of nineteenth-century America has become the story of a late-twentieth-century world defined by a vast migration of peoples across seven continents and as many oceans. Why, then, do we lose confidence in ourselves and grow fearful of our mongrel freedoms?

The politician who would lift us to a more courageous un-   38
derstanding of ourselves might begin by saying that we are all, each and every one of us, as much at fault as anybody else, that no matter whom we blame for our troubles (whether George Bush, or Al Sharpton, or David Duke) or how pleasant the invective (racist, sexist, imperialist pig), we still have to rebuild our cities and revise our laws. We can do the work together, or we can stand around making strong statements about each other's clothes.

Rev. Al Sharpton is a black activist in New York City who served as an adviser to Tawana Brawley, who charged that she had been raped by a Dutchess County assistant district attorney and others.

The last sentence issues a challenge to do the hard work of cooperation instead of taking the easy path of blaming others.

POSSIBLE ANSWERS

Meaning and Purpose

1. Some sentences and phrases that express Lapham's counterassertions: *Group 1:* "We were always about becoming, not being; about the prospects for the future, not about the inheritance of the past" (10); "We are a nation of parvenus" (11); "We were always a mixed and piebald company" (12); "A theme of metamorphosis recurs throughout the whole chronicle of American biography" (14); *Group 2:* "If America is about nothing else, it is about the invention of the self" (18); "a chronic revolutionary

Meaning and Purpose

1. Lapham's definition of "American" emerges from his refutations of each of what he calls "false constructions of the American purpose and identity." In each of his refutations he makes counterassertions about what Americans or American ideals really are. Find one or more sentences in each of his four refutations that best express his counterassertions.

2. Using the ideas expressed in the sentences you selected for question 1, fashion a definition of "American" that you believe reflects Lapham's view. You may have to change some phrasing and

and a born pilgrim" (20); *Group 3:* [Americans] insist on . . . decent and mutual respect across the lines of age, race, gender, and social class" (22); "We protect the other person's liberty in the interests of protecting our own . . ." "we value . . . helpfulness, forgiveness, kindliness, and above all, tolerance" (23); [we] "take part in the same idea" and [share] "a common temperament and habit of mind" (26); "the institutions of American government were meant to support the liberties of the people, not the ambitions of the state" and "it was the law that had to give way to the citizen's freedom of thought and action . . ." (27); "My love of country follows from its love of freedom, not from my pride in its fleets or its armies or its gross national product" (28); *Group 4:* "The climate of anxiety is the cost of doing business" and "a democracy places [burdens] on its citizens" (33).

2. Each person's definition will be different. You may wish to have the students discuss them in small groups.

3. The sponsors of political campaigns (7).

4. Briefly: to be honest with each other, to recognize our differences and accept them, and to work together without underestimating the challenge of the task. (34–38).

5. He believes in the value and strength of the culturally diverse society but decries the idea of defining ourselves by the group(s) we belong to. Noting that "We were always about becoming," and that we have always been a "mixed and piebald company," he urges us to protect each other's liberty, tolerate our differences, and reflect on what we have in common. He rejects the politics of blame that divides us into factions.

Strategy

1. He begins each section with a further (negative) amplification of the false construction and then refutes it with a barrage of examples.

2. The description of the political climate in his introductory paragraphs is disheartening to say the least. Lapham is establishing such a discouraging view to prepare his readers for his analysis of where our politics have gone wrong.

3. The sheer numbers and the diversity of individuals and examples used become overwhelming, and therefore convincing.

combine some ideas. Try to cover as many of Lapham's ideas as possible.

3. In Lapham's view, who is responsible for promoting these false constructions?

4. What does Lapham suggest are the means of overcoming the effect of these "false constructions"?

5. What is Lapham's attitude toward a culturally diverse society?

Strategy

1. What structure does Lapham use to develop his counterarguments to each of the "false constructions"?

2. Lapham presents a lengthy introduction to the four assumptions he attacks. What is he establishing in these introductory paragraphs?

3. What does Lapham achieve by naming so many people and giving so many examples?

4. How successful is Lapham in defining *American* by refuting the assumptions instead of using a more straightforward technique?

Style

1. What does the term *ur-American* in paragraph 18 mean?

2. Explain the difference between "centrifugal forces" and "centripetal forces" in paragraph 6.

3. If necessary look up the following words in a dictionary: *petulant* (3); *demagogue* (4); *parvenus* (11); *piebald* (12); *candor, cant* (34).

Writing Tasks

1. Reread paragraphs 25–28 of Lapham's essay. Do you think Lapham's position here is patriotic or nonpatriotic? Explain your

4. Opinions will differ, but we think he has been reasonably successful. This approach allows him to discredit opposing views as he advances his own. Readers may not be left with a definitive statement about the term *American* but they will have a clear "feeling" for the word. Such a definition may be superior to a more straightforward definition, which may leave readers unmoved. Clearly, too, Lapham's purpose goes beyond definition into argument.

Style

1. *Ur* is a combining form meaning earliest or original. As used here, *ur-American* refers to the people who are closest to the original spirit of America.

2. *Centrifugal*: moving outward from the center; *centripetal*: directed toward the center.

3. *Petulant*: showing sudden irritation; *demagogue*: a political leader who arouses the prejudices of the people; *parvenus*: persons who have acquired new wealth or position in society without having developed the appropriate behavior or manners; *piebald*: Having mixed patches of black and white or other colors; *candor*: being open and sincere; *cant*: insincere or hypocritical speech.

answer in an essay that offers an extended definition of the word *patriotic* or *patriotism* and then measures Lapham's paragraphs against the definition.

2. Select a group that has perhaps been misjudged by others: athletes, feminists, gays, teachers, motorcycle riders, gang members, lawyers, politicians, and so on. Write an essay defining the group's values, beliefs, or behaviors using Lapham's approach of stating the misjudgments first, then refuting them.

Touching a Snake

Symbols are visible objects or actions that communicate significance beyond their literal meaning. For example, the American flag might stir our patriotic feelings. A superstitious person might grow anxious if he breaks a mirror, predicting a streak of bad luck for himself. The flag, breaking a mirror—each is a symbol.

Often symbols have conventional meanings; for example, a heart sent on St. Valentine's Day is an emblem of affection. A wedding ring is an emblem of eternal commitment to another person. A Christian cross is an emblem of devotion. Many objects or actions do not have conventional meanings, but create significance form their context. For example, imagine you observe the following scene. You see a woman in black standing next to a tombstone, which reads:

539

Harold Ross
1930–1993
May He Rest in Peace

Next to the woman, with their heads bowed, stand three young children. From a few yards away you watch the scene, believing that this is a widow and her children in mourning. After all, the grave, the tombstone, the black dress, the bowed heads all suggest this interpretation. But then the woman turns from the grave and you see her face. She's smiling, joyfully smiling. The children begin to skip and sing, "Who's afraid of the big bad wolf/the big bad wolf/the big bad wolf? Who's afraid. . . ." Suddenly the significance of this symbolic scene has changed. To what? Well, that's open to interpretation, which is characteristic of symbolic experience.

Frequently, a symbolic dimension is at work in photographs. Photographers carefully compose the elements of their images so we sense a symbolic dimension in a photograph. "Touching a Snake" is such a photograph. With definition as the dominant development pattern, complete one of the following writing tasks. Before beginning the task, reread "Definition: Limiting Meaning" at the beginning of the chapter to review the conventions involved in writing a definition.

1. Begin by looking up the definition of *symbol* in an unabridged dictionary or other resource material in the library. From the information you gather and from information you glean from the introductory comments to this assignment, develop a full definition of symbol, using examples from your experience and reading. Next, interpret the symbolic significance of "Touching a Snake." Consider several elements: the snake itself, which has a rich conventional symbolic history; the teddy bear; the fact of the generational difference between the man and the boy; the image on the man's T-shirt. In the process of developing your material, you might decide that there are several ways to interpret the photograph. Try to accommodate them in your essay.

2. Research the symbolic significance of "snake" as it has appeared throughout history and in different cultures. Integrating the various symbolic meanings your research has uncovered, define

"snake" as a multidimensional symbol, integrating its various interpretations. Finally, using one or more views of the symbolic snake, interpret the meaning of "Touching a Snake."

❦ Additional Writing Tasks ❦

Definition

1. Write an essay that defines one of the following terms. Explore the subject beyond its dictionary meaning, using a variety of methods to develop your definition. As part of this or any extended definition, you can state what the subject *excludes* as a way to clarify your definition.
   a. humanity
   b. education
   c. Armageddon
   d. terror
   e. leadership
   f. honesty
   g. fad
   h. evil
   i. female liberation
   j. male liberation
   k. corruption
   l. intuition
   m. liberation theology
   n. social responsibility
   o. obsession
   p. team player
   q. sociopath
   r. maverick
   s. imagination
   t. tragedy
   u. confidence
   v. luck
   w. glamour
   x. scorched earth
   y. genocide
   z. blindsided
2. From the following list of seldom-used slang terms, select one and define it in several paragraphs. After you explain the term, create a situation in which it might apply, using the term in

several sample sentences as a speaker might. Also include current slang that has a similar meaning.

a. hoodwink
b. greenhorn
c. whoopee
d. scam
e. boob
f. folknik
g. bamboozled
h. boodle
i. macho
j. bonehead

3. As a representative of a student rights organization, you have accepted the responsibility to convince a campus grievance committee composed of students, faculty, and administrators that a sexual harassment policy should be adopted as official college policy. Your first task is to define "sexual harassment" and to illustrate at least three different ways it manifests itself in behavior.

4. a. You are an environmentalist living in a major metropolitan area. You have formed an action group committed to protect all the natural landscapes that still exist in your city, even to the point of taking militant action against developers. You have used the phrase "urban environmentalist" to describe people who think and act as you do. In an essay, define "urban environmentalists" and describe what developers can expect from them.

   b. A group of self-designated "urban environmentalists" are disrupting development in the city. They see themselves as saviors of natural settings that exist within the urban landscape, but you regard them as "environmental terrorists." In an essay, define "environmental terrorists" and predict what city officials can expect from them.

5. Look up the medical explanation of a debilitating ailment such as Alzheimer's disease, Down's syndrome, or Hodgkin's disease. Once you understand the medical terminology, write a definition essay that explains the disease to someone who has no background in medicine. Create a case study of a person who has the disease to further explain its debilitating effects.

11

Persuasion and Argument
Convincing a Reader

The Method

An argumentative essay is an attempt to change or reinforce someone's opinion or to move someone to take action. On the one hand, the essay may be emotionally charged, appealing to a reader's feelings with emotional detail and biased language. The writing is then called *persuasion* or *persuasive argument*. On the other hand, an argumentative essay may be highly rational, appealing to a reader's intellect with logical explanation. This writing is called *argument* or *logical argument*. Political writing relies heavily on persuasion, and scientific writing on argument. Rarely, however, does an argumentative essay appeal only to emotion or only to reason. Usually, writers appeal to both, striving to convince their readers that their position is valid.

Imagine that you want to convince your readers of the merits of a vegetarian diet. You might begin by appealing to reason. First, you might contrast the high cost of meat with the low cost of grains that provide comparable protein. Second, you might point out that the grains grown for animal feed would be better used to feed the world's hungry. You might continue by presenting the danger highly marbled meat poses to health. You might then shift the appeal to emotion. You might construct an emotional description of animals being raised in pens, relating examples of force feeding and chemical injections, and describing slaughterhouse procedures. While composing the essay, you would keep an eye on your readers, anticipating their responses to your appeals by asking yourself if you are being too emotional or even too rational.

Throughout an argumentative essay a writer must carefully balance reason and emotion. A writer whose essay is so self-righteous that it ignores reason or so rational that it ignores feelings will alienate most readers. A general rule to follow is that an argumentative essay should be primarily rational or it may fail to convince critical readers. Consequently, writers of effective arguments usually present their opinions persuasively but develop ample and strong evidence throughout their essays. This practice will impress upon readers that the writer is *ethical;* that is, a well-informed, reasonable person committed to his or her position—and, therefore, worthy of being believed.

Assertions and Evidence

An argumentative essay is predicated on an *assertion;* that is, the opinion you want a reader to accept or an action you want your reader to take. When stated in a sentence the assertion is referred to as a *proposition* or *thesis:* "The high-fashion fur industry should be curtailed"; "The state should resume capital punishment"; "Magazines featuring nudity, such as *Playboy, Penthouse,* and *Playgirl,* should be banned from community magazine stands." The writer then supports the proposition with evidence.

It is the quality of evidence that persuades the reader to agree with an assertion and reject an opposing assertion. Keep in mind that the evidence writers use in an argumentative essay is the same as that any of us uses in oral arguments: personal experience, the experience of others, and authoritative sources.

First, personal experience can be used to support a proposition. Suppose you wanted to develop the argument that police are harassing college-age drivers. You, yourself, have had firsthand experience. Several times a patrol car has pulled you over while you were driving near campus. Each time an officer initiated a search of your car. Once one even required you to take a field sobriety test, which you passed. At none of these times did any officer issue a traffic citation. These personal experiences could serve as legitimate evidence to support your opinion.

Second, the experience of others can also be used as evidence to support an argument. You might narrate a story of a friend who had a similar experience. You might also include observations by a passenger or bystander to corroborate your friend's experience. When using the experience of others, do all you can to be sure that the information is accurate. You know how accurate a description of your experience is because you lived it, but when you use the experience of others, you are, in effect, vouching for its veracity. It is wise, therefore, to include more than one account of the same event.

Finally, authoritative sources can also be used to support an opinion. An argument gains its strength from the quality of authoritative evidence a writer can marshal. You can develop some authoritative information yourself. Once again consider the argument supporting the proposition that police are harassing college-age drivers. To support your opinion even more thoroughly, you might research police records. If the research revealed that police stopped and searched a significantly larger number of college-age drivers than older drivers, then you would use the information as evidence.

Sometimes, however, you must rely on other authoritative sources, such as encyclopedias, dictionaries, handbooks, digests, journals, and scientific research as well as people who are recognized as having extensive knowledge about a subject. When citing knowledgeable people to support an argument, be sure their expertise is in the subject you are discussing. It will not do your argument much good to quote a well-known nuclear physicist's opinion on gun control; your reader won't accept that specialist's word as authoritative.

Facts and statistics from authoritative sources can lend a great deal of credibility to any argument. Facts are irrefutable. No matter what the source, a fact is a fact: The Earth revolves around the sun. John F. Kennedy, the thirty-fifth president of the United States, was assassinated on November 22, 1963. When facts are corroborated by statistics, they exert a powerful influence on a reader. The United States has more homicides each year than Japan, Taiwan, and the combined countries of Western Europe. But what does this statistical fact mean? Should the government execute all convicted murderers? Do we need stricter handgun laws? Should every citizen arm for self-protection? Answering these questions involves interpretations of fact based on personal feelings and beliefs—that is, it involves opinions.

Strategies

Writers of argumentative essays will use any rhetorical method that is appropriate to their presentations: narration, description, examples, comparison and contrast, cause and effect, process analysis, and definition. Generally, however, effective argumentative essays do have five elements:

1. A clear statement of the writer's assertion;
2. An orderly presentation of the evidence;
3. A clear connection between the evidence and the argument;
4. A reasonable refutation of evidence that is counter to the writer's assertion;
5. A conclusion that emphasizes the assertion.

No doubt the most important of these elements is clear presentation of the evidence. To be convincing, evidence in an argumentative essay must be arranged in logical sequence or readers will reject the writer's conclusion. When composing an argument, writers reason from evidence to a conclusion through one of two processes: induction or deduction.

Inductive Reasoning

Through *inductive reasoning* writers accumulate enough specific evidence to justify a *general conclusion*. In other words, inductive reasoning moves from the *specific* to the *general*. While growing up we all learned to use induction. A child may bite into a hard green apple and discover that it tastes bitter. When the child tastes a hard green pear, he finds that it, too, is bitter. At another time the child bites into a hard green plum and an apricot. Both are bitter. By induction, he draws the general conclusion that hard green fruit is bitter and should not be eaten.

Argumentative essays written with inductive reasoning follow a similar pattern but with one difference: they usually begin with a *hypothesis* or question that embodies the conclusion the writer wants the reader to accept as valid. To argue that a city named Glenwood is environmentally responsible, a writer will have to present evidence that leads directly to that conclusion.

Hypothesis:	Glenwood is an environmentally responsible city. (or: Is Glenwood an environmentally responsible city?)
Evidence:	Glenwood has instituted these environmental programs:
	Curbside recycling for glass, newspaper, aluminum, and plastics;
	Disposal of household toxic waste;
	Law prohibiting release of ozone-depleting chlorofluorocarbons from air conditioners;
	Refuse landfill designed to protect ground water from toxic pollution and to generate methane gas;
	A wetlands bird habitat preserved as open space.
Conclusion:	Glenwood is environmentally responsible.

Conclusions drawn from the inductive reasoning procedure are usually referred to as *probable conclusions,* or *inferences,* for they are reached with incomplete evidence. The reader's acceptance of a conclusion that follows from inductive reasoning is often referred to as the *inductive leap.* To establish a clear connection between the evidence and the conclusion, you must be sure that the evidence you present is *relevant, sufficient,* and *representative.*

To be relevant, the evidence must support the hypothesis and contribute directly to the conclusion. To be sufficient, the evidence must amply support the conclusion. And to be representative, the evidence must represent the full range of information related to the hypothesis, not just one side or the other. By following these criteria, a writer increases the probability that the conclusion is valid, thus bridging the distance from evidence to conclusion and making the reader's passage easier.

Deductive Reasoning

Deductive reasoning is the opposite of inductive reasoning. Deductive reasoning moves from general assumptions, called *premises,* to a specific conclusion that follows from the general premises. In formal logic, this deductive pattern is called a *syllogism,* a form of organization that includes a *major premise,* a *minor premise* and a *necessary conclusion,* one that is the logical result of the two premises. The classic example of syllogistic form comes down to us from Aristotle:

Major premise: All humans are mortal.
Minor premise: Socrates is human.
Conclusion: Therefore, Socrates is mortal.

The conclusion of a syllogism is always drawn from the major and minor premises, both of which must be accurate for the conclusion to be accurate. If the premises are drawn from relevant, sufficient, and representative evidence—the same criteria used to draw sound conclusions in inductive reasoning—the conclusion of a syllogism will probably be accurate. But syllogisms can be illogical. An inaccurate major premise may make the syllogism illogical:

Major premise: Professional gamblers carry large quantities of cash and drive expensive cars.
Minor premise: John Murphy is a professional gambler.
Conclusion: Therefore, John Murphy must carry large quantities of cash and drive an expensive car.

The major premise is inaccurate. Ask yourself, Are all professional gamblers successful enough to have large quantities of cash on their person and drive expensive cars? Because the major premise is inaccurate the conclusion is inaccurate.

Sometimes the language of a syllogism is deceptive. Consider the use of "good American," "accept," and "change" in this flawed syllogism.

Major premise: Every good American accepts the United States Constitution.

Minor premise: Martin Luther King did not accept the United States Constitution because he worked to change it.

Conclusion: Therefore, Martin Luther King was not a good American.

The phrase "good American" is vague, too vague to describe a class of people accurately. What do "accept" and "change" mean in this context? The United States Constitution has provisions for change. In fact, it has been amended many times. Anyone who accepts the Constitution accepts the possibility of changing it. Because language is used deceptively in the premises, the conclusion is meaningless.

Sometimes a syllogism is illogical because it is constructed improperly. First, examine this properly constructed syllogism:

Major premise: All artists rely on intuition.

In a properly constructed syllogism, the subject of the major premise, in this example "artists," must appear in the minor premise and be narrowed.

Minor premise: John is an artist.

The conclusion then follows necessarily from the major and minor premises.

Conclusion: Therefore, John relies on intuition.

This syllogism is properly constructed and is valid. Now examine this invalid syllogism:

Major premise: All artists rely on intuition.
Minor premise: All psychics rely on intuition.
Conclusion: Therefore, all psychics are artists.

This syllogism is improperly constructed because the minor premise does not repeat the subject of the major premise. The conclusion, therefore, is invalid.

Like inductive reasoning, deductive reasoning can help organize an argument. But using deduction is never quite as simple as the skeletal form of syllogisms used to illustrate it.

Imagine that the Sierra Club has established a *representative sample* of environmentally responsible cities. By extensive inductive reasoning, the Sierra Club finds several cities, including Glenwood, from our previous example, operating effective environmental programs. Based on its analysis of these programs, the Sierra Club defines the environmentally responsible city. A syllogism showing that a city is environmentally responsible might be constructed in this sequence:

Major premise:	Cities with ecologically beneficial programs for disposal of waste, conservation of energy, and preservation of open space are environmentally responsible.
Minor premise:	San Lorenzo has ecologically beneficial programs for disposal of waste, conservation of energy, and preservation of open space.
Conclusion:	Therefore, San Lorenzo is environmentally responsible.

In an argumentative essay, a syllogism seldom appears in such clear form, but often its deductive structure is embedded in the text. If a writer wanted to argue that San Lorenzo is environmentally responsible, he or she might first construct a syllogism such as the one above, analyze the evidence needed to support the proposition, and then arrange the argument, incorporating syllogistic reasoning in the structure.

In the first section of the essay, the writer would address the questions raised in the major premise.

1. What is an ecologically beneficial program for disposing of waste?

2. What is an ecologically beneficial program for conserving energy?
3. What is an ecologically beneficial program for preserving open space?

To answer these questions would take several paragraphs, and the writer would have to rely on the authority of the Sierra Club's definition. An ecologically beneficial program for disposing of waste would probably require recycling usable trash, disposing of toxic waste, and stringent restrictions on use of landfills. An ecologically beneficial program for conserving energy would probably mean reducing use of automobiles to save fuel and increasing use of solar energy to save electricity. An ecologically beneficial program for preserving open space would probably include protection for unique land formations and wildlife habitats. This discussion would be rather broad because the definition is based on a representative sample of many cities that may vary dramatically in size and geographic location.

To develop the second section of the essay, the writer would address the questions raised by the minor premise:

1. What specific actions has San Lorenzo taken to implement an ecologically beneficial waste-disposal program?
2. What specific actions has San Lorenzo taken to implement ecologically beneficial programs for conserving energy?
3. What specific actions has San Lorenzo taken to implement an ecologically beneficial program for preserving open space?

The purpose of this section is to present evidence that San Lorenzo does indeed meet the definition of environmentally responsible cities. In this section, which would also require several paragraphs to fully develop, the writer would present as evidence the specific environmental programs San Lorenzo has implemented, thus demonstrating the validity of the syllogism's minor premise.

In the last section of the essay, by far the shortest, the writer would conclude that San Lorenzo is an environmentally responsible city. The writer might choose to summarize the key points of the argument, but here the force of deductive reasoning would be irresistible, making it unnecessary to rearticulate the argument in abbreviated form. But whether to develop a conclusion fully or to leave it implied is the decision of the writer, who is responsible for the argument's coherence and consistency. Risks lie in both strategies.

Logical Fallacies in Writing

Logical fallacies are common mistakes in reasoning, and an argument tainted by them is ineffective. The word *fallacy* means "deception," or "a fault in reasoning." Fallacies deceive by distorting the truth and making logical conclusions unattainable. Using fallacies consciously signifies dishonesty; using them inadvertently demonstrates muddled thinking.

Study this list of eight most common fallacies. Remember that writers must scrutinize their arguments to avoid slipping into fallacious reasoning.

Overgeneralization.   Writers overgeneralize when they draw a conclusion from insufficient or unrepresentative evidence.

> During the last year, three of five award-winning films concentrated on family violence. An examination of family violence was just broadcast on national television. No doubt these events indicate that family violence is on the rise.

A handful of films and a television program do not constitute a trend. The conclusion that family violence is rising could be substantiated with statistics and reports from authorities such as psychologists, sociologists, and law-enforcement officers.

Oversimplification.   To oversimplify is to ignore essential information from which a conclusion is drawn. Be careful to avoid this fallacy when writing about complicated subjects. You might become too eager to offer a simple explanation to a complicated problem.

> The problems of air pollution, ozone depletion, and global warming are not really problems at all. They are merely manifestations of our educational system. We have too many scientists working in universities with nothing to do but study our environment.

Faulty either/or reasoning.   The either/or fallacy is a type of oversimplification in which a writer assumes only two alternatives, black or white, when there are others, including gray. The slogan, "America, love it or leave it," implies that love of country must be unqualified, which has the effect of excluding constructive criticism.

> Everyone would agree that America is being severely damaged by the sale and use of illegal drugs. The only two courses of action are these: the country's leaders can ignore the problem, or they can enforce the law to its maximum limits.

Of course, other actions are possible—initiate public education, fund rehabilitation for former drug users, develop agreements with other countries to curtail manufacturing of drugs, and even legalize use of drugs. The choice is not between doing nothing or joining a law-and-order crusade.

Post hoc **argument.**   The complete Latin phrase is *post hoc, ergo propter hoc,* which means "after this, therefore because of this." The assumption in this fallacious argument is that one event causes another event simply because the second follows the first in time.

> For more than a year, I have been meditating nightly for one hour. Although I usually have the flu at least once each year, I didn't have it last year. No doubt the meditation prevented me from catching the flu.

As stated, the only relationship between meditation and catching the flu is that one followed the other. Other explanations could be found: perhaps that year had no flu epidemic, or perhaps the person was lucky enough to avoid a deadly sneeze. Time sequence alone cannot prove that a cause-and-effect relationship applies.

Non sequitur.   In Latin, *non sequitur* means "it does not follow." A *non sequitur* is a conclusion that does not logically follow from its premises.

> The city in this county that has the most crime also has the highest-paid police force. The city with the least crime has the lowest-paid police force. It does not make sense for our city to pay higher salaries to our police when doing so will not reduce crime.

The reasons for high crime rates are many, a high incidence of poverty being one of them. But we doubt that high police salaries contribute to a rising crime rate. In fact, dangerous working conditions could lead to higher wages for police.

False analogy.   Someone using a false analogy assumes that if two things are similar in one or more characteristics, then they are similar in other characteristics.

> We should not forget the lessons of Grenada and Panama, when our leaders tried to negotiate settlements and failed. Once we sent in the Marines, peace and a working relationship were restored. The best way to deal with renegade countries who act against our interests is to invade them to show other hostile governments we will not be bullied.

We are not living in the same world we lived in even five years ago. The break-up of communist-bloc countries, the danger of renegade terrorist action, the proliferation of nuclear weapons, all make the international scene too complex for rash action based on a false analogy.

Ad hominem argument.   When a writer attacks a person

associated with an issue rather than the argument supporting the issue, then the writer is committing an *ad hominem* fallacy, which in Latin means "to the man."

> Councilman Hunt has made a strong argument against raising the gasoline tax for revenue to build more roads. Why shouldn't he? He takes the bus to work each day, and he has the money to fly to any part of the country where he might want to vacation.

This statement ignores the argument for a tax increase and concentrates instead on the person making the argument.

Association fallacy.   To commit the association fallacy is to claim that an act or belief is worthy or unworthy simply because of the people associated with it.

> Congressman Will is supported by some of Hollywood's leading figures. Because actors, directors, and producers know talent when they see it, you should support Congressman Will too.

Do Hollywood figures know any more about the qualities necessary to serve as an effective congressman than most other voters?

Argument in College Writing

Often you will be asked to take a position and convince a reader of its validity. In the next example, Rhonda Burris responds to an assignment in a mass-communications class. Her task is to convince a reader that movies featuring characters who smoke should carry a warning much like the one the law requires cigarette companies to place in magazine advertisements. She leads her reader to the general conclusion, which she states directly in the closing paragraph.

The opening is indirect but interesting. It ends with the author's hypothesis: films that feature appealing actors smoking may encourage viewers to smoke.

Among college students Humphrey Bogart is still a popular actor. Films he starred in, such as <u>The Maltese Falcon</u>, <u>The Harder They Fall</u>, and <u>To Have and Have Not</u>, still flicker every weekend in fraternity houses and dormitories across America. Just last Saturday my college sponsored a Bogart film retrospective. Probably for the fifteenth time in my life, I watched <u>Casablanca</u>, a film that could be classified as a cult favorite. It has become more romantic each time I view it, capturing an exotic place and time, featuring mysterious supporting characters, and concentrating on the dilemma the beautiful heroine faces when trying to decide between two men who love her, a political idealist and a world-weary cynic, whom Bogart plays. Bogart is suave, his style dominating the film, but during this viewing, I saw something I had not noticed before: No actor could handle a cigarette better than Bogart. Hanging from the corner of his mouth as he talks or held between two fingers as he drinks, the burning cigarette is part of the suave image Bogart projects to the viewer. The truth that is not part of the image is that he died, at the relatively young age of fifty-eight, of lung cancer. Toward the end of the film, I asked myself how many people Bogart's suave handling of a cigarette influenced in their decision to smoke?

Specific examples illustrate how one cigarette manufacturer associates its products with appealing actors. The assumption is that if Phillip Morris is willing to pay producers to feature Lark and Marlboro, then the association must have some influence on viewers.

Apparently the power of association to influence someone's decision to smoke has not been lost on cigarette manufacturers. Recently the Phillip Morris Company, the people who sell such popular brands as Benson and Hedges ("For people who love to smoke"), Virginia Slims ("You've come a long way, Baby"), and Merit ("For those who want marital bliss") paid $350,000 to have secret agent 007 James Bond smoke Lark Cigarettes in

<u>License to Kill</u>. Why? Many young men, Phillip Morris seems to believe, are too immature to make the obvious connection between smoking and death, and so they make the ridiculous connection between smoking and the adventurous life James Bond leads, even though that life is only a movie life, not a real one.

A couple of years earlier, it was the Phillip Morris Company who paid $42,000 to have Lois Lane smoke Marlboro cigarettes in <u>Superman II</u>. The payment went unnoticed until one movie critic raised the question that if characterization of Lois Lane required that she smoke, why feature a brand of cigarette so prominently? Now the answer is clear. Phillip Morris must have been counting on the power of association even then. Will every immature young woman who sees <u>Superman II</u> come to believe that if she smokes Marlboro cigarettes, sooner or later her own Man of Steel will arrive? Probably not consciously, but the subconscious might associate smoking and sex appeal. What more could a cigarette advertiser expect?

The reader is led to conclude that if viewers are warned that some films are violent then they should also be warned that smoking, an established health hazard, is also featured.

Movies are rated according to who should be allowed to see them. The National Coalition on Television Violence discovered that cigarette smoking appears in 100 percent of PG-13 films, which are approved for people over thirteen who have parental permission to view them. Clearly, young people who attend films (what young people do not?) are exposed to actors smoking in varied situations and from various stations in life. Even if they come from families who do not smoke, they are exposed to powerful images that show smoking as accepted behavior. But where is the warning that smoking is hazardous to health?

The writer draws a parallel between cigarette advertisements in magazines and indirect advertisements in movies. The reader will reasonably conclude that both should carry health warnings.

Cigarette advertisements have been banned from television and radio. When they appear in magazines, cigarette advertisements must by law include the Surgeon General's warning that smoking can result in cancer, heart disease, or fetal injury in pregnant women. This requirement is a sensible public-health policy, but where does such a warning appear in films that feature characters who smoke? Clearly one cigarette manufacturer believes that by associating its cigarettes with appealing characters it will influence a person's decision to smoke. Why else would Phillip Morris pay movie producers to feature their products?

Burris concludes with an emotional allusion to Bogart's death.

The practice of featuring characters who smoke in films is disturbing enough, but when cigarette manufacturers actually pay to have their brands featured in a film, the practice goes beyond being disturbing to being criminal. It is time government put a stop to this kind of indirect advertising, or at the very least, require that films featuring characters who smoke announce the dangers of smoking before the plot begins. Then the next time someone watches Humphrey Bogart raise a glass, squint through a cloud of cigarette smoke at Ingrid Bergman, and say, "Here's looking at you, Kid," the viewer will not concentrate on the romantic image but on the excruciating pain Bogart must have felt while dying of lung cancer.

Rhonda Burris begins her argument indirectly by discussing Humphrey Bogart. She refers to *Casablanca*, one of Bogart's most popular movies, and creates an impression of the suave Bogart style. In the closing sentences she sets up her hypothesis by revealing that Bogart, usually portrayed with a cigarette in hand, died of lung cancer. She maintains that films that feature appealing actors smoking may influence viewers by leading them to smoke.

In paragraphs 2 and 3, Burris develops her argument with examples of the Phillip Morris Company actually paying to have its cigarettes prominently displayed in films. The goal, she argues, is to associate its products with appealing characters, hoping that the association will benefit sales. In paragraph 4, Burris presents an interesting observation: movies are evaluated for the violence they display, but nothing is done to warn viewers that smoking, a clear hazard to health, is displayed in appealing ways. At the end of the paragraph she raises a question that echoes her conclusion: "Where is the warning that smoking is hazardous to health?"

In paragraph 5, Burris points out something we all know: cigarette advertisements in magazines must carry the Surgeon General's warning, a sensible public-health policy. Burris's reasoning clearly leads us to one conclusion. In the final paragraph, Burris completes the inductive sequence and states her thesis: "It's time the government put a stop to this kind of indirect advertising, or at the very least, require that films featuring characters who smoke announce the dangers of smoking before the plot begins." She closes with an emotional reference to *Casablanca* and Bogart's painful death from lung cancer.

This essayist argues against the radical side of recently debated questions. Should we become more aware of the arguments used by a radical group within a larger group, and should we more actively examine our own opinions about whether or not to use animals in medical research and scientific experimentation? In fact we "use" animals in many ways without thinking about their comfort or possible death.

A fruitful way to begin the discussion is with such provocative questions as "Should animals be captured, trained, and caged for the pleasure of circus audiences?" "Should seeing-eye dogs have their movements severely limited so that they can function as guides for the blind?" "Should chicks be dyed and sold as Easter gifts?" "Should sled-dog races be banned?" "Should people who want dogs and cats as pets be required to have a psychological evaluation before being permitted to have those pets?"

Can some animals be used for scientific research? Can some human beings better the world by doing scientific research that involves animals? These are the questions to ask after the class has established that the world of morality has more gray than first meets the eye.

MARGINAL NOTES

Karpati starts not with a declaration but with an exclamation. But then we see that he does not subscribe to his "confession"; he feels slandered, "vilified."

A chronic or acute disease causing unrestrained growth of white blood corpuscles. The patient develops anemia, infections, and fatigue, among other symptoms. An infant born at any time before completing the thirty-seventh week of gestation (time from conception to birth) is premature. *Trauma* is a physical injury or wound caused by external force or violence.

❦ Ron Karpati ❦

Ron Karpati is a pediatrician involved in cancer research. Born in Los Angeles, California, in 1961, he did his undergraduate studies at the University of California, Los Angeles, and then attended UCLA Medical School. He did his medical residency at Children's Hospital of Los Angeles. The essay reprinted here reflects his views about the use of animals in medical research. Employed by the National Cancer Institute in Bethesda, Maryland, he did research on using the body's immune system to fight cancer, known as the "immunotherapy" of cancer. In 1991 he became a clinical fellow at the University of California at San Francisco, where he works in pediatric oncology and transplantation of bone marrow.

A Scientist
"I Am the Enemy"

A physician reacting against animal-rights activists, Karpati attempts to convince the reader of the need for animal research. In this essay, first published in Newsweek's "My Turn" column in December 1989, he uses both factual information and emotional appeals to rouse the "apathetic majority" to action.

While reading Karpati's essay, note where the author uses factual information and where he uses emotional appeals to make his argument.

I am the enemy! One of those vilified, inhumane physician-scientists involved in animal research. How strange, for I have never thought of myself as an evil person. I became a pediatrician because of my love for children and my desire to keep them healthy. During medical school and residency, however, I saw many children die of leukemia, prematurity and traumatic injury—circumstances against which medicine has made tremendous progress, but still has far to go. More important, I also saw children, alive and healthy, thanks to advances in medical science 1 such as infant respirators, potent antibiotics, new surgical techniques and the entire field of organ transplantation. My desire to tip the scales in favor of the healthy, happy children drew me to medical research.

My accusers claim that I inflict torture on animals for the sole purpose of career advancement. My experiments supposedly have no relevance to medicine and are easily replaced by computer simulation. Meanwhile, an apathetic public barely watches, convinced that the issue has no significance, and publicity-conscious politicians increasingly give way to the demands of the activists.   2

We in medical research have also been unconscionably apathetic. We have allowed the most extreme animal-rights protesters to seize the initiative and frame the issue as one of "animal fraud." We have been complacent in our belief that a knowledgeable public would sense the importance of animal research to the public health. Perhaps we have been mistaken in not responding to the emotional tone of the argument created by those sad posters of animals by waving equally sad posters of children dying of leukemia or cystic fibrosis.   3

Much is made of the pain inflicted on these animals in the name of medical science. The animal-rights activists contend that this is evidence of our malevolent and sadistic nature. A more reasonable argument, however, can be advanced in our defense. Life is often cruel, both to animals and human beings. Teenagers get thrown from the back of a pickup truck and suffer severe head injuries. Toddlers, barely able to walk, find themselves at the bottom of a swimming pool while a parent checks the mail. Physicians hoping to alleviate the pain and suffering these tragedies cause have but three choices: create an animal model of the injury or disease and use that model to understand the process and test new therapies; experiment on human beings—some experiments will succeed, most will fail—or finally, leave medical knowledge static, hoping that accidental discoveries will lead us to the advances.   4

Some animal-rights activists would suggest a fourth choice, claiming that computer models can simulate animal experiments, thus making the actual experiments unnecessary. Computers can   5

Notice the radically opposite points of view in the last sentence in paragraph 1 and sentence 1 in paragraph 2.

Karpati distinguishes three groups in paragraph 2: his group, the activist-accusers' group, and the apathetic-public group.

"Animal fraud" is an example of emotive speech used to persuade an audience by appealing to its emotions.

"cystic fibrosis": An inherited, incurable disease that affects the pancreas, respiratory system, and sweat glands.

Paralleling the triangle in paragraph 2 comes this triangle of debatable choices: test on animal models of injuries, test on human beings, or hope for accidental medical discoveries.

Karpati anticipates and rejects the fourth choice, offering his argument against it.

simulate, reasonably well, the effects of well-understood principles on complex systems, as in the application of the laws of physics to airplane and automobile design. However, when the principles themselves are in question, as is the case with the complex biological systems under study, computer modeling alone is of little value.

One of the terrifying effects of the effort to restrict the use of animals in medical research is that the impact will not be felt for years and decades: drugs that might have been discovered will not be; surgical techniques that might have been developed will not be; and fundamental biological processes that might have been understood will remain mysteries. There is the danger that politically expedient solutions will be found to placate a vocal minority, while the consequences of those decisions will not be apparent until long after the decisions are made and the decision makers forgotten. 6

This is the status quo or "existing-condition" argument, which says that many of us now enjoy good health because of animal research.

Fortunately, most of us enjoy good health, and the trauma of watching one's child die has become a rare experience. Yet our good fortune should not make us unappreciative of the health we enjoy or the advances that make it possible. Vaccines, antibiotics, insulin and drugs to treat heart disease, hypertension and stroke are all based on animal research. Most complex surgical procedures, such as coronary-artery bypass and organ transplantation, are initially developed in animals. Presently undergoing animal studies are techniques to insert genes in humans in order to replace the defective ones found to be the cause of so much disease. These studies will effectively end if animal research is severely restricted. 7

In this paragraph he argues for compassion. Animals and human beings die, but some human beings live because some animals die.

Karpati attempts to dispose his audience toward his argument by pointing out that not everyone in the animal-rights movement is his accuser. On the contrary, the movement itself has done much good work. The fact remains that the more radical members of the movement might get their way.

In America today, death has become an event isolated from our daily existence—out of the sight and thoughts of most of us. As a doctor who has watched many children die, and their parents grieve, I am particularly angered by people capable of so much compassion for a dog or a cat, but with seemingly so little for a dying human being. These people seem so insulated from the reality of human life and death and what it means. 8

Make no mistake, however: I am not advocating the needlessly cruel treatment of animals. To the extent that the animal-rights 9 movement has made us more aware of the needs of these animals, and made us search harder for suitable alternatives, they have made a significant contribution. But if the more radical members of this movement are successful in limiting further research, their efforts will bring about a tragedy that will cost many lives. The real question is whether an apathetic majority can be aroused to protect its future against a vocal, but misdirected, minority.

With this question, he urges the audience to action.

POSSIBLE ANSWERS

Meaning and Purpose

1. Let students articulate their own opinions about animals used in research. Karpati, of course, does not believe that he is an "inhumane physician-scientist."
2. Karpati is not very tolerant of the extremists' opinion against using animals in medical research. He says activists misunderstand him and might succeed in their efforts to restrict animal research (2). Karpati says he is "particularly angered by people capable of so much compassion for a dog or a cat, but with seemingly so little for a dying human being" (8). He calls the activists' success "a tragedy that will cost many lives," and the activists themselves a "misdirected minority" (9).
3. He specifies the kind of activist in the animal-rights movement whom he argues against (3). He compliments many activists for the good they have done (9).
4. "Insulated" means placed in a detached situation. In this sentence it means such people are not in touch with "the reality of human life and death," and that they shut themselves off from understanding "what it means."
5. The first sentence of paragraph 2 implies that Karpati himself uses animals for medical research.

Meaning and Purpose

1. Do you agree or disagree with the animal-rights activist opinion that Karpati declares in the first two sentences? Why or why not?
2. How tolerant is Karpati of the animal-rights activist opinion that he presents in the first two sentences? What does he think might happen if the activists are successful? Support your answers with statements from the essay.
3. How do you know that Karpati is not totally against the animal-rights movement?
4. Paragraph 8 has a sentence that says people seem "insulated from the reality of human life and death and what it means." Define "insulated" as it is used in that sentence.
5. Can you find a sentence implying that Karpati himself uses animals for experiments relevant to medicine?

Strategy

1. What is one of Karpati's arguments for using animals in medical research?
2. What is one of the animal-rights activists' arguments against using animals for medical research?

Strategy

1. One argument is that "vaccines, antibiotics, insulin and drugs to treat heart disease, hypertension and stroke are based on animal research" (7).

2. One argument is sentence 1 in paragraph 4.

3. Karpati appeals mostly to reason when he says that stopping animal research will mean that drugs and surgical procedures will not be discovered (6), that much in medicine now is based on animal research (7), and that using computers instead of animals is often inadequate (5). Some of his words are emotional, such as "terrifying effects" (6) and "a tragedy" (9), but overall he appeals to reason.

4. Karpati's evidence is experience—"I also saw children alive and healthy, thanks to advances in medical science such as infant respirators, potent antibiotics, new surgical techniques and the entire field of organ transplantation" (1). He is an authoritative source because he is a physician-scientist.

Style

1. The emotional tone is apparent in description ("malevolent and sadistic nature"), in waving "sad posters of animals," and in accusing Karpati of inflicting "torture on animals."

2. The issues are not explained thoroughly for at least two reasons: (1) Most of the public has already heard of the issues, even though they are probably not "familiar" with them in any depth. (2) Karpati argues against radical animal-rights advocates more than he argues the animal-rights issue.

3. The first two sentences grab readers because the language is emotional and startling. First Karpati castigates himself as activists do, then he defends himself. His accusers cannot say worse of him than he's said of himself; the technique undermines their argument.

3. Does Karpati appeal mainly to emotion or reason in his argument? Find statements that illustrate his appeal.

4. What kind of evidence does Karpati offer to support his argument: personal experience, the experience of others, or authoritative sources? Is his choice effective for his argument?

Style

1. How do animal-rights activists give a strongly emotional tone to their argument against experimentation?

2. Modern essayists often follow a classical arrangement including a part called *explicatio,* in which they define terms and explain issues. Why aren't the issues explained thoroughly in Karpati's essay?

3. What is the effect on readers of Karpati's describing himself as the enemy in the first two sentences?

Writing Tasks

1. Whether you subscribe to this viewpoint or not, take the position of animal-rights activists against Karpati. Write an essay in response to "A Scientist: 'I Am the Enemy' " arguing against using animals in research. Be sure you respond to each of Karpati's arguments first.

2. Write a brief dramatic dialogue with an argument between two people: one is an animal-rights activist who has just toured a research lab where conditions for the animals are cruel, appalling. The other person is the parent of a child who is about to have surgery for a life-or-death ailment, a procedure that was made possible by animal research.

❦ Joy Williams ❦

Joy Williams, born in Massachusetts in 1944, was educated at Marietta College in Ohio and at the University of Iowa. She has written three novels, State of Grace *(1973),* The Changeling *(1978), and* Breaking and Entering *(1988), and two collections of short stories,* Taking Care *(1982) and* Escapes *(1991). She has also contributed nonfiction pieces to a number of magazines including* Esquire, *where the following essay was first published. She lives in Key West, Florida, and has written a history and guidebook about the Florida Keys.*

The Killing Game

Williams's essay, presented here in a shorter version than the original in Esquire, *argues passionately against hunting. She examines the traditional reasons advanced by hunters to explain the attraction of hunting and the arguments used to justify it, rejecting each in turn. Then she advances her personal interpretation of why humans hunt. Whichever side of the argument you are on, Williams's skillful use of language is sure to hold your interest and probably elicit a strong response.*

As you read the essay, be aware of your response to each para-graph. Which of her arguments do you accept and which do you reject?

Death and suffering are a big part of hunting. A big part. Not that you'd ever know it by hearing hunters talk. They tend to downplay the killing part. To kill is to put to death, extinguish, nullify, cancel, destroy. But from the hunter's point of view, it's just a tiny part of the experience. *The kill is the least important part of the hunt,* they often say, or, *Killing involves only a split second of the innumerable hours we spend surrounded by and observing nature . . .* For the animal, of course, the killing part is of considerably more importance. José Ortega y Gasset, in *Meditations on Hunting,*

1

wrote, *Death is a sign of reality in hunting. One does not hunt in order to kill; on the contrary, one kills in order to have hunted.* This is the sort of intellectual blather that the "thinking" hunter holds dear. The conservation editor of *Field & Stream,* George Reiger, recently paraphrased this sentiment by saying, *We kill to hunt, and not the other way around,* thereby making it truly fatuous. A hunter in West Virginia, one Mr. Bill Neal, blazed through this philosophical fog by explaining why he blows the toes off tree raccoons so that they will fall down and be torn apart by his dogs. *That's the best part of it. It's not any fun just shooting them.*

Paragraphs 2 and 3 continue the attack on lofty justifications for hunting, dismissing them as the "blather" of "apologists."

2   Instead of monitoring animals—many animals in managed areas are tagged, tattooed, and wear radio transmitters—wildlife managers should start hanging telemetry gear around hunters' necks to study their attitudes and listen to their conversations. It would be grisly listening, but it would tune out for good the *suffering as sacrament* and *spiritual experience* blather that some hunting apologists employ. *The unease with which the good hunter inflicts death is an unease not merely with his conscience but with affirming his animality in the midst of his struggles toward humanity and clarity,* Holmes Rolston III drones on in his book *Environmental Ethics.*

Ralston is a professor of philosophy at Colorado State University. *Environmental Ethics* was published in 1987.

3   There is a formula to this in literature—someone the protagonist loves has just died, so he goes out and kills an animal. This makes him feel better. But it's kind of a sad feeling-better. He gets to relate to Death and Nature in this way. Somewhat. But not really. Death is still a mystery. Well, it's hard to explain. It's sort of a semireligious thing . . . Killing and affirming, affirming and killing, it's just the cross the "good" hunter must bear. The bad hunter just has to deal with postkill letdown.

Paragraphs 4 and 5 reject the idea that hunting is done to provide food.

4   Many are the hunter's specious arguments. Less semireligious but a long-standing favorite with them is the vegetarian approach: you eat meat, don't you? If you say no, they feel they've got you— you're just a vegetarian attempting to impose your weird views on others. If you say yes, they accuse you of being hypocritical, of allowing your genial A&P butcher to stand between you and reality. The fact is, the chief attraction of hunting is the pursuit and murder of animals—the meat-eating aspect of it is trivial. If

the hunter chooses to be *ethical* about it, he might cook his kill, but the meat of most animals is discarded. Dead bear can even be dangerous! A bear's heavy hide must be skinned at once to prevent meat spoilage. With effort, a hunter can make okay chili, *something to keep in mind,* a sports rag says, *if you take two skinny spring bears.*

As for subsistence hunting, please . . . Granted that there   5
might be one "good" hunter out there who conducts the kill as spiritual exercise and two others who are atavistic enough to want to supplement their Chicken McNuggets with venison, most hunters hunt for the hell of it.

For hunters, hunting is fun. Recreation is play. Hunting is   6
recreation. Hunters kill for play, for entertainment. They kill for the thrill of it, to make an animal "theirs." (The Gandhian doctrine of nonpossession has never been a bit hit with hunters.) The animal becomes the property of the hunter by its death. Alive, the beast belongs only to itself. This is unacceptable to the hunter. *He's yours . . . He's mine . . . I decided to . . . I decided not to . . . I debated shooting it, then I decided to let it live . . .* Hunters like beautiful creatures. A "beautiful" deer, elk, bear, cougar, bighorn sheep. A "beautiful" goose or mallard. Of course, they don't stay "beautiful" for long, particularly the birds. Many birds become rags in the air, shredded, blown to bits. *Keep shooting till they drop!* Hunters get a thrill out of seeing a plummeting bird, out of seeing it crumple and fall. *The big pheasant folded in classic fashion.* They get a kick out of "collecting" new species. *Why not add a unique harlequin duck to your collection?* Swan hunting is satisfying. *I let loose a three-inch Magnum. The large bird only flinched with my first shot and began to gain altitude. I frantically ejected the round, chambered another, and dropped the swan with my second shot. After retrieving the bird I was amazed by its size. The swan's six-foot wingspan, huge body, and long neck made it an impressive trophy.* Hunters like big animals, trophy animals. A "trophy" usually means that the hunter doesn't deign to eat it. Maybe he skins it or mounts it. Maybe he takes a picture. *We took pictures, we took pictures.* Maybe he just looks at it for a while. The dis-

Beginning with paragraph 6, Williams shifts from refuting the hunters' arguments to advancing her own: Hunters pursue pleasure (thrills) and power (control or possession).

Mohandas K(aranchand) Gandhi (1869–1948), known for his ascetic way of life and his use of civil disobedience and nonviolence as political weapons in India.

Note the irony. Apparently the beauty of an animal adds to the thrill of destroying it.

Williams frequently uses the apparent words of hunters to convict them of unthinking cruelty.

position of the "experience" is up to the hunter. He's entitled to do whatever he wishes with the damn thing. It's dead.

Hunters like categories they can tailor to their needs. There are the "good" animals—deer, elk, bear, moose—which are allowed to exist for the hunter's pleasure. Then there are the "bad" animals, the vermin, varmints, and "nuisance" animals, the rabbits and raccoons and coyotes and beavers and badgers, which are disencouraged to exist. The hunter can have fun killing them, but the pleasure is diminished because the animals aren't "magnificent."

Then there are the predators. These can be killed any time, because, hunters argue, they're predators, for godssakes.

Many people in South Dakota want to exterminate the red fox because it preys upon some of the ducks and pheasant they want to hunt and kill each year. They found that after they killed the wolves and coyotes, they had more foxes than they wanted. The ring-necked pheasant is South Dakota's state bird. No matter that it was imported from Asia specifically to be "harvested" for sport, it's South Dakota's state bird and they're proud of it. A group called Pheasants Unlimited gave some tips on how to hunt foxes. *Place a small amount of larvicide* [a grain fumigant] *on a rag and chuck it down the hole . . . The first pup generally comes out in fifteen minutes . . . Use a .22 to dispatch him . . . Remove each pup shot from the hole. Following gassing, set traps for the old fox who will return later in the evening . . .* Poisoning, shooting, trapping—they make up a sort of sportsman's triathlon. . . .

Large predators—including grizzlies, cougars, and wolves—are often the most "beautiful," the smartest and wildest animals of all. The gray wolf is both a supreme predator and an endangered species, and since the Supreme Court recently affirmed that ranchers have no constitutional right to kill endangered predators—apparently some God-given rights are not constitutional ones—this makes the wolf a more or less lucky dog. But not for long. A small population of gray wolves has recently established itself in northwestern Montana, primarily in Glacier National Park, and there is a plan, long a dream of conservatists, to "reintroduce"

7

8

9

10

Irony again: These animals are predators, but so are the humans that hunt them.

A specific example of a concerted attack on a particular predator. The red fox is killed so hunters will have more ducks and pheasant to shoot.

Paragraphs 10 and 11 give another specific example of hunters protecting "their" game from natural predators.

the wolf to Yellowstone. But to please ranchers and hunters, part of the plan would involve immediately removing the wolf from the endangered-species list. Beyond the park's boundaries, he could be hunted as a "game animal" or exterminated as a "pest." (Hunters kill to hunt, remember, except when they're hunting to kill.) The area of Yellowstone where the wolf would be restored is the same mountain and high-plateau country that is abandoned in winter by most animals, including the aforementioned luckless bison. Part of the plan, too, is compensation to ranchers if any of their far-ranging livestock is killed by a wolf. It's a real industry out there, apparently, killing and controlling and getting compensated for losing something under the Big Sky.

Wolves gotta eat—a fact that disturbs hunters. Jack Atcheson, an outfitter in Butte, said, *Some wolves are fine if there is control. But there never will be control. The wolf-control plan provided by the Fish and Wildlife Service speaks only of protecting domestic livestock. There is no plan to protect wildlife . . . There are no surplus deer or elk in Montana . . . Their numbers are carefully managed. With uncontrolled wolf populations, a lot of people will have to give up hunting just to feed wolves. Will you give up your elk permit for a wolf?* 11

It won't be long before hunters start demanding compensation for animals they aren't able to shoot. . . .

Hunters' self-serving arguments and lies are becoming more preposterous as nonhunters awake from their long, albeit troubled, sleep. Sport hunting is immoral; it should be made illegal. Hunters are persecutors of nature who should be prosecuted. They wield a disruptive power out of all proportion to their numbers, and pandering to their interests—the special interests of a group that just wants to kill things—is mad. It's preposterous that every year less than 7 percent of the population turns the skies into shooting galleries and the woods and fields into abattoirs. It's time to stop actively supporting and passively allowing hunting, and time to stigmatize it. It's time to stop being conned and cowed by hunters, time to stop pampering and coddling them, time to get them off the government's duck-and-deer dole, time to stop thinking of wild animals as "resources" and "game," 12

The inductive arrangement of the essay leads to a strong assertion (thesis) in sentence 2 that is rephrased and amplified in the remainder of the paragraph.

Note the use of parallel structure and the repetition of the word *time* in sentences 5 and 6. "Time" is echoed in the last phrase of the essay, "check-out time."

POSSIBLE ANSWERS

Meaning and Purpose

1. Obviously, the essay is not addressed to hunters—it would only anger them—though we can easily imagine Williams enjoying the possibility that some hunters may read it. It is addressed to a broader group of nonhunters or only occasional hunters, presumably male, since it first appeared in *Esquire*. Like most argumentative essays it probably appeals most to those whose opinions it reinforces, but the passion of the argument suggests her desire to change opinions too. It's not a call to action except in the most indirect sense: Someone should make hunting illegal. Evidence to support this answer is in practically every paragraph: the emotional language; the sarcasm; the fact that she never addresses hunters, only refers to them; and the fact that she doesn't outline a plan of action for any reader to take.

2. Hunters say they hunt to relate to Death and Nature, to become a part of nature, for the nobility of the activity itself, and for the less "semireligious" reasons that man needs meat for subsistence and that hunting is a service (ridding an area of predators).

3. Williams says hunters hunt for fun, recreation, play, entertainment, thrills, to make the animals "theirs" (trophies), and to establish dominance and control.

4. The answer depends entirely on the readers, but probably most didn't know that the state bird of South Dakota was imported for "harvest" or about the political maneuvers behind the reintroduction of wolves to Yellowstone.

5. Here, too, the answer is personal. Some may complain that the essay is too intemperate in tone and would prefer a more thorough, logical argument. Others may more readily accept the emotional nature of the issue itself and find the essay convincing because it counters each of the hunters' arguments in turn.

6. The assumption is that life itself is of paramount value and should be left to its natural destiny. Williams comes closest to saying it directly in her last paragraph when she refers to animals as "sentient beings who deserve our wonder and respect." The series "put to death, extinguish, nullify, cancel, destroy" in the first paragraph and the repetition "dead, dead, dead" in paragraph 13 also reflect this assumption.

Strategy

1. She includes such quotations either to ridicule and dismiss them as she does with Ortega y Gasset, George Reiger (1), and Holmes Rolston III (2) or to let the words serve as self-convictions as she does with Bill Neal (1) and Jack Atcheson (11).

2. Williams has made little attempt to balance logic and emotion. Her argument is emotional, but it proceeds from the assumption mentioned in question 6 under Meaning and Purpose. If

and start thinking of them as sentient beings that deserve our wonder and respect, time to stop allowing hunting to be creditable by calling it "sport" and "recreation." Hunters make wildlife *dead, dead, dead.* It's time to wake up to this indisputable fact. As for the hunters, it's long past check-out time.

Meaning and Purpose

1. Is Williams's essay designed to change or reinforce a reader's opinion, to move someone to action, or both? Who is the intended audience? Support your answer with evidence from the essay.
2. According to the essay, what reasons do hunters use to explain why they hunt?
3. What are the real reasons hunters hunt according to Williams?
4. What information about hunting that you were previously unaware of has this essay given you? List specific items.
5. Do you find this essay convincing? Why or why not?
6. Underlying Williams's essay, though not directly stated, is an assumption about life and nature. What is that assumption?

Strategy

1. Williams frequently quotes the apparent words of hunters. What effect does she achieve by doing this? Point to at least one such quotation and explain why you think she included it.
2. On page 546 we say, "Throughout an argumentative essay a writer must carefully balance reason and emotion." Has Williams, in your opinion, achieved that balance? Support your answer by references to specific portions of the essay.
3. Where does Williams directly state her assertion (thesis)? Why do think she delays a direct statement for so long?

that assumption is accepted, her emotional defense of it is understandable and more acceptable.
3. The assertion is directly stated in the second sentence of the last paragraph: "Sport hunting is immoral; it should be made illegal." The essay is arranged inductively—all the previous paragraphs make this conclusion inevitable. To state her assertion at the outset would be to risk losing readers who, without having read the other paragraphs, might dismiss the essay out of hand.
4. The words of the hunters, some apparently hypothetical, some identified, some not, have been carefully selected to support her view that their arguments are fatuous, unthinking, or cruel, so she runs no risk using them.

Style

1. A variety of adjectives might be used to describe the tone: caustic, mordant, ironic, sarcastic, truculent, scathing, sardonic. Supporting examples will vary.
2. A few examples of each: *Irony:* the hunters' appreciation of beautiful creatures which they then destroy (6); hunters prey on predators, but not for food (8); the state bird of South Dakota, the ring-necked pheasant, was actually imported from Asia to be hunted (9). *Sarcasm:* Mr. Neal "blazed through this philosophical fog" (1); "it's just the cross the 'good' hunter must bear" (3); "supplement their Chicken McNuggets with venison" (5); "We took pictures, we took pictures" (6). *Emotional word and phrases:* "intellectual blather" (1); "pursuit and murder" (4); "rags in the air, shredded, blown to bits" (6); "conned and cowed" and "pampering and coddling" (13).
3. The series in sentence 5 emphasizes the finality and horror of what hunters do and discredits in advance the first quotation: "The kill is the least important part of the hunt." The repetition of "dead, dead, dead" at the end of the essay recalls the opening series and achieves the same effect even more starkly.
4. *fatuous:* foolish or inane; *precious:* seemingly plausible, but actually not valid; deceptive; *atavistic:* the reappearance of a characteristic after several generations of absence; *vermin and varmints:* disgusting or objectionable animals or insects; *abattoir:* a slaughterhouse; *sentient:* conscious, aware, having sense perceptions.

4. Williams devotes a considerable portion of her essay to the words and arguments of hunters. Why do you suppose she gives them so much space when she wants her readers to reject those ideas?

Style

1. How would you describe the tone of the essay? Point out specific examples that contribute significantly to that tone.
2. Point out examples of irony, sarcasm, and the use of emotional words and phrases.
3. What is the effect of the series of words for death in sentence 5 of the first paragraph and the three-word series in the third-to-last sentence of the essay? How do they work together?
4. If necessary look up these words in a dictionary: *fatuous* (1); *specious* (4); *atavistic* (5); *vermin* and *varmints* (7); *abattoir, sentient* (13).

Writing Tasks

1. Write an argumentative essay defending hunting. Refer to Williams's arguments as appropriate and/or quote her directly and answer her charges.
2. Write an essay calling for the abolishment of something. For example, the sale of handguns, the presidential primaries, a particular kind of tax, or athletic scholarships. Balance emotion and logic in your arguments.

At least since Aesop, people have been attracted to stories that have a moral, and this narrative has a kind of moral—an ethical argument that depends a great deal on the writer's credibility.

Indirect arguments are used for the sake of harmony. To avoid confronting readers directly, she disarms them first, here by telling about her experiences with Blue. Gradually, however, readers come to see her argument: all of us, other animals and human beings alike, have feelings and ability to communicate—and therefore have rights. It is dangerous and unethical to believe otherwise.

You could begin by asking students to think about pets. Do we "have" them or do we "own" them or do we "live with" them? How do we perceive our relationships with pets? How do we communicate with pets? How do they communicate with us? Do animals have feelings akin to ours, or is that a foolish belief?

Above all, do animals have rights? What sort of rights? And do we classify living things on a vertical line, with human beings at the top and microorganisms at the bottom, and every other living creature somewhere between? If we do, then human beings are in charge. What then are we charged with? Taking care of those "beneath" us, or are they simply here to serve us?

❦ Alice Walker ❦

Born in Eatonton, Georgia, in 1944, Alice Walker studied at Sarah Lawrence College. She has published short stories, novels, poetry, children's fiction, and two collections of essays. Though the themes of sexism and racism are predominant in her work, critics praise her writing for its universal relevance. She has taught literature and Afro-American Studies and has been writer in residence at several colleges and universities, including Wellesley College, Brandeis University, and the University of California, Berkeley. In 1983 she won both the Pulitzer Prize and the American Book Award for her novel, The Color Purple, *which was made into a feature film, directed by Steven Spielberg, in 1985. Her most recent book is a novel,* The Temple of My Familiar *(1989).*

Am I Blue?

In this essay Alice Walker uses narrative and description to further a very general argument in favor of freedom and justice. She chooses a horse as an example to illustrate her point, but her subject is all living things. This selection is from her book of essays, Living by the Word: Selected Writing 1973–1987 *(1988).*

First, skim this essay; then pause to think of how you yourself have perceived animals and other writing that includes animals. Then read the essay carefully, to see how Walker speaks of the horse and what it represents.

Walker opens with an idyllic description: the small house opens to a view of majestic unspoiled nature unobstructed by society; society is near, but it is not visible.

For about three years my companion and I rented a small house in the country that stood on the edge of a large meadow that appeared to run from the end of our deck straight into the mountains. The mountains, however, were quite far away, and between us and them there was, in fact, a town. It was one of the many pleasant aspects of the house that you never really were aware of this.   1

It was a house of many windows, low, wide, nearly floor to   2

575

ceiling in the living room, which faced the meadow, and it was from one of these that I first saw our closest neighbor, a large white horse, cropping grass, flipping its mane, and ambling about—not over the entire meadow, which stretched well out of sight of the house, but over the five or so fenced-in acres that were next to the twenty-odd that we had rented. I soon learned that the horse, whose name was Blue, belonged to a man who lived in another town, but was boarded by our neighbors next door. Occasionally, one of the children, usually a stocky teenager, but sometimes a much younger girl or boy, could be seen riding Blue. They would appear in the meadow, climb up on his back, ride furiously for ten or fifteen minutes, then get off, slap Blue on the flanks, and not be seen again for a month or more.

Feeding apples to Blue sparks Walker's reminiscence about her childhood experiences riding horses. Because of these experiences, she has an affinity for horses, recognizing their great qualities.

There were many apple trees in our yard, and one by the fence that Blue could almost reach. We were soon in the habit of feeding him apples, which he relished, especially because by the middle of summer the meadow grasses—so green and succulent since January—had dried out from lack of rain, and Blue stumbled about munching the dried stalks half-heartedly. Sometimes he would stand very still just by the apple tree, and when one of us came out he would whinny, snort loudly, or stamp the ground. This meant, of course: I want an apple.

3

It was quite wonderful to pick a few apples, or collect those that had fallen to the ground overnight, and patiently hold them, one by one, up to his large, toothy mouth. I remained as thrilled as a child by his flexible dark lips, huge, cubelike teeth that crunched the apples, core and all, with such finality, and his high, broad-breasted *enormity;* beside which, I felt small indeed. When I was a child, I used to ride horses, and was especially friendly with one named Nan until the day I was riding and my brother deliberately spooked her and I was thrown, head first, against the trunk of a tree. When I came to, I was in bed and my mother was bending worriedly over me; we silently agreed that perhaps horseback riding was not the safest sport for me. Since then I have walked, and prefer walking to horseback riding—but I had forgotten the depth of feeling one could see in horses' eyes.

4

I was therefore unprepared for the expression in Blue's. Blue

5

was lonely. Blue was horribly lonely and bored. I was not shocked that this should be the case; five acres to tramp by yourself, endlessly, even in the most beautiful of meadows—and his was—cannot provide many interesting events, and once rainy season turned to dry that was about it. No, I was shocked that I had forgotten that human animals and nonhuman animals can communicate quite well; if we are brought up around animals as children we take this for granted. By the time we are adults we no longer remember. However, the animals have not changed. They are in fact *completed* creations (at least they seem to be, so much more than we) who are not likely to change; it is their nature to express themselves. What else are they going to express? And they do. And, generally speaking, they are ignored.

The phrasing "human animals and nonhuman animals" and the reminder that children assume the ability to communicate with other animals express a natural link between human beings and animals. The link is too often broken as we grow older.

After giving Blue the apples, I would wander back to the house, aware that he was observing me. Were more apples not forthcoming then? Was that to be his sole entertainment for the day? My partner's small son had decided he wanted to learn how to piece a quilt; we worked in silence on our respective squares as I thought. . . . 6

In this transition and the next four paragraphs, Walker moves from the horse's ability to communicate with her to the larger consideration of human beings and their communication with one another, weaving an argument into her narrative: In many relationships we are not truly communicating because we are not truly listening; we are not sensitive to each other.

Well, about slavery: about white children, who were raised by black people, who knew their first all-accepting love from black women, and then, when they were twelve or so, were told they must "forget" the deep levels of communication between themselves and "mammy" that they knew. Later they would be able to relate quite calmly, "My old mammy was sold to another good family." "My old mammy was _____ _____." Fill in the blank. Many more years later a white woman would say: "I can't understand these Negroes, these blacks. What do they want? They're so different from us." 7

And about the Indians, considered to be "like animals" by the "settlers" (a very benign euphemism for what they actually were), who did not understand their description as a compliment. 8

And about the thousands of American men who marry Japanese, Korean, Filipina, and other non–English-speaking women and of how happy they report they are, *"blissfully,"* until their brides learn to speak English, at which point the marriages tend to fall apart. What then did the men see, when they looked into 9 the eyes of the women they married, before they could speak English? Apparently only their own reflections.

I thought of society's impatience with the young. "Why are   10
they playing the music so loud?" Perhaps the children have listened to much of the music of oppressed people their parents danced to before they were born, with its passionate but soft cries for acceptance and love, and they have wondered why their parents failed to hear.

Walker returns to her narrative about Blue. Only when the white horse has a mate does it see itself as free. The irony is that being alone is not the same as being independent.

I do not know how long Blue had inhabited his five beautiful,   11
boring acres before we moved into our house; a year after we had arrived—and had also traveled to other valleys, other cities, other worlds—he was still there.

But then, in our second year at the house, something hap-   12
pened in Blue's life. One morning, looking out the window at the fog that lay like a ribbon over the meadow, I saw another horse, a brown one, at the other end of Blue's field. Blue appeared to be afraid of it, and for several days made no attempt to go near. We went away for a week. When we returned, Blue had decided to make friends and the two horses ambled or galloped along together, and Blue did not come nearly as often to the fence underneath the apple tree.

When he did, bringing his new friend with him, there was a   13
different look in his eyes. A look of independence, of self-possession, of inalienable *horse*ness. His friend eventually became pregnant. For months and months there was, it seemed to me, a mutual feeling between me and the horses of justice, of peace. I fed apples to them both. The look in Blue's eyes was one of unabashed "this is *it*ness."

After the other horse has been taken back to her owner, Blue reacts much like a person whose loved one is taken away. Walker sees the affinity between the horse's feelings and how slaves must have felt—she compares the common features of relationships treated with callousness, which strengthens her later argument.

It did not, however, last forever. One day, after a visit to the   14
city, I went out to give Blue some apples. He stood waiting, or so I thought, though not beneath the tree. When I shook the tree and jumped back from the shower of apples, he made no move. I carried some over to him. He managed to half-crunch one. The rest he let fall to the ground. I dreaded looking into his eyes—because I had of course noticed that Brown, his partner, had gone—but I did look. If I had been born into slavery, and my partner had been sold or killed, my eyes would have looked like

Animals suffer, Walker argues. They share our temperaments and have joys and sorrows. Because we have forgotten that animals communicate, we do not bother to listen to them. We see them as beneath us on a vertical scale of animal life. Where we have cast animals, we have sometimes cast other people. How we treat animals parallels our way of treating other people, especially those who are seen as "beneath us." Subtly but inexorably, Walker has argued in this narrative essay that people and other animals alike are to be treated with compassion, empathy, and respect.

that. The children next door explained that Blue's partner had been "put with him" (the same expression that old people used, I had noticed, when speaking of an ancestor during slavery who had been impregnated by her owner) so that they could mate and she conceive. Since that was accomplished, she had been taken back by her owner, who lived somewhere else.

Will she be back? I asked.   15

They didn't know.   16

Blue was like a crazed person. Blue *was*, to me, a crazed   17
person. He galloped furiously, as if he were being ridden, around and around his five beautiful acres. He whinnied until he couldn't. He tore at the ground with his hooves. He butted himself against his single shade tree. He looked always and always toward the road down which his partner had gone. And then, occasionally, when he came up for apples, or I took apples to him, he looked at me. It was a look so piercing, so full of grief, a look so *human,* I almost laughed (I felt too sad to cry) to think there are people who do not know that animals suffer. People like me who have forgotten, and daily forget, all that animals try to tell us. "Everything you do to us will happen to you; we are your teachers, as you are ours. We are one lesson" is essentially it, I think. There are those who never once have even considered animals' rights: those who have been taught that animals actually want to be used and abused by us, as small children "love" to be frightened, or women "love" to be mutilated and raped. . . . They are the great-grandchildren of those who honestly thought, because someone taught them this: "Woman can't think" and "niggers can't faint." But most disturbing of all, in Blue's large brown eyes was a new look, more painful than the look of despair, the look of disgust with human beings, with life, the look of hatred. And it was odd what the look of hatred did. It gave him, for the first time, the look of a beast. And what that meant was that he had put up a barrier within to protect himself from further violence; all the apples in the world wouldn't change that fact.

Blue moves from center stage in an argument to an image in a narrative. At the very time he has come to symbolize freedom to Walker's friend, however, he has lost his own freedom. He is now an advertisement for freedom, not the real thing.

And so Blue remained, a beautiful part of our landscape, very   18
peaceful to look at from the window, white against the grass. Once a friend came to visit and said, looking out on the soothing

view: "And it *would* have to be a *white* horse; the very image of freedom." And I thought, yes, the animals are forced to become for us merely "images" of what they once so beautifully expressed. And we are used to drinking milk from containers showing "contented" cows, whose real lives we want to hear nothing about, eating eggs and drumsticks from "happy" hens, and munching hamburgers advertised by bulls of integrity who seem to command their fate.

As we talked of freedom and justice one day for all, we sat   19
down to steaks. I am eating misery, I thought, as I took the first bite. And spit it out.

The hypocrisy of discussing freedom and justice for *all,* while eating a steak, overwhelms the narrator.

POSSIBLE ANSWERS

Meaning and Purpose

1. Evidence that Walker is empathetic is in these statements, among others: "Blue was horribly lonely" (5); and "Blue *was*, to me, a crazed person" (17).
2. Walker's main point is that we are insensitive to animals, just as we are to people we think of as no more than animals. Her thesis is in words she ascribes to Blue: " 'Everything you do to us will happen to you; we are your teachers, as you are ours. We are one lesson' " (17).
3. The title questions whether people and animals are the same in having feelings and needs and being connected creatures on the same planet. She discusses how some animals and people are treated by those who have more power. The title is also that of an old blues song.
4. "*Horse*ness" means that Blue had become the most horse he could be and had all the horse identity he could have in being properly treated as a horse. "*It*ness" means that bliss and peace were achieved and Blue's life was what it should be, the ultimate, with no abuse or neglect.
5. These are false images. The reality is that cows are slaughtered and hens lay eggs to feed people. We like to imagine these animals "contented" and "happy" and not to be aware that they are treated cruelly for our advantage.

Meaning and Purpose

1. Have you ever felt empathy for an animal as Walker does for Blue? How do you know she is empathetic?
2. What is the main point Walker is making? Can you find a statement of it?
3. How does the title fit the meaning of the essay?
4. What does Walker mean by "*horse*ness" and "*it*ness" in paragraph 13?
5. In paragraph 18, what is the meaning of "contented" cows and "happy" hens?

Strategy

1. Both narration and description appear in Walker's argument. How do all three rhetorical strategies work together?
2. In paragraphs 7–10, Walker talks about a group of people with whom those in power have poor or misdirected communication, and about whom they have a low opinion. What is the connection between these paragraphs and the rest of the essay?

Strategy

1. Walker's argument is embodied in her narrative about Blue's life in the meadow. She uses the story to frame her argument and give it appeal and a familiar context. The description enhances the narrative and makes the scene real and alive—and this effect makes readers empathize with Blue as Walker does.

2. The people Walker refers to—enslaved Negroes, American Indians, foreign brides, young people—are considered like "lower" animals by some. This is what Walker thinks while she quilts and connects to the following thoughts: Blue depending on people's goodness for the quality of his life; how meaningful communication is possible between human beings and other animals; and how lack of empathy for other animals leads us also to the abuses she describes in paragraphs 7–10.

3. Walker makes an emotional appeal to readers: "Blue was lonely. Blue was horribly lonely and bored" (5); "It was a look so piercing, so full of grief, a look so *human*" (17); and "those who have been taught that animals actually want to be used and abused by us, as small children 'love' to be frightened, or women 'love' to be mutilated and raped" (17).

Style

1. That a white horse is an image of freedom is ironic because Blue is not free; he is trapped. It is ironic that our image of other animals is of " 'contented' cows," and "bulls of integrity who seem to command their fate," when really they are raised for slaughter.

2. "Anthropomorphize" means to attribute human form and traits to something not human, as when she says Blue is lonely and bored (5), he wonders "Were more apples not forthcoming then?" (6), and he had "the look of disgust with human beings, with life; the look of hatred" (17). This appeal to emotion is effective to the degree that readers identify with her feelings or think she is overly dramatic.

3. Freedom and justice are connected to Walker's purpose of recognizing the rights of animals and human beings. Her reaction to eating steak connects to the paragraph before, where she talks about image versus reality of animals' lives.

3. What kind of appeal does Walker make in her argument? Give evidence of it in the essay.

Style

1. Explain the irony in paragraph 18.
2. Look up the word *anthropomorphize* and comment on how Walker uses it, and how effective you think it is.
3. The last paragraph is about "talking of freedom and justice," and about Walker's reaction to eating steak. How is this paragraph relevant to the rest of the essay and Walker's purpose?

Writing Tasks

1. Develop an argument for or against something and write it into a narrative. Be sure the story illustrates the argument. You might argue for the rights of a group on campus while telling the story of their demonstrating or petitioning.
2. How do you think Walker would respond to Karpati's argument for using animals in medical research in "A Scientist: 'I Am the Enemy' "? How do you think Karpati would respond to Walker's assertions about animals' feelings and to her reaction to eating steak? In a paragraph or two for each, write what you think these responses would be, in a voice appropriate to each author.

TEACHING SUGGESTIONS

The first part of Gray's argument, paragraphs 1–6, should be fairly accessible to most students. She states her thesis in paragraph 1, establishes the idea of idleness as necessary for the highest human achievements as embedded in the historical thought of western civilization (culminating in Christ's "Sermon on the Mount" in paragraphs 2 and 3), suggests in paragraph 4 what could happen if St. Paul's work ethic were followed too seriously, and then establishes in paragraphs 5 and 6 why such results would occur. The reasoning, though accessible, logical, and well documented, is still difficult. We suggest a paragraph-by-paragraph analysis.

More difficult for the students will be the second part of Gray's argument, paragraphs 7–16. She plays with both ideas and language in this section of her essay, dealing with "the literary implications of good idleness." The main idea is that marketplace language is manipulative and is meant, ultimately, to make someone money. Serious writing, on the other hand, liberates language from the marketplace to plumb the depths of the human psyche and thus helps us to understand the world as it actually is. An even closer analysis may be justified here.

❦ Francine du Plessix Gray ❦

Born in France in 1930, Francine du Plessix Gray came to the United States at age eleven. She attended Bryn Mawr College and Barnard College and, in the summers, Black Mountain College, where she studied writing and painting. She was dedicated to both of these creative arts, but eventually decided to focus on writing. She has been a reporter for United Press International, an editorial assistant for a French magazine, Realités, in Paris, and a staff writer at The New Yorker. As a freelance writer since 1955, she has contributed stories and articles to major periodicals, including Vogue, The New Yorker, Saturday Review, New Republic, and New York Times Book Review. Her novels include Lovers and Tyrants *(1976) and* October Blood *(1985).*

In Praise of Idleness

Francine du Plessix Gray argues against a popular belief of Western culture, that idleness is the root of evil. Expressing solicitude for the health of the English language, she proposes that idleness may offer a source for its rejuvenation. The essay was first published in Harper's *in April 1990, but was written as a sermon delivered at the New York City Cathedral of St. John the Divine in November 1989.*

In this essay, Gray uses both logical arguments and emotional arguments. Look for each kind of argument, and ask yourself if the emotional arguments appeal more to you than the logical arguments.

MARGINAL NOTES

Gray immediately states her thesis.

Hold aloof from every Christian brother who falls into idle habits.

—From the second letter of Paul
to the Thessalonians

I plan this morning to challenge St. Paul to a public debate: 1
I shall counter the apostle's attack against idleness by exalting, in

582

Aristotle (384–322 B.C.), a Greek philosopher, pupil of Plato, and tutor of Alexander the Great.

She then immediately establishes her position, part of the mainstream of western thought.

Plato (427–347 B.C.), a Greek philosopher and a pupil of Socrates.

Gray concludes this section by quoting from Christ's "Sermon on the Mount": Matthew 6:26.

She states the possible consequences of taking St. Paul too seriously.

Now Gray spends two paragraphs explaining why taking the work ethic too seriously might be so disastrous.

Jiddu Krishnamurti (1895–1986), an Indian spiritual leader who attained fame by presenting a unique version of Hindu philosophy and mysticism. During a time of spiritual purgation that came to be known as "The Process," his "higher self" departed from his body and entered a state that to his followers appeared to be a transcendent state of consciousness.

the broadest possible way, the indispensable riches and rewards of leisure.

To begin with, let us recall that in Aristotle's *Ethics,* leisure is a far more noble, spiritual goal than work. Unlike work, which is pursued for our financial advancement or for our egos, leisure is pursued solely for its own sake. The Greek word for leisure is telling: It is *skole,* the pursuit of true learning, our absorption in activities desirable for their own sake—highest of these being the pleasures of music and poetry, the exchange of conversation with friends, and the joy of gratuitous, playful speculation. The same esteem of leisure prevailed among the Romans: The Latin words for leisure and work are also notable—leisure, the ultimate good, is *otium;* and the verbal opposite, formed by a negative prefix, is *negotium,* or gainful work.

Which leads me to think that St. Paul might well have freaked out at those symposia or banquets described by Plato that were the highest educational forums of ancient times, those indolent round-the-clock dinner parties at which—over the passing of the libation cup—some of our earliest definitions of freedom, liberty, and love were born. And how would he have reacted to Matthew's adage: "They sow not, neither do they reap, nor gather into barns; yet your Heavenly Father feedeth them"?

And so I ask you to consider the possibility that we have sought too much counsel in the proto-Calvinist work ethic preached by St. Paul and that many of us constantly run the risk of losing our compassion, if not our souls and our very selves, by channeling our energies too exclusively into useful, gainful toil.

For it is only during the cessation of work that we nurture our family bonds, educate our children, nourish our friendships; it is in "recreation" that we literally re-create, renew, restore ourselves after the wear of labor. And those of us who are painters, writers, and musicians know that it is in a particular form of idleness, in the suspension of everyday, routine work, in loafing and inviting our souls, that most of our innovations and breakthroughs, our best inspiration, come; only then can we enjoy what the Hindu philosopher Krishnamurti called a Blessed Freedom from the Known. It is in the essential lazing offered by the Sabbath ritual that prayer and recollection proceed; it is only in our ungainful unemployed time that we can tune in to God's Word by dimming out the static created by our egos and our drive to excel. And it is only in our moments of deepest repose and just plain loafing that we are offered those miraculous peak moments in which we're suddenly startled to realize that we exist, that anything exists in which the gift of existence suddenly shines out at us, like chalk on a blackboard, against the possibility of not existing at all.

Finally, one might also say that it is only in a certain kind of idling that true compassion begins. For compassion is the art of acute selfless listening, of becoming alert and mindful to the needs of others by listening to them unconditionally with what St. Benedict called the "ear of our hearts." Compassion is an acuteness of attention difficult indeed to cultivate at the workplace and most readily reached over leisurely talk or a shared walk or cup, or during visits to jails, shelters, hospitals, wherever our social concerns draw us during our time off. So I would argue against Paul that the routine of our daily work has too often served as deep, dumb, deaf sleep, a refuge from two of life's most crucial states of being—keen awakedness to the needs of others and equal awakedness to the transcendent, which only comes in some state of loitering, dallying, tarrying, goofing off.   6

I'd like to move on to the literary implications of good idleness. For beyond the human community, if there is one thing on our planet most oppressed by soul-killing labor, by a dearth of recreation, it is the medium of my craft and of all human communication—language—which has been subjected to a round-the-clock shift as a drudge of media hype and of mass communication.   7

For here I must comment on a dilemma central and unique to that terrifyingly versatile symbolic system we call language: Compared to the mediums of music and painting, language has precious little Sabbath time in which to renew and re-create itself. Unlike the serenely abstract, leisured notations of music, or those means as free from daily labor as the visual artist's paint, canvas,   8

St. Benedict (A.D. 480?–543?), an Italian monk who founded the Benedictine order about A.D. 530.

Gray shifts her argument to address the necessity of idleness for writing.

and clay, our poor medium of language works like a slave in a salt mine. Look how vast a spectrum is covered by that one entity "word": From denoting the Word of God, "word" descends to those menial symbolic signs with which we holler and whimper our most primitive needs and fears, with which we execute our crassest commercial transactions. Compare the tranquillity of the musician's or painter's means to the incessant laboring of that verbal idiom we might use, within the span of a few hours, to say such diverse things as I love you unto death; please pass the horseradish; the Dow Jones went up 17 points at closing; Winston tastes good like a cigarette should. This is the exhausted, plodding dray horse—language—we prose writers are stuck with, and our central task is to air it and freshen it and reinfuse it with playfulness and honor and integrity in order to spiritualize it into art. In sum, our vocation, as writers, is the vacation of language; our task is to liberate words from their mercantile, pragmatic, everyday labor and usher them into the frolicking idleness of a perpetual Sunday; and, hopefully, to craft them into units of sound and meaning as free from everyday toil as James Agee's phrase "His eyes had the opal lightings of dark oil," or Vladimir Nabokov's "I stared at the window whence the wounded music came," or Joyce's "riverrun, past Eve and Adam's, from bend of bay to swerve of shore . . ."

James Agee (1909–1955), an American author, scenarist, and film critic. Vladimir Nabokov (1899–1977), an American novelist and short-story writer born in Russia. James Joyce (1882–1942), an Irish novelist and short-story writer.

How to resuscitate the exhausted word after relieving it of the drudgery of full-time employment? Few writers have answered that question more eloquently than St. Augustine, whose entire process of conversion to Christianity was marked by his rebellion against the mass media of his time. For St. Augustine spent his early adulthood—when he was still a pagan—as a rhetorician, as a salesman of gross commercial language. And in late antiquity rhetoricians were the PR magnates and advertising tycoons and TV anchors of their society. Employed by politicians to write their speeches, using the techniques of eloquence to win friends and influence people, they were very dangerous precisely because they were so powerful.   9

St. Augustine (A.D. 354–430), one of the Latin fathers in the early Christian Church.

So a fair part of Augustine's conversion to Christianity is based on his realization that the art of rhetoric has turned his colleagues   10 into a society of corrupt hot-air artists, on his disillusionment with what he calls "the peddling of tongue science." And a crucial step in his spiritual progress was to drop out of the work force, to abandon his lucrative peddling job, to liberate himself and his language into the gratuitous idleness of reading and talking about philosophy. Eventually, during that famous conversion scene in the garden, St. Augustine picks up the book nearest at hand and happens upon the chapter from St. Paul's Corinthians telling him to put on the *word* of Christ. That is the moment when Augustine, former taskmaster of enslaved words, is reborn into the truth and freedom of the absolute Word, thereby liberating his own verbal idiom and crafting the "language of the soul" that he will use to write his great *Confessions*.

The implications of St. Augustine's conversion to the higher Word are as deeply literary as they are religious: Once he's given up the practice of commercial writing, he begins to see his former sin, in part, as an addiction to debased and fettered language, to any discourse in which sheer technique prevails over ethics or genuine emotion. 11

Those passages of St. Augustine's *Confessions* that deal with his conversion to a purified language intimate, as few moments in literature have, that there is a particular form of grace to be sought by all writers; that, as we parole words from their perennial salt mines, it is our spiritual duty to follow an ethic of the written sign—or, to use the phrasing of the Commandments, "Honor thy medium as thyself." St. Augustine suggests that all those devices that he and his predecessors in the art of rhetoric pioneered—simile, irony, metaphor—must be used with care and precision and never with excess or with undue striving for a flamboyant effect. 12

Flannery O'Connor (1923–1954), an American novelist and short-story writer.

Which is why I turn to another writer who saw the perils of any language engaged in daily gainful employment—our beloved contemporary Flannery O'Connor. In her book *Mystery and Manners*, O'Connor left us a small treasure house of literary ethics. And although her thoughts were often couched in theological terms, they have been decoded by even the most hardheaded agnostics as some of the most precious literary advice of our time. 13

Gray has totally turned the tables on St. Paul's work ethic. A writer must have leisure to work and that work is ultimately religious.

St. Thomas Aquinas (1225?–1274), an Italian scholastic philosopher, a major theologian of the Roman Catholic Church.

Father Thomas Merton (1915–1968), a Trappist monk, and an American poet and religious writer.

For instance, O'Connor believed that the highest purpose of literature is "the accurate naming of the things of God"—as good a metaphor as any for a fastidiously responsible, selfless, non-exploitative attitude toward language. She often turns to another injunction she has learned from St. Thomas Aquinas: The artist, she tells us, must solely be concerned with the good of that which he makes, not with the good that it can bring into his life, for only thus can his work enlarge the glory of God's creation. 14

O'Connor went on to remind us that whatever talent we have comes from the Holy Spirit. This gift is given to us to plumb the mystery of evil, the mystery of personality, the mystery of our incompleteness. It is a considerable responsibility, a mystery in itself, something gratuitous and totally undeserved whose real uses will probably always be hidden from us. 15

To which I would add: Like the spirituality of our Sabbath, our fragile, beleaguered, exhausted language—the preserver of our civilization and the vehicle for most of our gifts—thrives on attitudes of release, of labor suspended. It will best endure not on the work ethic preached by St. Paul but rather on that message expressed by Thomas Merton in the following words: "The Lord plays and diverts Himself in the garden of His creation, and if we could let go of our own obsessions with what we think is the meaning of it all, we might be able to hear His call and follow Him in His mysterious, cosmic dance. . . . For the world and time are the dance of the Lord in emptiness. The silence of the spheres is the music of a wedding feast." 16

POSSIBLE ANSWERS

Meaning and Purpose

1. Give students time to discuss the meanings of both work and leisure in their lives, and where their attitudes toward these come from.
2. The title announces the subject and the author's persuasion about it. The phrase "In Praise of Idleness" ties in stylistically to much of the

Meaning and Purpose

1. In your own life, and considering time for attending school, what has been the balance of work and leisure? Which are you encouraged to pursue?

2. Comment about the appropriateness and effectiveness of the title. What is the connotation of "idleness"? of "leisure"?

formal and religious writing quoted in the essay. "Idleness" usually has the negative connotation of time spent in unproductive laziness; "leisure" is more positive and connotes time spent at some recreational or relaxing activity.

3. The purpose is to debunk the Calvinist-like superior status of the work ethic over that of leisure time by showing the merits of and need for leisure, particularly for leisure spent raising language to an art. She states her purpose clearly in paragraph 1.

4. "Proto" means beginning or giving rise to. The Calvinist work ethic says that the measure of one's worth and productivity, and one's service to God, is in work, not leisure. Leisure time is the playground of the devil.

5. She means that language can be used for everyday purposes in society without people's ever seeing it as art; thus, the versatility is "terrifying" because it includes using language "like a slave in a salt mine" (8) and might mean the demise of language as art.

6. St. Augustine's conversion is an example of a person changing from a "salesman of gross commercial language" (9) to one who crafts the "language of the soul" (10). This discussion strengthens the author's point about the need for writers to use leisure time to raise language to an art, and so enrich us all.

Strategy

1. The author appeals to reason when she cites authorities, such as a Hindu philosopher (5) and St. Augustine (10). She also appeals to emotion, and to a higher spiritual state that she believes human beings are capable of, as in 5, and in her discussion of compassion (6). She appeals about equally to emotion and to reason.

2. The reasoning in 13 and 14 is deductive; that is, general to specific. The general premise is that language becomes drudgery with full-time "employment" and that it needs to be "resuscitated." Flannery O'Connor believes in this careful treatment of language and accomplishes it in her own writing.

3. Some references to religion and spirituality: "it is only in our ungainfully employed time that we can tune in to God's Word" (5); "equal awakedness to the transcendent" (6); " 'Honor

3. What is du Plessix Gray's purpose in the essay, and where does she state it?
4. What does du Plessix Gray mean by the "proto-Calvinist work ethic" in paragraph 4?
5. Why does du Plessix Gray call language "that terrifyingly versatile symbolic system" in paragraph 8?
6. How does the discussion of St. Augustine's "conversion to the higher Word" (11) serve the author's purpose?

Strategy

1. Do you think du Plessix Gray appeals more to reason or emotion in her argument? Show places in the essay that support your answer.
2. Explain whether the reasoning in paragraphs 13 and 14 is inductive or deductive.
3. Find some references to religion, spirituality, and religious people. How do these references serve du Plessix Gray's purpose, or strengthen her argument?
4. The essay begins and ends with quotations from religious leaders. How does this strategy help structure the essay?

Style

1. What is the tone of this essay? How do words like "the passing of the libation cup" (3) and "our task is to liberate words from their mercantile, pragmatic, everyday labor and usher them into the frolicking idleness of a perpetual Sunday" (8) work with words like "freaked out" (3), or "loitering, dallying, tarrying, goofing off" (6)? To whom does du Plessix Gray appeal?
2. In the language that she uses, du Plessix Gray tries to "spiritualize [language] into art" (8). Give some examples of figures of speech that illustrate this intent.

thy medium as thyself'" (12); and "Like the spirituality of our Sabbath" (16). Du Plessix Gray carries a religious theme throughout.

4. The beginning and ending quotations tie together the theme of spirituality in the use of leisure time. The first quotation is the work ethic that the author argues against, and the last is the one she argues for. The structure of the essay goes through refuting the first work ethic and comes out asserting the second.

Style

1. The tone is reverent, authoritative, and conversational, as seen in the varied formal and informal language. The essay is a speech (she addresses listeners directly in sentence 1) to a modern, well-educated audience probably disposed to agree with her.

2. Some "artistic language" in the essay itself is: "dimming out the static" (5)—*metaphor;* "our poor medium of language works like a slave in a salt mine" (8)—*simile;* "How to resuscitate the exhausted word after relieving it of the drudgery of full-time employment?" (9)—*personification.*

3. The fragments are effective transitions between paragraphs because they carry over unfinished thoughts. They also make the tone conversational and informal.

4. *Libation cup:* used for ceremonial drinking; *adage:* a saying that embodies a common observation; *resuscitate:* to revive from apparent death; *beleaguered:* beseiged or beset.

3. The first sentences in paragraphs 3, 9, 13, and 16 are fragments. How do these sentences work stylistically in the essay?

4. What do these words mean: *libation cup adage* (3); *resuscitate* (9); *beleaguered* (16)?

Writing Tasks

1. Write an argument titled "In Praise of _____" (fill in the blank). Address your audience directly, as if you were giving a speech. Organize the main points you want to both make and refute. Decide which kind of evidence to give in support of your argument: personal experience, experience of others, authoritative sources.

2. Illustrate each of these fallacies in a separate paragraph: faulty either/or reasoning; post hoc; false analogy. Consult the chapter introduction for explanations of the fallacies.

❦ Jonathan Swift ❦

Born in Ireland in 1667 to English parents, Swift attended Trinity College in Dublin and Oxford University in England and was ordained an Anglican priest in 1694. While in England he was active in both religion and politics and worked as a pamphlet writer for the Tory party. Frustrated for many years in his attempts to gain advancement in the church, however, Swift returned to Ireland in 1713 as Dean of St. Patrick's Cathedral in Dublin. Increasingly he devoted himself to writing satire that exposed England's injustices against the Irish. His Drapier Letters *(1724), in which he openly attacked the English for their abuses, made him a national hero in Ireland. The satirical allegory,* Gulliver's Travels *(1726), is his most famous work. When he died in 1745, three years after being declared of unsound mind, his estate went to found a hospital for the insane.*

A Modest Proposal

The barbaric conditions of English rule over Ireland in the 1720s and England's blatant refusal to help the Irish poor is the subject of this biting satire, first published anonymously in 1729. Logic, hard facts, tone, and emotional appeal all contribute to the power of this argument.

Before you read this essay, read the definitions of irony *and* persona *in the Glossary. Look for examples of irony in the essay and try to imagine what sort of person (persona) would write this essay.*

***

It is a melancholy object to those who walk through this great 1
town or travel in the country, when they see the streets, the roads, and cabin doors, crowded with beggars of the female sex, followed by three, four, or six children, all in rags and importuning every passenger for an alms. These mothers, instead of being able to work for their honest livelihood, are forced to employ all their time in strolling to beg sustenance for their helpless infants, who, as they grow up, either turn thieves for want of work, or leave

"Pretender": James Stuart. In 1718, many Irishmen joined an army dedicated to restoring Stuart to the crown.

"Barbados": Other Irish, wanting to emigrate, bound themselves as indentured servants to work for a number of years in the Barbados, a West Indies island, or other British colonies to pay for their passage.

"projectors": planners, people who develop projects or schemes. Swift takes on this persona in the essay.

"shilling": At the time a shilling was worth less than twenty-five cents in today's United States currency.

Swift uses process analysis here to develop his argument, describing his method of calculation.

their dear native country to fight for the Pretender in Spain, or sell themselves to the Barbados.

I think it is agreed by all parties that this prodigious number of children in the arms, or on the backs, or at the heels of their mothers, and frequently of their fathers, is in the present deplorable state of the kingdom a very great additional grievance; and therefore whoever could find out a fair, cheap, and easy method of making these children sound, useful members of the commonwealth would deserve so well of the public as to have his statue set up for a preserver of the nation.

But my intention is very far from being confined to provide only for the children of professed beggars; it is of a much greater extent, and shall take in the whole number of infants at a certain age who are born of parents in effect as little able to support them as those who demand our charity in the streets.

As to my own part, having turned my thoughts for many years upon this important subject, and maturely weighed the several schemes of other projectors, I have always found them grossly mistaken in their computation. It is true, a child just dropped from its dam may be supported by her milk for a solar year, with little other nourishment; at most not above the value of two shillings, which the mother may certainly get, or the value in scraps, by her lawful occupation of begging; and it is exactly at one year old that I propose to provide for them in such a manner as instead of being a charge upon their parents or the parish, or wanting food and raiment for the rest of their lives, they shall on the contrary contribute to the feeding, and partly to the clothing, of many thousands.

There is likewise another great advantage in my scheme, that it will prevent those voluntary abortions, and that horrid practice of women murdering their bastard children, alas, too frequent among us, sacrificing the poor innocent babes, I doubt, more to avoid the expense than the shame, which would move tears and pity in the most savage and inhuman breast.

The number of souls in this kingdom being usually reckoned one million and a half, of these I calculate there may be about two hundred thousand couples whose wives are breeders; from which number I subtract thirty thousand couples who are able to maintain their own children, although I apprehend there cannot be so many under the present distress of the kingdom; but this being granted, there will remain an hundred and seventy thousand breeders. I again subtract fifty thousand for those women who miscarry, or whose children die by accident or disease within the year. There only remain an hundred and twenty thousand children of poor parents annually born. The question therefore is, how this number shall be reared and provided for, which, as I have already said, under the present situation of affairs, is utterly impossible by all the methods hitherto proposed. For we can neither employ them in handicraft nor agriculture; we neither build houses (I mean in the country) nor cultivate land. They can very seldom pick up a livelihood by stealing till they arrive at six years old, except where they are of towardly parts; although I confess they learn the rudiments much earlier, during which time they can however be looked upon only as probationers, as I have been informed by a principal gentleman in the county of Cavan, who protested to me that he never knew above one or two instances under the age of six, even in a part of the kingdom so renowned for the quickest proficiency in that art.

"are of towardly parts": Have innate ability.

"Cavan": a county in north central Ireland.

I am assured by our merchants that a boy or a girl before twelve years old is no salable commodity; and even when they come to this age, they will not yield above three pounds, or three pounds and half a crown at most on the Exchange; which cannot turn to account either to the parents or the kingdom, the charge of nutriment and rags having been at least four times that value. 7

"three pounds and half a crown": A pound was twenty shillings, a crown five shillings.

I shall now therefore humbly propose my own thoughts, which I hope will not be liable to the least objection. 8

Paragraphs 8–16 present the proposal, more calculations to demonstrate its potential, and a few ideas about how it would work.

I have been assured by a very knowing American of my acquaintance in London, that a young healthy child well nursed is at a year old a most delicious, nourishing, and wholesome food, whether stewed, roasted, baked, or boiled; and I make no doubt that it will equally serve in a fricassee or a ragout. 9

"ragout": A highly spiced French stew.

I do therefore humbly offer it to public consideration that of the hundred and twenty thousand children, already computed, 10

Paragraphs 10–15 compose a process analysis, the workings of the proposal. Paragraph 10 itself is cause-and-effect analysis.

Instead of the narrator's voice here, we get the voice of Swift himself, evident because the narrator has no quarrel with landlords and no sympathy with tenants. The pun on "devour" ironically gives away the stratagem because the humorless narrator would never have punned.

"French physician": François Rabelais (1494–1553), Swift's favorite French writer and a broad humorist, and thus not a grave author at all.

"among us": The narrator addresses the chief landowners and administrators of Ireland, who are Anglo-Irish (Englishmen who became Irish citizens) and Protestant. His views of Catholicism in Ireland and abroad reflect theirs.

twenty thousand may be reserved for breed, whereof only one fourth part to be males, which is more than we allow to sheep, black cattle, or swine; and my reason is that these children are seldom the fruits of marriage, a circumstance not much regarded by our savages, therefore one male will be sufficient to serve four females. That the remaining hundred thousand may at a year old be offered in sale to the persons of quality and fortune through the kingdom, always advising the mother to let them suck plentifully in the last month, so as to render them plump and fat for a good table. A child will make two dishes at an entertainment for friends; and when the family dines alone, the fore or hind quarter will make a reasonable dish, and seasoned with a little pepper or salt will be very good boiled on the fourth day, especially in winter.

I have reckoned upon a medium that a child just born will weigh twelve pounds, and in a solar year if tolerably nursed increaseth to twenty-eight pounds.   11

I grant this food will be somewhat dear, and therefore very proper for landlords, who, as they have already devoured most of the parents, seem to have the best title to the children.   12

Infant's flesh will be in season throughout the year, but more plentiful in March, and a little before and after. For we are told by a grave author, an eminent French physician, that fish being a prolific diet, there are more children born in Roman Catholic countries about nine months after Lent, than at any other season; therefore, reckoning a year after Lent, the markets will be more glutted than usual, because the number of popish infants is at least three to one in this kingdom; and therefore it will have one other collateral advantage, by lessening the number of Papists among us.   13

I have already computed the charge of nursing a beggar's child (in which list I reckon all cottagers, laborers, and four fifths of the farmers) to be about two shillings per annum, rags included; and I believe no gentleman would repine to give ten shillings for the carcass of a good fat child, which, as I have said, will make four dishes of excellent nutritive meat, when he hath only some particular friend or his own family to dine with him. Thus the   14 squire will learn to be a good landlord, and grow popular among the tenants; the mother will have eight shillings net profit, and be fit for work till she produces another child.

Those who are more thrifty (as I must confess the times require) may flay the carcass; the skin of which artificially dressed will make admirable gloves for ladies, and summer boots for fine gentlemen. 15

"artificially": artfully.

As to our city of Dublin, shambles may be appointed for this purpose in the most convenient parts of it, and butchers we may be assured will not be wanting; although I rather recommend buying the children alive, and dressing them hot from the knife as we do roasting pigs. 16

"shambles": butcher shops or slaughter houses.

A very worthy person, a true lover of his country, and whose virtues I highly esteem, was lately pleased in discoursing on this matter to offer a refinement upon my scheme. He said that many gentlemen of his kingdom, having of late destroyed their deer, he conceived that the want of venison might be well supplied by the bodies of young lads and maidens, not exceeding fourteen years of age nor under twelve, so great a number of both sexes in every country being now ready to starve for want of work and service; and these to be disposed of by their parents, if alive, or otherwise by their nearest relations. But with due deference to so excellent a friend and so deserving a patriot, I cannot be altogether in his sentiments; for as to the males, my American acquaintance assured me from frequent experience that their flesh was generally tough and lean, like that of our schoolboys, by continual exercise, and their taste disagreeable; and to fatten them would not answer the charge. Then as to the females, it would, I think with humble submission, be a loss to the public, because they soon would become breeders themselves; and besides, it is not improbable that some scrupulous people might be apt to censure such a practice (although indeed very unjustly) as a little bordering upon cruelty; which, I confess, hath always been with me the strongest objection against any project, how well soever intended. 17

Paragraphs 17 and 18 present and reject a possible refinement of the proposal.

But in order to justify my friend, he confessed that this expedient was put into his head by the famous Psalmanazar, a native of the island Formosa, who came from thence to London above 18

"Psalmanazar": Georges Psalmanazar, a Frenchman who passed himself off as a native Formosan in a totally fictional *Description of the Isle of Formosa* (1705). He became a celebrity of sorts in a gullible English society.

"groat": a coin worth a few pennies. "chair": A sedan chair, on which a person is carried by two men. Swift's own voice surfaces again to attack the costs for "foreign fineries."

Paragraph 19 dispenses with a possible remaining problem.

Paragraphs 20–28 describe the proposal's numerous advantages.

Swift uses cause-and-effect development in paragraphs 21–28. The advantages of the proposal are the positive effects showing that the plan will benefit both the poor (24–26) and the rich (21–23, 25, 27–28). In paragraph 21 Swift attacks the current prejudice against Irish Catholics as well as the motives of many Protestant dissenters from the Church of England.

twenty years ago, and in conversation told my friend that in his country when any young person happened to be put to death, the executioner sold the carcass to the persons of quality as a prime dainty; and that in his time the body of a plump girl of fifteen, who was crucified for an attempt to poison the emperor, was sold to his Imperial Majesty's prime minister of state, and other great mandarins of the court, in joints from the gibbet, at four hundred crowns. Neither indeed can I deny that if the same use were made of several plump young girls in this town, who without one single groat to their fortunes cannot stir abroad without a chair, and appear at the playhouse and assemblies in foreign fineries which they never will pay for, the kingdom would not be the worse.

Some persons of a desponding spirit are in great concern about that vast number of poor people who are aged, diseased, or maimed, and I have been desired to employ my thoughts what course may be taken to ease the nation of so grievous an encumbrance. But I am not in the least pain upon that matter, because it is very well known that they are every day dying and rotting by cold and famine, and filth and vermin, as fast as can be reasonably expected. And as to the younger laborers, they are now in almost as hopeful a condition. They cannot get work, and consequently pine away for want of nourishment to a degree that if any time they are accidentally hired to common labor, they have not strength to perform it; and thus the country and themselves are happily delivered from the evils to come.

I have too long digressed, and therefore shall return to my subject. I think the advantages by the proposal which I have made are obvious and many, as well as of the highest importance.

For first, as I have already observed, it would greatly lessen the number of Papists, with whom we are yearly overrun, being the principal breeders of the nation as well as our most dangerous enemies; and who stay at home on purpose to deliver the kingdom to the Pretender, hoping to take their advantage by the absence of so many good Protestants, who have chosen rather to leave their country than to stay at home and pay tithes against their conscience to an Episcopal curate.

"liable to distress": subject to seizures by creditors.

Paragraphs 24–33 anticipate objections to the proposal and dispose of them.

"receipts": recipes.

Secondly, the poorer tenants will have something valuable of their own, which by law may be made liable to distress, and help to pay their landlord's rent, their corn and cattle being already seized and money a thing unknown.

23 Thirdly, whereas the maintenance of an hundred thousand children, from two years old and upwards, cannot be computed at less than ten shillings a piece per annum, the nation's stock will be thereby increased fifty thousand pounds per annum, besides the profit of a new dish introduced to the tables of all gentlemen of fortune in the kingdom who have any refinement in taste. And the money will circulate among ourselves, the goods being entirely of our own growth and manufacture.

24 Fourthly, the constant breeders, besides the gain of eight shillings sterling per annum by the sale of their children, will be rid of the charge for maintaining them after the first year.

25 Fifthly, this food would likewise bring great custom to taverns, where the vintners will certainly be so prudent as to procure the best receipts for dressing it to perfection, and consequently have their houses frequented by all the fine gentlemen, who justly value themselves upon their knowledge in good eating; and a skillful cook, who understands how to oblige his guests, will contrive to make it as expensive as they please.

26 Sixthly, this would be a great inducement to marriage, which all wise nations have either encouraged by rewards or enforced by laws and penalties. It would increase the care and tenderness of mothers toward their children, when they were sure of a settlement for life to the poor babes, provided in some sort by the public, to their annual profit instead of expense. We should see an honest emulation among the married women, which of them could bring the fattest child to the market. Men would become as fond of their wives during the time of their pregnancy as they are now of their mares in foal, their cows in calf, or sows when they are ready to farrow; nor offer to beat or kick them (as is too frequent a practice) for fear of a miscarriage.

27 Many other advantages might be enumerated. For instance, the addition of some thousand carcasses in our exportation of barreled beef, the propagation of swine's flesh, and improvements

in the art of making good bacon, so much wanted among us by the great destruction of pigs, too frequent at our tables, which are no way comparable in taste or magnificence to a well-grown, fat, yearling child, which roasted whole will make a considerable figure at a lord mayor's feast or any other public entertainment. But this and many others I omit, being studious of brevity.

Supposing that one thousand families in this city would be constant customers for infants' flesh, besides others who might have it at merry meetings, particularly weddings and christenings, I compute that Dublin would take off annually about twenty thousand carcasses, and the rest of the kingdom (where probably they will be sold somewhat cheaper) the remaining eighty thousand.

I can think of no one objection that will possibly be raised against this proposal, unless it should be urged that the number of people will be thereby much lessened in the kingdom. This I freely own, and it was indeed one principal design in offering it to the world. I desire the reader will observe, that I calculate my remedy for this one individual kingdom of Ireland and for no other that ever was, is, or I think ever can be upon earth. Therefore, let no man talk to me of other expedients: of taxing our absentees at five shillings a pound: of using neither clothes nor household furniture except what is of our own growth and manufacture: of utterly rejecting the materials and instruments that promote foreign luxury: of curing the expensiveness of pride, vanity, idleness, and gaming in our women: of introducing a vein of parsimony, prudence, and temperance: of learning to love our country, in the want of which we differ even from Laplanders and the inhabitants of Topinamboo: of quitting our animosities and factions, nor acting any longer like the Jews, who were murdering one another at the very moment their city was taken: of being a little cautious not to sell our country and conscience for nothing: of teaching landlords to have at least one degree of mercy toward their tenants: lastly, of putting a spirit of honesty, industry, and skill into our shopkeepers; who, if a resolution could now be taken to buy only our native goods, would immediately unite to cheat and exact upon us in the price, the measure, and the

Many of these proposals Swift himself had made in earlier works.

"Topinamboo": A district in Brazil inhabited by primitive tribes and notorious for barbarism and ignorance.

Refers to the fall of Jerusalem to the Romans (**A.D.** 70), during which time many prominent Jews were executed on charges of collaborating with the enemy.

28

29

goodness, nor could ever yet be brought to make one fair proposal of just dealing, though often and earnestly invited to it.

Therefore, I repeat, let no man talk to me of these and the like expedients, till he hath at least some glimpse of hope that there will ever be some hearty and sincere attempt to put them in practice.

But as to myself, having been wearied out for many years with offering vain, idle, visionary thoughts, and at length utterly despairing of success, I fortunately fell upon this proposal, which, as it is wholly new, so it hath something solid and real, of no expense and little trouble, full in our own power, and whereby we can incur no danger in disobliging England. For this kind of commodity will not bear exportation, the flesh being of too tender a consistence to admit a long continuance in salt, although perhaps I could name a country which would be glad to eat up our whole nation without it.

After all, I am not so violently bent upon my own opinion as to reject any offer proposed by wise men, which shall be found equally innocent, cheap, easy, and effectual. But before something of that kind shall be advanced in contradiction to my scheme, and offering a better, I desire the author or authors will be pleased maturely to consider two points. First, as things now stand, how they will be able to find food and raiment for an hundred thousand useless mouths and backs. And secondly, there being a round million of creatures in human figure throughout this kingdom, whose sole subsistence put into a common stock would leave them in debt two millions of pounds sterling, adding those who are beggars by profession to the bulk of farmers, cottagers, and laborers, with their wives and children who are beggars in effect; I desire those politicians who dislike my overture, and may perhaps be so bold to attempt an answer, that they will first ask the parents of these mortals whether they would not at this day think it a great happiness to have been sold for food at a year old in this manner I prescribe, and thereby have avoided such a perpetual scene of misfortunes as they have since gone through by the oppression of landlords, the impossibility of paying rent without money or trade, the want of common sustenance, with neither

30

31

32

"country": England. Swift again allows his own voice to intrude where he says the English may as well eat Irish children, for they are already glad to eat up the nation.

house nor clothes to cover them from the inclemencies of the weather, and the most inevitable prospect of entailing the like or greater miseries upon their breed forever.

I profess, in the sincerity of my heart, that I have not the least personal interest in endeavoring to promote this necessary work, having no other motive than the public good of my country, by advancing our trade, providing for infants, relieving the poor, and giving some pleasure to the rich. I have no children by which I can propose to get a single penny; the youngest being nine years old, and my wife past childbearing.   33

Meaning and Purpose

1. Swift uses the persona of a "projector," a person who suggests plans for social and economic change (see paragraph 9) to put forth a "modest proposal." Describe the character of this projector. How do his views differ from those of Swift? Where do you find Swift's voice and beliefs coming to the surface?
2. Exactly what is Swift's "modest proposal"? What problems is it designed to solve? In what ways would it solve those problems?
3. What, primarily, does Swift condemn in the essay?
4. Underneath all the irony, what is Swift arguing for?
5. What objections to Swift's proposal can you think of?

Strategy

1. What does Swift do in paragraph 1 to set the reader up for the text that follows?
2. What means does Swift use to establish the narrator as reasonable, ethical, and trustworthy?
3. Where does Swift first give the reader a clue that his plan is horrible, not modest?
4. What purpose does the final paragraph serve?

POSSIBLE ANSWERS

Meaning and Purpose

1. The persona writes as an efficient, rational man who sincerely wants to solve the problems of Ireland in a reasonable and humane way. Swift offers real solutions to the problems (29). He voices exasperation, however, that the real solutions have never been tried (30, 31).
2. The essay's persona proposes to kill one-year-old Irish infants and sell their flesh as meat to the wealthy. Because the Irish poor are oppressed by their landlords and have no reliable source of income, they have no way to escape their poverty. His proposal would remedy this social ill.
3. Swift condemns the cruel exploitation and oppression of the Irish by the English.
4. Underneath his irony, Swift pleads for charity and compassion. He sets forth reasonable and compassionate solutions (29).
5. Ask students to try to be serious about answering this question, perhaps in the same rational voice Swift uses.

Strategy

1. By vividly depicting poor women and their children, he creates sympathy for them so that the reader will react with horror to his proposal.
2. Swift, calling his proposal "modest," repeatedly describes the time and care he spent pondering the problem (4), and uses first person with verbs of consideration: "I calculate," "I subtract," "I apprehend," and so on (6). He cites authorities and experts, such as the "very knowing American" (9). He puts forth his proposal with modesty and humility (8, 10). His attitude is respectful throughout: "as I must confess," (15); "although I rather recommend" (16); "But with due deference" (17). He piously objects to cruelty (5, 17). He refers repeatedly to the good of the nation (2, 7, 19, 21, 23, 29, 33). He carefully lists the

advantages of the proposal (21–28). He fears the flesh would spoil if exported (31). And he ironically professes at the end that he wouldn't make a penny from the proposal.

3. The first clue is language that is too outrageous to be taken seriously.

4. The final paragraph serves at least two subtle purposes: Swift takes one last poke at those whose sole motivation is profit, and he aligns himself with the oppressed, the implication being that if he had infants they also would be for sale.

Style

1. The livestock expressions dehumanize the Irish poor, making the narrator's proposal more palatable—and Swift's satire more horrifying. These expressions also reflect and thus satirize English attitudes toward the Irish poor.

2. Some students undoubtedly will object to Swift's somewhat archaic language ("increaseth," paragraph 11; "how well soever intended," 17), to his formality, and to his often complicated sentences. Others may find that initial difficulties soon fade. Some others may recognize that Swift's formal style perfectly fits the narrator's rather pompous persona.

3. *Importuning:* pressing or besetting with solicitations; *prodigious:* extraordinary in amount; *rudiments:* elements or first principles of a subject; *fricassee:* meat browned lightly, stewed, and served in a sauce made with its own stock; *ragout:* a highly spiced French stew; *prolific:* producing abundant offspring; *papists:* Roman Catholics; *repine:* complain; *deference:* respectful submission or yielding to another's judgment, opinion, or will; *mandarins:* members of an elite or powerful class; *gibbet:* a gallows with a projecting arm at the top, from which the bodies of criminals were formerly hung in chains and left suspended after execution; *desponding:* depressed from loss of hope; *tithes:* the tenth part of agricultural products or income paid in support of the church or priesthood; *vintners:* people who make or sell wine; *farrow:* to bring forth young; *parsimony:* extreme or excessive economy or frugality; *animosities:* feelings of strong dislike; *disobliging:* giving offense or affront to; *inclemencies:* severities or harshnesses of weather; *entailing:* causing.

Style

1. How does Swift's choice of words enforce the barbarity of his proposal? Pay particular attention to his referring to Ireland's poor in language usually reserved for livestock, such as "breeders" (6) and "fore or hind quarter" (10). Find other such expressions or sentences.

2. How would you describe Swift's writing style? Support your opinion by giving examples. Do his style and diction inhibit your understanding and appreciation of the essay? Why or why not?

3. If necessary, check the meanings of these words in a dictionary: *importuning* (1); *prodigious* (2); *rudiments* (6); *fricassee, ragout* (9); *prolific, papists* (13); *repine* (14); *deference* (17); *mandarins, gibbet* (18); *desponding* (19); *tithes* (21); *vintners* (25); *farrow* (26); *parsimony, animosities* (29); *disobliging* (31); *inclemencies, entailing* (32).

Writing Tasks

1. Think of a personal, social, or economic problem that you have an opinion about, and write an outrageous solution to it in a rational and responsible voice. Share your essay with other students to see if you have made your point effectively with irony.

2. Take the same problem you discussed in task 1 and propose a real, not an outrageous, solution to it. Consider your audience and whether to appeal to emotion or reason.

Some students may have seen and heard King speak on television, particularly the "I have a dream" speech, but the 1950s and 1960s civil-rights movement will be ancient history to most. Give them some history of the movement before they read the essay.

In 1955, Mrs. Rosa Parks, a seventy-two-year-old black woman, was arrested for breaking Montgomery, Alabama's segregation laws by refusing to give up her seat on a city bus to a white passenger. The outraged blacks organized the Montgomery Improvement Association to boycott the city's public-transit system. King, pastor of a Montgomery Baptist Church, was elected leader of the Association. In a difficult year it successfully desegregated transportation. King, greatly influenced by the New Testament teachings of Jesus, Thoreau's views on civil disobedience, and Gandhi's principle of nonviolent civil disobedience, then formed the Southern Christian Leadership Conference, which was committed to using nonviolent resistance to accomplish desegregation.

King put Birmingham, Alabama, the most segregated city in the South, in world news in 1963 when he led a campaign to desegregate the city's lunch counters and hiring. To the demonstrations and sit-ins, the Birmingham police responded by turning firehoses and dogs on the demonstrators and jailing King and 2,400 other civil rights workers. Eight local clergymen issued a public letter agreeing with the aims of the movement but deploring the methods used. King's letter is a response to theirs. King uses both logical argument and persuasion to convince readers that his actions are morally compelling. And his argument is complex enough to warrant a paragraph-by-paragraph analysis. You or one of your students might read paragraph 14 aloud to demonstrate its rhetorical power.

In 1964, Martin Luther King, Jr., was awarded the Nobel Peace Prize, at 34 the youngest person ever to receive that prestigious honor. He was murdered on April 14, 1968, in Memphis, Tennessee.

❦ Martin Luther King, Jr. ❦

Born in Atlanta, Georgia, King was the son of a Baptist minister. At age eighteen he was an ordained minister himself. He went on to study at Morehouse College, Crozer Theological Seminary, and Boston University, where he earned a Ph.D. Until his assassination in Memphis, Tennessee, in 1968, he was the acknowledged leader of the American civil-rights movement, having gained national recognition in 1955 by organizing a successful boycott of the segregated busing system of Montgomery, Alabama. He was arrested and jailed more than a dozen times as a civil-rights leader, once for eight days, during which time he wrote the now-famous letter reprinted here. He founded and acted as president of the Southern Christian Leadership Conference, through which he promoted a philosophy of nonviolent resistance to racial discrimination that has often been compared to Gandhi's. In 1964 he was awarded the Nobel prize for peace.

Letter from Birmingham Jail

King's letter is written in response to a public statement by Birmingham clergymen who opposed the demonstrations King was leading to protest against the city's segregated transportation system. The argument is backed by examples from history, philosophy, theology, and literature, but the power of the writing lies equally in King's rich rhetorical style.

One of the strengths of King's style is that it is highly coherent, in the sense that the content in each paragraph flows into the content of the next paragraph. As you read this essay, notice the extraordinarily strong transitions from paragraph to paragraph.

MY DEAR FELLOW CLERGYMEN:

While confined here in the Birmingham city jail, I came across your recent statement calling my present activities "unwise and untimely." Seldom do I pause to answer criticism of my work and ideas. If I sought to answer all the criticisms that cross my desk, my secretaries would have little time for anything other than such

MARGINAL NOTES

Paragraphs 1–4 explain King's presence in Birmingham, proceeding from immediate and practical causes to more philosophical, ultimate causes.

The first reason for his presence in Birmingham, he explains, is that he is president of the Southern Christian Leadership Conference, an interstate organization that has business there. He was, therefore, invited.

The second reason he is there is that injustice is there, and like the Apostle Paul and other religious prophets, he must respond.

The third reason for his presence is that we are all inextricably related, and injustice anywhere in our society affects us all. King, therefore, cannot be an "outside agitator." He is there because he is needed.

correspondence in the course of the day, and I would have no time for constructive work. But since I feel that you are men of genuine good will and that your criticisms are sincerely set forth, I want to try to answer your statement in what I hope will be patient and reasonable terms.

I think I should indicate why I am here in Birmingham, since you have been influenced by the view which argues against "outsiders coming in." I have the honor of serving as president of the Southern Christian Leadership Conference, an organization operating in every southern state, with headquarters in Atlanta, Georgia. We have some eighty-five affiliated organizations across the South, and one of them is the Alabama Christian Movement for Human Rights. Frequently we share staff, educational, and financial resources with our affiliates. Several months ago the affiliate here in Birmingham asked us to be on call to engage in a nonviolent direct-action program if such were deemed necessary. We readily consented, and when the hour came, we lived up to our promise. So I, along with several members of my staff, am here because I was invited here. I am here because I have organizational ties here.

But more basically, I am in Birmingham because injustice is here. Just as the prophets of the eighth century B.C. left their villages and carried their "thus saith the Lord" far beyond the boundaries of their home towns, and just as the Apostle Paul left his village of Tarsus and carried the gospel of Jesus Christ to the far corners of the Greco-Roman world, so am I compelled to carry the gospel of freedom beyond my own home town. Like Paul, I must constantly respond to the Macedonian call for aid.

Moreover, I am cognizant of the interrelatedness of all communities and states. I cannot sit idly by in Atlanta and not be concerned about what happens in Birmingham. Injustice anywhere is a threat to justice everywhere. We are caught in an inescapable network of mutuality, tied in a single garment of destiny. Whatever affects one directly, affects all indirectly. Never again can we afford to live with the narrow, provincial "outside agitator" idea. Anyone who lives inside the United States can never be considered an outsider anywhere within its bounds.

King uses paragraphs 5–9 to dispose of the clergymen's first objection, their deploring that Birmingham is the site of the demonstrations. Blacks, he explains, had "no alternative." His argument in this section is circular: There must be direct action after three more moderate steps have been taken; those three steps have been taken; there must, therefore, be direct action. The major premise is stated as a given. The minor premise, that all necessary steps have been taken, King fully documents.

King outlines the "four basic steps" in paragraph 6 and demonstrates how the first step, establishing that racial injustices exist in Birmingham, has been taken.

The second step, negotiation, was a failure.

King describes the third step, self-purification.

You deplore the demonstrations taking place in Birmingham. But your statement, I am sorry to say, fails to express a similar concern for the conditions that brought about the demonstrations. I am sure that none of you would want to rest content with the superficial kind of social analysis that deals merely with effects and does not grapple with underlying causes. It is unfortunate that demonstrations are taking place in Birmingham, but it is even more unfortunate that the city's white power structure left the Negro community with no alternative. 5

In any nonviolent campaign there are four basic steps: collection of the facts to determine whether injustices exist; negotiation; self-purification; and direct action. We have gone through all these steps in Birmingham. There can be no gainsaying the fact that racial injustice engulfs this community. Birmingham is probably the most thoroughly segregated city in the United States. Its ugly record of brutality is widely known. Negroes have experienced grossly unjust treatment in the courts. There have been more unsolved bombings of Negro homes and churches in Birmingham than in any other city in the nation. These are the hard, brutal facts of the case. On the basis of these conditions, Negro leaders sought to negotiate with the city fathers. But the latter consistently refused to engage in good-faith negotiation. 6

Then, last September, came the opportunity to talk with leaders of Birmingham's economic community. In the course of the negotiations, certain promises were made by the merchants—for example, to remove the stores' humiliating racial signs. On the basis of these promises, the Reverend Fred Shuttlesworth and the leaders of the Alabama Christian Movement for Human Rights agreed to a moratorium on all demonstrations. As the weeks and months went by, we realized that we were the victims of a broken promise. A few signs, briefly removed, returned; the others remained. 7

As in so many past experiences, our hopes had been blasted, and the shadow of deep disappointment settled upon us. We had no alternative except to prepare for direct action, whereby we would present our very bodies as a means of laying our case before the conscience of the local and the national community. 8

Mindful of the difficulties involved, we decided to undertake a process of self-purification. We began a series of workshops on nonviolence, and we repeatedly asked ourselves: "Are you able to accept blows without retaliating?" "Are you able to endure the ordeal of jail?" We decided to schedule our direct-action program for the Easter season, realizing that except for Christmas, this is the main shopping period of the year. Knowing that a strong economic-withdrawal program would be the by product of direct action, we felt that this would be the best time to bring pressure to bear on the merchants for the needed change.

Then it occurred to us that Birmingham's mayoral election was coming up in March, and we speedily decided to postpone action until after election day. When we discovered that the Commissioner of Public Safety, Eugene "Bull" Connor, had piled up enough votes to be in the run-off, we decided again to postpone action until the day after the run-off so that the demonstrations could not be used to cloud the issues. Like many others, we waited to see Mr. Connor defeated, and to this end we endured postponement after postponement. Having aided in this community need, we felt that our direct-action program could be delayed no longer. 9

You may well ask, "Why direct action? Why sit-ins, marches, and so forth? Isn't negotiation a better path?" You are quite right in calling for negotiation. Indeed, this is the very purpose of direct action. Nonviolent direct action seeks to create such a crisis and foster such a tension that a community which has constantly refused to negotiate is forced to confront the issue. It seeks so to dramatize the issue that it can no longer be ignored. My citing the creation of tension as part of the work of the nonviolent-resister may sound rather shocking. But I must confess that I am not afraid of the word "tension." I have earnestly opposed violent tension, but there is a type of constructive, nonviolent tension which is necessary for growth. Just as Socrates felt that it was necessary to create a tension in the mind so that individuals could rise from the bondage of myths and half-truths to the unfettered realm of creative analysis and objective appraisal, so must we see the need for nonviolent gadflies to create the kind of tension in 10

The final step, demonstration, has become inevitable.

In paragraphs 10 and 11 King argues the need for direct action, basing his argument primarily on Socrates.

Socrates (469?–399 B.C.) was an Athenian philosopher.

society that will help men rise from the dark depths of prejudice and racism to the majestic heights of understanding and brotherhood.

The purpose of our direct-action program is to create a situation so crisis-packed that it will inevitably open the door to negotiation. I therefore concur with you in your call for negotiation. Too long has our beloved Southland been bogged down in a tragic effort to live in monologue rather than dialogue. 11

Paragraphs 12–14 refute the clergymen's second charge, that the demonstrations are untimely, by demonstrating the opposite.

One of the basic points in your statement is that the action that I and my associates have taken in Birmingham is untimely. Some have asked: "Why didn't you give the new city administration time to act?" The only answer that I can give to this query is that the new Birmingham administration must be prodded about as much as the outgoing one, before it will act. We are sadly mistaken if we feel that the election of Albert Boutwell as mayor will bring the millennium to Birmingham. While Mr. Boutwell is a much more gentle person than Mr. Connor, they are both segregationists, dedicated to maintenance of the status quo. I have hoped that Mr. Boutwell will be reasonable enough to see the futility of massive resistance to desegregation. But he will not see this without pressure from devotees of civil rights. My friends, I must say to you that we have not made a single gain in civil rights without determined legal and nonviolent pressure. Lamentably, it is an historical fact that privileged groups seldom give up their privileges voluntarily. Individuals may see the moral light and voluntarily give up their unjust posture; but, as Reinhold Niebuhr has reminded us, groups tend to be more immoral than individuals. 12

Reinhold Niebuhr (1892–1971), an American Protestant theologian and philosopher.

We know through painful experience that freedom is never voluntarily given by the oppressor; it must be demanded by the oppressed. Frankly, I have yet to engage in a direct-action campaign that was "well timed" in the view of those who have not suffered unduly from the disease of segregation. For years now I have heard the word "Wait!" It rings in the ear of every Negro with piercing familiarity. This "Wait" has almost always meant "Never." We must come to see, with one of our distinguished jurists, that "justice too long delayed is justice denied." 13

We have waited for more than 340 years for our constitutional 14
and God-given rights. The nations of Asia and Africa are moving
with jetlike speed toward gaining political independence, but we
still creep at horse-and-buggy pace toward gaining a cup of coffee
at a lunch counter. Perhaps it is easy for those who have never
felt the stinging darts of segregation to say, "Wait." But when you
have seen vicious mobs lynch your mothers and fathers at will
and drown your sisters and brothers at whim; when you have
seen hate-filled policemen curse, kick, and even kill your black
brothers and sisters; when you see the vast majority of your twenty
million Negro brothers smothering in an airtight cage of poverty
in the midst of an affluent society; when you suddenly find your
tongue twisted and your speech stammering as you seek to explain
to your six-year-old daughter why she can't go to the public
amusement park that has just been advertised on television, and
see tears welling up in her eyes when she is told that Funtown
is closed to colored children, and see ominous clouds of inferiority
beginning to form in her little mental sky, and see her beginning
to distort her personality by developing an unconscious bitterness
toward white people; when you have to concoct an answer for a
five-year-old son who is asking, "Daddy, why do white people
treat colored people so mean?"; when you take a cross-country
drive and find it necessary to sleep night after night in the uncomfortable corners of your automobile because no motel will
accept you; when you are humiliated day in and day out by
nagging signs reading "white" and "colored"; when your first name
becomes "nigger," your middle name becomes "boy" (however
old you are) and your last name becomes "John," and your wife
and mother are never given the respected title "Mrs."; when you
are harried by day and haunted by night by the fact that you are
a Negro, living constantly at tiptoe stance, never quite knowing
what to expect next, and are plagued with inner fears and outer
resentments; when you are forever fighting a degenerating sense
of "nobodiness"—then you will understand why we find it difficult to wait. There comes a time when the cup of endurance
runs over, and men are no longer willing to be plunged into the

With this biblical allusion to Psalms 23:4–6,
King reinforces his point that he is walking
"through the valley of the shadow of death" and,
because of his faith, "will fear no evil." He thus
uses a biblical reference to enforce the point that
he is impatient.

abyss of despair. I hope, sirs, you can understand our legitimate and unavoidable impatience.

You express a great deal of anxiety over our willingness to break laws. This is certainly a legitimate concern. Since we so diligently urge people to obey the Supreme Court's decision of 1954 outlawing segregation in the public schools, at first glance it may seem rather paradoxical for us consciously to break laws. One may well ask: "How can you advocate breaking some laws and obeying others?" The answer lies in the fact that there are two types of laws: just and unjust. I would be the first to advocate obeying just laws. One has not only a legal but a moral responsibility to obey just laws. Conversely, one has a moral responsibility to disobey unjust laws. I would agree with St. Augustine that "an unjust law is no law at all." 15

Now, what is the difference between the two? How does one determine whether a law is just or unjust? A just law is a man-made code that squares with the moral law or the law of God. An unjust law is a code that is out of harmony with the moral law. To put it in the terms of St. Thomas Aquinas: An unjust law is a human law that is not rooted in eternal law and natural law. Any law that uplifts human personality is just. Any law that degrades human personality is unjust. All segregation statutes are unjust because segregation distorts the soul and damages the personality. It gives the segregator a false sense of superiority and the segregated a false sense of inferiority. Segregation, to use the terminology of the Jewish philosopher Martin Buber, substitutes an "I-it" relationship for an "I-thou" relationship and ends up relegating persons to the status of things. Hence segregation is not only politically, economically, and sociologically unsound, it is morally wrong and sinful. Paul Tillich has said that sin is separation. Is not segregation an existential expression of man's tragic separation, his awful estrangement, his terrible sinfulness? Thus it is that I can urge men to obey the 1954 decision of the Supreme Court, for it is morally right; and I can urge them to disobey segregation ordinances, for they are morally wrong. 16

Let us consider a more concrete example of just and unjust 17

In paragraphs 15–22, King refutes the next objection by the clergymen, that he and the civil-rights demonstrators are breaking the law by arguing that it is their moral responsibility to break unjust laws.

St. Augustine (**A.D.** 354–430) was one of the Latin fathers of the early Christian Church.

In paragraphs 16–20, King distinguishes between just and unjust laws and offers substantial support to the idea that the laws they are breaking are unjust.

St. Thomas Aquinas (1225?–1274) was an Italian Catholic philosopher and a major theologian of the Roman Catholic Church.

Martin Buber (1878–1965) was a Jewish philosopher and theologian.

Paul Tillich (1886–1965), born in Germany, was an American Protestant philosopher and theologian.

laws. An unjust law is a code that a numerical or power majority group compels a minority group to obey but does not make binding on itself. This is *difference* made legal. By the same token, a just law is a code that a majority compels a minority to follow and that it is willing to follow itself. This is *sameness* made legal.

18   Let me give another explanation. A law is unjust if it is inflicted on a minority that, as a result of being denied the right to vote, had no part in enacting or devising the law. Who can say that the legislature of Alabama which set up that state's segregation laws was democratically elected? Throughout Alabama all sorts of devious methods are used to prevent Negroes from becoming registered voters, and there are some counties in which, even though Negroes constitute a majority of the population, not a single Negro is registered. Can any law enacted under such circumstances be considered democratically structured?

19   Sometimes a law is just on its face and unjust in its application. For instance, I have been arrested on a charge of parading without a permit. Now, there is nothing wrong in having an ordinance which requires a permit for a parade. But such an ordinance becomes unjust when it is used to maintain segregation and to deny citizens the First-Amendment privilege of peaceful assembly and protest.

20   I hope you are able to see the distinction I am trying to point out. In no sense do I advocate evading or defying the law, as would the rabid segregationist. That would lead to anarchy. One who breaks an unjust law must do so openly, lovingly, and with a willingness to accept the penalty. I submit that an individual who breaks a law that conscience tells him is unjust, and who willingly accepts the penalty of imprisonment in order to arouse the conscience of the community over its injustice, is in reality expressing the highest respect for law.

In paragraphs 21 and 22, King presents several historical examples to justify the idea that they not only have the right but indeed the responsibility to break unjust laws.

Shadrach, Meshach, and Abednego, Jews living in Babylon, refused to worship a golden idol as demanded by the King of Babylon, Nebuchadnezzar. For punishment they were thrown into a fiery furnace. Daniel 3:1–30.

21   Of course, there is nothing new about this kind of civil disobedience. It was evidenced sublimely in the refusal of Shadrach, Meshach, and Abednego to obey the laws of Nebuchadnezzar, on the ground that a higher moral law was at stake. It was practiced superbly by the early Christians, who were willing to face hungry lions and the excruciating pain of chopping blocks rather than

Socrates was tried by the Athenians for corrupting their youth with his skeptical, questioning method of teaching. He refused to change and was condemned to death.

In 1956, an anticommunist revolution in Hungary was put down quickly by the Soviet army.

In paragraphs 23 and 24, King digresses from his logical argument to criticize white moderates.

submit to certain unjust laws of the Roman Empire. To a degree, academic freedom is a reality today because Socrates practiced civil disobedience. In our own nation, the Boston Tea Party represented a massive act of civil disobedience.

We should never forget that everything Adolf Hitler did in 22 Germany was "legal" and everything the Hungarian freedom fighters did in Hungary was "illegal." It was "illegal" to aid and comfort a Jew in Hitler's Germany. Even so, I am sure that, had I lived in Germany at the time, I would have aided and comforted my Jewish brothers. If today I lived in a Communist country where certain principles dear to the Christian faith are suppressed, I would openly advocate disobeying that country's anti-religious laws.

I must make two honest confessions to you, my Christian 23 and Jewish brothers. First, I must confess that over the past few years I have been gravely disappointed with the white moderate. I have almost reached the regrettable conclusion that the Negro's great stumbling block in his stride toward freedom is not the White Citizen's Counciler or the Ku Klux Klanner, but the white moderate, who is more devoted to "order" than to justice; who prefers a negative peace which is the absence of tension to a positive peace which is the presence of justice; who constantly says, "I agree with you in the goal you seek, but I cannot agree with your methods of direct action"; who paternalistically believes he can set the timetable for another man's freedom; who lives by a mythical concept of time and who constantly advises the Negro to wait for a "more convenient season." Shallow understanding from people of good will is more frustrating than absolute misunderstanding from people of ill will. Lukewarm acceptance is much more bewildering than outright rejection.

I had hoped that the white moderate would understand that 24 law and order exist for the purpose of establishing justice and that when they fail in this purpose they become the dangerously structured dams that block the flow of social progress. I had hoped that the white moderate would understand that the present tension in the South is a necessary phase of the transition from an obnoxious negative peace, in which the Negro passively accepted his unjust plight, to a substantive and positive peace, in which all men will respect the dignity and worth of human personality. Actually, we who engage in nonviolent direct action are not the creators of tension. We merely bring to the surface the hidden tension that is already alive. We bring it out in the open, where it can be seen and dealt with. Like a boil that can never be cured so long as it is covered up but must be opened with all its ugliness to the natural medicines of air and light, injustice must be exposed, with all the tension its exposure creates, to the light of human conscience and the air of national opinion, before it can be cured.

In paragraph 25, King takes on the next charge, that the demonstrations "precipitate violence." He shows this position is illogical by again citing historical precedents.

25   In your statement you assert that our actions, even though peaceful, must be condemned because they precipitate violence. But is this a logical assertion? Isn't this like condemning a robbed man because his possession of money precipitated the evil act of robbery? Isn't this like condemning Socrates because his unswerving commitment to truth and his philosophical inquiries precipitated the act by the misguided populace in which they made him drink hemlock? Isn't this like condemning Jesus because his unique God-consciousness and never-ceasing devotion to God's will precipitated the evil act of crucifixion? We must come to see that, as the federal courts have consistently affirmed, it is wrong to urge an individual to cease his efforts to gain his basic constitutional rights because the quest may precipitate violence. Society must protect the robbed and punish the robber.

In paragraph 26, King addresses the issue of whether the time is right for demonstrations.

26   I had also hoped that the white moderate would reject the myth concerning time in relation to the struggle for freedom. I have just received a letter from a white brother in Texas. He writes: "All Christians know that the colored people will receive equal rights eventually, but it is possible that you are in too great a religious hurry. It has taken Christianity almost two thousand years to accomplish what it has. The teachings of Christ take time to come to earth." Such an attitude stems from a tragic misconception of time, from the strangely irrational notion that there is something in the very flow of time that will inevitably cure all ills. Actually, time itself is neutral; it can be used either destructively or constructively. More and more I feel that the people of

ill will have used time much more effectively than have the people of good will. We will have to repent in this generation not merely for the hateful words and actions of the bad people, but for the appalling silence of the good people. Human progress never rolls in on wheels of inevitability; it comes through the tireless efforts of men willing to be co-workers with God, and without this hard work, time itself becomes an ally of the forces of social stagnation. We must use time creatively, in the knowledge that the time is always ripe to do right. Now is the time to make real the promise of democracy and transform our pending national elegy into a creative psalm of brotherhood. Now is the time to lift our national policy from the quicksand of racial injustice to the solid rock of human dignity.

King now answers the final charge, that the demonstrators are extremists, by showing that they are, in fact, taking the middle road that will prevent a "racial nightmare" in the future (paragraphs 27–31).

You speak of our activity in Birmingham as extreme. At first 27 I was rather disappointed that fellow clergymen would see my nonviolent efforts as those of an extremist. I began thinking about the fact that I stand in the middle of two opposing forces in the Negro community. One is a force of complacency, made up in part of Negroes who, as a result of long years of oppression, are so drained of self-respect and a sense of "somebodiness" that they have adjusted to segregation; and in part of a few middle-class Negroes who, because of a degree of academic and economic security and because in some ways they profit by segregation, have become insensitive to the problems of the masses. The other force is one of bitterness and hatred, and it comes perilously close to advocating violence. It is expressed in the various black nationalist groups that are springing up across the nation, the largest and best-known being Elijah Muhammad's Muslim movement. Nourished by the Negro's frustration over the continued existence of racial discrimination, this movement is made up of people who have lost faith in America, who have absolutely repudiated Christianity, and who have concluded that the white man is an incorrigible "devil."

I have tried to stand between these two forces, saying that 28 we need emulate neither the "do-nothingism" of the complacent nor the hatred and despair of the black nationalist. For there is the more excellent way of love and nonviolent protest. I am grateful to God that, through the influence of the Negro church, the way of nonviolence became an integral part of our struggle.

If this philosophy had not emerged, by now many streets of the South would, I am convinced, be flowing with blood. And I am further convinced that if our white brothers dismiss as "rabble-rousers" and "outside agitators" those of us who employ non-violent direct action, and if they refuse to support our nonviolent efforts, millions of Negroes will, out of frustration and despair, seek solace and security in black-nationalist ideologies—a development that would inevitably lead to a frightening racial nightmare.   29

Oppressed people cannot remain oppressed forever. The yearning for freedom eventually manifests itself, and that is what has happened to the American Negro. Something within has reminded him of his birthright of freedom, and something without has reminded him that it can be gained. Consciously or unconsciously, he has been caught up by the *Zeitgeist,* and with his black brothers of Africa and his brown and yellow brothers of Asia, South America, and the Caribbean, the United States Negro is moving with a sense of great urgency toward the promised land of racial justice. If one recognizes this vital urge that has engulfed the Negro community, one should readily understand why public demonstrations are taking place. The Negro has many pent-up resentments and latent frustrations, and he must release them. So let him march; let him make prayer pilgrimages to the city hall; let him go on freedom rides—and try to understand why he must do so. If his repressed emotions are not released in nonviolent ways, they will seek expression through violence; this is not a threat but a fact of history. So I have not said to my people, "Get rid of your discontent." Rather, I have tried to say that this normal and healthy discontent can be channeled into the creative outlet of nonviolent direct action. And now this approach is being termed extremist.   30

But though I was initially disappointed at being categorized as an extremist, as I continued to think about the matter I gradually gained a measure of satisfaction from the label. Was not Jesus an extremist for love: "Love your enemies, bless them that   31

"Zeitgeist": German. The spirit of the time; the general trend of thought or feeling characteristic of a period.

Here King cites several precedents in the history of extremism that have now become respectable.

Amos was a prophet in the eighth century B.C. A book in the Old Testament bears his name. Martin Luther (1483–1546) was a German theologian who led the Protestant Reformation in Germany. John Bunyan (1628–1688) was an English writer and preacher. His refusal to bow to royal edicts banning nonconformist preaching led to his imprisonment from 1660 to 1672.

curse you, do good to them that hate you, and pray for them which despitefully use you, and persecute you." Was not Amos an extremist for justice: "Let justice roll down like waters and righteousness like an ever-flowing stream." Was not Paul an extremist for the Christian gospel: "I bear in my body the marks of the Lord Jesus." Was not Martin Luther an extremist: "Here I stand; I cannot do otherwise, so help me God." And John Bunyan: "I will stay in jail to the end of my days before I make a butchery of my conscience." And Abraham Lincoln: "This nation cannot survive half slave and half free." And Thomas Jefferson: "We hold these truths to be self-evident, that all men are created equal. . . ." So the question is not whether we will be extremists, but what kind of extremists we will be. Will we be extremists for hate or for love? Will we be extremists for the preservation of injustice or for the extension of justice? In that dramatic scene on Calvary's hill three men were crucified. We must never forget that all three were crucified for the same crime—the crime of extremism. Two were extremists for immorality, and thus fell below their environment. The other, Jesus Christ, was an extremist for love, truth, and goodness, and thereby rose above his environment. Perhaps the South, the nation, and the world are in dire need of creative extremists.

King's rebuttal of the clergymen's charge and his argument for direct action end here. Paragraphs 32–44 are primarily devoted to chastising white moderates and the Jewish and Christian churches for being defenders of the status quo.

I had hoped that the white moderate would see this need. [32] Perhaps I was too optimistic; perhaps I expected too much. I suppose I should have realized that few members of the oppressor race can understand the deep groans and passionate yearnings of the oppressed race, and still fewer have the vision to see that injustice must be rooted out by strong, persistent, and determined action. I am thankful, however, that some of our white brothers in the South have grasped the meaning of this social revolution and committed themselves to it. They are still all too few in quantity, but they are big in quality. Some—such as Ralph McGill, Lillian Smith, Harry Golden, James McBride Dabbs, Anne Braden, and Sarah Patton Boyle—have written about our struggle in eloquent and prophetic terms. Others have marched with us down nameless streets of the South. They have languished in filthy, roach-infested jails, suffering the abuse and brutality of policemen who view them as "dirty nigger-lovers." Unlike so many of their moderate brothers and sisters, they have recognized the urgency of the moment and sensed the need for powerful "action" antidotes to combat the disease of segregation.

Let me take note of my other major disappointment. I have been so greatly disappointed with the white church and its leadership. Of course, there are some notable exceptions. I am not unmindful of the fact that each of you has taken some significant stands on this issue. I commend you, Reverend Stallings, for your Christian stand on this past Sunday, in welcoming Negroes to your worship service on a nonsegregated basis. I commend the Catholic leaders of this state for integrating Spring Hill College several years ago. 33

But despite these notable exceptions, I must honestly reiterate that I have been disappointed with the church. I do not say this as one of those negative critics who can always find something wrong with the church. I say this as a minister of the gospel, who loves the church; who was nurtured in its bosom; who has been sustained by its spiritual blessings and who will remain true to it as long as the cord of life shall lengthen. 34

When I was suddenly catapulted into the leadership of the bus protest in Montgomery, Alabama, a few years ago, I felt we would be supported by the white church. I felt that the white ministers, priests, and rabbis of the South would be among our strongest allies. Instead, some have been outright opponents, refusing to understand the freedom movement and misrepresenting its leaders; all too many others have been more cautious than courageous and have remained silent behind the anesthetizing security of stained glass windows. 35

In spite of my shattered dreams, I came to Birmingham with the hope that the white religious leadership of this community would see the justice of our cause and, with deep moral concern, would serve as the channel through which our just grievances could reach the power structure. I had hoped that each of you would understand. But again I have been disappointed. 36

I have heard numerous southern religious leaders admonish their worshipers to comply with a desegregation decision because 37 it is the law, but I have longed to hear white ministers declare: "Follow this decree because integration is morally right and because the Negro is your brother." In the midst of blatant injustices inflicted upon the Negro, I have watched white churchmen stand on the sideline and mouth pious irrelevancies and sanctimonious trivialities. In the midst of a mighty struggle to rid our nation of racial and economic injustice I have heard many ministers say: "Those are social issues, with which the gospel has no real concern." And I have watched many churches commit themselves to a completely otherworldly religion which makes a strange, un-Biblical distinction between body and soul, between the sacred and the secular.

I have traveled the length and breadth of Alabama, Mississippi, and all the other southern states. On sweltering summer days and crisp autumn mornings I have looked at the South's beautiful churches with their lofty spires pointing heavenward. I have beheld the impressive outlines of her massive religious-education buildings. Over and over I have found myself asking: "What kind of people worship here? Who is their God? Where were their voices when the lips of Governor Barnett dripped with words of interposition and nullification? Where were they when Governor Wallace gave a clarion call for defiance and hatred? Where were their voices of support when bruised and weary Negro men and women decided to rise from the dark dungeons of complacency to the bright hills of creative protest?" 38

Yes, these questions are still in my mind. In deep disappointment I have wept over the laxity of the church. But be assured that my tears have been tears of love. There can be no deep disappointment where there is not deep love. Yes, I love the church. How could I do otherwise? I am in the rather unique position of being the son, the grandson, and the great-grandson of preachers. Yes, I see the church as the body of Christ. But, oh! How we have blemished and scarred that body through social neglect and through fear of being nonconformists. 39

There was a time when the church was very powerful—in the time when the early Christians rejoiced at being deemed worthy to suffer for what they believed. In those days the church 40 was not merely a thermometer that recorded the ideas and principles of popular opinion; it was a thermostat that transformed the mores of society. Whenever the early Christians entered a town, the people in power became disturbed and immediately sought to convict the Christians for being "disturbers of the peace" and "outside agitators." But the Christians pressed on, in the conviction that they were "a colony of heaven," called to obey God rather than man. Small in number, they were big in commitment. They were too God-intoxicated to be "astronomically intimidated." By their effort and example they brought an end to such ancient evils as infanticide and gladiatorial contests.

Things are different now. So often the contemporary church is a weak, ineffectual voice with an uncertain sound. So often it is an archdefender of the status quo. Far from being disturbed by the presence of the church, the power structure of the average community is consoled by the church's silent—and often even vocal—sanction of things as they are. 41

But the judgment of God is upon the church as never before. If today's church does not recapture the sacrificial spirit of the early church, it will lose its authenticity, forfeit the loyalty of millions, and be dismissed as an irrelevant social club with no meaning for the twentieth century. Every day I meet young people whose disappointment with the church has turned into outright disgust. 42

Perhaps I have once again been too optimistic. Is organized religion too inextricably bound to the status quo to save our nation and the world? Perhaps I must turn my faith to the inner spiritual church, the church within the church, as the true *ekklesia* and the hope of the world. But again I am thankful to God that some noble souls from the ranks of organized religion have broken loose from the paralyzing chains of conformity and joined us as active partners in the struggle for freedom. They have left their secure congregations and walked the streets of Albany, Georgia, with us. They have gone down the highways of the South on tortuous rides for freedom. Yes, they have gone to jail with us. Some have been dismissed from their churches, have lost the 43

"Ekklesia": The Greek New Testament word for the church.

support of their bishops and fellow ministers. But they have acted in the faith that right defeated is stronger than evil triumphant. Their witness has been the spiritual salt that has preserved the true meaning of the gospel in these troubled times. They have carved a tunnel of hope through the dark mountain of disappointment.

I hope the church as a whole will meet the challenge of this decisive hour. But even if the church does not come to the aid of justice, I have no despair about the future. I have no fear about the outcome of our struggle in Birmingham, even if our motives are at present misunderstood. We will reach the goal of freedom in Birmingham and all over the nation, because the goal of America is freedom. Abused and scorned though we may be, our destiny is tied up with America's destiny. Before the pilgrims landed at Plymouth, we were here. Before the pen of Jefferson etched the majestic words of the Declaration of Independence across the pages of history, we were here. For more than two centuries our forebears labored in this country without wages; they made cotton king; they built the homes of their masters while suffering gross injustice and shameful humiliation—and yet out of a bottomless vitality they continued to thrive and develop. If the inexpressible cruelties of slavery could not stop us, the opposition we now face will surely fail. We will win our freedom because the sacred heritage of our nation and the eternal will of God are embodied in our echoing demands. 44

In paragraphs 45–46, King responds to the clergymen's praise of the Birmingham police.

Before closing I feel impelled to mention one other point in your statement that has troubled me profoundly. You warmly commended the Birmingham police force for keeping "order" and "preventing violence." I doubt that you would have so warmly commended the police force if you had seen its dogs sinking their teeth into unarmed, nonviolent Negroes. I doubt that you would so quickly commend the policemen if you were to observe their ugly and inhumane treatment of Negroes here in the city jail; if you were to watch them push and curse old Negro women and young Negro girls; if you were to see them slap and kick old Negro men and young boys; if you were to observe them, as they 45 did on two occasions, refuse to give us food because we wanted to sing our grace together. I cannot join you in your praise of the Birmingham police department.

It is true that the police have exercised a degree of discipline 46
in handling the demonstrators. In this sense they have conducted themselves rather "nonviolently" in public. But for what purpose? To preserve the evil system of segregation. Over the past few years I have consistently preached that nonviolence demands that the means we use must be as pure as the ends we seek. I have tried to make clear that it is wrong to use immoral means to attain moral ends. But now I must affirm that it is just as wrong, or perhaps even more so, to use moral means to preserve immoral ends. Perhaps Mr. Connor and his policemen have been rather nonviolent in public, as was Chief Pritchett in Albany, Georgia, but they have used the moral means of nonviolence to maintain the immoral end of racial injustice. As T. S. Eliot has said, "The last temptation is the greatest treason: To do the right deed for the wrong reason."

I wish you had commended the Negro sit-inners and dem- 47
onstrators of Birmingham for their sublime courage, their willingness to suffer, and their amazing discipline in the midst of great provocation. One day the South will recognize its real heroes. They will be the James Merediths, with the noble sense of purpose that enables them to face jeering and hostile mobs, and with the agonizing loneliness that characterizes the life of the pioneer. They will be old, oppressed, battered Negro women, symbolized in a seventy-two-year-old woman in Montgomery, Alabama, who rose up with a sense of dignity and with her people decided not to ride segregated buses, and who responded with ungrammatical profundity to one who inquired about her weariness: "My feets is tired, but my soul is at rest." They will be the young high school and college students, the young ministers of the gospel and a host of their elders, courageously and nonviolently sitting in at lunch counters and willingly going to jail for conscience' sake. One day the South will know that when these disinherited children of God sat down at lunch counters, they were in reality standing up for what is best in the American dream and for the most sacred values

T. (Thomas) S. (Stearns) Eliot (1888–1965) was a British poet and critic born in the United States. He won the Nobel prize for poetry in 1948.

In paragraph 47, King makes the point that the demonstrators, not the police, should have been praised.

James Meredith was the first black to register at the University of Mississippi.

In paragraphs 48–50, King sarcastically apologizes to the clergymen for taking so much of their "precious time." He also goes through the appropriate formalities for his Jewish and Christian colleagues and "brothers."

in our Judaeo-Christian heritage, thereby bringing our nation back to those great wells of democracy which were dug deep by the founding fathers in their formulation of the Constitution and the Declaration of Independence.

48   Never before have I written so long a letter. I'm afraid it is much too long to take your precious time. I can assure you that it would have been shorter if I had been writing from a comfortable desk, but what else can one do when he is alone in a narrow jail cell, other than write long letters, think long thoughts, and pray long prayers?

49   If I have said anything in this letter that overstates the truth and indicates an unreasonable impatience, I beg you to forgive me. If I have said anything that understates the truth and indicates my having a patience that allows me to settle for anything less than brotherhood, I beg God to forgive me.

50   I hope this letter finds you strong in faith. I also hope that circumstances will soon make it possible for me to meet each of you, not as an integrationist or a civil-rights leader but as a fellow clergyman and a Christian brother. Let us all hope that the dark clouds of racial prejudice will soon pass away and the deep fog of misunderstanding will be lifted from our fear-drenched communities, and in some not too distant tomorrow the radiant stars of love and brotherhood will shine over our great nation with all their scintillating beauty.

Yours for the cause of Peace and Brotherhood,
Martin Luther King, Jr.

POSSIBLE ANSWERS

Meaning and Purpose

1. Jail usually silences and intimidates people, making them powerless. King is not silent or powerless as he puts pen to paper in his jail cell, working for civil rights.
2. King claims that, though mistaken, his critics are "men of genuine good will" and that their criticisms are sincere. They deserve an answer.

Meaning and Purpose

1.   Of what significance is it that King writes his letter from jail?
2.   In paragraph 1, King says that he seldom pauses "to answer criticism." Why does he do so here?
3.   How does King justify the demonstrations? Why does he claim that the time for negotiation is past?

3. King outlines the four steps a nonviolent campaign must take to effect social change (6). Negotiation, the second, has already failed. All three first steps have been accomplished, leaving only the inevitable fourth: direct action, or demonstrations.

4. He discusses waiting for racial equality (13, 14). Freedom must be demanded because it is never voluntarily given over by an oppressor (13). He catalogues segregationist human abuses that legitimate immediate action (14).

5. King distinguishes between just and unjust laws (15–22). An unjust law is "out of harmony with the moral law"; is not rooted in eternal and natural law; "degrades human personality" (16); "is inflicted upon a minority that, as a result of being denied the right to vote, had no part in enacting or devising the law" (18). He shows historical and biblical precedents for breaking unjust laws (21, 22). A person who breaks an unjust law but is willing to suffer the penalty expresses highest respect for the law (20).

6. King establishes himself as "in the middle of opposing forces in the Negro community" (27), each of which is an extreme. Then he cleverly puts himself in the same camp as other "extremists" admired by the clergymen he addresses (31).

Strategy

1. Emphasizing that he writes from a jail cell, King hopes to create sympathy. He further ingratiates himself by complimenting the audience. He also intimates their importance, for he answers their criticisms, which he would not normally do.

2. King structures his letter around rebuttals to the clergymen's charges. He answers the first in paragraphs 5–9, the second in 10–11, the third in 12–14, the fourth in 15–22, the fifth in 25, the sixth in 26, and the last in 27–31.

3. King appeals to both reason and emotion. He reasons that a law is unjust and democracy thwarted if the minority has no voice in "enacting or devising the law" (18). His language is rational, not emotional. The logic is deductive: if democracy means the people participate in making the law, and a large group of people is denied this right, then the law does not meet

4. How does King respond to the admonition that the time for racial equality is not now, that he should "wait" until the time is right?

5. Describe King's distinction between just and unjust laws. What justifications does he use to advocate breaking unjust laws?

6. How does King turn the accusation of being an extremist from a criticism to praise?

Strategy

1. In paragraph 1, King clearly establishes the setting in which he is writing the letter and addresses his intended readers as "men of genuine good will." Why?

2. Where does King address the clergymen's objections to his activities in Birmingham? How does he refute them? How do his refutations figure in the construction of his own essay?

3. Does King appeal to reason or emotion in his argument? Explain the effectiveness of his appeal, and give examples from the essay.

4. The last three paragraphs don't further King's argument. What do they do?

Style

1. Reread paragraph 14. The sentence beginning "But when you have seen" is more than 300 words long. Discuss its effectiveness and its emotional effect. What does King do to keep such a long sentence clear?

2. Find some metaphors in King's letter and explain how he uses them.

3. If necessary, check a dictionary for the meanings of these words: *provincial* (4); *gainsaying* (6); *gadflies* (10); *millennium, lamentably* (12); *abyss* (14); *anarchy* (20); *elegy* (26); *incorrigible* (27); *sanctimonious* (37); *interposition, clarion* (38); *laxity* (39); *mores* (40); *inextricably* (43); *scintillating* (50).

the terms of a democracy and is unjust. He appeals to emotion by listing the horrible injustices that blacks suffer every day; he says to whites that the time has come for change (14). His language here is laden with emotion.

4. With sarcasm and subtlety King apologizes to the clergymen for taking too much of their "precious time." And he goes through the formalities appropriate to his "Christian brothers," to reestablish a harmonious relationship with them.

Style

1. The periodic sentence that begins "But when you have seen" is masterful. He withholds its full meaning until the last words, keeping the reader in suspense about how the sentence will come out, both structurally and semantically. The 300-word catalogue is organized into eleven parallel subordinate clauses, enforcing order and clarity. Repeating "when" connects the clauses and contributes to the drama in the switch to "then" in the short independent clause concluding the sentence. The long sentence emphasizes how long blacks have waited for justice.

2. King uses metaphors to achieve an eloquent and poetic style and to enhance his appeal to emotion.

3. *Provincial:* having the manners, viewpoints, and so on considered characteristic of unsophisticated inhabitants of an outlying province; *gainsaying:* denying, disputing, contradicting; *gadflies:* people who persistently annoy or provoke others with criticism, schemes, demands, requests; *millennium:* a period of general righteousness and happiness; *lamentably:* unfortunately; *abyss:* a deep, immeasurable pit or cavity; *anarchy:* without government or law; *elegy:* a mournful, melancholy, or plaintive poem, especially a funeral song or lament for the dead; *incorrigible:* beyond correction or reform; *sanctimonious:* making a hypocritical show of religious devotion or piety; *interposition:* barrier or obstacle; *clarion:* clear and shrill; *laxity:* carelessness or negligence; *mores:* folkways accepted without question and embodying a group's fundamental moral views; *inextricably:* incapable of being disentangled; *scintillating:* animated, vivacious, effervescent.

Writing Tasks

1. Write a persuasive essay illustrating King's statement in paragraph 4: "Injustice anywhere is a threat to justice everywhere." Think of an example of injustice and argue that it has implications beyond that case.

2. Think of a situation in which you feel that some person or group is being unjustly opposed, such as freshman students not being allowed some privilege that upperclassmen are allowed. In a brief essay, argue for a course of action that resolves the injustice. Who is your audience? What kind of appeal will you choose, and with what kind of evidence will you support your argument?

If Pollitt is correct that most students have no reading life outside of college, it may indeed be difficult to get them to really understand why college and university faculty can become so impassioned about what books they choose for students to read. You might go through the works and authors Pollitt mentions and ask your students if they have read them, or even heard of them. This might lead to a discussion of differing assumptions about the nature of higher education. The underlying assumptions of the conservatives and liberals engaged in the canon debate obviously assume value in the life of the mind as it encounters great literature. The debate, therefore, is about what constitutes great literature. These assumptions may be totally alien to a student who perceives higher education as a series of hurdles on the way to a well-paying job. A lively debate could ensue.

A discussion of the essay's structure could also be profitable. Pollitt outlines the various positions on the debate in the first six paragraphs and then forcefully argues her own position.

Marginal Notes

"the literary canon": In this context, that group of books which is accepted as self-evident or universally required for the study of literature.

E(dward) M(organ) Forster (1879–1970) is the British novelist whose best-known work is *A Passage to India* (1924). Ask your students if they are familiar with the idea of writing to discover what one thinks or knows.

❦ Katha Pollitt ❦

Katha Pollitt (born 1949) is an American poet and critic. Her poems have appeared in many periodicals, including Atlantic Monthly, The Nation, The New Yorker, *and* Paris Review. *Her first poetry collection,* Antarctic Traveler, *won the National Book Critics Circle Award in 1982. She is also a well-known literary and political essayist, a winner of the 1992 National Magazine Award in Essays and Criticism, and a contributing editor of the political journal,* The Nation, *where this essay first appeared in the September 23, 1991, issue.*

Why Do We Read?

Over the past several years in higher education there has been an ongoing debate about "the canon," that is, what books should have been read by anyone claiming to be educated. Pollitt explores the various positions in the debate, finds a certain merit on all sides, but is disturbed by the underlying ills in our society that would cause the debate in the first place.

Be sure to clearly distinguish the differences among the three different positions on the canon that Pollitt describes. Pay particularly close attention in order to discern the causes she claims gave rise to the debate.

For the past couple of years, we've all been witness to a furious debate about the literary canon. What books should be assigned to students? What books should critics discuss? What books should the rest of us read—and who are *we*, anyway? Like everyone else, I've given these questions some thought and, when an invitation came my way, leaped to produce my own manifesto. But to my surprise, when I sat down to write—in order to discover, as E. M. Forster once said, what I really think—I found that I agreed with all sides in the debate at once. . . .

Take the conservatives. Now, this rather dour collection of

Allan Bloom. University of Chicago professor; author of *The Closing of the American Mind: Education and the Crisis of Reason,* 1987.

Hilton Kramer. Art critic for the *New York Observer.*

John Silber. President of Boston University; candidate for governor of Massachusetts, 1990.

All these authors were once unquestioningly included in the "literary canon" of American universities.

The author speaks from a sense of intellectual fatigue: How does one "explain" the obvious to a fledgling writer, that studying the poetry of others helps one to become a better poet?

scholars and diatribists—Allan Bloom, Hilton Kramer, John Silber, and so on—are not, to my mind, a particularly appealing group of people. They are arrogant, they are rude, they are gloomy, they do not suffer fools gladly—and everywhere they look, fools are what they see. All good reasons not to elect them to public office, as the voters of Massachusetts decided recently. But what is so terrible, really, about what they are saying? I too believe that some books are profounder, more complex, more essential to an understanding of our culture than others; I too am appalled to think of students graduating from college not having read Homer, Plato, Virgil, Milton, Tolstoy—all writers, dead white Western men though they be, whose works have meant a great deal to me. As a teacher of literature and of writing, I too have seen at first hand how ill-educated many students are and how little aware they are of this important fact about themselves. Last year, for instance, I taught a graduate seminar in the writing of poetry. None of my students had read more than a smattering of poems by anyone, male or female, published more than ten years ago. Robert Lowell was as far outside their frame of reference as Alexander Pope. When I gently suggested to one student that it might benefit her to read some poetry if she planned to spend her life writing it, she told me that yes, she knew she should read more, but when she encountered a really good poem it only made her depressed. That contemporary writing has a history which it profits us to know in some depth, that we ourselves were not born yesterday, seems too obvious even to argue.

But ah, say the liberals, the canon exalted by the conservatives is itself an artifact of history. Sure, some books are more rewarding than others, but why can't we revise the list of which books those are? The canon itself was not always the list we know today: Until the 1920s, *Moby-Dick* was shelved with the boys' adventure stories. If T. S. Eliot could singlehandedly dethrone the Romantic poets in favor of the neglected Metaphysicals and place John Webster alongside Shakespeare, why can't we dip into the sea of stories and pluck out Edith Wharton or Virginia Woolf? And this position too makes a great deal of sense to me. After all, alongside the many good reasons why a book might end up on the required reading shelf are some rather suspect reasons why it might be excluded—because it was written by a woman and therefore presumed to be too slight; because it was written by a black person and therefore presumed to be too unsophisticated or, in any case, to reflect too special an instance. By all means, say the liberals, let's have great books and a shared culture. But let's make sure that all the different kinds of greatness are represented and that the culture we share reflects the true range of human experience.

If we leave the broadening of the canon up to the conservatives, it will never happen because, to them, change only means defeat. Look at the recent fuss over the latest edition of the Great Books series published by the Encyclopedia Britannica, headed by that old snake-oil salesman Mortimer Adler. Four women have now been added to the series: Virginia Woolf, Willa Cather, Jane Austen, and George Eliot. That's nice, I suppose, but really! Jane Austen has been a certified great writer for a hundred years! Lionel Trilling said so! There's something truly absurd about the conservatives, earnestly sitting in judgment on the illustrious dead as though up in Writers' Heaven Jane and George and Willa and Virginia were breathlessly waiting to hear if they'd finally made it into the club, while Henry Fielding, newly dropped from the list, howls in outer darkness and the Brontës, presumably, stamp their feet in frustration and hope for better luck in twenty years, when *Jane Eyre* and *Wuthering Heights* will suddenly turn out to have qualities of greatness never before detected in their pages. It's like Poets' Corner over at Manhattan's Cathedral of St. John the Divine, where mortal men—and a woman or two—of letters actually vote on which immortals to put up a plaque to—complete, no doubt, with electoral campaigns, compromise candidates, and all the rest of the underside of the literary life. "No, I'm sorry, I just can't vote for Whitman. I'm a Washington Irving man myself."

Well, being a liberal is not a very exciting thing to be, and so we have the radicals, who attack the concepts of "greatness," "shared," "culture," and "lists." (I'm overlooking here the ultra-radicals, who attack the "privileging," horrible word, of "texts,"

4

5

"to reflect too special an instance": to be so culturally bound as not to have significant meaning for people outside its culture.

"snake-oil salesman": a traveling huckster who sold liquid concoctions of dubious value, as all-purpose curatives.

Mortimer Adler (born 1902), an American educator and writer, guided a team of scholars in the 1940s, at the University of Chicago, in the production of the Syntopicon, a synthesis of the great ideas of Western civilization that was published with the Great Books collection.

George Eliot was the pseudonym of Mary Ann (or Marian) Evans (1819–1880), whose works include *Adam Bede* (1859), *The Mill on the Floss* (1860), and *Silas Marner* (1861).

Lionel Trilling (1905–1975), a scholar and literary critic, wrote his well-known *The Liberal Imagination* in 1950.

An April 1992 issue of the British weekly newsmagazine *The Economist* said that of all Americans, Walt Whitman (1819–1892) "has the strongest claim to be called his country's national poet."

In this context, "deconstructing" refers to an attempt to expose powerful yet unspoken assumptions about the deceptive nature of speech and writing, as those assumptions affect human activities.

Television's *Leave It to Beaver* series concerned routinely exciting activities of the "typical" preteen boy.

self-esteem: This term can mean having a realistic respect for oneself *or* it can mean having an exaggeratedly favorable impression of oneself. Ask students to consider what the term means to them.

Anna Laetitia Barbauld (1743–1825) and her husband conducted a boys' boarding school in Suffolk (1774–1785), during which she wrote *Hymns in Prose for Children.*

Lady Anne Lindsay (1750–1825) wrote a greatly popular ballad, "Auld Robin Gray," but did not acknowledge that fact until two years before she died. Her journals, *Lady Anne Barnard at the Cape, 1797–1802,* provide important information about the first British occupation of Cape Town, South Africa.

Sir Arthur Quiller-Couch (1863–1944), probably best known personally for his two important volumes of lectures, *On the Art of Writing* (1916) and *On the Art of Reading* (1920), and for his *New Cambridge Shakespeare,* edited the first *Oxford Book of English Verse* in 1900, which enjoyed large sales and enormous influence.

as they insist on calling books, and think one might as well spend one's college years "deconstructing," i.e., watching reruns of *Leave It to Beaver.*) Who is to say, ask the radicals, what is a great book? What's so terrific about complexity, ambiguity, historical centrality, and high seriousness? If *The Color Purple,* say, gets students thinking about their own experience, maybe they ought to read it and forget about—and here you can fill in the name of whatever classic work you yourself found dry and tedious and never got around to finishing. For the radicals, the notion of a shared culture is a lie, because it means presenting as universally meaningful and politically neutral books that reflect the interests and experiences and values of privileged white men at the expense of those of others—women, blacks, Hispanics, Asians, the working class, whatever. Why not scrap the one-list-for-everyone idea and let people connect with books that are written by people like themselves about people like themselves? It will be a more accurate reflection of a multifaceted and conflict-ridden society and do wonders for everyone's self-esteem, except, of course, for living white men—but they have too much self-esteem already.

Now, I have to say that I dislike the radicals' vision intensely. 6 How foolish to argue that Chekhov has nothing to say to a black woman—or, for that matter, myself—merely because he is Russian, long dead, a man. The notion that one reads to increase one's self-esteem sounds to me like more snake oil: literature is not a session at the therapist's. But then I think of myself as a child, leafing through anthologies of poetry for the names of women. I never would have admitted that I needed a role model, even if that awful term had existed back in the prehistory of which I speak, but why was I so excited to find a female name, even when, as was often the case, it was attached to a poem of no interest to me whatsoever? Anna Laetitia Barbauld, author of "Life! I know not what thou art/ But know that thou and I must part!," Lady Anne Lindsay, writer of languid ballads in incomprehensible Scots dialect, and the other minor female poets included by chivalrous Sir Arthur Quiller-Couch in the old *Oxford Anthology of English Verse*—I have to admit it, just by their presence in that august volume they did something for me. And although it had nothing to do with reading or writing, it was an important thing they did.

Now, what are we to make of this spluttering debate, in which   7
charges of imperialism are met by equally passionate accusations of vandalism, in which each side hates the others, and yet each seems to have its share of reason? It occurs to me that perhaps what we have here is one of those debates in which the opposing sides, unbeknownst to themselves, share a myopia that will turn out to be the most interesting and important feature of the whole discussion, a debate, for instance, like that of our Founding Fathers over the nature of the franchise. Think of all the energy and passion spent debating the question of property qualifications, or direct versus legislative elections, while all along, unmentioned and unimagined, was the fact—to us so central—that women and slaves were never considered for any kind of vote.

While everyone is busy fighting over the canon, something   8
is being overlooked. That is the state of reading, and books, and literature in our country, at this time. Why, ask yourself, is everyone so hot under the collar about what to put on the required-reading shelf? It is because, while we have been arguing so fiercely about which books make the best medicine, the patient has been slipping deeper and deeper into a coma.

Let us imagine a country in which reading was a popular   9
voluntary activity. There, parents read books for their own edification and pleasure and are seen by their children at this silent and mysterious pastime. These parents also read to their children, given them books for presents, talk to them about books, and underwrite, with their taxes, a public library system that is open all day, every day. In school—where an attractive library is invariably to be found—the children study certain books together but also have an active reading life of their own. Years later, it may even be hard for them to remember if they read *Jane Eyre* at home and Judy Blume in class or the other way around. In college, young people continue to be assigned certain books, but far more important are the books they discover for themselves browsing in the library, in bookstores, on the shelves of friends,

---

"the nature of the franchise": Section 2, Article I of the Bill of Rights used the "three-fifths rule": For purposes of determining representation in the House of Representatives, which is based on population, "three-fifths of all other persons [slaves]" besides free men, apprentices, and indentured servants, would be counted. In other words, every slave equaled 60 percent of one free man, for the purpose of establishing a state's population. Article XV of the U.S. Constitution, passed by Congress in 1869 and ratified by enough states in 1870, granted Negro suffrage, even though the "three-fifths rule" had been abolished three years earlier. Women were guaranteed the right to vote under Article XIX, adopted in 1920.

"Let us imagine": An ironic comment follows. The people arguing "the canon" assume just such a happy country as Pollitt describes here. But, in fact, the average family in this country watches television far, far more than it reads books. (Ask your students to approximate how much time they spend watching television compared with how much time they spend reading books they are not required to read.)

The last sentence of this paragraph reinforces the ironic tone set forth in the first sentence of the paragraph.

Toni Morrison (born 1931), the African-American novelist, has written several critically received works, including *Song of Solomon* (1970), about a man's search for a place as an individual, despite a heritage of slavery and violence; and *Tar Baby* (1981), a story of motherhood and relationships between black and white cultures in the Caribbean and in America.

Not to be listed in "the canon" could well contribute to a writer's mark of distinction. For that matter, perhaps writers in the 1990s, like Anaïs Nin or Henry Miller in the 1930s, would have a larger audience if their works were too inspiring or stimulating to be considered for any "canon."

Pollitt attacks the "either/or" argument here: Either students are going to read approved books or they are not, on their own, going to read any books—so say the "highly educated people" arguing about establishing "the canon." The crux of Pollitt's argument is that trying to establish "the canon" of only several dozen books, while knowing full well that learning how to read books well takes years of practice reading hundreds of books, deflates the merit of the entire enterprise. The assumption that unless a student is told what to read, then she or he will read nothing at all, rubs raw against one's common sense.

one book leading to another, back and forth in history and across languages and cultures. After graduation, they continue to read and in the fullness of time produce a new generation of readers. Oh happy land! I wish we all lived there.

In that other country of real readers, voluntary, active, self-determined readers, a debate like the current one over the canon would not be taking place. Or if it did, it would be as a kind of parlor game: What books would *you* take to a desert island? Everyone would know that the top-ten list was merely a tiny fraction of the books one would read in a lifetime. It would not seem racist or sexist or hopelessly hidebound to put Hawthorne on the list and not Toni Morrison. It would be more like putting oatmeal and not noodles on the breakfast menu—a choice part arbitrary, part a nod to the national past, part, dare one say it, a kind of reverse affirmative action: School might frankly *be* the place where one read the books that are a little off-putting, that have gone a little cold, that you might overlook because they do not address, in reader-friendly contemporary fashion, the issues most immediately at stake in modern life but that, with a little study, turn out to have a great deal to say. Being on the list wouldn't mean so much. It might even add to a writer's cachet *not* to be on the list, to be in one way or another too heady, too daring, too exciting to be ground up into institutional fodder for teenagers. Generations of high-school kids have been turned off to George Eliot by being forced to read *Silas Marner* at a tender age. One can imagine a whole new readership for her if grown-ups were left to approach *Middlemarch* and *Daniel Deronda* with open minds, at their leisure.

But, of course, they rarely do. In America today, the underlying assumption behind the canon debate is that the books on the list are the only books that are going to be read and if the list is dropped, *no* books are going to be read. Becoming a textbook is a book's only chance—all sides take that for granted. And so all sides agree not to mention certain things that they themselves, as highly educated people and, one assumes, devoted readers, know perfectly well. For example, that if you read only twenty-five, or fifty, or a hundred books, you can't understand them,

10

11

however well-chosen they are. And that if you don't have an independent reading life—and very few students do—you won't *like* reading the books on the list and will forget them the minute you finish them. And that books have, or should have, other lives than as items in a syllabus—which is why there is now a totally misguided attempt to put current literature in the classroom. How strange to think that people need professorial help to read John Updike or Alice Walker, writers people actually *do* read for fun. But all sides agree, if it isn't taught, it doesn't count. What a peculiar notion!

Let's look at the canon question from another angle. Instead of asking what books do we want others to read, let's ask, why do we read books ourselves? I think it will become clear very quickly that the canon debaters are being a little disingenuous here, are suppressing, in the interest of their own positions, their own experience of reading. Sure, we read to understand our own American culture and history, and we also read to recover neglected masterpieces, and to learn more about the accomplishments of our subgroup and thereby, as I've admitted about myself, increase our self-esteem. But what about reading for the aesthetic pleasures of language, form, image? What about reading to learn something new, to have a vicarious adventure, to follow the workings of an interesting, if possibly skewed, narrow and ill-tempered, mind? What about reading for the story? For an expanded sense of sheer human variety? There are a thousand reasons why a book might have a claim on our time and attention, other than its canonization. I once infuriated an acquaintance by asserting that Trollope, although in many ways a lesser writer than Dickens, possessed some wonderful qualities Dickens lacked: a more realistic view of women, a more skeptical view of good intentions, a subtler sense of humor—a drier vision of life that I myself found congenial. You'd think I'd advocated throwing Dickens out and replacing him with a toaster. Because Dickens is a certified Great Writer, and Trollope is not.

Am I saying anything different than what Randall Jarrell said in his great 1953 essay, "The Age of Criticism"? Not really, so I'll quote him. Speaking of the literary social gatherings of the era,

12

13

Pollitt gives a number of reasons for why people read, including her own reasons for reading. Ask your students why they read voluntarily.

Those at such a literary gathering would be expected to have read Homer's *Ulysses,* Franz Kafka's *The Castle* (1926), Fëdor Dostoevski's *The Brothers Karamazov* (1880), F. Scott Fitzgerald's *The Great Gatsby* (1925), or Graham Greene's last novel, which in 1953 could be *The Power and the Glory,* for which Greene won the Hawthornden prize, because those works were part of "the canon" of the day.

Jarrell wrote: "If, at such parties, you wanted to talk about *Ulysses* or *The Castle* or *The Brothers Karamazov* or *The Great Gatsby* or Graham Greene's last novel—Important books—you were at the right place. . . . But if you wanted to talk about . . . any of a thousand good or interesting but Unimportant books, you couldn't expect a very ready knowledge or sympathy from most of the readers there. They had looked at the big sights, the current sights, hard, with guides and glasses; and those walks in the country, over unfrequented or thrice-familiar territory, all alone—those walks from which most of the joy and good of reading come— were walks that they hadn't gone on very often."

I suspect that most canon debaters have, in fact, taken those 14 solitary rambles, if only out of boredom—how many times, after all, can you reread the *Aeneid,* or *Mrs. Dalloway,* or *Cotton Comes to Harlem* (to pick one book from each column)? But those walks don't count, because of another assumption all sides hold in common. And that is that the purpose of reading is not the many varied and delicious satisfactions I've mentioned; it's medicinal. The chief end of reading is to produce a desirable kind of person and a desirable kind of society—a respectful high-minded citizen of a unified society for the conservatives, an up-to-date and flexible sort for the liberals, a subgroup-identified, robustly confident one for the radicals. How pragmatic, how moralistic, how American! The culture debaters turn out to share a secret suspicion of culture itself, as well as the anti-pornographer's belief that there is a simple, one-to-one correlation between books and behavior. Read the conservatives' list and produce a nation of sexists and racists—or a nation of philosopher kings. Read the liberals' list and produce a nation of spineless relativists—or a nation of open-minded world citizens. Read the radicals' list, and produce a nation of psychobabblers and ancestor-worshippers—or a nation of stalwart proud-to-be-me pluralists.

But is there any list of a few dozen books that can have such 15 a magical effect, for good or for ill? Of course not. It's like arguing that the perfectly nutritional breakfast cereal is enough food for the whole day. And so the canon debate is really an argument about what books to cram down the resistant throats of a resentful

---

Cotton Comes to Harlem (1965) was written by the African-American novelist Chester Himes (1909–1984), who began to write while serving a seven-year prison term for robbery in Ohio. He lived in France after 1953 and made a fortune writing a series of mystery thrillers. The movie *Cotton Comes to Harlem* (1970), directed by Ossie Davis, starred Godfrey Cambridge and Raymond St. Jacques.

"one book from each column": that is, one book from the conservatives' list, one from the liberals' list, and one from the radicals' list.

Pollitt points out importantly that "the canon" makers assume we do not read to enjoy; instead, we read to become molded into a preordained image, cast from the materials assigned to us.

These either/or statements are based on perceptions. But whose? Ask your students whether these cause-and-effect statements comprise strong arguments for carefully reconsidering the notion of having "the canon."

Ask your students why people read books. After all, if one believes what Pollitt says here, we have no sacrosanct reasons, intrinsic or otherwise. Can anyone in your class begin a discussion about the intrinsic value of reading books— of reading books "just for the fun of it"?

captive populace of students—and the trick is never to mention the fact that, under such circumstances, one book is as good, or as bad, as another. Because, as the debaters know from their own experience as readers but never acknowledge because it would count against all sides equally, books are not pills that produce health when ingested in measured doses. Books do not shape character in any simple way, if indeed they do so at all, or the most literate would be the most virtuous instead of just the ordinary run of humanity with larger vocabularies. Books cannot mold a common national purpose when, in fact, people are honestly divided about what kind of country they want—and are divided, moreover, for very good and practical reasons, as they always have been.

For these burly purposes, books are all but useless. The way books affect us is an altogether more subtle, delicate, wayward, and individual, not to say private, affair. And that reading, at the present moment, is being made to bear such an inappropriate and simplistic burden speaks to the poverty both of culture and of frank political discussion in our time. 16

On his deathbed, Dr. Johnson—once canonical, now more admired than read—is supposed to have said to a friend who was energetically rearranging his bedclothes, "Thank you, this will do all that a pillow can do." One might say that the canon debaters are all asking of their handful of chosen books that they do a great deal more than any handful of books can do. 17

When it comes to reading books, we have no common national purpose.

Samuel Johnson (1709–1784) was not only the maker of the modern dictionary (1755), but was also a fine poet, playwright, and essayist.

Meaning and Purpose

1. What reasons does Pollitt give for her argument against having a literary canon?
2. Why was it so difficult for Pollitt to teach a graduate seminar in writing poetry?
3. What three groups of people are arguing over which books

out that required reading never accomplished anything (15), and that reading is a private affair (16).

2. Her students had read so little poetry, they lacked the cultivated taste in literature that comes from extensive reading. Her frightening example of the student who became depressed whenever she read "a really good poem" points up the fact that students often avoid reading out of a sense of intimidation. With so little background in literature, especially poetry, Pollitt's students had nothing by which to gauge the merits of their own work.

3. The three groups are the conservatives, the liberals, and the radicals. Each group aims to establish a literary canon according to what it wants a specified group of books to do for (or *to*) the students.

4. The franchise that Pollitt talks about in paragraph 7 is the constitutional right to vote. Her analogy is that while the framers of the Constitution argued about the comparatively trivial, large groups of people were being denied their rights as human beings: While the framers of literary canons argue about the comparatively trivial, large groups of students are being disregarded.

5. As it is used in this essay, the term *literary canon* refers to a list of books that are selected according to a basic principle or standard. One connotation that arises from another definition of *canon*—"a law or code of laws established by a church council"—implies that a literary canon assumes the prestige of being official.

Strategy

1. Paragraph 8 is a transitional paragraph, moving the reader from the arguments about a canon to the idealism upon which those arguments are based.

2. Pollitt quotes Randall Jarrell as an appeal to an authority. Rather than to present her own views—which, after all, are reflections of Jarrell's—she chooses to quote Jarrell extensively because of his fine reputation, both as a poet and as a critic.

3. The "solitary rambles" in paragraph 14 refer to the extended analogy in paragraph 13, about a reader's "walking" through the unfamiliar territory of books that they had read cursorily or not at all.

should be included in the literary canon? Each group has the same aim. What is that aim?

4. What franchise is Pollitt talking about in paragraph 7? How is the franchise an analogy to forming a literary canon?

5. As it is used in this essay, what does the term *literary canon* mean? What is one connotation of the word *canon?*

Strategy

1. What function does paragraph 8 serve?
2. Why does Pollitt quote Randall Jarrell in paragraph 13?
3. What are the "solitary rambles" in paragraph 14?
4. How does paragraph 14 prepare the reader for paragraph 15?
5. What is the significance of Dr. Johnson's comment in the last paragraph of this essay?

Style

1. What is the tone of paragraph 9?
2. In paragraph 6, how do you know that Pollitt is presenting a personal opinion?
3. What does *spluttering* mean, in paragraph 7?
4. Pollitt's diction shows that this debate is vigorous. What five examples of diction can you find to show the vigor of the debate?
5. How do you know that the first sentence in paragraph 15 is a rhetorical question? (See the term *rhetorical question* in the Glossary.)

Writing Tasks

1. Construct your own "literary canon": List five books that you have read and argue why those works should be required reading

4. Paragraph 14 makes the point that the canon makers believe the purpose of reading is "medicinal," which stimulates interest, preparing the reader to accept, reject, or consider that point, which in paragraph 15 is flatly refuted.

5. As Dr. Johnson suggests by analogy in the final paragraph, anything is only so good as its intended purpose; no one can make something else of it. What is true of pillows in this context is also true of books.

Style

1. The tone of paragraph 9 is the irony of mockery: An incongruity exists between what might be expected and what actually occurs. By this time, the reader knows how Pollitt supports her argument against having a literary canon. Here, she invents the kind of country that her opposition uses to support its arguments.

2. Paragraph 6 is a personal anecdote; Pollitt ethically admits that having found the names of two women in the *Oxford Anthology of English Verse* somehow "did something" for her.

3. The word *spluttering* means "speaking hastily and unclearly, as when angry."

4. Examples abound, and students will list several different ones, depending on where they read. Some of the examples are "manifesto" (1), "terrible" (2), "dethrone" and "pluck" (3), "fuss" (4), "lie" (5), "awful" (6), "imperialism" (7), "fighting" (8), "racist" (10), "misguided" (11), "infuriated" (12), "spineless" (14), and so forth.

5. Immediately upon asking the question in paragraph 15, Pollitt begins to answer it. As seen in the Glossary, a rhetorical question is posed for effect. The writer, not the reader, is expected to answer it—if the question merits an answer at all.

for every member of your class. Point out how those books have changed you for the better, what they teach, and how they will help each student to become a better person.

2. Reread paragraph 9. Write an argument showing how the country described in that paragraph could or could not possibly exist in the 1990s.

Teaching Suggestions

This essay could effectively be used along with Pollitt's essay, which precedes it, and with Lapham's definition piece, "Who and What Is American?" Paragraphs 4 and 5 in Hughes's essay almost seem to have been distilled from Lapham's assertions about America as woven into his refutations of the "false constructions." If you had your students write a definition of "American" as suggested in question 2 under "Meaning and Purpose" while working with the Lapham essay, you might wish to have them compare their definitions with Hughes's paragraphs.

Pollitt's essay centers more specifically on the literary canon, but both she and Hughes find agreement and disagreement with those who would change the curriculum, though both agree that the debate is overheated.

Marginal Notes

W(yston) H(ugh) Auden (1907–1973). Anglo-American poet. One of the great literary figures of the twentieth century, his *Age of Anxiety* was awarded a Pulitzer prize in 1948. *For the Time Being* was published in 1944.

Herod the Great, King of Judaea, 37 B.C.–A.D. 4 gave orders that all boys age two or under be killed to prevent the fulfillment of a prophecy that a newborn child (Jesus) would become King of the Jews.

❦ Robert Hughes ❦

Robert (Studley Forrest) Hughes was born in Sydney, Australia, in 1938. He attended St. Ignatius College and Sydney University where he studied architecture. Early in life he developed a talent for art criticism and has published several books on art, most notably Heaven and Hell in Western Art *(1968) and* The Shock of the New *(1980), a history of modern art that became an eight-part television series in the United States in 1981. In 1987 Hughes published* The Fatal Shore, *a bestseller about the settlement of Australia by convicts, soldiers, and government officials of Great Britain. His most recent book is* Barcelona *(1992), a history of the Spanish city. The following essay appeared in* Time *magazine in 1992.*

The Fraying of America

Arguing that "separatism is the opposite of diversity," Robert Hughes attacks those in the multicultural movement who would throw out the old and bring in the new simply because it is new or because it soothes particular groups previously denied fair and equal treatment. While acknowledging that the historical and cultural record must be expanded to include the contributions of peoples previously ignored or oppressed, he urges that such contributions must meet tests of validity and value. He cautions that a certain kind of multiculturalism will fragment our society and asserts that a more healthy kind recognizes our differences but expands our understanding "across ethnic, cultural and linguistic lines."

As you read this essay, notice how much information Hughes has packed into his essay and what efforts he has made to keep the information from stifling a reader.

Just over 50 years ago, the poet W. H. Auden achieved what all writers envy: making a prophecy that would come true. It is embedded in a long work called *For the Time Being*, where Herod muses about the distasteful task of massacring the Innocents. He

The term *New Age* is now used to describe an eclectic movement of personal development and spiritual awakening.

Hughes evokes images of ancient Rome as analogous to present-day America.

The Roman augers interpreted the will of the gods by observing flights and songs of birds. Their interpretations were often matters of political convenience or attempts to influence policy, hence the implied similarity with modern pollsters and spin doctors. A poll taker can influence events through the nature of the questions asked or through the interpretation given to the results. The term *pollster* was first used by political scientist Lindsay Rogers in 1949 to imply a similarity between a poll taker and a huckster. A spin doctor is one who rushes to interpret an invent or a speech hoping to influence later interpretations.

A sarcastic allusion to Ronald Reagan and his wife, Nancy, who consulted an astrologer about the scheduling of some of President Reagan's activities.

A reference to the Gulf War, popularly known as Desert Storm (January 17–February 27, 1991)

Satraps were provincial rulers of the old Persian Empire, often noted for tyrannical rule. The allusion here is to Saddam Hussein of Iraq.

A reference to the recently developing "men's movement," one of whose gurus is Robert Bly, poet and author of *Iron John* (1990).

doesn't want to, because he is at heart a liberal. But still, he predicts, if that Child is allowed to get away, "Reason will be replaced by Revelation. Instead of Rational Law, objective truths perceptible to any who will undergo the necessary intellectual discipline, Knowledge will degenerate into a riot of subjective visions . . . Whole cosmogonies will be created out of some forgotten personal resentment, complete epics written in private languages, the daubs of schoolchildren ranked above the greatest masterpieces. Idealism will be replaced by Materialism. Life after death will be an eternal dinner party where all the guests are 20 years old . . . Justice will be replaced by Pity as the cardinal human virtue, and all fear of retribution will vanish . . . The New Aristocracy will consist exclusively of hermits, bums and permanent invalids. The Rough Diamond, the Consumptive Whore, the bandit who is good to his mother, the epileptic girl who has a way with animals will be the heroes and heroines of the New Age, when the general, the statesman, and the philosopher have become the butt of every farce and satire."

What Herod saw was America in the late 1980s and early '90s, right down to that dire phrase "New Age." A society obsessed with therapies and filled with distrust of formal politics, skeptical of authority and prey to superstition, its political language corroded by fake pity and euphemism. A nation like late Rome in its long imperial reach, in the corruption and verbosity of its senators, in its reliance on sacred geese (those feathered ancestors of our own pollsters and spin doctors) and in its submission to senile, deified Emperors controlled by astrologers and extravagant wives. A culture that has replaced gladiatorial games, as a means of pacifying the mob, with high-tech wars on television that cause immense slaughter and yet leave the Mesopotamian satraps in full power over their wretched subjects.

Mainly it is women who object, for due to the prevalence of their mystery-religions, the men are off in the woods, affirming their manhood by sniffing one another's armpits and listening to third-rate poets rant about the moist, hairy satyr that lives inside each one of them. Meanwhile, artists vacillate between a largely self-indulgent expressiveness and a mainly impotent politicization, and the contest between education and TV—between argument and persuasion by spectacle—has been won by TV, a medium now more debased in America than ever before, and more abjectly self-censoring than anywhere in Europe.

The fundamental temper of America tends toward an existential ideal that can probably never be reached but can never be discarded: equal rights to variety, to construct your life as you see fit, to choose your traveling companions. It has always been a heterogeneous country, and its cohesion, whatever cohesion it has, can only be based on mutual respect. There never was a core America in which everyone looked the same, spoke the same language, worshipped the same gods and believed the same things. 4

Paragraphs 4 and 5 describe fundamental ideals of being American.

America is a construction of mind, not of race or inherited class or ancestral territory. It is a creed born of immigration, of the jostling of scores of tribes that become American to the extent to which they can negotiate accommodations with one another. These negotiations succeed unevenly and often fail: you need only to glance at the history of racial relations to know that. The melting pot never melted. But American mutuality lives in recognition of difference. The fact remains that America is a collective act of the imagination whose making never ends, and once that sense of collectivity and mutual respect is broken, the possibilities of American-ness begin to unravel. 5

If they are fraying now, it is at least in part due to the prevalence of demagogues who wish to claim that there is only one path to virtuous American-ness: paleoconservatives like Jesse Helms and Pat Robertson who think this country has one single ethic, neoconservatives who rail against a bogey called multiculturalism—as though this culture was ever anything *but* multi!—and pushers of political correctness who would like to see grievance elevated into automatic sanctity. 6

Jesse Helms (born 1921). U.S. senator from North Carolina.

Pat Robertson (born 1930). American evangelist.

Big Daddy Is to Blame

Americans are obsessed with the recognition, praise and, when necessary, the manufacture of victims; whose one common feature is that they have been denied parity with that Blond Beast of the 7 sentimental imagination, the heterosexual, middle-class white male. The range of victims available 10 years ago—blacks, Chicanos, Indians, women, homosexuals—has now expanded to include every permutation of the halt, the blind and the short, or, to put it correctly, the vertically challenged.

Forty years ago, one of the epic processes in the assertion of human rights started unfolding in the U.S.: the civil rights movement. But today, after more than a decade of government that did its best to ignore the issues of race when it was not trying to roll back the gains of the '60s, the usual American response to inequality is to rename it, in the hope that it will go away. We want to create a sort of linguistic Lourdes, where evil and misfortune are dispelled by a dip in the waters of euphemism. Does the cripple rise from his wheelchair, or feel better about being stuck in it, because someone back in the early days of the Reagan Administration decided that, for official purposes, he was "physically challenged"?   8

Lourdes, in southern France: a Roman Catholic shrine known for miraculous cures of physical ailments. A "linguistic Lourdes" would heal by changing the name of the ailment (use of a euphemism).

Because the arts confront the sensitive citizen with the difference between good artists, mediocre ones and absolute duffers, and since there are always more of the last two than the first, the arts too must be politicized; so we cobble up critical systems to show that although we know what we mean by the quality of the environment, the idea of quality in aesthetic experience is little more than a paternalist fiction designed to make life hard for black, female and gay artists.   9

Since our newfound sensitivity decrees that only the victim shall be the hero, the white American male starts bawling for victim status too. Hence the rise of cult therapies teaching that we are all the victims of our parents, that whatever our folly, venality or outright thuggishness, we are not to be blamed for it, since we come from "dysfunctional families." The ether is jammed with confessional shows in which a parade of citizens and their role models, from LaToya Jackson to Roseanne Arnold, rise to denounce the sins of their parents. The cult of the abused Inner Child has a very important use in modern America: it tells you that nothing is your fault, that personal grievance transcends political utterance.   10

The all-pervasive claim to victimhood tops off America's long-cherished culture of therapeutics. Thus we create a juvenile culture of complaint in which Big Daddy is always to blame and the expansion of rights goes on without the other half of citizenship: attachment to duties and obligations. We are seeing a public recoil from formal politics, from the active, reasoned exercise of citizenship. It comes because we don't trust anyone. It is part of the cafard the '80s induced: Wall Street robbery, the savings and loan scandal, the wholesale plunder of the economy, an orgy released by Reaganomics that went on for years with hardly a peep from Congress—events whose numbers were so huge as to be beyond the comprehension of most people.

Single-issue politics were needed when they came, because they forced Washington to deal with, or at least look at, great matters of civic concern that it had scanted: first the civil rights movement, and then the environment, women's reproductive rights, health legislation, the educational crisis. But now they too face dilution by a trivialized sense of civic responsibility. What are your politics? Oh, I'm antismoking. And yours? Why, I'm starting an action committee to have the suffix -man removed from every word in every book in the Library of Congress. And yours, sir? Well, God told me to chain myself to a fire hydrant until we put a fetus on the Supreme Court.

In the past 15 years the American right has had a complete, almost unopposed success in labeling as left-wing ordinary agendas and desires that, in a saner polity, would be seen as ideologically neutral, an extension of rights implied in the Constitution. American feminism has a large repressive fringe, self-caricaturing and often abysmally trivial, like the academic thought police who recently managed to get a reproduction of Goya's *Naked Maja* removed from a classroom at Pennsylvania State University; it has its loonies who regard all sex with men, even with consent, as a politicized form of rape. But does this in any way devalue the immense shared desire of millions of American women to claim the right of equality to men, to be free from sexual harassment in the workplace, to be accorded the reproductive rights to be individuals first and mothers second?

Francisco de Goya (1746–1828). This painting, said to be of the Duchess of Alba, was done in two versions: one fully clothed for public viewing and one nude that was discovered after Goya's death.

The '80s brought the retreat and virtual disappearance of the 14
American left as a political, as distinct from a cultural, force. It
went back into the monastery—that is, to academe—and also
extruded out into the art world, where it remains even more
marginal and impotent. Meanwhile, a considerable and very well-
subsidized industry arose, hunting the lefty academic or artist in
his or her retreat. Republican attack politics turned on culture,
and suddenly both academe and the arts were full of potential
Willie Hortons. The lowbrow form of this was the ire of figures
like Senator Helms and the Rev. Donald Wildmon directed against
National Endowment subventions for art shows they thought
blasphemous and obscene, or the trumpetings from folk like David
Horowitz about how PBS should be demolished because it's a
pinko-liberal-anti-Israel bureaucracy.

The Battles on Campus

The middle-to-highbrow form of the assault is the ongoing 15
frenzy about political correctness, whose object is to create the
belief, or illusion, that a new and sinister McCarthyism, this time
of the left, has taken over American universities and is bringing
free thought to a stop. This is flatly absurd. The comparison to
McCarthyism could be made only by people who either don't
know or don't wish to remember what the Senator from Wisconsin
and his pals actually did to academe in the '50s: the firings of
tenured profs in mid-career, the inquisitions by the House Committee on Un-American Activities on the content of libraries and
courses, the campus loyalty oaths, the whole sordid atmosphere
of persecution, betrayal and paranoia. The number of conservative
academics fired by the lefty thought police, by contrast, is zero.
There has been heckling. There have been baseless accusations
of racism. And certainly there is no shortage of the zealots, au-
thoritarians and scramblers who view PC as a shrewd career move
or as a vent for their own frustrations.

In cultural matters we can hardly claim to have a left and a 16
right anymore. Instead we have something more akin to two
puritan sects, one masquerading as conservative, the other posing

While on furlough from a Massachusetts prison,
Willie Horton committed rape and murder. Horton was featured in some television commercials
by the Bush campaign in 1988.

Rev. Donald Wildmon, head of Christian Leaders for Responsible Television, organized boy-
cotts of companies that sponsored supposedly
offensive programs.

National Endowment for the Arts: an independent U.S. government agency established in 1965
to support the arts and humanities. Recently the
NEA has been under attack for giving financial
support to artists and works that have offended
some.

David Horowitz: co-director of Second Thoughts
Project of the National Forum Foundation, a
conservative organization dedicated to a strong
national defense, comprehensive welfare reform, and the preservation of the integrity of
the family.

McCarthyism: from the tactics of the former U.S.
senator from Wisconsin, Joseph McCarthy
(1909–1957) who made accusations of procom-
munist activities on doubtful evidence in the
late 1940s.

The House Committee on Un-American Activities investigated subversive activities in the
United States before and after World War II. Its
methods and results were highly controversial
and it was abolished in 1975.

PC: politically correct. A currently popular label
used to describe one side of a variety of racial,
ethnics and gender issues.

John Milton (1608–1674). English poet. His most famous work is *Paradise Lost.*

Titian (1488?-1576). Italian painter.

Michel Foucault (1926–1984). A French philosopher and cultural historian who studied the use of state power to control social deviance.

The scene of a Chinese student's protest in 1989.

Vaclav Havel (born 1936). A Czech playwright, imprisoned from 1979 to 1982 for opposition to the communist authorities. Following the ouster of the communists in 1989, Havel was unanimously elected president of Czechoslovakia by the new Federal Assembly.

Jacques Derrida (born 1930). French philosopher, a leader of the deconstructionist movement that questions the ability of language to represent reality.

Jean François Lyotard (born 1924). A leading voice of postmodernism. The term *postmodernism* is roughly synonymous with deconstructionism and poststructualism. Lyotard expresses scepticism about any possible attempt to make sense of history.

Charles Dickens (1812–1870). English novelist. Little Nell is the heroine of *The Old Curiosity Shop,* a novel in which she and her grandfather, reduced to poverty, are relentlessly pursued by the evil moneylender Daniel Quilp. Nell dies as a result of her troubles.

as revolutionary but using academic complaint as a way of evading engagement in the real world. Sect A borrows the techniques of Republican attack politics to show that if Sect B has its way, the study of Milton and Titian will be replaced by indoctrination programs in the works of obscure Third World authors and West Coast Chicano subway muralists, and the pillars of learning will forthwith collapse. Meanwhile, Sect B is so stuck in the complaint mode that it can't mount a satisfactory defense, since it has burned most of its bridges to the culture at large.

In the late '80s, while American academics were emptily theo- 17 rizing that language and the thinking subject were dead, the longing for freedom and humanistic culture was demolishing European tyranny. Of course, if the Chinese students had read their Foucault, they would have known that repression is inscribed in all language, their own included, and so they could have saved themselves the trouble of facing the tanks in Tiananmen Square. But did Vaclav Havel and his fellow playwrights free Czechoslovakia by quoting Derrida or Lyotard on the inscrutability of texts? Assuredly not: they did it by placing their faith in the transforming power of thought—by putting their shoulders to the immense wheel of the word. The world changes more deeply, widely, thrillingly than at any moment since 1917, perhaps since 1848, and the American academic left keeps fretting about how phallocentricity is inscribed in Dickens' portrayal of Little Nell.

The obsessive subject of our increasingly sterile confrontation 18 between the two PCs—the politically and the patriotically correct—is something clumsily called multiculturalism. America is a place filled with diversity, unsettled histories, images impinging on one another and spawning unexpected shapes. Its polyphony of voices, its constant eddying of claims to identity, is one of the things that make America America. The gigantic, riven, hybridizing, multiracial republic each year receives a major share of the world's emigration, legal or illegal.

To put the argument for multiculturalism in merely practical 19 terms of self-interest: though élites are never going to go away, the composition of those élites is not necessarily static. The future of American ones, in a globalized economy without a cold war, will rest with people who can think and act with informed grace across ethnic, cultural, linguistic lines. And the first step in becoming such a person lies in acknowledging that we are not one big world family, or ever likely to be; that the differences among races, nations, cultures and their various histories are at least as profound and as durable as the similarities; that these differences are not divagations from a European norm but structures eminently worth knowing about for their own sake. In the world that is coming, if you can't navigate difference, you've had it.

Thus if multiculturalism is about learning to see through borders, one can be all in favor of it. But you do not have to listen to the arguments very long before realizing that, in quite a few people's minds, multiculturalism is about something else. Their version means cultural separatism within the larger whole of America. They want to Balkanize culture. 20

To *Balkanize* is to divide something into small contending factions. The word comes from the Balkan Peninsula in Europe, which contains the countries of Yugoslavia, Rumania, Bulgaria, Albania, Greece, and part of Turkey.

The Authority of the Past

This reflects the sense of disappointment and frustration with formal politics, which has caused many people to look to the arts as a field of power, since they have power nowhere else. Thus the arts become an arena for complaint about rights. The result is a gravely distorted notion of the political capacity of the arts, just at the moment when—because of the pervasiveness of mass media—they have reached their nadir of real political effect. 21

One example is the inconclusive debate over "the canon," that oppressive Big Bertha whose muzzle is trained over the battlements of Western Civ at the black, the gay and the female. The canon, we're told, is a list of books by dead Europeans—Shakespeare and Dante and Tolstoy and Stendhal and John Donne and T.S. Eliot . . . you know, *them,* the pale, patriarchal penis people. Those who complain about the canon think it creates readers who will never read anything else. What they don't want to admit, at least not publicly, is that most American students don't read much anyway and quite a few, left to their own devices, would not read at all. Their moronic national baby-sitter, the TV set, took care 22

Big Bertha: a slang name for a long-range cannon used by Germany in World War I. Hughes is playing with the words *cannon* (artillery) and *canon* (an agreed upon reading list), implying that the traditional reading list is thought by some to be a weapon used against blacks, gays, and females.

William Shakespeare (1564–1616)
Dante Alighieri (1265–1321)
Leo Tolstoy (1828–1910)
Stendahl (pseudonym of Marie Henri Beyle) (1783–1842)
John Donne (1572–1631)
T(homas) S(tearns) Eliot (1880–1965)
    The works of the above are all firmly established parts of the traditional canon.

of that. Before long, Americans will think of the time when people sat at home and read books for their own sake, discursively and sometimes even aloud to one another, as a lost era—the way we now see rural quilting bees in the 1870s.

The quarrel over the canon reflects the sturdy assumption 23 that works of art are, or ought to be, therapeutic. Imbibe the *Republic* or *Phaedo* at 19, and you will be one kind of person; study *Jane Eyre* or *Mrs. Dalloway,* and you will be another. For in the literary zero-sum game of canon-talk, if you read *X,* it means that you don't read *Y.* This is a simple fancy.

So is the distrust of the dead, as in "dead white male." Some 24 books are deeper, wider, fuller than others, and more necessary to an understanding of our culture and ourselves. They remain so long after their authors are dead. Those who parrot slogans like "dead white male" might reflect that, in writing, death is relative: Lord Rochester is as dead as Sappho, but not so moribund as Bret Easton Ellis or Andrea Dworkin. Statistically, most authors *are* dead, but some continue to speak to us with a vividness and urgency that few of the living can rival. And the more we read, the more writers we find who do so, which is why the canon is not a fortress but a permeable membrane.

The sense of quality, of style, of measure, is not an imposition 25 bearing on literature from the domain of class, race or gender. All writers or artists carry in their mind an invisible tribunal of the dead, whose appointment is an imaginative act and not merely a browbeaten response to some notion of authority. This tribunal sits in judgment on their work. They intuit their standards from it. From its verdict there is no appeal. None of the contemporary tricks—not the fetishization of the personal, not the attempt to shift the aesthetic into the political, not the exhausted fictions of avant-gardism—will make it go away. If the tribunal weren't there, every first draft would be a final manuscript. You can't fool Mother Culture.

That is why one rejects the renewed attempt to judge writing 26 in terms of its presumed social virtue. Through it, we enter a Marxist never-never land, where all the most retrograde phantoms of Literature as Instrument of Social Utility are trotted forth. Thus

The Republic and *Phaedo* are dialogues by Plato. *The Republic* describes the ideal state. *Phaedo* describes the last hour of Socrates's life and discusses the immortality of the soul.

Jane Eyre (1847) is a novel by Charlotte Brontë (1816–1855).

Mrs. Dalloway (1925) is a novel by Virginia Woolf (1882–1941).

John Wilmot, second Earl of Rochester (1648–1680), a poet known for his satirical and often obscene verse.

Sappho (b. 612 B.C.). One of the most famous lyric poets of all time. Her work survives only in fragments.

Bret Eastin Ellis is the author of *American Psycho,* a controversial recent book about a fictional serial killer.

Andrea Dworkin, author of *Pornography: Men Possessing Women,* is a feminist writer who often campaigns against pornography on the grounds that it inspires violence against women.

Harriet Beecher Stowe (1811–1896). Her *Uncle Tom's Cabin* (1848) was the most popular book of the nineteenth century. It is credited with turning American attitudes against slavery.

Herman Melville (1819–1891). His *Moby-Dick* (1851), though not popularly received at the time, is now considered one of the greatest American novels. The *Pequod,* the whaling ship captained by the novel's monomaniacal character, Ahab, was named for the first Indian tribe exterminated by white Americans.

William Gropper (1897–1977). U.S. artist.

New Masses: a journal of left-wing politics (1926–1948).

Edward Hopper (1882–1967). U.S. artist.

the *Columbia History of the American Novel* declares Harriet Beecher Stowe a better novelist than Herman Melville because she was "socially constructive" and because *Uncle Tom's Cabin* helped rouse Americans against slavery, whereas the captain of the *Pequod* was a symbol of laissez-faire capitalism with a bad attitude toward whales.

With the same argument you can claim that an artist like 27 William Gropper, who drew those stirring cartoons of fat capitalists in top hats for the *New Masses* 60 years ago, may have something over an artist like Edward Hopper, who didn't care a plugged nickel for community and was always painting figures in lonely rooms in such a way that you can't be sure whether he was criticizing alienation or affirming the virtues of solitude.

Rewriting History

It's in the area of history that PC has scored its largest suc- 28 cesses. The reading of history is never static. There is no such thing as the last word. And who could doubt that there is still much to revise in the story of the European conquest of North and South America that historians inherited? Its basic scheme was imperial: the epic advance of civilization against barbarism; the conquistador bringing the cross and the sword; the red man shrinking back before the cavalry and the railroad. Manifest Destiny. The notion that all historians propagated this triumphalist myth uncritically is quite false; you have only to read Parkman or Prescott to realize that. But after it left the histories and sank deep into popular culture, it became a potent myth of justification for plunder, murder and enslavement.

Manifest Destiny: the nineteenth-century belief that the United States was destined to expand its boundaries to include all of North America.

Francis Parkman (1823–1893). American historian best known for *The Oregon Trail.*

So now, in reaction to it, comes the manufacture of its op- 29 posite myth. European man, once the hero of the conquest of the Americas, now becomes its demon; and the victims, who cannot be brought back to life, are sanctified. On either side of the divide between Euro and native, historians stand ready with tarbrush and gold leaf, and instead of the wicked *old* stereotypes, we have a whole outfit of equally misleading new ones. Our predecessors made a hero of Christopher Columbus. To Europeans and white

William Hickling Prescott (1796–1859). American historian. In his *History of the Conquest of Mexico* (1843), he examined the effects of European imperialism on native American culture.

Americans in 1892, he was Manifest Destiny in tights, whereas a current PC book like Kirkpatrick Sale's *The Conquest of Paradise* makes him more like Hitler in a caravel, landing like a virus among the innocent people of the New World.

30   The need for absolute goodies and absolute baddies runs deep in us, but it drags history into propaganda and denies the humanity of the dead: their sins, their virtues, their failures. To preserve complexity, and not flatten it under the weight of anachronistic moralizing, is part of the historian's task.

31   You cannot remake the past in the name of affirmative action. But you can find narratives that haven't been written, histories of people and groups that have been distorted or ignored, and refresh history by bringing them in. That is why, in the past 25 years, so much of the vitality of written history has come from the left. When you read the work of the black Caribbean historian C.L.R. James, you see a part of the world break its long silence: a silence not of its own choosing but imposed on it by earlier imperialist writers. You do not have to be a Marxist to appreciate the truth of Eric Hobsbawm's claim that the most widely recognized achievement of radical history "has been to win a place for the history of ordinary people, common men and women." In America this work necessarily includes the histories of its minorities, which tend to break down complacent nationalist readings of the American past.

C(yril) L(ionel) R(obert) James (born 1901). Journalist, historian, and political essayist. Born in Trinidad.

Eric Hobsbawm (born 1917). Emeritus Professor of Economic and Social History, University of London. Hobsbawm has written several books on Marxism and revolution.

32   By the same token, great changes have taken place in the versions of American history taught to schoolchildren. The past 10 years have brought enormous and hard-won gains in accuracy, proportion and sensitivity in the textbook treatment of American minorities, whether Asian, Native, black or Hispanic. But this is not enough for some extremists, who take the view that only blacks can write the history of slavery, only Indians that of pre-European America, and so forth.

33   That is the object of a bizarre document called the Portland African-American Baseline Essays, which has never been published as a book but, in photocopied form, is radically changing the curriculums of school systems all over the country. Written by an undistinguished group of scholars, these essays on history,

social studies, math, language and arts and science are meant to be a charter of Afrocentrist history for young black Americans. They have had little scrutiny in the mainstream press. But they are popular with bureaucrats like Thomas Sobol, the education commissioner in New York State—people who are scared of alienating black voters or can't stand up to thugs like City College professor Leonard Jeffries. Their implications for American education are large, and mostly bad.

Was Cleopatra Black?

The Afrocentrist claim can be summarized quite easily. It says the history of the cultural relations between Africa and Europe is bunk—a prop for the fiction of white European supremacy. Paleohistorians agree that intelligent human life began in the Rift Valley of Africa. The Afrocentrist goes further: the African was the *cultural* father of us all. European culture derives from Egypt, and Egypt is part of Africa, linked to its heart by the artery of the Nile. Egyptian civilization begins in sub-Saharan Africa, in Ethiopia and the Sudan. 34

Imhotep: an official in Third Dynasty Egypt, Imhotep contributed to the founding of astronomy and architecture and was the first to build a pyramid entirely of stone.

Euclid (c.300 B.C.). Greek educator and geometrician.

Hence, argued the founding father of Afrocentrist history, the late Senegalese writer Cheikh Anta Diop, whatever is Egyptian is African, part of the lost black achievement; Imhotep, the genius who invented the pyramid as a monumental form in the 3rd millennium B.C., was black, and so were Euclid and Cleopatra in Alexandria 28 dynasties later. Blacks in Egypt invented hieroglyphics, and monumental stone sculpture, and the pillared temple, and the cult of the Pharaonic sun king. The habit of European and American historians of treating the ancient Egyptians as other than black is a racist plot to conceal the achievements of black Africa. 35

Arnold Toynbee (1889–1975). British historian. His *A Study of History,* in twelve volumes written between 1934 and 1961, argues that history is an ever recurring cycle of growth and decay.

No plausible evidence exists for these claims of Egyptian negritude, though it is true that the racism of traditional historians when dealing with the cultures of Africa has been appalling. Most of them refused to believe African societies had a history that was worth telling. Here is Arnold Toynbee in *A Study of History*: "When we classify mankind by color, the only one of the primary races 36

. . . which has not made a single creative contribution to any of our 21 civilizations is the black race."

No black person—indeed, no modern historian of any race— 37 could read such bland dismissals without disgust. The question is, How to correct the record? Only by more knowledge. Toynbee was writing more than 50 years ago, but in the past 20 years, immense strides have been made in the historical scholarship of both Africa and African America. But the upwelling of research, the growth of Black Studies programs, and all that goes with the long-needed expansion of the field seem fated to be plagued by movements like Afrocentrism, just as there are always cranks nattering about flying saucers on the edges of Mesoamerican archaeology.

Mesoamerican: an archeological term used to describe the civilization of central America that flourished before the time of Columbus.

To plow through the literature of Afrocentrism is to enter a 38 world of claims about technological innovation so absurd that they lie beyond satire, like those made for Soviet science in Stalin's time. Afrocentrists have at one time or another claimed that Egyptians, alias Africans, invented the wet-cell battery by observing electric eels in the Nile; and that late in the 1st millennium B.C., they took to flying around in gliders. (This news is based not on the discovery of an aircraft in an Egyptian tomb but on a silhouette wooden votive sculpture of the god Horus, a falcon, that a passing English businessman mistook some decades ago for a model airplane.) Some also claim that Tanzanians 1,500 years ago were smelting steel with semiconductor technology. There is nothing to prove these tales, but nothing to disprove them either— a common condition of things that didn't happen.

Horus: sun god of ancient Egypt.

Tanzania: a republic in East Africa formed by the merger of Tanganika and Zanzibar in 1964.

The Real Multiculturalism

Nowhere are the weaknesses and propagandistic nature of 39 Afrocentrism more visible than in its version of slave history. Afrocentrists wish to invent a sort of remedial history in which the entire blame for the invention and practice of black slavery is laid at the door of Europeans. This is profoundly unhistorical, but it's getting locked in popular consciousness through the new curriculums.

Periclean Athens: the flowering of Greek civilization, named after the statesman Pericles (c.495–429 B.C.).

Augustan Rome: the golden age of Latin literature, named after the first Roman emperor, Augustus (63 B.C.–A.D. 14).

Roots (1976) by Alex Haley won a Pulitzer Prize Special Citation and became a popular television mini-series the following year. In the book Haley traces his family's roots to Kunte Kinte, an African ancestor who was made a slave and brought to the New World.

Djibouti: a former French overseas territory in East Africa. Gained independence in 1977.

Mauritania: the Islamic Republic of Mauritania in West Africa. Formerly a French colony. Independent since 1960.

"the Sudan:" a region in North Africa south of the Sahara extending from the Atlantic Ocean to the Red Sea.

Nigeria: a republic in West Africa formerly a British colony. Independent since 1960.

Rwanda: a republic in Central Africa formerly a British Trust Territory. Became independent in 1962.

Niger: a republic in North West Africa formerly part of French West Africa. Became independent in 1960.

It is true that slavery had been written into the basis of the   40
classical world. Periclean Athens was a slave state, and so was Augustan Rome. Most of their slaves were Caucasian. The word slave meant a person of Slavic origin. By the 13th century slavery spread to other Caucasian peoples. But the African slave trade as such, the black traffic, was an Arab invention, developed by traders with the enthusiastic collaboration of black African ones, institutionalized with the most unrelenting brutality, centuries before the white man appeared on the African continent, and continuing long after the slave market in North America was finally crushed.

Naturally this is a problem for Afrocentrists, especially when   41
you consider the recent heritage of Black Muslim ideas that many of them espouse. Nothing in the writings of the Prophet forbids slavery, which is why it became such an Arab-dominated business. And the slave traffic could not have existed without the whole-hearted cooperation of African tribal states, built on the supply of captives generated by their relentless wars. The image promulgated by pop-history fictions like *Roots*—white slavers bursting with cutlass and musket into the settled lives of peaceful African villages—is very far from the historical truth. A marketing system had been in place for centuries, and its supply was controlled by Africans. Nor did it simply vanish with Abolition. Slave markets, supplying the Arab emirates, were still operating in Djibouti in the 1950s; and since 1960, the slave trade has flourished in Mauritania and the Sudan. There are still reports of chattel slavery in northern Nigeria, Rwanda and Niger.

But here we come up against a cardinal rule of the PC attitude   42
to oppression studies. Whatever a white European male historian or witness has to say must be suspect; the utterances of an oppressed person or group deserve instant credence, even if they're the merest assertion. The claims of the victim do have to be heard, because they may cast new light on history. But they have to pass exactly the same tests as anyone else's or debate fails and truth suffers. The PC cover for this is the idea that all statements about history are expressions of power: history is written only by the winners, and truth is political and unknowable.

The word self-esteem has become one of the obstructive shib-   43
boleths of education. Why do black children need Afrocentrist
education? Because, its promoters say, it will create self-esteem.
The children live in a world of media and institutions whose
images and values are created mainly by whites. The white tradition is to denigrate blacks. Hence blacks must have models that
show them that they matter. Do you want your children to love
themselves? Then change the curriculum. Feed them racist clap-
trap à la Leonard Jeffries, about how your intelligence is a function
of the amount of melanin in your skin, and how Africans were
sun people, open and cooperative, whereas Europeans were ice
people, skulking pallidly in caves.

It is not hard to see why these claims for purely remedial   44
history are intensifying today. They are symbolic. Nationalism
always wants to have myths to prop itself up; and the newer the
nationalism, the more ancient its claims. The invention of tradition, as Eric Hobsbawm has shown in detail, was one of the
cultural industries of 19th century Europe. But the desire for self-
esteem does not justify every lie and exaggeration and therapeutic
slanting of evidence that can be claimed to alleviate it. The separatism it fosters turns what ought to be a recognition of cultural
diversity, or real multiculturalism, tolerant on both sides, into
a pernicious symbolic program. Separatism is the opposite of
diversity.

The idea that European culture is oppressive in and of itself   45
is a fallacy that can survive only among the fanatical and the
ignorant. The moral and intellectual conviction that inspired
Toussaint-Louverture to focus the rage of the Haitian slaves and
lead them to freedom in 1791 came from his reading of Rousseau
and Mirabeau. When thousands of voteless, propertyless workers
the length and breadth of England met in their reading groups
in the 1820s to discuss republican ideas and discover the significance of Shakespeare's *Julius Caesar,* they were seeking to unite
themselves by taking back the meanings of a dominant culture
from custodians who didn't live up to them.

Americans can still take courage from their example. Cultural   46
separatism within this republic is more a fad than a serious pro-

Toussaint Louverture (1743–1803). Haitian political and military leader.

Jean-Jacques Rousseau (1712–1778). French
social reformer and philosopher.

Honoré Mirabeau (1749–1791). An orator and
statesman of the French Revolution.

posal; it is not likely to hold. If it did, it would be a disaster for those it claims to help: the young, the poor and the black. Self-esteem comes from doing things well, from discovering how to tell a truth from a lie and from finding out what unites us as well as what separates us. The posturing of the politically correct is no more a guide to such matters than the opinions of Simon Legree.

Simon Legree: a brutal slave owner in Stowe's *Uncle Tom's Cabin.*

Meaning and Purpose

1. Hughes says the public is not taking an active role in politics. What does he say is the reason?
2. Is Hughes antifeminist? Find passages of the essay to support your answer.
3. What aspects of multiculturalism does Hughes support? Which does he oppose?
4. In paragraphs 21–27, Hughes writes about the "canon." What does he say about the validity of the canon and about possible additions or changes?
5. Is Hughes for or against the rewriting of history?

Strategy

1. What does Hughes achieve by beginning with the long quotation from W. H. Auden?
2. What is the purpose of comparing America in the 1980s to ancient Rome?
3. Paragraphs 4 and 5 serve as a kind of definition of America. Why do you think these paragraphs are included?
4. Paragraph 15 explains the McCarthyism of the 1950s. Why is it important for Hughes to include this discussion?
5. Near the end of the essay Hughes cites the example of Toussaint-

But he does not think that each group should be the only one to write its own history or that you should remake the past to please any group or add to its self-esteem. Every new work of history must meet traditional standards of scholarship and veracity. He objects to attempts to label "absolute goodies and absolute baddies." He says the last ten years have already brought great improvement in textbooks treating American minorities. See paragraphs 28–32.

Strategy

1. Probably he is expecting that readers will begin to see parallels with life today even before he says this is just like America. If so, they will be prepared for the critical statements of paragraph 2.

2. Ancient Rome inevitably brings to mind the "fall" of the empire, and thus the comparison allows him to communicate the seriousness of his criticism.

3. They serve as a model against which to measure the coming discussion. They emphasize diversity and mutual respect and much of what follows is seen by Hughes as a falling away from these principles.

4. Hughes rejects the comparison of political correctness to McCarthyism, so he wants to inform his readers of the vast difference in scale between the two phenomena.

5. Toussaint-Louverture is a black leader who developed his moral convictions from reading white Europeans, thus illustrating that the works of these writers is not oppressive.

Style

1. The tone is difficult to pin down. Sometimes Hughes is outrageous, sometimes sarcastic, sometimes humorous, sometimes vituperative, but mostly the tone is serious and direct.

2. To separate into contending fragments.

3. A membrane is pliable; a fortress is rigid. Hughes is saying that the canon changes with time.

Louverture. Why is he a particularly good example for Hughes's essay?

Style

1. How would you characterize the tone of this essay?
2. What does the phrase "to Balkanize culture" in paragraph 20 mean?
3. Explain the meaning of "the canon is not a fortress but a permeable membrane."
4. If necessary, look the following words up in a dictionary: *cobble* (9); *scanted* (12); *divagations* (19); *moribund* (24); *caravel* (29); *shibboleths* (43).

Writing Tasks

1. Hughes's essay is full of provocative statements. As you read them, you may be nodding your head in agreement, or shaking it in dismay or anger. Select one such statement and write an argument paper supporting or refuting the statement. Use examples to illustrate your point. Some possibilities:

   a. "The contest between education and TV—between argument and persuasion by spectacle—has been won by TV" (3).

   b. "We want to create a sort of linguistic Lourdes, where evil and misfortune are dispelled by a dip in the waters of euphemism" (8).

   c. "The cult of the abused Inner Child has a very important use in modern America: it tells you that nothing is your fault" (10).

   d. "Thus we create a juvenile culture of complaint in which Big Daddy is always to blame and the expansion of rights goes on without the other half of citizenship: attachment to duties and obligations" (11).

4. *cobble*: to put together roughly; *scanted*: treated slightly or inadequately; *divagations*: digressions; *moribund*: stagnant or near dead. Hughes is saying that some dead authors' works are more alive than those of some current authors; *caravel*: a small sailing ship used in Spain and Portugal in the Middle Ages; *shibboleths*: pet phrases.

e. "We are seeing a recoil from politics, from the active, reasoned exercise of citizenship" (11).

f. "The future of American [elites], in a globalized economy without a cold war, will rest with people who can think and act with informed grace across ethnic, cultural, linguistic lines" (19).

g. "Most American students don't read much anyway and quite a few, left to their own devices, would not read at all. Their moronic national baby-sitter, the TV set, took care of that" (21).

2. Read the headlines and at least a portion of each article in the first section of a daily newspaper in your area. Then write a paper on either side of this statement: The (name of newspaper) accurately reflects daily life in (name of town, city, state, or country). Use plenty of evidence to support your view.

🦃 *Responding to Photographs* 🦃
Persuasion and Argument

Saturday Morning—USA

What is the impact of television violence on children? Does television violence cause aggressive behavior? Research has not conclusively proven that it does or does not teach children to use force or violence in their relationships with other children. But most researchers agree that when children watch hours of television they participate in "imitative learning" or "modeling." In simple terms—watching television creates a "monkey-see, monkey-do" effect.

Research has even shown that onetime exposure to televised aggressive behavior can be repeated in children's play by as many as 88 percent of the children who have seen it. Moreover, a single experience viewing a dramatic aggressive act can be recalled and reenacted by children six months after the viewing. Earlier studies indicate that the average child between 5 and 15 will witness during this ten-year period the violent deaths of more than 13,400 humans. Surely the accumulated impact of television violence must influence monkey-see, monkey-do behavior. Or does it?

"Saturday Morning—USA" captures a moment when television generates "imitative learning." Drawing on details from the photograph and from the discussion here, compose an argument based on one of the following assignments. Before beginning your first draft, reread "Persuasion and Argument: Convincing a Reader" at the beginning of the chapter to review the conventions of a sound argument.

1. Compose an inductive or deductive argument which leads your reader to conclude that children should be curtailed from watching television violence. Here are a few suggestions to get you started. Include a description of "Saturday Morning—USA" which leads to the conclusion that television has a powerful modeling effect. You might also include some of your own observations of children modeling violent television behavior. You might then point out what research suggests about the effect of television violence on play, thus leading your reader to an obvious conclusion.

2. Compose an inductive or deductive essay that takes the opposing position called for in option 1; that is, the viewing of television violence should not be curtailed because it, like all television viewing, stimulates creative play. Here are a few suggestions to get you started. In this approach you will describe the contents of "Saturday Morning—USA" but interpret the photograph as an indication that television stimulates imaginative play, not actual violent behavior. You might also draw on your own experience modeling television violence during play, but point out that you and your friends are not criminals or violent people. You might state and agree with the research alluded to in the opening discussion of the writing task, but you would interpret it in a way that supports your point; that is, modeling is a powerful teacher, but children have the ability to separate television behavior from reality.

❦ Additional Writing Tasks ❦

Persuasion and Argument

1. Write an argument in which you express one of your own deeply felt opinions. If the subject you select has undergone extensive public discussion, assume that your reader is familiar with the general elements of the debate and develop specific evidence based on your own observations, reading, and experience. Use the following list to stimulate your thinking, but do not feel bound by the subjects.

   a. Fraternities
   b. Sororities
   c. Hiring quotas
   d. Euthanasia
   e. Prayer in schools
   f. Giving birth control advice to teenagers
   g. Sex education
   h. Legalized drugs
   i. Capital punishment
   j. Smoking in public buildings
   k. Public profanity
   l. Disruptive behavior in public places
   m. Requiring people on public assistance to work for the city
   n. Animal rights
   o. Student code of conduct
   p. Violence on television
   q. Movie ratings
   r. Subliminal messages in music
   s. Emotional advertising in political campaigns
   t. Censorship

2. Plastic disposable diapers are becoming a significant problem. Each year Americans toss approximately eighteen billion diapers—containing an estimated 2.8 million tons of excrement and urine—in the trash. Every one of these disposable diapers takes up to five hundred years to decompose. Aside from the solid waste issue, there are also growing concerns about infectious material seeping into our soil and ground water, wasted

653

natural resources, the rising costs of diaper production, "disposal," and increasing risks of severe rashes and toxic shock syndrome in children.

Write an argument essay in opposition to disposable diapers. Direct your essay to new parents.

3. Many people find junk mail entertaining, something to thumb through during a leisure moment. You, however, believe junk mail is not only a nuisance but also a hazard. For example, all the junk mail you receive this year will have consumed the equivalent of one and a half trees. One year's junk mail sent in the United States amounts to a hundred million trees.

Write an essay arguing against junk mail. Here are some commonly known facts you might want to use:

a. Almost two million tons of junk mail are sent each year.
b. Over 40 percent of all junk mail is never opened.
c. Junk mail receives special postage rates—currently 10.1 cents per piece if arranged in presorted batches.
d. The average American will spend eight months of his or her life just *opening* junk mail.
e. The junk mail sent to a million people means the destruction of 1.5 million trees.

4. A radical counterculture has emerged in Germany's inner cities. They are the *autonomen,* a term that means the same as "autonomous" in English. The *autonomen,* who wear masks at demonstrations, are composed of squatters and street people. They see themselves as the last hope of revolutionary activism. The group refuses to participate in any political or social system, and its brand of activism is usually spontaneous, unorganized, and often violent.

The *autonomen* have no counterpart on the American social scene, but some social psychologists predict our government's failure to solve the problems of homelessness, drug abuse, and street gangs will lead to the formation of groups like the *autonomen* to express the anger and alienation the inner-city underclass already feels.

Write an essay in which you argue that inner-city life must be improved or city governments will soon be dealing with groups like Germany's *autonomen*. You might begin by using the *Reader's Guide to Periodic Literature* to find background information on these groups.

Glossary

Abridgment A shortened version of a work, but one in which the compiler attempts to include all pertinent parts of the longer work.

Abstract Abstract words or terms describe ideas, concepts, or qualities, as opposed to **concrete** entities. Sample abstract words and expressions are *philosophy, remorse, happiness, beauty, honor, peace, organizational climate, achievement motive,* and *burden of proof.*

Acronym A word formed by combining the first letters or syllables of words, to form a new word. An example is BASIC, the word that names a computer language; it is an acronym meaning "Beginner's All-purpose Symbolic Instruction Code."

Ad hominem argument *See* **Logical fallacies.**

Allusion An allusion briefly and often casually refers to something the writer believes is common knowledge. If you write that your neighbor's fence "looks like the Berlin Wall," you allude to the state of the Berlin Wall, which is in ruins. "Future Schlock," the title of the Neil Postman essay in Chapter 3, is an allusion to Alvin Toffler's *Future Shock,* a book about what to expect in the future. A Robert Frost poem about the sudden death of a boy is titled, " 'Out, Out—,' " an allusion to lines from Shakespeare's *Macbeth:*

> Out, out, brief candle!
> Life's but a walking shadow, a poor player
> That struts and frets his hour upon the stage,
> And then is heard no more (V,v,23).

Analogy An analogy is an imaginative comparison between two things, one less familiar than the other, usually intended to clarify a description of the less familiar one. In his novel *The Red and* *the Black,* the French author Stendhal (Marie Henri Beyle) wrote, "A novel is a mirror that strolls along a highway. Now it reflects the blue of the skies, now the mud puddles underfoot," clarifying his concept of the novel by imaginatively comparing it to a common, familiar item.

Analysis   In an analysis, a writer examines a piece of writing by paying special attention to its elements of thought. An analysis is based on the premise that some ideas or concepts are actually combinations formed of other ideas or concepts. An analysis of an idea or concept as incorporated in an extended piece of writing often shows that many smaller thoughts have been combined into larger thoughts. Analyzing the Pledge of Allegiance to the Flag shows that it includes a definition of an ideal republic, which has its roots in classical Greek philosophy.

Anecdote   An anecdote is an incident, or **narration,** which reveals a facet of character, most often about a well-known person.

Argument   An argument is meant to persuade an audience to accept the qualities of a proposition (a statement to be supported), so that the audience will be convinced of the proposition's truth or falsity. In his commentary on rhetoric, Aristotle spoke of "artistic proofs," so called because they are invented in the sense of being thought up or devised for the specific purpose of swaying an audience to an orator's point of view.

Aristotelian proofs as they are used when writing arguments appeal to the audience in one of three ways: rationally, emotionally, or ethically. A rational appeal (*logos*) appeals to the audience's reason: an emotional appeal (*pathos*) appeals to the audience's emotions or passions; ethical appeal (*ethos*) appeals to the audience's confidence in the writer's character or credentials. Today, an argument commonly includes more than one of these proofs, and may also embody such nonartistic proofs as statistics, results of polls, scientific data, and other scientifically verifiable statements.

Association fallacy   *See* **Logical fallacies.**

Audience   An audience is a reader or a class of readers whom writers keep in mind while they write and particularly while they revise their writing. Writers determine as much as they can about their audiences, including their expertise, their education, their biases, their political and cultural background, their assumptions, and their interests. Writers deal with many kinds of audiences, including those who already share the writer's convictions. Each audience affects the writer's way of casting the writing.

Knowing as much as they can about their audiences helps writers determine which **strategies** to use, such as sentence structure, reasoning, **definition, emphasis,** organization, and **style.**

Audiences also affect writers' **diction.** A writer aiming at an audience of experienced amateur sailors would use words like *pulpit* and *roach,* but for an audience knowing nothing of nautical terminology, the writer would use "the platform on the forward part of the ship from which sailors handle and change sails," instead of *pulpit,* and "the curved portion of a sail closest to the rear end of the ship," instead of *roach.*

Body The main part of a piece of writing is its body. Here, events are dramatized, dialogue is sustained, **conflicts** are developed, and other **strategies** are applied to sustain the reader's involvement.

Categories Classes or divisions in an organized **classification.** Under the classification *general education requirements,* a writer could list the categories humanities, foreign languages, and sciences. Further, the writer could subcategorize by listing *foreign languages* such as French, Latin, German, and Japanese.

Cause and effect A cause is that which came before an effect, the effect being the result of that cause. Combined, *cause and effect* is a useful way of analyzing reasons for actions and for the results of those actions. In the sentence, "Because Gwen did not study, she failed the calculus examination," one can see the immediate cause and the immediate effect. But what ultimate cause was behind Gwen's not studying? Not even Gwen can be absolutely sure, because most causes in our daily lives are probable, not certain. Aware of this uncertainty, writers use with caution the cause-and-effect strategy.

Circumlocution Circumlocution in writing fails to make a point clearly or evades a point because many words are used where fewer would have sufficed. The sentence, "What is the cause of the source of his pain cannot be other than his appendix, which seems to be less than healthy," illustrates circumlocution. The sentence could have been recast as, "His pain is probably caused by appendicitis."

Claim   The philosopher and rhetorician Stephen Toulmin devised a model of reasoning similar to the **syllogism**. One of the Toulmin model's primary elements is *claim,* which is the conclusion. The other two elements are *data,* which form the evidence, and *warrant,* which is the supporting argument. This sentence briefly illustrates the Toulmin model: Jasmah is a physicist *(data);* therefore, Jasmah is intelligent *(claim)* because all physicists are intelligent *(warrant).*

Classification   Classification is a system for sorting things into distinct categories, or classes. A music lover might want to organize her cassettes. After sorting them, she sees that she can classify them into these categories, according to types of music: jazz, classical, and country and western. Later, perhaps when she wants to write a paper about her jazz cassettes, she can classify them into categories according to the musical styles of the featured artists on her tapes, making sure that each category is described clearly so that it is distinct from other categories.

Cliché   In French, the *cliché* is an outmoded system for making metal printing plates with which to print the same thing again and again. In English, the name describes words and phrases that have been used again and again so that they have become worn out, tired. Examples abound: A person can be "as old as the hills." A night can be "as black as coal." We can be "afraid of our own shadow." Someone can have "an ax to grind." A child can be "a chip off the old block," "here today; gone tomorrow," "a square peg in a round hole," "start from scratch," and so on. When revising, writers "keep an eye peeled" for clichés so that they can replace those with fresh, colorful expressions of their own **invention**.

Climax   In a **narration** essay, the climax is the conclusion, the highest point of interest. In other kinds of writing the climax, or peak of interest, marks the turning point in the action.

Coherence   Coherence clearly, consistently, and logically connects the parts in a piece of writing. It is the glue that holds together all vigorous, effective writing. Among other techniques, coherence invokes **transitions** to show introductory relationships among ideas, paragraphing to signal shifts in thought, sentences that follow reasonably from those which came before them, and **diction** appropriate to the **audience.**

Colloquial expressions   Colloquial expressions, such as "Don't even try to psych out Professor Sherman," and "Ralph crammed all his stuff into his closet" characterize informal (and often playful) speaking and writing. Therefore, they have limited use in formal writing because their very casualness can distract readers.

Comparison and contrast   A comparison involves similarities; a contrast, differences. Combining these two ways of judging qualities can lead to discoveries about two things formerly thought to be ordinarily alike or unalike. A writer who compares and contrasts an electric typewriter and a computer discovers that whatever an electric typewriter can do, a computer with a word-processing program and printer can do more efficiently (a comparison). The writer will also discover the many things that a computer, equipped with various programs, can do that a typewriter cannot possibly do, such as maintaining a continuous record of household expenditures (a contrast). On the other hand, the writer will discover that both machines can be used for writing brief informal notes, but a computer can also retain easily correctable copies of those notes on a disk (comparison and contrast).

Conclusions   Conclusions are ways of ending essays. The way in which an essay is concluded depends in great part on the content of the essay itself. An essay arguing for or against gun control is likely to end by restating the reasons for taking one position or another. An essay explaining one of the complex relationships between human beings and nature might conclude by warning the reader that the relationship is endangered. An essay with several examples of how the world's economies are intertwined might end with one sterling example of an economy that is vitally connected to our own. An essayist offering information about an inexpensive medicine for a common disease might conclude by recommending that readers consult their personal physicians for more information.

Conclusions do not drift into other topics, nor do they shift an essay's emphasis away from its own topic. A writer would not end an essay taking a firm stand against showing pornographic movies on television by writing something like, "It all depends on each person's tastes."

So-called cute conclusions suggest to the audience that the writer was not deeply involved in thinking about the essay's content. They should be avoided.

Conclusions grow logically and sufficiently from the essay, and they should content the **audience.**

Concrete Concrete words or expressions refer to things experienced by the senses, as opposed to **abstractions.** These words and expressions are concrete: *chair, perfume, music, automobile, bitter, cardboard box, dictionary, window,* and *refrigerator.*

Conflict In writing, a conflict is a struggle that grows from two opposing beliefs, values, characters, and so on, which are developed in the **body** of the piece.

Connotation The word "connotation" describes the implied meanings that become attached to words, *Skinny* and *slender* both mean thin or slight, but the first has negative connotations (emaciation and perhaps ill health), and the latter implies grace, even elegance.

The descriptive phrase *cheap furniture* carries connotations of shoddy workmanship and poor quality. The phrase *inexpensive furniture,* however, implies only the furniture's low cost. Although *cheap* and *inexpensive* are dictionary synonyms, the meaning implied in *cheap* sets it apart from *inexpensive.* Careful writers keep in mind what words mean according to dictionaries and what those same words may imply beyond their dictionary definitions.

Data The proofs in Stephen Toulmin's model of reasoning are *data.*

They are the evidence that supports the model's **claim**, or conclusion.

Data are also nonartistic proofs (see **argument**) used in other models of reasoning. These kinds of data come from scientific observations, record keeping, or statistics—facts or figures from which conclusions can be inferred, and information from credible, reliable sources.

Deduction   A deduction is the result of reasoning from a general statement to a specific instance. If your college requires that all prospective students be tested in a foreign language before they are enrolled, then you can reason that Pat, who sits next to you in English class, has taken a test in a foreign language. Deductions are not always that clear-cut, though.

One might think that all small cars get good gas mileage and then buy a small car to save money on fuel, only to find that this car gets poor mileage. The original assumption, then, was false.

Definition   A definition outlines, limits, or states the meaning of a word, term, phrase, or concept.

A formal definition puts a term into a class and then shows how it differs from other members of the same class. A trumpet (term) is a brass musical wind instrument (class) consisting of a tube in an oblong loop or loops, with a flared bell at one end, a curved mouthpiece at the other, and three valves for making tonal changes (difference).

An extended definition, a form of **exposition**, not only defines in the senses above but also explains issues by including **strategies**, such as **narration**, **description**, **example**, and **evidence**. One example of an extended definition in this book is Paul Theroux's "Being a Man."

Denotation   The term *denotation* applies to the literal, lexical meaning of a word—that which is explained in a good dictionary.

Description   The technique of making pictures with words is *description*. An effective description includes clear evidence that appeals to one or more of the senses—sight, touch, taste, smell, or hearing—as well as **explanation**. Henry David Thoreau's "The

Battle of the Ants," in Chapter 4, demonstrates this combination of description and explanation: "his own breast was all torn away, exposing what vitals he had there to the jaws of the black warrior, whose breastplate was apparently too thick for him to pierce; and the dark carbuncles of the sufferer's eyes shone with ferocity such as only war could excite."

Diction   Diction is deliberate choice of words. Writers conscientiously choose words and the ways in which they use them, being guided by their audience and their purpose. Writers make their selections from various levels of usage, including **standard English, slang**, conversational expressions, regionalisms (choosing among "spigot," "tap," and "faucet"), and scientific and technical **jargon**.

Consider these sentences:

1. "Christine resigned her position."
2. "Chris quit her job."
3. "Chris told him he could take his job and shove it!"

What determines which of these sentences is correct? The audience and the purpose.

Sentence 1 is appropriate for a formal audience and a formal purpose: perhaps the writer's audience was college-level readers and the purpose was to describe her best friend's employment difficulties.

Sentence 2 might have been for a semiformal audience and a semiformal purpose, such as writing an essay for the readers of a college alumnae newsletter to help graduates keep track of their classmates.

Sentence 3 might have been for an informal audience and purpose, such as writing an essay for other members of a composition class to explain how one of them had reacted to being treated poorly by the manager of a local pizza parlor.

Whoever the audience and whatever the purpose, writers are guided by their own sense of propriety and by dictionaries and a thesaurus. They rarely use a thesaurus, however, without also consulting a dictionary to be sure that the words they have chosen from the thesaurus are in fact appropriate for their audience and purpose.

Directive process analysis   A directive process analysis tells how to do something. It is a sequence of directions to guide a reader who wants to complete a specific task. Such an analysis tells how to plant a tree, but *not* how a tree grows, the latter topic being an **informative process analysis.**

Division Division is a subclass of **classification.** Writers divide a classification into logical parts, usually for description or explanation. Let's say that a writer wanted to describe a personal computer. First, you would classify it, telling how it differs from mainframe computers, from large industrial computers, and from laptop computers. Then you would divide the home computer into its logical parts: the keyboard, the central processing unit, and the video monitor. After making that division, you would describe each of these components. By your division, you help the reader to see one component at a time, rather than try to imagine an entire home computer all at once.

Dominant impression The dominant impression is the main sensation or conception that the author strives to fix in the reader's mind, by carefully shaping the details of a **description.**

Effect It is part of **cause and effect,** the result or outcome of an occurrence or action, but the word *effect* also refers to the impression that writing—whether a word, sentence, paragraph, essay, or larger work—makes on its audience.

Emphasis With emphasis, writers stress or highlight the things they want their readers to see as most important in their writing. Writers use such **strategies** as **diction,** sentence structure, position, active voice, repetition, and mechanics to emphasize their main points.

> *Diction:* A writer who wanted to emphasize a negative opinion of a newly opened restaurant could write, "This restaurant has food fit to eat only if you are starving."

> *Sentence structure:* If you wanted to emphasize your opinion of the food itself, you could write a periodic sentence, which moves from supporting details to the main idea. "With lukewarm coffee, half-cooked cold chicken, salty mashed potatoes, and burned vegetables, my meal was barely edible." You could emphasize your description of the food by writing a loose sentence, in which the supporting details follow the main idea: "I had a

barely edible meal of lukewarm coffee, half-cooked cold chicken, salty mashed potatoes, and burned vegetables."

Position: That which we read last, we remember longest, whether chapters in a book, groups of words in a sentence, or paragraphs in an essay. Commenting on an unsavory experience in a restaurant, you might begin a paper by describing how you had read about the restaurant in a respectable tourist guide, where it had been awarded three stars. Then you might devote a short paragraph to the small problem you had in finding the place because it was in a part of the city unfamiliar to the taxicab driver, who had been profusely apologetic. You then might describe the restaurant's décor, a delightful amalgam of French Provincial and Early American, and your waitress, a pleasant young lady dressed in a peasant frock, who was also attending law school at the nearby university. Finally, because you had been shocked at the poor quality of the food, in utter contrast to the treat you had been expecting, you might conclude the essay with a paragraph meant to shock your readers as well, thus emphasizing the most important point in your experience by putting it last.

Active voice: Verbs in active voice—"This restaurant serves poorly prepared food"—are more emphatic than those in passive voice: "Poorly prepared food is served by this restaurant."

Repetition: "I spent a valuable hour of my vacation sipping the lukewarm coffee at Harry's Restaurant, chewing Harry's half-cooked chicken, tasting the salty mashed potatoes at Harry's, and staring at the vegetables Harry burned. Never again will I eat in Harry's Restaurant."

Mechanics: Usually the least appropriate way to emphasize formal writing, mechanics include underlining, quotation marks, and exclamation points: "When I was served the 'food' I had ordered in this 'restaurant,' I was *shocked* to see how *poorly* it had been prepared!" Such devices must be used sparingly. Your emphasis will be more successfully communicated with diction, sentence structure, position, active voice, and repetition.

Essay   The word *essay* is from the French *essai,* meaning "attempt" or "experiment." In English, an essay is a relatively short piece of nonfiction prose on a specified topic. It is an attempt by a writer to persuade, inform, explain, argue, describe, narrate, expose, or in some other way organize and develop a topic to interest an **audience.**

Essays are occasionally defined as informal or formal, although the definitions admittedly are vague. Generally, however, a formal essay includes **diction** appropriate to a serious audience, has a serious **tone,** and is focused on a serious topic. An informal essay, on the other hand, often has a light, perhaps humorous tone and informal language, and is focused on a personal, perhaps frivolous topic.

Evaluation An evaluation determines the worth or quality of a work. If you are revising your own work or reading someone else's, you try to evaluate it objectively, to see how well it fulfills its purpose. Usually, those who evaluate a work look to see how well its thesis is stated and supported, how strongly its proofs support its claims, how clearly it is organized, whether or not its language is clear, and whether or not it is appropriately written for its intended audience.

Evidence Evidence is support for a theory, claim, or **thesis.** The commonest kinds of evidence are obvious evidence, manifest evidence, and clear evidence. Obvious evidence, usually scientific, is readily perceived or easily inferred. If $6 + 2 + x = 9$, then the evidence is obvious that $x = 1$. Manifest evidence is immediately clear to the understanding, often by intuition. If you see water in its solid state, then you know almost without thinking that it is frozen. Clear evidence, the kind essayists use most often, supports and clarifies a reader's understanding of the writer's thesis. If the writer's thesis is that marriage vows are hopelessly outmoded, then you must offer clear evidence to support that thesis. You must examine and clarify the vows, compare them with the spousal responsibilities in modern marriages, illustrate how those vows conflict with reality, and so on.

Examples An example is an instance that follows and illustrates the content of your statement. Among the more usual are specific examples, typical examples, and hypothetical examples. Specific examples amplify one experience, event, incident, or fact. They clarify in detail your earlier statement. Typical examples illustrate many experiences, events, incidents, or facts. They clarify generally your earlier statement, so that they will be representative. Hypothetical examples are imagined or supposed representations. They clarify the probability of your earlier statement.

Exposition   An exposition is a detailed explanation of the content of an idea, an object, an attitude, or a position. An exposition exposes, makes something accessible to a reader, by using any of a number of **strategies**, including examples, comparisons and contrasts, analogies, and classifications. Most essays in this book are expository, as are most essays written in college.

False analogy   *See* **Logical fallacies.**

Faulty either/or reasoning   *See* **Logical fallacies.**

Figures of speech   Tropes, or figures of speech, make a clear style vivid by adding **connotations** to statements, which appeal to the reader's imagination. The most used figures of speech are metaphor, simile, personification, hyperbole (overstatement), litotes (understatement), synecdoche, metonymy, and paradox.

A *metaphor* is an implied comparison between two dissimilar things: "Jamie is the tiger on the team." Tigers are noted for their speed, intelligence, and strength—the attributes that this metaphor gives to Jamie.

A *simile* is an explicit comparison between two dissimilar things, using the word *as* or *like*: "Jamie is as southern as Georgia."

Personification gives human qualities to inanimate objects or abstract ideas: "Six tall, menacing pine trees guard our campus at night."

Hyperbole (overstatement) is deliberate exaggeration used for emphasis: "It was raining so hard that I almost drowned while driving to school."

Litotes (understatement) is deliberate understatement used for emphasis: "Getting a D on my history test was not my greatest birthday present."

Synecdoche substitutes part of something for the whole: "Two hands left the ship just before it sailed." In this example, *hands* substitutes for "sailors."

Metonymy substitutes the whole for a part of something:

"The Pentagon said today that, except for Near Eastern flareups, fewer troops will be needed in the next decade." In this example, *The Pentagon* substitutes for "a spokesperson for the army."

A *paradox* appears to be contradictory, but in fact carries some truth: "The wealthier you are, the poorer you may be." Wealth is not always measured by money. It is also measured by wisdom, knowledge, morality, love, and other qualities.

Focus   In photography, a subject that is in focus is sharply defined. That is also true in writing. Writers who focus on their subject bring it into sharp detail. They begin by thinking about a large unfocused topic, such as "crime in the streets." Then they may decide to focus on some part of crime in the streets—"street crime in our city." After they have found their focus, they may narrow it even more—to "street crime in my neighborhood." How sharply they focus on a subject often depends on their **audience** and **purpose.**

General and specific   General words are names for broad classes of things, from which you can move to words that designate members of those classes. One broad class is *automobiles*. A term that designates a member of that class is *sports car*. A designation for a more specific member of the sports-car class is *Alfa Romeo*. Writers are guided by their **audience** and by their **purpose** when they choose among general and specific names.

Generalization   A generalization is a broad statement that rests on personal observation or acquired information. The sentence "Children usually follow their parents' advice" suggests that its writer has experience with raising children and from that experience has written a generalization that includes all children.

Writers sometimes begin with generalizations and then move toward conclusions based on their generalizations. But to avoid hasty generalizations, they often use qualifiers in their conclusions: "She has a degree in English, and so she *probably* knows a lot about Shakespeare." Or, "She has a degree in English, and so she *might* know *something* about Shakespeare." See also **induction.**

Hyperbole   *See* **Figures of speech.**

Hypothetical examples *See* **Examples.**

Image An image appeals to the imagination through the senses. It is a **strategy** many writers apply to help readers "see" what they are reading. The sentence, "Her ancient face was a sheaf of small etched road maps to nowhere," is an image that describes an old and wrinkled countenance. The sentence, "He sings the songs of an old man's childhood, the golden past that never was," describes a person who reminisces about former times, which seem far more attractive now ("the golden past") than they were then.

Induction An induction is the result of reasoning that interprets limited evidence to arrive at a general truth. A person who has owned three or four friendly and alert cocker spaniels over the years may reason that all cocker spaniels are friendly and alert.

Inductive reasoning is useful in writing because it is a powerful persuader. Writers who want to persuade readers of a general truth use enough sound evidence to make their claims reasonably acceptable. If you wanted to persuade readers of the benefits in jogging, you might offer as evidence all your healthy friends who jog, newspaper articles that endorse jogging as a healthy activity, well-known athletes who jog, your doctor's saying that jogging promotes health, and so on. The more sound evidence you present, the more apt the reader is to accept your persuasive **argument.**

Informative process analysis With an informative process analysis, you tell how something is done. You describe sequentially the steps in a natural procedure that does not involve intervention. An informative process analysis might tell how a tree grows, but *not* how to plant a tree, the latter topic being a **directive process analysis.**

Introduction An introduction begins a piece of writing. An effective introduction establishes the essay's topic, tone, and territory. It leads directly into the main idea or issue discussed in the **body** of the paper. Its purpose is to engender readers' interest. To achieve that purpose, writers include such **strategies** as **rhetorical questions**, unusual facts, **anecdotes**, and personal comments.

The length of an introduction depends on the essay's **purpose** and its intended **audience**.

Invention   Writers use invention to develop their subjects. It includes planning the piece of writing, thinking of ways of organizing material, of presenting material, and of deciding how to handle questions that you anticipate readers will raise.

Irony   A difference between appearance and reality creates irony. When it compliments, it is ironically condemning. When it condemns, it is ironically complimenting. The sentence "What a magnificent car," when used to describe a rusting hulk sitting in a junkyard, is ironic. The sentence "It's not a bad paint job," when used to describe Michelangelo's Sistine Chapel ceiling, is ironic. When the irony is not subtle but is intended to cause deliberate harm, it is called **sarcasm.** If someone says, "Thank you. It's just what I've always wanted," when reacting to the ketchup stain you accidentally put on her new blouse, she is using sarcasm.

When they are contrary to our anticipation, situations can also be ironic. You might discover that you were not hired for a job because you failed a company's mandatory typing test, only to learn that the job for which you applied required no typing at all.

Jargon   Jargon is technical vocabulary that is appropriate only among experts in a field. As a kind of shorthand, it saves time in their communication. Among themselves lawyers use such expressions as "caveat," "entrapment," "estoppel," "the M'Naghten Rule," and "mens rea," knowing that they all understand legal jargon. To a lay listener, however, the words mean little. For lay audiences, writers use jargon sparingly, and when they do use it, they include definitions.

Another kind of jargon, sometimes called bureaucratese, is nothing more than pompous **diction** used more to impress readers than to inform them. The sentence "Our consumer demand analysis precludes our implementation of the proposed planning stage"—which means, by the way, "We don't need to plan to produce something that no one wants to buy"—typifies the jargon of pomposity.

Litotes   *See* **Figures of speech.**

Logical fallacies   Mistakes in reasoning that lead to faulty conclusions are logical fallacies or fallacious reasoning.

An *ad hominem argument* attacks a person rather than the issue that is being considered.

The *association fallacy* suggests that an act or belief is worthy or unworthy merely because of the people who are associated with it.

A writer falls into *false analogy* by presuming that if two things are alike in one or more ways, then they must be alike in other ways as well.

The *either/or fallacy* is a type of oversimplification in which a writer assumes only two alternatives are possible when in fact many others should be considered.

A *non sequitur* is a conclusion that does not follow from the premise.

A writer making an *overgeneralization* draws a conclusion from insufficient or unrepresentative evidence.

With an *oversimplification,* we draw a conclusion while ignoring information essential to the subject.

Someone who accepts the *post hoc* argument assumes that if one event occurred before another, then the second event was caused by the first.

Metaphor   *See* **Figures of speech.**

Metonymy   *See* **Figures of speech.**

Narration   A narration tells a story and often includes extensive **description.** Narrations, usually chronological, include among their purposes entertaining, informing, and instructing. Some narrations have a plot, a story line that moves toward an insight about the principal character in the narration.

Narrative effect   The main **effect** from reading a **narration** is named the *narrative effect.* Each narration incorporates a reason for being. Writers decide the main effect that their narrative should have on their readers, and then form the narrative so as not to depart from their decision.

Non sequitur   *See* **Logical fallacies.**

Nonstandard English   Words and expressions that are often spoken but rarely written except when the writer has a clear reason for using them sometimes include nonstandard English. Some examples are *ain't, nohow, irregardless, theirselves, hisself, we'uns, could care less* (for "could not care less"), and *them* (instead of *those*), as in *Them people ain't got no smarts,* instead of "Those people do not seem intelligent."

Objective and subjective   Objective writing is designed to be a distanced, factual account presented in language that is plain, direct, and free of value judgments. Pure objectivity is hard to achieve because people's perceptions are almost always colored by their experiences, their values, and their biases. But in writing such as scientific papers and technical reports, authors strive for objectivity. Subjective writing is more personal, more indicative of the writer's thoughts, feelings, and attitudes. The emphasis here is on the writer's relationship to the topic rather than the topic itself. Very few essays are exclusively objective or subjective. Most often, writings combine the two.

Opening   An opening is the first part of a three-part narrative essay. The other two parts are the body and the climax. The beginning sentences usually capture the reader's attention without giving away the outcome. The opening may hint at the purpose of the story about to unfold, but may not actually reveal it.

Order of ideas   Ideas can be arranged in various ways, but all are derived from the subject and the writer's purpose. The order may be spatial, moving from top to bottom, side to side, or background to foreground. Or the order may simply be chronological, as in a narrative. The writer may work from least important to most important. The sequence of ideas should always be well thought out, chosen for its greatest effect.

Overgeneralization   *See* **Logical fallacies.**

Oversimplification   *See* **Logical fallacies.**

Paradox   *See* **Figures of speech.**

Paragraph   The paragraph is the basic unit in an essay. It is composed of a group of closely related sentences that together develop one of the essay's main ideas. The main or unifying idea of a paragraph is often stated in a topic sentence, often found at the beginning of the paragraph. All other sentences in the paragraph relate directly to the topic sentence, thus establishing unity and coherence. But occasionally a unified and coherent paragraph has no topic sentence. The paragraph then undoubtedly has a leading idea that is strongly implied in every sentence. Paragraphs also work visually in an essay, graphically demonstrating the progress of ideas and also providing visual relief to the reader.

Parallel structure   The repetition of similar grammatical elements within or between sentences makes a parallel structure. Logic dictates that grammatical elements with equal value in a sentence be constructed in the same grammatical form. Thus, "I prefer running, jumping, and to swim" does not exhibit parallelism, but does have awkwardness. "I prefer running, jumping, and swimming" demonstrates parallelism and logic. Parallel structure is also a stylistic technique often used to create emphasis and drama. The long fourth sentence in paragraph 14 of Martin Luther King's "Letter from Birmingham Jail" (Chapter 9) is a particularly effective example of parallel structure.

Paraphrase   A paraphrase is a restatement of another person's words in your own words. This technique is particularly necessary when writing any essay in which you use others' ideas or words as evidence supporting your own argument. Often, you paraphrase instead of using a direct quotation in order to more easily mold the idea to fit your argument. The sense of the original, as well as the tone and order of ideas, remains the same. In either a paraphrase or a direct quotation you must give credit to your source. In a more informal paper you incorporate the credit into your text: "According to Charles Neerland, being a Minneapolitan means being cold much of the year." In more formal writing, such as a research paper, footnoting is required.

Person   The grammatical distinction between the speaker (first person: I, we); the person spoken to (second person: you, singular and plural); and the subject spoken about (third person: he, she, it, or they) is labeled *person*.

Persona   A fictional speaker in an essay or the fictional narrator of a story is its persona. The character, attitudes, and ideas of the persona are often different from those of the author. In fact, it is often the persona's character, attitudes, and ideas that are held up for criticism. The persona of Swift's "A Modest Proposal" voices ideas that Swift obviously finds abhorrent.

Personification   *See* **Figures of speech**.

Persuasion or persuasive argument   Persuasive writing is an attempt to win readers to a point of view and, often, move them to action. It appeals primarily to the emotions, as opposed to *argument*, which is meant to win the reader by reason and logic. Most often, the two are used together.

Plagiarism   Presenting someone else's words or ideas as if they were your own is plagiarism. It is a serious offense in the academic world and can lead to consequences such as failure and expulsion from school. Whenever you use someone else's words or ideas you must give that person credit in your own text or by footnoting (see **paraphrase**).

Point-by-point and subject-by-subject development   These are the two basic methods for developing a comparison-and-contrast essay. Point-by-point development alternately presents each point being considered. Subject-by-subject development presents all the details about one side of the argument first and follows with all the details about the other side.

Point of view   In an argumentative essay the point of view is the author's opinion or the thesis the writer hopes to advance. In expository essays it is the physical or mental vantage point from which the author views the subject. An essay on professional football told from a player's first-hand experience would be approached differently from that of the team's owner (whose interest may be exclusively financial) or from that of a newspaper reporter. Each would approach the subject with a different kind of authority. And that authority would mean a difference in vocabulary, style, and tone. The player might use first **person** to capture immediacy. The owner might want to involve the reader in experiencing her financial woes and so use second person. Or, to create a mood of objectivity, the reporter might use the third person. The point of view in an essay must remain consistent. An inconsistent point of view can leave the reader confused and disconcerted.

Post hoc argument   *See* **Logical fallacies.**

Premise   A deductive **syllogism** is composed of two premises and a conclusion. The first or major premise is an assumption and the second or minor premise is a fact or another assumption based on evidence: All mammals are animals (first premise is an assumption). Raccoons are mammals (second premise is a fact). Therefore, all raccoons are animals (conclusion is logically deduced from the two premises).

Prewriting   All the activities a writer goes through before actually beginning to write are part of *prewriting*. These might consist of brainstorming for a subject, doing background reading, narrowing the subject, devising a thesis, planning the essay—everything, in other words, that leads to the actual writing.

Probable conclusions   Conclusions arrived at by inductive reasoning and from incomplete evidence are *probable conclusions*. The reader's acceptance of a conclusion that follows from inductive reasoning is often referred to as the *inductive leap*. To establish a clear connection between the evidence and the conclusion, the writer must be sure to present **relevant evidence, sufficient evidence,** and **representative evidence.**

Proposition or thesis   In argument, the proposition or thesis is a written assertion, the opinion the writer wants a reader to accept, or an action the writer wants a reader to take.

Psychological time   Arranging events in a narrative so as to show how they are connected in memory, shifting back and forth in time while keeping a sense of forward movement, creates *psychological time.*

Purpose   The goal the writer wants to achieve is the *purpose*. The clearer the writer's purpose, the more clarity, coherence, and unity the essay will have. If the writer's purpose is muddled, the essay too will be muddled. All kinds of purposes are possible:

to entertain with an amusing story; to inform; to convince readers of a point of view and move them to action. These purposes can be achieved by using the modes of prose: narration, description, exposition, and argument. In an essay you may use them alone or in combination.

Qualification   Tempering broad statements to make them more logically acceptable is the technique called *qualification*. In qualifying a statement the writer admits that exceptions to that assertion are possible or probable, thereby indicating that the statement is not oversimplified. In these days with much emphasis on physical fitness, the statement "Physical exercise is good" might, at first blush, seem valid. But exercise may, in fact, be detrimental to some people. Therefore the statement needs qualifying. "Exercise is good for most people" might be a more acceptable statement.

Reason and result   Another way of saying **cause and effect**.

Refutation   The attempt to counter an opposing argument by revealing its weaknesses is called *refutation*. You must refute the opposition's argument if it is obvious and is strong or logical enough to be a real alternative to your own. The refutation usually is done early in an argumentative essay to get it out of the way so that you can proceed with your own argument. The three most usual strategies are pointing out weaknesses in the opposition's evidence, questioning the argument's relevance, and pointing out errors in logic. Refutation indicates that the writer is aware the issue is complex and is willing to consider opposing opinions. To be effective, refutation must always be done in a moderate tone and must always be accurate in representing the opposing argument. To do otherwise is to risk being judged harshly by the reader for sounding intemperate and for treating the opposition unfairly.

Relevant evidence   You can directly support the essay's thesis and contribute directly to its conclusion with relevant evidence (see **representative evidence** and **sufficient evidence**).

Representative evidence   Representative evidence covers the full range of information related to an essay's thesis, not just one side or the other. An argument cannot be convincing unless evidence from every point of view is admitted (see **relevant evidence** and **sufficient evidence**).

Representative sample   A representative sample is a typical example chosen from among examples that exhibit similar characteristics.

Rhetoric   Rhetoric is the study and art of using prose effectively. The various methods of prose discourse described and exemplified in this textbook—narration, description, exposition, and argument—are rhetorical forms.

Rhetorical question   A rhetorical question is posed for effect and no answer is expected. It is a question meant to provoke thought or to launch the writer into the subject to be discussed in the writing.

Satire   The form of writing using wit, irony, and ridicule to attack foolish and vicious human behavior and the institutions and customs that promote such behavior is *satire*. Two main types of satire are at the writer's disposal: social satire, which is used to attack foolish, but not dangerous, behavior and does it by invoking laughter and sympathy; ethical satire, which is far sharper and points with anger and indignation at social corruption and evil (see Jonathan Swift's "A Modest Proposal" in Chapter 9).

Sentimentality   Sentimental writing overemotionalizes its subject and thus becomes ineffective. Sentimentality is often emotion displayed for the sake of emotion, losing connection with the actuality of the thing that supposedly caused the emotion. Sentimental writers risk readers' ridicule because they don't fully acquaint the reader with the actuality and thus appear to overreact.

Simile   *See* **Figures of speech.**

Slang   Colorful and humorous expressions, mostly short-lived and often peculiar to a group of people, are called *slang*. Almost always informal, slang is unacceptable in formal writing except in quotations and for creating special effects.

Specific examples   *See* **Examples.**

Standard English   The English language in its most widely accepted form, written and spoken by educated people in both formal and informal contexts, and having universal currency though it incorporates regional differences, is *standard English*.

Strategy   The means by which writers effectively accomplish their purpose in a piece of writing form their *strategy*. This planning includes evaluating the audience, narrowing the subject, choosing a dominant rhetorical pattern such as narration, description, examples, comparison and contrast, and definition, among others.

Style   The distinctive way in which a writer writes creates an individual *style*. Choice of words, structure of sentences, use or nonuse of figurative language—all contribute to a writer's style. Two writers may write about the same subject, have the same attitude toward the subject (see **tone**), and yet "sound" distinctly different. Style is a writer's writing personality and can be developed with practice.

Subject-by-subject development   *See* **Point-by-point development**.

Sufficient evidence   In an argumentative paper you must supply ample evidence to convincingly support your conclusion (see **relevant evidence** and **representative evidence**).

Summary   A summary is a comprehensive and usually brief recapitulation of previously stated facts or statements. Summarizing your main points is one way of concluding a paper.

Suspense   The pleasurable uncertainty or excitement we feel when anticipating what will happen next as we read a story is *suspense*. This tactic is most evident in mystery or detective stories but is less dramatically present in much narration.

Syllogism   A form of deductive reasoning composed of two premises and a conclusion is the *syllogism*. The first premise (major premise) is an assumption and the second (minor premise) is a fact or another assumption based on **evidence**. The conclusion is logically deduced from the two premises: All human beings are animals (major premise is an assumption). Ephraim is a human (minor premise is a fact). Therefore, Ephraim is an animal (conclusion is logically deduced from the two premises).

Symbol   A symbol is any concrete thing that means something beyond itself. Many symbols are, on the surface, clear-cut and readily acceptable. The flag, of course, represents country and elicits patriotic feeling. But ideas and attitudes differ about what constitutes patriotism and what things conjure patriotic feelings. Some people become proud when their country asserts itself militarily. Others find their patriotic values in freedom, tolerance, fairness, and compassion. The flag, a rather simple symbol as symbols go, therefore has a complex of powerful meanings beyond itself. Symbols are employed most in fiction and poetry, less in exposition and argument. But they can be used in the latter to express meaning concisely and palpably.

Synecdoche   *See* **Figures of speech.**

Thesis   The thesis is the main point in any piece of prose writing, an idea that all the other ideas and facts in an essay should point to and support. A thesis can be either clearly stated or implied. It is most commonly found at the end of an early paragraph. A thesis cannot be a statement of fact, because facts do not need proving. A thesis, therefore, must have an argumentative edge, a point of view that will be proven or demonstrated in some way somewhere in the paper.

Tone   Diction, sentence variety, figurative language, and anything else that establishes the writer's attitude toward the subject forms the tone, which can vary extensively. The writing's tone can be amused, angry, exasperated, approving, surprised, sarcastic. It can, in other words, run the gamut of human emotions. But tone should be consistent, for it must inform the entire essay and lead the reader to the response the writer desires.

Topic sentence   A topic sentence states the main idea of a paragraph. All other sentences in the paragraph support the topic sentence. Most often it appears at the beginning but can be placed anywhere in the paragraph.

Transitions   Transitions are words, phrases, sentences, and paragraphs that link ideas. Because a reader cannot get into the writer's head, it is the writer's responsibility to make sure that the ideas are clearly stated and that relationships between the ideas are clear. The first way to ensure that clarity is to organize ideas so that they flow logically from one to another. But even sturdier bridges are needed to carry the reader from sentence to sentence and from paragraph to paragraph. For this continuity you will need to use transitional devices such as these:

1. In the first sentence of a paragraph repeat some words or phrases from the last sentences in the preceding paragraph.
2. Use pronouns to refer to nouns in the preceding paragraph. You must be careful here to make precisely clear which words the pronouns refer to.
3. Use transitional expressions to carry the reader.

   Addition: also, in addition, too, moreover, and besides, further, furthermore, equally important, next, then, finally.

   Example: for example, for instance, thus, as an illustration, namely, specifically.

   Contrast: but, yet, however, on the other hand, nevertheless, conversely, in contrast, on the contrary, still, at the same time.

   Comparison: similarly, likewise, in like manner, in the same way, in comparison.

   Concession: of course, to be sure, certainly, naturally, granted.

   Result: therefore, thus, consequently, so, accordingly.

   Summary: as a result, hence, in short, in brief, in summary, in conclusion, finally, on the whole.

   Time sequence: first, second, third, fourth, next, then, finally, afterward, before, soon, later, during, meanwhile, subsequently, immediately, at length, eventually, in the future, currently.

   Place: at the front, in the foreground, at the back, in the background, at the side, adjacent, nearby, in the distance, here, there.

Two-part classification   Often called *binary,* two-part classification is the simplest way of breaking a subject down. This pattern divides the subject in two, usually into positive and negative categories, such as vegetarians, nonvegetarians; smokers, nonsmokers; television viewers, nonviewers of television, and so on. But two-part classification is usually inexact and skirts the edge of comparison and contrast. Most classification systems, therefore, have at least three categories.

Typical examples   *See* **Examples.**

Understatement (Litotes)   *See* **Figures of speech.**

Unity   In a paragraph, every idea and every sentence relates directly to and helps support the main idea, usually stated in the topic sentence. Likewise, in the essay as a whole, every unified paragraph points to and supports the essay's main idea expressed in the thesis.

Warrant   Warrant is the supporting argument in Toulmin's model of reasoning (see **Claim**).

Writing process   The various tasks a writer must perform to produce a piece of writing are called the writing process. **Prewriting** entails a series of activities that pave the way for the actual writing. Only after this stage can the writer make the first draft, revise it into a number of subsequent drafts, and then polish it to achieve the final product.

A Guide to Editing and Revising Sentences

This guide will help you revise your sentences to make them more readable and interesting. Unfortunately, no one has invented a clear procedure to follow when editing and revising prose. Some writers revise as they carefully work their way through a first draft; others swoop through the first draft and then revise during a second or third draft. Each writer, it seems, devises his or her own approach.

Two preliminary steps in revision do seem to be adopted by all writers. First, they must learn what makes writing effective. We offer this guide as a source of suggestions you can use to gain that knowledge. Second, they must pick up a pencil and go to work on their sentences. We must now stand aside and wish you the best of luck.

Eliminate pretentious language.

Pretentious writing draws attention to itself. The vocabulary is unnecessarily complex, perhaps because the writer has thumbed through a thesaurus replacing simple words with difficult words. Always try to select simple words over fancy ones. If you want to indicate that dogs make good pets, do not write, "Domesticated canines will contribute felicity to anyone's life."

The earthquake ~~struck with a malignant force that~~ *killed* ~~destroyed the lives of~~ more than than four thousand villagers.

Children ~~frolicking~~ *playing* with ~~their companions exhibit~~ *friends demonstrate* these fears.

683

Eliminate obsolete, archaic, and recently invented words.

Over the years some words and their meanings change or fall from common use. A good dictionary labels these words and meanings "obsolete" or "archaic." Obsolete words or meanings should not be used at all. "Yestereen," meaning last evening, is obsolete. Archaic words still occur in special contexts, especially in literary or religious works. "Thou" and "thee," "brethren," and "kine" appear in the King James version of the Bible and are identified as "archaic" in dictionaries. Unless you have a special reason for using archaic words, they too should be eliminated from your writing.

Recently invented words, or *neologisms,* are so new to the language that they may be unacceptable in college writing. Often neologisms, such as "teleplay," "floppy disk," and "aerobics" become part of our common vocabulary because they are the clearest way of referring to the things they stand for. But neologisms may quickly fall from use, as "usership," "time frame," and "palimony" may do any day. If a neologism is in common usage, then feel free to use it, but if it was created very recently, then use another word or phrase or risk confusing your reader.

Eliminate sexist language.

Rid your sentences of sexual bias. Traditionally, the masculine pronouns "he," "him," and "his" have been used to refer to members of either sex when gender is indefinite. Today, such usage leads to gender stereotyping, and we have a number of simple ways of eliminating sexist language in writing. One option is to change "his" to "his or her."

Faulty: Every attorney must prepare *his* closing remarks with care.

Revised: Every attorney must prepare *his or her* closing remarks with care.

This solution may generate wordiness and become awkward if applied throughout a longer passage. An alternative solution is to revise the sentence with the plural "attorneys," which would call for the plural pronoun "their" and eliminate the suggestion of gender.

> *Revised:* Attorneys must prepare their closing remarks with care.

"Man" and "men" are used to refer to both men and women. With some thought you can change this practice in your writing. "Policeman" can be changed to "police officer"; "mailman" to "mail carrier"; "congressman" to "member of Congress"; "mankind" to "humanity," "people," or "human beings."

Eliminate slang and regional expressions.

Slang can be the colorful vocabulary that arises from the experience of a group of people with common interests, such as teenagers, rock stars, jazz musicians, actors, baseball fans, street gangs, and truck drivers. Unfettered by dictionary definitions, slang changes rapidly, reflecting each group's perceptions. Most slang expressions, such as "awesome," "bummer," "downer," "sleezoid," "rad," "bro," and "stoked" appear, increase in use, and then either become trite or shift in meaning. When slang words such as "jazz" and "A-bomb" become part of the general vocabulary, you may use them freely. Generally in college writing, however, revise your sentences to eliminate slang because it is imprecise and may be confusing.

As a type, comedians are ~~trippy, bummed~~ *unpredictable, depressed* out one moment and ~~flying~~ *elated* the next.

The reviewers ~~ragged on~~ *criticized* Kaufmann's poetry collection for

being sentimental.

Regional expressions are associated with a geographical area. A "soda pop" in one part of the country is a "tonic" in another.

A "skillet" in one region is a "frying pan" in another. Generally, you should eliminate regional expressions from your college writing for the same reason as you should avoid slang: you may confuse the reader.

The vice squad had been ~~fixing~~ *preparing* to arrest Hawkins for months.

Use technical language, or jargon, with care.

When writing for a group of computer specialists, you may use such terminology as "hard disk," "modem," "user area," and "megabyte" with confidence that your readers will understand; these are technical terms, or jargon, which computer specialists use freely.

Most occupations and special activities have technical vocabularies. A person in advertising uses "story board," "outsert," "keyline," and "live tag" with ease. A ballet dancer feels equally at ease with "adagio," "barre," "sickle foot," and "pointe." Such language, however, is inappropriate for most readers.

Technical language is especially insidious when taken from its proper field and used in a broader context. Technical vocabulary from psychiatry is inappropriate when used to describe the behavior of any animals other than human beings.

The whale seemed ~~traumatized~~ *stunned* as it floundered in the

shallow surf, struggling to beach itself and ~~fulfill~~ *die*.

~~its unconscious death wish.~~

Consider the denotation and connotation of words.

Denotation is a word's literal definition, found in a dictionary. *Connotation* describes the emotional colorings that surround the word and influence how a reader might respond to it.

According to one dictionary, the word "apple" denotes "a round, firm, fleshy, edible fruit with a green, yellow, or red skin and small seeds." For some of us the word "apple" also connotes health ("an apple a day keeps the doctor away") and knowledge (the apple is often referred to as the forbidden fruit in the Garden of Eden, and the apple is the gift left on the teacher's desk). No wonder the name "Apple" seemed appropriate for the country's first popular personal computer (the logo even features an apple with a bite taken from it, "a little bite (byte) of knowledge is healthy for you"). It became "the apple of the consumer's eye"!

As a writer you must consider both the denotation and connotation of the words you use. If you do not, you may create a meaning you did not intend, as the writer of the next sentence does in attempting to describe how the company president moved through a crowded room to sit down and start a meeting.

> *Faulty:*   Robert Rice, the company president, maneuvered himself to the chair at the head of the table.

Inadvertently, the writer creates a feeling that Robert Rice manipulated his way into the presidency of the company.

> *Revised:*   Robert Rice, the company president, sat in the chair at the head of the table.

When selecting one of several words that have nearly the same meaning, you must take special care. Consider the words "emulate," "copy," and "mimic." Their denotations are similar, but they differ in connotation.

Beginning writer Jane West ~~mimics~~ *emulates* romance novelist

Rosemary Rogers's style.

The connotation of "mimic" is too negative for the sense this writer wants to convey, which is that West strives to achieve quality equaling that of Rogers.

Select concrete and specific words rather than abstract and general ones.

Abstract words name qualities, ideas, and concepts we experience in our feelings and our thoughts: "freedom," "love," "hate," "hope," "democracy," "honesty," and so on. Concrete words label things we experience through our senses: "smack," "kiss," "laugh," "smoke," "dance," "shout," and so on.

General words cover relatively large groups of things: "food," "places," "people." Specific words name specific things, a more limited segment of a large group: "pizza," "Boston," "Tom Cruise." "General" and "specific" are relative words. Language becomes more specific as it moves from the general group to a unique example of the group, as from "athlete" to "professional athlete," to "baseball player," to "Babe Ruth."

General	Specific	More specific
weapon	pistol	.45 automatic
fish	shark	hammerhead
food	pasta	linguini
music	popular music	rock and roll
Native Americans	Plains Indians	Sioux

College writers are inclined to overuse abstract and general words. Their sentences, therefore, can be vague, leaving their writing drab and lifeless. As you revise your sentences, replace vague wording with more concrete and specific wording wherever you can.

The subway ~~was frightening.~~ *smelled of fear.*

A crowd ~~waited~~ *restlessly milled* in the square.

The night ~~was dark.~~ *turned black as clouds swept in from the north.*

Envy ~~brings out the worst in people.~~ *makes people scheme, manipulate, and steal.*

You should also replace *euphemisms* with specific language. A euphemism is a word or phrase substituted for another word that is harsh or blunt. The funeral industry substitutes "loved one" or "the deceased" for "corpse," "vault" for "coffin," and "final resting place" for "grave site."

Euphemisms often may be necessary for tactfulness. No doubt most of us prefer to ask a stranger to guide us to the restroom rather than the toilet. Euphemisms may, however, distract us from the realities in experiences such as poverty, unemployment, and war. We have become accustomed to the euphemism of "low income," "inner city," and "correctional facility" as substitutes for "poor," "slum" or "ghetto," and "jail." Euphemisms are pervasive in the language of "polite society" and so you must guard against their slipping into your finished papers. If you find euphemistic phrasing when revising your sentences, consider rewriting the phrase in more specific language.

> decline
> The ~~deterioration of his economic status~~ began when he
> *lost his job, car, and house*.
> ~~became unemployed.~~
>
>   lying
> Military officials seem to believe that ~~misrepresenting the~~
>
> ~~facts~~ is acceptable ~~behavior.~~

Use figurative language with care.

Figurative language draws a comparison between two things that are essentially different but alike in some underlying and surprising way. The two commonest figures of speech are simile and metaphor.

A *simile* expresses a comparison directly by connecting two ideas with "like" or "as."

His face was like the sky, one minute overcast, the next minute bright.

—*Joseph Conrad*

The bowie knife is as American as the half-ton pickup truck.

—*Geoffrey Norman*

A *metaphor* expresses a comparison indirectly, with neither "like" nor "as."

Roads became black velvet ribbons with winking frost sequins.

—*Hal Borland*

A sleeping child gives me the impression of a traveler in a very far country.

—*Ralph Waldo Emerson*

To be effective, a simile or metaphor must create a verbal image or clarify a writer's thought by making it understandable in other words. When a simile or metaphor is trite or overblown, it must be revised.

When he leaned toward the audience and smiled, his gold tooth ~~shined like a bright star.~~ *reflected the light*.

Mixed metaphors create confusion by combining two or more incompatible comparisons.

Thought is restless, soaring and diving before ~~coiling~~ *circling* ~~around~~ an idea.

"Soaring" and "diving" suggest a bird in flight. "Coiling" suggests a snake, leaving the metaphor mixed and in need of repair.

Eliminate trite expressions.

Trite expressions are phrases that have become stale by overuse. They include clichés ("He ran around the neighborhood *like a chicken without a head*"), wedded adjectives and nouns ("They made a *lifelong commitment*"), and overused phrases ("We all know that *the rich get richer and the poor get poorer*"). Many trite phrases appear in early drafts of college papers, especially if the writing has been rushed. When revising, strike out trite expressions and reword them in a more direct way.

He was guilty~~beyond a shadow of doubt~~. *undeniably*

The business was ~~sinking in a sea of red ink~~ *almost bankrupt*.

~~To make a long story short,~~ The widow married the banker.

To make you more aware of trite phrases, here are some of the most exhausted ones.

a crying shame	in the final analysis
a thinking person	in the nick of time
after all is said and done	last but not least
at this point in time	method in his madness
depths of despair	never a dull moment
drop in the bucket	none the worse for wear
face the music	pay the piper
flat as a pancake	quick as a flash
in this day and age	sadder but wiser

Eliminate wordiness.

Empty phrases make your writing unnecessarily wordy. Often one word will do the work of an entire empty phrase.

Barthes ~~is of the opinion~~ *believes* that culture can be understood

by reading the "signs" it generates.

~~It is usually the case that~~ *D* diet books *usually* encourage the dieter's

fantasies about being slim.

Study this list to become familiar with common empty phrases and substitutes for them.

Empty phrase	*Substitute*
at all times	always
at this point in time	now
at any point in time	then
by means of	by
due to the fact that	because
for the purpose of	for
give consideration to	consider
give encouragement to	encourage
in order to	to
in the event that	if
in the final analysis	finally
make contact with	call
of the opinion that	that
regardless of the fact that	although
the fact that	that
until such time as	until or when

Repetition of key words is often necessary for parallel structure or for emphasis, but needless repetition leads to boring, wordy sentences.

The Pacific ~~rattlesnake~~ *rattler* is California's most dangerous

snake.

I ~~continue to~~ *still* believe that government will not survive

unless the Attorney General acts.

Redundancy is similar to needless repetition in that it conveys the same meaning twice, as in the phrases "visible to the eye" and "large in size." Like needless repetitions, redundancies make your sentences wordy and should be eliminated during revision. At times, an entire sentence or passage may need to be rewritten.

If researchers probe the fact~~ual truth deeply~~s, they

will find the solution.

Millions of ~~people who~~ vote support national health

insurance.

Though suffering from malaria, he continued ~~on~~ his journey

to the Mayan temple.

These are some common redundancies.

advance forward
autobiography of her life
basic fundamentals
circle around
close proximity
combine together
consensus of opinion

continue to go on
disappear from sight
factual truth
important essential
refer back
repeat again
round in shape

Eliminate unnecessary expletive constructions.

The word "there" followed by a form of the plain verb "to be" is an *expletive,* a word used to fill out a sentence. An expletive signals that the subject of the sentence will follow the verb. This construction is unnecessarily wordy and lacks the vigor of subject-verb constructions.

~~There are~~ <u>T</u>wo horses trott~~ing~~ *ed* in the meadow.

~~There is no hope for~~ <u>T</u>he rain forests, *face destruction*.

The pronoun "it" often functions as an expletive in similar constructions.

~~It is difficult to~~ *A*nalyz~~e~~ *ing* poetry, *is difficult*.

At times, however, "it" often is needed as an expletive, as in "It is raining."

Revise passive sentences.

Voice is the quality in verbs that shows whether a subject is the actor or is acted upon. "The arroyos were flooded by rain" is a passive sentence because the subject, "arroyos," is acted upon. In contrast, "Rain flooded the arroyos" is an active sentence because the subject, "rain," is the actor. Active constructions are more concise, direct, and forceful than passive constructions.

The tornado left death
~~Death~~ and despair ~~was left by the tornado.~~

~~The western world's attention was captured by~~ Nelson

Mandela's speeches, *captured the western world's attention*.

Scientists consider astrology
~~Astrology is considered by scientists~~ to be a mere

superstition.

Although generally in revising you should eliminate unnecessary passive constructions, at times the passive may be necessary. Passive constructions are appropriate when the subject is ambiguous or when you wish to emphasize the receiver of an action.

The mysterious rumor was received from New York.

In this example, the writer does not know who started the rumor.

His self-esteem was damaged by years of severe criticism.

In this example, the writer wishes to emphasize the thing that received the action, "self-esteem."

Revise for proper coordination.

Clauses that have equal importance in a sentence are *coordinate* and should be connected by a coordinating word or punctuation mark. To show the relationship between equal clauses you need to select the proper coordinator.

Coordinating conjunctions

and   but   for   nor   or   so   yet

Correlative conjunctions

both . . . and   either . . . or   neither . . . nor
not only . . . but also   whether . . . or

Conjunctive adverbs

consequently	furthermore	however	meanwhile
moreover	nevertheless	therefore	thus

Different coordinators show different relations. The common kinds of relations are addition, contrast, choice, and result.

Addition: Reviewers criticized his paintings, *and* collectors stopped buying them.

Contrast: Once novels were the primary home entertainment, *but* today television predominates.

Choice: *Either* we human beings will stop polluting the earth, *or* we will perish amid our waste.

Result: Advertising campaigns sell products; *therefore,* manufacturers are willing to pay for them.

Writers sometimes use semicolons to give equal emphasis to main clauses when the main clauses they connect are closely related in meaning and structure.

In Irish folklore, spirits sometimes appear as men or women; at other times they appear as birds and beasts.

When revising a paper, correct faulty coordination that gives equal emphasis to unequal or unrelated clauses.

Faulty: John Fowles is the author of three bestsellers, and he lives in England.

The clause "he lives in England" has little connection to the clause "John Fowles is the author of three bestsellers." These two clauses therefore should not be coordinated. Still, the writer might want to include the information, even though it does not relate directly to the main idea.

Revised: John Fowles, who lives in England, is the author of three bestsellers.

Revised: John Fowles, an English writer, is the author of three bestsellers.

You should also revise to eliminate excessive coordination; that is, stringing main clauses together for no apparent purpose. This practice can become monotonous for the reader and fails to show the proper relation between clauses. A sentence with excessive coordination must be untangled and rewritten.

Excessive: Americans desire heroes, and they find them in films, sports, and politics, but sometimes the real-life behavior of hero figures is disappointing, and then they must find new ones.

Revised: Americans desire heroes, whom they find in films, sports, and politics, but sometimes the real-life behavior of hero figures is disappointing, which means they must find new ones.

Revised: Americans desire heroes, whom they find in films, sports, and politics. Sometimes the behavior of real-life hero figures is disappointing, which means they must find new ones.

Revise for proper subordination.

Clauses deserving less emphasis in a sentence are dependent and should be introduced by a subordinating word. To establish the correct relation between a main clause and a dependent clause, you must use the proper subordinating word.

Common subordinating conjunctions

after	although	as	as if
as soon as	because	before	if
in order that	since	so that	though
unless	until	unless	when
whenever	where	wherever	while

Relative pronouns

that	what	whatever	which	whichever
who	whoever	whom	whomever	whose

Choosing which clause to subordinate depends, of course, on your intention, but writers commonly subordinate a clause to show concession, identification, time, cause, condition, and purpose.

Concession ("as if," "though," "although")

> *Although the evidence clearly called for a guilty verdict,* the jury found him innocent.

Identification ("that," "when," "who")

> Medical researchers, *who came from around the world,* gathered in San Francisco for the convention.

Time ("before," "while," "as soon as")

> The attacks continued *as soon as the troops withdrew.*

Cause ("because")

> *Because historians know how events turned out,* they study the causes of those events.

Condition ("if," "unless," "provided")

> *If bombastic masculinity hides fear of inferiority,* many police officers lack feelings of self-worth.

Purpose ("so that," "in order that")

> Following a catastrophe, people must accept reality *so that healing can begin.*

When revising your sentences, check to see if you have faulty or excessive subordination. If so, rewrite the sentences.

Professor Clark, ~~who is~~ noted for her work in *reproductive cell* ~~the~~ chemistry ~~of cells when they reproduce has~~ received the *prestigious* Louis Pasteur Award, ~~which is highly prestigious.~~

Place modifiers with care.

A writer can confuse a reader by misplacing a modifier in a sentence. When revising your sentences, be sure to place modifiers so that a reader will be certain which words they modify.

Revise sentences with a *dangling modifier,* a phrase or clause not clearly attached to any word in the sentence. To correct a dangling modifier, see that it clearly relates to the intended word.

~~Running~~ *As he ran* through the meadow, his breathing made steamy clouds.

To complete a screen play, *a writer must keep* a daily schedule ~~must be kept.~~

After six months in therapy, ~~the~~ *he spent* psychiatrist pronounced *his* him cured.

When a student at Reed, *I was* Ken Kesey was the student body's favorite writer.

For clarity, revise sentences to place modifiers as close as possible to the words they modify.

Many beginning actors wait on tables *in Hollywood restaurants* to support themselves ~~in Hollywood restaurants.~~

An aging athlete who exercises (occasionally) hurts himself.

Be particularly aware of where you place limiting modifiers, such as "only," "hardly," "just," "nearly," "almost," and "ever." They can function in many positions in a sentence, but they modify the expression immediately following them. As these limiting modifiers change position in a sentence, the meaning of the sentence also changes.

I will go *only* if he asks me. [Otherwise I will stay.]
Only I will go if he asks me. [The others will stay.]
I will go if *only* he asks me. [Please ask!]
I will go if he asks *only* me. [If he asks others, I will stay.]

Revise sentences with lengthy modifiers placed between important sentence elements.

~~Inner-city crime,~~ ß̶ecause of the increase in drug
inner-city crime
use and reduced law-enforcement budgets, is rising.

~~The winning candidate appeared,~~ t̶o the surprise
the winning candidate appeared
of his supporters, unprepared.

~~The rescue team has been,~~ ẃith the help of local
the rescue team has been
scouts, searching for the lost teenagers all night.

Revise sentences with modifiers that split infinitives awkwardly. An infinitive consists of "to" plus the simple form of a verb: "to dance," "to moan," "to study," and so on. Usually, a split infinitive can be revised effectively by placing the modifier more accurately.

When oil was discovered, even conservative bankers began

to (frantically) invest in land.

Sometimes a sentence with a split infinitive cannot be revised without creating a misreading. Rewrite the sentence.

Faulty:	His inability to *clearly* explain the issues cost him the election.
Faulty revision:	His inability to explain the issues *clearly* cost him the election.
Rewritten:	His inability to explain the issues *in clear language* cost him the election.

Eliminate faulty pronoun reference.

Pronoun reference is the relation between a pronoun and its *antecedent*—that is, the word to which it refers. If a pronoun's reference is unclear, the sentence will confuse or misinform a reader. Revise sentences so that a pronoun refers clearly to one antecedent.

After Duff had studied Shakespeare for a decade,
he realized that ~~he~~ *Shakespeare* was a master psychologist.

Revise sentences that use "this," "that," or "it" to make a broad reference to an entire sentence.

While *I* watch~~ing~~*ed* Friday *the 13th* on television, my cat howled and sprang onto my lap, ~~This~~ *which* frightened me.

Revise sentences that use "it," "they," and "you" without specific antecedents. In conversation these pronouns are often used to make vague reference to people and situations in general. In writing, this practice should be avoided.

During the "Six O'Clock News," ~~it~~ *one reporter* gave a

special report on intelligence testing.

~~They do~~ *School policy does* not allow soliciting on campus.

In law enforcement, ~~you~~ *a police officer* must stay alert to a

community's changing values.

Using "you" to refer to "you the reader" is perfectly appropriate in all but the most formal writing.

If *you* major in accounting, then *you* should find a job easily.

Revise sentences with pronouns ending in "-self" and "-selves" in place of other personal pronouns.

The philosophy professor tried to convince Robin and ~~myself~~ *me* that Albert Camus was fundamentally an optimist.

Pronouns ending in "-self" and "-selves" should refer to words within the sentence.

To stay calm, *I* talked to *myself*.

Nick Ufre is such a sly character, *he* tricked *himself*.

Eliminate inconsistencies in sentences.

Revise your sentences for faulty shifts that indicate your thinking is not clear. Often a faulty shift in consistency takes place in pronoun reference.

If students properly prepare for their tests, ~~you~~ *they* will

not fear failing.

If you stretch your muscles before a workout, ~~a runner~~ *you*

will not face injury.

Faulty shifts also afflict verb tenses, which can confuse time sequences.

The dancer rehearsed for six months, but finally master*ed*

the movement and was ready to perform.

Sometimes shifts in the *mood* of a verb confuse a writer's intent.

Study the causes of World War I, and then ~~you should~~ study

World War II.

A common inconsistency befalls a writer who shifts from active to passive voice, thus dropping from the sentence someone or something performing the action.

In the game of curling a player slides a heavy stone

over the ice toward a target, and *a teammate sweeps* the ice in front of

the stone ~~is swept~~ to influence its path.

You should also revise sentences with shifts between direct and indirect discourse. *Direct discourse* includes a direct quotation: "Dr. Jones said, 'Life, my friends, is boring.' " *Indirect discourse* rephrases a direct quotation and therefore does not require quotation marks: "Dr. Jones had indicated that life is boring."

Faulty shift:	The judge said to pay the fine and "Never return to my court again."
Revised:	The judge said to pay the fine and never return to his court again.
Revised:	The judge said, "Pay the fine and never return to my court again."

Finally, revise sentences with *faulty predication,* which occurs when the information that follows a linking verb does not rename or describe the subject of the verb. In the sentence, "Dr. Brown is a full professor," both "Dr. Brown" and "full professor" refer to the same person. And in the sentence, "Dr. Brown is short," "short" clearly describes "Dr. Brown." In both sentences the predication is logically consistent; that is, the information following the linking verb "is" clearly renames or describes the subject. When the sentence's predication is faulty, however, you must revise it.

> *Faulty:*   The issue of gun control is an easy solution to a complicated problem.

The predication is faulty because the subject "issue" is not a "solution," as the sentence indicates. The "issue," however, is "complicated."

> *Revised:*   The issue of gun control is complicated.
> *Revised:*   Gun control is an easy solution to a complicated problem.

Sometimes predication is faulty because "when" is misused; the word should be used to indicate time.

> *Faulty:*   Nepotism is when officials appoint their relatives to desirable positions.
> *Revised:*   Nepotism is the appointing of relatives to desirable positions.
> *Revised:*   Nepotism takes over when relatives are appointed to desirable positions.

Complete your sentences.

Some sentences are incomplete because they lack words a reader needs to understand them. Often comparisons are not complete. Revise your comparisons to make them clear and logical.

Dr. Casey treats students better/ *than other professors.*

Mystery novels are easier to read than romance novels/ *are*.

The silence of the streets was more frightening
a wail from
than a siren.

In some sentence constructions writers omit words that are understood, and this practice is correct.

> *Correct:* Two people control the city government: one is the
> mayor; the other, the mayor's wife.

But if omitted words do not fit consistently into the structure, the omission is faulty and the sentence must be revised.

In the woods I feel the peace of nature; now/ the *I feel*

violence of the city.

in
Humans have a strong belief and desire for love.

Maintain parallelism.

When you revise a paper, maintain *parallel structure* by keeping similar ideas in the same grammatical form. In a pair or a series, you must make items parallel to avoid awkward shifts in construction. A noun must be matched with a noun, a verb with a verb, a phrase with a phrase, and a clause with a clause. Revise your sentences to make coordinate ideas parallel.

Anne Sexton's
She loved reading Anne Tyler's novels and ~~the~~ poetry ~~of~~

~~Anne Sexton.~~

dancing
His summer activities were ~~the dances~~ at Hotspur's

and sleeping until noon.

Words such as "by," "in," "to," "a," "the," and "that" should usually be repeated when they apply to both elements in a parallel construction.

By not developing their land and ~~by~~ ignoring tax-reporting

requirements, the family found itself bankrupt.

Revise your sentences to make compared and contrasted ideas parallel.

Ms. Lauko would prefer ~~to~~ work*ing* on her physics project rather

than playing chess.

Zen masters are materially poor, but they are rich *spiritually* ~~in spirit.~~

Revise correlative constructions to make them parallel. The ideas joined by correlative conjunctions, such as "either . . . or," "rather . . . than," and "not only . . . but also," should be parallel.

The law applies not only to people but also *to* corporations.

Cosmo is either dreaming about the future or ~~in a deep~~

examin*ing* ~~ation of~~ the past.

Provide variety in your sentences.

One way to create varied sentences is to revise sentence beginnings. Most inexperienced writers start their sentences with a subject. Unyielding repetition of this pattern can become monotonous, but if you frequently vary your sentence beginnings, you can offset the monotony.

Begin with an adverb.

*t*The answer came (*Unexpectedly*) in a dream.

a A low moan (*suddenly*) echoed through the empty mansion.

Begin with a prepositional phrase or verbal phrase.

v~~V~~ictory ~~for~~ ^F^ most politicians, justifies any behavior.

a~~A~~ banker ~~who wants~~ ^T^o be successful, must speak Japanese
and "computerese."

Allen Bates ~~rubbed~~ *Rubbing* his hands together, ~~and~~ studied the
photograph.

Begin with descriptive phrases.

Hanging in the air like a heavy mist,
v~~V~~iolence, ~~which~~ was the only solution left, ~~hung in the~~
~~air like a heavy mist.~~

His hand trembling, he
~~He~~ picked up the pencil ~~and felt his hand tremble.~~

~~The~~ basics necessary for a secure childhood, ~~include~~ ^F^ood,
shelter, and love, *these are the*.

You can also vary sentences by mixing their structures. In an
early draft you might rely too heavily on one kind of structure.
When you revise your paper, include varied structures.

Simple sentences have only one main clause and no dependent clauses, although they may have several modifiers and modifying phrases.

A crucial function in writing advertisements is manipulating
clichés. They help involve consumers.

Compound sentences have two or more main clauses but no
dependent clauses.

Puns are said to be the lowest form of humor, but ad writers breathe new life into them.

Consumers must analyze an ad writer's techniques, and ad writers must create new ones.

Complex sentences have one main clause and at least one dependent clause.

When ad writers sit at their word processors, they must rely on their understanding of the popular imagination.

Ad writers who work at major advertising firms are dramatically influencing public perceptions.

Compound-complex sentences have at least two main clauses and at least one dependent clause.

If you are curious about commercial influences in society, examining advertisements critically will reveal the desires ad writers stimulate, but be careful because the examination may stimulate your desire for a new car, a trip to exotic islands, or merely time with "people who like beer."

You should also consider revising your sentences to vary their form. You might include an inverted sentence now and then, but not often. Inverted sentences reverse typical subject-verb structures by moving the verb ahead of the subject.

~~The vault is at~~ *At* the bottom of a winding staircase

that leads into the cellar, *is the vault*.

Occasionally use a question to create sentence variety.

~~The~~ *What does the* word "persona" mean*s* *?* ~~"mask."~~ *means "mask" and* It refers to a

theatrical mask that Greek actors wore on stage.

(Acknowledgments continued from page iv. Constitutes an extension of the copyright page.)

"Finishing School" from *I Know Why the Caged Bird Sings* by Maya Angelou. Copyright © 1969 by Maya Angelou. Reprinted by permission of Random House, Inc.

"A Hanging" from *Shooting an Elephant and Other Essays* by George Orwell, copyright 1950 by Sonia Brownell Orwell and renewed 1978 by Sonia Pitt-Rivers, reprinted by permission of Harcourt Brace Jovanovich, Inc.

"Trapped in Another Life" by Art Harris, (©) 1990 The Washington Post. Reprinted with permission.

"Los Pobres" from *Hunger of Memory* by Richard Rodriguez. Copyright (c) 1982 by Richard Rodriguez. Reprinted by permission of David R. Godine, Publisher.

"Barba Nikos" from *Reflections: A Writer's Life, A Writer's Work* by Harry Mark Petrakis. Reprinted by permission of Lake View Press.

"Photographs of My Parents" from *The Woman Warrior: Memoirs of a Girlhood Among Ghosts* by Maxine Hong Kingston. Copyright © 1975, 1976 by Maxine Hong Kingston. Reprinted by permission of Alfred A. Knopf, Inc.

"Once More to the Lake" from *Essays of E. B. White* by E.B. White. Copyright 1941 by E. B. White. Reprinted by permission of HarperCollins Publishers.

"The War Room at Bellevue" by George Simpson. Copyright © 1992 K-lll Magazine Corporation. All rights reserved. Reprinted with the permission of *New York* magazine.

"The Emma Chase" from *PrairyErth* by William Least Heat-Moon. Copyright © 1991 by William Least Heat-Moon. Reprinted by permission of Houghton Mifflin Co. All rights reserved .

"Cyclone" by Peter Schjeldahl. Copyright © 1988 by *Harper's Magazine*. All rights reserved. Reprinted from the June issue by special permission.

"On Natural Death" from *The Medusa and the Snail: More Notes of a Biology Watcher* by Lewis Thomas. Copyright © 1979 by Lewis Thomas. Reprinted by permission of the publisher, Viking Penguin, a division of Penguin Books USA Inc.

"Mother Tongue" by Amy Tan. © Amy Tan. First published in *The Threepenny Review,* 1990. Reprinted by permission of the author.

"Tools of Torture" from *Never Say Goodbye* by Phyllis Rose. Copyright © 1991 by Phyllis Rose. Used by permission of Doubleday, a division of Bantam Doubleday Dell Publishing Group, Inc.

"Future Shlock" from *Conscientious Objections* by Neil Postman. Copyright © 1988 by Neil Postman. Reprinted by permission of Alfred A. Knopf, Inc.

"Sexism in English: A 1990s Update" by Alleen Pace Nilsen. Copyright © 1990 by Alleen Pace Nilsen. Reprinted by permission of the author.

"Grant and Lee: A Study in Contrasts" by Bruce Catton. Copyright) © U.S. Capitol Historical Society. Reprinted with permission.

"For All Those Who Were Indian in a Former Life" by Andy Smith. Copyright © 1991. Reprinted by permission of *Ms. Magazine*.

"Los Otros, Mis Hermanos" from *Hunger of Memory* by Richard Rodriguez. Copyright © 1982 by Richard Rodriguez. Reprinted by permission of David R. Godine, Publisher.

"Intercultural Misunderstandings: Crossing the Threshold", Chapter 1 from *Cultural Misunderstandings: The French-American Experience* by Raymonde Carroll. Translated by Carol Volk, 1988. Reprinted by permission of The University of Chicago Press and the author.

"My Wood" from *Abinger Harvest,* copyright 1936 and renewed 1964 by Edward Morgan Forster, reprinted by permission of Harcourt Brace Jovanovich, Inc.

"Baby, Take a Bow," excerpt from "Waiting for Miss America" © 1989 by Gerald Early. From *Tuxedo Junction* by Gerald Early, first published by The Ecco Press in 1989. Reprinted by permission.

"Severing the Human Connection" by H. Bruce Miller from the *San Jose Mercury News,* August 4, 1981. Reprinted with permission from *San Jose Mercury News.*

"Kids in the Mall: Growing Up Controlled" from *The Malling of America* by William Severini Kowinski. Copyright © 1985 by William Severini Kowinski. By permission of William Morrow & Company, Inc.

"Who's Afraid of Math, and Why?" reprinted from *Overcoming Math Anxiety* by Sheila Tobias, by permission of W. W. Norton & Co. Inc. Copyright © 1978 by Sheila Tobias.

"Binding Decisions" by Joan Gould. First published in *Memories* Magazine, Feb/March, 1989. Reprinted by permission of Harold Ober Associates Incorporated. Copyright © 1989 by Joan Gould.

"Symbols of Mankind" by Don Lago, originally printed in *Science Digest,* March, 1981. Reprinted by permission of the author.

"On Keeping a Notebook" from *Slouching Towards Bethlehem* by Joan Didion. Copyright © 1966, 1967, 1968 by Joan Didion. Reprinted by permission of Farrar, Strauss, and Giroux, Inc.

"The Maker's Eye: Revising Your Own Manuscripts" by Donald M. Murray. From *The Writer,* October, 1973. Reprinted with permission of the author.

"How Books Helped Shape My Life," Copyright © 1980 by Judith Viorst. Originally appeared in *Redbook.*

"American Regional Costume" from *The Language of Clothes* by Alison Lurie. Copyright © 1981 by Alison Lurie. Reprinted by permission of Melanie Jackson Agency.

"Three Kinds of Discipline" from *Freedom and Beyond* by John Holt. Copyright © 1992 by Holt Associates, Inc. Reprinted with permission.

"Territorial Behavior" reprinted from the book *Manwatching: A Field Guide to Human Behavior* by Desmond Morris. Published in 1977 by Harry N. Abrams, Inc. New York. Copyright © 1977 by Desmond Morris. All rights reserved.

"Notes on Class" from *The Boy Scout Handbook and Other Observations* by Paul Fussell. Copyright © 1982 by Paul Fussell. Reprinted by permission of Oxford University Press, Inc.

"The Need for Secrecy" from *Secrets: On the Ethics of Concealment and Revelation* by Sissela